AN UNKNOWN JEWISH SECT

by

LOUIS GINZBERG

THE JEWISH THEOLOGICAL SEMINARY OF AMERICA

NEW YORK CITY

5736 — 1976

Prepared and published with the aid of the
Stroock Publication Fund
of The Jewish Theological Seminary of America

© Copyright 1970 by

THE JEWISH THEOLOGICAL SEMINARY OF AMERICA

Library of Congress Catalog Card Number: 76-127636
ISBN 0-87334-000-0

Library of Congress Cataloging in Publication Data

Ginzberg, Louis, 1873–1953.
    An unknown Jewish sect.
    (Moreshet Series; v. 1)
    Revised and updated translation of the author's
Eine unbekannte jüdische Sekte, 1922 ed.
    Includes bibliographical references and indexes.
    1. Zadokite documents. I. Title. II. Series:
Moreshet (New York); v. 1.
BM175.Z3G5613   1976   296.8′1   76-127636

Distributed by KTAV Publishing House, Inc.
New York, New York 10013

PRINTED IN THE UNITED STATES OF AMERICA

PRESS OF *Maurice Jacobs*, INC.

1010 ARCH STREET, PHILADELPHIA, PA. 19107

Moreshet Series, Vol. I
Studies in Jewish History,
Literature and Thought

The **Moreshet** [Heritage] Series represents the atest venture of The Jewish Theological Seminary of America in the dissemination of Jewish scholarship and thought. Under its imprint will appear the works of Seminary faculty and alumni in all areas of Jewish scholarly and theological endeavor including works on Bible, rabbinics, history, philology, law, theology, philosophy and ethics. Among them will also be translations of classics, commentaries — ancient as well as modern — and books reflecting the whole spectrum of Jewish activity and expression. The timeliness of such a new series under the auspices of a major center of Jewish scholarly and theological endeavor in the most populous Jewish community of the world requires no elaboration. Hopefully, this series will serve to illuminate afresh to both scholar and layman the wealth and variety of Jewish activity and thought from ancient times to the present.

Table of Contents

Foreword

It might be wise to present this book without explanation or apology. However, since the world of scholarship confronts sufficient enigmas, there is no point in deliberately adding to them. Therefore this foreword will tell what I myself know and what I have learned from experts about this scholarly effort of my father, which was started shortly after Dr. Solomon Schechter published *Fragments of a Zadokite Work*, Cambridge, 1910.

In the years immediately after Dr. Schechter's book appeared (1911–1914) my father wrote a series of articles which were published in the *Monatsschrift für Geschichte und Wissenschaft des Judentums*, Vol. LV to LVIII. In 1922, this series was published as a book with the following title page: *Eine Unbekannte Jüdische Sekte*, von Louis Ginzberg, Erster Teil, New York, 1922, Im Selbstverlage des Verfassers. The back of the title page carried the notation: Karl Angermayer, Pressburg (Tschecho-Slowakei).

From the preface to this volume we learn that my father "had planned to add to this book a critical text of the fragments and a translation, as well as further studies of their language and authenticity and of the various strata of source material, and last but not least, a critical bibliography. Unfortunately I have been obliged to give up this plan because in the present state of things it is almost impossible for an author living in America to have his works published in Europe. Let us hope that peace so yearningly awaited by millions will come soon." The preface was dated January 1916.

A postscript dated July 1921 stated, "I have nothing to add to the foregoing other than that the entry of the United States into the World War made it impossible for this book to be published before peace was concluded. For the further delays neither the author nor the political situation is responsible. I trust there will not be an equal delay in the publication of the second part."

Publication of the second part was delayed not five years but for more than fifty years. One thing led to another. My father had decided to print his *Monatsschrift* articles in book form without waiting to complete the additions which he considered desirable. But much of what he expected to add was complete by the outbreak of World War I. In fact there is no evidence that what is published here for the first

time as Chapters 8, 9, and 10 was written after that time. The war
brought a halt to his intensive research into the "Unknown Sect." In
addition, it must be noted that this manuscript was written in German; all of his later work was in English or Hebrew. It may well be
that Dr. Schechter's death in 1915 — the published volume is dedicated to his memory — also served as a deterrent. My father was willing to argue with a man who was at once his chief and his friend. But
he was not willing to return to the battlefield after his colleague had
died. Louis Ginzberg, like the rest of the scholarly world, lost interest
in the fragments. This is confirmed by the fact that he made only
six brief entries on his interleafed copy of the printed volume.

I personally recall that during the early 1930's Dr. George A.
Kohut extracted from my father a promise to permit the Kohut Foundation to publish this manuscript. Kohut became a frequent visitor
at my father's home in the 1930's as he expanded his efforts on behalf
of Jewish scholars and scholarship. My father liked him a great deal
and appreciated his efforts. Although prompted on repeated occasions
to release the manuscript for publication, my father refrained. He
had doubts about releasing for publication materials on which he had
stopped writing two decades earlier; moreover, he had no inclination
with Hitler on the scene to publish in German. The only alternative
was to translate Part Two into English, as I believe Kohut suggested,
but then part of the work would be in German and part in English —
clearly an anomaly. So my father procrastinated and, while affirming
his promise, he did not release the manuscript.

The discovery of the "Dead Sea Scrolls" in 1947 was one more
reason to hold back the manuscript. He early appreciated the tre-
mendous significance of the scrolls for biblical and post-biblical studies,
but he went out of his way to avoid becoming entangled in this complex arena which earlier had exercised so deep a hold on his interest
and imagination. As he wrote to his friend Ralph Marcus, "I do not
belong to the Jewish 'cave dwellers.' All that I know is that a good
deal of trash has been written on the scrolls found in the caves — so
that I decided not to read anything bearing on this subject." (quoted
in *Keeper of the Law: Louis Ginzberg*, by Eli Ginzberg, Jewish Publication Society, 1966, p. 279). But he surely read enough to appreciate
that his manuscript on the "Unknown Sect" would have to take account of the scrolls. At the time of his death in November 1953 he
had made no move to release the manuscript of Part Two, to alter or
add to it, or to leave instructions about its eventual disposition.

The Kohut Foundation reaffirmed its interest in and commitment
to publish the manuscript. But a consensus of interested scholars was
that with the German edition of Part One out of print and out of

sight — it appeared only infrequently in book catalogues — and with the new interest in the subject awakened by the Dead Sea Scrolls, it would be wise to translate the published as well as the unpublished section into English. This was the plan that was adopted shortly after my father's death. Now, more than two decades later, it has been completed.

Professor Ralph Marcus of the University of Chicago undertook to translate the printed volume. At the time of his premature death in 1956 he had translated considerably more than half. The remainder of Part One was translated by my father's colleague, Professor H. L. Ginsberg and Rabbi Zvi Gotthold of Jerusalem, Israel, who also translated the whole of Part Two. In addition, Professor Ginsberg reviewed Professor Marcus' translation.

Dr. Arthur Hertzberg, a favorite student of my father in his later years, undertook the arduous task of checking the Gotthold translation against the German original as well as for English usage. In addition he read through the entire translation and made certain changes for clarification and simplification. In the penultimate stage of the undertaking he was continually available to me for counseling and advice.

Many questions arose about what effort should be made to bring this work "up to date" in accordance with the canons of scientific inquiry. A final decision was made to do as little as possible, rather than as much as possible, since even a minimum program would result in additional years of delay.

Here, in brief, are the questions that were raised and the solutions that were reached. Since the translation was the work of four men — Marcus, Ginsberg, Gotthold and Hertzberg — it was inevitable that the final product would contain differences in style and editorial preferences. But since each of the translators had sought to remain faithful to the original, it was decided not to strive for uniformity.

Consideration was given to transliterating all Hebrew and other non-English words, but this appeared to be unduly burdensome and in fact unnecessary since the scholars and students who will use the book will have some knowledge of foreign languages, particularly Hebrew.

Since critical editions of various Rabbinic texts have been published during the intervening sixty years, it was decided to refer the reader to them rather than to the editions available to the author, a task to which Professor C. Z. Dimitrovsky and Dr. Hertzberg contributed.

Rabbi Gotthold described his additions as follows: "I have taken the liberty of relegating notes and long cross-references which oc-

casionally appear in the text to the notes ... I have also occasionally
quoted more extensively from the manuscript for the sake of clarity ... I have also introduced more paragraphing ... I have also referred to elaboration on some points by the author in subsequent
works." These several editorial revisions by Rabbi Gotthold were an
attempt to make it easier for the reader to follow the author who had
left an unedited manuscript.

We also considered whether it would be desirable to prepare a
critical edition of Schechter's text with Louis Ginzberg's corrections
and emendations supplemented by other readings accepted today.
But we had decided against this on the ground that it was not
necessary.

The Zadokite Documents, 2nd Edition, by Chaim Rabin, Oxford,
1954, provides such a critical edition together with parallels from the
Dead Sea Scrolls, particularly the Discipline Scroll, the Habakkuk
Commentary, and the Thanksgiving Scroll. Consequently there appeared that few gains would accrue from altering Louis Ginzberg's
basic text and notes. Professor H. L. Ginsberg did add notes which
have been included in brackets, sometimes with his initials, sometimes
without, on matters on which Rabin should be consulted. Professor
Saul Lieberman also added a few clarifying notes. These are designated [S.L.]

One basic question remains. How much of Louis Ginzberg's reconstruction of "An Unknown Jewish Sect" has been confirmed by
later scholarship, including the new knowledge gained from the last
two decades of deciphering and interpreting the scrolls? He ended his
work by stating:

> The sect whose history and doctrine are revealed in this docu-
> ment emerged around 76–67 B.C.E. within the Pharisees' colony
> of Judeans at Damascus whither they had fled from Alexander
> Jannaeus' persecutions. In the beginning the Damascus refugees
> differed only on political grounds from their fellow Pharisees in
> Judea. Gradually there evolved, however, also religious and par-
> ticularly halakhic distinctions which set them more and more
> apart until a schism and rift consolidated the sect of exiles. The
> Damascene sect branded both Pharisees and Sadducees as back-
> sliding sinners and considered only its own sect as divinely elected
> true Israel.

Since I am a layman without knowledge or control over the sources,
I asked my father's colleague and my friend, Professor H. L. Ginsberg,
to help me answer the foregoing question. He told me that the Dead
Sea Scrolls unequivocally confirm the historicity, language, law,
customs, and theology of the "Unknown Jewish Sect" that Louis

Ginzberg delineated on the basis of the Zadokite Fragments. Louis Ginzberg had decided that the dissidents of the wilderness had been a true sect because of their fundamental disagreements with the Pharisees with respect to the laws of incest which precluded their intermarrying with the backsliding majority.

The Scrolls present further evidence that the dissidents were a sect since they followed a different calendar which led them to observe holidays on days different from those observed by their coreligionists. While the origins of the sect and the stages in its differentiation from the main body of the community remain obscure, the evidence points to initial conflict about priestly succession which led to further differentiation growing out of the eschatological teachings of the leader of the sect, the Teacher of Righteousness. These led the sect to develop distinctive views about laws of purity, observance of the Sabbath, property ownership, sex, relations to gentiles, and these differences came to be expressed in thought, law, and custom.

Louis Ginzberg ended his study of the sect with firm views about the time of its emergence and its domicile. With respect to timing, he dated its emergence at 76–67 B.C.E. Professor Frank Moore Cross, Jr. in *The Ancient Library of Qumran*, Anchor, 1961, defined the time period as follows: "The upper limit while not certain, is suitably drawn around 150 B.C.; the lower limit which I would regard as definitely fixed falls not far from 100 B.C.; in other terms, from the priesthood of Jonathan (160–142 B.C.) to the reign of Alexander Jannaeus (102–76 B.C.)" According to Cross, Ginzberg's timing is tenable.

With regard to locale the author postulated that the sect, while originating in Palestine, eventually settled in the land of Damascus. It is Cross' view (*op. cit.*, pp. 81 ff.) and that of most contemporary scholars that the "land of Damascus" is the "prophetic name" applied to the desert of Qumran. It is clear that the sect had its headquarters in the wilderness near the Dead Sea. The only question that remains moot is whether, at some time, some of its members relocated at or near Damascus. But no weighty issues hang on this answer. It is now certain that most of the sectarians lived in the desert, not in Damascus. This correction can be made without altering Louis Ginzberg's basic scaffolding. Interestingly enough, Ginzberg points out (p. 271) that the Talmud notes that certain dissenters moved to the south; and (p. 397) he takes note of the "correspondence between our document and the Essene doctrine." How much closer could he have come?

The reasons for the decision to translate and publish *An Unknown Jewish Sect* with a minimum of corrections and additions should now be clear. The discovery of the Scrolls confirmed most of the hypotheses that Louis Ginzberg advanced forty years earlier on the basis of his studies of the Zadokite Fragments. It is not often in the history of scholarship that texts are found which describe a group about whom little or nothing was previously known. It is unusual in the history of scholarship for a researcher to venture upon a detailed reconstruction of the life and thought of a largely unknown group from the minute study of a limited number of fragments. It is rare indeed that archeological and paleographical discoveries two generations later provide definitive evidence in support of most of the earlier reconstructions of a venturesome scholar.

While Louis Ginzberg was willing to let his imagination roam when the Zadokite Fragments were discovered, most scholars preferred to eschew the subject especially after the initial excitement following the publication of the text. There were too many puzzles that could not be answered by the materials at hand. There was ample room for speculation but little opportunity to reach firm conclusions. And so the matter would have remained had it not been for the discovery of the Dead Sea Scrolls.

While pieces of the puzzle are missing even after the rich discoveries of the recent past, it is no longer correct to talk about the "unknown" Jewish sect. We now know the Jewish sect which lived in the wilderness of the Dead Sea in the first century before the Common Era and which was in fundamental conflict with both the Sadducees and the Pharisees.

While the decision to translate and publish the whole of my father's *Unbekannte Jüdische Sekte* was made by me as executor of his estate, it was really determined by fate. The Dead Sea Scrolls confirmed so large a part of his work that it seemed only right that his entire work be made available to scholars. Two decades have passed since that decision was made and in the interim much of the initial excitement engendered by the discovery of the Scrolls has receded. But scholarship, while not free of fashion, has a life of its own. And all those who helped to bring the present undertaking to fruition believe that Louis Ginzberg's contribution of the 1910's has enough lasting value to justify its second debut in the mid-1970's.

This was the advice that my father's colleagues and my friends — Louis Finkelstein, H. L. Ginsberg, Saul Lieberman and Shalom Spiegel — gave me. This is the advice that I have followed, not without trepidation, but I know that these scholars would not have encouraged this project if they had seriously doubted its value.

This work is neither a finished nor a polished product, but we hope that the reader will focus on its strengths and overlook its shortcomings.

Many others helped during the years required to complete the translation and to see the work through the press. Dr. Abraham Goldberg and Dr. Moshe Davis provided an important bridge between Dr. Gotthold in Jerusalem and me.

Dr. Edward Gershfield undertook the arduous task of reading proof and worked out with Dr. Menahem G. Glenn the stylistic and editorial problems that arose when the book was set in type. Further, through a combination of dedication and ingenuity, Dr. Glenn was able to fill in many cross references including those in the last three hitherto unpublished chapters. The Maurice Jacobs Press is responsible for seeing through to a successful conclusion a difficult publishing task, an accomplishment made possible by the special efforts of Dr. Maurice Jacobs, Mr. Arnold Fisher, and Mr. David Skaraton.

Dr. Louis Finkelstein provided encouragement and support all along the way and arranged that the work be published under the auspices of the Stroock Publication Fund of the Jewish Theological Seminary. The Kohut Foundation, the American Academy for Jewish Research, and the Jewish Theological Seminary made contributions to help cover the costs of translation.

Dr. Saul Lieberman was always ready to help. Once the translation had been completed, he assumed the responsibility for seeing that the various scholarly efforts which were required to turn the manuscript into a book were forthcoming. He also helped to clarify many conundra. Above all he recruited and provided counsel for Prof. Tovia Preschel.

In addition to preparing the index, which in Dr. Lieberman's opinion is critical for making the book useful to scholars, Prof. Preschel served as anchor man. He was the last of the many through whose hands the proofs passed. Prof. Preschel considered it an obligation to the author to free the page proofs of a great many errors that had crept in as a result of the many who assisted in preparing the text for publication. All readers are indebted to him for the conscientious and skillful manner in which he performed this difficult task.

But I finally called a halt. I felt that it was better to publish the book even with its remaining rough spots, than to continue the endless task of polishing a manuscript that the author himself had not revised.

My mother's interest in seeing the task completed was a stimulus to many who helped to bring it about.

The final arrangements about the financing and publishing of the work rested with Dr. Gerson Cohen, the Chancellor of The Jewish Theological Seminary of America.

New York   ELI GINZBERG
April, 1976

Preface

The greater part of the present study of the work published by Solomon Schechter under the title *Fragments of a Zadokite Work* (Cambridge, 1910) appeared in volumes LV to LVIII (1911–1914) of the *Monatsschrift für Geschichte und Wissenschaft des Judentums*. Although this sectarian writing has given rise to a considerable literature in the interim, I have not seen any reason to modify my treatment of it, and therefore reproduce it here without change. Numerous theories concerning the origin of these enigmatic fragments, some probable, some improbable, some even bizarre, have been proposed by qualified persons, and even more by unqualified. However, exceedingly little of real value has been done for the interpretation of the very obscure text and the understanding of the problems raised by the fragments in the fields of both Halakah and Haggadah. In this instance too the wise saying of Humboldt is confirmed, that unless serious attention is given to details, all theories about the whole can only be castles in the air.

The application to *Jüdische Wissenschaft* of the contrary principle, accepted by many, that a general impression is sufficient and one need not bother about the details, has resulted in nothing less than disaster for a number of writers who have sought to evaluate the fragments. A famous historian of religion has declared in the chief organ of German Oriental studies that the fragments should not be attributed to a particular sect in as much as their discovery in the Genizah of the community of Cairo shows that they were there regarded as canonical. Following out this line of reasoning, the begging letters, the prescriptions for gout and anaemia, the invoices of merchandise and the exercises of schoolboys learning their ABC's, which are all abundantly represented in the Genizah, must have enjoyed canonical status in the Cairo community. All that now remains is for the genizah of a community in Lithuania to come to light, and our historians of religion will make the happy discovery that Karl Marx's *Das Kapital* and Eugene Suë's novel *The Mysteries of Paris* enjoyed a canonical dignity among the Lithuanian Jews of the nineteenth century. Fragments of these works will inevitably be found in the genizot, which are the ultimate repositories of everything that is written or printed in Hebrew characters; in the eleventh century it may be a sectarian book, and in the nineteenth a novel translated from the French.

That the sectarian Halakah is completely ignored by those who think that a knowledge of details can be dispensed with in judging Jewish history and literature is not surprising. For the Halakah regulates and makes normative only the individual acts of human life, the understanding of which is alleged to have no significance for the total religious life. It is just those details that are of the very greatest importance for the circles in which this sectarian writing originated, but that is regarded as irrelevant. Attaching importance to such trivial things was only a Jewish prejudice. So, in accordance with the ancient prescription *ex lege discere quod nesciebat lex*, the primary is made secondary, and the secondary primary. I have therefore considered it an especially important task to attain clarity about the Halakah in these fragments, for this alone is capable of dispelling the darkness that surrounds them. Beside numerous observations on the halakic principles in the fragments, which are found scattered in Section III (pp. 5–104), I have made a comprehensive survey of the sectarian Halakah and its relation to the standard Halakah and to that of the other sects in Section IV (pp. 105–154). The results of these detailed investigations of the Halakah in the fragments can be summarized in the following words. The Halakah of the sect represents the Pharisaic view in all essential questions of law and contains nothing that can be traced to the influence of Sadducean, Dosithean, or any other heresy.

The theology of the sect forms the content of the fifth section (pp. 155–208), in which I believe I have proved that it basically agrees with that of the Pharisees.

The Messianic idea does not, to be sure, occupy a central position in the theology of the fragments, but it is upon a correct understanding of the Messianic passages therein that our judgment concerning the nature and origin of the sect depends. I have therefore made a thorough investigation of the Messianic doctrines of the sect in the sixth section (pp. 209–256), and in this connection have dealt with the problem whether "the excellent teacher" or "the teacher of righteousness" is identical with the expected Messiah. The result to which I have come is that in these fragments, in agreement with Pharisaic writings, the work of salvation is awaited from Elijah and "the son of David," and the latter bears the title "the Messiah of Israel," the former "the Messiah of Aaron."

On the basis of the special studies on the Halakah, theology, and Messianic doctrines I have sought in the last section (pp. 257–303) to understand the genesis of the sect from whose midst these written remains arose. This effort resulted in the working hypothesis that these fragments are the deposit of a movement which went through three phases. It began in Palestine in the time of Alexander Jannaeus as a covenant of zealous Pharisees in opposition to the Sadduceeism of this king, developed in "the land of Damascus" into a party of intransigents who found the concessions made to the Pharisees by Queen Alexandra insufficient, and ended as a sect whose slogan was: Let us have done with the false Pharisaism of the Palestinians.

I had planned to add to this book a critical text of the fragments and a translation, as well as further studies of their language and authenticity and of the various strata of source-material, and, last but not least, a critical bibliography. Unfortunately I have been obliged to give up this plan because in the present state of things it is almost impossible for an author living in America to have his works published in Europe. Let us hope that the peace so yearningly awaited by millions will come soon.

In the first essay that Schechter published about the Genizah he remarked: "I cannot overcome a sad feeling stealing over me that I shall hardly be worthy to see all the results which the Genizah will add to our knowledge of Jews and Judaism." These prophetic words have, alas, been fulfilled all too soon. It is with a feeling of deepest sadness and indescribable grief that this book, which I had hoped to present to the discoverer of the fragments and their gifted interpreter as an offering in honor of his seventieth birthday, has now been dedicated to his memory. David, the Rabbis state, implored God to let him live in both worlds, saying, "May my words be read in the houses of prayer and the houses of learning, and this will assure me eternal life in this world as in the other." So long as there are Jewish houses of learning the name of Solomon Schechter will be mentioned in them, and even though he may no longer be among us, yet he is with us.

L. G.

New York, January, 1916

Postscript. I have nothing to add to the foregoing other than that the entry of the United States into the World War made it impossible for this book to be published before peace was concluded. For the further delays neither the author nor the political situation is responsible. I trust there will not be an equal delay in the publication of the second part.

New York, July 1921

I

Introduction

"Israel did not go into exile until it had split into twenty-four sects." Apart from the number twenty-four, which we may well regard as haggadic license,[1] this saying of Rabbi Joḥanan[2] contains a profound truth. The fall of the Jewish state is to be ascribed not only to the Roman policy of conquest[3] but also to the party feuds and sectarian hates of the Jews, which tore their state apart long before a Roman soldier set foot on the soil of Palestine. The conflicts between the Pharisees and the Sadducees are the only incidents in the internal history of the Jews during the century preceding the destruction of the Temple in 70 C. E. which can be dated with certainty. The antagonisms which provoked these conflicts, however, are most imperfectly known to us. Rabbinic tradition sees in Sadduceeism nothing but an apostasy from the true religion, the bearers of which were the Pharisees. For the modern historian, on the other hand, the opposition between Pharisees and Sadducees is that between a church party and a worldly power. And since the Talmud and Josephus, hitherto the only sources of our knowledge of the parties, represent Pharisaic tendencies, their reports would not suffice for a true evaluation of the relations between the parties even if they were more definite and extensive than they are. *Audiatur et altera pars* is the first requirement for a correct decision to be made by a judge as well as an historian, and so long as we cannot fulfil this requirement, we must withhold judgment.

While our knowledge of the three great sects, the Pharisees, the Sadducees, and the Essenes, must be described as imperfect, the many undercurrents and parallel movements about them are not even known to us by name. The followers of these tendencies appear in Talmudic literature under the collective designation of מינים or חיצונים so that

---

[1] *Cf.* Hai Gaon in *Aruk*, s. v. עסר; he has already noted: ודקאמר כ׳ד בלשון הבאי ונוזמא; *cf.*, however, *Responsa*, ed. Harkavy, 281.

[2] TP Sanhedrin x, 29c.

[3] R. Joḥanan, to be sure, is speaking of the first exile but those who know the Haggadah need no proof that the Haggadah uses biblical material in its description of the second exile.

we have no means of being acquainted with the individualities of these various movements.[4] Nothing would be more calculated to bring our ignorance of the nature of these sects into relief than for at least a few connected leaves from the hand of an ancient sectarian to come into our possession.

This unexpected event has now actually been realized. The Genizah in Cairo, that great repository of literary treasures, has preserved a writing[5] in which we hear the words of a sectarian for the first time, and which from now on must be consulted before one undertakes any discussion of Jewish sectarianism.

Professor Schechter, the fortunate discoverer of this treasure, calls this writing "a Zadokite work," and in his Introduction to it gives the reasons for this name. In a separate section I shall speak about the sect whose creed is embodied in this fragment. Because of the poor condition of the document, however, I consider it proper first to examine the text in some detail and then to go on to a discussion of its contents.

---

[4] That מין sometimes means "Jewish Christian" is an established fact, but it is just as certain that the same word frequently means something quite different.

[5] The full title is: *Documents of Jewish Sectaries*, vol. 1. *Fragments of a Zadokite Work*, edited from Hebrew Manuscripts in the Cairo Genizah collection ... and provided with an English translation, Introduction and Notes by S. Schechter, Cambridge University Press, 1910.

II

Orthography of the Fragments

Several of the emendations to our text[1] proposed in the following sections presuppose the orthography peculiar to it, and for that reason it seems advisable to note its peculiarities very briefly.

A) ו is used for tone-long *o* in the following instances:

1. The infinitive construct of the kal is almost always[2] written ולבחור, ולמאוס 2,15 ולנדול 6,16 ולדרוש 6,21; ולשמור 6,18; ונוקם ונוטר 8,5; לשפוט 10,8. לרחוץ 11,1 לשפוך 12,6; ושנוא 8,6 עמוד 5,5; בעמוד 1,14; לירוש 1,7.

2. Segolate nouns sometimes have ו where the Masorah usually has only the defective spelling: 4,12 חוק; 12,1 קודש; 4,6 הקודש 25, כוח; 24, ורוב; 1,7 שורש.

3. The imperfect kal is almost always written *plene*:[3] 8,3 תשפוך. ימכור 12,10; תרמוש 12,13 ימשול 13,12 ידור 16,13; וימסור 3,3; תקום תמור 9,2.[4]

B) In the following instances י is found for tone-long *e* [or for *e* which other texts do not indicate by a vowel letter]: 3,15 עידות; ביצי 5,14 ביצים 5,14; ומיאיות 13,1; סורירה 1,13; שאירית 2,6; פליטה 2,7; ופירוש 4,6 כפירושיהם 6,20; אשימים 1,9; עידים 9,23.

C) ו is used for short *o* in cases like the following: 11,1 עומדו; שלושתם 14,6;[5] במועלם 1,3; מגורנו 12,9; לפוקדם 8,2.[6]

D) We have ו for short *u* in 2,11 ובכולם; 11,23 כולה; 5,12 חוקי 2,9 תומם, but it is to be noted that in all these cases *dagesh forte* follows.[7]

Similarly we have י for short *i* with a following *dagesh forte* in: וגיבוריהם 3,9 נימול (ניצל?) 16,6; לתיתו 1,6; הניצל 4,18

---

[1] Only Fragm. A is considered here, since B follows the Masoretic orthography in most cases.

[2] Only 6,10 עמד and 7,9 בפקד are exceptions.

[3] *Cf.* however 14,6 יפקד.

[4] By the side of ימכר, which, however, should perhaps be read יִמָּכֵר, *cf.* further below the interpretation of this passage.

[5] Against the Masorah in Num. 5:6, Sifre and Sifre Z. have למעול for למעל.

[6] At the same time, however, 14,4 has שלשתם.

[7] In Ben Sira also ו is written for short *u* in numerous instances; *cf.* Smend, *Einleitung*, p. 15.

In one case,[8] 4,20 ניתפשים, it occurs even though *dagesh forte* does not follow. Noteworthy but not unexampled are 1,9 וכימנששים and 8,5 ניטור where י is used for short *i* and for *shewa* respectively.

In spite of this preference for full spelling we also find *scriptio defectiva* writings where the Masorah has always or preponderantly *scriptio plena* as in: 9,10 השפטים; 10,18 רק; 11,21 צדקם and similarly 10,9 ימו as well as 11,2 חפצו. Among the further orthographic peculiarities of our fragments is the omission of pronominal suffixes and of plural and feminine endings of nouns: 5,7 מבדיל=מבדילים; 5,13 יזק= ; 2,9 מעמד = ;חבורת=חבור 12,8 ;חבלה=חבל 2,6 ;טמאת=טמא 4,18 ;זיקות מעמדם. In accordance with Aramaic orthography בפי is written for בפה in 6,7 while in 2,3 תושייה is the usual late Hebrew way of writing תושיה.

---

[8] *Cf.* also 13,11 ושוכלו, for which שיכלו is to be read.

[9] The text has ויקי, but this probably goes back to ויק׳, the stroke over ק being a sign of abbreviation, which was mistaken by later copyists for a י.

III

Textual and Exegetical Notes

1,2: ומשפט יעשה בכל מנאציו. Schechter's reference to Gen. 18:25 יעשה משפט is not quite exact since עשה משפט in this biblical passage means "to do justice" while in our passage it is to be translated with "to execute judgment." The biblical parallel to this use of עשה משפט is Ps. 149:9 לעשות בהם משפט, in agreement with which it is construed with ב in our passage.

1,5: שנים שלש מאות וכו'. In spite of שנים עשרים in 1,10 and שנים ארבעים in 20,15 the use of שנים in this verse is very puzzling since the number is defined by the following phrase לתיתו אותם, and one would therefore expect שנת.

1,7: ויצמח...שורש מטעת. Schechter would read נצר מטעו in the light of Isa. 60:21.[1] But our author probably was thinking of Jer. 12:2 נטעתם גם שרשו, and we should therefore translate, "and He caused to sprout from Israel and Aaron the root which He had planted." In the years of suffering, Israel could not develop but existed only as a root without branches or fruit. Only at the end of the years of suffering could it spread out. Our author here speaks not of a specific person, as Schechter assumes, Introduction 12, such as the founder of the sect, but of the people as a whole, which he designates more particularly as Israel and Aaron. Hence the expression ויצמח מישראל ומאהרן whereas the Messiah is משיח מאהרן ומישראל. On the expression ויצמח מישראל ומאהרן it should also further be noted that Talmudic מטעה = biblical מטע, and further that in this fragment suffixes are frequently not indicated, so that מטע is equivalent to מטעתו.

1,12: את אשר עשה בדור אחרון. Schechter is quite right in explaining the words בדור אחרון as a scribal error, since it can hardly be assumed that our author wrote, "and He proclaimed to the later generations what He did to the later generation," where "the later generation" certainly represents a period of time earlier than that of "the later generations." Nevertheless Schechter's emendation בדור ראשון is hardly tenable since, apart from the fact that it is hard to explain how אחרון rose from ראשון, בדור ראשון can hardly mean "former generation," as

[1] So the Ketib; the Qere has מטעי.

5

Schechter translates, since this would be expressed by בדור אשר היה
מלפניהם. We should therefore read בדור חרון, "the generation of wrath."
The time of suffering is for our author the time of "wrath," as in 1,5,
and the generation upon which God sent suffering was the generation
of wrath, since suffering, to our author, is only explicable as the consequence of divine wrath. The expression דור חרון corresponds exactly
to the biblical דור עברתו Jer. 7:29,[2] while the א in אחרון (for חרון) owes
its existence to the preceding אחרונים. Conceivably בדור אחרון could be
a doublet to לדורות in as much as beside the reading ויודע לד' אח'
there may have been another which read ויודע בד' and both may have
been admitted into the text. The miswriting of דור חרון as דור אחרון is,
however, very easy to understand, and we may therefore regard
דור חרון as the correct text.

1,15: מימי כזב. Similar expressions for false doctrines are מים
הרעים "bad water" in the saying of Abtalion, Avoth 1,12, and מים עכורים[3]
"troubled water," Sifre Deut. 48 = Midrash Tannaim p. 42. As in the
Rabbinic sources, so in our text "deceitful water" is to be understood
as the false doctrines of Jewish teachers and not something like pagan
doctrines. Accordingly the איש הלצון is certainly a Jewish opponent
of the sect and not somebody like Antiochus Epiphanes, who forced
the Jews to abandon their religion. Also the expression הטיף indicates
that the מטיף (cf. 4,19) is a false teacher, since in Scripture too הטיף
is used only of the prophets, both false and true.

1,15: להשח גבהות עולם. This expression is not taken from Isa.
2:11, 17, as Schechter assumes, since in these passages גבהות אדם
means the pride of man, which would make no sense here, but is a
paraphrase of Hab. 3:6 שחו גבעות עולם. It is not necessary, however, to
emend גבהות to גבעות, since our author fairly frequently allows himself
small changes in biblical quotations. Moreover, we should not err by
reading גְּבָהוֹת from גִּבְהָה "height," rather than גַבְהוּת, although both in
Bible and Mishnah גֹבַה is used in this sense.

1,16: ולסיע גבול. In view of the fact that the expression used in
Scripture is always and only הסיג גבול (Deut. 19:14; 27,17; Hos. 5:10;
Prov. 22:28), and that our author himself speaks of מסיני הגבול (5,10)
one might be inclined to emend ולסיע to ולסיג. Not impossibly, however,
הסיע is here deliberately used instead of הסיג because it expresses the
thought of the author, who reproaches his opponents with "tearing
down firmly established teachings," better than the biblical הסיג גבול
which means "to move boundary (signs)." An interesting parallel to

---

[2] *Cf.* also Ps. 95:10–11.
[3] This reading of Midrash Tannaim is cited by Meiri Avoth *ad loc.* from the Sifre.

our verse is the *derash* of R. Simon[4] on Prov. 22:28; he explains the words of Scripture, "Remove not the ancient landmarks which thy Fathers have set" to mean מנהג שעשו אבותיך אל תשנה אותו "do not change a custom which was established by your forefathers." This midrashic passage is probably the source of the comment in ספר חסידים, p. 207, ed. Wistinetzki, לא תסיג גבול ... ראשונים שלא יאמר ניגון של תורה לנביאים ... אלא כל ניגון כמו שהוא מתוקן, "Do not remove the landmark ... which your forefathers set. This means that one should not employ the cantillation which has become established for the Pentateuch in reading the Prophets but should employ in the different parts of Scripture the melodies which have long been fixed for them." R. Simon's *derash* is also the source of Midrash Aggadah, Deut. 199 — a fact which escaped Buber.

1,19: ויבחרו בטוב הצואר. The phrase טוב הצואר is biblical (Hos. 10:11),[5] and our passage must accordingly be translated "and they wished for a stout neck"; the adversaries are reproached with being intent only upon stuffing themselves full. The mockers in Israel, observes the Midrash (Tanḥuma, ed. Buber, II, 129), said ראו צואר "See the fleshy neck of Moses; what he eats belongs to the Jews, and what he drinks belongs to the Jews." In this Midrash passage too, צואר stands for the entire body, and similarly in a Medieval saying, מי שמתעסק בתורה ובעבודה לא יתכן שיהיה צוארו עב וגופו שמן (מבחר הפנינים I,29); "He who is devoted to the study of the Torah and to pious deeds cannot have a fat neck or a fat body." The reproach that our author directs at his adversaries is that they are slaves to earthly pleasures, and this characterization has a parallel in the Assumption of Moses VIII, 4, "Since they will *be* deceitful men, living only to please themselves ... loving to feast at every hour of the day and glutting themselves."

2,2: ואלה אזנכם בדרכי רשעים. There is absolutely no reason to emend אזנכם to עיניכם as Schechter suggests, since the author did not wish to call his readers' attention to something that was happening or had happened before men's eyes, as in 2,14, but wishes to proclaim

---

[4] Midrash Mishle, *ad loc.*, ed. Buber 93. *Cf.* also Sifre Deut. 188, p. 227 where the passage in Deut., ... לא תסיג, is applied to the correct transmission of the teachings of individual scholars; the text is probably to be emended in accordance with Midrash Tannaim, *ad loc. Cf.* also the Slavonic Book of Enoch LII, 9, "blessed be he who keeps the foundations which the Fathers laid down in the most ancient time," where a *derash* on Prov. 22:28 is likewise present. In the Ethiopic Enoch XCIX, 2, 14, this *derash* is obscured.

[5] *Cf.* Ehrlich, מקרא כפשוטו, *ad loc.* He translates עברתי "erfassen"; "to consider" would probably be more correct.

the punishment of the godless, and that, not on earth but in a future life. He is expounding a doctrine, and אגלה אזנכם is the only proper expression. One should not, to be sure, on taking this view, fall into the error of translating דרכי רשעים as "the ways in which the wicked walk." The "ways" are rather the להבי אש (2,5) Gehenna, for which the wicked are destined, where they receive their punishment. The biblical verse, Ps. 1:6 כי יודע י"י דרך צדיקים ודרך רשעים תאבד, of which our author was probably thinking in this passage, is explained in Midrash Tehillim, *ad loc.* (ed. Buber, 24), to mean, והוא דן את הצדיקים ומוליכן לגן עדן ודן את הרשעים ומחייבן לגיהנם, "He (God) sits in judgment on the righteous and thereupon *leads* them *to* Paradise; He also judges the godless, and sentences them *to* Gehinnom." This Midrash, therefore, understands by דרך צדיקים and דרך רשעים the "ways" on which the righteous and the godless proceed to their appointed places. Rabban Joḥanan b. Zakkai also spoke on his deathbed[6] "of two ways, one leading to Paradise and the other to Hell."

2,4: עד ודעת. As Schechter has already remarked, ערמה here does not mean "cunning" but, as in Prov. 8:12,[7] "insight," "understanding." And I should like to add here that in the Talmud too ערמומית is "understanding," not "cunning," as can be seen from Niddah 45b.

2,4: ארך אפים עמו. Schechter refers to Ex. 34:6 but there ארך is an adjective, while here it is a noun, as עמו shows, so that אֹרֶךְ is perhaps to be read, even though the Masorah in Jer. 15:15 reads אֶרֶךְ and not אֹרֶךְ. Another possibility is that the text should be read ארך אפים ועמו רוב סליחות[8] "He is long-suffering, and with Him is abundance of forgiveness(es)." In favor of this assumption may be cited the fact that in rabbinic Hebrew one speaks of אריכות אפים and not of ארך אפים, but this could be countered with the argument that in accordance with the orthographic practice of our fragment ארך can also stand for אריכות. *Cf.* also Ben Sira XVI, 11, עמו ואף רחמים כי.

2,6: מלאכי חבל. In view of the frequency of the term in Talmudic-Midrashic literature it is very improbable that our author spoke of מלאכי חבול or חבל. The absence of a ה at the end is not a scribal error but agrees with other spellings in our fragment, in which the feminine ה is not always expressed.

---

[6] *Cf.* Berakhoth 28b; Avoth de R. Nathan XXV,79, ed. Schechter.

[7] A better parallel to our text is Prov. 1:4, where דעת and ערמה are combined, as in our fragment.

[8] An echo of Isa. 55:7, כי ירבה לסלוח. In the liturgical formula רב סליחות ובעל הרחמים, on the other hand, רב is probably to be translated "master," as the parallelism of בעל requires.

2,8: וַיְתָעֵב את דורות מדם. That this sentence is corrupt requires no proof. But the correct text can easily be restored; for it is a paraphrase of Ps. 5:7 איש דמים ומרמה יתעב ה' so that the correct reading is דורות דמים, "generations laden with bloodguilt." It is blood-guilt that causes the ruin of sinners. It would also be possible to read דורות אדם, "the generations of man," or דורות קדם, "generations of old," as parallels to the second half of the verse מן הארץ. But the Psalm passage cited speaks for דמים.

2,9: מי עד תומם. There is no reason to assume, with Schechter, that there is a lacuna here. Read מועד תומם and translate, "and He (God) hid His face from the earth at the time that was appointed for their (the wicked's) destruction."

2,9–10: וידע . . . לכל שני עולם. "And he knew the years of existence, the number and the precise end of all that exists and has existed, and also that which will come at the end of the years (=times) of the world." God's omniscience extends to all things, to the present הֹוִי, the past [נִהְיָית] נִהְיָה and the future מה יבוא and indeed to all individual events. There is nothing remarkable about the orthography מעמד for מעמדם and מספר for מספרם as well as הוי for הויה (Exod. 9:3!) after what was noted in Section II, since the suffix is frequently omitted in this fragment.

2,12: ויודיעם ביד משיחו רוח קדשו. Schechter translates, "And through His anointed He made them know His holy spirit." If, however, we were to accept Schechter's view[9] that the Messiah of this sect had lived on earth and vanished only for a time, and was to appear again, it would be impossible to translate משיחו as "his Messiah" in this passage, since ויודיעם refers to past generations in the course of history, whereas the appearance of this Messiah took place only at the time when this sect arose. Now if we bear in mind that this sentence corresponds to Neh. 9:30, ותעד בם ברוחך ביד נביאיך it follows that מְשִׁיחָו "His anointed ones" stands for נביאיו. And indeed our author, in accordance with his view[10] of the great importance of the patriarchs for the true doctrine, deliberately uses משיחו instead of נביאיו, therein following the example of Ps. 105:15, אל תגעו במשיחי where "My anointed ones" means the same thing as "the patriarchs,"[11] and where furthermore משיחי

---

[9] Cf. below, Section V.

[10] Cf. Schechter, Introduction 29. This view also appears prominently in the Book of Jubilees. Moreover, rabbinic tradition (Seder Olam XXI) considers "The Fathers" as prophets, and this is also the view of Philo, Quis rerum div. her. sit LII, who even follows rabbinic tradition in counting Noah as a prophet.

[11] Cf. Midrash Tehillim, ad loc., במשיחי אלו האבות " 'My anointed ones': these are the Fathers."

stands as a parallel to נביאי (ולנביאי אל תרעו). If, however, we wish to keep the reading משיחו, we must read להודיעם and translate: "And during all these years He caused to arise . . . that He, at the end of times, might make known His holy spirit through His Messiah." Against the view that משיחו means "His Messiah," however, militates the fact that our author always speaks only of the Messiah as משיח מאהרון ומישראל and not of the משיח י"י.

Very characteristic are the words רוח קדשו והוא אמת, which not only give us the Hebrew equivalent of πνεῦμα τῆς ἀληθείας but also are of significance for the development of this concept.[12] In Jubilees XXV, 14, the spirit of truth רוח אמת is identical with the infallible prophetic spirit, for which reason we also read "holy spirit" in some manuscripts instead of "spirit of truth." For our author, on the other hand, the spirit of truth is the spirit that leads men to morality and piety, that reveals itself most clearly in the good and pious deeds of "the anointed of God" but nevertheless dwells in every man, so that sinners defile this holy spirit through their sinful acts (5,11) in resisting its guidance. Exactly the same view is found in Test. XII Patr. where the following passage (T. Judah XX, 1) is especially instructive: "Know that two spirits go about with men, that of truth and that of error, and in the midst is the spirit of insight, of understanding, to incline wherever he will." Similarly it is said in the Wisdom of Solomon VII, 27, "And from generation to generation passing over to holy souls, she endows the friends of God and prophets with spirit."

2,13: ובפרוש שמו שמותיהם. Schechter considers שמו the result of a scribal error because of the following שמותיהם, but admits that even if we delete שמו the clause gives no sense. In reality, however, there is no good reason for any such emendation. The clause ובפרוש . . . התעה refers to the שם קרואי in line 11, and one should translate, "And they (those chosen by God) left behind imperishable names,[13] but those whom He (God) hated, He led astray." "To make a name for himself" as the meaning of שָׂם שֵׁם is, to be sure, not a biblical sense, but a Talmudic one, as can be seen from Berakhoth 7b, where שָׂם שָׁמוֹת in Ps. 46:9 is explained as שָׁם שֵׁמוֹת.

[12] *Cf.* more fully on this Bousset, *Religion des Judentums*, pp. 343 and 375 ff., although his arguments require correction. His statement that according to the view of the Testaments of the Patriarchs the Messiah will pour out this spirit upon the pious is based on an error, since in T. Judah XXIV, 3 it is "the spirit of grace" and not "of truth" that is spoken of. But the idea is to be found in John 15:26, where, however, πνεῦμα τῆς ἀληθείας probably designates a degree of prophecy.

[13] Literally, "with distinctness they set their names." Our author uses שָׂם שֵׁם in the sense in which שם עשה is used in Scripture.

2,18: בה נאחזו. There is no reason to emend בה to בם, as Schechter does. For though the author uses בם in the preceding line, here it is primarily a question of "a" sin which caused the fall of the angels, namely זנות; for which reason the singular בה is quite in order; this sin is referred to by בה in 3,1.

2,19: וכהרים גויותיהם. Legend[14] relates that the descendants of the fallen angels were 3,000 cubits tall (Enoch VII, 2); some go still further and assert that Og, the least of these giants,[15] was of such great stature that his leg measured more than three parasangs (Niddah 24b). Our text probably refers to such views in saying "And their bodies were like mountains." Test. XII Patriarchs, T. Reuben V, 7 even goes so far as to say that the fallen angels reached to heaven.

2,19–20: כי נפלו...כי גבע. Schechter emends גם כן both times for כי but without valid reasons. The construction in this sentence depends on line 16 כי רבים, "One should not follow sinful thoughts and unchaste eyes (i. e. looks), for many[16] were led astray thereby . . . for their (the fallen angels') sons fell, and all flesh that was on dry land perished."

2,21: ולא שמרו את מצות עשיהם. This sentence is a reminiscence of Isa. 22:11 and is found almost literally in the Slavonic Enoch VII,3, where the fallen angels are described as "those who fell away from the Lord, did not hearken to the commandments of God and acted in accordance with their own will." Another reminiscence of these words of Isaiah is found on page 3, lines 6–7.

3,1: ומשפחה הם בה הם נכרתים. Schechter reads ומשפחותיהם,[17] which, however, is hardly acceptable since we cannot assume that our author would have said, "The families of the sons of Noah were destroyed," inasmuch as the whole of mankind is after all only the posterity of the sons of Noah. We should read משפחת חם "the family of Ham," the Canaanites,[18] who were destroyed, precisely because of their immoral behavior (Lev. 18:27–29: כי את כל התועבות האל עשו...ונכרתו), for which reason our author, in agreement with this biblical passage, asserts בה תעו...בה הם נכרתים, where בה refers to זנות in 2,16, as was noted above. Like our author, so also the Book of Jubilees says, XX, 4 and XXII, 21, of the destruction of Canaan, "The seed of Canaan will be destroyed from the land, for in the sin of Ham has Canaan trans-

---

[14] *Cf.* the legends about the posterity of the fallen angels in my *Legends of the Jews*, I, 125, 150, 160; III, 268, 343–346.

[15] *Cf.* my *Legends of the Jews*, III, 346.

[16] Perhaps in this passage רבים should be translated "great ones."

[17] [This Rabin has found in the manuscript.]

[18] [This is modified by Ginzberg on p. 167, n. 59.]

gressed;[19] and all his seed will be destroyed from the earth and all his descendants, and no descendant therefrom will be saved on the day of judgment."

3,2: ויע...הב בשמרו. Schechter reads ויעשה אוהב, which in my opinion, however, is hardly admissible on linguistic grounds. At most one might say ויעשהו לו אוהב, "and God made him His friend," as the Mishnah (Avoth I, 6) says עשה לך רב. If we are to retain the letters ויע we can only read ויעידהו אוהב, "And He praised him as His friend";[20] probably, however, we should simply read ויקראהו "And He called him His friend," in which case there would be a reference to Isa. 41:8 אברהם אהבי, just as the Book of Jubilees, XIX, 9 and XXXI, 19 and the Apocalypse of Abraham IX speak of Abraham the friend of God. No doubt the designation of Abraham as in Mekilta, Bo 18, p. 70, l. 3 also goes back to the biblical verse just cited.[21]

3,4: ובעלי ברית לעולם. Schechter translates, "And men of the Covenant for ever." But "men of the Covenant," without further specification gives no sense, and if we are not to emend the text more radically, we must at least explain ברית as an abbreviation of בריתו; the Patriarchs are men of his (God's) Covenant. However, I do not believe that לעולם is in place here, since we expect a parallel to לאל, and therefore the reading בעלי ברית עליון might commend itself. The appellation of God as אל עליון was, as we know, very popular in the period of the Hasmonaeans, who officially described themselves as priests לאל עליון.[22] Perhaps use has been made here of Ben Sira XLIV,20, where it is said of Abraham אשר שמר מצות עליון ובא בברית עמו.

3,5: במצרים...להיעץ על מצות אל. The view that Israel fell away from God in Egypt is represented in the Bible only by Ezekiel (20:7–8,36), and the Apocrypha take no note of the fact. The Haggadah,[23] on the other hand, makes no secret of Israel's sinfulness in Egypt, and it is instructive that our text agrees therein with the rabbinic

---

[19] In the Book of Jubilees the reason for the destruction of Canaan is different from that given in our text, which depends more closely on Lev. 18:29. On the licentiousness of the Canaanites see also Pesaḥim 113b.

[20] Cf. Job 29:11.

[21] This passage has escaped both Beer, *Leben Abrahams*, 431 and Malter, *Monatsschrift* 1907, 713.

[22] Cf. Rosh Hashanah 18b כהן לאל עליון, Assumpt. Mos. VI, 1, "sacerdotes summi Dei"; and Book of Jubilees XXXII, 1, "And Levi dreamed that they had ordained him and made him priest of the most high God." Even Ben Sira also uses it frequently, cf. 46:5a, 5c and 47:5a.

[23] Mekilta, Bo 5, p. 15, "Israel was given over to idolatry," and *loc. cit.* Cf. my *Legends* II, 362.

sources. The special reproach for the eating of blood that our author directs against Israel in Egypt similarly agrees with the assertion in Sifre Deut. 76, p. 141, שהיו שטופין בדם קדם מ'ת, "They were addicted to the eating of blood before the revelation of the Torah." In the view of Sifre, to be sure, the eating of blood was as a matter of fact not forbidden before the revelation of the Torah, whereas in the view of our author the eating of blood was forbidden earlier, probably since the days of Noah.[24]

3,6–7: ויכרת זכורם. The term זכורם contains more than the biblical passage, Num. 14:29, to which our passage alludes: Not improbably the latter, perhaps in agreement with an Aggadah, implies that only the men — זכורם — but not the women died in the wilderness.

3,7: במדבר להם בקדש עלו ורשו את רוחם. This undoubtedly corrupt text is probably to be emended as follows ויכרת זכורם במדבר דבר להם בקדש עלו ורשו ורעו את רוחם ולא שמעו וכו', "He spoke to them in Kadesh, saying, Go up and take possession of the land, but they pursued vanity, and did not hearken etc." The words דבר and ורעו have fallen out through homoioteleuta, since similar letters precede not only דבר but also ורעו for ע and ש are similar enough to be confused. It is also possible that the original text read עלו והקשו את ערפם (cf. Neh. 9:16–17) but graphically the text before us cannot easily be divined from such a prototype.

3,14: שבתות קדשו ומועדי כבודו. The expression is biblical (Neh. 9:14). It is also rabbinic; for example, in the liturgy for Friday evening, in the Qiddush, where the formula ושבת קדשך probably belongs to the oldest elements of this prayer, since it is found in all versions of the Qiddush. Schechter's note, "It is, however, not clear what is meant by the Holy Sabbath," is therefore quite incomprehensible to me.

3,16: פתח לפניהם וכו'. Of this verse it is first to be noted that already in Scripture (Isa. 41:18, אפתח על שפיים נהרות) פתח means "Create a source of water."[25] It is further to be noted that for רבים one should certainly read חיים to which the following clause ומואסיהם לא יחיה very clearly refers, and the whole passage therefore reads, "He caused a spring to arise, for them which they (the pious in Israel) dug as a source of living water." What the author means by this

---

[24] *Cf.* Gen. 9:4 and the Book of Jubilees VII, 28. In the view of the Halakah, the eating of blood is not forbidden to Noachides [i. e. gentiles]; *cf.* Tosefta Avodah Zarah, end.

[25] רועה רוח is biblical: Hos. 12:2, and there is no reason to question the transmitted text as do several modern scholars. It is another question whether the verb is connected with רעה "to pasture, graze" or רעה "to take pleasure."

statement is explained below, 6,4, הבאר היא התורה וחופריה הם שבי ישראל, God gave Israel the Torah — He brought into being a store of water — and the chosen among them made of this store of water a source of living water by rightly interpreting and teaching the Torah.

3,17: והם התגוללו. The verb התגולל in this passage, as in 8,5, is probably a denominative from גלל, "excrement," and has nothing to do with גלל, "to roll." One should therefore translate "And they besmirched themselves," just as in Ben Sira XII,14 ומתגולל בעונותיו, "and besmirches himself with his sins." Linguistically it is also possible to take התגולל as a by form of התגאל from גאל "to make unclean."

3,17: בפשע אנוש. Schechter translates "transgression of man" and refers to Prov. 29:6, which, however, is no parallel at all to our passage; since this reads בפשע איש רע, "because of the sin of a wicked man," which indeed gives good sense, whereas "the sin of man" is quite impossible. There is no doubt in my mind, however, that we must read not אֱנוֹשׁ but אָנוּשׁ; פשע אנוש is "incurable sin." According to biblical usage divine forgiveness is healing (Isa. 6:10, ושב ורפא and elsewhere), and a sin that is unforgivable is described as "incurable." But God, continues our author, was so gracious that He forgave even their unforgivable sins.

3,18: ברוי פלאו. The miswriting of ברוב as ברוי can easily be explained as a graphic error, especially as רוב is written with ו in our fragment (2,4), but from the standpoint of content the expression "abundance of wonders" fits very badly. One would expect ברוב חסדו, "abundance of His grace," or ברוב אהבתו, "abundance of His love," or a similar expression but not "wonders," for divine forgiveness כפר בעד עונם is the outpouring of His grace and mercifulness but not of His wonder-working. I conjecture that behind ברוי פלאו lies an expression like ברבבות אלפים or something similar. The author meant to say that God has forgiven their sins not once but tens of thousands of times.*

4,2: מעליהם. Schechter translates, "from them." There can be no doubt, however, that we must read מעלי הם corresponding to the words of Ezekiel מעלי המה in the cited passage (Ezek. 44:15). The only doubt is whether הם is merely another way of writing המה which is quite

---

*[It is now known that the manuscript reads ברזי פלאו, "by the mysteries of his grace," and numerous parallels in the Qumran scrolls confirm both the reading ברזי and the sense of "grace," or "graciousness" for פלא. This meaning, which Ginzberg rightly desiderated in the context, is borne by פלא not only in this sectarian literature but already in the Bible, namely in Isa. 9:5; 25:1; Ps. 88:11,13; 89:6 — See Kaplan Jubilee Volume, New York 1953, English Section, pp. 247–8. H.L.G.]

possible in view of the fragment's peculiar orthography, or our author really wrote הם since he also quotes not quite literally in other places.

4,2: הם שבי ישראל. Schechter decides in favor of the reading שבי "captivity" but it seems to me that the only correct reading is שבי "the penitent ones," "those who return to God." This view is particularly favored by 8,16, "And this is the law for the שבי of Israel, who turned from the way of the (sinful) people," where שבי is explained by "those who turned from etc.," which gives satisfactory sense only if we read שָׁבֵי and not שְׁבִי. In support of his interpretation, Schechter refers to 6,5, but in that passage שָׁבֵי gives at least as satisfactory sense as שְׁבִי. "Those who return to God" is only another expression for באי הברית, as the followers of this sect were called. At first they went astray like the rest of the people but were led back to God by "the teacher of righteousness" (1,11; 20,32), for which reason they are rightly called שבי ישראל.[26]

4,3: ובני צדוק הם בחירי ישראל. This sentence does not mean, as Schechter claims, that the Sons of Zadok are the chosen ones of Israel but that the chosen ones of Israel were designated by the prophet Ezekiel (44:15) as בני צדוק, "sons of righteousness." In genuinely midrashic style our author declares that the prophet includes an allusion to the history of the sect; by "priests" he means the fathers of the sect, those who returned to God; by "Levites," those who attached themselves[27] to the fathers of the sect; and by "the sons of Zadok,[28] the chosen ones of Israel who will arise at the end of times. After he has given this midrash on Ezekiel's words, he adds: this is the explanation of their names, namely of those of the כהנים לוים ובני צדוק mentioned by Ezekiel, in accordance with their history, the periods[29] of their existence, the reckoning of their suffering, and the years of their sojourn in a strange land. This sentence therefore, does not constitute an introduction to a history of the sect, as Schechter assumes, but refers back to what precedes, pointing out that the prophet includes an allusion to the history of the sect. On this view, a new sentence begins with ופרוש מעשיהם, "And this is a statement — literally, interpretation — of their deeds," which is followed by a brief characterization of the pious.

[26] Cf. also 20,7 שבי פשע.

[27] A word-play on לוים and נלוים; Esther 9:27 would lead one to expect והנלוים עליהם and not עמהם; however, נלוה is construed with עם in Ps. 83:9.

[28] The Midrash, Lev. R. I, p. 12, understands צדוק in this verse to be the high priest Aaron, taking צדוק in the sense of צדיק, "the righteous one," and a similar derash underlies our passage.

[29] On this meaning of קץ, see below on 6,10.

4,6: הקודש שונים . . . רשע. This sentence contains an antithesis to
1,19, and since, as has already been noted on that passage, the words
ויבחרו בטוב הצואר reproach the opponents of this sect with addiction
to sensual indulgence, הקודש שונים must conceal a eulogy for the ad·
herents of the sect, who, in contrast to their opponents, are dedicated
to spirituality and holiness. I therefore strike out the ש in שונים as a
dittography of the preceding ש, and read אוהבים,[30] "They love holiness"
as a suitable contrast to the words "They find pleasure in a well-fed
neck." [See author's emendation on p. 297 to שוגים]. The following אשר
כפר אל בעדם should accordingly be translated, "which God counted as
an atonement[31] for them"; meaning that a holy life,[32] a life according
to the Law, is considered an atonement for their earlier sins.

4,8–9: שלום הקץ השנים. For הקץ we must read קץ since הקץ השנים is
not Hebrew. The error is probably due to the presence of ובשלום הקץ
in the following line. Alternatively, we ought perhaps to read לשנים
for השנים corresponding to למספר השנים in the following line, in which
case הקץ is to be retained.

4,10–12: ובשלום הקץ . . . רחק החוק. For the understanding of this
very obscure sentence it should be noted that for our author Jerusalem
is and remains the holy city. The time of God's anger began with the
destruction of Jerusalem by Nebuchadnezzar (1,5), and the adversaries
are reproached for polluting the Sanctuary in Jerusalem (5,6). The
desecration of the Temple, of course, compelled the adherents of this
sect to withdraw from the Temple of Jerusalem so long as those in
control of it were men who did not observe the Law[33] and as the
situation then was, they did not expect an early improvement. Their
only hope was that the Messiah upon his appearance would again
enter Jerusalem and restore its Temple to its pristine holiness. Our
author therefore says: "And during the course of this period of years,[34]
no one shall attach himself to the house of Judah but every one shall
stand upon his rampart; the wall (of separation) has been erected,
the (Messianic) time is far off." In these words a warning is sounded
against any attempt to bring about a reconciliation with Jerusalem;
the separation of the sect from the mass of the people must continue
until the coming of the Messiah, which, however, still lies in the far

---

[30] אוים would be graphically closer to ונים but the kal אוה does not occur elsewhere.

[31] We should read either כֻּפַּר or כִּפֶּר in the sense of "count as an atonement."

[32] It is also possible that here, as often, הקודש is the Sanctuary and that it is
stated by the founders of the sect that they love the Sanctuary, while their opponents are indifferent and are concerned only about their own welfare.

[33] From the standpoint of our author, of course.

[34] On this meaning of קץ cf. below on 6,10.

distant future. The expression לעמוד איש עלי מצורו [35] is based on Hab. 2:1 נבנתה הגדר רחק החוק על משמרתי אעמודה ואתיצבה על מצור is a para- phrase of the words of Micah (7:11) ירחק חק . . . יום לבנות גדריך.

4,16: אשר הוא תפש בהם בישראל. Schechter correctly remarks that our author here uses Ezek. 14:4 למען תפש את בית ישראל but misled by the usual interpretation of this passage in Ezekiel, he believes it is necessary to translate, "by which Levi took Israel in their hearts." But there cannot possibly be any doubt about the meaning of תפש in our fragment, since it is clear from יתפש בזה in line 18 and from הם נתפשים in line 20 that תפש can only mean the trapping of sinners by Satan. Accordingly Belial is also the antecedent of הוא, and it is he who traps the house of Israel (for בישראל[36] read בית ישראל) by means of his three nets. In Ezekiel too, according to the view of the Talmud (Qiddushin 40a and parallels), one should interpret, "that I may seize the house of Israel, that is, hold it responsible, for that which they have in their thoughts (heart)." It makes no difference whether this Tal- mudic interpretation is the correct one or not.[37] That the ancients understood this verse of Ezekiel in this way adequately explains why our author quotes it here.

4,16: ויתנם פניהם. Schechter translates, "and directed their faces to the three kinds of righteousness," but even if we read ויתן for ויתנם this interpretation is still beset by difficulties. In the first place it ought to read ויתן פ' אל של' , as in Gen. 30:40, and not לשלושת; and furthermore the change of subject is very peculiar, since, as has already been remarked, אשר הוא can refer only to בליעל while only לוי can be the subject of ויתנם. I therefore read and translate, "The three nets by means of which he (Belial) trapped the house of Israel so that they turned away from the three chief virtues." What the three virtues are is not stated. Perhaps our author was thinking of the saying of Simon the Just in Avoth I, 2, "The world rests upon three things, upon the Torah, worship and good deeds." It is not impossible, however, that the teaching of the three virtues is a Jewish transformation of the four virtues posited by Plato for his ideal state, *sophia*, *andreia*, *sophrosyne* and *dekaiosyne*. The inclusion of bravery (*andreia*),* rep-

---

[35] I read מצורו and not מצודו as Schechter does; ד and ר are hardly to be dis- tinguished in the ms. of this fragment. Perhaps, however, the manuscript really has מצודו but as a result of contamination by מצודות in line 15.

[36] The original was probably בית ישראל — ב' ישראל which was then contracted by the copyists into one word.

[37] Ehrlich, מקרא כפשוטו, *ad loc.*, explains this verse as the Talmud does, without, however, citing the Talmud.

* Ginzberg inadvertently wrote *dekaiosyne* for *andreia*. — [R.M.

resented by Plato's warrior-class, had no justification from the Jewish point of view, for which reason only three virtues were named instead of the original four.

4,17: ‏הראשונה היא הזנות . . . המקדש‎. The three cardinal sins are also spoken of in rabbinic literature, for example in Mekilta, Yitro 1, p. 189, ‏והיא אומרת רבש"ע בג' דברים חטאתי‎,[38] "And she (Rahab) said, I committed three sins." The three sins are not specified,[39] but we shall probably not err in claiming that they are idolatry, immorality and murder — sins which according to Jewish teaching no one may commit even at the risk of his own life (Sanhedrin 74a *et al.*), and may therefore be described as cardinal sins. This view is supported by the Baraita in Arakhin 15b, where the ‏ג' עבירות‎ are explicitly designated as the three aforementioned, and similarly Tosefta, Peah I, 2. Instructive for this problem is also Sifra on Lev. 16:16 where "the uncleannesses of the people of Israel" are identified as these three vices.[40] One is therefore led to surmise that for his purposes our author was not able to list the usual three cardinal sins because he could not very well reproach his adversaries with idolatry and murder, and that he therefore substituted dishonestly acquired property[41] and the pollution of the Temple for idolatry and murder.

4,19: ‏הצו הוא . . . הטף יטיפון‎. Our author explains the obscure ‏צו‎ in Hos. 5:11 as ‏מטיף‎, "The speaker," whom he describes more fully as the speaker to whom the people call out, "Speak!," in contrast to the true teacher and prophet, to whom the people will not listen, of whom it is said in Mic. 2:6, ‏אל תטיפו יטיפון‎. This ‏מטיף‎, the leader of the opponents of our sect, is probably identical with the ‏איש הלצון‎ mentioned in 1,14, and this same person is here described not without irony as a favorite of the people because he speaks to them only about that which they are eager to hear. This sentence reads literally, "The

[38] *Cf.* the parallel passage, Mekilta R. Sim. Epst., p. 128, where the gloss found in the editions but not in the Oxford manuscript of the Mekilta, ‏בנדה חלה הדלקת הנר‎ is rightly missing.

[39] The idolatress Rahab who was, besides, a ‏זונה‎ up to the time of her conversion, naturally confessed to idolatry and immorality. As regards murder, perhaps that is to be understood as abortion, which according to the Talmudic theory is accounted to pagans as murder. *Cf.* Sanhedrin 57b and Geiger, *Urschrift* 437 f.

[40] *Cf.* also Tosefta, Nedarim XI, 15, ‏ע"ז ומגלה ע' ושופכי דמים‎; Mekilta Yitro, Baḥodesh 2, p. 207, ‏ושמרני . . . מע"ז‎; ‏הם חייבין על ע"ז ועל ג"ע ועל שפיכת דמים‎; Gen. R. 70, p. 801, where, ‏ג' עבירות נ"ע שפיכות דמים וחלול ש‎ and Giṭṭin 6b end, ‏מגלוי עריות משפיכות דמים‎ however, with R. Ḥananel (see Tosaphot *ad loc.*) instead of ‏חלול שבת‎ we should probably read ‏חלול השם‎ which is a variety of ‏עבודה זרה‎.

[41] There is an empty space in the ms. after ‏ההון‎ which, in the light of 6,15 is to be filled with something like ‏הרשעה‎ or ‏רשע‎.

commander, this is the speaker of whom it is said, they say [to him],
'Speak!' "

4,20–21: לקחת שתי נשים בחייהם. These words contain a paraphrase
of the biblical prohibition (Lev. 18:18), ואשה אל אחותה לא תקח לצרר
לגלות ערותה עליה בחייה, where according to our author the first three
words are to be translated "a wife together with an other one," which
is linguistically quite possible and indeed occurs in Scripture several
times with this meaning, e. g. Exod. 26:5, 6, 17. We can also account
for the fact that the adherents of this sect rejected the traditional
interpretation of this verse as given in the Mishnah (Yevamoth I, 1),
in the Septuagint and in Philo (*De Spec. Leg.* III, V, 27–28). As our author explicitly states (5,9), the forbidden degrees of marriage relation,
although the relevant passages of Scripture are addressed only to
men, apply to women as well, and as, for example, a man is forbidden
to marry his aunt, so also a woman is forbidden to take her uncle as
husband. And since Scripture (Lev. 18:16) forbids a man to marry the
wife of his brother even after the latter's death[42] it follows, according
to the sect's principle which has just been expounded, that neither may
a woman marry her brother-in-law even after her sister's death.
Therefore the words אשה אל אחותה וגו' could not be taken literally,[43]
since Scripture expressly qualifies this prohibition of marriage by
בחייה, "while the first (wife) is still alive," whereas marriage with a
brother-in-law is permanently forbidden. The simplest way of resolving
the difficulty was to take אשה אל אחותה in the sense of "a wife together
with an other one." The Karaites, who maintain the same principle
as our author with reference to marriages between relatives, similarly
declare that אשה אל אחותה in Lev. 18:18 is not to be taken literally,[44]
and the various ways in which the verse has been interpreted by
Karaites include the view that it is directed against polygamy. The
Karaites, to be sure, assert that the biblical prohibition is not an absolute one but, as the addition of the word לצרר shows, applies only when

---

[42] Among the Jewish sects there is no difference of opinion as to the fact that
the marriage-relations prohibited in Lev. 18:11–17 are in force after the death of
the husband too, which certainly accords with the true intention of Scripture.

[43] Aside from this, verse 18 would be quite superfluous as well, since it is contained in 16. *Cf.* the passage from Anan's law book, cited below.

[44] The first Karaite who is known to have interpreted this biblical prohibition
differently from the Rabbanites is Anan. *Cf.* the passage in his law book in Harkavy,
Studien und Mittheilungen, VIII, 105, 109. Closely related to Anan's view is that
of Hadassi, אשכל 118b–118d, a fact which escaped Harkavy, and furthermore
Anan's view was accepted by Qirqisani (Harkavy, *op. cit.*, 129) and Daniel Alkumsi
(*op. cit.*, 191). Other Karaites, however, rejected Anan's as well as the Rabbanite
interpretation of אשה אל אחותה, as can be seen from Aaron of Nicomedia (*loc. cit.*).

the second marriage is injurious to the first one, that is, when it is the husband's intention to evade his marital duties toward his first wife; otherwise, however, polygamy would be permitted. The one who expresses himself most clearly on this question is Aaron ben Elijah of Nicomedia in his גן עדן[45] (Nashim IX, 146d), whose words I cite herewith: שהכתוב ראה לאסור לשאת איש שתים נשים בעת שיהיה שם צרור ואין הכוונה שאם לא תהיה רוצה הראשונה יהיה אסור לשאת השניה שכבר הכשיר הכתוב נשיאת שתי נשים... אלא על מנת שלא יגרע שאר כסות ועונה אבל אם לא ימנע ממנה חקה... אין זה צרור... ובעבור שהיו האסורים הראשונים בחיים ובמות על כן התנה הנה בחיים... אבל אם תהיה גרושה אין מניעת חוק ממנה לא יהיה שם אסור.

From this statement it follows very clearly that there is no question in our text of prohibiting divorce, as Schechter claims, but that our author merely went a step further than the Karaites and forbade polygamy, so long as the first wife was alive, even if her rights were not impaired. Naturally, however, he is permitted to marry a second woman after he is divorced from his first wife, since he thus has only one wife. The addition of בחייהם (=בחייהן) in our text is borrowed from Scripture and means only that this prohibition of marriage differs from all the others in so far as it is in force only so long as a man lives with his first wife in marital union. Thus Anan remarks (*op. cit.* 106) explicitly... וקא אמא עליה בחייה בהדה הוא דאסירא ליה למנסבה אבל אי מגריש שרי ליה למנסב בת אחתה וכו'.

5,3–4: מיום מות אלעזר... אשר עבדו את העשתרות. Schechter translates, "Eleazar and Joshua and the Elders who worshipped Ashtaroth," and refers to Judg. 2:13; but there (7–13) just the opposite is asserted, namely that the worship of the Ashtaroth began only after Joshua, Eleazar and the Elders had passed away. It would be highly improbable in itself that our author regarded Israel's apostasy from the Torah as having begun with Joshua and Eleazar, but this assumption becomes an impossibility when the author refers to a biblical passage that contains the very opposite of this assertion. Furthermore, if Joshua and his generation had been idolaters, why מיום מות, "since their death," and not earlier? Accordingly there is no doubt that the antecedent of אשר is not אלעזר ויושע[46] but the preceding בישראל and the passage reads, "for (the holy ark) was not opened in Israel from the death of Joshua, Eleazar and the Elders because they (the Israelites)

---

[45] Also in his כתר תורה, *ad loc.*, he briefly mentions it.

[46] According to Samaritan legend Eleazar died after Joshua (*cf.* the Samaritan book of Joshua XL); however, the mention of Eleazar before Joshua in our text is no proof that our author placed the death of Eleazar before that of Joshua.

worshipped the Ashtaroth" and this agrees with the passage cited from Judges. To be sure there is no reference in this passage to the Torah's being forgotten but only to the worship of idols after the death of Joshua and the Elders, but our author seems to have combined this passage with II Kings 23:22 and Neh. 8:17, where it is said of the festivals of Passover and Sukkoth respectively that they were not observed during the period of the Judges and Kings except for Joshua's time. On the basis of these biblical passages our author asserts that after the death of Joshua not only did the worship of idols begin but also the Torah fell into oblivion.

5,4: ויטמון נגלה עד עמוד צדוק. Schechter's proposal to read מגלה for נגלה is hardly acceptable since Scripture is never called מגלה, "scroll," and our author himself a little earlier has spoken of ספר התורה. His second suggestion to add לא before נגלה, is also somewhat awkward since, though there are many scribal errors to be found in our fragment, no words have fallen out, so far as I can discover, except as a result of homoioteleuta, which is not, however, the case here. We have therefore to read, והטמון נגלה עת עמוד צדוק, "and that which was hidden (the Torah) was revealed at the time when Zadok arose." That these words refer to the discovery of the Torah in the time of Josiah (II Kings c. 22) there can be no doubt, especially if one bears in mind what was said in the preceding note in our author's view of the neglect into which the Torah fell during the period of the Kings. It is very strange, to be sure, that here the discovery of the Torah is ascribed to Zadok whereas in Scripture (II Kings 22 and II Chron. 34) it is Hilkiah who found the book of the Torah. It is to be noted, however, that this Hilkiah was a grandson of Zadok according to I Chron. 5:38–39, and the assumption is probably justified that our author spoke of this high priest as בן צדוק[47] and that later בן fell out or was purposely omitted by the copyists because צדוק indeed was known to them but not בן צדוק.

5,5: ויעלו מעשי דויד מלבד דם אוריה. Schechter reads ויעלימו and translates, "But they concealed the deeds of David save only the

[47] That he was not, however, called בן שלום after his father is not surprising since the name of the grandfather is given instead of the father's in some other passages in Scripture. Cf., for example, I Sam. 9:1 where Kish appears as the son of Abiel although he was properly his grandson, and similarly Neh. 12:23 where the high priest יוחנן appears as בן אלישב although he was his grandson; cf. Graetz, Geschichte II, part 2, 393. Cf. also Naḥmanides on Exod. 2:16 and Ibn Ezra on Num. 10:29, who adduce many instances of this usage from Scripture. For similar designation in the Middle Ages we may call to mind the famous Masoretes, Ben Asher and Ben Naphtali; the former's name was Aaron ben Moses ben Asher, the latter's Moses ben David ben Naphtali, cf. Baer-Strack, דקדוקי הטע' x–xi.

blood of Uriah." I believe, however, that for more than one reason this interpretation, according to which our author expels David from the community of the pious, is quite untenable. First of all, it is quite impossible to tell at whom the reproach that they kept secret the deeds of David is aimed; is it to the authors of the books of Samuel, Kings, and Chronicles? Can it be that these books are not regarded by our author as holy that he reproaches their authors with falsifying history? It surely requires no proof that these books were considered canonical by our author, as his use of them shows. But even if we grant that he did not take literally the accounts of David or put no faith in them, how did he come to cite in support of his statement about the sinful career of David words of Scripture that state just the opposite, for it is admitted by Schechter also that the sentence ויעלו . . . אוריה is based on I Kings 15:5. Furthermore, it would be more than out of place for our author to pronounce David's marriage with many women sinful and then to add that this sin is hushed up by those who wrote the biblical books, when the only source for David's polygamy are just those books. From all this it follows that our passage finds no fault with David but, on the contrary, the statement that David "did not read the Torah" is supplemented with another to the effect that otherwise his deeds were good and pious, aside from shedding Uriah's blood. And this is in keeping with the words of Scripture in I Kings 15:5. We should therefore translate וַיַּעֲלוּ, "And the deeds of David were excellent."[48] Alternatively we might read ויעלימו with Schechter, but in that case מעשי would have to be taken as the subject, and the sense would be that these (sinful) deeds of David were committed in ignorance,[49] because, as was stressed above by our author, David was not familiar with the contents of the Torah.

5,6: ויעזבם לו אל. Schechter: "And God abandoned them to him." This, however, gives absolutely no sense. One should therefore translate, "And God forgave him them." עזב has already the sense of "to remit a debt" in the Bible, Neh. 5:10 נעזבה נא וגו'. In our passage it refers either to דם אוריה (where דם probably stands for דמי hence the plural ויעזבם) or to מעשי דויד the sins that David committed unwittingly; cf. the preceding note.

5,7: הרואה את דם זובה. What halakic controversy is alluded to here one cannot say with certainty, but it is surely not to the dispute

---

[48] Biblical נעלה, "to be exalted," Ps. 47:10; 97:9; mishnaic and especially frequent מעולה, "excellent."

[49] נעלם, the biblical as well as mishnaic expression for a sin committed in ignorance.

between the "Pharisees and Samaritans"[50] concerning דם טהור, for in
that case the text here would read either הרואה את דם לדתה (so already the
Schools of Shammai and Hillel, Niddah IV, 3) or דם נדתה (Lev. 12:2).[51]
The Halakah involved here concerns a זבה and not a נדה or יולדת and
is mentioned in the Mishnah, Horayoth I, 3. We read of a dispute
between Pharisees and Sadducees over הלכות זבה the details of which
are not clear[52] (cf. the Talmudic discussion thereon). But this much is
clear: that the Pharisees adopted the stricter view. Accordingly, the
standpoint of our author agrees with that of the Pharisees, since he
also reproaches his opponents for declaring דם זבה to be clean.

5,7: ולוקחים איש את בת אחיהם. As Schechter has already noted, our
author agrees with the Samaritans and Karaites, who declare a marriage between uncle and niece incestuous. The view of Estori Parchi[53]
that in this these two sects follow Arab custom is refuted by our own
text, from which we see that we have to do with an old Halakah which
is at variance with that of the Pharisees. A further proof of the antiquity
of this halakah is the fact that the Falashas also forbid such marriages.
Thus the Pseudepigraph of Baruch published by Halevy,[54] fol. 120r,
tells of a section of Hell in which those who have had intercourse with
their nieces abide. Indeed it can be shown from Talmudic sources that
there existed an opposition to these marriages, for only in this way
can we explain why the Talmud (Yevamoth 62b, end) commends
precisely such marriages as acts especially pleasing to God.[55] The
Pharisees would probably never have carried their more lenient decisions through if they had simply and solely declared such marriages
permissible; for few would have been found ready to conclude marriages that were regarded by many as incestuous. Only when the
Pharisees stamped such marriages as an act pleasing to God did the
opposition to them disappear. On the one hand, an act commended by
the Pharisees as pleasing to God, on the other hand an heretical view
that held this act to be a sin — in such a case, the majority of Jews

[50] On this dispute see below in Section IV.

[51] Cf. Aaron ben Elijah of Nicomedia in his כתר תורה, Lev., loc. cit.: על כן אמר
שלא תקרא זבה ולא תתחייב ספירה.

[52] The interpretation of the Talmud (Horayoth 4a) can hardly be made to fit
the plain literal meaning of the Mishnah.

[53] כפתור ופרח, V end; Zunz, Ges. Schrift., II, 303; Steinschneider, Polemische
Lit. 398, Note 1, and Wreschner, Samar. Tradit., XIV.

[54] Appearing as an Appendix to Teezaza Sanbat, Paris, 1902.

[55] Schorr, החלוץ VII,34 believes that Persian influence is to be found here, but
in the Persian sources cited by him, marriages of kin are recommended that the
Jews regard as prohibited. On the problem whether the Talmud speaks only of
בת אחותו or also of בת אחיו, cf. Tosafoth ad loc., and Maimonides, Issure Bi'ah, II, 14.

would not find it hard to decide.[56] An opposition to these marriages of
kin seems to have existed even in Pharisaic circles. At any rate such
an assumption makes it possible to explain the following story from
the life of R. Eliezer ben Hyrcanus most simply. R. Eliezer's mother,
we are told (TP Yevamoth XIII, 13c), strongly urged him to marry his
niece (his sister's daughter), whereupon R. Eliezer urged this niece
several times to get married. Only when she said to him, "Behold,
I am thy slave to wash the feet of the servants of my lord" (I Sam.
25:41), could R. Eliezer make up his mind to marry his niece; whom,
however, he only "recognized" when she showed signs of puberty.
The Talmud seems to ascribe R. Eliezer's hesitation to the minority
of his niece,[57] but we should then be unable to understand how R.
Eliezer could advise her to get married if he opposed marriages with
minors. R. Eliezer's attitude can be explained most simply by assuming
that he, who was often the exponent of the old halakah, in this case
too was following the view that held marriage between uncle and
niece to be prohibited; for that reason he did not at first wish to yield
to the urging of his mother, and so advised his niece to look for another
man. When, however, he saw that his niece also shared his mother's
wish, he thought it advisable to give up his objections to such a
marriage and thereupon married his niece, although she was not
sexually mature, but abstained from all marital intercourse until she
was of age.[58] It is highly instructive for the attitude of official Judaism
on this question that even in the Middle Ages voices were raised
against such marriages. R. Judah the Pious of Regensberg (died
1217 C. E.) forbids them in his ספר חסידים, ed. Wistinetzki, p. 282, and
also in his Testament,[59] which is probably to be attributed to Karaite
influence, since R. Judah and his circle also betray Karaite influence[60]
in other ways.

[56] Of such rabbinic institutions, which owe their existence to the Sadducees,
there are quite a few; cf., for example, Ḥagigah 2:4 and Menaḥoth 10:3.

[57] This, to be sure, is not expressly stated in the Talmud but the context in
which this anecdote is mentioned in the Talmud speaks clearly for the interpretation given by the commentators.

[58] Although the Halakah recognizes the father's right to marry off his minor
daughter, there are nevertheless some strong words against marriages of minors in
the Talmud; cf., for example, Niddah 13b, Qiddushin 41a.

[59] This צואת ר"י החסיד has several times been published separately and also as
an appendix to his ספר החסידים.

[60] Karaite influence is revealed in the statement, ספר החסידים 283, that marriage
with a sister-in-law brings misfortune. The Karaites forbid it outright, as was noted
above on 4,20. Interesting also is the remark, ספר החסידים 334, that the prayer-

5,11: וגם את רוח קדשיהם טמאו. With this sentence a new section begins. What preceded was directed exclusively at those who pervert and misinterpret the Law. What follows is addressed to those "who with blasphemous tongue open their mouth against the laws of the covenant, saying 'They are not right.' " Hence the admonition to keep far from these sinners, who do not recognize the authority of the Law. Interesting is the expression "They polluted their holy spirit" or literally "the spirit of their holiness"; according to rabbinic usage רוח הקדש, "the holy spirit," is a divine gift to those especially chosen, like prophets and other holy men, whereas our author speaks of a holy spirit that is present in every person and, as remarked above on 2,12, designates thus the moral force of man. A related concept is found in the Baraita in Shabbath 152b and Eccles. R. XII, 7: והרוח תשוב אל האלהים אשר נתנה לו כמו שנתנה לך בטהרה אף אתה בטהרה, " 'and the spirit returns to God who gave it' (Eccles. 12:7); give it back to God in the same condition in which He gave it to thee; as He gave it to thee pure, so give it back to Him pure." There it is further explained that the souls of the godless, because they are stained and polluted, cannot return to God but are tossed back and forth by the angels. Also in an ancient prayer that is already cited in Berakhoth 60b, and still forms part of the daily liturgy today, it is said: אלהי נשמה שנתת בי טהורה היא, "O God, the soul that thou gavest me is a pure one." Here too the thought is expressed[61] that the human soul came from God holy and pure and that it is man's duty to keep it in holiness and purity. In another Talmudic passage it is said (Berakhoth 10a), מה הקדוש ב"ה טהור אף הנשמה טהורה, "As God is pure, so too the soul is pure." It is further to be noted that the theological concept of purity, טהרה,[62] is closely related to that of holiness, קדושה, so that in Talmudic passages one can be used in place of the other. But since in later usage רוח הקדש assumed a quite special meaning, one avoided speaking of the human soul, נשמה, or spirit, רוח, in connection with קדש, whereas our author, in agreement with Ps. 51:13, speaks of the holy spirit of every man.[63] I conjecture, moreover, that there is some connection or other between the words of our fragment concerning "The blasphemers who defile the

houses of the Karaites should be treated with respect; cf. further Epstein in the Hebrew periodical החוקר II, 1–11, 38–48. Naturally it was only an unconscious opposition to such marriages, since a man like R. Judah was wholly attached to rabbinic Judaism.

[61] Cf. the fuller interpretation of this passage in my Geonica II, 109.

[62] Cf. Mishnah, Soṭah, end, and the parallel passages in Bavli and Yerushalmi.

[63] Cf. the expression רוח טהרה in a saying of R. Akiva, Sanhedrin 65b.

holy spirit"[64] and Mark 3:29, where it is said, "But he who blasphemes the holy spirit shall never be forgiven."

5,15: כהר ביתו יאשם כי אם נלחץ. For these meaningless words read: עכר ביתו ואשם כי אין לחש, "he brings misfortune upon his house and burdens himself with guilt;[65] for conjuring avails nothing against it." Sinners are described in the preceding verse as harmful serpents, צפעונים, an expression which our author probably owes to Jer. 8:17, from which he has also borrowed the addition, אין להם לחש or אין לחש. It is also possible that our author substituted גם אם נלחשו for the words of the prophet, since he also likes to make slight changes elsewhere in phrases borrowed from the Bible.[65]

5,18: שר אורים. Schechter reads שר הפנים. I believe, however, that if the text is to be changed, שר העירים, "Prince of the Watchers," is much closer to the transmitted text both graphically and phonetically. The term עירים for angels occurs elsewhere in our fragments (2,18); and as the opponent of Belial, the leader of the Satans and demons, we should expect the prince of the angels, presumably Michael, who, with his colleague Gabriel is described in Rabbinic literature[66] as מלכיהון דמלאכיא, "the princes of the angels." It is very doubtful, however, whether any emendation at all is needed here, since שר האורים can very well be the name of an archangel, for example, of the one called אוריאל in rabbinic and pseudepigraphic literature. In rabbinic angelology, to be sure, Uriel is the fourth of the four great archangels, who always appear in this order: Michael, Gabriel, Raphael and Uriel. In the pseudepigraphic literature (Enoch XX, 1), however, Uriel is the first of the angels and their prince, so that the name שר האורים, "prince of the fiery beings," would be very suitable for him. Furthermore, it was this angel who was sent by God to save Noah from the flood (Enoch X, 1), so that the task that our author assigns to the שר האורים, namely to assist Moses and Aaron in their fight against Belial and his envoys, is exactly the same as Uriel's. What is more, in IV Esdras IV, 1 Uriel is the angel of the revelations of guardian-angel.[67]

---

[64] In Isa. 63:11 רוח הקדש is more like the later usage.

[65] [But see Rabin — H.L.G.].

[66] Cf. Pesiqta, ed. Buber 45b [ed. Mandelbaum, p. 84], and parallel passages.

[67] Blau, Jewish Encyclopedia, s. v. "Uriel," refers to Num. Rabbah II, 10, according to which Uriel would be the angel who transmitted the Torah to Israel; however, in spite of Machiri, Isaiah 73, which agrees with the reading of the editions, this passage is probably to be read ומכפר עליהם, not ומכפר עליו, "through him," as Blau translates. It is therefore very doubtful that the interpretation of the name in the Midrash has anything to do with the functions of the angel. Zohar II, 78a and 78b, states that Uriel rules in the month of Sivan, and for that reason the revelation of the Torah took place in that month. In another passage of the Zohar, III, 32b–33a, Uriel is identified instead with the heavenly fire that appears on the altar.

In general this arch-angel seems to have played a much more important
role in the older angelology than in the later. So, for example, in the
Vita Adae,[68] XLVIII, he functions together with Michael as one of the
two angels whom God sent down to bury Adam and Abel. Significant
for the high place of Uriel in the old angelology are the following words
which Origen cites (Commentary on John, II, 25, ed. Lommatosh
I, 147) from the Prayer of Joseph, a pseudepigraph held in high regard
by the Jews of his time: "My name," said Uriel to Jacob, "has precedence over thine and all other angels." Jacob, to be sure, it is said in
this source, rebuked Uriel by making clear to him that he, Jacob, was
the prince of angels, while Uriel was eighth in rank below him. But
Uriel's assertion reflects the old concept that this archangel was the
prince of all heavenly beings, שר האורים.

Furthermore it is highly probable that the archangel Suriel סוריאל
is none other than Uriel, אוריאל (שר =) סר having quite according to
rules become סוריאל. As for the position of Suriel, he is described in
the Talmud Berakhoth 58a, as שר הפנים, "angel of the presence," but a
little further on the same is said of the angel of death that was previously said of Suriel. We shall not err, therefore, if we identify Suriel
with the angel of death; this identification becomes a certainty when
we consider that among both the Mandaeans and the Falashas
(Faitlovich, *Mota Muse*, Paris, 1906, p. 13) the angel of death is called
Suriel. In the book of Enoch, however, (*loc. cit.*) Uriel is described as
the angel who is set over Tartarus; and even though the angel of death
is not identical with the angel of the realm of the dead, the identification of the two functions, which are similar, can easily be understood.
We probably have a reminiscence of Uriel as the angel of death in
Midrash Aggadah, ed. Buber I, 132, where Uriel is described as the angel who sought to swallow Moses in the form of a serpent. In view of all
this, it is not unlikely that in שר האורים we have merely another name
for the archangel Uriel. If, however one prefers to read שר העירים,
one should probably understand it to refer to Michael, since, according
to the view of the Midrash (Exod. Rabbah II, 5), he was the angel of
God who spoke to Moses out of the burning bush.

6,1: וגם במשיחו הקודש. One must not infer from these words that
"the holy Messiah" was a contemporary of these seducers of Israel.
"They preached apostasy from his holy anointed one"[69] means only

---

[68] In the parallel text in the Greek Apocal. of Moses, XLIII, on the other hand,
it is three angels who bury the corpse of Eve, probably Michael, Gabriel and Uriel,
as in the rabbinic legend of the death of Moses. *Cf.* Deut. Rabbah, end, where
the role of Uriel is assigned to זגנזאל.

[69] The verb דברו סרה.

that the opponents of this sect in their Messianic doctrine held views that our author regarded as apostasy from the Messiah.

6,3: וישמעם. Schechter wavers between the readings וישמיעם and וישביעם but the text requires no emendation; one should read וישמעם, "and he summoned them," like וישמע in I Sam. 15:4 and 23:8, and Semaḥoth I, 6. Similarly, the Palestinian texts of Sheqalim I, 1 have מְשַׁמְּעִין עַל הַשְּׁקלים and not משמיעין, which occurs only in the Babylonian texts.[70]

6,6: כי דרשוהו ולא הושבה פארתם בפי אחד. The text is not so incurably corrupt as is believed, and requires no very radical emendation to give satisfactory sense. First of all, Isa. 20:5, ויבושו מכוש . . . תפארתם, shows that instead of הושבה פארתם, which is quite meaningless, we must read הובשה תפארתם. They are called princes, says our author in his haggadic interpretation of Num. 21:18, because the object of their pride did not become a cause of shame to them. And if, furthermore, we take into account the peculiar orthography of our fragment, we shall, even if we do not prefer to read בפה, probably have no objection to taking בפי אחד as an aramaizing writing of בפה אחד, in which case the meaning of the clause would be, "They were named princes because the object of their pride did not become a cause of shame, and that was because they sought him (God) with one accord." The phrase דרשוהו בפי[ה] אחד is in essence identical with בלב שלם דרשוהו (1,10), as our author describes the efforts of the fathers of the sect. A parenthetic clause like ולא הובשה תפארתם would hardly be permissible in a simple prose, but in the elevated style of our text its insertion is not surprising.

6,7: והמחוקק הוא . . . כלי למעשהו. An interesting parallel to this characterization of the lawgiver as the vessel which God uses to accomplish His work is the description of Moses in the opening passage of the Mekilta[72] as כלי לדברות, the vessel for the words of God. In Zohar II, 218 the general rule is established that "The pious are called the vessels of God."

6,10: להתהלך במה. There is no reason for changing במה to בהם, since במה (=במו) is quite in place here.[73]

---

[70] [The manuscript reading is now known to be וישמעם. — H.L.G.]

[71] Cf. Ps. 89:18 where God appears as the pride תפארת of Israel.

[72] For כלל לדברות of the editions we must read כלי with Midrash Haggadol on Lev. 1:1. Cf. Lewy, Ein Wort über die Mechilta d. R. Simon, 38n. Probably in the Hebrew original of the Apocal. of Moses XVI, end, there similarly stood היה כלי לדבר.

[73] [מה for masoretic ם is now familiar from some manuscripts of the Qumran library which includes copies of the work which is the subject of Ginzberg's study. Cf. below the bracketed addition to n. 152. — H.L.G.]

6,10: ‏בכל קץ הרשיע וזולתם לא ישיגו‎. In order to understand this sentence correctly we must be clear about the meaning of ‏קץ‎ in our fragment. It occurs in 1,5 ‏שלים הקץ‎; 4,8–10 ‏ובקץ חרון‎; 4,5 ‏וקץ מעמדם‎; ‏לקץ הרשע 6,14;[74]קץ הרשיע 6,10‎; ‏ובקץ חרבן הארץ‎; 5,20 ‏ובשלום הקץ‎; 7,21 ‏בקץ הפקדה 19,10‎; ‏בכל קץ הרשע 15,7‎; ‏בקץ הרשעה 12,23‎; ‏בקץ הפקודה הראשון‎; ‏בקץ מעל ישראל 20,23‎; ‏ובקץ ההוא 20,15‎. Although the reading ‏הרשעה‎ is found only once over against ‏הרשע‎, which occurs in three passages, I nevertheless consider ‏הרשעה‎ to be the correct form, whereas ‏הרשע‎ derives from the orthographic peculiarity of our fragment, which has already been mentioned several times, of not expressing the feminine ‏ה‎ in writing. That ‏קץ הרשע‎ or ‏קץ הרשעה‎, however, does not mean something like "the end of wickedness" is clearly shown by all the four passages in which the expression occurs. "The laws that the lawgiver enacted to be observed during the whole ‏קץ הרשע‎ (6,10)" gives sense only if "the period of wickedness" is meant thereby, since we cannot assume that the laws are to be observed only "at the end of wickedness." "The period of wickedness," on the other hand, is a term for ‏עולם הזה‎ in contrast to ‏ימות המשיח‎. One is to to keep the prescriptions of the Torah in accordance with the interpretation of the True Teacher during "the whole period of wickedness," that is, until the coming of the Messiah. In one place (12,23) "the period of wickedness" is even explicitly contrasted with the Messianic period, ‏בקץ הרשעה עד עמוד‎ ‏משיח אהרן וישראל‎. The contrast between this sinful world, which is ruled by the evil power of Satan,[75] and the future world, in which only goodness and purity will rule, is the central idea of apocalyptic literature, so that no further argument is necessary for making clear what our author understands by ‏קץ הרשעה‎. We may, however, make the added observation that both ‏קץ‎ in the meaning of "period" and ‏רשעה‎ as a designation of the pre-Messianic period are found elsewhere in Rabbinic literature. The plural ‏קצים‎ means "periods" in many passages of the Babylonian and Palestinian Talmuds, cf. e. g., TP Bikkurim III, 65c, ‏שהוא אחד לקיצים‎, "it (the bringing of first-fruits to the Temple) is only in season once"; Berakhoth I, 3a, ‏ואתי לקיצים‎, "Who comes from time to time"; Gen. Rabbah LXVIII,10, p. 781 reading ‏קצים‎ with Midrash Hag. Schecht. 447 instead of ‏פרקים‎ as in the edi-

---

[74] The ‏י‎ indicates the reading ‏הרשעה‎ which can also be written ‏הרישעה‎ and then through error became ‏הרשיע[ה]‎, but cf. the note on 8,17.

[75] In view of this attitude, which prevails in the apocryphal literature, one might be inclined to take ‏קץ הרשע‎ to mean "the period of the wicked one," especially as Samael (=Satan) is often called ‏סמאל הרשע‎. However, ‏רשע‎ never occurs alone as a designation of Satan, and furthermore the term which our author uses for Satan is ‏בליעל‎.

tions. Especially instructive for this meaning of קצים is Avodah Zarah
61b, ממונה הבא לקצין, "an official who appears at certain times," where
קצים is used in exactly the same sense as by our author. As for further
references to this world as the period of wickedness, we may cite the
ancient prayer ובכן תן פחדך, which prays for the coming of the Messiah
so that evil may disappear from the world, וכל הרשעה כלה כעשן תכלה.
As in קץ הרשע, the meaning "period" is certainly present. "The completion of the period of these years" gives satisfactory sense but not
"the completion of the end of these years." We shall therefore not go
astray if we further assign to קץ the sense of "period" in passages
where the sense of "end" would also be suitable.

6,11: יורה הצדק. The reading יורה is not confirmed by מצות יוריהם
(3,8) since what we have in the latter passage is not a substantive
מורה=יורה but a regular imperfect יורה, whereas יורה צדק can only be
a noun יורה from the Hiphil הורה, it is probable that מורה is to be read
for יורה, in agreement with 1,11; 20,1 and 20,32.[75a] As for the meaning
of the clause, Schechter remarks, "זולתם, that is any new things not
included in בהם as dictated by the lawgiver shall not be reached before
the end of the days." But there is nothing said in the entire book about
"new things." The view that prevails throughout is that the teachings
of the מחוקק[76] are the only true ones and in the time of the Messiah
will be recognized as such by all. Translate therefore: "To follow these
laws (of the מחוקק) for the whole period of wickedness until the Teacher
of Truth shall arise, and apart from these (laws) they cannot achieve
anything." In the last words it is emphasized that the laws of the lawgiver are the only true ones, and that therefore those who fancy
that they can arrive at the truth without the law will not achieve
anything.

6,11: וכל אשר הובאו בברית וכו'. By מקדש is usually understood the
sanctuary of the sect in Damascus,[77] entrance to which is denied all
those who do not live in accordance with the teachings of the sect.
But the quotation from Mal. 1:10 shows very clearly that the temple
in Jerusalem is meant here. Translate: "And all those who entered
the Covenant not to go into the temple, not to kindle any fire on the
altar, so that its doors must be closed in accordance with the words of
God: 'Oh that there were among you one that would close its doors
and not kindle mine altar for nought.' " The Covenant entered into

---

[75a] [The author retracts this suggestion on p. 219, n. 56.]

[76] On the problem whether the מחוקק is identical with the Messiah see below,
Section V.

[77] There is, however, no direct evidence in the text of the Fragment that such
a sanctuary existed!

was therefore a Covenant to avoid the temple because those in control of it defiled it, in the opinion of this sect, so that God preferred (Mal. 1:10) to have the pious keep away from the sanctuary altogether. The author then goes on to remind the adherents of the sect that God expects more than this from His servants, namely to keep away from property dishonestly acquired, to observe the laws concerning the Sabbath, holy days and fast-day in accordance with the Law. If, then, they do not keep the second part of the program, they are no better than their opponents, who defile the sanctuary. This thought is introduced by the words אם לא . . התענית במצ׳ except that at the end some such conclusion is missing as באי עון פקד כאשר והיה [78] הברית הראשונים עליהם כן יפקד עונותיכם עליכם.

6,16: ובהון המקדש. The emendation ומהון is superfluous since בהון depends upon the preceding הטמא, "to keep from the possessions of wickedness, which are defiled by a vow or ban or its belonging to the sanctuary." That is, הון הרשעה is more fully described by these three examples and the following ולגזול, wherein טמא is naturally to be taken in an ethico-religious and not a ritual sense.[79]

6,19: בארץ דמשק . . . באי הברית. As has already been noted on 6,11, the apodosis to אם לא (6,14) is missing before this section, and it is not impossible that more than this apodosis is missing. At any rate it is highly probable that באי . . . בארץ דמשק is the title[80] of the following section. Indeed, before באי one should insert מצות or the like, "The commandments for those who entered the new covenant made in the land of Damascus." Note the difference between הובאו בברית (6,11) and באי הברית . . . דמשק. The former are those who made a covenant in Jerusalem not to visit the Temple, whereas those who later left Jerusalem and established their community in Damascus are termed באי הברית החדשה.

7,1: ולא ימעל. For ימעל one reads below, in 8,6 and 19,18, ויתעלמו which, in view of Isa. 58:7, ומבשרך אל תתעלם is probably the original text and is not to be altered to וימעלו or the like, since both A and B read ויתעלמו. The meaning is that they were unfriendly and were not in the least concerned about their blood-relatives.[81] It is not incon-

---

[78] Cf. 3,10, בו חבו באי הברית הראשונים.

[79] The use of טמא in this sense occurs very frequently in rabbinic literature. Cf., for example, Shabbath 104a בא ליטמא פותחין לו, where ליטמא means "to sin." [Comp. the interpretation of the passage by Lieberman, *Greek in Jewish Palestine*, p. 135.]

[80] Such titles also occur in 9,8; 10,10; 10,14; 16,10.

[81] Already the Targum, *ad loc.*, interprets ומבשרך as מקריב בשרך, and Tosefta Soṭah VII, 2 and Talmud Kethuvoth 52b interpret the passage similarly. Cf., however, R. Abraham ben Hiyya in his הגיון הנפש 15a, who takes בשר literally, supposing

ceivable, to be sure, that our author, in his love for the cento-style and in dependence on the phrase cited from Isaiah, uses וימעלו בשאר בשרכם in the sense of "and they offended with their blood-relatives," referring to the incestuous marriages which have been contracted by their opponents.[82]

7,1: להזיר מן הזונות. The reading זונות instead of זנות as Schechter reads, is assured by זונות in 8,5. Our author was probably thinking of עם הזונות יפרדו Hos. 4:14 and therefore used זונות as Hosea does.

7,2: ולא לנטור מיום ליום. Schechter refers to Romans 12:19, where, however, only the biblical injunction (Lev. 19:17) is mentioned. An interesting parallel to our passage is the saying of R. Neḥunyah ben Haqqanah (Megillah 28a), לא עלתה על מטתי קללת חברי, "The insult offered me by my neighbor never mounted my couch" (i. e., "had been forgiven by the time I retired"). In the same Talmudic passage it is related about Mar Zutra that every night before getting into bed he spoke these words שרי ליה לכל מאן דמצערן, "Forgiven is everyone who has insulted me." From these statements of the Talmud it follows that the command ולא לנטור מיום ליום was not unknown to the Pharisees.[83] The expression מיום ליום is modelled on the biblical מיום אל יום (Num. 30:15), which verse our author (9,7) actually cites with this variant.

7,5: כל יסודו ברית אל. A ברית has fallen out through haplography. Read: כל יסודי הברית, ברית אל "in accordance with all the principles of the (new) covenant; for them the covenant of God is maintained for ever." [See, however, p. 289.]

7,6: ואם מחנות ישבו. The preceding section contains the rules for those who live around the sanctuary built by the sect in the land of Damascus. These men lived in celibacy, since marital intercourse was forbidden in the city of the sanctuary according to the views of this sect (12,1). Our author then continues, "And if they settle in settlements, as is customary, they shall marry etc." Celibacy is not enjoined

---

that the prophet is denouncing excessive fasting! Aggadat Shir Ha-Shirim, ed. Schechter 27 (=Midrash Zuta ed. Buber 23) similarly takes בשר in the sense of "body."

[82] Cf. 5,8–11 where our author in reference to the marriage between uncle and niece which is permitted by the opponents of the sect remarks והיא שאר. Hence שאר בשרו in the present passage!

[83] Cf. also TP Taanith III, 67a and Makiri on Psalms, CI, 122, where קללתי means "the insult offered me." In the Midrash אלה אזכרה (Jellinek, Beth Hamidrash, II, 68) it is said of the Meturgaman R. Ḥuzpit, ומעולם לא עלה קללת חבירו על מטתו, which is exactly the same as that which the Talmud reports (loc. cit.) of R. Neḥunyah. Jellinek misunderstood this passage and emended מטתו to שפתו. In most editions of the Prayer Book there is found before the evening prayer the direction to begin it with the words שרי לכל וכו'.

forever but only so long as one lives near the sanctuary. *Cf.* however
below on 11,18–20; 12,1; 16,13, and p. 281.

7,6: כסרך הארץ. How the סרך, "consequence," of the Babylonian
and Palestinian Talmudim developed that particular sense is hard to
trace. It should be noted, however that Rabbenu Ḥananel in his
commentary on Yoma 30a explains סרך as מנהג, which is exactly the
sense it has in our fragment; and in the Aramaic text of the Testament
of Levi (Charles, *The Greek Versions of the Testaments of the Twelve
Patriarchs*, p. 250) סרך is twice used in the sense of Greek ταξις,
"order, rule." Accordingly סרך doubtless means "manner" in our
fragment too. This סרך is probably from a different root (with *sin*
in Arabic) from that of the Talmudic סרך which probably corresponds
to Hebrew שרך.

7,8: כאשר אמר . . . ובין אב לבנו. This expression is probably based
on Num. 30:17, as Schechter notes. In content, however, this biblical
verse has nothing to do with our passage. If the believers marry, says
our author, they must guide themselves by the words of the Torah
in their new relations, whether in those between man and wife or
between father and son. The phrase בין אב לבנו includes מצות הבן על
האב[84] as well as מצות האב על הבן and naturally represents something
quite different from בין אב לבתו in the biblical passage quoted.

7,9: וכל המואסים בפקד אל את הארץ. That something has fallen out
after מואסים hardly requires any proof. The parallel text in B reads,
וכל המואסים במצות ובחקים, which may well be right in substance but does
not represent the original text. We should read, וכל המואסים בפִקֻדֵי
אֵל בְּפָקֻד אֶת הָאָרֶץ, "And those who scorn the laws of God when God
visits punishment on the earth etc." The present text owes its defective-
ness to the circumstance that the copyists omitted בִּפָקֻד and wrote
only בְּפָקֻד אֵל which followed; which was all the more liable to happen
in ancient texts because matres lectionis were not used, and these two
groups of words have exactly the same consonants. As for בפקודי אל,
which is missing in our text, it is found in Ps. 19:9 (our text usually
has אל for י״י) and is also used by our author in 20,2.

7,13: שר אפרים. For שר probably שבט is to be read. The clause
בהפרד . . . יהודה is our author's interpretation of the verse cited by
him, Isa. 7:17. We should, of course, read אשר לא באו instead of אשר באו
as Schechter has already noted, whereas י״י after יביא was probably
omitted by our author deliberately, since he does not use the Tetragrammaton on principle.[85]

---

[84] *Cf.* Mishnah, Qiddushin I, 7, where both these terms are mentioned.
[85] He usually writes אל instead, but not consistently. *Cf.* note on 9,5.

7,13: והמחזיקים ... וכל הנסוגים. In this clause too י״ is to be supplied both after הנסוגים (cf. Isa. 59:13, ונסוג מאחר אלהינו) and after והמחזיקים: "Those who turned away from him (God) were delivered to the sword, and those who held fast to him escaped to the land of the North."

7,15: מאהלי דמשק. The text, is not to be corrected according to Amos 5:7, to read מהלאה instead of אהלי(מ); for even if it be assumed that our author found no other reading in his copy of Amos, he interpreted מהלאה as אהלי(מ) in Midrashic fashion,[86] in order to find in these prophetic words an allusion to the headquarters of the sect in Damascus.[87]

7,16: כאשר אמר והקימותי את וכו'. The proof-text from Amos 9:11 shows first of all that the king can represent the entire people, since the tent of David is the same as the tent of Israel. But how our author came to identify סוכת with ספר תורה he does not say. He probably derives it from סכת "to take note of"[88] (הסכת "to give heed to"), and takes סכת מלככם as "that to which the people shall give heed, that is the Torah."

7,17: וכינוי הצלמים וכיון הצלמים. Schechter deletes the first two words which he regards as scribal errors for וכיון הצלמים. I consider it more probable, however, that this was the original text, which was later emended out of ignorance in order to find in it the words alluded to in Amos. The author says וכנוי הצלמים "And the epithet[89] צלמים represents books of the Prophets, whose words Israel scorned like idols." [The author revises his view of צלמים on p. 365.] In view of the Midrashic character of this section it is not impossible that we have here an interpretation of כיון as "make straight" or "direct." The Prophetic writings (to use a Talmudic expression) מכוונים לבם לאביהם שבשמים "direct hearts to the heavenly Father."

7,18–20: והכוכב הוא דורש התורה ... השבט הוא נשיא כל העדה. For our author the "star of Jacob" is not identical with the comet[90] of Israel. By the former he understands the founder of the sect or, as he calls

---

[86] Such interpretations are very frequent in both haggadic and halakic sections of the Talmud. Cf. more fully Waldberg, דרכי השנוים, 4b ff.

[87] אהל, "tent," is equivalent to "sanctuary" in the Bible, Ps. 15:1 and elsewhere, and in post-biblical literature to "house of study"; cf., for example, Targum Onqelos to Gen. 25:27. [The author revises his view on p. 196, n. 182.]

[88] Cf. also Ibn Ezra ad loc., who similarly derives סכות from סכת and translates it as רצון!

[89] From the root כנה which already occurs in the Bible, the Mishnah forms the word כנוי, "periphrasis."

[90] This, as already noted by R. Hai Gaon, cited in the 'Arukh, sub voce, is the meaning of שבט in Num. 24:17, which our author cites on his proof-text.

him, "The searcher of the Torah," while the comet is "the prince"[91] of the whole community," that is, the Messiah who will someday ובעמדו destroy all the sons of Seth. In rabbinic tradition, on the other hand, כוכב is explained as a term for the Messiah; *cf.*, for example, the words of R. Akiba, TP Taanith IV, 68d. Shahrastáni, ed. Cureton, I, 170, relates that the followers of Dositheos applied this biblical verse to him. It is still very doubtful, however, whether Dositheos set himself up as a Messiah.

7,21: אלה מלטו בקץ וכו'. This sentence forms the transition from the section on the past, the time of the sect's settling in Damascus, to that on the future, God's final reckoning with sinners in the time of the Messiah. In contrast to "the future day of God" on which He will punish sinners, היום אשר יפקד אל, the punishment of sinners at the time of the founding of the sect is described as the first one, פקודה הראשונה.

8,1: אשר לא יחזיקו באלה. The parallel text B has באלה החקים, which at the most proves that the copyist of B already had באלה before him but not that החקים belonged to the original text. I therefore conjecture that באלה is short for באלות הברית (Deut. 29:20): "So will it befall all those who entered the covenant but did not hold fast to the oath of the covenant" gives much more exact meaning than the colorless באלה החקים. Besides, there are no חקים in what immediately precedes to which באלה could refer.

8,4: יחלו למרפא וידקמום כל מורדים. The text requires no emendation; but it should be realized that וידקמום combines two readings, namely the *scriptio plena* וידקום and the *defectiva* וידקם: "And they (the princes of Judah) hoped for healing,[92] but they were crushed by the rebels." The historical events here alluded to were perhaps the sufferings of the Jews under Demetrius and the other pretenders to the throne of Antiochus Epiphanes. The expulsion of Alcimus and the death of Judas Maccabaeus fall in the time of Demetrius and his army commanders, of whom it can rightly be said that they crushed the princes of Judah. The parallel text B has nothing that corresponds to this passage, a further proof of the later date of this text, whose redactor no longer understood the allusions to historical events and therefore omitted them.

8,6: ויתעלמו איש וכו'. *Cf.* the note on 7,1.

8,8: ולא נזרו מעם. Schechter supplies from B ומחטאתם, but in line 16 B also has סרו מדרך העם, from which it appears that ומחטאתם is an

---

[91] The rabbinic sources occasionally speak of "King Messiah," but our author uses "prince," נשיא, for "king," מלך, in other places. Also, *cf.*, 5,1.

[92] *Cf.* Jer. 8:15 and 14:19 קוה . . . לעת מרפא, where קוה is used of hoping for מרפא as יחל is here.

explanatory gloss. The sense of the clause, however, is clear and does not require this addition. The author reproaches the princes of Judah for being no better than the common people in that, instead of leading them to the fear of God and the observance of the Law, they followed their bad example and turned away from God.

8,10: התנינים הם מלכי העמים וכו'. In Sifre (323, on Deut. 32:33, p. 374) two opinions are cited.[93] According to one, represented by R. Judah, this verse refers to the Israelites who act as if they were poisonous serpents, and whose leaders (ראש) are as pitiless as the adder. According to the other view, all this is said of the Gentiles, and it is with this view, represented by R. Neḥemiah, that our author agrees. The interpretation of ראש as "head" in Sifre and in our fragment is of course only haggadic explanation.

8,12: בוני החיץ וטחי התפל. Below in line 18, as above, in 4,19, the opponents are called only בוני החיץ; our passage, however, shows that this is merely an abbreviation of the complete expression בוני החיץ וטחי הטפל. It is not for building a wall that the opponents are reproached but for working their wall over with nothing but whitewash, so that it has no durability; so also in Ezek. 13:10–15, the false Prophets are reproached for being טחי תפל but not for being בוני חיץ. There is therefore no reason to see in בוני חיץ any allusion to the Pharisees, whose activity consisted in "building a fence around the Law."

8,13: אשר חרה אף וכו'. The meaning of the clause is doubtful, since אשר can mean "so that" as well as "because." In the first case, God became angry with Israel because of the false teachings of the "confused spirit."[94] In the other case, God permitted these false teachers to spread their teachings because he was angry with Israel. But the further comment of our author, ובשונאי את . . . חרה אפו (line 18), speaks for the former interpretation.

8,14: ואשר אמר משה. The text is correct and requires no emendation. The author attempts to refute any future objection to his statement that God is angry with Israel because of its sins. The objection consists in a reference to Deut. 7:8 and 9:5, where Moses says that God supports Israel not because of its good deeds but because of the oath that He swore to the fathers according to which God would always have to be on Israel's side regardless of its merits. The answer to this objection

---

[93] This difference of opinion also applies to the interpretation of vs. 32, for which reason Sifre does not repeat R. Neḥemiah's words in commenting on the following verse. In Midrash Tannaim 200 the *derash* on vs. 33 comes in the wrong place; for it is the continuation of R. Judah's words and not of R. Neḥemiah's.

[94] Schechter is probably right in identifying this "confused spirit" with "the mocker" (1,14), although we cannot rule out the possibility that it means the spirit of false prophecy.

is וכו' המשפט וכן: "This (promise given in Scripture) refers to those in Israel who return to God . . . for whom the covenant with the Fathers is binding, whereas He hates the builders of the wall and is angry with them and similarly with all those who despise the laws of God."

8,16: סרו ישראל לשבי. Although B also reads thus אשר is certainly to be supplied before סרו. What סרו מדרך הע' means has already been explained above in the comment on line 8.

8,17: אחריו הועירו אשר. B shows that אחריו appeared in its *Vorlage* too. Since, however, אחרי העיר is hardly possible, we may confidently say that B misunderstood its source. We should read הֶעֱרוּ,[95] "who gave themselves over to him." ערה, originally meaning "to pour out," is occasionally employed in the sense of "to be closely attached to",[96] this suggests that our הערו אחריו corresponds to the biblical דבק אחרי (Jer. 42:16) and in rabbinic Hebrew simply expresses the devotion of the Fathers to God; cf. however, Ben Sira IV, 11, ותעיד לכל in place of which, to be sure, I read ותעיר in my *Randglossen* on the passage.

8,20: הוא הדבר אשר אמר ירמיה. It is extremely probable that we have here a reference to the Syriac Apocalypse of Baruch LXXXIV, 5, where we read: "Moses once said to you that (dispersion and other suffering) will not come upon you, and yet it has come upon you, for you have abandoned the Law . . . If you comply with that which has been commanded you, you will receive from the Almighty all that which has been set aside and preserved for you." These words of Baruch exactly agree with the view of our author that Israel can count on God's love only if it observes the Law; otherwise the promise made to the Fathers is of no help to it.[97] It should be noted here that the letter of Baruch to the 9½ tribes, in which the passage cited occurs, has only a loose connection with the original Apocalypse of Baruch, and is very probably an independent composition, and since in the Bible it is Jeremiah who sent a letter to the Diaspora in Babylonia (Jer. 29:1), it is a natural assumption that this letter was originally ascribed to Jeremiah; hence the wording in our fragment, הוא הדבר אשר אמר ירמיה לברוך.[98]

[95] In view of the peculiar orthography of our fragment (*cf.* above, Section II) the reading הָיְעֲרוּ (so probably in the ms.) for הָעֱרוּ is quite possible, so that no emendation at all is necessary.

[96] *Cf.*, *e. g.*, Yoma 54b, כאיש המעורה בלוייה שלו, on which Aruch, *s. v.* ער III correctly remarks שהמיעור הוא הדיבוק.

[97] Among the Tannaim there is a difference of opinion as to whether the final redemption is dependent upon Israel's repentance or not; *cf.* Sanhedrin 97b and further below, Section V.

[98] It is also possible that originally this letter was considered to be one from Jeremiah to Baruch for the Babylonian Diaspora, whereby the difference between

8,20: ‏ואלישע לגחזי נערו‎. The words of Elisha to Gehazi are otherwise unknown, but it is worthwhile to note that according to rabbinic legend[99] Elisha made vain efforts to cause his disciple to repent
after his fall. The passage here referred to fits very well into an
exhortation to repentance, namely that "God's anger is directed
against those who despise His laws and follow the lusts of their heart,"
like Gehazi who turned away from his God because of greed for
money. It is also noteworthy that according to rabbinic legend[100]
Damascus was the scene of Gehazi's sinful behavior, and if it should
be the case, as it seems to be, that we are here dealing with a local
legend, it would hardly be surprising that our author, who was a
Damascene,[101] was acquainted with it. At any rate the association of
Jeremiah with Baruch and of Elisha with Gehazi in our fragment
seems to indicate that for our author Gehazi was no sinner but in a
certain sense the successor of Elisha, as was Baruch of Jeremiah. In
view of the above-mentioned legend, which places Gehazi in Damascus, it would not be at all strange if he had been elevated to the
position of a holy man[102] by our sect, as one who first preached the
word of God in the place which was later the residence of the sect.
The statement of the Talmud (Sanhedrin 107b) that Gehazi by magical
tricks gave the appearance of divine origin to the golden calves set up
by Jeroboam is perhaps the answer of Pharisaic Judaism to the
glorification of Gehazi by our sect. Gehazi, say the former, was not
the founder of the true religion in Damascus but was a second Jeroboam, in that he widened the breach made by Jeroboam between
Judah and Israel, between the supporters of the Temple in Jerusalem
and those of the one in Beth-el.

9,1: ‏כל אדם אשר יחרים וכו׳‎. The view that these words prohibit
having a Jewish criminal executed by Gentile authorities encounters
material and linguistic difficulties. Not only must one delete ‏מאדם‎
but the phrase ‏בחוקי הגוים‎ is also very inappropriate. The text would

---

our fragment and the Apocalypse of Baruch can easily be explained. That Baruch
lived in Babylonia is asserted in Rabbinic tradition, cf. Megillah 16b.

[99] TP Sanhedrin X, 29b, TB ibid. 107b. In the latter source Gehazi's answer to
Elisha is actually given, explaining why he did not wish to change his sinful ways,
and this may go back, though indirectly, to the Pseudepigraph cited by our author.

[100] TP and TB loc. cit.

[101] Whether he lived in Damascus cannot be stated positively, but at least this
city was of so great importance to him that he knew its history as well as its legends.

[102] The view of some scholars that Gehazi, like the other names mentioned in
the Mishnah of Sanhedrin, stood for Jesus or his disciples (cf. ‏החלוץ‎ X, 32–46) is
untenable in my opinion.

have to be על ידי שופטי גוים or, in accordance with later usage, על ידי
בית דין של גוים, but not בחוקי הגוים. Furthermore, with this interpretation, the concluding clause ואשר א' לא תקום וכו' can hardly be explained;
for the reason for the prohibition is certainly something quite different[103] from the unlawfulness of revenge, since the punishment of a
lawbreaker is not always motivated by revenge. In view, moreover, of
the very exclusivist outlook of the adherents of this sect it would be
very surprising if they, in contrast to the Rabbis,[104] should have
permitted suits which involved no penalty of death for the guilty to
be brought before Gentile courts. I therefore read כל אדם אשר יחרים
מאדו מאדם בחוקי הגוים מיתהלך, "Every one who declares his property
consecrated for anyone, acts in accordance with the laws of the
Gentiles." In explanation of this statement the following comment
may be made. Anyone who is refused a favor by any person can get
revenge by declaring his property "consecrated," חרם, for that person,
who may under no circumstances have any use of the object declared
חרם.[105] Warning is here given against such vengeful treatment of an
acquaintance, and it is pointed out that this is not the Jewish way,
for even if one is badly treated by one's neighbor, Scripture commands
us: "Take no revenge and bear no grudge against any of thy people."
It is interesting that in a midrash (Jellinek, *Beth ha-Midrash* III, 113)
it is remarked on this biblical verse cited by our author, ולא יהיה נוקם
ונוטר שנאמר לא תקום ולא תטור וזה דרכן של ישראל הקדושים אבל הכותים[106]
האכזרים וערלי לב נוקמין ונוטרין ועברתם שמורה נצח, "One must not be vengeful or bear a grudge, for it is said (Lev. 19:18), 'Thou shalt not take
revenge nor bear a grudge'; this is the way of the Israelites who are
holy,[107] but the Gentiles, who are merciless and are uncircumcised in
heart, take revenge and bear a grudge, and their anger is preserved
for ever." In these words we have an exact parallel to our text, in which
revenge and rancor are characterized as Gentile traits. So far as the
linguistic aspect of the reading proposed by me is concerned, the
following may be said. מאד meaning "power," "possessions" is used a

---

[103] *Cf.* the passages cited by Schechter, to which may be added Mekilta de R.
Simon, Hoffm. 117, לפניהם ולא לפני גוים. The judgment can be given only by the competent authorities, whereby gentile judges are naturally excluded.

[104] The sources cited in the preceding note deal with civil cases; *cf.* also Bava
Meẓi'a 83b.

[105] The usual formula for נדר חרם הנאה was הריני עליך חרם; *cf.* Mishnah Nedarim V, 4 and
below, the note on 16,15.

[106] For הכותים one should certainly read הגוים.

[107] The adjective קדושים, "holy," is here used because the biblical law here referred to belongs to the laws of holiness (Lev. 19:2 ff.).

few lines below in our text (line 11, and 12,10); the miswriting אדם
for מאדו is due to the preceding אדם and the following מאדם while the
phrase בחוקי הג' מיתהלך is modeled on the biblical לא תלכו בחקת הגוי
(Lev. 20:23). Whether the concluding clause begins with ואשר or with
הוא cannot be stated with certainty; the latter supposition is the more
probable one, and one should therefore read, הוא אשר אמר, "This is
what Scripture means in saying etc." If, however, we connect הוא
with the preceding מיתהלך, it would seem best to regard the clause
beginning with ואשר as an introduction to the law וכל איש מבאי הברית
וכו': "And as for what Scripture says . . . therefore every one of those
who enter the covenant etc."

9,4:   והביאו בחרון וכו'. The text is correct and should not be emended
to והכהו. The meaning is: if anyone in anger or vexation accuses one
of his fellows of a sin committed secretly, he transgresses the biblical
commandment not to take revenge. The object of והביאו is, of course,
דבר inasmuch as יביא ע' ר' דבר in the preceding line are more fully
explained to mean that the denunciation was made in anger. To
understand this precept one should have the additional information
that the statement of a single witness has no validity in law,[108] so
that the statement of a single person can only have the purpose of
lowering the prestige of another person, which is equivalent to slander.
The same precept, moreover, is also found in the Talmud (Pesaḥim
113b), where it is reported that R. Papa caused to be whipped a man
who came before him to accuse someone of a crime, and justified the
whipping in the following way. "It is written (Deut. 19:15) that a
single witness may not testify against a person, yet you appeared as an
only witness with the intention of giving this man a bad reputation."

9,5:   נוקם הוא . . . ונוטר הוא. That our author does not cite the
words of Nahum (1:2) quite literally in twice omitting יהוה is in keeping with his fundamental principle of never using the name of God.
Not even in an oath does he consider the use of the divine name
permissible, as is clear from 15,1. Ordinarily he uses אל for יהוה, while
in this passage הוא appears as an equivalent of the tetragrammaton.
Instructive for this use of הוא is the statement in the Mishnah, Sukkah
IV,5, that הוא was sometimes used as a paraphrase of יהוה in the Temple
liturgy.[109] There is a parallel to the haggadic interpretation of Nah. 1:2

---

[108] Cf. Deut. 19:15 and further below in our fragment, where this law is somewhat modified. This דבר, by the way, can mean something which is unseemly but
not exactly a violation of the law.

[109] Geiger, *Nachgelassene Schriften* V, 102 and קבוצת מאמרים, ed. Poznanski, 101,
asserts that in this Mishnah אָנְיהו is to be read instead of אני והו, but the use of הוא
as כנוי for יהוה in this fragment shows that there is no reason to emend the text of

in the New Testament, Romans 12:19, where men are warned against vengefulness, since God has said, "Vengeance is Mine," and it must therefore be left to Him. The author of our fragment, however, cites the Nahum passage and not, as Paul does, Deut. 32:35, because the words of the prophet contain a twofold teaching. Vengeance is only for God, and He uses this only against His enemies and those who hate Him, wherefore no one may let himself be led by desire for revenge, least of all in dealings with one's coreligionists, with Jews, the friends of God. Moreover it should be noted that the Samaritan version and the Septuagint of Deut. 32:35 read ליום instead of לי and that if our author had the same reading, it would have been impossible for him to refer to this passage in support of his teaching that vengeance belongs only to God.

9,6: החריש לו מיום ליום. *Cf.* above on 7,2.

9,6: בדבר מות. In rabbinic phraseology this would have appeared as חייב מיתה, if the seriousness of a sin was to be stressed. Our author bases his statement on the fact that the sinner acts contrary to the word of God if he bears a grudge against his neighbor for a long time. *Cf.* also the note on 16,9.

9,8: על השבועה. As in 10,14; 14,10 and probably 16,10 too (*cf.* the note *ad loc.*), so too in this passage we have a superscription that gives the content of the following laws. Whether this was written by the author himself cannot be definitely stated.

9,10–11: וכל . . . ממאד המחנה. The emendation מֹעֵד for מאד is untenable since, in the first place, מועד cannot stand for אהל מועד and, second, the meaning of אהל מועד in Scripture is so constant that it is inconceivable that our author should have given it a different one from that of the Bible. Nor will anyone be prepared to assert that we are here dealing with a theft in the Sanctuary.[110] But מאד does not need to be emended at all, since the meaning of this rule is quite clear: "If a man has lost something and does not know who has stolen it — the lost article — from the property of the camp, he shall adjure the camp in which the thief abides." The meaning "property" for מאד is both biblical and rabbinic and is, moreover, found elsewhere in this fragment, while one המחנה has been omitted, probably through haplography. The complete text would read, מי גנבו ממאד המחנה המחנה אשר . . .

---

the Mishnah. *Cf.* my notes on קב מא', *loc. cit.*, and on p. 143. Chajes, *Markus-Studien*, 61–62, refers to LXX, Prov. 24:7 which renders פיהו by στόματος κυρίου; *cf.* also Perles, *Analekten*, 17. [Ginzberg corrects the above explanation of הוא on p. 163, n. 34.]

[110] In the concluding clause, בעליו is explicitly mentioned.

9,13: והתודה המושב לכהן. As Schechter rightly conjectures, המשיב is to be read instead of המושב,[111] but it does not mean "the man who repays the debt" but, as is clear from 15,4, והתודה והשיב, "the penitent." Instead of the full expression השיב אל לב "repent" our author uses the shorter form השיב "repent" and משיב "the penitent." Very important for the history of penitential confession is the statement that the sinner must confess his trespass before the priest לכהן. In the passage of Scripture that is here used, Num. 5:7, there is not the slightest allusion to this, and in the Talmud one who publicly confesses his sins is actually severely blamed.[112] In view of this fact I was at first inclined to take לכהן as the object of כל אשם in agreement with the words of Scripture, Num. 5:8 האשם המושב לכהן, while והתודה המשיב as an interpolated clause adds the condition that the sinner must acknowledge his sin at the same time. But though there are no linguistic difficulties in the way of this interpretation, it still seems better to keep the usual one since Midrash Tadshe, which, as we know,[113] used the pseudepigraphic literature, similarly, states that the sinner should confess his sins to the priest. This passage reads, למה גזר הקב״ה לשרוף פר החטאת בפרהסיא חוץ למחנה אלא רצה הקב״ה ללמד שלא יהא אדם מתבייש להתודות חטאתו לפני כהן[114] שכן כתיב והתודה אשר חטא עליה שיאמר כהן גדול לא נתבייש ממני אני לא אתבייש ממנו, "Why did God command that the bull which the high priest offers as a sin offering shall be publicly burned outside the camp? God wished to teach thereby that a man should not be ashamed to confess his sins to the priest, as is written, 'and he shall confess his sin'[115] (Lev. 5:5). The sinner will say, 'The high priest was not ashamed to confess his sins before me (publicly), and so I will not be ashamed before him' " (Midrash Tadshe XXXV, ed. Epstein). The older sources, like Bavli and Yerushalmi, cite the prescriptions of the Torah concerning the offering of the sin-offering to support their view of the objectionableness of public confession of sin, cf. Soṭah 32b and TP Yevamoth VIII, 9c. The first of these passages, to be sure, does admit that כהן הוא דידע, "The priest knows

---

[111] המושב is due to the preceding אשם המושב.

[112] Cf. Yoma 86b; Berakhoth 34, end of Perek: "He who publicly confesses his sins is to be considered impudent. Cf. also Rashi on Yoma 21a, שלא ישמע איש ודוי של חברו, "that the one may not hear the confession of sin of his fellow." Did Rashi read ודוי for תפלה in Gen. Rabba V,7? Cf. also מחזור ויטרי, p. 539 on Avoth V,5.

[113] Cf. Epstein, pp. 4 ff.

[114] The editions have כהן גדול and after שיאמר only כהן whereas the opposite is alone correct, as Epstein has already noted. At the end of the sentence ממנו is not to be taken literally and is used only for the sake of contrast with ממני.

[115] But in this Scriptural passage it is not said that he shall confess his sin to the priest. For Talmudic formula for the confession of sins see Tosefta Menaḥoth X, 12.

whether the sacrifice is a sin-offering or not," although the law has taken precautions that sinners shall not be publicly declared to be such, שלא לפרסם החטאים. *Cf.* also ספר חסידים, ed. Wistinetzki, 50–51, where sinners are advised to mention their sins to a scholar in order that he may prescribe for them the penitence suitable to their sins. It is not impossible, however, that the author of ספר חסידים was influenced by the Christian doctrine of confession.

9,14: והיה לו לבד מאיל האשם הכל. The words איל האשם are not to be emended to איל הכפורים after Num. 5:8, since our author does not wish simply to cite the words of Scripture but to explain them as well, and for that reason he writes האשם instead of הכפורים, in agreement with Lev. 5:25 where this sacrifice is described as an אשם. It is also probably with this passage in mind that he adds הכל to the words of Scripture, by which he means that the priest receives not only the repayment of the money owed but also an extra fifth, as in Lev. 5:25 and Num. 5:7. This is also the view of the Mishnah, Bava Qamma IX,11, whereas the Karaites state that when the money owed is repaid to the priest, he receives only the principal sum and not the extra fifth.[116]

9,14–16: וכן כל אבדה . . . הם ישמרו. As the text now reads, it contains a contradiction. First it says that if an object is found and its owner cannot be ascertained,[117] it shall belong to the priests, but then it says that the priests shall have it in safekeeping if the lawful owner cannot be found. Nor do we understand how the words כי לא ידע מוצאיה את משפטה, "for its finder does not know what to do with it," can be cited as a basis for the prescription that it shall belong to the priests. That היתה לכהנים, however, is to be taken absolutely and is not limited by הם ישמרו standing at the end of the sentence, is clear from the word וכן, which makes sense only if the unclaimed find really belongs to the priests, exactly as in the case mentioned earlier. I suspect, therefore, that the concluding clause כי לא . . . ישמרו did not belong to the original text. The older view was that unclaimed finds are given to the priests whereas later the law was modified in the sense that the priests acted only as guardians for the unidentified owner because the ordinary man does not know what to do with a found object. What is meant by the last words we learn from the Mishnah, Bava Mezi'a 2:8, which gives a number of instructions as to what use the finder may make of a found object, if its owner cannot be ascer-

---

[116] *Cf.*, for example, Aaron Nicomedia in his כתר תורה, *ad loc.*; this Karaite, to be sure, follows rabbinic tradition, as so often is the case.

[117] There is no warrant whatever for making a distinction between אין לה בע' and לא נמצאו לה בע', since we are here dealing only with unclaimed finds, and the first expression is influenced by the preceding one (אשם . . . אין בעלים).

tained. That is what is to be understood by משפטה, which in the view
of our author is not within every man's competence. The latter view
is, as we see, essentially the same as that of the Rabbis, except that
according to our author the priests hold the find in safekeeping
whereas the Rabbis assign this duty to the finder.

9,17: אם דבר מות. This is usually translated, "if it is a capital
case," but this is quite impossible, since the beginning of the sentence
reads כל דבר אשר ימעל, "any transgression." אם is therefore to be
understood in the sense of "even if," that is, even if capital punishment is involved, this testimony is sufficient to condemn the sinner:
שלם משפטו. The stress laid on the fact that this law applies to cases
involving the death penalty also is not superfluous, since the Halakah
admits such evidence only in cases involving money but not in those
involving the death penalty.[118]

9,19: אם ישוב וניתפש וכו'. Schechter takes this clause to mean that
the sinner must have committed the act before three witnesses. There
can be no question of this, however, since further on (lines 22 f.) it is
explicitly stated with emphasis that two witnesses suffice in all cases.
The meaning of this clause is rather the following: if a witness observes
someone committing a sin, he must report it to the Censor;[119] the latter
then writes down this report in order that he may consult it if a similar
report should come to him from a second person; if, continues the
author, the sinner should be caught by a second witness, and the latter
reports this to the Censor, the charge against the sinner is complete.
It is also highly probable that the words ושב והודיע למבקר have been
misplaced, that is, they belong after the second לפני אחד while the
copyists have placed them after the first לפני אחד.

9,20–21: ואם שנים הם והם מעידים על דבר אחר. Schechter admits that
the meaning of this and the following clause is not clear to him. For
their understanding, the following may be noted. If someone commits
a forbidden act twice, each time in the presence of a single witness, he
is subject to punishment, since two witnesses can testify to the forbidden act. This is the case which is dealt with in lines 16–20, where
in view of the possibility of a conviction the first witness is charged
with the responsibility of making an immediate report. If however,
a person commits two different offenses, each in the presence of a single
witness, he cannot be held for trial, since in each case there is only

---

[118] Makkoth, Mishnah I, 9 and Gemara, *ibid.*, 6b; Sanhedrin 30, where a view is
cited that such evidence is not valid even in money matters.

[119] *Cf.* Aaron Nicomedia, כתר תורה on Lev. 5:1, where a similar view is cited, and
the fuller discussion below in Section IV.

one witness to testify to the punishable act. However, the joint statements of both witnesses do suffice to cause such a person to be regarded as untrustworthy in matters of clean and unclean, that is to
determine that such a person deserves no credence when he declares
something to be pure.[120] According to this view the clause והם מעידים
הראשון מעיד על דבר אחד והשני על דבר אחר is equivalent to על דבר אחר
and the words ואם שנים הם is to be translated, "even if there are two
witnesses, but their testimony refers to different things, the man shall
be excluded only in respect of purity."

9,22: ועל החוק כלו.[121] After what has been observed on the preceding
line, this clause offers no difficulty. It is to be translated, "The rule
that two witnesses are given credence applies to all laws; however,
one witness is sufficient to cause a man to be excluded from 'the
purity.' "[122]

10,1–2: אשר לא מלאו ימיו וכו'. According to the accepted Halakah,[123]
a male reaches his majority at the end of his thirteenth year; however,
it can be shown from both the Haggadah and the Halakah that the
age of majority was originally twenty years. That the heavenly court
punishes no one under twenty years[124] is stated in both the Palestinian
and Babylonian Haggadah (TP. Bikkurim II, 64c; Sanhedrin XI, 30b;
Bavli Shabbath 89b; and cf. also Gen. R. 58 beginning), and is
therefore probably an old tradition. If a male at the completion of his
thirteenth year or a female at the completion of her twelfth year shows
no signs (סימנים) of puberty, they are legally considered minors but in
any case they reach adulthood in their twentieth year. This is a Halakah
about the details of which the schools of Hillel and Shammai argue
(Niddah V, 9), and we may therefore see in it traces of the old Halakah.
That the old Halakah continued to exert an influence at a still later
period can be seen from the fact that according to Talmudic law no one
under twenty years of age may dispose of real estate (Bava Bathra

---

[120] According to the Halakah one who has been convicted of transgressing a
commandment may not appear as a witness, and is פסול לעדות, as the expression
goes; cf. Sanhedrin 26b and Maimonides, Yad, Eduth, X, 3. It is possible and not improbable that טהרה means an unblemished reputation and one's position in the
community. One loses טהרה when one becomes suspected; cf. also 10,3.

[121] So in the manuscript, cf. Schechter, p. 58.

[122] For להבדיל הטהרה in line 23 we should probably read מן הטהרה as in line 21,
if the explanation given in note 120 is correct.

[123] Niddah, Mishnah V, 6 and many other passages; cf. also Löw, Lebensalter
142 ff., though his statements require corrections in some details.

[124] Cf. also Maimonides in his commentary on the Mishnah, Sanh. 7:4; it is
probably with the words עונשין וכורתין, used in the Yerushalmi in mind that he states
that this applies only to the penalty of Kareth.

156a) — which probably indicates that some business circles are often more conservative than judges. Esoteric Halakah also recognizes the twentieth year of life as the age of majority, as can be seen from the Book of Jubilees XLIX, 17, where it is said with reference to the Passover lamb that "everyone . . . shall eat it in the Sanctuary from twenty years old and upward." Our author on the other hand, seems to follow the later Halakah in the main, but he insists that the testimony of a young man who has not yet reached his twentieth year is not of sufficient force to cause a person to be sentenced to death. Similar to this is the teaching of the Talmud (TP Sanhedrin IV, 22b) that a judge who has not reached the twentieth year of his life may not impose the death penalty. Instructive for the history of Karaism is the fact that Anan agrees with the old Halakah, as can be seen from two passages of his Lawbook, published by Harkavy. Thus it is stated in this Lawbook (p. 22) כל בן עשרים שנה דעייל לבית כנישתא כי שאתי מיחייב קטלא, "if anyone who is twenty years old enters a synagogue when intoxicated he is guilty of a capital crime." Similarly Anan states (*id.* 59), כל דלא האוי בן עשרים שנה לא מטמיא ליה נבלתה, "so long as a person has not reached his twentieth year, he is not made unclean by eating the carrion of a clean animal." In both cases the twenty-year old person is treated as one who has reached his majority.[125]

10,2: ירא את אל. Schechter remarks that לא has fallen out here, but I do not believe that the addition of לא restores the text to its original form. In my opinion it is quite out of the question that our author should exclude one who does not fear God as a witness in criminal cases only but should declare his testimony valid in other cases, especially since the sinner is declared in the following sentence to be incompetent to testify in all cases, and to try to make a distinction between עובר דבר מן המצוה and [לא] ירא את אל would be a counsel of despair. The text, however, will be seen to require no emendation at all if it is observed that though the expression עובר על הפקודים is borrowed from Scripture, our author understands it in a quite different sense from that which it had originally. In the Bible it is the man fit for military service who is to be over twenty (Num. 1:3) whereas in our book the adult[126] member of the sect is to be taken into its camp, as 14,3 clearly shows: The עובר על הפקודים was a יוצא צבא (*ibid.*) while the latter was recruited in order to be received as a ירא את אל. The expression ירא את אל which is formed on the model of biblical ירא את ה'

---

[125] Cf. also Anan's *Sefer ha-Miẓwoth*, ed. Harkavy, pp. 131, 159. [See also below, p. 396, n. 166.]

[126] Since our author uses the biblical term, we probably should assume that according to him also the "recruiting" is to be done in the twentieth year of life.

or rather ירא יי, corresponds in many respects to the rabbinic חייב
במצוות later בר מצוה, by which the adulthood of a person was indicated.
The members of the sect were therefore (20,19) called ירא אל.

10,3: עד זכו לשוב. I cannot imagine anyone using an expression
such as "until he is worthy of doing penitence." Moreover the text
has זכו and not זכה. According to the Halakah a disqualified witness,
פסול לעדות, can be again admitted as a witness only when there are
proofs at hand that he is no longer committing the transgression for
which he was disqualified.[127] Something similar probably lies behind
the words זכו לשוב. The Talmudic expression[128] for this is חזר בו, and it
is not improbable that in our text too we should read עד חזרו בו לשוב,
"until he gives up his sinful way of life to return to God." Another
possibility is that עד זכו is a miswriting for עד זנחו, "until he aban-
dons"=עד חזרו בו.

10,4: עד עשרה אנשים ברורים. In the time of Josephus[129] the court
consisted of seven judges; in the time of the Mishnah[130] of three judges.
Of a court of ten judges there is no trace in either of these sources.[131]
The prescription of our fragment that the court must consist of ten
judges can be explained most simply by supposing that this sect
wished to see its panel of judges composed like the boards of higher
magistrates, which had ten members; on these *cf.* below on 13,1.

10,4: אנשים ברורים. Schechter refers to TP Qiddushin IV, 66a (also
Sifre Deut. 21, p. 33, Num. R. IX, 7), according to which all officials
must be מן הברורין, but in our passage ברורין means "chosen from" as
the following מן העדה לפי העת shows, whereas in the Yerushalmi it
means only those of blameless origin. A linguistic and substantive
parallel to our passage is found in the Mishnah, Sanhedrin III, 1. From
this Mishnah and the corresponding Tosefta, V, 1, we learn that even
ordained judges did not have the right to summon litigants before
them but the plaintiff and the defendant* is each to choose a judge
and these two are then to coopt a third.[132] The term used by the

---

[127] Sanhedrin 25b; Maimonides, *Yad*, Eduth XII, 4.

[128] Sanhedrin, *loc. cit.*, Tosefta V, 2.

[129] Antiq. IV,8,14 *et al.*, *cf.* Weyl, *Die jüd. Strafgesetze bei Fl. Josephus* 12–16.

[130] Sanhedrin I, 1 *et al.*; on the view of the Karaites, *cf.* below and Section IV.

[131] The only instance in which the Halakah speaks of a court of ten judges is
Sanhedrin I, 3 = Megillah IV, 4, with reference to a board of appraisers, which,
strictly speaking, is not relevant here.

[* The author has inadvertently written "der Kläger und der Ankläger" (="the
plaintiff and the complainant") instead of "der Kläger und der Angeklagte" (="the
plaintiff and the defendant")].

[132] In the Mishnah and the Tosefta there is a difference of opinion between
R. Meir and his colleagues as to the method of choosing judges, but the Mishnah
and the Tosefta do not agree in the details, *cf.* Duenner's הגהות *ad loc.*

Mishnah for this method is בורר corresponding to ברורים, "chosen," used in our fragment. The difference between the Mishnah and our author consists merely in the fact that according to the former the judges are chosen by the litigants in every individual case, whereas according to the latter the community chooses the judges for a fixed period of time. The elders named by Moses were ברורים, "chosen," according to a remark in Sifre Num. 92, p. 93.

10,5: לפי העת. Schechter renders, "according to the age," *i. e.*, according to the age prescribed further on. But apart from the fact that "age" in the sense of "time of life" can never be expressed by עת but only by ימים as in 10,1, the information, according to this interpretation, would be quite superfluous, since the required age of the judges is stated exactly in the following lines. Fortunately the expression used by our author is found in the Hebrew text of Ben Sira, vi,8:[133] כי יש אוהב כפי עת ולא יעמד ביום צרה, "There are those who are friends so long as it is convenient and do not remain so in time of trouble." Accordingly, לפי העת is to be translated "so long as they are fit," and thus at the very beginning of this law it is pointed out that judges are not to serve for life but only for the period of their fitness, *i. e.*, till their sixtieth year, since they lose their fitness in advanced age, as is explained more fully later. *Cf.* also Ben Sira XX, 6–7, where עת is used in a similar sense.

10,5: ארבעה למטה לוי ואהרן. The Halakah[134] requires only that judges be of pure Jewish descent in capital cases but not that there must be Levites or priests among them. Nevertheless it is clear from the Talmudic sources themselves that ordinarily every Synhedrion, even the small one of 23 members, had priests in it, even though their presence was not legally required.[135] The observation of the Talmud (Yoma 26a), לא משכחת צורבא מרבנן דמורי אלא דאתי משבט לוי, "Only sages of the tribe of Levi are wont to give correct decisions,"[136] means only that the presence of priestly judges in court guarantees a correct decision. The court attendants, שוטרים, were always Levites according to a statement in Josephus. Every authority (=court), he reports (*Ant.* IV,8,14), was provided with two men of the tribe of Levi as

---

[133] *Cf.* my *Randglossen zum hebräischen Ben Sira*, p. 7.

[134] Mishnah, Sanhedrin IV, 2. *Cf.* more fully Hoffmann, *Der oberste Gerichtshof*, pp. 26–28. The priestly courts ב"ד של כהנים mentioned in the Talmudic sources had jurisdiction chiefly over priests; *cf.* Sifre Deut. 144, p. 198. שממנין ש' לכל שבט, which later could be done only in the case of priests. A different view is held by Büchler, *Synhedrion*, p. 102 ff.

[135] [Sifre Deut. 153, p. 206. S. L.]

[136] What is said there in regard to ש' יששכר has only theoretical value, since the tribal distinctions were effaced in the Talmudic period.

attendants. And Josephus is found to agree with the Tannaitic Halakah (Sifre Deut. 15, p. 25; Midr. Tann. 9), which similarly states that the שוטרים must be Levites. When this law was changed we do not know. The Amora R. Ḥisda (d. ca. 300) seems to date this change in the law in the time of Ezra,[137] but this is hardly tenable in view of the statements in Josephus and Sifre, both of whom probably spoke of conditions in their own time. According to the interpretation given above, the prescription in our fragment that the court must include priests, Levites[138] and Israelites among its members is not only based upon Biblical examples (cf. 2 Chron. 17:7) but also is found to be in agreement with the conditions that existed in the post-biblical period. It is characteristic of the standpoint of our author that the proportion of Israelite members to Levite and priestly ones redounds to the advantage of the first group, for while in the biblical passage referred to the officials appointed by Jehoshaphat consisted of nine Levites, two priests and five Israelites, the court described by our author consists of six Israelites and four descendants of Levi.

10,6: בספר ההגו. The uses of הגה in Talmudic-Midrashic literature and in Geonic writings leave no room for doubt as to the meaning of the expression ספר ההגו. A pedagogic rule of the Amora Rava (Berakhoth 63b) reads, לעולם ילמוד אדם ואחר כך יהגה, and, as is clear from Bava Bathra 21a, יהגה in this sentence corresponds to the Aramaic דייק,[139] wherefore we should translate, "First one should learn the material mechanically and then try to understand it fully." In Eruvin 21b and 54b ההוגה בהן probably likewise means "one who tries to explain the words of Torah" and not "one who studies them." The word טעם following contains a play on words, since טעם means both "taste" and "explanation of a biblical passage." In Palestinian sources הגה is used as an equivalent of בֵּאֵר "to explain." Thus for example, it is said of Moses (Ber. Rabba 49,2, p. 498, in the variae lectiones, and Tanḥuma, ed. Buber, I, 79) that "he interpreted (שהוגה) the Torah in seventy languages,[140] as it is written (Deut. 1:5), 'Moses began to interpret'

---

[137] Yevamoth 86b. It is not, to be sure, directly said in the Talmud that this disqualification of the Levites took place in the time of Ezra but the connection of this statement with what precedes permits of no other interpretation. Moreover the text appears not to be quite in order, since a biblical verse is there cited which is not to be found therein! Cf. Berliner-Hoffmann, *Magaz.* V,37, where an attempt is made to explain this passage. Probably, however, we should read עכשיו מעמידין אפילו ישראל.

[138] How many of these were to be priests and how many Levites is not stated.

[139] Bacher, *Terminologie*, mentions דייק but not הגה!

[140] The "seventy languages" is to be understood in the light of Mishnah Soṭah 32a and parallels, which Buber has failed to note.

(בְּאֵר)." In the light of this meaning of הגה one cannot be surprised to find that for Saadya Gaon הגא is the same as the oral law or the Mishnah, since this represents only the official interpretation of Scripture. This Gaon describes (*Saadyana*, p. 5) the composition of the Mishnah in the following words, בראות הורינו את ההמון כי נפץ בכל הארץ ויגורו על ההגא לבלתי השכח ויאספו כל מלה אשר העתיקו מני קדם... ויקראו את שמם משנה, "When our forefathers saw that the people (of Israel) was scattered throughout the whole world, they feared that the interpretation (הגא) would be forgotten. They therefore collected every word that had been handed down from ancient times ... and called this collection Mishnah."

Closely related to this הגות or הגא in הגיון in the well-known saying of R. Eliezer, ומנעו בניכם מן ההגיון (Berakhoth 28b). This Tanna, who was described by his teacher as "a well plastered cistern that does not lose a drop" (Avoth II, 8), and prided himself on "never having taught anything that I did not learn from my teacher" (Sukkah 28a), gave his disciples the advice to keep away from teachers who did not base their teaching on tradition but on הגיון, "logical inference."[141]

From the preceding it follows that ספר ההגו is nothing other than "the book of interpretations," that is, the authoritative interpretation of Scripture as given by our sect, accordingly a kind of "sectarian Mishnah."

In view of the occurence of הגא in Saadya Gaon one would actually be inclined to read הגי for ההגו;[142] nevertheless the writing הגות=הגו offers nothing unusual. On the other hand הָגוּ is, in spite of שָׂחוּ in Ezek. 47:5, hardly Hebrew (בהו and תֹהו are not related forms), so that this nominal form can only be explained as the Aramaic absolute state of הגותא.

We may perhaps also recall the statement in Megillath Taanith IV that the Sadducees used a ספר גזירתא, "a book of decisions," and that the day on which this law book was declared null and void was of such importance to the Pharisees that they appointed it a festival day. Accordingly ההגי (=ההגים) is perhaps to be read, inasmuch as הֶגֶה would be the same as מאמר, "judical decision."[143] Or is ס' ההגו the same as סֵפֶר מֻגֶּה, an expression that occurs not infrequently in the Talmud and means a correct copy? The Torah of this sect may have

---

[141] *Cf.* also Avoth de R. Nathan, ed. Schechter, 67, כופו את הילדים מנאון and the observation of Brüll in *Jahrb.* IX, 137, who also refers to Ber. Rabba XII, beg. p. 97, for והגיונו, "interpretation."

[142] *Cf.* above, the note on 6,6–7 where פי stands for פה.

[143] *Cf.* above, 9,10 או מאמרם and Gen. Rabba XLIX, 2 (Theodor-Albeck, p. 501) where the statement is made ואין הגא אלא תורה.

differed from the received text of Scripture in many passages, and our author may therefore have described their text as ספר מוגה "correct text."

10,6: מבני חמשה ועשרים . . . ששים. It is somewhat surprising that our author, in contrast to Num. 8:25, sets the age-limit at sixty and not at fifty. Dare one conclude from this[144] that our author read ששים instead of חמשים in the passage mentioned?

10,9: אמר לסור את דעתם. A well known[145] Tannaitic saying reads, תלמידי חכמים כל זמן שמזקינין חכמה נתוספת בהם, "The older that scholars become, the greater their wisdom becomes," and only of the 'Amme ha-'Areṣ is it said, כל זמן שהן מזקינין דעתן מטורפת עליהן, "The older they become, the more confused their mind becomes." It should be noted that the expression דעתן מטורפת corresponds exactly to the expression לסור דעתם employed by our author. It is also deserving of mention that according to the Halakah (Horayoth I, 4; Sanhedrin 36b; cf. however Tosefta VII, 5 where זקן is omitted) an old man may not serve as a judge in cases of capital crimes.

10,10–11: אל ירחץ איש במים צואים. This, as everyone knows, is not the view of the Halakah, according to which unclean water may very well be used for an immersion. It should be noted, however, that according to the Halakah also, there are circumstances in which water which has not its natural color may not be used (Miqwaoth VII, 3) and that the Halakah likewise prescribes that water used for washing the hands shall be clean (Tosefta Yadayim I, 10; Ḥullin 106a). Rashi (Zevaḥim 22a) even states that this prescription also applies to the water for immersion; cf. however Tosafoth, rubric למעוט.

10,11: מדי מרעיל. The emendation מטביל for מרעיל is hardly acceptable since in the first place מרעיל is graphically difficult to explain as an error for מטביל and in the second place טבל can be used of partial as well as total immersion.[146] Since, therefore, our author wishes to stress that there must be enough water for the bather to

---

[144] Cf. also Lev. 27:7; according to Avoth V end, old age begins at sixty, similarly Mo'ed Qaṭan 28a and Yerushalmi Bikkurim II, 64c.

[145] This saying has been handed down in various forms: Qinnim, end; Shabbath 152a; Sifre Deut. 48, p. 111 and Cant. Rabba on 1:2 near end.

[146] Cf. for example Josh. 3:15 נטבלו "were wetted," and in Talmud Pesaḥim 115a טבולו במשקה "moistened with a liquid." Naturally this is not to say that טבילה does not mean "submersion," but this does not lie in the word טבל but in the fact that according to the Halakah all ritual ablutions must be made by total immersion, and for this reason רחץ and טהר in such uses in the Halakah can also mean only "total immersion." [Comp. Lieberman, Greek in Jewish Palestine, p. 135, p. 151.]

immerse himself wholly, there must be something else behind these words than מדי מטביל. I therefore conjecture that מגעיל is to be read for מרעיל and in this fragment הגעיל has indeed the same meaning as in the Talmud, where it means "to cleanse" and not "to abominate" as in biblical Hebrew. Accordingly the sentence reads, "Nor shall anyone take his (ritual) bath in dirty water or in water not sufficient to wash a person clean." In the Talmud indeed the rule prevails הגעלה בחמין, "Only cleansing with warm water is denoted by הגעלה," but this specializing of the idea of הגעלה (Mishnah Avodah Zarah, end; Talmud *idem*, 76a) does not lie in the term itself but is a *terminus techni-cus* coined by the Halakah which our author does not know or use. The real meaning[147] of הגעלה, געל and מגעיל is "cleansing" and the Halakah indeed uses it exclusively in a ritual sense, whereas for our author the ritual cleansing must also be an actual washing clean. That the entire body of the person cleansing himself must be covered with water is also required by the Halakah, as Schechter observes, and we may add that Anan prescribes this law as is expressly stated in his Book of Laws, ed. Harkavy, 52.[148] The Samaritans, on the other hand, state מקוה מטהר כל שהוא[149] (Yerushalmi Avodah Zarah V, 44d).

10,12: אל יטהר במה כלי. Schechter emends במה to במי and finds in this sentence the prescription of the unfitness for use of "drawn water" מים שאובים for a ritual bath. That our author should know of the prohibition of מים שאובים would not be strange inasmuch as, accord-ing to the Talmud (TP Avodah Zarah V, 44d), even the Samaritans,[150] who, as was remarked above, adopted a very lenient view with respect to the quantity of water, disqualified מים שאובים. Nevertheless the interchange of ירחץ and יטהר speaks against this interpretation, for if this prescription, like the preceding one, referred to the ritual bath of a person, our author would certainly have said, אל ירחץ במי כלי. Now in Halakic terminology טהר means the ritual cleansing of vessels[151]

---

[147] Rashi on Avodah Zarah 76a and on Lev. 26:11 takes the basic meaning of הגעיל to be "to throw out"; this view is followed by Kimḥi שרשים, *s. v.* געל, but it is an unfounded opinion. הגעיל can be explained most simply as the primitive Hiphil form of געל, "to be impure," so that הגעיל means "to make pure," "to cleanse."

[148] Harkavy, *ad loc.*, does not call attention either to the Talmudic view as being in agreement with Anan nor to the variant view of the Samaritans.

[149] On the distinction between מקוה and מעין *cf.* below on 10,12.

[150] Qirqisani in Harkavy, *op. cit.*, 130, cites the view of Anan that טבילה must take place in מים שאובים. It is possible, however, that Qirqisani made a slip and wished to say the opposite, since he then points out that in this matter Anan agrees with the Talmud in contrast to the Karaites, who, as is well known, declared מים שאובים to be fit for use.

[151] *Cf.*, for example, TP Shabbath II,4d in re טהרת כלים.

while רחץ is used of persons, and exactly the same terminology is
used in our fragment. The prescription in lines 10–11 deals with the
bathing of a person, אל ירחץ איש, whereas the following line deals with
the cleansing of vessels, for it is remarked that the water which is unfit
for the bath of a person is also unusable for the cleansing of vessels.
We should therefore read במה, "therein," or, more probably, בהם.[152]
And this view agrees with that of the Halakah, which does not permit
a מקוה "body of water" containing less than forty *seahs*, the amount
required to cover the body of the average person,[153] to be used for the
ritual cleansing of either persons or things.[154]

10,12: וכל גבא בסלע. The Mishnah also speaks very frequently
of the use of a pool, גבא, for ritual baths; *cf.* for example, Beẓah II,3
and Miqwaoth I, 1 and similarly Tosefta, Miqwaoth I, 3–4. The usual
designation in rabbinic literature for the ritual bath is, to be sure,
מקוה; nevertheless it is not without good reason that our author speaks
of גבא. According to the Halakah the water of a מקוה[155] is not susceptible
of uncleanness, whereas a pool, גבא, does become unclean if an unclean
vessel touches it, though not by contact with an unclean person. It is
this Halakah, embodied in Mishnah Miqwaoth I, 1–2, that is taught
by our author in this passage. It reads, "If a pool does not contain
enough water for a purifying bath and that water comes into contact
with an unclean object,[156] its water is made unclean by the water of
the (unclean) object." In this sentence הטמא is not an unclean person
but, as כלי at the beginning and הכלי at the end show, an unclean
object. Uncleanness is established by our author on the same basis
as in the Mishnah, namely that the water that comes into contact
with an unclean object, is made unclean thereby and conveys uncleanness to the whole body of water. This, however, applies only to a cistern
that does not contain enough water for an immersion. Otherwise the
water that has the power to cleanse is not made unclean by anything,

---

[152] *Cf.* above 6,10 להתהלך במה, where similarly either במה (=במו) or בהם is to be
read. [As is well known, מה(ה) regularly takes the place of ם(ה) as the suffix of the
third person plural masculine in an Isaiah scroll which was part of the library which
this sect used to own near the Dead Sea and of which extensive remains have been
recovered since the year 1947. *Cf.* above, n. 73. — H.L.G.]

[153] *Cf.* Eruvin 4b מים שכל גופו עולה בהן ... ושערו ... מ' סאה.

[154] Nazir 38a and the other passages in the Talmud which are cited by Rashi,
ad loc.

[155] This means a quantity of water that can be used for a ritual immersion or,
as the Mishnah, Miqwaoth I, 7, expresses it, מקוה שיש בו מ' סאה, corresponding to
יש בה די מרעיל in our passage.

[156] Miqwaoth I, 2 and הלך בהן הטמא טהור, *ibid.*, I, 4; *cf.* the reasoning in support of
this Halakah in Maimonides, Okalin, XV,1.

as was remarked above. A מקוה is just this kind of pool and is never made unclean. For במימי הכלי, Schechter reads כמימי הכלי and translates, "like the water in a vessel." But in that case one would expect כלי not הכלי, which alone is justified according to our interpretation, since what is spoken of is *the* vessel that causes the uncleanness.

It should be noted herewith that the view of our author that unclean water makes vessels unclean is in agreement with that of the Halakah, which recognizes such an uncleanness, even though, in the opinion of many, this is only a "rabbinic" (i. e., not a biblical) law; *cf.* Pesaḥim 16a–17b. On the other hand Anan states in his Book of Laws, 48–49, that only beverages manufactured by men, like wine, beer and the like, are susceptible of uncleanness, whereas water can never be made unclean at all. This view of Anan is referred to by Qirqisani (*op. cit.*, 130) in the following words: ואמר כי הטומאה אינה חלה על המים, "and he (Anan) stated that water is not susceptible of uncleanness." Harkavy, remarkably enough, has completely misunderstood this statment of Qirqisani, and instead of referring to Anan's words in his Book of Laws, 48, top, and 49,22, he cites Mishnah Yadayim IV,7, where the statement is made that the Sadducees declare a brook in a cemetery to be clean. This, Harkavy then explains, is based on the Sadducees' doctrine, also accepted by Anan, that water cannot be made unclean any more than earth can. For anyone who has even a superficial knowledge of the Halakah this completely false interpretation needs no refutation. The correct state of things will therefore be indicated here only briefly. In the Mishnah Yadayim it is not only the Sadducees who state that a brook in a cemetery[157] is clean but also the Pharisees; or more exactly, even the Sadducees, who otherwise state that when water is poured from a clean vessel into an unclean one, the water that remains in the clean vessel also becomes unclean because the stream of poured water unites the two vessels — even the Sadducees admit that a brook in a cemetery does not become unclean, simply because water cannot be made unclean so long as it is flowing, במחובר. This principle is also accepted by the Pharisees, but they go even further and state that a stream of poured water does not produce a union of two vessels. Accordingly it follows from this Mishnah that on this question Anan and his followers (*cf.*, for example, גן עדן 98d and אדרת אל' 126c) were further removed from the view of the Sadducees than from that of the Pharisees, since the

---

[157] *Cf.* R. Solomon Adeni in his commentary *ad loc.*, who is inclined to assume that what is here spoken of is a brook that is *beside* but not *in* a cemetery. But this distinction can hardly be justified from the standpoint of the Halakah.

former declare even the water that comes into contact with something unclean through a stream of pouring to be unclean in some circumstances.

10,14: על השבת וכו'. As was remarked above on 9,8 this clause is the title of the following section.

10,15: גלגל שמש. In Tannaitic literature חמה and not שמש is used in expressions of time, cf., for example, שקיעת החמה, גלגל החמה and so on.[158] Nevertheless it is highly instructive that in a saying of the Hillelites, which the Mishnah has probably transmitted to us in its original form, שמש and not חמה is used, just as in our author; cf. Shabbath I,8 בית הלל מתירין עם שמש, "The Hillelites permit it to be done so long as the sun has not yet set."[159]

10,16: רחוק מן השער. According to the Book of Enoch, LXXII, 3 ff., there are twelve heavenly gates, six in the East, through which the sun rises, and six in the West, through which it sets. A different view is found in the rabbinic sources (TP Rosh Hashanah II, 58a; Pirqe R. Eliezer c.VI), which speak of the 365 windows of heaven, through which the sun rises and sets. Which of these two views was held by our author cannot be definitely stated but the use of the word שער, "gate," and not חלון, "window," indicates that he followed the former view. The function of the "sun-window" in the Book of Enoch, on the other hand, is a different one, namely to diffuse warmth, while light "comes through the gate."

10,16: מלואו. Usually בְּמִלּוּאוֹ, "in its fullness," is read, that is, when the whole sphere of the sun is above the horizon. I do not think, however, that מלא can be used of the sun, since in Talmudic literature[160] it is used only of the waxing of the moon. If the text is to be altered at all, it is best to read מלבוא;[161] "when the sun is still distant from the gate through which it sets" gives very satisfactory sense, especially if one bears in mind what was said in the preceding comment, that is, the sun is רחוק מן השער in the evening as well as in the morning but with the difference that in the morning it is ר' מ' השער and in the evening השער מלבוא מ' 'ר. This reading too, to be sure,

[158] Cf. the dictionaries sub voce and further, Mishnah Rosh Hashanah II, 6, רואי השמש=רואי החמה, Eccles. 6:1. לפני החמה and Nedarim III, 7,

[159] This expression is perhaps based on the biblical עם שמש (Ps. 72:5). In any case it means only מבעוד יום. The conclusions drawn from this expression by R. Elijah of Wilna in his commentary to Oraḥ Ḥayyim 261 are unwarranted.

[160] Cf. Ben Sira L, 6; TP Berakhoth IX, 13b and the prayer קדוש לבנה where similarly the expression שתמלא פגימת הלבנה (Sanhedrin 41b; Pesiqta R. 179a) is found.

[161] Cf. 3,18, ברבוי=ברוי where ו is similarly used for ב. [But see the bracketed note to the discussion of 3,18 — H.L.G.]

has its difficulty, since nothing is said to indicate how high the sun still is above the horizon when the Sabbath begins and this is so essential a point that it could hardly be omitted here. It therefore seems advisable to separate מלואו into two words: מל "mile" and וא"ו "six"; therewith the beginning of the Sabbath is precisely determined, that is, as an hour and 48 minutes before sunset.[162] Time is reckoned in the Talmud, as is well known, by giving the distance that can be covered during the interval, and is always used as the measure of distance; thus our author would be using the usual method of reckoning time. As for the determination of the beginning of the Sabbath, our author comes very near to the view of the Rabbis, for whom the Sabbath begins something more than an hour and a half before nightfall,[163] and the difference between them and our author amounts to about a quarter-hour, but here it is further to be noted that the Rabbis also regard it as an act pleasing to God, a מצוה, if one begins to observe the Sabbath earlier than is absolutely necessary, that is, even earlier than an hour and a half before nightfall.[164]

10,16: לקדשו ... את שמור אמר אשר הוא כי. A *derash* to Exod. 20:8 and Deut. 5:12, which is found in various Tannaitic sources,[165] reads, זכור עד שלא יכנס להוסיף עליו מן החול בתחלתו, שמור משיכנס להוסיף עליו מן החול ביציאתו, "Be mindful of the Sabbath — that is, begin the Sabbath even before its time has come and when it is still a workday. And keep the Sabbath — that is, continue to observe the Sabbath even when it is over and the workday has already begun." Like the Tannaitic Midrashim, so also our author finds in שמור a reference to תוספת שבת, "the prolongation of the Sabbath." Whereas the former, however, refer to the prolongation at the end of the Sabbath, the latter refers to the prolongation at the beginning of the Sabbath, therein partially

---

[162] One mile = 18 minutes; *cf.* Pesaḥim 93b, where 40 miles = 12 hours.

[163] There are three ways of reckoning the beginning of night in the Talmud: (a) sunset, שקיעת החמה; (b) appearance of the stars, צאת הכוכבים; (c) twilight, בין השמשות. The time between sunset and the appearance of the stars comes to 90 minutes (Pesaḥim 93b). The Sabbath is supposed to begin shortly before sunset (Rosh Hashanah 9a), whereas the end of the Sabbath does not come until the stars appear. The statements of the Talmud about these time-reckonings cause great difficulties. The most plausible explanation of these passages is that given by R. Elijah of Wilna in his commentary on *Oraḥ Ḥayyim* 261; the statements in Zuckermann's *Materialien zur Zeitrechnung*, 65–68, are to be corrected in accordance with this explanation.

[164] Rosh Hashanah, *loc. cit.*, [See now Rabin on 10,16.]

[165] Mekilta, Yethro 7 (p. 229); Mek. de R. Simon (Hoffmann, p. 107), and Midrash Tannaim 21 (from which the citation in the text is taken). [ed. Epstein-Melamed, p. 148, n. 30. Comp. Brüll, *Jahrbücher* IV, p. 85–86. — S. L.]

agreeing with the Karaites, who find in the words of Scripture (Lev. 19:3) ואת שבתותי תשמרו a reference to the prolongation at the beginning of the Sabbath; cf. Bashyazi, 'אדרת אל 44c. Of interest for the development of the תוספת שבת is the view of the Falashas,[166] for whom the Sabbath begins as early as the ninth hour on Friday, that is, at three o'clock in the afternoon. The esoteric Halakah, as, for the sake of brevity, I designate the Halakah contained in the Pseudepigrapha, often differs from the canonical Halakah, as represented in the Talmud in that the latter draws a sharp line between "law," חוב, and "pious deed," מצוה, whereas this distinction does not exist for the former. To begin the Sabbath early and to end it late is regarded by the Halakah as a pious deed without, however, being required as a duty.[167] In our fragment, on the other hand, it is said that one may not do any work 108 minutes before the beginning of the Sabbath.[168] Thus the "prolongation of the Sabbath" becomes a duty. Further, it is said in the Talmud:[169] He who does any work on Friday after three o'clock will not see any blessing come therefrom; and this recommending of a pious deed developed into a formal prohibition among the Falashas. The great antiquity of this custom is evident from the fact that already in an edict of Augustus in favor of the Jews, they were excused from having to appear in court on Friday after three o'clock; cf. Josephus, Antiq., XVI,6,2.

10,17: אל ידבר איש דבר נבל ורק. Schechter reads וְרַק and takes it with the following sentence, but this is quite impossible. Not only do we have in what follows something like fifty sentences that begin with אל and it would be very curious if this one sentence should begin with אל ורק, but there is absolutely no apparent connection between the two sentences joined together by ורק. There can therefore be no doubt that ורק belongs to the preceding, and is in fact to be read וָרֵק; דבר נבל ורק is "empty prating," which in our fragment as in the Talmud, Shabbath 150a, is forbidden on the Sabbath. If one further reflects that הבל וריק is a biblical phrase (Isa. 30:7), one may well assume that נבל is a miswriting of הבל.

---

[166] Cf. Halevy, Teezaza Sanbat 42b: "The Sabbath came down from heaven to earth on Friday at the ninth hour and remained until sunrise on Sunday"; cf. also ibid., pp. 13a, 14b.

[167] Cf. the proof-texts for this statement in R. Elijah Gaon's commentary on Oraḥ Ḥayyim 261,11.

[168] [Comp. L. Ginzberg, Commentary on TP, Berakhoth I, p. 33, and 'Arugath Habosem I, p. 86: בספר הכבוד שצריך להוסיף שעה — S. L.]

[169] Pesaḥim 50b, and the comment of the Talmud, שמותי לא משמתינן; cf. also Pesaḥim 99b concerning eating after three o'clock.

10,18: אל ישפוט על הון בצע. Usually one sees in this prescription the rabbinical prohibition of holding a trial on the Sabbath, but שפט על cannot possibly mean "to pass judgment on" but as in Jer. 2:35 must mean "to plead" or "dispute about," so that we should probably read יִשָּׁפֵט; "one must not dispute about money or property on the Sabbath." An almost verbal parallel to this is found in the Falasha pseudepigraph *Teezaza Sanbat* 19a, "He who is involved in a dispute on the Sabbath, and especially he who buys or sells, shall die." The dispute here mentioned is one about money matters, as is clear from the juxtaposition of this prohibition and the one concerning trade.

10,19: אל ידבר ... למשכים. Exactly the same prohibition is found in a Baraita,[170] Shabbath 150b, לא יאמר לו ... כך וכך אני עתיד להוציא, "One shall not say to his neighbor on the Sabbath, I am thinking of spending such and such a sum." With למשכים[171] is to be compared מחשיך, Mishnah Shabbath XXIII, 3. So far at least as content is concerned, this prohibition coincides with that of the Mishnah except only that the Mishnah speaks of an activity to be undertaken the same evening while our author speaks of one on the following morning. May we conclude from this that for our author, as for the Falashas (*cf. Teezaza Sanbat* 42b), the night from Saturday to Sunday is regarded as a continuation of the Sabbath?

10,20: לעשות את עבודת חפצי השבת. The emendation חפצו ביום השבת, though 11,2 might seem to favor it, is entirely unwarranted. For it is so self-evident that one may not cultivate a field on the Sabbath that no special mention of such a prohibition is necessary. And further, what need is there of the long-winded sentence אל יתהלך איש בשדה לעשות, "No man shall go into the field to do the necessary work"? Would it not be sufficient to say, אל יעש איש עבודת חפציו בשבת, "No man shall undertake work on the Sabbath"? A Baraita[172] cited in Eruvin 38b gives an almost verbal parallel to our passage and enables us to grasp its real meaning. The Baraita reads, לא יהלך אדם בתוך[173] שדהו לידע מה היא צריכה, "A man shall not go into his field (on the Sabbath) in order to see what work is necessary (after the Sabbath)." Exactly the same thing is forbidden in our fragment.[174] We should therefore either read לדעת for לעשות or insert אחר before השבת. It is also possible,

---

[170] *Cf.* also the other Baraita there cited and Tosefta Shabbath XVII (XVIII), 9.

[171] [See Lieberman, *Greek in Jewish Palestine*, p. 135, n. 151.]

[172] The second half of this Baraita is found in Tosefta Shabbath XVII (XVIII),10, where the first half was probably originally included.

[173] The editions read לסוף but *cf.* Rabbinowitz *ad loc.*

[174] How strictly this law was observed is shown by the anecdote in TP Shabbath XV,15a; TB 150b is to be corrected in accordance with TP.

to be sure, that in this passage השבת means "week," and accordingly חפצי השבת denotes the work of the week. It should further be noted that the expression עבודת חפצו is taken from the biblical ממצוא חפצך (Isa. 58:13) and is also used in the Talmud; *cf.*, for example, Shabbath 150a, חפציך אסורים וכו', "You may not attend to your affairs on the Sabbath but only to the affairs of Heaven;" that is, one may not speak of business matters on the Sabbath but may speak of the care of the poor, etc.

10,21: עד על אלף אמה. The first, partly illegible, word is probably to be read as עדף, "more than," *i. e.*, the prescribed Sabbath limit (of movement). In view of the peculiar orthography of this fragment, which frequently omits the plural ending, the writing אלף for אלפים is not strange, and the occurrence of אלפים in 11,6 shows quite clearly that our author recognized the same Sabbath limit as did rabbinic tradition.

10,22: כי אם המוכן. Schechter rightly remarks that מוכן is here to be taken in the sense of "prepared for this purpose," just as the Halakah insists that only that which has been prepared before the Sabbath for use on that day may be eaten. The early Karaites were divided in their opinions about this matter;[175] some of them followed rabbinic tradition in respect of הכנה, while others permitted the enjoyment of fruits that fell from the tree on the Sabbath, although in the nature of the case they had not been prepared before the Sabbath for use on that day. From a remark in the Mishnah, Pesaḥim IV end, we learn that the inhabitants of Jericho did not take this rabbinic prescription too literally, and if the statement[176] is true that this practice of the people of Jericho is attributable to Sadducean influence we should here have an instance in which our author agrees with the Pharisees against the Sadducees.

10,22–23: ומן האובד בשדה. Schechter translates, "of that which is perishing in the field." I consider it quite impossible, however, that

[175] Anan's view on the subject is difficult to state exactly. In his Book of Laws he twice gives his opinion (pp. 70, 73). Both passages, however, can be understood to mean that actual work must be done before the Sabbath, and on p. 73 we should perhaps read ומטוי, "what is roasted," instead of ואצנעי. At any rate the Karaites appeal to Anan as one who required הכנה, whereas Benjamin Nahawendi did not consider it necessary. *Cf.* Harkavy, *Anans Gesetzbuch*, pp. 136, 152 (he, however, has not noticed that Anan's words in this Book of Laws can be interpreted differently) and Nicomedia, נן עדן XIX, 35a. As for the distinction that Anan makes (p. 70) between the Sabbath and a festival-day, Harkavy has overlooked the fact that Anan himself (p. 74) has given fuller reasons for this.

[176] *Cf.* Büchler, *Priester und Kultus*, pp. 164 ff.

our author with his extraordinary rigorism would permit fruits to be picked or grain to be cut because they might otherwise suffer damage from rain or from any other cause. In general the context shows quite clearly that in אובד there must lie a synonym for מוכן. We should read האגור, "that which has been stored away," and the illegible word at the beginning is not בשדה but באצרה[177] "in the storeroom." Similarly in the Mishnah, Shabbath 18:1, the question is discussed under what circumstances food may be taken from the storeroom.[178] The reading האוכר, denominative from אִכָּר, "farmer," is also possible and the meaning would be that on the Sabbath one may use only that which the farmer has already prepared for use, in which case fruits or grain may be eaten if they are still in the field, בשדה, and are not found in the house as מוכן. To be sure in the following sentence it is said, אל יאכל ואל ישתה כי אם היה במחנה, "One shall not eat or drink that which was not in the camp, מחנה, already at the beginning of the Sabbath,"[179] but this does not exclude what is in the field; for it means only, that if a non-Jew has brought something from outside the camp, that is, the Sabbath limit, on the Sabbath, this may not be used, and this is in agreement with the Halakah, which similarly forbids it.[180]

11,1: בדרך וירד לרחוץ. Schechter reads היה בדרך, and the omission of היה could be explained by the fact that in the sentence היה במחנה היה בדרך the copyists erred in omitting the second היה. One does not, however, understand why just the man who was "on the way" should bathe, and it seems much better to read הבא מן הדרך, just as there is frequent mention in the Talmud of bathing on returning from a journey; cf., for example, TP Yoma VIII, 44d, הבא מן הדרך והיו רגליו קיהות עליו שמותר להרחיצם במים, "R. Acha permitted a man (on the Day of Atonement) who returned from a journey and whose feet hurt to bathe them in water." This reading also disposes of the difficulty of someone being "on the way" on the Sabbath, since in 10,21 it was expressly forbidden to go more than two thousand cubits away from the city. But with the proposed reading we are here dealing with someone who has returned from a journey late on Friday and bathes on the Sabbath to wash away the dust of travel. That our author should speak of the occasion for bathing at all is due to the fact that in his view not every kind of bathing is permitted on the Sabbath, and the words בא מן הדרך are meant to indicate that it is not permitted

---

[177] The writing באצרה for באצרו is not strange, cf. 10,12.

[178] Cf. the explanation of this Mishnah in the Talmud ad loc., 126b f.

[179] It is in this sense that אם היה "that was" is to be explained.

[180] Cf. Beẓah III,2, and the explanation of this Mishnah in TB 24b and Yerushalmi 62a.

to take a ritual bath, this being in agreement with the view represented by the Shammaites (Yom Tov II,2), whereas the Hillelites permit it. In *Teezaza Sanbat*, bathing on the Sabbath is described as a serious sin (21b), and this is probably the view of the Book of Jubilees also, as will be shown in the following remarks.[181]

11,1–2: ישתה על עומדו ואל ישאב אל כל כלי. Schechter refers to the Book of Jubilees, L, 8 (*cf.* also 11,29) where it is said, "and also he who draws water on it (the Sabbath) that he has not prepared beforehand on Friday . . . shall die." But if one looks at our text more closely, it appears that its author agrees not with the Book of Jubilees but with the rabbinic Halakah. The prohibition is motivated in the Book of Jubilees by the words "that he has not prepared beforehand" or, if we use the terminology of the Halakah,[182] because water is מוקצה דהכנה and such a thing may not be used on the Sabbath *under any circumstances*, whether drawn in a vessel or with the hands. The Karaites, who in this matter agree with the Book of Jubilees, similarly give הכנה as the reason for this, as the words of Hadassi, *Eshkol* 56a, clearly state, פלני מים . . . אסור לנו לשלוח יד בהם לשתות או להתרחץ מהם גופנו מצואה . . . יען כי אינם מוכנים לנו ברשותינו, "We are forbidden to use brooks whether to drink from them or to bathe in them, since their water was not already in our houses before the Sabbath." To be sure, Hadassi adds, אף מעיני מים שהם בבתים אסור לנו לשאוב מהם מים ויעלו כי היא מלאכה,[183] "also from water-tanks that are in our houses we are forbidden to draw water for this is a labor (prohibited on the Sabbath)." We must not, however, ascribe this Karaite view to the Book of Jubilees, where the drawing of water is forbidden because the water has not been "prepared beforehand,"[184] from which it appears that drawing itself was not work. The view of our author, to be sure, can be made to agree in part with that of the Karaites, namely that the drawing of water is forbidden but not its use. On closer examination, however, this view proves to be untenable since then the words על עומדו, "where he stands," would simply have no meaning. For the correct understanding of our passage it is first necessary to know that וירד לרחוץ means "and he entered the bath." The question here discussed, however, is whether a person who stands on the bank of a stream in

---

[181] At least with respect to bathing in rivers and comparable bodies of waters.

[182] According to the Rabbinic definition of the concept of הכנה water is, to be sure, always to be considered מוכן.

[183] In this sentence מעין does not mean "spring" but "water-tank." It is also possible that בית is equivalent to "private property," רשות היחיד.

[184] Similarly in *Teezaza Sanbat* 19 V, where only the drawing of "flowing water" is forbidden.

order to enter the water is first permitted to drink a little water from the stream. The rule laid down in our fragment reads, "He may drink in the place where he finds himself but he may not draw water in a vessel." Accordingly this view corresponds in every detail to that of the Halakah. First it is presupposed that a place where one bathes is an area, רשות, out of which one may not carry anything, as the Halakah[185] also teaches (Eruvin VIII,7). Moreover, it is taught in our fragment, in further agreement with the Halakah,[186] that one who stands on the bank of a stream may stretch out his upper body and without leaving his place, על עומדו, may put his mouth to the stream and drink. He is not, however, permitted to stretch out his arm from his place on the bank and draw water in a vessel because then it is to be feared that he may draw back his arm with the filled vessel, thereby bringing the water from the stream to the bank, which is forbidden.

11,3: מובאים בגו. Schechter translates "that were brought by a gentile" and refers (Introduction, p. xxv) to the custom of the Falashas, who pronounce unclean anything touched by a gentile. Now there can, of course, be no doubt that in the period when rabbinic Judaism adhered to the observance of the laws of ritual purity, this law, which is now observed only by the Falashas, was generally regarded as an undisputed Halakah.[187] Nevertheless the interpretation given by Schechter of מובאים בגו is quite impossible on both linguistic and material grounds. In the first place מובאים בגו, "brought by a gentile," is not Hebrew,[188] since this would have to be expressed either by מובאים מן גוי or, in accordance with Mishnaic usage, by על ידי גוי. Strange too is the omission of the י in גוי, when one considers that this letter belongs to the root and therefore could hardly be omitted. More

---

[185] The Mishnah speaks of a body of water which is located on private property and which nevertheless is regarded as כרמלית. With reference to streams, lakes, etc. cf. Tosefta Shabbath I, 4 and the parallels, according to which a body of water is under all circumstances a כרמלית.

[186] Cf. Eruvin X, 6 and the explanation of this in the Talmud, 99a, בחפצין הצריכין לו, which can best be understood with Rashi ad loc. (against Maimonides, Hilkoth Shabbath XIV, 2) to mean that there is a difference between drinking without the use of a vessel, which is permitted, and drinking from a vessel, which is forbidden. TP X,26b seems to interpret the Mishnah differently from Bavli, but the meaning is very obscure. Dünner's explanation of the passage is untenable since למעלה מי is no רה"ר but a מקום פטור.

[187] Sifra on 15:2 Zavim, begin. ed. Weiss 74d; Tosefta Zavim II,1; Niddah 34a; cf. also John 18:28 and Acts 10:28.

[188] Such a construction is reminiscent of the Arabic جاءَب "to bring someone something," "to come with someone."

important than these linguistic objections are those connected with the subject matter. In the section 10,14 to 11,18 we have a brief compendium of Sabbath laws,[189] and one is amazed to find this law of ritual purity[190] among them. To be sure, it does appear from II Macc. XII, 38 that it was the custom to purify oneself for the Sabbath, whereas on weekdays only those who intended to visit the Temple or to take part in sacred activities kept themselves pure.[191] In view of this, the prescription in question would be very much in place among the Sabbath laws. But not even if we should ascribe this view to our author would all the difficulties vanish, for the question still remains unanswered, how can the ritual impurity which is caused by contact with a gentile be removed by rubbing with incense, שופם בלבונה,[192] when the Bible and the whole of post-biblical literature recognizes water[193] as the only means of purification, and not rubbing with incense?[194] All these difficulties disappear if we read סואבים בגל[195] instead of מובאים בגו. "Soiled by excrement" is exactly what we expect after בגדים צואים, "dirty clothes." In both cases we are dealing not with

[189] As will be shown below, the sentence (11,21) וכל הבא has nothing to do with the Sabbath, any more than the preceding ואל ישלח; accordingly, the Sabbath laws extend only to מלבד שב'.

[190] "And when the seventh day came round, they purified themselves, as was their custom, and kept the Sabbath." According to Sifra on Lev. 11:8 ed. Weiss 49a (=Rosh Hashanah 16b) non-priests were bound to observe the obligation of purifying themselves only on the three pilgrim-festivals; cf., however, Hadassi, Eshkol 56a, who speaks of the obligation to purify oneself on Friday for the Sabbath, and this is also the view of the Samaritans.

[191] This, of course, was only the minimum, whereas "the chosen ones" spent their whole life in a state of purity. Maimonides (Okalim 16,9) asserts that even priests had to avoid only corpses but not other unclean things; his source is probably Pesaḥim 113a, כהנא ... נבילה פשוט. Cf., however, Sifra on 5,3, ed. Weiss 22d seq., where it is expressly stated that all priests must "avoid" all forms of uncleanness. In Pesaḥim, loc. cit., כהנא does not mean "priest" but is a personal name. [The reference to the Sifra is not understandable. For Maimonides' source, see TB Bekhoroth 29b. — S. L.]

[192] So we must read instead of שופים; "he rubs them," namely his clothes.

[193] At best fire might be considered, cf., Num. 31:23; but there the main thing is the voiding of the contents of vessels; at least this is the interpretation of the Halakah. Cf. Avodah Zarah 75a; Yerushalmi, end of the tractate, and Section IV, below.

[194] For a parallel to this kind of purification one could at best refer to Herodotus I, 198 where it said of the Babylonians that they purified themselves with incense after sexual intercourse. [But Herodotus adds that afterwards both men and women bathed. — R.M.]

[195] מסואבים in the Mishnah, but also the qal is used in the Targums. Perhaps, however, we should read מסואבים.

ritual impurities but with actually soiled clothes, which were not to be worn on the Sabbath until they had been cleaned (before the Sabbath, of course) with water or incense, and both the dirt and the bad odor had been removed. מ and ס are graphically so close, as are ו and ל, that the miswriting of סואבים בגל as מובאים בגו is easily explained. The prescription of wearing only clean clothes on the Sabbath is also found in Tannaitic literature.[196]

11,4: אל יתערב ... מרצונו. It seems best to follow Schechter in reading יתרעב for יתערב in accordance with Mishnaic הרעיב עצמו[197] "to starve oneself," whereas the qal רעב means "to be hungry." Josephus, *Vita* 54, relates that a crowd of people, gathered in the house of prayer on a Sabbath, and in such agitation, that it was on the point of raising the banner of revolution, dispersed when the sixth hour (11 a.m.) came, since as Josephus remarks, "our Law requires that we eat at this hour on the Sabbath." In this Josephus agrees with the statement of the Talmud, Yerushalmi Taanith III, 67a, that it is forbidden to fast later than the sixth hour on the Sabbath, אסור להתענות עד שש שעות בשבת. The Book of Jubilees, L, 12 and also *Teezaza Sanbat* 21a decree the death penalty for fasting on the Sabbath, whereas the Halakah not only allows this offense to go unpunished[198] but even permits fasting under certain circumstances.[199] Instructive is the custom, still observed by the Falashas,[200] of partaking of a small meal on the Day of Atonement that falls on a Sabbath because in their opinion complete abstinence from food and drink on the Sabbath is a greater sin than eating on the Day of Atonement.

11,5–6: אל ילך כי אם אלפים אמה. This prescription adds something not found in 10,21, namely that one is not permitted to let cattle graze outside the Sabbath limits even if the herdsman stays within the limit of two thousand cubits,[201] and this is also the view of the Halakah as formulated in the Mishnah Bezah 5:3: הבהמה כרגלי הבעלים, "Cattle may go only so far as their owner."

---

[196] *Cf.*, for example, Mekilta de R. Simon 107 [ed. E-M, p. 149]; Sifra on Lev. 23:35, ed. Weiss 102b, and parallel midrashim on this verse.

[197] In a saying of R. Akiva, Sanhedrin 65b.

[198] Fasting on the Sabbath is, to be sure, forbidden on biblical grounds according to the views of both Talmuds (Rosh Hashanah 19a; TP Nedarim VIII, 40d, לוקה ואי'צ היתר), but only because the commandment of קדוש is not fulfilled, and since this is only a מצוה עשה, no punishment is possible.

[199] *Cf.* Pesahim 68b and *Shulḥan Arukh, Oraḥ Ḥayyim* 288,2.

[200] *Cf.* Faitlovich, *Quer durch Abessinien*, p. 86. That this sect violates the teaching of the Talmud need not be specially emphasized, *cf.* Menaḥoth XI, 7.

[201] The death-penalty is decreed for the violation of this prohibition also in *Teezaza Sanbat* 19a.

11,6: אל ירם את ידו להכותה באגרוף. These words can be interpreted in various ways. They may contain a prohibition of causing pain to animals on the Sabbath because, according to Scripture (Exod. 20:10), this day was given to animals as a day of recuperation. Or they may mean that one may not strike animals on the Sabbath to force them to move because it is a day of rest for them and their rest may not be disturbed. The concluding clause, "if it is unruly, he shall not take it out of the house," speaks for the second interpretation; an unruly beast must be forced to move, and this is forbidden. The Halakah[202] does not contain such a prohibition and expressly allows one to drag an unruly beast by a rein or a rope. The rest prescribed for animals on the Sabbath by Scripture relates, according to the Halakah,[203] only to one's not burdening them with a load. In agreement with our fragment, on the other hand, is the pseudepigraph Baruch,[204] which is highly regarded by the Falashas, where a special place is reserved in Hell for the priests and Levites who did not say to the people, "On these days (Sabbaths) do not drive into their stalls asses, mules, oxen, sheep, goats or even chickens." It should be noted, moreover, that according to the Book of Jubilees, L, 12, striking an animal[205] is to be punished with death, which corresponds to the prohibition, found in our fragment, of striking an animal with one's fist. I have a suspicion, I must admit, that in the Hebrew original of the Book of Jubilees there appeared the expression והכה ומת "struck fatally," which in the translation became "to strike and kill." This assumption is supported by the prescription in *Teezaza Sanbat* 21a, "He who strikes and kills . . . shall die," and this is also the view of the Halakah, Mishnah, Shabbath VII, 2.

11,7: אל יוציא איש . . . ומן החוץ אל בית. According to a statement in the Talmud, Horayot 4a, the Sadducees forbade only carrying something out of the house (on the Sabbath) but not carrying something into it. Accordingly our author, who forbade both acts, would seem to be in agreement with the Pharisees as against the Sadducees. Nevertheless it is clear from the Talmud itself that this statement has no basis in fact but is purely scholastic speculation and is offered only

---

[202] *Cf.* Shabbath 52a on חמור שעסקיו רעים "an ass with bad habits."

[203] Mishnah, Shabbath V, *passim*. *Cf.* also Talmud, *ibid.* 154a.

[204] Printed in Halevy, *Teezaza Sanbat*, 100. The text is, I confess, not wholly intelligible to me.

[205] So we should probably interpret this passage and not "whoever strikes or kills someone," since homicide is a capital crime even on weekdays and it would be pointless for the author to include the punishment of homicide among Sabbath laws.

as a hypothesis by the Talmud itself. It is instructive that our author uses יוציא for both acts (carrying in and carrying out), as the very ancient Mishnah, Shabbath I, 1, also does,[206] whereas the later terminology designates the former as הכנסה and the latter as הוצאה. In the following sentence our fragment has אל יוצא . . . ואל יבא.

11,9: אל פתח כלי טוח בשבת. Schechter remarks that rabbinic Halakah is not so strict in this instance, while the Karaites agree with the strict view of our author. It should be noted, however, that the Karaites (Hadassi, *Eshkol* 56a) even forbid the opening and closing of a door, which is certainly not the view of our author, who forbids only the breaking open of a vessel sealed with pitch, and this is also the view of the Halakah, which permits the breaking only in an exceptional case.[207] Moreover, in our passage it is probably not the breaking of the vessel that is discussed but making an opening in it, and this is forbidden as a matter of course in the Mishnah, Shabbath XXII,3.

11,10: אל יטול בבית מושבת סלע ועפר. Schechter would like to read יום השבת[208] for מושבת but in my opinion this is quite impossible since in that case it would have to stand either before בבית or after ועפר. In the Additions (p. ix) Schechter seems to have given up this emendation, inasmuch as he refers to the term מקום מושבת used by the Karaites,[209] meaning "the place inhabited by Jews who observe the Sabbath in accordance with the Law," and the term מקום מחולל, "the place inhabited by gentiles[210] who desecrate the Sabbath." One might cite 11,14 in support of this interpretation, where it is prescribed that one may not spend the Sabbath in a place near which gentiles reside, that is, in a מקום מחולל. But this interpretation is nonetheless untenable, since in the first place the text would have to read מקום and not בית, as our author himself in the passage cited speaks of a מקום in the neighborhood of gentiles, and in the second place one would

---

[206] The term יציאות in this Mishnah as well as the formulation of the Halakoth therein indicate the beginnings of fixed Halakoth, *cf.* Frankel, *Darke ha-Mishnah*, 13. The interpretative part of this Mishnah, beginning with כיצד, which does not belong to the body of the Halakah, already uses the term.

[207] *Cf.* Beẓah 33b, where it is expressly said that the Mishnah speaks only of a case where the vessel was broken open before the Sabbath and only temporarily sealed; *cf.* further *Ṭur Oraḥ Ḥayyim*, 314.

[208] This is probably a printer's error for ביום.

[209] Since Schechter gives no reference for this, we may here refer to Hadassi, *Eshkol* 54c and Nicomedia, *Gan Eden* 30d.

[210] The Karaites are not agreed among themselves whether one may reside with Jews who do not observe the Sabbath in accordance with the Law; *cf. Gan Eden* 30a.

expect יטלטל and not יטול, which means "remove" or "take away" and not "move." This interpretation also has difficulties of a material kind. The term בית מושבת presupposes that one may spend the Sabbath in such a place only, so that it would be quite superfluous to stress in connection with any particular Sabbath laws that it is forbidden in a בית מושבת since it is to be assumed that on the Sabbath Jews are to be found only in such places. It is furthermore strange that of the many varieties of מוקצה[211] only rock and earth are mentioned, that is just such objects as one would be least likely to carry out on a day of rest.[212] Now, if we read מַגְבֵשֶת for מושבת, which is certainly not a drastic emendation in view of the fact that ו and נ are easily confused, and furthermore that there are numerous examples of transposition of consonants in our fragment, we find in this prescription a material and linguistic parallel to Shabbath 73b: היתה לו גבשושית ונטלה בבית חייב משום בונה, "If a man has a heap of earth in his house and removes it, he is guilty of a capital offense because he has constructed something (on the Sabbath)." Accordingly our passage should be translated, "A man shall not remove a heap[213] of rock and earth from his house." To be sure, the Talmud in the same passage also forbids the removal of such a heap in a field as well, but it should be noted that this applies only to newly broken land, ניר, and not otherwise (*ibid.*, 81b בשדה ניר), whereas in a house it is forbidden under all circumstances, which is why our fragment has בבית.

11,12: אל ימרא איש. Schechter translate, "No man shall provoke," which is linguistically permissible even though מרא for מרה occurs only once (Zeph. 3:1), since we also find ירפא for ירפה in 12,5. However, מרא is probably a denominative verb from Aramaic מרא, "master" or "lord," and one should therefore translate, "No one shall give his slave . . . commands on the Sabbath." The first interpretation is supported by *Teezaza Sanbat* 21a, where cursing and swearing are forbidden on the Sabbath. The other interpretation finds support in Philo, who states (*De Spec. Legibus* II, 67, ed. Mangey 283) that on the Sabbath masters must do without the services of their slaves, and must perform all necessary work themselves. This, to be sure, is not in agreement with the view of Talmudic Halakah, but Philo probably did not invent the law.

---

[211] How strict they were in this respect in earlier times is shown by Shabbath 123b and Josephus, *Bellum* II, 8, 19.

[212] Note that the text speaks of rock and not of small stones.

[213] For גבשושית of the Talmud the form נבוש is found in Tosefta, Oholoth XVII, 9, so that a third form מנבשת is not at all strange.

11,14: ‏אל ישבו²¹⁴ איש במקום קרוב לגוים‎.²¹⁵ Schechter refers to the views of the Karaites and Samaritans, according to which it is forbidden to spend the Sabbath anywhere else but among Jews. If, however, this had been the view of our author, he would have said ‏במקום גוים‎ and not ‏במ' קרוב לגוים‎, since it is difficult to see how the ‏מקום מושבת‎²¹⁶ could be defiled by the proximity of gentiles. It is more probable that our author held the opinion that the Sabbath must be spent in a state of ritual purity, ‏טהרה‎. For that reason he warns against staying in the neighborhood of gentiles, since one thereby incurs the danger of being made unclean. In the Mishnah, Shabbath I, 7,²¹⁷ it seems to be assumed that gentiles are not permitted to stay among Jews on the Sabbath. Anan in his Book of Laws, p. 6, forbids living with gentiles altogether, whereas in the Talmud it is reported of prominent scholars that they spent the Sabbath with gentiles, though this, to be sure, was only in exceptional cases.²¹⁸

11,15: ‏אל יחל ... על הון ובצע בשבת‎. The formulation of this enactment agrees both in content and in form with Tosefta Eruvin IV, 5: ‏גוים שבאו על עיירות ישראל ... לא באו על עיסקי נפשות ... אין מחללין עליהן את השבת‎, "In the case of gentiles who attack Jewish cities with no intent against the lives of the inhabitants — i. e., that they have come only to rob and plunder — the Sabbath is not to be desecrated in order to repel their attack." The special emphasis in our text on ‏על הון ובצע‎ shows that our author well knew the Halakah that the Sabbath could be desecrated where there was danger to life. ‏פקוח נפש דוחה שבת‎; he must therefore have lived after the time of the Maccabean revolt, for this Halakah was first taught by Mattathias.²¹⁸ᵃ

11,17: ‏אל יעלה איש וכו'‎. That our author would forbid saving a human being from drowning is quite impossible from what has been said in the preceding remarks and also contradicts the statement in line 13 that one may not lift an animal from a ditch, which certainly

²¹⁴ See Schechter for ‏ישבית‎ of the text.

²¹⁵ ‏בשבת‎ can hardly stand after ‏ישבות‎ and is probably due to the copyist, influenced by the preceding and following sentences that end with ‏בשבת‎.

²¹⁶ Cf. above, p. 66.

²¹⁷ ‏עד שיגיע למקום קרוב‎, "until he (the gentile) reaches the nearest settlement of gentiles." Rashi and Maimonides give a very forced explanation of ‏מקום קרוב‎, as R. Samuel Strashun has noted ad loc.

²¹⁸ Eruvin 65b; cf. the correct observation of the Poseqim (Magen Avraham 244,8), ‏אין דרך ישראל לשבות אלא אצל יהודים‎, "a Jew usually spends the Sabbath only among Jews," and cf. below, Section IV.

²¹⁸ᵃ I Macc. II, 32 ff. This passage has been thoroughly discussed by Geiger, Urschrift, p. 217. I hope to describe the evolution of this Halakah elsewhere.

implies that one must[219] help a human being in a similar situation. This sentence, therefore, also begins with נפש אדם in contrast to the case mentioned in line 15; accordingly, here something is permitted and not forbidden. We should therefore read, וְאַל מקום אל יַעַל יַעֲלֶה and translate, "If a person has fallen into a body of water[220] or any place from which he cannot extricate himself, one shall pull him up by means of a ladder, a rope or some other instrument." The confusion in our text arose from the fact that the scribes considered יעל superfluous and therefore wrote only יעלה. The composition אל יעל is a formation similar to the biblical בליעל, so that perhaps מקום אל יעל means just "a dangerous place."

11,18: כי כן כתוב מלבד שבתותיכם. The biblical passage here referred to is certainly Lev. 23:38, where, to be sure, the text has י"י שבתות. Since, however, our author never uses the tetragrammaton and in this passage it was probably not convenient to use אל, the equivalent of י"י elsewhere employed by him[220a] — שבתות אל would hardly be permissible — it became שבתותיכם in accordance with the words מתנותיכם, נדריכם etc. which follow in this verse. Moreover, the proof from Scripture is not adduced for the first half of the statement, that the burnt-offering of the Sabbath, עולת שבת, is to be offered on the Sabbath, since that is expressly prescribed in Num. 28:9–10,[221] but, Lev. 23:38 proves rather, in the opinion of our author, that no other kind of offering may be brought on the Sabbath. It follows from the fact that in connection with the festivals it is stated that the Sabbath-offerings and peace-offerings are to be brought in addition to the festival offerings, but nothing is said about oblations other than the Sabbath burnt offering[222] in connection with the Sabbath. It is most probable that our author's opposition is directed against the rule proposed by Hillel[223] that the Passover lamb must be offered on the Sabbath even though it is not a Sabbath-offering. Nevertheless one may not ascribe an anti-Pharisaic tendency to our author on the basis

[219] I say "must" in accordance with the Halakah, Yoma 84b, הזריז הרי זה משובח.

[220] Schechter emends מקום מים to מקוה מים, which is indeed probable but not absolutely necessary.

[220a] See p. 197, n. 184.

[221] Hadassi, *Eshkol* 4a top, reports that the sectarian Meshvi Baalbeki taught that no offering might be brought on the Sabbath at all; such a view, however, is hardly conceivable at the time when the Temple stood, and no opposition to such a view is to be expected in our fragment.

[222] Anan too (*Book of Laws* 76) makes an effort to prove from Scripture that no sacrifice may be brought on the Sabbath except the עולת שבת [and, of course, the daily offering, Num. 28:10 — H. L. G.].

[223] Pesaḥim 66a and many other places; *cf.* the detailed discussion of this in Chwolson, *Das letzte Passahmahl*, pp. 18 ff.

of this opinion since it is quite clear from the talmudic accounts of this ruling of Hillel that at first it met with opposition from the Pharisees too.[224] The Book of Jubilees, L, 10–11, also seems to be opposed to Hillel's view inasmuch as it specially stresses the point that only the daily sacrifice, תמיד, and the Sabbath-offerings, מוסף, may be brought on the Sabbath.

11:18–20: אל ישלח ... לטמא. These prescriptions, like the two following, do not, it is true, deal with the Sabbath but are given as an addition to the rules about the Sabbath sacrifices since they refer to the sanctifying of the sacrifices and the Temple. This first prescription, to be correctly understood, must be read in connection with 6,11 ff. As is clear from this passage, the motive for the founding of this sect was not its opposition to the sanctity of the Jerusalem Temple but precisely the great veneration shown the legitimate Temple by these people, which was the occasion of their breaking away. They blamed their opponents for not treating the holy place in Jerusalem as holy enough, and their first step was to shun the Jerusalem Temple in order to avoid being involved in its profanation.[225] We may therefore assume that among the members of the sect were some who kept away from the Temple but nevertheless sent their sacrifices through others,[226] and it is this practice that is forbidden in this passage. If someone was convinced that the laws of ritual purity were not observed in the Temple, he was the abettor of those who defiled the Temple, and for that reason every form of participation in the Temple-service, whether direct or indirect, was a sin. From the concluding words, "and the prayer of the righteous is like a gift acceptable to God," ותפלת צדיקים כמנחת רצון,[227] it appears that the followers of this sect did not possess a sanctuary where they could sacrifice, and for that reason many of them sent their sacrifices to the Temple in Jerusalem, and these persons are here reminded that their prayer is just as acceptable to

---

[224] That the Bene Bathyra, who refused to accept Hillel's view, were not Sadducees is in my opinion certain.

[225] Cf. also 5,6, where their opponents are reproached with defiling the Temple in entering it while in a state of impurity, for which reason it becomes impossible for followers of the sect to visit the Temple, for thus they would be offering "unclean sacrifices," מקריב קרבן בטומאה, which is strictly forbidden.

[226] Josephus reports the like about the Essenes, who did not visit the Temple but still had their sacrifices brought there; cf. Ant. XVII,1,5.

[227] A deliberate alteration of the expression in Prov. 15:8, תפלת ישרים רצונו, in that "the upright," ישרים, is changed to צדיקים, "the righteous," not because our author is a Sadducee and because צדיקים reminds one of צדוקים but because in post-biblical times the conflict of parties was a legal-ecclesiastical one, and therefore "righteous" and "unrighteous" were the usual names.

God as sacrificial offerings.[228] Schechter is inclined to assume on the basis of 11,17 ff. that the sect had an altar. But, as was said above, this passage merely contains a protest against the teaching of Hillel that one should sacrifice the Passover lamb on a Sabbath. The altar that is mentioned must therefore be the one in Jerusalem, and this law, so far as our sect is concerned, must be of a more theoretical nature than many other laws in this fragment.[229]

11,21–22: וכל הבא אל בית השתחות. By בית השתחות Schechter understands some kind of prayer-house in contrast to the central sanctuary of the sect in Damascus. That the unclean are forbidden to enter synagogues is of course not surprising since this is in agreement with the Halakah as it was observed in the period of the Mishnah and in many lands down to the late Middle Ages.[230] However the name "house of prostration" is extremely odd for the synagogue because although השתחויה, "prostration," was usual even in synagogues in earlier times and was not limited or discontinued until the Amoraic period,[231] still it was never so essential a part of the service that it could have given prayer-houses their name.[232] On the other hand it is out of the question that בית השתחות should mean the Temple since our author several times speaks of מקדש (cf., 5,6; 6,12 et al.), and it is surely highly improbable that he would use so unusual a name in place of the latter. If then we do not wish to change the text and read וכל הבא אל בית אל להשתחות, it seems simplest to identify the ב' ה' with the central sanctuary in Damascus; this was neither a מקדש nor an ordinary prayer-house, but was designated as בית השתחות. Cf. also below on 20,10.

---

[228] Although the Pharisees never thought of doubting the obligation to sacrifice, they did state that "Prayer is more important than any sacrifice," Berakhoth 32b. This and similar remarks in the Talmud should not be overlooked by those who are too ready to discover conflicts between priests and prophets; cf. also the Slavonic Enoch LV.

[229] Such, for example, as those on capital punishment, which are just as theoretical as the corresponding statements in Maimonides' *Yad*; cf. below, Section IV.

[230] Mishnah, Berakhoth III, 5 and Talmud, *ibid*. 22; in Babylonia this old prohibition was not taken so seriously later while in Palestine (TP *ibid*. III, 6c) the old practice survived. For the Middle Ages cf. *Tur* and *Beth-Yosef, Oraḥ Ḥayyim* 88, as well as the very interesting remark in a letter of Maimonides, ed. Leipzig, 1840, p. 25b; cf. also the excerpt from the works of his son in the *Lewy Festschrift*, p. 45. Perhaps the Babylonian custom, attested in the Talmud, of building synagogues outside the city was motivated by a desire to have them near water for ablutions. Cf. also Schürer, *Geschichte* II, 519.

[231] Cf. Megillah 22b.

[232] The *Mesged* of the Falashas is probably borrowed from the Arabs, although, to be sure, מסגד occurs in the Elephantine Papyri. [See p. 374.]

11,22: טמא כבוס. Schechter is of course right in stating that this expression denotes "an unclean person who must wash," but since every unclean person must wash, the addition of כבוס after טמא would be quite superfluous. I see in this expression a euphemism for בעל קרי, which form of uncleanness is the only one here discussed, in agreement with the Halakah.[233] And טמא כבוס of course, means "he who must wash himself" in contrast to one who must immerse himself. That is to say, whereas every other form of uncleanness can be removed only by an immersion-bath, a בעל קרי need only have nine *kabs* of water poured over him in order to be admitted into a synagogue,[234] for which reason he is called טמא כבוס. It should, however, be noted that in the ברייתא דנדה the word כבוס occurs fairly often with the meaning of טבילה.

11,22–12,1: ובהרע הצוצרות... קודש הוא. Schechter refrains from explaining this passage, which he regards as completely unintelligible. But on closer inspection, it yields quite satisfactory sense. As we learn from Tamid VII,3 the Temple service proper concluded with the final blowing of trumpets by two priests, whereupon the choir of Levites began its singing and the people prostrated themselves in prayer to God. Ben Sira describes the conclusion of the sacrifices in the following sentences. "Until he concluded the service at the altar ... then the sons of Aaron sounded their trumpets ... with a powerful blast ... all men hastened and fell prone upon the ground to prostrate themselves before the Most High, the Holy One of Israel."[235] It is this same custom, mentioned by Ben Sira and the Mishnah, of beginning prayer[236] after the trumpet-blast, that is mentioned here; and our passage is to be translated as follows: "and when the trumpets sound, the congregation must already have taken its place (יתקדם), or else it must appear, after the trumpet blast is over (יתאחר), so that people

---

[233] Berakhoth 22b, where it is explicitly stressed that the בעל קרי is not allowed to pray but not one who is unclean in some other way. Only the Karaites (*Gan Eden* 70a) forbid all unclean persons to pray. With reference to נדה, *cf.* תוספתא עתיקא, ed. Horowitz, pp. 30–33, and the note of the editor; we are here probably dealing with a work influenced by the Karaites.

[234] In the Talmud he is forbidden only to pray but not to enter a prayer-house, *cf.*, against this, תוספתא עתיקתא 26, "No Jew may enter a prayer-house so long as he is unclean."

[235] 50,14–17. *Cf.* my *Randglossen zum hebr. Ben Sira*, p. 17.

[236] The prostration was more than an external ceremony, as the words of Ben Sira clearly show, "and all the laymen broke into prayer before the Merciful One," so that one may rightly regard the trumpet-blast as a signal for prayer. For this reason also in the synagogue service (Megillah 22b; Bava Meẓi'a 59b) the Amidah, which, as is well known corresponds to the sacrificial service in the Temple, is followed by the ceremony of נפילת אפים for the performance of private devotions.

do not disturb the service, for it is a sacred service throughout, „כולה עבודת237 קודש היא". What is stressed here is the requirement that people shall not appear for the saying of prayers during the sounding of the trumpets and thus disturb the priests in the performance of this ceremony, and it is then indicated that "the whole service" in the sanctuary, that is, including the sounding of trumpets, is a sacred act and may therefore not be disturbed. We now also understand the connection between this clause and the preceding. The trumpet blast was the signal for the השתחויה so that the words ובהרע חצוצרות continue the clause וכל הבא אל הבית השתחות. Now since it is out of the question that our author should give instruction for visitors to the Temple in Jerusalem, we must assume that in the prayer-houses of this sect, or at least in the one in Damascus, the trumpets were blown by the priests at the end of certain ceremonies and that thereupon the people prostrated themselves and prayed to God. That the trumpets at the beginning of the service do not necessarily prove the existence of a sacrificial service is clear from the use formerly made of them by the Samaritans as a signal for prayer even after they had discontinued their sacrificial service on Mt. Gerizim. Originally the trumpets served the same purpose among the Samaritans as in the Temple of Jerusalem, being used at the end of the service to summon the people to prayer.238 But this passage has nothing to do with the trumpet blasts for the cessation of work on the Sabbath (on this see below, Section IV), since it says expressly, ולא ישבתו, "and they shall *not* interfere with their work."

12,1: אל ישכב איש עם אשה בעיר המקדש לטמא. There is absolutely no reason to understand by "the city of the sanctuary" any city other than Jerusalem. In 5,6 as in 6,12 (*cf.* also 20,22, where Jerusalem is described as "the holy city," עיר הקדש) המקדש certainly means the Temple in Jerusalem, so that "the city of the sanctuary," עיר המקדש, can mean no other place than Jerusalem. In view of the rigorous laws of holiness in this sect, this prescription is not so surprising, especially if one considers that according to the Halakah too a בעל קרי is forbidden to set foot on the Temple Mount (Kelim 1:8, according to the interpretation of the Talmud, Pesaḥim 67b). In the view of our author the entire city possesses this degree of holiness, while according to the Halakah only the Temple Mount does so. As a matter of fact, the

237 Of this word only the *taw* is preserved in the ms., *cf.* Schechter *ad loc.*, who, to be sure, reads שבת. For הוא at the end of the sentence read היא since it refers to the עבודה.

238 *Cf.* Kirchheim, כרמי שמרון, p. 20 top.

Halakah also states that Jerusalem is "more holy" than the rest of the Holy Land (Kelim, *loc. cit.*), and the Karaite Anan (*Book of Laws* 29,30) goes even further than the Halakah in directing the בעל קרי[239] to keep a certain distance away from the sanctuary.[240] It is interesting that in the pseudepigraph of Baruch (101 V.), which is highly regarded by the Falashas, terrible torments in Hell are predicted for those who have sexual intercourse in prayer-houses. Conceivably the rigorousness of our author is dictated by a policy of making a sojourn of some time in Jerusalem very difficult for the adherents of the sect and thus removing them from the influence of their opponents. Probably, however, עיר המקדש here corresponds to the biblical עיר דוד which coincides with the הר הבית, "Temple Mount," of the rabbinic sources. In that case, there is no difference here at all between the Halakah and our fragment, since, as was remarked above, the Halakah also forbids the בעל קרי to set foot on the Temple Mount. This assumption is especially attractive in the light of 2 Chron. 8:11, which passage, לא תשב אשה..., probably served as our author's source for the prohibition stated by him.

12,2: בנדתם. As the context shows, this word does not here mean the uncleanness of נדה but the uncleanness that results from sexual intercourse, just as already in the Bible נדה by itself means simply "uncleanness."

12,2: רוחות בליעל. For this expression compare the Book of Jubilees, 11:4, "and the evil spirits helped and seduced them, so that they committed sins and uncleanness;" also *ibid.*, 11:2, "and ... unclean demons began to seduce the children of Noah"; *cf.* below, Section V.

12,3: וכל אשר יתעה לחלל את השבת ואת המועדות לא יומת. This statement contradicts not only rabbinic tradition, which imposes the death-penalty for specific desecrations of the Sabbath, and the data in the Book of Jubilees[241] but also the law, several times repeated in Scripture, that he who desecrates the Sabbath shall be put to death. It would therefore seem in order to read יַתְעֶה, "lead astray," and not יִתְעֶה, "go astray," as Schechter reads. It refers not to those who desecrate the Sabbath but to those who cause others to desecrate it. Naturally, this refers to those who in contrast to the strict Sabbath laws of the sect hold many things to be permissible, and not to those

---

[239] Halakically, the effect of קרי and תשמיש המטה is the same with reference to the laws of purity.

[240] The distance away depends on the extent of the sanctuary. It is doubtful, to be sure, whether the sanctuary was thought by Anan to begin with the Temple Mount.

[241] Mishnah, Sanhedrin VII,4 *et al.* Book of Jubilees, L, 8, 12.

who declare the Sabbath laws of Scripture to be not binding. For this reason we have the juxtaposition of the case of "one who being dominated by evil spirits, preaches apostasy" and the case of "one who (in the opinion of the sect) advises others to desecrate the Sabbath." In both cases we are dealing not with forbidden acts but with sinful teachings. The Halakah agrees with our author in saying the seducer, מסית,[242] shall be punished for the attempt to cause others to apostatize even if he himself has not committed any such unlawful act (Sanhedrin VII, 10) whereas causing others to desecrate the Sabbath or any other thing is not punishable.

12,5: משמרו. There is no reason to read משמרו; לשמרו, "his guarding," gives just as good sense as לשמרו, "to guard him."

12,5: ואם ירפא. It is highly improbable that our author regarded sinfulness as illness although in the Talmud (Soṭah 3a) there is a statement that "no one commits a sin without having first become foolish." One should therefore read יְרְפָּא as simply another way of writing, יְרְפֶּה, "he desists."

12,7: אל ישא מהונם כל. These words are probably to be translated, "one shall not accept anything from them," that is one shall not accept any contributions for charitable purposes from gentiles. In rabbinic literature there are frequent references to the objectionableness of this practice,[243] and it is even possible that the prohibition of accepting alms from gentiles is one of the famous "eighteen ordinances" that the Shammaites enforced against the protest of the Hillelites.[244] Whether the acceptance of gifts and sacrifices for the Temple is also forbidden here is questionable. The Pharisees were very tolerant in this respect; cf. the fuller treatment of this by Lerner in the Berliner-

---

[242] It is true that the words ודבר סרה refer to the נביא שקר (Deut. 13:6) but when it is said that like the sorcerer he is to be put to death, our author is not contradicting the Halakah, which rules that the latter is to be punished by stoning, the former by strangling; for according to the Halakah the false prophet also is punished by stoning if he preaches idolatry. "The spirits of Belial" also favor the view that the false prophet is here meant; cf. below, Section IV, and Philo, De Spec. Leg. I, XI, who expressly restricts the law about false prophets to the case of one who preaches idolatry.

[243] Bava Bathra 10b; one who takes alms from gentiles is disqualified as a witness, Sanhedrin 26b, according to the interpretation of R. Hananel, Rashi and the Arukh, s. v.

[244] TP Shabbath 1, 3c. Graetz, Geschichte III, 807 observes: "The improbability of this explanation is obvious," but he does not say why, and his interpretation of מתנותיהן is certainly untenable, as I have shown in Notes to the Yerushalmi, which are soon to be published. Moreover, he, like Lerner, loc. cit., has overlooked Tosefta, Soṭah XIV, 9 as well as the saying of R. Eleazar of Modein in Bava Bathra 10b, which make the great antiquity of this prohibition quite clear.

Hoffmann *Magazin* IX, 121, although, to be sure, he has overlooked the very interesting passage in Pesiqta Rabbati 192a. From this passage it is clear that after the destruction of the Temple, when the whole question had only theoretical value, a much harsher view prevailed.

12,8: בעצת חבור ישראל. There is no occasion to assume a masculine חבור here, since חבור of our text can very well stand for חבורת from חבורה, which occurs often in rabbinic literature. A ת has to be supplied at the end of this word, as of many others in our fragment. Of course חבורה here does not mean simply "gathering" or "company" but "high council," a meaning which this word also has in some of its occurrences in Talmud and Midrash.[245] The explanation of מהונם given by me above thus gains in plausibility: the high council of the sect can under certain circumstances permit them to accept gifts from gentiles, whether for the building of prayer-houses or the support of the poor. It is unlikely, on the other hand, that anyone approached the high council to ask whether he might steal from or rob a gentile.

12,8–9: אל ימכר . . . בעבור אשר לא יזבחום. According to the Mishnah, Pesaḥim IV, 3 and Avodah Zarah I, 6, it is forbidden to sell large cattle to gentiles, while the sale of small cattle (sheep and goats) is legally permitted. The Amoraim had no tradition about the reason for this prohibition, as is clear from the discussions in both Talmuds,[246] whereas the argument in our fragment is a very plausible one. It does not, to be sure, suffice to explain the distinction between large cattle and small cattle that is made in the Halakah, since both kinds were offered as sacrifices by Jews as well as gentiles. It appears, therefore, that in the Mishnah we have the second phase in the development of this Halakah. Originally, that is at a time when the Temple was still standing, it was forbidden to sell to gentiles such animals as were used as sacrifices in the Temple, since animals that were offered to God were not supposed to be sacrificed to idols.[247] After the destruction of

---

[245] *Cf.* Halevy, *Doroth ha-Rishonim* II, 42,45 on the חבורה as the high council under the direction of the Nasi, and *cf.* further Lev. Rabba II end, p. 52, and Shir ha-Shirim Rabba on 7:14, where the חבורה of Moses and other great leaders is mentioned. In Lev. Rabba for ר' מאיר we should probably read ר' גמליאל, since only kings, judges and patriarchs are here named.

[246] *Cf.* TP Pesaḥim IV, 30d, 31a and Bavli Avodah Zarah 15a, where various reasons are first given and then refuted until finally this prohibition is connected with resting on the Sabbath, but in such a forced manner that the argument can hardly be accepted.

[247] The qualification טהורים refers of course to such animals as were considered טהורים, that is, suitable for sacrifice, by the Jews.

the Temple the real reason for this prohibition ceased to exist. But the Tannaim now had a quite new and in a certain sense far more important reason for maintaining this old prohibition, at least in a modified form. In the year 70, as a result of the war, a considerable part of Palestine came into the possession of the gentile population, and since the Jews could not rescue it from them by force, they sought by means of a strict boycott[248] to make the pagans' stay in their midst as unpleasant as possible. The Tannaim forbade the selling or renting of houses and fields to gentiles, and every kind of business dealing with them was forbidden on certain days. In addition, one might not sell them anything that might be expected to be used by them for idol-worship.[249] Now since the soil cannot be cultivated without large cattle, the old prohibition of selling animals to gentiles was maintained, but since the reason for this prohibition was now quite different from before, it was modified. On the one hand the sale of small cattle (sheep and goats), was permitted, since these were useless for agricultural labor, but on the other hand all species of animals that could be used for agricultural labor were included in the prohibition, even the "unclean ones," although originally only the "clean ones" had been forbidden. In many places, however, the old law survived, at least in its more rigorous aspects, in the shape of the local custom, מנהג המקום, which the Mishnah mentions, of not selling even small cattle (sheep and goats) to gentiles. The difference between the Halakah and our fragment is thus conditioned by differences in circumstances at different times.

12,9–10: ומגורנו . . . אל ימכר להם בכל מאדו. In contrast with the preceding law, no explanation is given for this one, which is the more surprising since we are dealing here with a law that contradicts the Halakah. For according to the Halakah,[250] one is permitted to sell grain and wine to gentiles. However, it should be noted that our author speaks not of דגן ויין but of גרן וגת. That is because he is speaking of grain and wine from which the priest's portion has not been put aside, for this was done only after the grain was brought home from the threshing-floor and the wine from the wine-press.[251] The reason for the prohibition will then be that selling these products to gentiles

[248] For the details of these laws cf. Mishnah, Tosefta and Talmud, Avodah Zarah I.

[249] In agreement with the view of our author, אשר לא יובחום; in this respect, however, the Halakah is not so strict.

[250] Cf. Avodah Zarah I, 8 and especially, TP Pesaḥim IV, 30d, where it is quite simply assumed that grain, wine and oil may be sold.

[251] Maasroth I, 5; Bava Meẓi'a 87b.

before the holy part thereof, תרומה ומעשר, has been set aside would be equivalent to a desecration, and in this respect the Halakah might very well agree with our author.[252] Conceivably, however, our passage contains nothing other than what is taught in the Mishnah, Avod. Z. I,1, namely that one may not sell anything to gentiles on their festivals, אידיהן של גויים; in which case, בכל יום אידן, "on any of their festival days," is to be read, in accordance with the Mishnah instead of בכל מאודו.

12,11: אשר באו עמו. This means, not "who enter with him into the Covenant of Abraham" but "because they enter etc." In this passage, as also in several places in Scripture, אשר has the meaning of יען "because."

12,11: בברית אברהם. The "Covenant of Abraham" is probably nothing but "circumcision," as often in the Mishnah and Talmud,[253] and properly refers only to עבדו and not to אמתו.[254] The view of our author agrees with that of the Halakah, according to which one may sell slaves to gentiles so long as they are still uncircumcised.[255] Similarly it is noted in Mekilta on Exod. 20:10 that the rest which is commanded for male and female slaves applies only to those who are "members of the Covenant," בני ברית, but not to "uncircumcised slaves." Cf. also the very old Mishnah (Weiss, *Dor Dor we-Doreshaw*, I, 69), Baba Qamma I, 3, where בני ברית is similarly used as a term for Israelites.

12,12: לאכל מהם. There is no reason to delete מהם. We may not of course refer מהם to what follows, since it belongs to לאכל, "one shall not defile oneself through any animal or insect, from bees to the animals, by eating of them."

12,12: מעגלי הדבורים. The assumption that our author forbade the eating of bees' honey is highly improbable, for not only would he thereby be found to disagree with Scripture[256] (Judg. 14:8–9) but also the use of the word עגלי for דבש would be very strange. The Syriac

---

[252] This is nowhere stated explicitly but *cf*. TP Pesaḥim IV, 30d, where it is presupposed that offerings for the priests have been set aside at the time of sale, as has already been noted by R. David Frankel *ad loc*. At any rate, this passage proves nothing because it may be a hypothetical supposition that does not take actual law into account. With regard to טבל of which our passage perhaps treats, *cf*. Demai V, 8.

[253] Avoth III, 2; Tosefta, Berakhoth VII, 12; Shabbath 137b and many other passages.

[254] To the circumcision of male slaves corresponds to the baptism, טבילה, of female slaves.

[255] *Cf*. for full discussion, Yevamoth 48b.

[256] *Cf*. also Ben Sira 11:3, וראש תנובות פריה.

term עגלי דבריתא, "little worms,"[257] leaves no room for doubt that in
our passage nothing other is meant than the prohibition (Lev. 11:29)
against (eating) insects, which in the opinion of our author, who in
this respect agrees with the Halakah, includes even the smallest
insects. In the Talmud (cf., for example, Makkoth 16b) the ant is usually cited as the insect that is forbidden in spite of its diminutiveness.
while our author calls special attention to "the small worms." It is also
possible that these עגלי הדבורים belong to the winged insects, שרץ העוף
(loc. cit., 20), which Targum Jonathan ad loc., paraphrases as זני זיבורי
but with the explicit comment that bees' honey may be eaten. In
reference to the prohibition of honey for (offerings to) the Temple
(Lev. 2:11) Philo, to be sure, remarks (De Spec. Leg., I, LIII, 291;
I, 255 M.) that this is based on the fact that honey comes from an unclean animal. In another passage, however, (De Congressu 30; I, 543)
Philo gives as the reason for this prohibition the fact that it is difficult
to consecrate what is sweet and pleasant to taste. According to the second explanation, therefore, the prohibition applies not only to the
offering of bees' honey but also to fruit juices, and this is also the view
of the Halakah (Shevuoth 12b top). It should also be noted that Anan
also permits the use of bees' honey (Book of Laws, beg.).

12,13–14: כי אם נקרעו חיים ונשפך דמם. The statement that the "tearing" of fish is here a ceremonial act[258] corresponding to the slaughtering
of cattle has no support in the text itself. For even though the Samaritans and Karaites insist upon "the Scripturally prescribed gathering,"
the Talmud (Pesaḥim 49b; Ḥullin 21a) uses the expression קרעו כדג
for any kind of killing. What is here meant is that the blood of fish
is forbidden, and therefore fish may be eaten only if they are torn
while still alive and their blood has been removed, but not otherwise,
because blood cannot be removed from a dead body; and this is also
the view of the old Halakah, as Epstein has shown in his Introduction
to Eldad, 38. Our author, therefore, agrees with the view that the blood
of fish is forbidden,[259] on which all Karaites are agreed though there are
differences of opinion among them about the ritual gathering of fish.[260]

[257] [See now S. Lieberman, Proceedings of the American Academy for Jewish
Research XX, 1951, p. 397, n. 21. — H. L. G.]
[258] Schechter refers to Wreschner, Samarit. Traditionen, pp. 51–52, in regard
to this view of the Samaritans and the Karaites; cf. also Hadassi, Eshkol, 89c–89d.
[259] Cf., for example, Hadassi, Eshkol 89c bot. and Nicomedia, Gan Eden 93c.
[260] Wreschner's assumption that this view was influenced by the Arabs is quite
unfounded, even assuming that our author does not also prescribe the killing of
fish in a particular manner, for a heretical view, according to which fish must be
slaughtered is already cited in Gen. Rabba VII, 2 (ed. Theodor, 50). Cf. also the
Shammaite Halakah, Oqazin III, 8.

In Pirqe de R. Eliezer IX דמן נשפך is opposed to ד' לכסות, which also means only that the blood need not be covered but not that it is unlawful to partake of it. However, the Halakah also forbids the use of fish blood when it is not outwardly recognizable as such; cf. Kerithoth 21b and Tanna de-Be Eliyahu Rabba XVI, 73.

12,14–15: וכל החגבים . . . עד הם חיים. Whereas fish must first have their blood removed before they may be cooked or baked, for which reason they must be killed before they are prepared for eating, as is stressed in the preceding sentence, locusts may without further ado "come into water or fire," that is, be cooked or roasted, while they are still alive, since they have no blood that needs to be removed or, as the author expresses it, "for this is the nature[262] of their creation, כי הוא משפט בריאתם.[263] Whether, however, our author permitted the eating of live locusts or not cannot be definitely stated, for the words יבואו באש או במים עד הם חיים, "they shall be roasted in fire or cooked in water while they are still alive," mean only that in contrast to fish they may be prepared alive but not that they must first be killed by water or fire. Anan states (Book of Laws, 67) that the prohibition against eating live animals, אבר מן החי, includes locusts too, while the Halakah (Tosefta, Terumoth IX, 6) does not include these in the prohibition.[264] Very instructive is the fact that none other than the Gaon R. Saadya, the foremost opponent of Karaism, cannot escape their influence in this respect, since he forbids the eating of locusts if they die of themselves,[265] which, as was noted above, is a Karaite doctrine.

[262] משפט is used in this sense in Scripture also; cf., for example, II Kings 1:7 and Judg. 13:12.

[263] Schechter tries to explain these words in the light of the Haggadah, Ḥullin 27b; cf. also Pirqe R. Eliezer IX, where two views on the creation of birds are given. At the beginning of the chapter, the words מן המים must be deleted, whereby the difficulty of the text אלו שנבראו, which R. David Luria vainly tried to explain, disappears. But it is quite out of the question that our author thought that locusts have been created from fire. Midrash Konen (Jellinek, Beth Hammidrasch, II, 26) states that fish were created from a mixture of light (אש is not to be read for אור) and water. Fire, on the other hand, is the element of heavenly, not earthly creatures, least of all such insignificant ones as locusts.

[264] According to Shabbath 90b, however, this is forbidden on other grounds, but cf. Maimonides, Yad, Sheḥitah I, 3.

[265] Cf. my Geonica II, 45. From the Responsum there published it is clear that this Karaite Halakah found proponents among the Rabbanites as well. The information about Saadya's view given by the Samaritan writer refers to fish and not to locusts, and thus Wreschner's question (loc. cit.) is answered.

12,15–16: וכל העצים והאבנים והעפר. According to the Halakah,[266] vessels made of stone or earth are not susceptible to uncleanness, and it would be very surprising if our author were to consider stone and earth in their natural state[267] among the things that can be made unclean. I therefore conjecture that either כלי has fallen out after וכל (as in the next sentence) or that וכל stands for וכלי, since here we are dealing with vessels made of wood, stone or earth. Thus the only difference between the Halakah and our author would be in the כלי אבנים, which the latter considers unclean, while the former considers them clean. Under כלי עפר we have probably to understand such earthen vessels as can become unclean according to the Halakah as well.[268] We may, however, refer to the quite exceptional statement of the apocryphal ברייתא דנדה concerning an unclean woman, which says[269] that the ground on which she walks, as well as the stone on which she sits[270] are unclean, אסור לאדם להלך אחר הנדה ולדרוס את עפרה שהוא טמא. In spite of the relatively late date of this Baraitha (it probably dates from the second half of the Geonic period), it contains a good many ancient views, and in the present case we are probably dealing with an old Halakah. This assumption has in its favor the fact that Targum Jonathan also represents a view that diverges from the accepted Halakah. The words in Num. 19:14, וכל אשר באהל יטמא, are paraphrased in this Targum as follows, מכל דבמשכנא ואפילו קרקעיתיה ואבנוי וקיסוי ומנוי יהי מסאב, "and everything that is in the tent, even its floor, its stones, its wood and its vessels, shall be unclean." Our author seems to agree with the Targum rather than with the above mentioned Baraitha, since whereas the latter speaks of the uncleanness of the ground on which the menstruating woman walks, the former recognizes such uncleanness only in case of defilement through a corpse, which, as is known, represents the highest degree of uncleanness and is, to borrow a phrase of Kalir (in the Silluq to פרה 'פ; cf. also Rashi on Bava Qamma 2b), "the grandfather of uncleanness." That our author, however, is speaking of this case is very clearly shown, first of all, by the words בטמאת האדם, since this expression is certainly the same

---

[266] Kelim X, 1; Sifre Num. 126.

[267] The so-called פשוטים remain clean even if they consist of material that is otherwise susceptible of uncleanness, cf. Kelim XV, 1.

[268] Cf. Kelim II, 1, כלי חרס וכלי נתר. Thus our author does not employ the Biblical term חרס but subsumes נתר and perhaps glass, זכוכית, too under כלי עפר.

[269] Ed. Horowitz, p. 13.

[270] Loc. cit., אפילו ישבה על האבן אסור ליגע בו מפני שהוא בולע ואינו פולט. The reason given is very strange.

as the biblical טמא לנפש אדם, and further by the explicit statement in
the following line אשר יהיו עם המת.

12,16: אשר יגואלו בטמאת האדם לגאולי שמו בהם. Seemingly badly
corrupted, this text can easily be emended. It will be helpful to our
understanding of it, if we remember that many things can be made
unclean themselves without imparting their uncleanness to other
things.[271] Such a thing is, to use the terminology of the Mishnah,
נטמא but not מטמא.[272] For נטמא our author uses the word גאל in which
he follows biblical usage.[273] He therefore terms an object that imparts
its uncleanness to others as one that is possessed of גאול טומאה, "the
defiling power of uncleanness." The statement about the defiling of
wood, stone and earth through any form of uncleanness, וכל ... אשר
יגואלו בטמאת האדם, is therefore explained by the addition of the words
לגואלי טמאה בהם,[274] "by entities which have the power of making unclean,"
indicating that the objects specified, namely עצים אבנים ועפר, can be
made unclean only when they come into contact with such unclean
objects בטמאת אדם, as possess the property of transmitting their uncleanness further, גאולי טמאה. Translated into the terminology of the
Halakah, this clause would read וכל העצים ... אשר נטמאו באב הטומאה.

12,16–17: כפי טמאתם יטמא. This addition becomes intelligible only
when one takes into account the explanation given for וכל העצים.
Wooden, stone and earthen vessels are all made unclean by contact
with unclean objects of the first grade, אב הטומאה, but there are differences among them. For example,[275] wooden vessels can again be made
clean by immersion, whereas earthern pots, כלי חרס, can never again
be made clean once they have become unclean. Our author therefore
remarks, "they are unclean in accordance with the respective commandments relating to their uncleanness."

12,17–18: וכל כלי מסמר ... יטמא. Schechter translates, "every instrument, nail or pillar in the wall [i. e., peg]," and finds in this sentence a view contradictory to that of the Halakah, since according to
the latter the nails or pegs fastened into a wall never become unclean

---

[271] *Cf.* on this the first Mishnah in Kelim and its interpretation in Bava Qamma,
beginning.

[272] These concepts partly coincide with אב and ולד הטומאה.

[273] Though the biblical גאל has no ritual connotation.

[274] The meaningless שמו is a miswriting of טמ'=טמאה; ש and ט are often confused, and similarly the stroke that serves as a sign of abbreviation is not infrequently
mistaken for a ו. [For טמ' the original has, erroneously, שמו. See also p. 351, n. 32.]

[275] In addition, there are still a number of respects in which these forms of uncleanness differ from one another.

anymore than does the wall itself, into which they are fastened.[276]
Nevertheless there is no occasion for finding a difference between the
Halakah and our fragment unless one accepts the second interpretation
of line 15 given by me; in that case, of course, our author cannot
recognize the Halakah of מחובר since he makes the קרקע itself become
unclean. But translate: "and every vessel that is made out of a nail
or a peg that is used near the wall . . . shall be unclean." This is also
the view of the Halakah, as is clear from the Mishnah, Kelim XI,3;
XII,5.

12,18: בטמאת אחד כלי מעשה. There is no reason to emend בטמאת
to כטמאת since יטמא בטמאת is quite correct. It is not as if a tool, כלי מעשה
(*cf.* German *Werkzeug*) were unclean in and by itself, so that one could
say כטומאת כלי מעשה as one might say כטומאת הנדה.[277] What is meant is
rather that the laws of unclean and clean that apply to nails and to
the other objects enumerated here, are the same as those prescribed in
Scripture for כלי מעשה, for which reason the expression "They are in
(i. e. subject to) the uncleanness of tools" is quite correct. We may
not, of course, connect אחד with בטמאת,[278] since, apart from all other
objections to such a use of אחד in the sense of "the same," we should
have to read בטמ' אחת and thus there is nothing left but to suppose that
אחד has got into the wrong place, since it belongs to בית; "that are
found in the same house with a dead body," אשר יהיו עם המת בבית אחד,
gives satisfactory sense.

12,18: כלי מעשה. Schechter correctly remarks that this expression
is taken from Num. 31:51, but since our author speaks only of the laws
about the uncleanness of the כלי מעשה, which is not mentioned at all
in the biblical passage referred to, we must assume that this expression,
borrowed from the Bible, paraphrases the condition found in Scripture,
Lev. 11:32, in reference to the uncleanness of vessels, כל כלי אשר
יעשה מלאכה בהם, and this assumption is both substantively and linguistically correct, since כלי מעשה is certainly nothing else than כלי
אשר יעשה מלאכה בו.[279] The meaning of the whole passage would then be

---

[276] *Cf.* moreover Kelim XII, 4, where R. Zadok's view is cited, which diverges
from the generally accepted one and can be harmonized with that of our author, if
we understand by מסמר a nail which also has another use.

[277] *Cf.*, for example, Ezek. 36:17.

[278] Schechter has no note on אחד and the word is completely ignored in his
translation.

[279] Modern scholars have varying views about the meaning of the expression
כלי מעשה but in any case it is clear from our fragment that it is meant to have the
sense of "worktool," which may well be the correct one; *cf.* also Ehrlich, *Randglossen* on Num. l. c.

that if other utensils are made with nails or pegs, that are in themselves not susceptible of uncleanness, these are to be considered like
any כלי אשר יעשה מלאכה בו and therefore unclean.

12,21: להשכיל ... Schechter reads למשכיל להתהלך בם עם כלהו.
עם כלהו, "to instruct and thus to guide all the people," but יתהלכו
זרע ישראל in the following clause shows very clearly that first only the
משכיל, that is, "the censor" (*cf.* 13,6) was spoken of and then all the
people, so that עם כלהו is quite impossible. Perhaps we should read
עד עולם instead of עם כלהו; "to all eternity" fits in very well after
להתהלך especially as this follows חקים which are frequently described
in Scripture as חקת עולם "an eternal law." It is also possible that
להתהלך עד עולם is modeled on 1 Sam. 2:30, יתהלכו לפני עד עולם. The
whole sentence accordingly would read, "And these are the laws
which the man of understanding is to follow for all eternity in his
judicial and legal decisions.[280] After למשפט we should probably supply
a word like לדין or להורות, which is graphically closer to ועת. The
following sentence וכמשפט etc. further develops the thought that if
the seed of Israel obeys such decisions, וכמשפט הזה יתהלכו, they are
sure of not being struck by any such curse, ולא יוארו, as will fall upon
those "who do not fullfil the word of the Torah."[281]

12,23: תהל ... בקץ הרשעה. The words missing before and after
תהל can be supplied with considerable certainty thus, וזה סרך מושב
המחנות להתהלך בו בקץ הרשעה[282] "and this is the regulation for the settlement of the camps that is to be followed during the period of wickedness."[283] That here the סרך "of the camp," מחנה, is given can be seen
quite readily from the following laws, where constant reference is made
to the camp (13,4; 13,5; 13,7; 13,13; 13,16. 13,20, מושב המחנות; 14,3
מושב כל המחנות and 14,9) while the expression להתהלך בו בקץ הרשע
is also found in 6,10.

13,1–2: עד עשרה ... וחמשים ועשרות. In spite of 10,4, where עד עשרה[284]
also occurs, I consider עד in this passage to be an abbreviation of עדה,
"congregation," since "up to ten at least" contains a *contradictio in
adjecto*, for ע ד is a *terminus ad quem* and not one *a quo*, which could
only be expressed by מן. This passage, moreover, offers an instructive
example of our author's predilection for using biblical phrases. For,
properly speaking, ועשרות is quite superfluous at the end, since עד עשרה

[280] [See Rabin.]

[281] *Cf.* 20,8, ארריהו וכו', and Deut. 27:6.

[282] [This surmise is substantially correct; see Rabin.]

[283] On this "period" *cf.* my note on 6,10.

[284] But in this passage it is probably to be regarded, with Schechter as a dittography of the preceding עדה.

has already appeared at the beginning. The author, however, would not forgo citing the biblical verse (Exod. 18:25) . . . מאות . . . אלפים [שרי] עשרות . . . חמישים as soon as he has the opportunity to do so. As for the number ten as a minimum for the establishment of a congregation, this prescription reminds us of the rule so frequently invoked by the Tannaim and Amoraim,[285] "no congregation of fewer than ten members," עדה שהיא עשרה. Even the number of ten prescribed for the panel of judges in 10,4 is not altogether without parallels. That the administration of synagogues was in the hands of a board of ten persons is a groundless assertion,[286] it is true, but it is also true that Jewish cities with a constitution of Hellenistic type had a governing body of ten men,[287] so that Hellenistic influence is probably to be seen in the court of ten judges. We should not, of course, ignore the fact that although according to the literal wording of the law three judges suffice to constitute a lower court, דיני ממונות בשלשה (Sanhedrin I, 1), it was nevertheless customary to have a court of ten judges. At any rate we have the express testimony of the Talmud (Sanhedrin 7b) to the fact that in the third century this was the usual practice in Palestine and Babylonia. The Palestinian R. Jehoshua ben Levi speaks of the responsibility that "rests" upon each of the ten judges, and it is expressly attested of the head of the Academy of Sura, R. Huna, that whenever he had to decide a civil case he set up a court of ten judges. This custom never became established as a law, to be sure, but nonetheless it was considered a rule that כל עדות נאמנות לישראל בעשרה, "every public ceremony must be executed in the presence of ten men" (Pirqe R. Eliezer XIX; Midrash Tehillim XCII, 406), and the ceremony of drawing off the shoe, חליצה, and similar ones, are cited as examples.

13,7: ישכיל את הרבים. The designation of the community as רבים is very strange, since our author otherwise uses עדה for this, and moreover, רבים does not occur elsewhere in this meaning.[288] It is therefore perhaps not altogether improbable that רבים in this passage, as

[285] Sanhedrin I, 6; cf. also Megillah IV, 3.

[286] Cf. Schürer, Geschichte⁴ II, 316, who correctly rejects the view that the בטלנים were officials, but he is wrong in holding that the בטלנים were only persons who also attended the synagogue on weekdays because they had nothing to do. The Baraitha TP Megillah I, 70b, explains בטלנים as בטלים ממלאכתם לבה״כ, "who give up their work to be present in the synagogue." Cf. the correct explanation by Maimonides, Responsum 17. [ed. Freimann 13, p. 14. Comp. notes ibid.]

[287] These δέκα πρῶτοι. are frequently mentioned in Josephus, cf. Schürer, op. cit. 228. I have referred to a similar office in Geonic times in Geonica I, 207; cf. also the שליטים in Eccles. 7:19.

[288] In rabbinic Hebrew רבים is used only in contrast to יחיד and is synonymous with צבור.

already in Scripture, denotes "the leading men," who are instructed by the Censor, as, according to the Talmud (Eruvin 54b), the elders, זקנים, were instructed by Moses and they in turn instructed the people.[289]

13,8: נהיות עולם בפרתיה. Fatal to the assumption that בפרתיה is a miswriting of בתורת יה is the fatal objection that our author *never* uses the name of God and therefore could not possibly have written תורת יה. Hardly acceptable also is the second emendation proposed, namely to read בפרטיה for בפרתיה, for it would be beyond the powers even of a professional historian to narrate the events of world history, נהיות עולם, "in their details." We should therefore read בפתריה[ן] "in their explanations," the sense will then be that the history of the world, which for our author is identical with that of Israel, is to be taught with the right commentary.

13,9: לכל מרחובם. Schechter translates, "all their rebellions." There is no reason, however, to emend מרחובם to מרדותם.[290] We should rather read מרי חובם, "the rebelliousness of their sins." The sins are, of course, not those against God, which no man can forgive, but those against the "Censor," for which reason חוב, properly "obligation," is used, and not חטא or עון, which without further specification means transgression against God.

13,10: יתר כל חרצובות קשריהם. As the preceding כרועה עדרו shows, it is quite out of the question to read רשעותיהם for קשריהם, since a shepherd does not loosen "the bonds of sinfulness." The text requires no emendation, however. "The bonds with which they are bound" here gives very satisfactory sense, and it is not without interest to note that the Gaon R. Saadia (*cf.* Schechter, *Saadyana*, 6) also uses the expression קשר חוצב. The expression יתר קשר[291] reminds us of the rabbinic התר, "loosen," and אסר, "bind," in the senses of "permit" and "forbid," since our passage probably says that the leader of the community has the power to permit what the individual members accept as forbidden to themselves, in agreement with the Halakah that a recognized scholar, יחיד מומחה, has the authority to release

---

[289] ישכיל את הרבים], echoes Dan. 11:33; cf. Dan. 12:3. On the source of Dan. 11–12, in turn, see *Vetus Testamentum* 3 (1953), pp. 400–404. *Enziqlopedia Miqra'it* II, cols. 949–52. On רבים in the sense of "community" see S. Lieberman, *JBL* LXXI, 4, 1952, p. 203.]

[290] מרדות, "rebellion," occurs neither in the Bible nor in the later literature, where מרדות is connected with רדה, "discipline" as the Geonim (*cf.* שערי תשובה no. 15) and Rashi on Ḥullin 141b already observed. In the dictionaries this explanation is credited to Lagarde! [For other suggestions on מרחובם see Rabin *ad loc.*]

[291] *Cf.* also line 19 נקשר.

persons from vows.[292] However, the following עשוק ורצוץ does seem to indicate that "the bonds with which they are bound" refer to the wrongs suffered by the oppressed.

13,12: כפי יהותו בגורל. The י in יהותו is a dittography of the preceding י in כפי, and we should therefore read כפי הויתו "in accordance with his position." הוָיָה, a verbal noun from היה, literally "being," occurs several times in the Talmud,[293] though with a meaning different from that which it has here.

13,14–15: אל יתן . . . [294]אל ישא . . . בני השחר . . . אם. After יתן we should probably supply עם, while כי is to be read after השחר, as Schechter has already conjectured; and שחר is to be emended to שחת as in 6,15. The meaning of the whole clause is, "One shall not buy from or sell to the sons of Hell except from hand to hand." The "sons of Hell"[295] are, of course, the opponents of the sect, the pagans, and the warning is given not to place any trust in them but to deal with them only "from hand to hand." Here we may recall the Halakah[296] that a gentile can become the rightful owner of an object only by actually taking possession of it, by משיכה, that is to say taking it into his hand, whereas a Jew acquires the object so soon as he pays the consideration.

14,4–6: ויכתבו בשמותיהם . . . והגר רביע. Josephus (*Contra Apionem* 1,7) gives a very interesting account of the care with which the priests guarded their genealogical records. But not only the priests but also the Israelites, at least the distinguished families among them, possessed such registers, as is clearly to be seen from the stories about מגלת יוחסין and ספר יוחסין[297] in the Talmudic sources. That proselytes were included in the registers, is not, to be sure, expressly stated in the Talmudic sources, but very probably this was the case. For though it was not regarded as a mark of distinction to be the descendant of a proselyte,[298] there were nonetheless certain strata of the Jewish popu-

---

[292] *Cf.* Bekhoroth 36b–37a. What is the meaning of Josephus, *Bell.* I, 5,2 where it is said of the Pharisees that they have the power to bind and to loose? Cf. Matt. 16:19.

[293] *Cf.* Qiddushin 5a and parallel passages.

[294] So in MS.; *cf.* Schechter, Appendix.

[295] According to Eruvin 19a שחת is a synonym for גיהנום. Pagans are frequently called "sons of Hell"; *cf.*, for example, Pesikta R. X, 36b.

[296] Bekhoroth 13b, לעמיתך בכסף ולעכו'ם במשיכה, where, to be sure, we have also an opinion that is just the opposite of the one expressed here.

[297] Yevamoth 49b and Pesaḥim 62b. The latter passage shows that the registers existed as late as the period of the Amoraim. Schürer, *Geschichte* I, 525, does not know of this passage or of PT Taanith IV, 68a.

[298] Aside from the fact that marriages between priests and proselytes were forbidden (Yevamoth VI, 5; Josephus, *Contra Apionem* 1, 7), the latter could not hold any office, M. Qiddushin IV, 5 and Talmud *ibid.*

lation that were far lower in status than the proselytes,[299] and it was worth their while to possess a legitimation that made it possible to prove that they did not belong to the "rejected ones of the community," פסולי קהל. Julius Africanus, according to the report of Eusebius, *Hist. Eccl.* I, 7, 5, even states expressly that proselytes were entered in genealogical registers. A full discussion of this statement of Africanus is contained in the article of Rosenthal in the *Monatsschrift* XXX, 118 ff.; *cf.* also below, the citation from R. Judah on "the four communities." It is not impossible that "the book of remembrance for those who feared the Lord," alluded to in Mal. 3:16, is nothing else than the books in which the names of proselytes were entered, for "the Godfearers," "φοβούμενοι τὸν θεόν" or "σεβούμενοι τὸν θεόν," is the usual designation for proselytes in Hellenistic literature.[300] Thus the prescription in our fragment that in every settlement there should be a register[301] for priests, Levites, Israelites and proselytes corresponds to a custom observed by all Jews.

14,5–6: הכהנים לראשונה ... והגר רביע. Compare with this rule the passage in Mishnah, Qiddushin, IV, 1, where the order of rank among the Jewish population is given as priests, Levites, Israelites, "disqualified priests" and proselytes. Since the fourth division includes only a very small class, who were not even to be found in many places, they could readily be passed over by our author. Sifre Deut. 247, p. 276, reports the view of R. Judah according to which the Jewish nation consists of "four communities, of priests, Levites, Israelites and proselytes," exactly as our author describes them. According to a tradition mentioned in the Talmud (Yevamoth 37a), the Mishnah here cited originated with Hillel, and it is therefore not unlikely that the Mishnah at the end of Horayoth, where the proselyte is placed one degree below the נתין,[302] belongs to a later time. For it is an undeniable

---

[299] *Cf.* Qiddushin IV, 1 and Horayoth end. As is clear from Nedarim III, 11, a proselyte still belonged to "the seed of Abraham" and Schürer, *Geschichte* III, 187, is to be corrected accordingly. The opposite view, cited by Schürer, is not in accord with the accepted Halakah, since it is expressly stated in PT Bikkurim I, 64a that proselytes may pray "to the God of Abraham, Isaac and Jacob."

[300] *Cf.* Schürer, *op. cit.*, III, 174, and Israel Lévi in *REJ* LI, 1 ff.

[301] *Cf.* Josephus, *loc. cit.*, who explicitly states that such registers were also carefully preserved in the Diaspora, as is also stated in the Baraitha, Kerithoth 25a.

[302] The Talmud (Horayoth end) justifies the preference for the *nathin* over the proselyte on the ground that the former has lived as a Jew from birth on, while the latter does so only since his conversion. That the proselyte is named directly after the Israelite in Qiddushin *et al.* is probably due to the further fact that among the classes there mentioned only the proselyte can contract marriage with an Israelite. *Cf.* also Rosenthal, *Monatsschrift* XXX, 118 ff.

fact that the attitude of official Judaism toward the problem of the proselyte was considerably altered when Christianity began to flourish. "The Godfearers," like the various grades of proselytes, were those who were readily disposed to exchange a legally rigorous Judaism for a form of the same religion that left them the Bible but did not insist upon the observance of the laws. Whereas earlier the Pharisees "compassed sea and land to make one proselyte,"[303] it was later said, "proselytes are a scab on the body of Israel."[304] It is therefore not to be wondered at that in later times the rights of proselytes were restricted, so that we have no right to regard the disqualification of proselytes for public office, for example, as an old Halakah.

14,6: וכן ישבו וכן ישאלו לכל. An interesting parallel to this prescription is found in Tosefta, Sanhedrin VI, 7: חכם ותלמיד נזקקין לחכם תלמיד ועם הארץ נזקקין לתלמיד, "when a scholar and a student address a question to the Synhedrion, the question of the scholar is considered first; when a student and an 'am ha-areẓ address a question to it, the question of the student is considered first."

14,8: בכל משפטי התורה לחברם כמשפט. As Schechter notes in his Corrections, only the upper stroke of ה can still be read in the manuscript, for which reason we should probably read לסברם, "to explain the laws of the Torah." The use of the Hiphil הסביר or rather its Aramaic form אסבר, is first attested in the Babylonian Talmud,[305] to be sure, but since סבור already belongs to the Tannaitic terminology, there can be no objection to the reading here proposed.

14,9–10: בעול בכל סוד אנשים. A married woman is called בעולה, i. e., "one who has a wedded lord," but it is quite impossible[306] for a married man to be designated as בעול, he is either a בעל אשה or, as in Mishnaic usage, a נשוי, so that בעול cannot possibly be translated as "married." We cannot read בחון (as in 13,3) or נבון (as in 10,6) because of the graphic difference for which reason it seems quite proper to read בלוע "experienced" (cf. Arabic بَلَغَ).[307] The leader must be a

---

[303] To this passage, Matt. 23:15, there is a parallel in Midrash Gen. Rabba 28, p. 264, to which Jellinek, *Beth ha-Midrash* V, 46, has called attention.

[304] Yevamoth 47b. Schürer, *loc. cit.*, has given a completely distorted picture of the attitude of the Pharisees to proselytes because he has wholly ignored this factor.

[305] *Cf.* also Midrash Tehillim V, ed. Buber 55, note 57, where the reading לסבור מעשה מרכבה is cited from a manuscript, for which we should read לַסְבִּיר.

[306] One cannot, of course, cite as a counterargument the Latin *maritus*, "spouse," as this derives from *mas*, "male."

[307] This בלע is not attested in Aramaic. Berakhoth 31b מובלע בין אנשים does not mean "superior," as Kohut and Levy explain s. v., but literally "swallowed up," i. e. one

man who is "experienced in the counsels of men." Possible also is בלול, properly "mixed," i. e., "initiated."

14,10: לכל לשון רמיה פרך.[308] The interpretation of this passage offers no particular difficulty. פרך, literally "crushing," is already used in the Talmud in the figurative sense of "refute." It is required of the leader that he have the further qualification of "being able to refute the false tongue," that is that he be able to cope with the discussions and arguments of opponents.[309]

14,12: וזה סרך הרבים להכין כל חפציהם. As has already been noted above on 13,7, הרבים means "the leaders," and our passage should therefore be translated, "This is the regulation for leaders, who are to manage the affairs (of the people)." Because of the bad state of the following text it is no longer possible to determine in detail what the leaders were to do. Apparently they were charged with taking care of the poor and aged.[310]

14,15: לאיש אשר ינע[311] ולא . . . ישבה לגוי נכר. Schechter reads ולאשר יִשָּׁבֶה[312] לגוי נכר, which he translates, "who was captured by a strange people," but this would have to be ולאשר נִשְׁבָּה מן גוי נכר, and even if we should emend the text in this manner, there remain difficulties of content. All those who are here mentioned as being in need of support are members of a certain settlement, מחנה, whereas "the captive" is certainly among the gentiles. The ransoming of captives, פדיון שבוים, is of course regarded in the Talmud as a very pious deed,[313] but nothing is said here about ransoming. Strange too is the expression גוי נכר instead of the briefer הגוים, which would have been quite sufficient. It is therefore tempting to read ולאיש אשר יש בה לגוי נכר; the poor and the aged of the community, as well as beggars who come from outside, לאיש אשר ינע,[314] are to be supported, and even a man

---

who is not distinguished from his fellows either by conspicuously good qualities or conspicuously bad ones, as the Talmud itself notes in this passage. Still less have expressions like עיירות המובלעות anything to do with this בלע. "Enclaves" are "swallowed" by their surroundings.

[308] Cf. Schechter, *Corrections*, p. lviii.

[309] [But see Rabin on this passage.]

[310] [But see editorial note on 13,7.]

[311] Cf. Schechter, LIV, note 7, where he gives ינוע as the exact reading.

[312] Thus Schechter vocalizes the word.

[313] Cf. Bava Bathra 8b top.

[314] Schechter translates it as "homeless," but already in Ps. 59:16 and 109:10 נוע means "to beg alms," as Ehrlich correctly observes in his commentary *ad loc.*; he also points out that in Hebrew and Aramaic verbs of motion like סבב, חזר, סחר, are used to indicate begging alms.

from a foreign people, who resides there, לאיש אשר יש בה לגוי נכר,[315] is not to be allowed to go away empty-handed. One may further refer to the Tosefta[316] (Gittin V, 4), where a similar rule is stated, מפרנסין עניי גוים מפני דרכי שלום, "one must support poor gentiles for the sake of peace."[317]

14,19: אהרון וישראל ויכפר עוננו. Schechter rightly assumes that משיח is to be supplied before אהרון, but still we cannot refer the following ויכפר ע' back to משיח. A "messiah forgiving sins" is conceivable only in a Christian work. Even the author of the Testaments of the Twelve Patriarchs, in spite of his highly developed messianology, did not go so far as to ascribe forgiveness of sins to the Messiah.[318] I conjecture that the text read somewhat as follows: עד אשר ישלח אל משיח מאהרון וישראל ויכפר עוננו, where "and he will forgive our sins" refers to אל, God. The same thought, though in different words, is found at the end of our fragment (20,31–34), where the messianic age is described as that in which people will hearken to the teacher of righteousness, and God will forgive their sins. It is also possible that ויכפר עוננו is equivalent to על עוננו. The "anointed of Aaron," that is, the high priest, is of course the one who will carry out the rites of atonement in the messianic period; on this cf. more fully Section VI.

15,1: כי אם שבועה הב ... . Schechter reads שבועת הברית and finds himself compelled to supply או in the following line, but we have probably to read שבועה הכתובה באל' הבר', "the oath that is written in the curses of the covenant." What is here stressed is that one may not use any of the names of God in taking an oath, neither the name אֵל nor אדני, but the oath must follow the form of the curse in Deut. 28:15 ff. The expression used by our author, שב' הכת' וכו' is probably based on Deut. 29:20 אלות הברית הכתובה בספר and II Chron. 34:24 האלות הכתובות על הספר. It is very noteworthy that the form of oath prescribed by our author is not identical with the one that is usual in the Talmudic period,[319] but with the one that is prescribed by the

[315] In this sense לגוי is biblical, as בן לישי and other examples show.

[316] TB Gittin 61a, TP V, 47c.

[317] The Mishnah, Gittin V, 8 enumerates a number of regulations motivated by דרכי שלום; in many respects these correspond to what are called "laws of equity" in English law.

[318] Charles, to be sure, would read εἰς μεσίτην τῶν ἐθνῶν in Test. Levi VIII, 14, but in that case the Messiah would be only the "intercessor," מליץ, for the gentiles. However, Charles' assumption that the Greek translator wrongly read לצלם instead of מליץ is hardly tenable, since κατὰ τύπον can hardly refer to לצלם. Did the Hebrew text have לעיני? [See p. 231, n. 99.]

[319] The form of oath then usual (cf. also Test. Reuben I, 6; VI, 9) was "I swear by God, the Lord of heaven," although, according to the views of the scholars it

Geonim,[320] which consists in an announcement by the court in the presence of the person on whom the oath is imposed that "פלוני shall be smitten by such and such curses if he does not speak the truth." In view of the aversion to swearing by the name of God that already existed in the Talmudic period, which made people prefer to suffer monetary loss rather than take the oath required of them by the court, one may well assume that the Geonim with their form of oath merely formally fixed as law a custom that had already existed in talmudic times.[321] Cf. also Philo, *Special Laws*, II, I, 2 (II, 270); *On the*

---

was sufficient to swear "by the Merciful One" or "by the Almighty"; cf. Shevuoth 35a.

[320] Cf. the responsum published in *Geonica* II, 154 and the references there given by me, pp. 147–8; cf. further Ṭur and Beth Yoseph, *Ḥoshen Mishpaṭ* 87, 35.

[321] The Jewish sages, to be sure, did not go so far as the New Testament in forbidding every kind of swearing, but nonetheless pious persons refrained from taking an oath in which the name of God was mentioned, cf. Naḥmanides, השגות to Maimonides *Sefer ha-Miẓwot*, Commandment VII, who refers to Tanḥuma (ed. Buber, III, 10; IV, 157), where true oaths are already forbidden; cf. on this subject Schmiedl in *Beth Talmud* I, 245–47, who has, however, not exhausted the sources in which the true oath is forbidden, for which reason I here add the most important among them. In Tanḥuma, end of the section ויצא it is said in reference to the Scriptural passage Gen. 31:53, וישבע יעקב בפחד א' יצחק, "Far be it! That righteous man (Jacob) did not swear by the name of the King (God), but rather by the life of his father, like one who says, to give force to his words, 'by the life of my father, I will not do it.' And even this oath Jacob would not have taken if it had not been for his fear (of Laban)," וישבע בפחד אביו יצחק חס ושלום לא נשבע אותו צדיק בשמו של מלך אלא בחיי אביו כאדם הרוצה לאמת דבריו ואומר חי אבא אם אעשה זאת ואף אותה שבועה לא נשבע לולי הפחד כדכתיב בן יכבד אב. It is highly instructive to note that these words of the Midrash are almost the same as those used by Philo (*De Spec. Leg.* II, I, 3) to interpret the biblical verse in question, "In the Law (Gen. *loc. cit.*) it is stated of one of our forefathers that he swore by the fear of his father, for the benefit and edification of future generations ... in order that they might properly honor their parents, and not be so readily inclined to call on the name of God." In view of these words of Philo I should even be inclined to translate the final sentence in the Midrash as follows, "Even this oath Jacob would not have taken, if it had not been that he wished to express his respect (his fear) for his father, as it is written (Mal. 1:6) 'the son honors his father'." In the Midrash on the Decalogue (Jellinek, *Beth Hammidrash* I, 72) an even stricter view is taken of true oaths. "One may not swear even a true oath ... and if anyone desecrates the name of God by swearing falsely or even when he swears in accordance with the truth, God reveals his hiding place (read מסתורו for משכורתו), and his wickedness is made known to all men. Woe to him in this world and woe to him in the future world ...'' אפילו באמת אין אדם רשאי לישבע וכל המחלל שמו של הקב"ה ונשבע לשקר או אפילו באמת סופו הקב"ה מגלה משכורתו בעולם הזה אוי לו בעולם הבא. From an unknown Midrash R. Yoḥanan Treves in his work קמחא דאבישונא (on the Shavuoth פיוט: אל' בהנחילך) cites the following statement about a true oath, "This verse (Jer. 4:2) teaches you how serious the sin of swearing is, for even if one were compelled to swear by the name of God in court, he should give alms as a penance for taking the oath, בא הכתוב

Decalogue XVII–XVIII (II, 195–196), *Allegor.* III, LXXIII, who similarly strongly condemns the use of God's name in swearing.

15,2: ואת תורת משה אל יזכור. To this prescription also a parallel is found in the Gaonic ruling[322] that an oath in the name of the Torah cannot be invalidated by any authority, אין התר לשבועה זו, and, as already remarked by the Poseqim,[323] the Gaonim issued this decree in order to keep the people from taking such oaths. Presumably the oath[324] by משה used in the Talmud is only an abbreviation of בתורת משה which was not uttered completely out of reverential fear.[325] *Potztausend*

להודיעך כמה חמורה השבועה שאפילו הוצרך להשבע בבית דין באמת בשם י"י יתן צדקה על השבועה. Significant of the reluctance to take an oath, even a truthful one, is the anecdote in Bava Bathra 32b, bottom, about the man who stakes his reputation and even speaks an untruth only to avoid taking an oath. It is probably also on the basis of these statements in the Talmudic-Midrashic literature that in the *Sefer Ḥasidim*, 341, (p. 137, ed. Wistinetzki) complete abstinence from swearing is recommended. But that this reluctance to swear is older than primitive Christianity is shown not only by Philo and the Essenes, who, according to the testimony of Josephus (*Bell. Jud.* II, 8,6), considered an oath worse than perjury, but also by the Pharisees of the time of Herod. These men, Josephus reports (*Ant.* XV, 10, 4) refused to take an oath of allegiance but were not punished out of consideration for Pollio (certainly הלל not אבטליון), whom Herod highly esteemed. This refusal to take an oath of allegiance could have had no other basis than the Pharisee aversion to swearing by the name of God; otherwise Herod would have been the very last person to release them from the oath of allegiance. It was certainly for this reason that the Essenes refused to take an oath of allegiance, for Josephus reports explicitly of them that they never swore. And the difference between the Pharisees and the Essenes in this matter was that the former, as people occupied with practical life, retained the oath in trials, even though they themselves never took such an oath, whereas the latter completely rejected it. It is to be noted moreover that even the Essenes condemned only the oath taken in the name of God, whereas they used other forms of oaths and curses, as Josephus expressly states (*Bell. Jud.* II, 8,7), and this is exactly the standpoint taken by our author. In the Test. XII Patriarchs, on the other hand, oaths taken in the name of God are very frequent.

[322] *Cf.* my *Geonica* II, 153 and the literature there given on p. 146, to which should be added the Responsum of R. Meir of Rothenburg, ed. Bloch (Budapest) No. 120.

[323] *Cf.*, for example, the Responsum of R. Meir of Rothenburg, 122, R. Nissim on Nedarim 22b, and the אור זרוע (recently published by Freimann) on Shevuoth, where there is a detailed Responsum of R. Isaac ben Abraham, who shows that in Talmudic times this oath could be invalidated exactly like any other oath under certain circumstances.

[324] *Cf.* the lexicons and Nedarim 10b, where מוהי is probably a popular mutilation of משה.

[325] As is clear from Pesiqta R. XXVI, 129b, the custom, mentioned in the Talmud, of holding the Torah in one's hand while taking an oath, is only an impressive form of swearing "by the Torah" which, to be sure, was later used in other formulas of swearing as well.

in German and *Sacrebleu* in French illustrate the alterations to which oath formulas are subjected by the people.

15,3: ואם באלות הברית . . . השפטים. Schechter rightly supposes that before השפטים something like והובא לפני is to be supplied, and that this is a reference to the Halakah that perjury is legally punishable although otherwise only "acts" and not "words" are punishable.[326]

15,4: והתורה והשיב. *Cf.* above on 9,13.

15,5: את בניהם אש . . .. The missing words can easily be supplied from 10,1 את בניהם אשר מלאו ימיהם לעבור וכו', "whose sons, as soon as they reach the age of passing muster," that is, as soon as they are twenty years old, not thirty, as Schechter states.[327]

15,8: אשר לרבים יפקדוהו. If our interpretation of 13,7 is correct, this passage is to be translated, "on the day on which he speaks with the overseer, he (the overseer) shall give him (the penitent) over to the leading men with the oath of the Covenant."

15,10: לעשות בם[328] . . . ץ . . . ואל. I would restore the missing words as follows, לעשות בם כחפץ אל "in order to fullfil them (the laws) in accordance with the wish of God." Since, however, ון very frequently becomes ץ perhaps instead the more usual כרצון is to be read instead of כחפץ; for ידיעיהו read יודיעהו.

15,11: המבקר א. יתפתה. Schechter reads המבקר אשר. Since, however, there is a lacuna before א in the manuscript, אשר cannot be the missing word, for which reason ואו is probably to be supplied. For the following יתפתה, of which the reading is very doubtful, as Schechter remarks, I should like to read יתפתח[329] "be initiated into the understanding of this." Accordingly, the prescription here given reads, "Let no one impart to him (the new member) the teachings of the sect. Only when he stands before the overseer, is he to be initiated by him into the understanding of this."

16,1: יקום איש על נפשך. The text absolutely requires נפשו, which is actually found in line 4, and נפשך is probably only a printer's error; similarly יקום for יקים.

16,2: ופרוש קציהם . . . ובשבועותיהם . . .. This sentence interrupts the continuity, and its genuineness is very suspect. It probably comes from a reader for whom the Book of Jubilees possessed high authority and

---

[326] *Cf.* Mekilta, Yitro VII, p. 227; Shevuoth 21a.

[327] The age of officials is set higher than that of ordinary members, which fact Schechter has overlooked, for לעבור על הפקודים can only denote the age of twenty.

[328] If בם is read, it refers to the laws of the Torah, while בה refers to the Torah itself.

[329] The use of פתח in the meaning of "initiate into a text," "explain to" is Mishnaic, *cf.* Sheqalim V, 1. For the special use in our fragment *cf.* Yerushalmi Moed Qatan III, 83b שפתח לו תחלה, wherefore we should perhaps read, ואו יפתח לו.

called attention to the fact that the words of our fragment, "for everything is exactly given in it (the Torah)," כי בה הכל מדוקדק, are not to be taken literally, for in respect of the "calendar,"[330] פרוש קציהם, one must be guided by what is written on this subject in the Book of Jubilees. To the מדוקדק connected with the Torah is opposed the מדוקדק connected with the pseudepigraphon here mentioned.[331]

16,6: על כן נימול אברהם ביום דעתו. What this sentence on the circumcision of Abraham has to do with the preceding observation of the author is absolutely impossible to see. Schechter refers to the Book of Jubilees XV, 26, 32, but there is not a single word about his being saved from the power of Maṣṭema through his being circumcised, aside from the fact that our author speaks of the resolve to observe the Torah and not of circumcision. Furthermore, ביום דעתו can hardly mean "on the day of his knowing it" but means literally "on the day of his knowing." It seems proper, therefore, to read נִיצֵּל[332] for נימול. What our author is saying is that Abraham was saved (from the snare of Maṣṭema) on the day of his knowing, that is, so soon as he came to know God and was firmly resolved to walk in His ways. Our author is probably alluding to the legend, found in the Book of Jubilees XI, 16 ff. and in the Apocalypse of Abraham, cc. III–VIII,[333] in which Abraham by himself comes to recognize the vanity of idol-worship and is therefore rewarded by God in that He saves him from the sufferings that He has inflicted upon other men and finally reveals Himself to him, so that Maṣṭema has no power over him and his descendants.

16,8: עד מחיר מות. This expression is the equivalent of the expression, used in both Halakah and Haggadah, יהרג ואל יעבור "one should let oneself be killed rather than transgress (a commandment)." If these words of our author are to be taken literally, his view differs from that of the Halakah,[334] which sets up the rule that where life is endangered, all prohibitions may be disregarded with the exception of idolatry, sexual immorality, and murder. Probably, however, עד מחיר מות is not to be taken literally, just as similar expressions are also used in the Talmud (cf. for example, Bava Meẓi‘a 59a; Eruvin 21b; Lam. Rabbati I, 62,[335] and the parallels cited by Buber) in order to make a particular prohibition more impressive. Nevertheless it should be

---

[330] Cf. above on 6,10 (pp. 29–30).

[331] [See now Rabin.]

[332] [Rather the post-biblical ניצול, with Rabin.] [But see below, p. 302, n. 103.]

[333] A similar story is told also in rabbinic sources, cf. my Legends of the Jews, I, 209 ff.

[334] Cf. Sanhedrin 74a et al.

[335] That חייב מיתה there is not to be taken literally is obvious from the parallel, Pes. R. Kahana 99b, where first the same sin is likened to the eating of for-

noted that according to Philo[336] perjury is punishable with death, and
it would not be at all strange if our author agreed with the Karaites
(*Aderet El* 87a) in holding the view that a prohibition, for the transgressing of which the penalty of death is set, must not be disregarded
under any circumstances, even if it is in order to save one's life.[337]
In rabbinic sources also there are found statements that show very
clearly that the view that perjury is to be punished with death was a
fairly common one. Thus it is said in Pesiqta Rabbati XXVI, 131a,
that Nebuchadnezzar had the following message sent to Zedekiah,
"By the law of your God you are deserving of death, for you swore
falsely by His name," בדין אלהיך חייב אתה להרג שנשבעת בשמו לשקר. The
possibility that a man might risk death in order to fulfill a vow seems
to be presupposed also in PT Nedarim II, 37b, as R. David Frankel
correctly observes in his glosses *ad loc.* in שירי קרבן. The author of
ספר חסידים justifies his unqualified prohibition of swearing by the
statement that "the ancients remained faithful to their oaths even if
they were killed" and that for this reason they were permitted to
swear. Although no source is given for this assertion, it may well be
assumed that the author of the ספר חסידים had one before him. In
Tanḥuma, ed. Buber, III, 9–10, it is indeed said that only very pious
men like Abraham, Joseph and Job were permitted to swear, and this
agrees with the view of the ספר חסידים, but nothing is said there about
the pious men who remained faithful to their oaths until death.
Cf. also Ben Sira IV, 28, עד המות היעצה, which reminds one vividly of
עד מחיר מות.

16,8: אל יפדהו. Schechter would read יפרהו, "make it void," and
if one takes into account that the question whether one can be absolved
of an oath is a matter of controversy between the schools of Shammai
and Hillel,[338] one might be inclined to accept this emendation and

---

bidden food and then is emphatically connected with ח' מ'. Maimonides, M. Assur.
X, 20, therefore does quite right to leave this Haggadic exaggeration out of account,
cf. Schwarz, *Mishneh Torah*, 139.

[336] *De Spec. Leg.* II, VI, 28 and II, XLVI, 252. In Philo the oath is in principle
sinful (*loc. cit.*, II, I, 2), and in this he is in essential agreement with our author (*cf.*
on 15,1). In *De Spec. Leg.* II, III, 9; it is said in a merely general way that a person
should seek with all his might and in every way to keep his oath, so that he may not
be hindered by anything from carrying out his intention.

[337] *Cf.* Pirqe Rab. Hak., ed. Grünhut, 43 (also cited by רמב"ן and רא"ה on
Kethuvoth 19a as a non-canonical Baraita), where the opinion is stated that robbery,
גזל, also belongs to the sins that one must not commit even to save one's life.

[338] *Cf.* Nedarim 28a. It should be noted here that the view of the Shammaites
(Nazir V, 1), הקדש טעות הקדש "an offering vowed to the Temple must be made even
if the vow was made in error," is similarly to be atrributed to this school's aversion
to the "annulment of oaths," which they sought to reduce to a minimum.

characterize our author as a Shammaite, for they assert אין שאלה
בשבועה, "an oath cannot be annulled."[339] Nevertheless there is no
reason to depart from the text given to us, for, as is clear from 1 Sam.
14:45, there was a time when it was considered possible to disregard
a vow provided that a certain sum was given to the Temple.[340] Accordingly אל יפדהו would be quite correct; an oath is binding for our author
as it is, moreover, for the Halakah, and one cannot get a dispensation
from it by "paying a ransom."

16,8–9: עד מחיר מות ... כל אשר .... איש על נפשו ל . Schechter recon-
structs this line as follows, כל אשר יקים איש על נפשו לסור מן התורה עד
מחיר מות אל יקימהו so that we should first have a prescription relating
to an oath having as its object the fulfillment of a law or a neutral
action, and then one relating to an oath aiming at transgressing a law.
In support of this interpretation one might cite the Halakah (Nedarim
II, 2; Philo, *De Spec. Leg.* II, III, 9) אין נשבעין לעבור על מצות, "no oath is
valid if its fulfillment is a breach of a commandment," but in that
case it would seem proper to supply the missing words in somewhat
the following way, כל אשר יקים איש על נפשו לעבור עברה עד וכו' for not
only would לעבור עברה then correspond to the Mishnaic לעבור על
המצות[341] but also, as is clear from 15,3, this use of עבר is known to our
author. Nevertheless I do not believe that this interpretation is the
correct one since it is very hazardous to explain the expression עד
מחיר מות as a dittography from the preceding verse, as would be
absolutely necessary with this interpretation. It is therefore not
unlikely that our author makes a distinction between "oath," שבועה,
and "vow," נדר.[342] The former is binding under all circumstances,
עד מחיר מות אל יפדהו, while the obligation to fulfill a vow is removed in
certain circumstances. We should then read, כל אשר ידור איש על נפשו
לעשות יקים דברה[343] ואם עד מחיר מות אל יקימהו, "whatever vow a man takes
on himself, he shall fulfill it but if it is at the cost of his life, he shall
not fulfill it."

---

[339] *Cf.* above on 15,2.

[340] At any rate this is the traditional interpretation of ויפדהו in this biblical
passage, *cf.* Midrash Shemuel *ad loc.*, ed. Buber, 96; *cf.* also Sifre Zuṭa, Breslau,
1910, p. 171 [Leipzig, p. 326], where Hillel opposes the "redemption" of an oath.

[341] The letters still preserved in the manuscript make it impossible to read
לעבור על המצות in our fragment too.

[342] *Cf.* the view of the Shammaites cited in the text above, which refused to
recognize any annulment of an oath but probably permitted this in the case of
a vow.

[343] The writing דברה for דברו is not strange in view of the peculiar orthography
of the fragment.

16,10: אשר אמ . . . שה להניא. Schechter reads אמר משה, but it is
highly improbable that the biblical laws would be cited as the words of
Moses[344] when they are the laws of God. We should read על שבועת
[345]האשה אשר אמר על אישה להניא את שבועתה, "Concerning the oath of a wife,
of which it is said (in Scripture, Num. 30:8 ff.) that her husband shall
revoke it."

16,11: שבועה אשר לא. דע . . . דם להקים הוא. Schechter completes the
defective words as לא ידע אדם without, however, giving an explanation
of these obscure words,[346] for it is obvious that a man must know that
his wife has taken an oath before he can annul it. It is, indeed, possible
that what is given here is the Halakah mentioned in Nedarim X,7 to
the effect that a man may revoke only an oath that has already been
made but has not the power to declare, "The oaths that my wife may
make shall be invalid," כל הנדרין שתדורי . . . הרי הן מופרין אינו מופר.
However, in that case one would expect לא ידע אישה and not לא ידע
אדם, since it is quite immaterial whether other people had any knowledge of her taking an oath or not. I therefore read אשר לא להרע אדם,
"A husband shall not revoke an oath that contains nothing harmful
to anyone." The expression להרע אדם in the sense mentioned above is
very often used in the Halakah,[347] and in our passage it is the equivalent
of לענות נפש in Num. 30:14. The Mishnah, Nedarim XI,1, states that
the husband may revoke only "vows of abstinence" or "affliction"
נדרים שיש בהם ענוי נפש, for which reason our author also says that vows
that contain no afflictions[348] remain valid in spite of the protest by the
husband.

16,11–12: ואם להניא אם לעבור ברית . . . ואל יקימנה. Schechter renders,
"As to disallowing if it is to transgress the Covenant then he shall
disallow it and not confirm it." This interpretation of the text, however, is quite impossible, since aside from the fact that אם להניא can

---

[344] The case is different in 8,14 where אמר משה refers to a statement made by
Moses and not to a law; cf. below, Section V.

[345] Under שבועות are of course included נדרים as well. The Halakah usually speaks
of the נדרים that the husband annuls, and includes שבועות among them.

[346] Schechter translates איש as "man" although here "husband" is meant, since
only he can annul the oath of his wife. Perhaps איש is only an abbreviation of אישה
"her husband."

[347] More exactly this expression is given as להרע אחרים in rabbinic literature,
Sifra to Lev. 5:4 ed. Weiss 23, and Shevuoth 27a, but cf. Sifre Zuṭa Breslau, 1910,
p. 171 [Lipsiae, p. 326].

[348] In Scripture in לענות נפש the נפש of the wife is meant, but our author adds
that even if the vow contains no affliction for the wife, it is still valid only when it
is not להרע אדם "likely to harm anyone." Otherwise it is invalid, as the Halakah
also holds, Sifra and Shevuoth, ad loc.

hardly mean "as to disallowing," which could only be correctly expressed by ואשר להניא, it is also out of the question, from the point of
view of content, that the husband's power to annul his wife's oath
should be limited to those cases in which the oath involves the violation of a law. It was explicitly and forcefully stated in the preceding
regulation[349] (line 9) that no oath has any validity at all if it aims at
the violation of a law. I read ואם לוא להרע and take it to refer to the
preceding. If the oath was not "an oath of abstinence," the wife must
fulfil it; otherwise her husband has the right to annul it. Apart from
oaths of abstinence, נדרים שיש בהם עני נפש, the Halakah[350] recognizes
a second class of vows which the husband may annul, namely those
that encroach upon the marital rights of the husband, נדרים שבינו לבינה,
and these are the ones described by our author as לעבור ברית, where
ברית means "marriage," as it does several times in Scripture,[351] and
לעבור ברית means "violate marital obligations." It should also be noted
here that the Geonim limited the husband's right to vows, נדרים,
whereas the wife's oaths, שבועות, could not be annulled; cf. הלכות פסוקות,
ed. Müller, No. 122. [This is also the view of Resh Lakish in TP
Nedarim XI,1, 42c. S.L.]

16,13: אל ידור איש למזבח מאום אנוס. Schechter renders, "No man
shall vow anything for the altar under compulsion." This law,[352] however, would then be addressed to the wrong person, for no one wishes
to be compelled but many like to compel others. [This law is, however,
clearly stated in Sifra, Mekilta d'Miluim, Ẓaw, 15, ed. Weiss 41d. S.L.].
We should therefore translate מאום אנוס as "anything that is taken
with force." God "hates robbery for burnt offering," said Isaiah long
ago (61:8), and Malachi (1:13) reproaches his contemporaries for bringing as offerings animals taken by robbery, and Ben Sira (XXXII, 14)
admonishes, ואל תבטח על זבח מעשק, "do not rely upon a sacrifice of

---

[349] If the interpretation of this verse given by me is accepted, namely that it
deals with something quite different from oaths violating a law, it is quite impossible that our author should have limited the husband's right of annulling oaths
to those cases in which Scripture expressly mentions לענות נפש.

[350] Sifre Num. 155, p. 206, Nedarim 79b et al. Philo, De Spec. Leg. II, VI, 24 seems
to hold the view that the husband has the right to annul his wife's vow only when
it encroaches upon his rights. Perhaps line 11 should be read as אשר לא לענות נפש
נד' שבינו לבינה=לעבור ברית ,גד' שאין ב' ע' נ'=אדם, after which comes. As Schechter
remarks in his footnote, a ו is still visible after ע, which supports the reading
לענות נפש.

[351] In Ezek. 16:8 the expression ואבוא בברית is actually used for "into marriage."

[352] The Halakah too (Sifra on Lev. 1:3, ed. Weiss 5c) knows this regulation, but
still under certain circumstances one can be compelled to bring a sacrificial offering.
It is perhaps this that our author opposes.

robbery." Moreover, one must not infer from this verse that the sect was in possession of an altar, for it is essentially the second half of this law, namely that the priests may not forcibly seize the offerings which are their due,[353] that our author is concerned with, and this is not dependent upon the existence of a temple. Since, however, our author had biblical proof-texts only for the first half of the law, as has already been noted,[354] he introduces the regulation about priests with that concerning sacrifices, although the latter has only theoretical meaning for him and his readers.

16,12: וכן המשפט לאביה. The Halakah also (Sifre Num. 155, p. 207, and PT Nedarim XI, 42c top) states that the father's right to annul (a woman's vow) is exactly the same as that of her husband,[355] but Philo (*De Spec. Leg.* II, VI, 24) does not know of any limitation of the father's right in this respect.

16,14: אל יקחו מאת ישראל. We should probably supply after ישראל the words תרומתם בזרוע, to which Tosefta Menaḥoth XII, 18 ff. offers a verbal as well as factual parallel. We learn from this source that in the period shortly before the destruction of the Temple the ruling priests used to send their slaves to the threshing-floors to take by force the offerings that were due them.[356] The Halakah (Ḥullin 133a) not only forbids the personal appropriation of offerings but also the request for them. Similarly, the individual priests are forbidden to help with work in the fields in order to have the owner of the field assign him the offerings out of gratitude. Such a priest is called המסייע בבית הגרנות, "a priest who helps at the threshing-floor."[357]

16,14: י . . . ל . י . י הוא אשר. I read אל יקדש איש את יקדש איש את מאכל. מאכל פעלו כי הוא אשר, "One shall not declare the food of his hired worker to be 'holy,' for of this it is said (in Scripture) etc." For the understanding of this regulation we must first note that in the Halakah,[358] a hired worker may eat any produce on which he works without

---

[353] *Cf.* below on 16,14.

[354] The Targum does indeed seem to have read גזל ועולה in the passage cited but for the Masoretic reading בעולה we have the authority of the Tanna R. Simon ben Yoḥai (*cf.* Sukkah 30a), who deduces from this verse the Halakah that stolen property must be kept away from the altar. *Cf.* also Philo, *De Plantatione* XXV, who makes fun of people who dedicate to the altar property which has been acquired in a dishonest way.

[355] The explanation given by Friedmann, *ad loc.*, (p. 58b), from the commentary of R. Hillel, according to which the view of the Sifre would be the direct opposite, is so forced as to require no refutation.

[356] Josephus, as is well known, reports the same thing in *Ant.* XX, 8,8; 9,2.

[357] *Cf.* Qiddushin 6b, for example.

[358] Bava Meṣi'a VII, 2–8 on Deut. 23:25–26.

being in any way hindered by the owner. Now we may well assume that many a miser, in order to circumvent this law, would announce to his workers that what they were going to eat was consecrated to the Temple, קדש,[359] and naturally no one then dared to touch anything. It is against such evasions of the Law that a warning is given here, and in genuinely Midrashic style the verse from Mic. 7:2 את איש אחיהו יצודו חרם, "one catches the other in the net," is alluded to, with חרם being taken in the sense of "consecrated"=הקדש, and further עבדו being used for אחיהו, so that this verse reads, "The owner[360] catches his worker through what is consecrated," that is, by declaring "holy"[361] what is due the worker.

19,2–3: כחוקי הארץ אשר היה מקדם. Ms. B paraphrases the brief wording of Ms. A (7,6), כסרך הארץ, rather awkwardly as "in accordance with the laws that formerly obtained in the land," but this can hardly be correct, since סרך הארץ probably means nothing different from the Mishnaic דרך הארץ (biblical דרך כל הארץ) that is, "the usual manner of living." In its preference for biblical idioms Ms. A uses מחנה and מחנות but without referring to the "camps" mentioned in Scripture; rather it refers to any kind of settlement. Ms. B, on the other hand, took מחנה in its technical sense and was therefore compelled to ascribe to the following כסרך הארץ a meaning of which the author never thought.

19,4: וכמשפט היסודים. The reading יסודים, "foundations," as against יסורים, "instructions," is favored by the following sentence in the Slavonic Enoch LII, 9, "Blessed is he who observes the foundations of his fathers." Accordingly our passage also seems to speak of the יסודים that is, the teachings of the Fathers,[362] and then of the סרך התורה, the Mosaic teachings; cf. TP Eruvin V, 22c מיסדין ההלכה.

19,5: כאשר אמר. The usual form of the citation of biblical passages in Talmudic literature is שנאמר, but beside this there is also אמור, and this latter form probably lies behind כאשר אמר as well, although it is not impossible that אמר is an ellipsis for אמר הכתוב; cf. below, Section V.

19,9: והשומרים אותו. Schechter renders, "and they that watch him are the poor of the flock." Now it is true that, as Schechter assumes, this is an allusion to Zech. 11:11, עניי הצאן השמרים אותי; nevertheless a

---

[359] Similarly, in the New Testament the Pharisees are reproached for evading their duties to their parents by declaring their property "holy"; cf. also p. 38 on 9,1.

[360] So our author probably understood איש in this verse, cf. above 13,2 איש כהן and Yoma I,7.

[361] In view of the Midrashic method of our author it would not be at all surprising if in replacing אחיהו by עבדו he had thought of the rule that even a slave, עבד, is our brother, since אחיו הוא במצות, "he is our brother (like us) in the obligation to observe the commandments"; cf. Bava Qamma 88a.

[362] These teachings form the real Halakah of our document.

literal reproduction of the biblical text here gives absolutely no sense. We should therefore read אותם for אותו and translate, "and those who keep them (the commandments of God) are the poor flock that will escape etc." The contrast is between those who despise the laws, המאסים במצות (line 5), and those who keep the laws, השומרים אותם, and will therefore escape when judgment comes.

19,11–12: אשר אמר יחזקאל ביד יחזקאל. This is a conflation of two readings: אשר אמר יחזקאל (cf. above, 3,21; 7,11; 8,14) and אשר אמר ביד יחזקאל. Both methods of citing are also found in talmudic literature.[363] A biblical passage is either ascribed to the Prophets — אמר ישעיהו, ירמיהו etc. — or it is introduced by על ידי . . . הוא אמר, where הוא probably means הקדוש ברוך הוא.[364] Originally the latter formula was probably intended to stress the high degree of inspiration, by expressing the idea that the prophet was only the instrument employed by God, so that the words are not the prophet's but God's. Later, however, both formulas were used indiscriminately.

19,29: סרו מדרך. If we do not supply אשר before סרו, we shall have to read סָרֵי for סרו: the repentant ones in Israel, who turn aside from the (evil) way of the people.

19,35–20,1: לא יחשבו בסוד עם . . . עד עמוד משיח. Whereas those who lived before the appearance of the unique teacher[365] may allege ignorance as an excuse for their sins, those who directly or indirectly learned the true teachings of this teacher are without any excuse. For this reason a verdict of guilty is pronounced by our author upon those who first heeded the call of the unique teacher but then rejected his teachings, as it is upon all who despise the Law; they shall not be admitted into the council of the people and shall not be registered in its book.[366] This applies to all sinners from the time of the unique teacher to the appearance of the Messiah.

20,7: אל יאות איש עמו. Neither in biblical nor in mishnaic Hebrew does אות mean "to unite," so that it seems best to read יֵאָח from אחה,

---

[363] Cf., for example, Makkoth 24a, משה אמר . . . ישעיהו אמר and Eruvin 21a, אמרו דוד אמרו איוב אמרו יחזקאל. Bacher, Terminologie II, 19 ff. has not a single example of this usage from the Babylonian Talmud.

[364] Bacher, Terminologie I, 68, assumes that הוא stands for הכתוב, but this is not probable, for then there would be no motive for the substitution, whereas the replacing of the name of God by a pronoun is very common as was shown above on 9,5. The full form, אמר הקב"ה על ידי probably occurs in Lev. Rabbah XXXI, 10, p. 732 et al.

[365] On מורה היחיד see below, Section VI.

[366] As Schechter rightly observes, this passage is taken from Ezek. 13:9, which probably had special importance for our author, since it was the practice of the sect (14,3 ff.) to have all the members of the community registered in a book.

"unite," "bind together," which frequently occurs in the Talmud and, according to some,[367] is even used once in the Bible as well.

20,8–9: לכל המאס בראשונים ובאחרונים. The "first" are those who lived before the rise of the sect, and the "last" are those who lived after that momentous event. The correctness of this interpretation is assured by 3,10 which speaks of the באי הברית הראשונים, "the first members of the Covenant," that is, those who lived before the rise of the sect; but *cf.* below, Section VII, p. 265, n. 25; p. 272, n. 54.

20,9: אשר שמו גלולים על לבם. This expression is taken from Ezek. 14:3 and is not, of course, to be taken literally. In our fragment opponents are never reproached with idolatry.

20,10: בבית התורה. By בית התורה are probably to be understood the headquarters of the sect in Damascus, where the "authentic Torah" was to be found. The fact is also stressed in another passage of our fragment (7,15 ff.) that in Damascus the scrolls of the Torah as well as the books of the prophets found a safe shelter, which is probably meant to stress the authority of the Torah text used by the sect; but *cf.* below, Section VIII, p. 298.

20,15: ובקץ ההוא. The translation "and at the end of these" is quite impossible, for the text would then have to be ובקץ שנים אלה or ובקץ זמן זה. As has already been observed, on 6,10, קץ means "period" and we must therefore translate, "and during this period the wrath of God will be visited on Israel."

20,17–18: או...ניד...איש אל רע.... This is to be restored (partly after Mal. 3:16) as אז נדברו איש אל רעהו למען[368] איש, "then spoke one to another, that one might support the other etc."

20,22: מבית פלג. The usual translation, "The house of Peleg" gives no sense. If, however, we translate בית פלג as "house of separation," the text offers no difficulty at all. The fathers of the sect are described as "The house of separation" and this is later explained by saying that in reliance upon God, וישענו על אל, they left Jerusalem when Israel became unfaithful to its God, בקץ[369] מעל ישראל, and their meritorious deeds will be reckoned to the benefit of their descendants until the thousandth generation. Accordingly, nothing has been lost between לאלף דור and מבית פלג, but the latter explains that "the thousandth generation" must be reckoned from "the house of separation."[370]

---

[367] *Cf.* Targum on Isa. 7:2, which renders נָחָה by אתחבר.

[368] [The text actually has להצדיק. See Rabin.]

[369] Not "at the end" but, as was already noted on 20,15, "during the period."

[370] Perhaps this description is chosen with reference to Gen. 10:25: these pious men did the same thing that Peleg did in his time when he separated himself from the sinful builders of the Tower (of Babel); *cf.* Book of Jubilees X, 18.

20,23: וטמאו את המקדש. A verb is impossible after בקץ so that we must read either וטומאת המקדש or וטמאו, "during the period of the unfaithfulness of Israel and the defiling of the Temple." This sin of טמאת המקדש is several times made a reproach against adversaries in our fragment; *cf.* 4,18 and 5,6.

20,28: ויתודו לפני אל ... אנו. Before אנו we should supply ואמרו.[371]

20,29: רשענו ... אנחנו גם. The word missing before אנחנו is גם;[372] *cf.* Gen. 46:34; 47:3 גם אנחנו גם אבותינו.

20,32: ולא ישיבו אל חקי הצדק. If we do not read יסירו מעל חקי הצדק the miswriting of אבל as לא is easily explainable, especially as the preceding sentence begins with ולא so that hardly any one will object to this emendation.[373]

[371] [See Rabin.]
[372] [The text actually has it; see Rabin.]
[373] [See now Rabin.]

IV

The Halakah of the Fragments

"We, the Rabbanites, do not repel the Isawites, even though they ascribe prophetic power to those who were no prophets — Jesus, Muhammad and Abu Isa — because they agree with us about the festival calendar."[1] These words of the Palestinian Jacob ben Ephraim are not only characteristic of the attitude of the Synagogue toward its undercurrents and tributary streams at the end of the first Christian millennium but also valid for much earlier centuries during which the Synagogue had to reckon with various tendencies. It was not dogma but law that was apt to produce lasting schisms in Judaism. It was not theological differences that created the Karaite schism in the eighth century but differences of opinion about matters of law, and one may confidently assert that so long as Jewish-Christianity was not distinct from the bulk of the people in its attitude to the Law, it was regarded as a normal part of it in spite of its peculiar dogmas. Accordingly, for the correct understanding of the circle in which the fragments that here engage our attention originated, the Halakah contained in them is much more important than their theological position. It is in place, therefore, to investigate what is characteristic of the legal parts of the fragments before we attempt to form a judgment about them.

The questions that we have to answer here are: Is the Halakah of the fragments distinct from that found in the rabbinic sources, and if it is, what is the nature of this difference? We must not, however, lose sight of the fact that not every variation in law is to be taken as an indication of sectarianism. The well known words of R. Yose,[2] "Until the appearance of the schools of Shammai and Hillel there were no controversies in Israel," must of course be taken with a grain of salt. For aside from the fact that legal controversies have come down

[1] *Cf.* Harkavy in the Appendix to the Hebrew translation of Graetz, *Geschichte* III, 501, and the article of Poznanski, "Jacob ben Ephraim," in the *Gedenkbuch für D. Kaufmann.*

[2] Tosefta, Ḥagigah II, 9 and parallel passages.

to us from the time of the older "pairs," זוגות[3] this statement cannot
be accepted as a generality, since otherwise instead of the two schools
mentioned, we should have had two sects, the Shammaites and the
Hillelites. A certain independence and freedom in the interpretation
of Scripture and respecting the authority of tradition — those two
chief pillars of the Halakah — always prevailed in Pharisaic circles,
so that a "sectarian Halakah" requires something more to characterize it than its divergence from the "standard Halakah." It therefore
seems best to start with the Karaite Halakah in defining what is
sectarian. Karaism is distinguished from Rabbinism in that it denies
the authority of the Talmud, which is the fundamental source of
rabbinic law. It is not the many hundreds of Halakoth about which the
Rabbanites and Karaites have differences of opinion that justify us
in speaking of Karaite in contrast to Rabbanite Halakah (among the
Rabbanites themselves there were many disputed points of law) but
it was the Karaites' rejection in principle of the Talmud as a source
of law that created the "Karaite Halakah." To be sure, the exact same
criterion does not apply to the old sectarian Halakah, for even though
particular Halakoth were written down in very ancient times, nevertheless the unanimous tradition of trustworthy sources is that Pharisaic
Judaism[4] knew no "authoritative lawbook" outside of the Pentateuch.
We shall not, however, be in error if we state that in the very earliest
period of Pharisaism a number of Halakoth had acquired such authority
that the deliberate ignoring of them was regarded as the hallmark of
a sectarian. In general this essential component of rabbinic law can
still be determined today even though there were disputes at an early
time about certain details. From the three important parts of the law,
those on the Sabbath, ritual purity, and marriage, I will chose an
example of each to illustrate these primitive components of rabbinic
law. In spite of the many differences of opinion between the schools of
Shammai and Hillel about details of the *eruv*, this institution is regarded
as something not to be shaken, so that the term "*eruv*-denier" is
equivalent to "Sadducee."[5] In no fewer than eighty-three instances do
these two schools differ about "clean" and "unclean," but the funda-

---

[3] Aside from the controversy over סמיכה (Ḥagigah II, 2) that had begun as early as
the pre-Maccabean period, still other differences of opinion among the older "pairs"
are cited; *cf.*, for example, Tosefta, Makhshirin III, 4, where, to be sure, Estori
Parḥi in כפתור ופרח, ed. Luncz, 64, reads פרידא for פרחיה.

[4] The Sadducees, on the other hand, are thought to have possessed a written
lawbook; *cf.* the note on 10,6, p. 50. Is the prohibition against writing down the
Halakah perhaps to be regarded as anti-Sadducean? *Cf.* Joel, *Blicke*, I, 58.

[5] Eruvin VI, 1; *cf.* below, pp. 135 ff.

mental rabbinic concepts such as מים שאובים, טמאת משקין and the like are presupposed by both schools without further question. The first Mishnah in Qiddushin cites a difference of opinion between the Shammaites and the Hillelites about the value of the object which a man must give to a woman in order to effect a marriage.[6] But no one disputes the authority of the old Halakah as to the three forms of consummating marriage, האשה נקנית בשלוש דרכים, which is a basic constituent of rabbinic law.

A third question which we must answer in discussing the Halakah contained in our fragments is: What is its relation to heretical Halakah? I must indeed confess that the longer and the more exhaustively I study the development of the Halakah, the more convinced I am of the untenability of Geiger's theory that seeks to establish an historical connection between Sadduceeism and Karaism. In spite of the סבל הירושה which the Karaites recognize, their Halakah bears so individual and arbitrary a character that it would be very hazardous to base upon it any conclusions concerning Sadducean Halakah. Of this, however, we know so pitifully little that it would be very risky to take it into consideration as a serious factor in the development of the Halakah. Nevertheless, however little light may be expected from the Karaite Halakah for the understanding of our document, it is worthwhile to investigate further the relation between them. That is to say, it is not altogether improbable that this document or one similar to it was known to the ancient Karaites, and it is not without importance for the history of Karaism to determine how much it drew from these sources. I therefore give at the end of this section a summary of the relation of our document to Karaite Halakah.

*

* *

In the short program of the First "Covenant" (6,11 ff.) the members are obligated with special emphasis to observe strictly the laws of the Sabbath[7] and ritual purity. It is therefore not a matter of chance that in the extant fragments these legal regulations occupy the most space, since it is on the strict observance of precisely these that our sect lays so much weight. If we except the regulations about the

---

[6] On the motivation of this difference of opinion see my remarks in the addenda to Geiger's קבוצת מאמרים, ed. Poznanski, p. 387.

[7] Cf. also 3,14 where "the holy Sabbath" is similarly spoken of.

communal organization of the sect,[8] the Sabbath laws[9] take up more than a third of the legal portion, and we are probably justified not only in beginning our inquiry into the character of the Halakah in our document with these but also in regarding them as the essential part of it.

The regulation about the "extension" of the Sabbath, תוספת שבת, (10,14) is often mentioned in the Talmud and already in Tannaitic passages (cf., for example, B. Yoma 81b). According to a statement of the Bavli (Shabbath 148b), this "extension" is a biblical commandment, and this is certainly the view of our document, which cites a proof-text for it from Scripture. In the Yerushalmi, on the other hand, it is stated (Shevi'ith 33a beg.) that "One may work on Friday until sunset," ערב שבת בראשית את מותר לעשות מלאכה עד שתשקע החמה which, of course, means only that the extension is rabbinic and not biblical; cf. Tosaphoth on Rosh Hashanah 9a bot. and Maimonides, Yad שביתת ע' I, 6. Noteworthy is the statement of Josephus (Bel. Jud. IV 9, 12) that the signal for the cessation of work was given at twilight* on Friday, which contradicts the sources quoted above, according to which the signal had to be given before twilight, since all work was forbidden during twilight. The Tannaitic sources[10] on the other hand, quite correctly state that the signal was given before the inauguration of the Sabbath, and we probably have a slight inaccuracy in Josephus.

The regulation that "one's conversation on the Sabbath must be different from that on weekdays," לא יהא דבורך של שבת כדבורך של חול, Shabbath 113b (the correct interpretation of this is given in Tosaphoth ad loc., which refer to TP Shabbath XV, 15a bot., where idle talk is expressly forbidden), is illustrated in our document by four concrete examples. One is not to speak of any idle matter,[11] warn a debtor,

---

[8] The section 12,22–16,6 treats of this exclusively; the laws proper are given in 9,1–12,18.

[9] Much of what is given as Sabbath law also applies to the Day of Atonement (6,19, יום הצום=יום התענית Menaḥoth XI, 9) and to the festivals.

*[Possibly deile here means "late afternoon." — R. M.]

[10] Tosefta, Sukkoth IV, 12; Shabbath 35b; cf. more fully on this Elbogen in Festschrift Lewy, 173 ff., whose attention this passage in Josephus has escaped, so that he discusses only the signal given at the beginning of the Sabbath, although Maimonides (Yad, Shabbath V, 20), whose view Josephus splendidly supports, gives the correct information. It is probably to this trumpet-signal at the end of the Sabbath and the Day of Atonement that the Shofar-signal, still given at the end of the Day of Atonement, is to be traced.

[11] R. Moses of Tachau in his כתב תמים (Oẓar Neḥmad III, 62) cites from TP Shabbath XV the sentence, אסור אדם לאשתעויי מותר מילי בשבת "It is forbidden to speak of idle matters on the Sabbath." In our text of the Yerushalmi this sentence is not found.

quarrel about money-matters[12] or speak of the work that one plans to do on the following day. Perhaps the statement of Agatharchides (Josephus, *Con. Ap.* I, 22)[13] that the Jews in the time of Ptolemy I spent the whole Sabbath in "prayer" is based on the fact that nothing concerning everyday living was discussed on the Sabbath. As a gentile Agatharchides spoke of "praying," he could not know that for the Jews it was not prayer that was the chief part of their cult but the study of the Torah. Jewish sources, however, speak with greater precision. Thus it is said in Yerushalmi, Shabbath XV, 15a, "The Sabbath and the festivals were given by God only that they might be used for the study of the Torah," לא ניתנו שבתות וימים טובים אלא לעסוק בהן בדברי תורה. Similarly Philo speaks (*De Spec. Leg.* II, XV, 62) of the many houses of study "that are open on the Sabbath, and in which instruction is given about useful things, through which the whole of life is ennobled." That the prohibition of "idle talk"[14] was not merely a pious wish can be seen from the fact that even the *'am ha-'arez*, whose word was not otherwise trusted, was above the suspicion of lying on the Sabbath because, in the words of the Palestinian Talmud, (Demai IV, 23d) "The fear of the Sabbath is on him, and he speaks the truth," אימת שבת עליו והוא אומר אמת. If then even the *'am ha-'arez*, out of "fear (of desecrating) the Sabbath" was careful of his words, how much more careful must have been the "law-abiding man" who certainly chose and weighed his words on this day.

Just as speech was limited on the Sabbath, so was walking, which, though in itself not a forbidden activity,[14] still should not serve business

---

[12] So, according to my interpretation of 10,18, whereas Schechter takes אל ישפוט to be the commandment forbidding the holding of court-trials on the Sabbath, which is known from the Mishnah (also Philo, *De Migrat. Abrahami* XVI). That ישה, however, is not to be translated "lend" is clear from the context, which here certainly requires forbidden "words" and not "actions." Moreover, it would be inexplicable that the creditor should be forbidden to lend but not the debtor to borrow. ישה, however, can be used only of the former, not of the latter. Exod. 22:24; Ps. 89:23; Neh. 5:7 *et al.*, show clearly that נשא as well as נשה (originally, perhaps, two distinct roots) can be used in the sense of "press a debtor." When Charles, *ad loc.*, expresses surprise at Schechter's "false" translation of ישה as "exact debts" he shows that he was venturing to interpret a Hebrew text with an inadequate knowledge of Hebrew.

[13] *Cf.* also *Ant.* XVI, 12,3.

[14] Beside the Baraita cited above cf. also Lev. Rabba XXXIV near end, and Pesiqta Rabbati XXIII, 116b ed. Friedmann. I note belatedly that Friedmann has already juxtaposed the comparison Bavli Shabbath 150b and TP XV, 15a as is done above on p. 58, note 174. However, I consider his attempt to read into Bavli the missing elements במוצאי שבת and לעולם on the basis of Yerushalmi to be quite unsuccessful. Most probably the Babylonians had the Palestinian Baraita before them in a defective form.

purposes or extend beyond two thousand cubits.[15] As has already been remarked, all this agrees with the view of the Halakah, and I should only like to add that as in the Halakah (Eruvin V, 8 et al.) the two thousand cubits begin from the end of the city,[16] so too do they do according to the teaching of our document, as is clear from 11,5.

The regulations in 10,22–23 illustrate the Halakah about הכנה which is familiar from Tannaitic source. It will be seen that the statement of Josephus (Bel. Jud. II, 8, 9)[17] that the Jews prepare their food on Friday because they do not use fire on the Sabbath is not quite accurate, for even foods that do not require cooking must also be set aside on Friday for use on the Sabbath.

In agreement with the Halakah and in contrast to the Book of Jubilees and the Karaites, the use of flowing water for drinking and bathing is permitted by our sect (11,1), and only the "carrying of water outside" is forbidden, because according to the view of the Halakah[18] every stream is a "domain," רשות, by itself, and for this reason the carrying of water from a stream to its bank is forbidden.

Whereas the Bible only requires that one allow his slave to rest on the Sabbath, the Halakah goes far beyond the biblical commandment in respect of the work performed on the Sabbath by others in stating that "whatever one is not permitted to do on the Sabbath oneself, one may not let a gentile do either." As is clear from Shabbath I, 8 this prohibition was generally recognized as early as the time of the schools of Shammai and Hillel, but still the prevailing view was that it had only rabbinic sanction.[19] It is doubtful whether our document knows of any difference between rabbinic and biblical prescriptions, and the authority of Scripture seems to be the only one recognized by our sect; nevertheless it is instructive to observe that in this document (11,2) the performance of any work through the agency of a gentile is forbidden. The very strict interpretation of the commandment about the resting of slaves in our document (11,12), according to which even operations which one may perform on the Sabbath oneself may not be attended to by a slave, is probably connected with this "rabbinic prohibition."

[15] At any rate this is the view of the Halakah, cf. below.

[16] Schürer, Geschichte II, 475, inexactly gives it as two thousand cubits from one's dwelling place.

[17] The first part of the sentence does not refer exclusively to the Essenes but to all Jews.

[18] In regard to "drawing water," see also Eruvin X, 15.

[19] Cf. Mekilta, Pisḥa IX (Friedmann, p. 96, Horovitz, pp. 30–31), and the parallels cited by them. In Bavli (Shabbath 150b and parallels) the rule obtains that "it is rabbinically forbidden to assign work to a gentile (on the Sabbath)." אמירה לעובד כוכבים שבות.

The talmudic sources state that the only difference between a slave and a gentile in respect of performing work on the Sabbath lies in the fact that it is *biblically* forbidden to permit a slave[20] to do work, whereas there is only a *rabbinic* prohibition against permitting gentiles to work. Now since this difference between "rabbinic" and "biblical" probably did not exist for our author, he had to explain why Scripture (Exod. 20:10) mentions only the slave if even a gentile may not do any work for a Jew. His explanation is as follows: The master may not let his slave perform even such a service on the Sabbath as does not involve any "work," since the latter is to enjoy complete rest, whereas a gentile may very well perform a service for a Jew but not any "work."

This exposition of the views of our document in respect of the resting of slaves [on the Sabbath] is based on the explanation given of מרא in 11,12 (cf. above, p. 67), according to which this means the same as "to master" and is cognate with Aramaic מרא "master." From the context the translation "to upbraid," from מרה = מרא,[21] would be perfectly possible, because already further back, in agreement with the Halakah,[22] even idle talk has been forbidden on the Sabbath. Still the prohibition against upbraiding slaves is not superfluous. In the passage scolding is forbidden not because "profane words" are not in place on this holy day but because it interferes with the slave's rest, which may not be disturbed even if the upbraiding is justified. On linguistic grounds, however, I do not believe that ימרה = ימרא could be used of a master's unkind treatment of his slave, since in both biblical and post-biblical literature this verb denotes only the disobedience of a subordinate to his superior. As has already been remarked, *ad loc.*, the Halakah knows no prohibition against the performance of all services by a slave on the Sabbath. But just this view, as appears from the passage in Philo which is there referred to, was held not only by the Alexandrian philosopher but, as his words imply, the strict conception of the resting of slaves was the one generally held in Alexandria. In full agreement with the Halakah,[23] on the other hand, is the extension (11,12) of the rest which Scripture prescribes for slaves to (gentile) "laborers."

---

[20] By "slaves" our document (*cf.* 12,11) probably understands, in agreement with the Halakah, Mekilta, Baḥodesh VII, p. 230, slaves who have become part of the Jewish community, בני ברית.

[21] Pirqe de R. Eliezer [XIII] considers תמריא in Job 39:18 a by-form of תמרה.

[22] *Cf.* pp. 57, 108–109. R. Baḥya in his book כד הקמח, Section שבת, 76, ed. Lemberg, finds in the Talmudic passage, Shabbath 113b the precept to speak only softly on the Sabbath, and similarly זהר 'ת, [448, 85b].

[23] Mekilta, Kaspa, p. 331; Midrash Tannaim, p. 22.

Rather peculiar too is the view of our document about the Sabbath rest to be granted to animals. Of the two regulations (11,5–6) concerning this, only the first one, as was noted *ad loc.*, corresponds to the Halakah, while the second one is at variance with it. Nevertheless, it is to be noted that although, according to the Halakah, only the performance of work by animals is forbidden, the principle is recognized that "The Sabbath was given for the refreshment of animals and not for their discomfort," אין זה נייח אלא צער,[24] for which reason it is permitted, on the one hand, to let animals graze on the Sabbath, even though they are doing work thereby, and, on the other hand, it is forbidden to hinder their freedom of movement.[25] Our document goes a step further still and forbids anyone to cause animals any pain at all, just as it forbids (11,12) the performance of any service at all by slaves.

In complete agreement with the Halakah are the regulations (11,9–11) about "carrying" on the Sabbath. Carrying objects out from the house into the street or, as the case may be, bringing an object from the street into the house, is forbidden. The Book of Jubilees, however, speaks (2,30) of carrying objects from one house to another, which is not at all forbidden by the Halakah.[26] Our document also agrees with the Halakah in extending the prohibition against carrying objects to include the private (blind) alley, מבוי, although this is biblically permitted according to rabbinic tradition; the prohibition was in fact not recognized by the Samaritans and the Sadducees.[27] To supplement the prohibition against carrying objects, two special cases are mentioned, and these, to be sure, are ones that are often discussed in the Mishnah since, strictly speaking, they cannot be described as "carrying a burden" and are therefore only rabbinically prohibited. The first case concerns the carrying of aromatic herbs, סמנים, which are really a part of the toilette, particularly of that of women,[28] and as such are biblically permitted; the Rabbis forbade them

---

[24] Mekilta, Kaspa, *ibid.*

[25] Shabbath V, 3, and the interpretations of these Halakoth in the Talmud, 54; *cf.* also Bashyatzi, Shabbath VIII, 44b, אמנם ב'ה (= בעלי הקבלה) אסרו . . . כדי שלא תהיה הבהמה מצטערת "The Rabbanites forbid everything that causes these animals discomforts."

[26] Tosefta, Shabbath, I, 3; Talmud Shabbath 6a. Even the carrying of an object from one house to another through the street is only a rabbinic prohibition, *cf.* Shabbath, *loc. cit.*

[27] *Cf.* below, pp. 136 ff.

[28] In the Mishnah, Shabbath VI,3, this case is discussed only in connection with women; for since aromatic matter was not regarded as belonging to the toilette of

(Shabbath VI, 3) because[29] one might forget and take the perfume-bottle, צלוחית של פלייטון, from one's neck, to which it is fastened with a ribbon, and carry it in one's hand, which of course would be biblically forbidden.[30] It should be noted that our document also speaks of carrying aromatic herbs סמנים, "on one's person," עליו, whereby the peculiarity of this case is stressed. The second case which is separately mentioned concerns the carrying of a small child. The carrying of a grown child is not forbidden, at least not biblically, according to the Halakah (Shabbath X,5), but the carrying of a child which cannot yet walk[31] is definitely forbidden, for which reason this is particularly stressed in our document, just as the Mishnah (Shabbath XVIII, 2) also more fully describes the circumstances in which "walking" the baby is permitted.

A form of work which according to the Halakah falls into the category of building, בונה, and is therefore forbidden is the opening of a vessel which is sealed fast. Similarly our document (11,9), whereas the Karaites forbid the opening and closing of any vessel. Closely related to this prohibition is the regulation (11,10) אל יטול בבית, which, according to my interpretation ad loc., forbids clearing away, an act which according to the Halakah (Shabbath 73a) is similarly to be regarded as belonging to the category of "building" and is therefore forbidden. In Schechter's view, however, this regulation contains the the prohibition of מוקצה,[32] which is well known from rabbinic sources (and Josephus, cf. Bel. Jud. II, 8, 9). If one seek to support this interpretation by appealing to the context, since both the preceding and the following laws deal with the prohibition of "carrying," to which מוקצה is closely related,[33] we must not fail to note, on the other hand, that a little before our regulation a quite certain case of בונה is mentioned.

---

men, they are even biblically forbidden to carry it on their person on the Sabbath. Our document, on the other hand, speaks of men, perhaps because it uses the formula אל . . . איש in most of the Sabbath laws. Perhaps, too, a reason for the distinction was that the Pharisees opposed the use of scent by men; cf. Geiger, Jüdische Zeitschrift VI, 105–121.

[29] Shabbath 62a.

[30] Tosefta, Shabbath VII, 11 has בשם for which our text uses סמנים.

[31] Cf. the explanation of this law in Shabbath 94a and 141b; in the latter passage תינוק means a child that has learned to walk.

[32] Stones and rocks are of course מוקצה; cf. Yom Tov 12a.

[33] At least this is the view of Rashi on Yom Tov 36a, and Rabad on Maimonides, Yad, Shabbath, XXIV, 12. However, Maimonides has probably given the correct explanation in his account of the origin of this prohibition, loc. cit.

In regard to all activities forbidden on the Sabbath, our document, in agreement with the Halakah[34] sets up the principle that the Sabbath may be profaned where human life is at stake but not for the sake of avoiding loss of money or because of compassion for animals. It is very probable that the prescript (11,14) "one should not spend the Sabbath in a place near the settlement of gentiles" is connected with this principle. The proximity of a gentile settlement may under certain circumstances lead to desecration of the Sabbath, such as a Jew being attacked and being forced to defend himself with weapons, for which reason it was prescribed that such eventualities were to be avoided. The Talmud in fact (Eruvin 62a) states explicitly that Jews are not forbidden to dwell among gentiles since they avoid this of their own will because of their fear of being murdered by gentiles. Similarly it is said in the Mishnah, Avodah Zarah II, 1, that "gentiles are suspected of committing murder." Whether this suspicion was justified is a problem which does not concern us here, but at any rate it existed and was sufficient reason for the regulation, mentioned above, that one should not spend the Sabbath in a place where one might be forced to defend oneself with weapons.

Aside from the forbidden kinds of work, our document has two regulations (11,3–5), treating of the correct sanctification, קדוש, of the day of rest, and in this matter too it is in full agreement with the Halakah. The clause . . . אל יקח, as was shown in greater detail *ad loc.*, contains nothing else than the very well known regulation about "wearing clean clothes on the Sabbath."[35] I should like to add that the reading שופים, which I proposed to emend to שׁוּפָּם, can be retained, that is to say, taken as the passive participle of שׁוּף,[36] and accordingly vocalized as שׁוּפִים. The interpretation given by Schechter of the clause אל יתערב is in my opinion the only correct one. It contains the prohibition against fasting on the Sabbath, which is known from rabbinic sources, the Book of Jubilees, 1,12 and Josephus, *Vita* 54. From a linguistic

---

[34] The principle of פקוח נפש דוחה שבת is not only frequently mentioned in rabbinic sources (*cf.*, for example, Mekilta, Ki Tissa I, p. 343), but also in Josephus, as Schürer has already noted, *Geschichte* II, 460 (*cf.*, however, *Bel. Jud.* II, 16,4 and *Ant.* XVIII, 9,6) and Philo, *De Somniis* II, XVIII.

[35] *Cf.* above on 11,3, where it was shown that there is no trace in our document of the idea that the Sabbath must be spent in a state of purity, but this view is held by the Karaites (Hadassi 56b) and the Samaritans (Petermann, *Reisen*, I, 276, 2nd ed.); from Elephantine papyrus 6, on the other hand, it is clear that the Egyptian Jews, in agreement with the Halakah, maintained a state of purity only during the three pilgrims-festivals.

[36] The plural שופים is, to be sure, rather strange after כיבסו, and we probably should read כיבסם.

point of view יתערב, "mingle together," might well be considered a euphemistic term for sexual intercourse, and as a substantive parallel one might refer to the Book of Jubilees, 50,8 but the following מרצונו makes such an explanation impossible. It is quite out of the question to take יתערב מרצונו as an expression of opposition to the rabbinic institution of the *eruv*, for not only would יתערב be very strange for יערב but also the addition of מרצונו could hardly be explained. It is, however, possible that יתערך (in the old orthography יתערכ can hardly be distinguished from יתערב) is to be read in place of יתערב. This prohibition would then be directed against voluntary participation in battle on the Sabbath. The "voluntary," מרצונו, is particularly stressed, since the gentile authorities probably often forced a Jewish soldier to commit such a profanation of the Sabbath. The use of the *hithpael* form is not elsewhere attested, it is true, but התערך is the form one would expect from מערכה "battle-order."

In comparison with the Sabbath regulations, the rest of the law is treated in a very cavalier manner, unless we have only inconsiderable fragments of the law book of the sect before us. In the pronunciamento against opponents (5,6), they are reproached for "having intercourse with those who menstruate," ושוכבים עם הרואה את דם זובה. Because of the vagueness of this complaint, however, the underlying halakic difference between the sect and its opponents cannot be determined.[37] In another passage (12,1) sexual intercourse is forbidden in "the city of the Sanctuary," by which the Temple-mount is probably meant, for which place the Halakah also requires this degree of holiness, as was noted *ad loc*. Important for the history of the Halakah is the teaching of our document (12,15–18) that stone, wood and earth acquire Levitical uncleanness, in which it indeed agrees with the Targum Jonathan, but not with Talmudic sources. What Charles *ad loc*. cites from the Mishnah, however, has nothing to do with the question that concerns us. Kelim XII,6 (not 7, as Charles writes) speaks of vessels of wood which are not quite finished, whereas our document speaks of עצים, that is, of wood as raw material. Kelim VI,1 has as its subject the biblical law about the uncleanness of an oven (Lev. 11:35). According to the Halakah, stone with clay as base or top is subject to the laws of uncleanness because such objects are regarded as vessels of clay, כלי חרש. But אבנים in our document cannot, of course, mean "stoves." Incidentally, Charles has had the mis-

---

[37] Of course what is involved here is only a difference about the interpretation of the biblical law of זבה and not about the binding power of this law; *cf*. further below in Section V.

fortune to misunderstand the expression פטפוטים ג' in the Mishnah
loc. cit., since what is there discussed is not "three stones" but a tripod
made of clay. Just as wood in its natural state or stone vessels cannot
become unclean, so also according to the Halakah, an object attached
to the wall, to say nothing of one attached to the ground, cannot
become unclean. Kelim XIV,3 contains the rule that objects that are
only temporarily fixed in the ground, like tent-pegs (יתדות אהלים, not,
as Charles states, יתדות המשׁחות, which means the pegs used by sur-
veyors) and the like are susceptible to uncleanness. Our document,
however, declares יתד בכותל "a peg in the wall" (not "in the house,"
as Charles has it) unclean, which is decidedly against the Halakah.
As pegs do not become unclean because they are fixed in the ground,
neither do nails that are fixed to the wall, whereas our document
declares these to be unclean too. In Kelim XII, 5 there is a difference
of opinion between Rabbi Akiva and his colleagues as to whether nails
drawn from the wall to be used as keys and the like still retain their
original character. That nails that are driven into a wall for hanging
something on them are unclean is a statement cited by Charles from
the Mishnah *loc. cit.*, but it is not found either there or elsewhere in
rabbinic literature. For those familiar with the Halakah the above
detailed explanation is, of course, superfluous, but unfortunately it
has become common in recent times to write about the Halakah
without any knowledge of its most elementary concepts, and I have
therefore thought it in place to throw a little light on the learning of
these "halakists." Essentially in agreement with the views of the
Halakah are the regulations (10,10–13) about "the cleansing of an
uncleanness," which is a fact the more noteworthy in that there are
ordinances among them that are described in Talmudic tradition as
being rabbinic.

Of the dietary laws there are only three in our document (12,11–15),
including, first of all, the general rule that the biblical prohibitions
against eating certain animals include even the smallest species among
aquatic and land animals. We shall probably not be wrong if we find
in this rule the Halakah (Makkoth 16b) that the eating of a forbidden
animal, even if it is only an ant, is a punishable transgression, whereas
in the case of other forbidden foods, like blood, fat, etc., only one who
eats as much as the amount of an olive, כזית, has committed a sin.
The statement that our author, in contrast to the Halakah, forbids
the eating of honey because it comes from forbidden animals, is quite
gratuitious. No less untenable is the statement that our document, in
agreement with the Karaites and in contrast to the Halakah, prescribes
a particular form of killing fish; in reality it teaches only that the blood

of fish is forbidden. This is not the view of the Halakah, to be sure, but, as was noted *ad loc.*, the Halakah also forbids using the blood of fish, when it is not outwardly recognizable as such, and this "rabbinic ordinance" is raised to the status of an absolute prohibition in our document. The simple wording of the Mishnah, Kerithoth V, 1, favors the view (cf. Tosafoth *ad loc.*) that the blood of fishes is forbidden, even though the drinking thereof is not punished. Cf. also below, p. 126.

In several passages of our document reference is made to the sacrificial cult; it is, however, very probable that our sect had no sacrificial cult at all, for the regulations concerning this are all directed against the usual practice of the Temple in Jerusalem. Thus it is especially stressed (11,17) that only "the burnt offering of the Sabbath" may be brought on the Sabbath, whereby the teaching of Hillel, according to which the Passover lamb, which is not a burnt-offering, must be offered on the Sabbath, is rejected in unequivocal terms. It severely censures (11,18) those who permit sacrifices to be offered by "unclean men," whereby, as was more fully explained *ad loc.*, the adherents of the sect are forbidden to have any part in the Temple-service at Jerusalem because the priests there do not observe the sect's rules of ritual purity and as "unclean men" desecrate the temple with their sacrifices. The regulation (16,13–14) "not to dedicate to the altar anything acquired by force" contains the further clause, "neither shall the priests compel anyone to offer a sacrifice," which is probably a thrust chiefly at the violent procedure of the Sadducean priests, about which we read bitter complaints in the Talmud and Josephus,[38] but perhaps also at the teaching of the Pharisees (Arakhin V, 2) that one can be compelled to fulfill his vow to offer a sacrifice. The regulation (9,13) concerning the penalty offering, אשם, seems at first to speak against the assumption that the sect did not recognize any sacrificial cult, but on closer examination it favors this view. It is the only law in our document that is taken almost literally from Scripture without adding anything thereto. If, however, one assumes that the sect had no sacrificial cult, this regulation contains the important teaching that the priest keeps recovered property in spite of his not being able to offer the penalty offering. This is in agreement with the view of the Halakah (Bava Qamma IX, 12), according to which the restitution of property is independent of the sacrifice, whereas the Karaites (Nicomedia, חיוב שבועה 193b bot.) state that the priest may keep the money only if he brings the sacrifice.

---

[38] These accounts describe conditions shortly before 70 C. E. Similar things must have happened earlier; *cf.* Eccles. 5:5, where וחבל perhaps means "to pledge."

Most probably the provisions about capital crimes (12,2–5) are also of purely theoretical nature, for we have no reliable evidence that the right to inflict punishment was exercised by the sectarian community.[39] In agreement with the Halakah,[40] stoning is mentioned as the penalty inflicted on a false prophet who preaches "apostasy." Scripture, of course, did not specify the kind of death penalty inflicted in such a case. The second provision, that a prophet[41] who attempts to seduce the people to desecration of the Sabbath shall not be punished with death contravenes the Halakah and is probably a concession to the conditions that then existed. This is a case of one who does not recognize the strict Sabbath laws of the sect and not of one who rejects the biblical regulations concerning the Sabbath. Since it would not do to consider the bulk of Jewry, which rejected these laws, to be liable to the death penalty, our document had to accommodate itself to a certain leniency.

The few ordinances concerning courts and their procedure are on the whole in agreement with the Halakah. The courts, which, as has been remarked before, had no power of life and death, consisted (10,4; 13,1) of ten[42] members. Theoretically, to be sure, the Halakah states that three judges suffice for civil cases (criminal cases must be judged by at least twenty-three judges!), but in actuality the court of ten members was the usual one in the time of the Amoraim, as was shown more fully on 13,1. The judges were chosen by the community (10,4), a procedure somewhat modified from that mentioned in the Mishnah, as was noted *ad loc.*, but this seems to have been the usual procedure in Geonic times, as the term ברורים "chosen" for judges shows; cf. R. Saadya's Epistle in Bornstein, מחלקת, pp. 61, 64, and Alfasi's *Responsa*, no. 80, p. 131. The calling in of priests and Levites, which is recommended[43] by the Halakah for a criminal case,

---

[39] If the usual interpretation of 9,1 were the correct one, one might cite this passage as proof of our statement, for it implies that the execution of a transgressor is only possible through gentile authorities; however, *cf.* my explanation of this. In 9,6 ד' מות denotes the seriousness of the offense, whereas in 10,1 it is penal authority that seems to be spoken of.

[40] Sifre Deut. 86, p. 151. Midrash Tannaim 64 and Sanhedrin 67a.

[41] *Cf.* the sources cited in the preceding note, where the following Halakah is established: seduction to any sin whatever is punished with death when the seducer is a prophet, whereas another person is merely punished for seduction to apostasy, and it is possible that the second provision in our document does not speak of a prophet at all, for which reason the offense is not a capital crime.

[42] Perhaps a ten-member court of the Essenes is also implied in Josephus, *Bel. Jud.* II, 8,7.

[43] As for the passage in Yevamoth 86b, referred to on p. 49, we should probably there read הָרַבָּם for הרבים. The proof for the assumption that the court-officials,

and prescribed[44] for the high court, is required by our document for the court of ten members (for civil cases!) as well. The judges might not (10,6) be younger than twenty-five years old and not older than sixty, as the Halakah also requires for members of the criminal court that they must reach a ripe age[45] without, however, being really old men.[46] The fixing of the age of witnesses (10,1) also agrees essentially with the view of the Halakah, as was shown *ad loc.* The moral qualifications of the witness (10,2) are the same as those required by the Halakah;[47] the witness who transgresses the Law "with a high hand" is disqualified. Nevertheless the Halakah and our document differ in respect of the reliability of various witnesses, for whereas the latter (9,16–20) says that "joined together testimony," עדות מצורפת, suffices to convict one of a capital crime, such testimony, according to the Halakah, suffices for this in property cases at best but not in criminal cases. It is interesting to observe in what way our document arrived at this view. It is based upon a *derash* of Lev. 5:1, where, according to the view of the Halakah,[48] Scripture prescribes the duty of bearing witness. In this passage, however, we read והוא עד "and he is a witness," and since, according to the Halakah,[49] the statement of a single

----

שוטרים, need not be Levites exclusively, lies in the fact that in Deut. 1:15 the reading is ושוטרים and that the ו in this word "includes" (הרבם), these men in the category of the previously mentioned "heads," ראשיכם of whom it is explicitly stated that they were of *all* tribes.

[44] Sifre Deut. 153, p. 206. Among the Essenes too the priests were the leaders, *cf.* Josephus, *Ant.* XVIII, 1, 5.

[45] The expression בעלי זקנה in Sanhedrin 19a means "of ripe age," since old men are out of the question. According to Yerushalmi Sanhedrin IV, 22b a twenty-year old man can be a member of the Lesser Sanhedrin; in Midrash Mishle I, 4, on the other hand, it is said that up to the age of 25 one is still a youth, נער. [The conclusion of Rabbi Ishmael *ibid.*, is that a נער is up to the age of twenty. — S. L.] According to Maimonides, *Yad*, Sanhedrin II, 6 ripe age is no *conditio sine qua non* for a judge.

[46] This regulation is given not only in the Baraita, Sanhedrin 36b but already in Mishnah Horayoth I, 4, where with Maimonides (שגגות XIII) we must read either או or ו after זקן. That in this passage זקן is not a title, as some commentators assume, is clear from the preceding אחד מהן, according to which זקן is quite excluded.

[47] Sanhedrin 26b, from which Maimonides (Eduth XII, 1) rightly infers that the transgression of a commandment disqualifies a witness only when there is no doubt that he has committed it out of contempt for the Law (יד רמה in our document!).

[48] Tosefta, Shevuoth III, 4 expressly insists that although only an expiatory sacrifice is prescribed for one who refuses to give such testimony and thereby causes property loss, it is still the duty of a witness to testify against murderers, adulterers and idolaters, and this is also the view of our document, as the expression דבר מות shows.

[49] The Halakah finds this principle expressed in the words of Scripture in Deut. 19:15. *Cf.* Sifre Deut. 188, p. 228; Midrash Tannaim and Targum Jonathan *ad loc*

witness is of no weight in court, Scripture can only have imposed the
duty of giving testimony upon a single witness because this testimony
is important if the transgressor again commits the same sin in the
presence of a second witness.[50] According to the fundamental principle of the Halakic midrash[51] that עד everywhere means two witnesses, the Tannaim and Amoraim found no difficulty at all in the
words והוא עד, and therefore state[52] that two witnesses are meant in
this passage too. In complete agreement with the Halakah, on the
other hand, is the principle (9,22) that although in all cases it is the
rule that only two[53] witnesses deserve to be believed, still a single
witness suffices to declare something clean or unclean, that two
witnesses are necessary in all[54] cases, both criminal can civil, is also
stated by the Halakah, but at the same time it is regarded as an
undisputed rule[55] that "one witness suffices to declare whether something is permitted or forbidden," עד אחד נאמן באיסורין, for which our
document uses the biblical[56] expression ועל אחד להבדיל הטהרה. With the
Halakah[57] that witnesses may not retract the statements that they
have made in court, כיון שהגיד שוב אינו חוזר ומגיד, the regulation (9,9)
may be connected that witnesses are not to be adjured outside the
court, because they can retract their earlier testimony in court.

---

[50] However, when, in agreement with the Halakah it is forbidden, in 9,3, to
accuse a man of a sin so long as he is not convicted by witnesses, this means only
that the single witness merely reports to the "censor" but he is not to speak further of it.

[51] Sifre Num. 7, p. 12; Yerushalmi Soṭah VI, 20d; Bavli Soṭah 2a.

[52] Shevuoth IV, 2 et al.; cf., however, ibid., 32a.

[53] It has already been shown that three witnesses are not required by our
document in certain circumstances. The rule "two witnesses are as good as a
hundred," תרי כמאה, is a principle (Shevuoth 42a) that was disputed by no one.
It is noteworthy that in the pseudepigraphic Testament of Abraham XII (on the
Jewish origin of which see my discussion in the Jewish Encyclopedia I, 93 ff.) the
statement is made that only through three witnesses can a fact be established with
certainty.

[54] Sifre Deut. 188, p. 228, where two exceptions are also given.

[55] Giṭṭin 3b; cf. also Yevamoth 87b.

[56] Cf. Lev. 10:10 and 11:47. Our document uses this biblical expression also in
6,17. For another explanation of להבדיל הטהרה cf. above ad loc. For ועל read ועד.

[57] Kethuboth 18b.

[58] Cf. Shevuoth IV, 1, where R. Meir's view is cited that when witnesses have
testified under oath outside of court that they knew nothing about a certain case,
they need not bring an (expiatory) sacrifice in the event that they have sworn
falsely. Even R. Meir's opponents (IV,3) admit that if witnesses swear falsely outside of court, they need not bring a sacrifice so soon as they testify in court. As is
clear from the explanations of the Talmud, Shevuoth 32a, the basis of these
Halakoth is the assumption that so long as the witnesses can still give their testimony,
their denial of it is not punishable.

Connected with the testimony of witnesses in our document is the regulation (9,11) that if someone's property is missing, he shall impose an "oath of cursing," שבועת האלה, upon all those who know something about the theft. This way of investigating the theft is superfluous, according to the Halakah, it is true, since it is the duty of a witness to report the guilty person without more ado, but yet down to the present day[59] the custom has been observed of making a witness give testimony by threatening to announce a חרם. What our document means by "an oath of cursing" is made plain in 15,1 where a warning against the use of the divine name in oaths is given. If the court imposes an oath, this is to consist merely in the threat of heavenly punishment for one who speaks a falsehood, and this, as was noted *ad loc.*, corresponds to the oath-formula that was customary in court during the Geonic period, whereas in the talmudic period, in spite of the decided aversion to swearing in the name of God[60] among a large circle, this solemn oath-formula was retained in court. At any rate it appears from Yerushalmi, Qiddushin II, 62a[61] that as early

[59] Maimonides, *Yad*, Gezelah IV, 8 on the basis of Geonic tradition, and *Beth Yoseph*, Ḥoshen ha-Mishpat XVIII. Not only Lev. 5:1 but also Judg. 17:2 shows that in biblical times it was customary to compel a witness to give testimony through an oath and the same was customary in the Talmudic period, as can be seen from Shevuoth IV *passim* (particularly Mishnah X).

[60] Apart from the sources on the objectionableness of the 'true' oath cited for 15,1 (pp. 91–93 ff.), *cf.* also Sifre Deut. 330, p. 380, where it is stated that God does not like to swear, and further, Zohar I, 165a, where the passage from Tanḥuma on Jacob's oath, cited by me, *loc. cit.*, is probably used. *Cf.* also the Slavonic Enoch XLIX, 1 and L, 4 where a particularly sharp attack on swearing is made. In reference to the incident, cited by me, *loc. cit.*, from Josephus on the Pharisees' refusal to take an oath of loyalty, one should also compare Josephus, *Ant.* XVII,2,4, where the incident mentioned is reported for the reign of Herod in a version hostile to the Pharisees.

[61] There it is stated that a witness is to be considered "interested," נוגע, when through his testimony he gets out of taking a "biblical" oath but not when it is a "rabbinic" one. The commentators (*cf.*, for example, Adret on Bavli Qiddushin 43b) admit that this distinction is quite inexplicable. If, however, we assume that only the biblical oath was sworn in the name of God, the matter becomes quite clear. The aversion to such an oath was so great that a witness under certain circumstances would rather be convicted of a falsehood than take such an oath even truthfully (*cf.* pp. 91–92); as against this, people were not too much concerned about "being cursed"; cf. also *Beth Yoseph, loc. cit.*, LXXXVII, where the various opinions of the Poseqim about שבועת היסת are given, although this passage in the Yerushalmi escaped their notice. [The entire preceding discussion is based on the usual method of the commentaries to interpret the Yerushalmi in accordance with the Bavli (see Bavli *ibid.* 43b). In the Yerushalmi *ibid.*, there is no hint to an oath, either biblical or rabbinic. Moreover the existence of a שבועת היסת was unknown in Palestine at that time. The correct explanation of נוגע בדבר is available in ספר ניר *ad. loc.* — S. L.]

as the period of the Amoraim, the name of God was used in oaths only
in those cases in which an oath was demanded on the basis of biblical
law, שבועה מן התורה, but not in the case of a rabbinic oath, שבועה
מדרבנן, in which case only a curse was pronounced. Although the use
of God's name was never permitted in an oath, the sanctity of an oath
was very great in our document (16,8) and yet, as was noted *ad loc.*,
it could hardly have taken the view that the punishment of death was
to be inflicted for perjury or that danger of loss of life was no justification for the non-fulfillment of an oath. Such views were occasionally
held by individuals among the Pharisees.[62] But the prevailing view
is that for perjury only "stripes," מלקות,[63] are inflicted, and that in
spite of its sanctity an oath must be violated to save a human life.
And this is probably the view of our document. It is in full agreement
with the Halakah in the matter (16,11) of the authority of the father,
as over against the husband to annul the vows and oaths of a woman,
as was shown in greater detail *ad loc.* In agreement with the divergent
view of Philo, cited there, is that of Maimonides (Nedarim XII, 1),
although he concedes that Sifre decides otherwise, *cf.* his Responsum
No. 35, 9a; ed. Leipzig.

The regulations (12,6–11)[64] concerning relations with gentiles
belong, it is true, more to the constitution of the sectarian community
than to the realm of law proper, that is binding on all alike, but they
nevertheless also correspond to the rules laid down in rabbinic sources,
as was remarked *ad loc.*[65] It is especially to be noted that our document,
in agreement with the Halakah (Mekilta, Mishpatim, IV, p. 263), permits the killing of a gentile only in self-defense.[66] It is also of interest
that it is forbidden to take alms and gifts for charitable purposes from

---

[62] *Cf.* more fully on this pp. 95–96 ff. According to Philo the penalty of death is
inflicted not only on the perjurer but also on those who neglect to inform against
the perjurer, *De Spec. Leg.* II, VI, 26, ed. Mangey II, 275. That it is the duty of a witness to inform against a perjurer is also the view of the Halakah. Tosefta, Shevuoth
II, 14 (only the three cardinal sins are mentioned by name) but the penalty of
death is not, of course, imposed for failure to denounce the perjurer. *Cf.* also Targum Jon. on Lev. 5:1, which, like Philo, sees in this verse a reference to the testimony of a perjurer. Is perhaps אוריתא to be read instead of מומתא in the Targum?

[63] Shevuoth III, 11.

[64] *Cf.* also 13,14 and the explanations of this passage, p. 87.

[65] There can hardly be any doubt that according to the Halakah neither grain
nor wine may be sold to gentiles before the prescribed amounts for Temple-offerings
and tithes, such as תרומה and מעשר, have been set aside, since the Halakah permits
the sale of these products to Jews only in exceptional cases and then only to a
ḥaber but not to an *'am-ha'areẓ*; *cf.* Demai V, 8 and Yerushalmi *ad loc.*

[66] *Cf.* 11,15 where הון ובצע in contrast to נפשות, and so too in this passage, as
Schechter rightly observes.

gentiles, just as the Talmudic sources regard this as an "inexpressible sin."[67] More related to administrative procedure than to the law is also the regulation (9,15) that lost objects, of which the legal owners can not be located, are turned over to the priests. Rabbinic tradition, to be sure, knows no such ordinance.[68] However, in the light of the principle[69] הפקר בית דין הפקר there is nothing objectionable from the viewpoint of the Halakah in such a communal ordinance, especially since it was fashioned after the pattern of a law of the Bible (Num. 5:8).

It is instructive, for the relationship of our text to the Halakah, that both the rules relating to the divine service which were prescribed in the sectarian document parallel comparable usages in the Temple and the synagogue. The ritually impure[70] are excluded (11,22) from participating in the service of the synagogue [of the sect]; this rule exists in the rabbinic tradition and it is reported as having been first ordained by Ezra.[71] Secondly, in imitation of a ceremonial usage of the Temple the sounding of the trumpet was prescribed at the end of the divine service.[72] Also for many of the essential properties of the community's constitution one can find parallels in the ordinances of other Jewish Communities. "The priest learned in the book of interpretation," כהן מבונן בספר ההגו, who stands at the head of the court (13,2), has his counterpart in the "expert of the court," מופלא של בית דין, whose presence is absolutely necessary (Horayoth I, 4) to give authority to judicial decisions. Even the "censor," מבקר, the real leader of the community, certainly owes his name to the Temple officials who had to examine sacrificial animals for defects and have

---

[67] Cf. Sanhedrin 26b, where, according to an ancient interpretation (Aruk s. v. דבר), this sin is described as דבר אחר.

[68] The Karaites, however, do have such a one; cf. below.

[69] Giṭṭin 36b; [Tosefta Sheqalim I, 3. — S. L.] This principle made it possible for the rabbis to legislate most widely, as long as they did not invade the realm of religious law.

[70] Regarding the expression טמא כבוס, see Pesiqta Rabbati XII, 58b, top, where כבוסים 'ז are discussed; cf., however, R. Elijah of Wilna, his commentary on Num. 19:4, according to which the meaning of this passage is that seven washings, כבוסים, are mentioned in Scripture with regard to the red heifer. That our text perhaps prescribes only washing but not bathing, thus paralleling Karaite practice, is highly unlikely in the light of 10,10 ff. Moreover, we would expect the phrase to be טמא רחיצה and not טמא כבוס, just as the Karaites use רחיצה in contrast to טבילה.

[71] Cf. Berakhoth 22b and the extensive discussion in Bloch, שערי תורת התקנות, I, 120–137.

[72] For the correct explanation of this passage cf. pp. 72 ff. This usage here certainly has nothing to do with the sounding of the trumpet at the beginning and the end of the Sabbath (cf. above, p. 108), for it is stated directly ולא ישביתו את העבודה. Moreover יתקדם can no more mean "the beginning" than יתאחר can mean "the end"

the name of מבקרי מומין.[73] These had the task to discover whether the animals were free of physical defects, while it was the duty of the מבקר of the sect to see to it that the members of the community were free of spiritual defects. Indeed several of the functions of the מבקר are nothing else than what are described in the rabbinic sources as the tasks of the scholar. At the direction of the מבקר the priest declares the leper to be clean or unclean (13,5), and similarly it is the scholar who, according to a statement of Hillel,[74] gives the priest instructions upon which the latter declares the leper to be clean or unclean as the case may be. As the leaders of the community are like those whom we meet elsewhere among the Jews, so too the division of the community into four classes, priests, Levites, Israelites and proselytes (14,5) contains nothing new, as was more fully shown in the notes on that place.

The results reached in these detailed studies of the relation of our document to the Halakah, can be briefly summarized as follows. In respect of the very numerous and important Sabbath regulations our sect is in full harmony with the Halakah and what is especially noteworthy in this connection is the fact that most of these regulations are of the kind that Halakic tradition regards as rabbinic. Whether

---

[73] Kethuvoth 106a; *Midrash Shir ha-Shirim* R. on 3:7; P.T. Sheqalim IV, 48a; Philo, *De Spec. Leg.* I. 166, ed. Mangey II, 238. Particularly instructive for the relation of the מבקר to these מ' מומים are the statements of Philo that an elite of the noblest and most respected priests held this office, according to which מבקר was probably a higher title and therefore used with special liking by our sect. With the Roman Censor the מבקר has a name in common only by chance; their offices are completely different; *cf.* also I Clement V, 41, probably based on Philo. The head of the community is also called משכיל, as has been shown in detail on 12,21, and though this first appears as a scholarly title among the Karaites, it is not to be overlooked that already the Talmud (Bava Bathra 8b) takes משכילים in Dan. 12:3 to mean just judges. In connection with the ברורים discussed on pp. 47, 118, we may also refer to I Chron. 9:22 and 16:41 where the word already occurs with the meaning used in our document.

[74] Or rather his teachers, *cf.* Tosefta, Negaim I, end and Yerushalmi Pesaḥim VI, 33a. The words ואם פתי in our document correspond to the שוטה in the rabbinic source, and we should accordingly translate, "even if the priest is a simpleton." It is also possible that פתי, like שוטה, is a "literal" translation of הדיוט, ἰδιώτης, which in Jewish Aramaic means "layman" in contrast to חכם. [Comp. also *MGWJ* CVII, 1913, p. 289. But it is obvious that the author quoted from memory. The text should read: "Who, according to Sifra (on Lev. XIII.2, ed. Weiss 60b) gives the priest instructions etc." This is clear from the note of the author who mentions "to the שוטה in the rabbinic source" which can mean only the above mentioned Sifra (it does not occur anywhere else). The statement of Hillel and the references to Tosefta Negaim and Yerushalmi Pesaḥim apply to the case where the priest made a mistake. — S. L.]

the distinction between biblical and rabbinic laws that is sharply drawn in the rabbinic sources was also recognized by our author may, of course, be doubted but still it may be pointed out that the reproach levelled at opponents in our document, namely that they "remove the landmarks that the ancients set up" (1,16), probably expresses nothing else than the charge that their opponents rejected "the tradition of the fathers," παράδοσις τῶν πατέρων, παράδοσις τῶν πρεσβυτέρων. Thus the biblical command against removing landmarks was applied to the disregard of ancient customs not only in Midrashic sources, as was mentioned earlier (p. 6); Philo also remarks, with reference to this biblical law: "But this law, it seems, is made not only for estates and the boundaries of the field but also for the observance of ancient customs. For customs are unwritten laws, ordinances of the men of antiquity, which . . . live in the souls of citizens, and children are also in duty bound to take possession of the legacy of their forefathers and not to despise the usages and customs of their fathers . . . and their traditions because they are unwritten."[75] To be sure, the Saddu-cees also had their traditions, for the Pentateuch could not have been used as a book of law without an authoritative interpretation. If however we do not wish, out of pure arbitrariness, to throw aside the unanimous tradition of rabbinic sources, Josephus and the New Testa-ment about the Sadducees, we must recognize that for the Sadducees *their* traditions were binding not as "teachings of the ancients" but as their own interpretations of the Mosaic law. Our document, how-ever, not only speaks of the "landmarks that the ancients set up and that one must not remove" but there is also very clear reflection in its legal portions, particularly in its Sabbath laws, of a conscious classi-fication of the laws as "biblical" and "rabbinic." Unless, of course, someone wants to argue that it is pure chance that in connection with the Sabbath laws our document merely says that such and such a kind of work is forbidden whereas in the Book of Jubilees and in the *Teezaza Sanbat*, the Falasha book of law that is dependent upon the Book of Jubilees, to almost every Sabbath regulation is added the remark, "whoever does this shall die the death." The simplest explana-

---

[75] *De Spec. Leg.* IV, 149; ed. Mangey II, 360–61. As so often in Philo, there is here a mixture of Jewish and Greek ideas. That the idea of the unwritten law was not taken wholly from Greek philosophy, as Hirzel asserts (*Abhandl. Sächs. Ges. d. Wiss.*, Phil-Hist. Series, vol. XX; 16 ff.), is shown by Philo's agreement with the Rabbis in the interpretation of the law in Deut. 19:14 concerning the binding force of the oral law. In Geonic literature also the "removing of landmarks" is equivalent to "changing customs"; *cf.* Ben Meir (ed. Bornstein, 47, 95) and the Responsum of R. Sherira in אשכול, ed. Auerbach, 54.

tion of the complete silence maintained by our document about the
punishment for the violation of the Sabbath laws is that such violation
is merely a "rabbinic" prohibition, and for that reason our document,
in agreement with the Halakah,[76] imposes no punishment for this.
Now even if we must grant that in respect of the Sabbath rest of slaves
and animals our document takes a more rigorous view than the Halakah, still this difference is of the kind that we often find among the
Tannaim themselves, and we may confidently state that *there is
nothing in the Sabbath laws of our document that could not have come
from the hand of a Pharisee.* Moreover, it has already been observed
that Philo agrees with our document in the rigorous view of the resting
of slaves (on the Sabbath), and we are here probably dealing with an
old Halakah that was modified later.

In the regulations about "uncleannesses" (12,15) our document is
in disagreement with the Talmudic Halakah, but as was shown above
ad loc., in full agreement with Targum Jonathan. Here again we are
dealing with a case in which our document has preserved an old
Halakah and not with an heretical teaching any more than with
heretical teaching in Targum Jonathan.

The view that fishes' blood is forbidden (12,13) is not, to be sure,
advanced anywhere in the rabbinic sources but still it is not impossible that this is the view of the Mishnah,[77] although the violation of
this prohibition is not punished (perhaps because it is only rabbinically
prohibited?). However that may be, the enjoyment of fishes' blood
is, as was remarked *ad loc.*, permitted by the Talmud only when it is
recognizable as such, and it would not be at all surprising if some
rigorous Pharisees forbade it altogether.

The sacrificial laws in our document reveal a decidedly dissenting
character, as was shown more fully above, and this is to be expected
of our sect. But they contain nothing anti-Pharisaic, even though the
offering of a Passover lamb on the Sabbath was forbidden according
to the view of our sect, as was shown to be probable, above, p. 69,
whereas according to rabbinic tradition Hillel proved from Scripture
that it was permitted or, more correctly, that it was commanded.

---

[76] Shabbath 3a, where the rule is that in reference to acts forbidden only rabbinically the Mishnah uses the expression פטור, "free from punishment."

[77] *Cf.* Kerithoth V, 1. As the Tosafoth have already observed, on דם דגים, the words
of the Mishnah show that fishes' blood is probably forbidden, and it is very doubtful whether the interpretation of Rav's view given by the Talmud, 21b, is the
correct one, since his words can most simply be explained in the following way:
the blood of fishes need not be drawn out (by using salt, etc.) but so soon as it is
no longer in the fish, it is forbidden.

Hillel's teaching met with opposition not only among the Sadducees[78] but also among the Pharisees.[79]

Like the religious regulations so also the ordinances on civil and criminal matters are in essential agreement with the views of the Pharisees. The constitution of the court, the norms for the qualifications of judges and witnesses, the doctrines of judicial oaths and many others in the field of procedural law bear the stamp of the Pharisaic Halakah so clearly that one might believe himself to have a Tannaitic book of law before him. The divergences from the official Halakah, on the other hand, are so unimportant, as was shown more fully above, that one must be astonished at the stability of the Halakah at so early a period.

We have seen further that even such regulations as do not belong to the field of law in the proper sense, such as those about the constitution of the community and relations with the gentile world, correspond to the norms of the Halakah, and one may well assert without fear of contradiction that the legal part of our document, which has been discussed up so far in this study, represents the standpoint of a correct albeit somewhat rigorous Pharisaism. And since we have now adduced the entire content of the legal part, with the exception of a single passage, in our study, we may state the *certain result of this to be that in our document we have a Pharisaic book of law*. We must, to be sure, add "with the exception of one passage," since the application of the rule of analogy, הקש, to forbidden degrees of relation is, according to everything that we know of the history of the Halakah, a decidedly heretical teaching, which was therefore espoused only by the Samaritans, Falashas, and Karaites.[80] The biblical laws about incestuous marriages, עריות, belong to the most essential components of the Torah, according to the Rabbis,[81] and we should probably assume that that so important a question as that of marriage with one's niece[82]

[78] At any rate this was stated by the Karaites; *cf.* below near the end of this section.

[79] *Cf.* p. 70. For some Pharisees, on the other hand, Hillel did not go far enough, since they also required the bringing of the festival offering חגיגה on the Sabbath; *cf.* Pesaḥim 70b and Horovitz, *Sifre Zuṭa*, p. 63, n. 4. [Leipzig, p. 257, n. 11.]

[80] *Cf.*, p. 23.

[81] Apart from the many haggadic passages referring to this subject (see, for example, my *Legends of the Jews* IV, 238), it should be noted that גלוי עריות is the only ceremonial law that one may not violate even to save a life, *cf.* p. 18.

[82] Since this marriage connection is forbidden on the basis of the argument from analogy, this sect may well have forbidden many other forms of marriage that were permissible from the Rabbis' point of view. The Karaites extend analogy *ad infinitum*.

was decided at a very early time. The divergence from such a decision, therefore, could have been regarded only as a heresy and not merely as something like an exaggerated rigorousness. When there was a question of family purity, the Rabbis knew no compromise: either a particular marriage connection is forbidden or it is not. In the latter case even the most decided rigorist dared not allow himself a divergent opinion, for otherwise the offspring of such a marriage would incur the stain of bastardy, ממזרות.[83] It is for this reason that in the entire Halakic literature, in spite of the many thousands of differences of opinion among the scholars, there is *not a single case* of incestuous marriage on which they are not unanimous, and we also understand the reason why the talmudic sources recommend marriage with a niece as a particularly pious deed.[84] Expressive of the stability of the law in respect of incestuous marriages is the fact that the difference of opinion between the Shammaites and the Hillelites about a special case of Levirate marriage, the so-called צרות, made a more lasting impression on later generations than all the many hundreds of other differences between these two schools put together.[85] Later[86] it could not be explained how the Halakic tradition could have been so vacillating on so vital a matter.

[83] *Cf.* Yevamoth 14b bot. הולד פגום; in this case, however, we are not dealing with real ממזרות that excludes one from "the congregation of God" (Deut. 23:3).

[84] *Cf.* pp. 23 ff. Concrete examples from the tannaitic period are the marriages of R. Eliezer ben Hyrcanus (*cf.* above on 5,7) and his brother-in-law Abba (*cf.* below) and his younger contemporary R. Jose of Galilee (Gen. Rabbah XVII, 3, p. 152, bottom) in the light of which the statement by Krauss in the Kohler *Festschrift* (*Studies of Jewish Literature*, p. 170) is to be corrected. The expression צרת הבת speaks clearly enough for the frequency of marriage with a niece (not only with one's sister's daughter, as Krauss states *loc. cit.*) since it is only on that account that this term for Levirate marriage in cases of blood relation was chosen. Büchler (*JQR* 1913, 439) has, strange to say, misunderstood this expression צרת הבת and believes that בת is everywhere to be taken literally.

[85] Mishnah Yevamoth I, 4: Tosefta I, 9–10; Bavli 14a–16a; Yerushalmi 1, 3a. On the basis of this Tosefta passage one would be inclined to assume that originally the Ḥaliṣah ceremony was performed in the case of a צרה (co-wife) in order to satisfy the differing views, for though it was superfluous according to the Hillelite view, it was not forbidden. It should here be noted at the same time that from this difference between the two schools Geiger's statement (קבוצת מאמרים, 88) that the Shammaites, as supposed representatives of the old Halakah, sought to restrict Levirate marriage is clearly without foundation, for it is precisely the scholars of this school who, in contrast to the Hillelites, included the צרות in Levirate marriage; *cf.* also below, note 89 on the Sadducees, who, as we show there, agree with the Pharisees in the use of the Levirate marriage and did not restrict this to ארוסה, as Geiger states.

[86] But relatively early, for as early as around 100 C. E. the attempt was made to decide this controversy definitely; *cf.* the sources cited in the preceding note.

The argument from analogy, however, had further consequences than the mere prohibition of marriage with one's niece, for the prohibition of polygamy (not of divorce!) is, as was shown on pp. 19–20, a direct result of the argument from analogy. How widespread polygamy was in the period with which we are concerned[87] can no longer be determined with certainty. Decidedly wrong, however, is Frankel's[88] statement that "in the period of the Second Temple the educated and learned class recognized only monogamy." The controversy of the schools, mentioned above, concerning the Levirate marriage of the צרות presupposes polygamy and we even have direct evidence that it was practiced both in high-priestly families[89] and among the descendants of Hillel,[90] and yet these families certainly belonged to the representatives of culture and learning! We first meet the attempt to restrict polygamy around 300 C. E., in the teaching of a Palestinian Amora[91] that a woman may insist upon a divorce if her husband wishes to marry a second wife. The absolute prohibition of polygamy, however, was, as is well known, first decreed by R. Gershom of Mainz, "the light of the Exile," around the middle of the 11th century. It is nevertheless interesting that, as in our document (5,2) so also in a later midrash, David is reproached, though mildly to be sure, for his having had many wives. It is said in Midrash Tehillim VII, 63: "God said to David, How canst thou compare thyself with

[87] The *Terminus a quo* for our document is the Maccabean revolt, the *Terminus ad quem* the destruction of the Temple; *cf.* further under Section VII.

[88] *Grundlinien des mosaisch-talmud. Eherechts*, p. 10.

[89] Tosefta Yevamoth I, 10 and the parallels in Bavli 15b and Yerushalmi I, 3a. These families are עלובאי and קיפאי = Caiaphas. This passage, moreover, shows the untenability of Geiger's assertion (קבוצת מאמרים, 83 ff.) that the Sadducees restricted Levirate marriage to ארוסות, for we know in fact that Caiaphas belonged to a Saducean family, and it would have been senseless for R. Joshua to refer to the practice of the Sadducees if they had not in the first place recognized Levirate marriage in the case of נשואות. As for the difficulty that the Talmud finds in the words of R. Joshua, who in answer to a question about the statute of the צרות gives an answer that applies to their descendants (instead of them), it should be noted that both the Tosefta and the Yerushalmi have בני צרות in the question, and thus the difficulty vanishes.

[90] Abba, a son of the Patriarch Rabban Simon ben Gamaliel I and a brother of the Patriarch R. Gamaliel II and probably a prominent member of the Synhedrion in Javneh, was married both to his niece, the daughter of R. Gamaliel (II), and to a second woman at the same time, and when he died childless, the question was raised whether R. Gamaliel might marry the "co-wife" of his daughter (Yevamoth 15a); *cf.* also my article "Abba" in the *Jewish Encyclopedia* I, 29.

[91] Yevamoth 65a. This view is disputed by the Babylonian Rava, whereas the Karaites (*cf.* above, p. 20) accepted this restriction of polygamy and even considered it to be biblical, something this Amora never even thought of.

Saul? Saul had only one concubine but thou hast taken many wives and many concubines."[92] Beside David, however, another prominent biblical personality was reproached for polygamy, namely Elkanah, whose prophetic office[93] was of no avail against the sharp censure of the Haggadah.[94] Even the appeal (4,21) of our document to Gen. 1:27 as proof of the Bible's prohibition of polygamy is found not only in the New Testament, as Schechter has already pointed out,[95] but also, in rather different form, in the Midrashic literature, where the immorality of polyandry is proved from this verse. "Joseph," it is said in Midrash Abkir,[96] "said to Potiphar's wife, 'When God created the world, he did not create two men and one wife but he created a male and a female.' " The statements referred to from the Midrashim do not, of course, provide any proof for the rejection of polygamy at a time that is separated from the time of origin of these writings by several centuries but what they do prove is that we may not look for any heretical tendency in the very mild rebuke of David found in our document.

Our inquiry has shown that the prohibition of marriage with one's niece and the closely related one of polygamy are to be regarded as heretical Halakoth, and thus it is very natural to consider our document as a Sadducean one. The only heretics[97] of antiquity of whom we know anything more than the name are none other than the Sadducees. In his very learned and penetrating introduction to our document Schechter attempts to justify the title of "Zadokite Work" that he has given it on the basis of positive evidence. He appeals in particular to the testimony of the Karaite Qirqisani, who lived in the tenth

---

[92] The copyists shrank from letting harsh words be used against David and therefore sought to emend the text of the Midrash; cf. the variants in Buber's edition.

[93] Seder Olam Rabba XX end; Sifre Deut. 342, p. 393 and Midrash Shem. VIII, 69. The tannaitic sources strangely escaped the notice of Buber in his notes to Midrash Shem., ad loc.

[94] Midrash Shem. I, 45 and Pesiqta Rabbati XLIII, 181b. The only excuse brought forward for Elkanah is the long childlessness of Hannah, which induced her husband to marry a second time; cf. Midrash Shem. and Pesiqta loc. cit., 181 a,b.

[95] Note 5 on Chap. VII, where Matt. 21:3 is a printer's error for Matt. 19:4 = Mark 10:6.

[96] Cf. Neubauer, REJ XIV, 110, who gives this quotation from the lost Midrash Abkir on the basis of a manuscript excerpt.

[97] The Essenes, who, moreover, were no heretics but hyper-Pharisees, certainly do not come into question, since our document not only permits marriage, as many among the Essenes also did, but contains absolutely nothing of an ascetic nature, whereas it is precisely that which is the fundamental trait of the Essenes.

century,[98] who in his *Book of Lights* speaks of Zadok and says of him that he fought against the Rabbanites in his writings; Zadok sought to refute them in only a single instance by using the mode of analogy, namely, in the matter of marriage with one's niece, whereas in other cases he gave his views without using any arguments in support of them. This description of the Zadokite book fits our document so well that Schechter has no hesitation to identify it with the Zadokite work used by Qirqisani. On closer examination, however, this identification is doubtful. In the first place it should be noted that it is not only for the prohibition of marriage with one's niece that a scriptural warrant is cited in our document but also for five other regulations (in 4,21; 9,9; 10,16; 11,18; 16,15), whereas in the Zadokite book mentioned by Qirqisani the first prohibition was the only one supported by proof from the Scripture. Schechter interprets the words of Qirqisani to mean that he mentioned only the passage about marriage with one's niece because here Zadok opposed the Rabbanites in a matter of law on which the Karaites also differed with them. But even if one were to agree with this interpretation, although in my opinion the plain meaning of Qirqisani's text speaks against it, the objection raised by us would still remain, since in 11,18 there is certainly opposition expressed, as was pointed out *ad loc.*, to the view of the Rabbanites, which was also disputed by the Karaites, that the Passover lamb must be offered on a Sabbath.

A further proof of the identity of our document with the Zadokite book of Qirqisani is found by Schechter (Introduction, p. 17) in the statement of this[99] Karaite that the Zadokites forbid divorce, and the same view is supposed to be taken in our document. But as was more fully explained in pp. 19–20 our sect forbids polygamy but not divorce, and if we do not wish to blame Qirqisani for misunderstanding his source, as we have no reason whatsoever to do, it follows that the Zadokite book in which divorce is forbidden cannot be identical with our document. Indeed we might go still further and say that not only is divorce not forbidden anywhere in our document but also that one might adduce indirect evidence that it actually permits divorce. Opponents are reproached (4,20) for living in an immoral way because they marry several wives in violation of the Scriptural prohibition (Lev. 18:18). If it had been the author's view that divorces are not

[98] The number 637 in Schechter, p. 18 is a printer's error for 937, the year in which Qirqisani wrote the work mentioned.

[99] As Schechter has already noted, the same statement is found in Hadassi, but since he knew Qirqisani's work, his words have no independent value.

permitted by the Law, and accordingly that one who marries a divorced woman commits adultery, he would have reproached his
opponents with adultery rather than polygamy, which is actually a
less serious sin than the former, if one accepts his interpretation of
Lev. 18:18. This indirect proof gains in force if one compares the words
of our document with similar statements in the Synoptic Gospels.[100]
The biblical verse "male and female created He them" is cited in our
document as well as in the Synoptic Gospels to prove that the marriage
laws of the Pharisees offend against the teaching of Scripture. The
Synoptics, however, add the very important clause, "He who divorces
his wife and marries another, commits adultery against her; and if a
woman is divorced and marries another, she commits adultery."[101]
If our author had taken the same disapproving attitude toward
divorce, it would be very strange if he did not mention the remarriage
of the divorced persons, and we may safely assume that our document
forbids only polygamy but not divorce, whereas the Zadokite book
probably forbade the latter but not the former (if one may so interpret
Qirqisani's silence on this point).

A third reason for assuming the identity of our document with the
Zadokite book is found by Schechter in the agreement between the
two writings in the matter of the calendar. It is true that our document
contains nothing calendrical but (Schechter argues) the Sadducees
according to Qirqisani have a solar year and twelve months of thirty
days each. Similarly in the Book of Jubilees, the authority of which
in calendar-reckoning is expressly recognized in our document (16,3),
the solar year is accepted in contrast to the lunar year of the Pharisees:
consequently Qirqisani took his statement from a complete version of
our document in which the calendar-system of the Book of Jubilees
was given in detail. The weakness of this argument, however, is obvious,
for the words of our document, "in the Book of Jubilees the calendar
is exactly expounded," ופרוש קציהם . . . הנה הוא מדוקדק על ספר מחלקת
העתים[102] ליובליהם . . . (16,3), make sense only if we assume that our
document never contained anything more about the calendar than
this passage, for which reason the author saw himself obliged to call
his readers' attention to the fact that this matter was carefully treated

---

[100] Matt. 19:3–10; Mark 10:2–12; Luke 16:18.

[101] Mark 10:11–12.

[102] Therefore this sentence is not to be translated, "the explanation of their
ends," which makes no sense at all. In rabbinic literature קצים is frequently used
to denote periods of the calendar; cf., for example, Shir ha-Shirim Rabba II, 8;
Pesiqta Rab. XV, 70b; Lev. Rabba XIX, 5, p. 431; Pirqe R. Eliezer VIII; Soferim
XIX; cf. also pp. 94–95.

in the Book of Jubilees and could be consulted by those interested. But that in any book a description of the calendar should first be given and then in a quite different part of the book a reference should be made to another source by which one can be oriented in this subject, I consider to be quite impossible. It is true that, as was noted on 16,3, this reference to the Book of Jubilees that is found in our document is highly suspicious on the basis of internal criticism; if we deleted this passage, there would be no ground left for assuming that our document agrees with Qirqisani's Sadducees in the matter of the calendar. But even if we should grant that in its original form our document contained the calendar-system of the Book of Jubilees, it would still have to be proved that the Zadokite calendar in Qirqisani is identical with that in the Book of Jubilees. The agreement between the two systems in respect of the thirty-day month proves nothing, since the thirty-day month is found in many calendar-systems, whereas the most characteristic feature of the time-reckoning of the Book of Jubilees, that is, the intercalation of four days every year, is not even mentioned by Qirqisani and therefore in all probability was not customary among the Zadokites.

The grounds for identifying the Zadokite book of Qirqisani with our documents have been shown to be untenable. We should, however, like to go still further and assert that even if these grounds were established beyond all doubt, they would be of absolutely no value for the evaluation of the document with which we are concerned. The Karaites at the end of the first Christian Millennium, even the "Father of Karaism" who flourished in the eighth century, certainly did not know any more about Jewish history (in most cases they knew less) than did their teachers, the Rabbanites. In other words their historical sources were the Bible and Talmud. Now the Samaritans and the Sadducees (the latter include the Boethusians) were the only schismatics who are mentioned by name in the Talmudic-Midrashic literature. What could be more natural than that the Karaites should ascribe to the Sadducees a document that was not recognized by the Rabbanites and contained elements that from the standpoint of Rabbanism were at once recognized as heretical? A medieval historian[103] would never have been capable of assuming a Samaritan origin for a document in which, to select only a few characteristic

---

[103] This remained for a "modern critic" to do, cf. "Dositheos, the Samaritan Heresiarch" in *Amer. Jour. of Theology*, 1912, pp. 404 ff. Only in a period that witnesses a dejudaized Judaism as well as a Christless Christianity could an exponent be found for the notion of a Samaritanism without Gerizim and all other specifically Samaritan elements.

traits of our document, the words of the Prophets are cited together with the Pentateuch as divine revelation, and in which the "Time of divine wrath" begins with the destruction of Jerusalem by Nebuchad-nezzar, and in which the worst reproach that is directed at opponents is that they do not strictly observe (that is, according to the sect's teachings) the laws of ritual cleanness in the Temple of Jerusalem. If, therefore, Qirqisani had really had our document before him, he could not have declared it to be anything but a Sadducean one,[104] and therefore the problem of its origin is not a step nearer solution.

*
*   *

The inquiry into the relation of our document to Sadduceeism must proceed from the reliable data in Josephus and the Tannaitic sources concerning this sect and not from the more than doubtful medieval authors. First we may regard it as certain that there is not to be found in our document *a single Halakah that we are justified in pronouncing Sadducean.* The attempt to discover in the condemnation of opponents (5,7) as זובה דם את הרואה עם שוכבים a Sadducean protest against Pharisaic Teaching in the matter of טהר דם was shown, in the note *ad loc.*, to be misguided even if one were to agree with Geiger's view about a difference between Sadducees and Pharisees concerning טהר דם, though I have shown elsewhere[105] that it is quite unwarranted; in fact, our document very probably polemizes against the more lenient view of the Sadducees.[106] More important than this negative consideration is the positive fact that the prohibition of polygamy

---

[104] Hadassi states, on the basis of data furnished by al-Qumisi that "the Sad-ducees believed that God had a corporeal form," *cf.* אשכול 41d. These צדוקים, however, are certainly not to be identified with the ancient Sadducees but with some sect or other of later anthropomorphists whom the Karaites identified with the Sadducees.

[105] *Cf.* my comment on Geiger, מאמרים קבוצת, p. 385.

[106] *Cf.* above, pp. 22–23. That the Sadducees took a more lenient stand than the Pharisees in *all* details connected with regulations about נדה is also clear from the statements of the Tannaim (Tosefta, Niddah V, 3 and parallels) that the wives of the Sadducees brought their questions about these regulations to the Pharisaic scholars for their decisions. Since we cannot assume that these women were doing this behind their husbands' backs and that the latter were not so indifferent to the observance of the law that they followed the decision of the Pharisees with an un-troubled conscience, even when their opponents permitted something that was forbidden according to their views, it follows that in *all* these cases the Pharisees held more rigorous views, which the Sadducees had to follow for the sake of living in peace, for their own wives sympathized with their opponents.

THE HALAKAH OF THE FRAGMENTS

and marriage with one's niece, the only heretical Halakoth in our document, are as anti-Sadducean as they are anti-Pharisaic. If furthermore we take into account the fact that the Pharisaic Halakah was not nearly as stable as the Sadducean, there is nothing to hinder us from assuming that in these matters our document represents an early Pharisaic point of view,[107] which was given up by the later Pharisees, whereas the stability of Sadducean Halakah[108] makes it highly improbable that it was the latter which changed. And that the later Sadducees did not reject polygamy is shown by the statement of R. Joshua, who as a Levite officiating in the Temple[109] was certainly familiar with the state of affairs in the high priestly families, that polygamy was common in the family of the Sadducean high priest Caiaphas.[110] Similarly it can be shown that marriage with one's niece was found among the Sadducees, as is known, for instance, from Josephus' account of such a marriage entered into by Joseph, the head of the Tobiad family. For no one will doubt that these aristrocrats, who were, moreover, closely related to the ruling family of high priests, belonged to the Sadducees.[111]

We can, however, go still further and assert that several Halakoth in our document are not only anti-Sadducean but also Pharisaic. Such a Halakah is the one mentioned in 11,8, according to which it is forbidden to "carry" anything from or, as the case may be, to the blind alley known as מבוי. This prohibition, already known to the schools of Shammai[112] and Hillel (Eruvin I.2), was not recognized by the Sadducees, according to the express statement of the Mishnah

---

[107] Cf. p. 24, where it was shown to be probable that in a very early period marriage with one's niece was considered forbidden by many Pharisees as well.

[108] Pharisaic Halakah was rather fluid in the Tannaitic period as the result of a liberal use of Midrash, while this quickening factor was almost wholly missing among the Sadducees.

[109] Sifre Num. 116, p. 132, and Arakin 11b.

[110] Tosefta Yevamoth I, 10 and parallels; cf. the detailed discussion above, pp. 129 ff.

[111] Cf. Josephus, Ant. XII, 4,6. The problem of the historical value of this narrative is irrelevant for our purposes. In any case Josephus saw nothing strange in the story of a prominent Sadducee marrying his niece, and that should satisfy us. It may be noted, incidentally, that Jewish legend (see my Legends of the Jews IV, 81) surrounds the birth of David with features similar to those of the birth of the Tobiad Hyrkanus in the account of Josephus.

[112] Cf. my note on Geiger, קבוצת מאמרים, p. 387, where I showed that both these schools had before them an ancient Halakah on the legal definition of the מבוי. The scribal form מובה in our document, 11,8, is to be explained from Ezek. 43:11. [The correct reading, however, is בסוכה; see Rabin. — H. L. G.]

in Eruvin VI.1.[113] Accordingly they rejected the Pharisaic institution
of עירוב because of their view that the מבוי was to be regarded as
רשות היחיד, private property, for which reason no special regulations
were necessary to make it possible to carry things into them (on the
Sabbath). Geiger, to be sure, in keeping with his theory[114] about the
"conservative Sadducees" and "progressive Pharisees," argues that
the formers' rejection of the עירוב is due to their not considering the
prohibition of "carrying" into the מבוי as annulled by the עירוב.[115] He
had the misfortune, however, of failing to read the cited Mishnah to
the end, for otherwise he would easily have been convinced of the
untenability of this position. It is there stated that Rabban Gamaliel[116]
had a Sadducean neighbor with whom he shared a מבוי, and *since*

---

[113] As R. Immanuel Ricchi already in his commentary הון עשיר, *ad loc.*, quite
correctly pointed out, there can be no doubt that the expression "Eruv-denier,"
מי שאינו מודה בעירוב, in the Mishnah includes the Sadducees, and if the Samaritans
are meant thereby (Eruvin 31b) this means only "Samaritans and other sectarians."
In Babylonia there were hardly any Sadducees but there were indeed Samaritans (*cf.*
Qiddushin 72a, Giṭṭin 45a: בי כותאי, a Samaritan settlement) so that for the Babylonian
R. Ḥisda, who, moreover, shows familiarity with Samaritan matters (Pesaḥim 51a,
Giṭṭin, *loc. cit.*, Sanhedrin 21b), it was natural to use the Samaritans as an example of
the heretics mentioned in the Mishnah. The question of the Talmud (Eruvin 68b)
צדוקי מאן דכר . . . only raises the difficulty that it is not clear from the first part of
the Mishnah that the Tannaim had divergent views about the status of the Sadducees in this matter, whereas in the second paragraph of the Mishnah this is
assumed as a matter of course. The difficulty found in this Talmudic passage by
Ricchi and, before him, by R. Yom Tob of Seville, *RYṬBA*, never really existed.

[114] *Urschrift*, pp. 147–148; *Nachgel. Schriften* III, 290; *Jüd. Zeitschrift* II, 24
and קבוצת מאמרים, p. 67. He reproaches the Amoraim for misunderstanding the
Mishnah because they did not realize that in it מי שאינו מודה בעירוב stands for the
Sadducees. In the light of the preceding note, the misunderstanding is one by
Geiger, not by the Amoraim. Moreover he has overlooked the above-mentioned
notes of Ricchi and *RYṬBA* explaining that צדוקי is included among the Eruv-
deniers. *Cf.* also Halevy, *Doroth Rishonim* Ic, 436.

[115] But Geiger does not tell us how such a rigorous observer of the Sabbath
can be named by the Mishnah in the same breath with the gentile. It should be
noted at this point that Geiger does not keep the different forms of the עירוב distinct, since his view about the strict Sabbath-rest of the Sadducees, who do not
permit any extention of Sabbath-limits (עירוב תחומין), by no means necessarily en-
tails the rejection of "the cleaning of the courtyards," of which our Mishnah speaks;
cf. also my note on Geiger, קבוצת מאמרים, p. 387.

[116] The readings vary (see *Var. Lect. ad loc.*) between R. Gamaliel and R. Simon
ben Gamaliel. If the latter reading is correct, we must assume that R. Simon ben
Gamaliel I is meant, not R. Simon ben Gamaliel II, since the incident occurred in
Jerusalem, where no Jews lived after the destruction of the Temple. R. N. Ch. Z.
Berlin in his work עצי אלמוגים, 191a, offers the ingenious suggestion that this Sadducean neighbor of R. Gamaliel was the Apostle Paul. It is not very probable,
however, that Paul maintained neighborly relations with his former teacher after
he became a Christian.

his neighbor used the מבוי *on the Sabbath without participating in the eruv*, it would have been almost impossible for R. Gamaliel to use the מבוי. It was therefore the Pharisees who forbade the carrying of something into a מבוי without an *eruv*, while the Sadducees permitted it, and it is with the former that our document agrees, at least in respect of the prohibition of carrying. Moreover it is highly probable that the Sadducees did not recognize the prohibition of carrying at all. At any rate such an assumption is favored by the plain language of the Mishnah, Horayoth I.3,[117] even though the Talmud (4a) considers it unthinkable that the Sadducees should not recognize the prohibition of carrying, which is mentioned in Jer. 17:21, and seeks to interpret the Mishnah in an extremely forced manner. Apart from its still being very doubtful whether the Sadducees recognized the authority of the Prophets[118] (the Church Fathers assert that they did not), there is so essential a difference between "carrying a burden," ואל תשאו משא, of which Jeremiah speaks, *loc cit.*, and the Halakah's view of what may not be carried on the Sabbath that one might very well recognize the authority of Jeremiah without having to agree with the Pharisees' view that one commits a capital offence by carrying "a seed."[119]

I also doubt that the "Sabbath-limit" of two thousand cubits laid down by the Halakah and our document was recognized by the Sadducees. Josephus, *Ant.* XII. 8, 4, and even writings which are extremely rigorous in the matter of Sabbath observance, like the Book of Jubilees (50,8) and *Teezaza Sanbat* (19b), know only of a prohibition of traveling on the Sabbath but no definite Sabbath limit, which is probably a specifically Pharisaic regulation. There is perhaps a recollection of this difference between the Sadducees and the Pharisees in the statement of the Yerushalmi, Eruvin III, 21b, that travelling (the minimum is twelve miles!) is biblically prohibited, and the Sabbath-limit of two miles is only rabbinic. The latter was observed only by the Pharisees, the former by all Jews.

---

[117] The Mishnah does not, it is true, expressly say that those who rejected this law were Sadducees, but in view of Sanhedrin XI, 3 it is not to be doubted that the Mishnah was thinking of the Sadducees, as indeed the Talmud correctly explains.

[118] See below, Section V, p. 161.

[119] *Cf.* below, p. 145, where the views on this passage in Jeremiah of the Karaites, who did not share the rigorous views of the Rabbanites in respect of carrying, are cited. Moreover it is well to be reminded that according to the view of the Talmud (Bava Qamma 2b) legal principles may not be derived from the Prophets, דברי תורה מדברי קבלה לא ילפינן, so that it would not be at all surprising if the Sadducees did not regard this prophetic passage as a binding norm; *cf.* also my *Geonica* I, 81 on the biblical authority for the prohibition of carrying, which caused the Amoraim many difficulties.

If the assertion of the identity of our book with the Zadokite book
mentioned by Qirqisani were true, we should have further proof for
our assumption that it is not of Sadducean origin. For Qirqisani states
that in his Zadokite source it was taught that the Sabbath falling
during the week of Tabernacles did not belong to this seven-day
festival. As against this, a Baraita states (Sukkah 43b; Tosefta III,3)
that the Boethusians, whom I would identify as none others than the
"scribes of the Sadducees,"[120] opposed the "willow procession"
(חבוט ערבה) performed by the Pharisees on the seventh day of the
Festival of Tabernacles if it fell on a Sabbath (שאין ביתוסים מודים שחבוט
ערבה דוחה שבת). This is pointless unless the Boethusians did regard
such a Sabbath as part of the festival of Tabernacles.[121] To say that
the Boethusians opposed the procession of the willows on the Sabbath
is the same as saying that they observed the other festival ceremonies
on this day. But, as has already been noted above, the supposed
identity of our document with the Zadokite book of Qirqisani has
not only not been proved but is also improbable, so that the character
of this Zadokite book cannot determine that of our document.

*

*   *

Schechter, who realized very clearly that, aside from other difficulties, our document takes too rigorous a stand in its legal portions
for a Sadducean author, attempts to characterize this Sadduceanism
as that of the Dositheans, whose heresy allegedly sprang from Sadduceeism.[122] He also finds in our document much that is cited by the
Church Fathers and Arabic authors as characteristic of the Dositheans.
We shall now examine more closely these points of contact between the
Dositheans and our document. The first concerns the calendar. These
heretics had a solar year, and so did the Zadokite book mentioned by
Qirqisani, which, according to Schechter, is identical with our document. After all that was said above about this identification and about
the calendar of the sect, a second discussion of this point is superfluous.
A further point of contact is found by Schechter between the prohibition of eating honey (12,12), for which the reason is supposed to be
that tiny parts of the bodies of the bees are found in the honey, and
the statement of Epiphanius that the Dositheans ate nothing that

[120] See my article "Boethusians" in the *Jewish Encyclopedia* III, 284.
[121] Anan, on the other hand, seems to have shared the Zadokite view, *cf.*, his
Book of Laws, p. 130.
[122] As Schechter has already correctly observed, the reports about this sect are
so contradictory and confused that hardly anything certain can be said about it.

came from a living animal, אבר מן החי. But, as was remarked *ad loc.*, the eating of honey is in no way forbidden in our document, and furthermore this Church Father says nothing at all about the Dositheans forbidding any אבר מן החי (which was regarded as forbidden by all Jewish sects and even by the primitive Christians[123]) but only that they ate nothing that came from animals. That our sectarians, however, were not vegetarians like the Pythagoreans, Therapeutes, and Ebionites[124] is quite clear from our document (12,11–15); so that if Epiphanius' statement is based on facts, we have direct proof that our document is not the work of a Dosithean. What Epiphanius means by saying Ἐμψύχων ἀπέχονται ἀλλὰ καί τινες αὐτῶν ἐγκρατεύονται ἀπὸ γάμων μετὰ τοῦ βιῶσαι ἀλλὸ δὲ καὶ παρθενεύουσεν is not quite clear, but even if we assume that he means that many among them (the Dositheans) do not marry again after the death of their wives, our document contains nothing that can be adduced as a parallel to this, since in 4,21 it is expressly made clear that after the death of a man's wife (or after a divorce[125]) he may marry another woman. Most probably Epiphanius means only that the Dositheans, following the ascetic teaching of the Essenes[126] (Josephus, *Bel. Jud.* II.13, 13) suspended conjugal relations with their wives during their pregnancy, since for them marriage was permitted only to insure the continuance of the human race. If anything at all can be considered with certainty a teaching of the Dositheans, it is the extremely strict observance of the

---

[123] *Cf.* Acts 15:20, 29; 21:25 and the detailed discussion thereof by Joel in the *Graetz-Jubelschrift*, pp. 172 ff.

[124] Perhaps also the Essenes; *cf.* Schürer, *Geschichte*, II, 664, the statement of Abul-Fatḥ, *Annal.*, ed. Vilmar, p. 82, that the Dositheans ate only eggs that were found in an animal slaughtered according to the law has nothing to do with vegetarianism. Indeed one would be justified in concluding from these words that the Dositheans were no vegetarians, since we can hardly assume that animals were slaughtered only for the sake of the eggs. This restriction on eating eggs is also found among the Karaites. *Cf.* also pp. 148–149.

[125] *Cf.* above, p. 20.

[126] Anan also, *Book of Laws*, p. 60, forbids marital relations with pregnant women. *Cf.* more fully on this Geiger, *Jüd. Zeitschrift* VII, 167 ff., who on the basis of this passage in Anan's *Book of Laws* claims that Karaism was dependent on Essenism, a view in which Harkavy follows him (without mentioning him!). However, it should be noted that such a prohibition is also considered in the Talmud (Yevamoth 12b; *cf.* also ספר חסידים, p. 282); and although it did not prevail, it is still much more probable that Anan took his doctrine from this talmudic passage than from Essenism. It is not without interest that the Kabalah partially adopted this Karaite teaching. It is also possible that the Karaites came to adopt this view only in consequence of their strict application of the principle of עובר לאו ירך אמו; R. Akiva Eger argues similarly against this principle in his Responsa, No. 172.

Sabbath rest, but in this they went much further not only than the Talmudic authorities but also than our sect. Thus Abul-Fath, *loc. cit.*, reports that they did not permit their cattle either to graze or to be watered[127] on the Sabbath but prepared fodder and water on Friday to which the animals could help themselves. Our document, on the contrary, expressly permits (11,5) animals to be pastured and, of course, to be watered, in agreement with the Halakah. Furthermore Origen reports[128] that the Dositheans rejected the Sabbath-limit, תחם, and spent the whole day in the place where they found themselves at the beginning of the Sabbath, whereas in our document the Sabbath-limit is mentioned in two places (10,21 and 11,6). Also the laws of ritual cleanness ascribed to the Dositheans are stricter than those in our document. The Dositheans, reports Abul-Fath, pronounce unclean a spring into which an unclean creature has fallen, whereas our document (10,13) expressly states that a cistern can become unclean. As was fully explained *ad loc.*, the purpose of this is to stress the Halakah, also found in the Mishnah, that a cistern can become unclean but not a spring. When, however, Schechter appeals to the passage 11,3 in our document to establish a point of contact between it and the Dositheans, of whom Epiphanius says that "they have no intercourse with those of a different belief, because they despise the whole human race," there are two things to be said in rebuttal. In the first place, according to our interpretation of the passage, it deals with something quite different from the impurity of pagans; but even if the interpretation given by us *ad loc.*, were not the correct one, it is impossible to suppose that Epiphanius described as a specific peculiarity of the Dositheans that which they had in common with all Jews, for, as has already been observed, the pagans were regarded as unclean by all Jews. If, therefore, Epiphanius reproaches the Dositheans for their strict exclusiveness and misanthropy, what is meant is not their relation to the gentile and Christian world (*Adversus omnes alios hostile odium* is regarded by Tacitus, *Hist.* V, 5 as a characteristic of all Jews) but their unfriendly attitude toward Jews and the Jewish sects. And that just the regulation in 11,14, about not spending the Sabbath in the neighborhood of gentiles should have been the occasion for the reproach of misanthropy is quite out of the question, for as has already been pointed out above on p. 68 and p. 114, Talmudic Judaism went even further than this in its effort to prevent Jews from living together with gentiles; so that if Epiphanius' statement had no other

---

[127] This probably means watering with running water; *cf.* pp. 61, 110.
[128] *Adv. Celsum* I, 57 *et al. Cf.* J. Montgomery, *The Samaritans*, p. 256, n. 3.

basis than the Sabbath regulation, he would be giving a common Jewish peculiarity[129] as a characteristic of the Dositheans.

As an assured result of our investigation we establish the following: *Nothing in our document (at least nothing in its legal portion) can be regarded as the specific teaching of the Dositheans. On the contrary it contains a number of legal regulations that are in outspoken contradiction of the religious praxis of the Dositheans.*

While our preceding investigation has furnished proofs that our document has no points of contact either with Sadduceeism or with the teachings of the Dositheans, Schechter[130] had made it extremely probable that the Book of Jubilees was used by it. It is therefore doubly interesting to note that, in spite of this relation between the two documents, their legal standpoints are essentially different. The sanctification of the Sabbath is indeed of quite paramount importance for both works, as is shown externally by the very fullness of detail with which they both treat Sabbath regulations, and yet the differences are quite important. The prohibition of transporting objects, הוצאה והכנסה, is prescribed in our document (11,7) in complete agreement with the Halakah. It forbids carrying anything from the street (including a blind-alley, מבוי[131]) into a house and carrying anything from a house into the street, whereas the Book of Jubilees[132] (II, 30) states, "And on this day they shall neither bring in nor bring out anything from house to house." In the view of our document (11,12) which agrees with the Halakah,[133] Sabbath rest extends to hired workers also. In the Book of Jubilees, however, only slaves are mentioned, in the words of Scripture, Exod. 20:10. Also the prohibition found in our document and in the Halakah against having work done by a gentile (on the Sabbath) is missing in the Book of Jubilees, and this can hardly be accidental. An essential difference exists between the two documents in respect of the limiting of movement on the Sabbath, which, as was more fully shown above, p. 137, is unknown to the Book of Jubilees. The latter knows only the prohibition of traveling (50,8, and 12), whereas our document has exactly the same limits as the Halakah. It was also shown on p. 61 that our document agrees with the Halakah

---

[129] Even the Karaites share this view, as was observed on p. 68.

[130] *Cf.* the parallels adduced by him in the Index, which, however, apart from the very questionable passage 16,3, make this assumption only probable but not certain.

[131] *Cf.* above, p. 112.

[132] I:8 is also to be interpreted on the basis of this passage; "to bring out of his house" is the same as "to bring out of his house into another's."

[133] *Cf.* above, p. 111.

against the Book of Jubilees in respect of "the drawing of water." Still more important than these details is the difference in respect of the punishment for the violation of Sabbath laws. In the Book of Jubilees the penalty of death is threatened for the violation of any of these laws, whereas no punishment is mentioned in our document. The explanation of this was given on p. 125: it is "rabbinic" Sabbath regulations that are given in both these works, and these do not entail punishment according to the Halakah,[134] with which our document agrees, whereas the Book of Jubilees does not share this view. In light of these many and essential differences with regard to the Sabbath laws, one may well claim that the prohibition of marital intercourse, for which the death penalty is fixed in the Book of Jubilees L,8, was not recognized by our sect; otherwise the silence of our document about this matter would be very strange. Yet it is just this prohibition which most sharply distinguishes the Book of Jubilees from Pharisaic Halakah in respect of the Sabbath rest.

There are other differences between the two documents in respect to the following laws. The biblical prohibition of consuming blood is extended to the blood of fish in our document (12,13–14), whereas in two passages of the Book of Jubilees (6:12 and 21:6)[135] it is expressly stated that "the blood of animals, cattle and birds" is forbidden, which certainly means that other blood, דם דגים ודם חגבים, is permitted.[136] In view of the close relation that exists between the Test. XII Patr. and the Book of Jubilees, it may be assumed that the oath-formula of oath by God employed in the former pseudepigraphon[137] is not regarded as forbidden in the latter either, and therefore we can establish another difference between the Book of Jubilees and our document. For in the latter (15,1) swearing by the name of God is strictly forbidden. If, however, in the Book of Jubilees all the Patriarchs from Mahallalel to Noah marry their cousins, it is not permissible to infer from this that marriage with one's niece was held to be forbidden. For since these Patriarchs were the first-born sons of their parents, one could not very well have their siblings marrying and procreating before them. The next legally permitted

---

[134] But that 12,3 does not declare *every* desecration of the Sabbath, even such as is forbidden in Scripture, to be not subject to punishment was shown *ad loc*.

[135] When, however, it is said in 21:18 (*cf.* also 6:10) "eat no blood," we must not see therein a reference to the prohibition of fish blood, since it is based on a literal quotation from Lev. 7:26.

[136] This agrees with the view of the Halakah; *cf.* above, pp. 80 and 116.

[137] *Cf.* above, p. 91.

marriage relation,[138] however, is that between cousins. Moreover it is to be remembered that among the Arabs[139] the first cousin has prior right to his female cousin, and the Book of Jubilees perhaps presupposes such a custom among the Jews. At any rate, it cannot be proved that the two documents agree about marriage with a niece.[140] Only on one point, in forbidding the offering of a paschal lamb on a Sabbath,[141] do they agree in opposition to the Halakah, which permits this. But as has already been pointed out,[142] this prohibition is not to be considered anti-Pharisaic, since the Pharisees disagreed among themselves about this, at least in early times.

And so we find in the matter of the relation of our document to the Book of Jubilees a confirmation of the very noteworthy fact that *the legal standpoint of our sect is the same as that of the standard Halakah in all those cases in which the heretics, Sadducees, and Dositheans differed from it.*

In view of the close relations between the teachings of the Falashas and those of the Book of Jubilees, what we found to be true of the relation of this pseudepigraphon to our document is also true of its relation to the Halakah of the Falashas,[143] so that we do not need to

---

[138] The special emphasis on the fact that all the Patriarchs married their cousins was certainly meant to underline the merit of such a marriage, which is also recommended in the Book of Tobith. With regard to the corresponding custom among the Arabs (*cf.* following note), the statement of Kohut in Geiger's *Jüdische Zeitschrift* X, 61–2, who attributes it to Persian influence, is to be rejected. Whether the rabbinic advocacy of marriage with nieces is connected therewith is doubtful; *cf.* above, p. 23.

[139] *Cf.* Burckhardt, *Bemerkungen über die Beduinen*, pp. 91 and 219, and Yahuda in the *Nöldeke Festschrift*, p. 414.

[140] It is difficult to answer the question why this marriage with cousins begins with Mahalalel and not earlier with Kenan, since the latter certainly had a cousin. That Seth and Enosh married sisters and not their cousins is correct from the standpoint of the Haggadah, which will not hear of any marriage relation between these pious men and the accursed posterity of Cain (*cf.* my *Legends of the Jews*, I, 152), but Kenan could have married a granddaughter of Seth. We may here refer to the curious misunderstanding of a critic who in the *Amer. Journal of Theology* 1911, 428, states that the Book of Jubilees prescribes marriage with a niece.

[141] *Cf.* above, p. 69. One should note that in the Book of Jubilees L, 11 the offering of the Sabbath sacrifices is justified on the ground that they are regarded as an "expiation" for Israel, which implies that "peace-offerings," שלמים, to which class the paschal lamb belongs, may *not* be offered on the Sabbath because they are in no sense expiatory offerings.

[142] *Cf.* above, p. 69–70.

[143] In reference to the uncleanness of gentiles according to the Falashas and our sect, see above, pp. 62–63 and 140.

go into the matter further. The prohibition of marriage with a niece among the Falashas,[144] if it is not to be ascribed to foreign influence (Christians, Muhammedans, and Samaritans similarly forbid it), is the only point in which our document agrees with a Falasha teaching, and surely that is not sufficient reason to assume an historical connection between our sect and these African Jews. Or else there would also have to be a relation between Philo and our sect, since an agreement can certainly be shown to exist between them in respect of an Halakah.[145]

The total result of our investigation of the character of the Halakah in our document can be summarized as follows. *The Halakah of the sect in all essential questions of law* (with the exception of polygamy and marriage with a niece) *represents the Pharisaic standpoint, and contains nothing that can be ascribed to Sadducean, Dosithean or any other heretical influence.*

*

*   *

The claim that the Karaite Qirqisani knew our document has been shown in the course of our investigation to be highly improbable if not quite erroneous. However, that is not to say that it remained quite unknown to the early Karaites. We know that heretical writings did circulate among them.[146] In fact the Rabbanites accused them of having forged these for purposes of propaganda,[147] which is perhaps a not altogether baseless accusation, but such remarks do provide indirect evidence for the actual existence of anti-Rabbanite writings of non-Karaite provenience. It might therefore be of some interest to examine the relation of Karaite Halakah to our document more

---

[144] *Cf.* above, p. 23.

[145] *Cf.* above, pp. 67 and 111.

[146] *Cf.* Poznanski, *REJ* XLV, 176 ff., where the literature on this point is collected.

[147] R. Moses Tachau in his work אוצר נחמד (כתב תמים, III, 62) refers to "information" received from his teachers," וכבר שמענו מרבותינו, to the effect that Anan and his colleagues were guilty of such forgeries. This accusation was not limited to mystical writings like שעור קומה and the like, mentioned shortly before, but was generally to the effect that the Karaites forged writings in order to give authority to their teachings. Forgeries of writings by the Karaites for the purpose of embarrassing the Rabbanites by the monstrous character of these works are also mentioned by Maimonides, נטעי נעמנים 17.

closely in order to determine whether the Karaites may not have taken some Halakoth from our document.

We begin with a comparison of the Karaite Sabbath laws with those of our document. The question of the correct interpretation of biblical ordinances concerning the Sabbath is one of the most important matters of dispute between Rabbanites and Karaites; this part of the law is treated in greatest detail in our document and it is therefore most characteristic of the standpoint of the sect.

The old Karaites interpret the law in Exod. 16:29 "one shall not leave his place," אל יצא איש ממקומו, almost literally, and permit people at the most to leave the house for the purpose of attending the synagogue or to perform some other pious deed.[148] Our document, on the other hand, agrees with the Rabbanites in this and permits free movement within the Sabbath limit (which the Karaites reject), even for the purpose of leading cattle to pasture (11,5). In agreement with the Rabbanites against the Karaites[149] is the prohibition in our document against "carrying," and it is extremely rigorous. On the other hand, the conception of מוכן[150] is such that the use of flowing water is permitted, whereas the Karaites forbid it. In reference to bathing also, our document shares the view of the Rabbanites in contrast to the Karaites, who forbid it even on festivals.[151] As can be seen from our discussion of 11,9, our document, in agreement with the Halakah, forbids only the opening of a "sealed" object, whereas the Karaites

---

[148] Cf. Anan's Book of Law 69, 128–29, 139, 157; Hadassi, Eshkol 54c; Nicomedia, Gan Eden, Shabbath XIII, and Bashyatzi, Adderet XIII. The two last-named teachers, as so often, approach the Rabbanites closely and even permit the Sabbath limit to prevail, whereas Hadassi, 134d, attacked the Rabbanites because of it.

[149] Cf. the citations from old Karaite writings in Bashyatzi XIV, to which we may now add Anan, op. cit., 69, according to whom it is forbidden only to carry a real burden. The extension of this prohibition to the מבוי in our document and among the Rabbanites is unknown to the Karaites. Cf. also in Pinsker, לקוטי קדמוניות, Add. 21, the polemical poem of Yephet ha-Levi, whose words about carrying a burden are almost the same as those ascribed to Levi ben Yephet by Bashyatzi.

[150] Cf. Hadassi 56a and 56b and my explanation of these passages above, pp. 59, 61, from which it appears that the Karaites are much stricter in their definition of מוכן. Only Nahawendi (cf. above, p. 59, Nicomedia XIX and Bashyatzi XII) represents a very lenient viewpoint in this matter and even permits fruit which dropped. That, however, in 10, 22, האובד does not mean נשר is apparent from the preceding words כי אם מן המוכן, according to which fruit which dropped are forbidden.

[151] Cf. the sources cited in the preceding notes; cf. further Ṣahl b. Mazliaḥ, לקוטי קדמוניות, Add. 30 top; Hadassi 135a; 56b; and Bashyatzi XI, 46b.

forbid the opening of even a closed vessel.[152] The unrestricted prohibition of fasting in our document (11,4) similarly agrees more closely with the view of the Rabbanites than with that of the Karaites, who permit "religious fasting."[153] In the Middle Ages this view of the Karaites seems to have found exponents among the Rabbanites too.[154]

The Karaite laws of ritual purity differ even more from those in our document. The rule,[155] found as early as Anan (*Book of Laws*, 48, 1; 49, 22), that only a drink prepared by human hands can become impure but not water, very clearly contradicts the statement in our document[156] that even cisterns used for purifications can become unclean. In reference to other things, that are neither food nor drink (אוכלין ומשקין), the Karaites maintain the same point of view as the Rabbanites,[157] who assumed that such substances cannot become unclean in their natural state, so that earth, stones, and the like cannot become unclean; even vessels, כלים, escape uncleanness when they are attached to the earth. Of the rigorous Halakah preserved in our document (12,15), whereby the uncleanness of a corpse is extended to wood, stone, and earth, no trace can be found in Karaite literature; such a belief is, however, found in Targum Jonathan, as was remarked above *ad loc.* Hadassi[158] is the only Karaite who (perhaps under the

---

[152] Bashyatzi, V, 41b, permits only locking and unlocking the doors of a house, but not of a vessel.

[153] *Cf.* the long discussion on this in Bashyatzi, Shabbath XI.

[154] *Cf.* the sources cited by Müller, הלכות פסוקות, 192, and my *Geonica* I, 96, n. 2; II, 261, No. 10.

[155] It is accepted by *all* Karaites; *cf.*, for example, Hadassi, 107d, who excepts Anan's words (a fact overlooked by Harkavy *ad loc.*); further, Nicomedia, Tumah XII, and Bashyatzi XIII, 126d. Harkavy's statement that Anan took this doctrine over from the Sadducees has been shown above, p. 54, to be based on a misunderstanding.

[156] *Cf.* more fully on this p. 53. Perhaps the statement of Abul-Fatḥ about a similar teaching of the Dositheans (*cf.* p. 140) is based on a confusion of the cistern נבא with the spring מעיין, in which case, however, these heretics would be in agreement not only with our document but also with the Halakah.

[157] *Cf.* on this pp. 81, 115–116. Only in reference to stone vessels did the Karaites differ from the Rabbanites, in that the latter made no distinction between stones and stone vessels, while the former (Nicomedia X; Bashyatzi IV and VI) regard such vessels as similar to earthen ones, כלי חרס. If the emendation וכלי for וכל proposed by me on p. 81 is correct, our document would agree with the Karaites on this point, but I no longer entertain any doubt that the second explanation given there is the correct one.

[158] *Eshkol* 109b ff.; *cf.* also 109d on the uncleanness of earth and stones on which a corpse is found. According to the Halakah a grave imparts uncleanness only while a corpse is in it; the removal of the corpse removes the cause of the uncleanness. since the grave itself is not unclean.

influence of the Targum?) states that the house in which a corpse is found becomes unclean and does not become clean again until a sprinkling of it, הזיה, takes place. All other Karaites,[159] however, reject this rigorous ruling and declare that the house, being something attached to the earth, imparts uncleanness only so long as a corpse is found in it, but does not itself become unclean. Some of them go even further and take the view that only a tent, אהל, because it is movable, can impart uncleanness, whereas a house never does so. When, therefore, in a letter ascribed to Maimonides,[160] the Jews of Berber lands are reproached on the ground that in spite of their reverence for the Talmud they are to be regarded as Karaites because of their heresies, and their custom of considering as unclean the ground trod by a נדה, which is at variance with the Halakah, is cited as an example, this does not mean that they followed the Karaites in this respect, since, as we have seen, there is no such Karaite doctrine. Rather, these "Rabbanite" Jews are accused of caring for the authority of the Talmud in practical life as little as do the Karaites; and as an example of their religious practice which is at variance with the Halakah, a custom taken over from gentiles[161] is cited.

There are also essential differences between the Karaites and our document on the subject of the purification, טהרה, of objects and persons that have become unclean.[162] According to the former, every ritual purification must also be a physical one, for which reason such purification varies, so far as objects are concerned, in accordance with their various natures. Linens, clothes and similar things get their ritual cleansing through water, because they actually are cleaned in this manner, so that the absorbed material that causes uncleanness is really removed, whereas metal vessels must be purged in fire,[163] because the uncleanness absorbed by them cannot be rinsed off with

---

[159] Aaron the Elder in מבחר on Num. 19:14; Nicomedia, Ṭumath hammeth III; and Bashyatzi, Ṭumah XX; all of these decisively reject Hadassi's view.

[160] Known under the name מהרמב'ם...מוסר נאה in אגרות הרמב'ם, ed., Leipzig, 38–40; on its spuriousness cf. my note in the Jewish Encyclopedia I, 408.

[161] The people from which they took this custom is described as בני מאום והם אומה מן האומות הדרים בארץ ישמעאל. This statement is probably not taken from the thin air; cf. Munk on Moreh III, 47. Of course מגוס "The Magi" must be read for מאום.

[162] Hadassi 107b; Bashyatzi, Ṭumah IV.

[163] Hadassi 90a; 107b; מבחר on Num. 19:15; and Bashyatzi, Ṭumah IV. The Karaites cite Num. 31:23 to prove that cleansing by fire is necessary. According to the view of the Halakah, however, even in the case mentioned in Scripture an immersion-bath was required after cleansing by fire; cf. Avodah Zarah 75b and Yerushalmi Avodah Zarah, end.

water. Unclean persons, especially the נדה, are not made clean by immersion in water but by having water poured over them, רחיצה, because in this way a higher degree of physical cleanness is attained.[164] Furthermore objects, like persons, can preserve their ritual purity only if the stains caused by the substance that imparts impurity — by blood, for example, — are removed, but not otherwise.[165] Our document, however, in agreement with the Halakah, recognizes only one method of purification, namely immersion (10,10–14), for both persons and objects.[166] Again the regulation about the degree of purity required for sojourning in the holy city (12,2) — unless one accepts the interpretation given by me, namely that only the Temple Mount is meant — contradicts not only the view of the Halakah but also that of the Karaites, who likewise permit a בעל קרי to enter the holy city.

In regard to dietary laws there is an agreement between the Karaites and our author. They forbid fishes' blood,[167] which is permitted by the Halakah, although, as was remarked on p. 116, it is not improbable that the older Halakah also took this more rigorous view. On the other hand our document knows nothing of a special kind of "ingathering," אסיפה, for fish, such as the Karaites insist on, and just as little does it know of any prohibition of locust's blood, דם חגבים, which is forbidden by the Karaites.[168] It is also noteworthy that there is nothing in it about eggs being prohibited, whereas the early

---

[164] Against this teaching of the Karaites the Rabbanites fought very vigorously so that it was customary for women entering marriage to swear not to follow this sinful practice of the Karaites; cf. Maimonides' interdict against this heresy in תשובות הרמב׳ם, No. 149 and the Arabic original in Friedländer, Monatsschrift LIII, 469 ff. The later Karaites (cf. Nicomedia, Ṭumah III, 110b, and Bashyatzi VIII, 128a) also insist upon the pouring of water, stating that for a נדה it is just as essential as immersion is for other forms of uncleanness. On Anan's position in this matter see above, p. 52.

[165] But according to the Halakah, this is not necessary.

[166] According to the explanation given above for 10,11 our document insists that ritual purification be a physical one at the same time, but this now seems to me very doubtful. מרעיל probably means "wholly covered up with water"; a similar view is also presented in Yoma 78a. The statement of Rogers in Journal of Theol. Studies 1912, pp. 437 ff. that immersion in baths of lustration is of recent origin is definitely wrong. What is meant by טמא כבוס in 11,22 is explained more fully above.

[167] Cf. p. 79.

[168] Cf. more fully on this, p. 80. About דם חגבים there is a difference of opinion among the Karaites themselves. Anan, Book of Laws, 67, forbids it although he admits that it is not real blood, and this seems also to be the view of Hadassi 89c, who in his formulation of the prohibition of actual blood mentions fish, to be sure,

Karaites declare[169] that the eggs of a living animal are to be regarded as אבר מן החי and are therefore forbidden.

In the criminal and civil law of the Karaites, both agreements with the teachings of our document and essential differences from it are to be found. The punishment of the false prophet whose sin is preaching defection from God is the same in our document as in the Halakah, namely stoning, whereas among the Karaites it is strangling.[170] On the other hand, the Karaite view resembles that of our document in that, like the latter (12,3), it knows of no death penalty for the false prophet who teaches the desecration of the Sabbath or any other violation of the Law, whereas the Halakah prescribes death for this case too. This resemblance seems to be merely external, to be sure, since, as was explained on p. 118, this leniency in our document is to be ascribed to a special consideration. In principle, it certainly agrees with the Halakah that a prophet who preaches any transgression of the Law commits a capital offense. The disqualification of witnesses under twenty years in criminal cases (10,1) is closely related, as was remarked on p. 46, to the view of Anan that adulthood begins with the age of twenty. One should not, however, overlook the fact that this view was completely ignored by the other Karaites, for whom the legally recognized period of maturity is the twelfth year.[171] The age-requirement for witnesses in our document reads (*loc. cit.*): "Who has not attained the age of passing among those who are matured," which one is probably justified in regarding as an indication that women cannot appear as witness. This indeed corresponds to the view of the

---

but not locusts; while Nicomedia, *Sheḥiṭah* XVIII, and Bashyatzi, XVII, compare it with the blood of mammals, in which they have probably been influenced by the view of the מבחר on Lev. 7:27. On the view of the Gaon Saadya respecting "the ingathering of locusts" (*cf.* p. 80), compare further the quotation from Jacob ben Reuben's ספר העושר in Pinsker's לקוטי קדמוניות, Add. 84, where it is explicitly stated that, according to Saadya, אסיפה . . . מצטרכים אינם הארבה.

[169] Hadassi 89a; similarly the Dositheans; *cf.* p. 139.

[170] Nicomedia, תורה כתר on Deut. 13:6. Among the Rabbanites this view was exposed by R. Simon, Sifre Deut. 86, p. 151 (*cf.* Targum Jonathan). When Aaron the Elder in מבחר on Deut. 18:20 makes the statement that the false prophet suffers only "divine punishment" he does not refer to a case in which such a person preaches defection from God; *cf.* pp. 74–75.

[171] Nicomedia, *Gan Eden*, Nedarim 172b, where the views of several teachers of the Law are cited according to whom there is no age-limit at all, and only the intellectual development of the individual is taken into account. *Cf.* also Hadassi 11d. We may here refer to Philo. *Allegories of the Law* I,4, who (probably following the Greek view) makes the twenty-first year the age of maturity.

Halakah (Bava Qamma I, 3; Shevuoth V, 1), but not to that of the Karaites,[172] who permit women to be witnesses. The emphatic stressing of the point that a single witness may not testify (9,22) under any circumstances is also contrary to the view of the Karaites, who, in contrast to the Halakah, declare in many cases a single witness to suffice.[173] As our document agrees with the Halakah against the Karaites in respect of the number of witnesses, it also agrees in respect of the number of judges. Theoretically,[174] to be sure, the Halakah rule states that one judge suffices in civil cases but, as shown above, p. 85, a panel of ten judges, such as our document positively required (13,1) was normal for the Rabbanites. The Karaites, however, merely insist that the verdict must be pronounced publicly, for which reason they require the presence of at least ten persons, but not of more than one judge. Nahawendi therefore remarks, in connection with Ruth 4:2, that the ten men before whom Boaz and the unnamed man brought their litigation comprised the judges and the witnesses.[175] Similarly Anan (*Book of Laws*, 112) find in this biblical verse an indication that at least ten men must be present at the performing of the ceremony of *Ḥaliẓah*.[176] When, therefore, this Karaite in another passage[177] says,

---

[172] Hadassi, 133a, inveighs in his accustomed fashion against this disqualification of women by the Rabbanites and at the same time passes over in silence the inconvenient fact that Nahawendi (משאת בנימין) agrees with the Rabbanites. The later Karaites also approach the Rabbanite view; *cf*. Nicomedia, *Edim* 194a and Bashyatzi, *Qiddush ha-ḥodesh* XII.

[173] Great diversity of opinion, to be sure, exists among the Karaite scholars about this matter; *cf*. Hadassi 149b; מבחר and כתר תורה on Lev. 5:1; Nicomedia, *Edim* 194c; and Bashyatzi, *loc. cit.*, XII. The commentator on מבחר has misunderstood its language. It does not dispute the validity of the rule of the Halakah, עד אחד נאמן באסורין, but the teaching of the ancient Karaites that one witness suffices to convict a person of transgressing a religious commandment.

[174] *Cf*. Sanhedrin 3a, but *cf*. Avoth IV, 8, "do not judge alone, for only one (i. e. God) judges alone."

[175] משאת בנימין 1b, according to which the sentence והסר מעשרה לא ישפוט כן הוא אומר cannot mean (so Poznanski, *REJ* XLV, 69) that a court must consist of ten members but that a public of at least ten men must be present during the court's proceedings, for which reason also the singular ישפוט and not ישפטו is used, which alone would be correct if the number of judges were in question. The saying cited from the Mishnah in the preceding footnote is also found in Nahawendi in the form כי שופט יחיד שדי, but in saying this he probably requires only the presence of a public; otherwise it would be strange not to have anything said about the required number of judges.

[176] Like the Karaites the Talmud, Kethuvoth 7b, also cites this verse to prove that the blessing over a bridal couple, ברכת חתנים, can be pronounced only in the presence of ten persons. Anan requires this number to be present for *Ḥaliẓah* as for

in reference to *Ḥaliẓah*: וי' זקנים מותבינן בבית דינא דכת' גבי בעז ויקח עשרה אנשים מזקני העיר ובעז בבית דינא היא דסדר מילתיה, "and ten elders made up the court (for performing a *Ḥaliẓah*), for it is said of Boaz, 'and he took ten men of the elders of the city,' and it was to a court of law that Boaz submitted his case,"[178] we have here only a rather inexact wording. What he means is that ten men must be present at a ceremony of *Ḥaliẓah* conducted by a court,[179] but not that these ten men are members of the court. At any rate, not a single passage in Karaite literature is known to me in which a court of ten members is required.[180] An important difference between the Karaites and our document in matters of law is also found in the fact that the latter (9,1) forbids Jews to make use of a "gentile authority" in order to deliver a Jewish lawbreaker to appropriate punishment, whereas the former permit this in a case where a Jewish court has no power to enforce its decisions.[181] On the other hand, the Karaite view approaches that of our document (9,17) when it imposes upon the witness to a crime the duty of giving information about it even if since the conviction of an accused person is possible only with two witnesses,[182] his testimony is not

the marriage ceremony (112–113), while the later Karaites decide, as do the Rabbanites, that two witnesses are sufficient for a marriage-ceremony (Nicomedia, *Nashim* VI), without, however, troubling to refute Anan's view. Perhaps he considers the presence of ten persons to be not required, מעכב, but merely desirable. *Cf.* also Maimonides, *Moreh* III, 49.

[177] This is very strangely missing in the *Book of Laws* although the part treating of חליצה is extant, but was known to an anonymous Karaite writer; *cf.* Poznanski, *op. cit.* 67, and Harkavy, *Book of Laws*, 172.

[178] For דפרישין Harkavy reads, correctly, דפרשינן and adduces *Books of Laws* 111, where שער was interpreted to show that Boaz came before a court; *cf.* also Hadassi 64, bottom, which citation escaped Harkavy's attention in his comment on this passage.

[179] *Cf.* also Pirqe R. Eliezer XIX, where it is similarly taught that *Ḥaliẓah* must be performed in the presence of ten men (not necessarily judges; *cf.* R. D. Luria *ad loc.*); in the parallel, Midrash Tehillim XCII, 407, ed. Buber, Ruth 4:2 is referred to as proof, as is done by Anan. That this is not a scribal error as Luria and, following him, Buber think is shown by Anan's statement.

[180] *Cf.* Hadassi 146d, l. 22, whose wording certainly presupposes a single judge.

[181] Nahawendi, משאת בנימין 1b, where אין must be deleted; *cf.* also Anan, *Book of Laws* 116, who, however, probably speaks of a case in which Jews go to gentile courts with their litigation when there is no necessity for it; *cf.* also שערי צדק 84b.

[182] Hadassi, 104c, remarks that the truth is also served by the testimony of a single witness, and justifies this view in 131c by saying that it can lead to a confession by the accused, in which case justice takes its course. Nahawendi, 1b–1c, teaches that a single witness may not testify (similarly the Halakah); but that if he is required by the court to do so, he must do it; probably in his case too the reason

directly useful. According to the Halakah,[183] the single witness is not obliged to do so, but various reasons that are given for this duty by the Karaites, make it reasonably certain that they did not make any use of our document in this case.[184] But again, the view of the Halakah approaches that of our document (15,1) in the matter of the objectionableness of an oath by the name of God,[185] as against the Karaites, who even introduced this form of oath in cases where the Rabbanites held any form of oath at all to be superfluous and therefore objectionable, as, for example, in the marriage ceremony.[186] On the other hand, the Karaites rule that perjury is to be punished with death,[187] which is perhaps also the view of our document.[188]

If the statement made by us on p. 43 is correct, our document would agree with the Halakah against the Karaites[189] in reference to גזל הגר, while, on the other hand, the closely related regulation concerning lost property the ownership of which cannot be determined (9,15), is found only among the Karaites.[190]

Among the instances of agreement between our document and the Karaites the following are especially to be noted. The paschal lamb must not be offered on the Sabbath,[191] and the Karaites appeal to "the older generations of Tannaim," חכמי המשנה הראשונים, who, in contrast

---

is to be sought in the possibility of a confession. According to the Halakah, however, such a confession would have no value, since the rule is that "no one can be made a sinner by his own confession"; *cf.* Kethuvoth 18b. [This law is already prevalent in Tannaitic times, see Tosefta Shevuoth V, 4, and Sifre II, 188, p. 228. — S. L.]

[183] *Cf.* above, pp. 119–120; *cf.*, however, Shevuoth 32a, for the view of R. Eliezer ben Simon, who partly agrees with our document.

[184] Hadassi *loc. cit.*; *Mivḥar* and *Keter Torah* on Lev. 5:1; Nicomedia, *Edim* 194a, and Bashyatzi, *Shevuah* XII, 219.

[185] *Cf.* above, pp. 91 ff. and p. 121.

[186] Hadassi, 11c, 115c and 128c. In the last passage it is expressly stated that the marriage vow is to be in the name of God whereas in Nicomedia (who, moreover, gives numerous citations about this subject from the old Karaite writings), *Nashim* VI, the oath is *not* in the name of God. The Karaites, of course, know the difference between an oath and a curse, אלה (Nahawendi 2b, 2d, 3a; Hadassi 128c) but the latter is also by the name of God, *cf.* Nicomedia, *Shevuah*, and Bashyatzi, *Shevuah* IV.

[187] Hadassi 128c, מבחר on Exod. 20:7, and Bashyatzi, *loc. cit.*

[188] *Cf.* above, p. 96, where it was shown that this view also has its proponents among the Rabbis.

[189] As so often happens, however, there is great diversity of opinion among them on this subject; *cf.* מבחר and כתר תורה on Num. 2:8.

[190] Nicomedia, עבודה 185b; Nahawendi 2d, in connection with גזל הגר, has the addition that it goes to the high priest, but נדול after כהן is probably a scribal error.

[191] *Cf.* more fully on this above, pp. 69, 117.

to the latter Tannaim,[192] also forbid it. The rabbinic sources knew only of the Bene Batira, who lived in the time of Hillel, as exponents of this view, and it is probably they who are described by the Karaites as חכמי המשנה הראשונים.[193] It is further very probable that the reason for the prohibition (11,7) against letting any ill tempered animal run about freely on the Sabbath is to be found in the doctrine of the Karaites that it is an owner's duty to see to it that the animals belonging to him do not do any harm on the Sabbath, and "if they are vicious, they must be tied with ropes, in order that they may not desecrate the Sabbath." שור נגח ובהמה וחיה רעה יקשרום בחבלים וישמרום ולא יחללו ימות קדשך.[194] However, the interpretation of 11,6–7 is not quite certain, since the clause אם סוררת היא may just as well belong to the preceding sentence אל ירם ידו ...; in which case only restraining a refractory animal with blows would be forbidden, and the purpose of confining such an animal on the Sabbath would be to avoid the temptation to strike it.

Instructive for the relation of Karaite doctrine to that of our sect is their agreement in the matter forbidding marriage with a niece, which appears very clearly in our document as a Halakah which is quite peculiar to it, and which we also found to be the only "heresy" among its many laws.[195] In the Karaite literature[196] also there is hardly any legal distinction that is so frequently and so exhaustively treated as that of the prohibition of marriage with a niece, or more exactly, the use of analogy in cases of marriage with relatives, on the basis of

---

[192] Hadassi, 80a, to which the statements in Nicomedia, Pesaḥ VI, and Bashyatzi VIII go back. As is clear from these passages and also from Anan's *Book of Laws*, 72, 132, there was agreement among the ancient Karaites on this Halakah. The view of Alqumsi and Abu Ali that on the Sabbath a single paschal lamb was to be offered for all Israel is probably connected with the similar view of the Tannaim, Mekilta, פסחא V, p. 17.

[193] Since the Bene Batira performed a teaching function similar to Hillel's, this description is not at all unsuitable. On the other hand I consider it quite out of the question that the Karaites had at their disposal pre-Mishnaic works of Halakah that were unknown to the Rabbanites (so Chwolson, *Passahmahl*, p. 1, n. 2); this would be difficult to believe even if the Karaites had expressly asserted it, which, however, is not the case. Hadassi, 41d, states, moreover, that the Sadducees also shared the view of the Karaites.

[194] Hadassi, 56d, goes even further and states that it is forbidden to leave a well uncovered since someone may fall into it, and desecration of the Sabbath by causing an accident would be the guilt of the owner.

[195] *Cf.* pp. 127 ff.

[196] From Anan's *Book of Laws* to Bashyatzi's אדרת almost every Halakic work that appeared among the Karaites dealt exhaustively with this point of law.

which the Karaites, like our document, forbid this kind of marriage. But it would be quite unjustified to conclude from this agreement that the Karaites made use of our document. The use of הקש belongs to the oldest parts of rabbinic hermeneutics,[197] and the Karaites, like our document, did no more than consistently carry through a hermeneutic rule that was also used by their opponents.[198] The prohibition of polygamy was shown above to be a direct consequence of this doctrine of analogy, whereas the Karaites do not know of this prohibition.[199]

Our inquiry into the relation between Karaite Halakah and that of our document resulted in the discovery of a number of agreements between the two but still more differences, so that the problem whether the ancient Karaites were acquainted with this sectarian document must remain an open one.

[197] Rabbinic tradition attributes this to Hillel (Yerushalmi Pesaḥim VI, 33a, Bavli 66a; Tosefta IV, 1). In the two last-mentioned parallels the term הקש is not used but this mode of deduction itself does appear.

[198] A reproach frequently made by Karaite scholars to their opponents is that through the restriction of הקש — בעריות אין מקישין — they incur the fault of gross inconsistency.

[199] The Rabbanite R. Tobiah b. Eliezer in his Bible commentary לקח טוב, on Lev. 18:18 and Deut. 21:15, is mistaken when he states that the Karaites forbid polygamy, since even the most rigorous among them (with perhaps a single exception) only limit polygamy but do not forbid it, as was more fully shown on p. 19. Hadassi, 119d, 135b and 140d, appeals, exactly as R. Tobiah does, to the example of Elkanah to prove the admissibility of polygamy. Moreover, it should be noted here that this Karaite teacher contradicts himself in respect of the interpretation of Lev. 18:18; *cf.* his words on pp. 118c, 119d and 135b with those on p. 140d.

V

The Theology of the Fragments

It surely requires no exceptional powers of perception to see that the major interest of our document is the Law, or more accurately, the correct interpretation thereof. The sect attributed its origin to "the interpreter of the Torah," דורש התורה[1] (7,18), and the highest title of honor that it knows for its leader is מורה צדק,[2] "he who makes legal decisions in accordance with the truth." The first program[3] of the sect (6,11 ff.) obligates its members "not to enter the Temple so long as its service is not performed in accordance with the instructions of the Torah; to renounce sinful possessions, be they goods that have been set aside by a vow, or proscribed, or goods belonging to the Temple, or be they the proceeds of the despoiling of the poor, of widows, and of orphans; to distinguish between clean and unclean, as also between holy and profane; to observe the Sabbath properly, and to keep the festivals and the fast-day (the Day of Atonement) as has been commanded," לבלתי בוא אל המקדש . . . אם לא ישמרו[4] לעשות כפרוש התורה . . . ולהנזר מהון הרשעה[5] הטמא בנדר ובחרם ובהון המקדש ולגזול[6] את עניי עמו . . . ולהבדיל בין הטמא לטהור ולהודיע בין הקודש לחול ולשמור את יום השבת כפרושה ואת המועדות ואת יום התענית כמצוה[7]. The same keen interest

[1] As is clear from a comparison of 7,15 with 7,18, תורה in our document means the Pentateuch.

[2] *Cf.* below, Section VI, on the use made of מורה in our document. Here it will only be noted that the expression מ׳צ is synonymous with the rabbinic מורה הלכה, in which מורה similarly denotes the person who decides what religious praxis is, in contrast to רבי, "The Teacher."

[3] *Cf.* below, Section VII, on these two programs.

[4] The subject of ישמרו is not the members of the covenant but their opponents, who are described as בני השחת, *cf.* also above *ad loc.* [and below, p. 261, n. 11].

[5] This phrase probably was used in the Hebrew original of the Testaments of the XII Patriarchs, Gad VII, where the Greek (—A!) has πλοῦτον ἐν κακοῖς; *cf.* also the Book of Enoch 103:5.

[6] More accurately it ought to be ובגזול, since it qualifies טמא (*cf. ad loc.*), but בגזול got corrupted to וגזל under the influence of the following phrase beginning with ל.

[7] The MS. has במצא, which I emend, in accordance with 7,2 to כְּמִצְוָה. This expression is especially frequent in the liturgy. Charles' מוֹצָאֵי is not Hebrew.

155

in the Law is shown in the second program, which the sect drew up upon settling in Damascus after its migration from Palestine. It obligates the members to set aside the sacred dues as agreed upon; to love their fellows as themselves; to assist the poor, the needy, and the proselytes; to seek peace; to avoid incest, to shun harlots in accordance with the Law; to admonish one's fellows, as has been commanded, but not to prolong enmity from one day to another; and to keep far from all uncleanness in accordance with their regulations, so that no one will defile his holy spirit, . . . להרים את הקדשים ולא ימעל איש בשאר בשרו⁸ להזיר מן הזונות⁹ . . . . ולהבדל מכל הטמאות כמשפטם. For the "members of the covenant" in Damascus too, as we see, the strict observance of the ceremonial laws is the important matter and if along with this they are admonished to love their neighbors and take care of their poor, it is not the ethical content of these regulations that is considered but their practical value. It was only through the close and inward association of members with one another that they could hope to realize their ideal of the strict observance of the Law, wherefore love and concord were very specially commended. The paraphrasing of the biblical command to love one's neighbor[10] by לאהוב איש את אחיהו is very characteristic; the biblical "neighbor" is replaced by אח "brother"; it is not love of one's fellow-national countryman[11] that is commanded but of one's fellow-covenanter. Whereas the Halakah[12] would have this commandment to love one's neighbor apply even to the worst criminal, for our sect Jewishness begins only with one's covenant-brother. Characteristic for the standpoint of the sect is the description of "sinful possessions" or something the use of which is forbidden not by morality but by ritual law,[13] ההון הרשעה הטמא בנדר ובחרם. Most probably, too, the further description of "sinful possessions" as robbery of the poor and of widows and

---

[8] The combination of בשאר . . . ימעל — להזיר מן הזונות supports the interpretation given ad loc., p. 32; according to which marriage with a niece and similar unions are forbidden.

[9] The reading זונות is indirectly confirmed by Psalms of Solomon II, 11, ἀντὶ πορνῶν.

[10] Much more universal is the wording of this commandment in the Pseudepigrapha; Test. XII Patriarchs, Issachar V, VII; Dan V; Slavic Enoch LXVI, and Didache I,1; cf. below.

[11] At any rate this was the original meaning of the word רע, even though the idea of love of one's fellow was later understood in a much more universal sense.

[12] Cf. below.

[13] Probably there is in this some opposition to the dissolution of vows, התרת נדרים, whether our sect rejected it outright or had divergent Halakoth in particular instances; cf. Nedarim 28a and Nazir V,1, where the Shammaites and Hillelites still have differences of opinion about important questions in this rabbinic institution.

orphans contains an allusion to juridical differences between the sect and its opponents. The "covenant-brothers" bound themselves to give judgment in accordance with the teachings of the sect and through their (from their point of view) legally proper decisions to help the poor and widows and orphans obtain their rights.

The laws of inheritance, as is well known,[14] were an important element in the differences between the Sadducees and Pharisees. To the latter, the equality of rights of daughters with sons was nothing else than "the robbing of orphans," whereas the former were no less justified, from their point of view, in describing the disinheritance of daughters in the same language. In the case of "the robbing of widows" we probably also have to suppose that a juridical difference is involved; to Simeon ben Shatah, the earliest Pharisaic personality to emerge a little more concretely from the obscurity of tradition, rabbinic tradition[15] ascribes far reaching changes in the כתובה, and this new Pharisaic legislation could have been described by their opponents as a robbing of widows, while the Pharisees would have reproved the rejection of this legislation in the very same words. In view of the many[16] legal differences between the Sadducees and Pharisees, the complaint about robbing the poor should not appear particularly strange. A judicial decision against the Halakah of any party was considered by its adherents to be plain robbing of the poor.

Very characteristic of the legal coloring that our document gives to various moral teachings is the elaboration on the apocryphal vision of Levi (4,15 ff.) of the three snares of Belial. The text used speaks quite clearly of the three cardinal sins: sexual immorality,[17] dishonest acquisition of property, and defiling of the Temple, הראשונה היא הזנות השנית ההון[18] הש' טמא[19] המקדש; of these only the last is a ritual transgression, and then only in a limited sense, since sinners are not reproached for transgressing a particular law of cleanness or the like but for their

---

[14] Cf. Tosefta, Yadaim end.

[15] Cf. Shabbath 14b; Kethuvoth 82b; Tosefta Kethuvoth XII, 1; Yerushalmi Kethuvoth VIII, 32c. Tradition is unanimous in stating that this leader of the Pharisees substantially modified the rights of women, even though the sources mentioned above give different accounts of the details of these rights which can be harmonized only in a very forced manner. Cf. Fischer, Die Urkunden im Talmud, I, 77.

[16] Consider, for example, the Sadducee principle that the owner of slaves is responsible for damage done by them; cf. Yadayim IV, 7.

[17] Cf. Test. Reuben IV, 11: "For if fornication does not enthrall your mind, then will Belial also not enthrall you."

[18] Supply: הרשעה, cf. above ad loc.

[19] Since we have וְטִמְּאוּ אֶת המקדש, above in 20,23 טִמֵּא המקדש is probably to be retained and not to be emended to טִמְאַת המקדש.

contemptuous attitude toward the Temple, from which they withhold the reverence that is its due.[20]

In our document, however, we read that "the builders of the wall" will be caught in two snares[21] of Belial: They live in polygamy, which is forbidden by the precepts of the Torah (according to the interpretation of our sect, naturally), and they defile the Temple in that they permit intercourse with a זבה, and so they enter the Sanctuary in a state of uncleanness. The ethical-religious exhortation of the Testament of Levi is used in our document to justify the legal viewpoint of the sect! By "the snare of immorality," we are taught in our document, Levi meant "polygamy and marriage with one's niece,"[22] which the

---

[20] When in Ezek. (5:11; 23:38–39), the defilement of the Temple is made the reason for the divine judgement upon Israel, that is to be understood not as cultic but, as is particularly clear from 36:17 ff., moral impurity. There is also frequent reference in the Apocryphal literature to the defilement of the Temple by sinners, which primarily means the moral corruption of the priests. Thus it is said in Test. Levi IX (cf. especially the Aramaic and Greek fragments in Charles), where sexual immorality is warned against, "Beware of the spirit of fornication; for it is this that . . . will pollute the Sanctuary," and XVI, 1 is also to be understood in this sense. This idea of the defilement of the Temple through sinning appears quite clearly in the Assumption of Moses V, 3: "They will desecrate the house of their service through pollutions, for they will go awhoring after strange gods." It then, to be sure, goes on to say, "Some will defile the altar with unclean offerings," which means that the desecrating of the Temple will be a twofold one. Cf. also Psalms of Solomon, I, 8; II, 3, where it is said of the Sadducees that they desecrate the Sanctuary through their moral sins and godlessness, while in VIII, 2, as in our document, the reproach is made against them that they desecrate the sacrifices through cultic uncleanness. Cf. Schechter, Aspects, p. 205.

[21] Charles deletes בשתים without noticing that it is absolutely necessary; in Test. Levi three snares of Belial are mentioned, and our document stresses the fact that the opponents of the sect will be caught in two of these, in sexual immorality and defilement of the Temple, and then proceeds to describe these two snares more fully as polygamy and disregard of the law about זבה, while the third snare, הון הרשעה, remains unmentioned because in this respect there were no legal differences between the sect and its opponents. Cf. also below, Section VIII.

[22] Marriage with one's niece, which our document regards as forbidden, is certainly meant to be a further illustration of the זנות of opponents, and it is therefore extremely odd that this does not appear until after טמא המקדש. I therefore conjecture that either the whole passage on marriage with one's niece is a later addition or the biblical justification for it was added at a later time and to avoid interrupting the text of Scripture the clause ולוקחים . . . אחותו was moved from its place after אל (line 6) to the end of the section; cf. below, Section VII. As has already been noted ad loc., 5,11 begins a new section which is directed not so much against the opponents of the sect as against sinners and atheists in general. When Gressmann in ZDMG LXVI, 503, remarks that בשתים cannot mean "through two things" because three sins are enumerated in what follows, he overlooks the fact that our document uses Test. Levi, which speaks of three snares, זנות הון טמא מקדש, as a model, and that of two of these snares, בשתים, it is said that they can be applied to opponents.

opponents of the sect permit, and "the snare of defilement of the Temple" indicates their laxer view in certain cases of blood flow.[23]

In view of this rigorously legal orientation of our document it cannot seem strange to anyone that more than half of it is devoted to minute regulations about the Sabbath, ritual purity, and other religious observances. These were the things that chiefly interest the author. And even though some legal regulations in his work are very probably of later origin, still there is no reason to doubt that the Halakah formed a substantial or even the most substantial part of the original document. We should therefore hardly expect, in this document of preponderantly legal character, new theological doctrines, but we might expect it to take a position on the theological problems of the day. In a time when partisan hatred and sectarianism were rife, no polemical writing could appear that failed to take account of the differences between the Sadducees and Pharisees; in effect our document tells us in no uncertain terms where it stands in relation to the theological differences between those parties.

Josephus, the early Christian writings, and the rabbinic sources speak of the following dogmatic controversies between the Sadducees and the Pharisees.[24] "The Pharisees," says Josephus,[25] "entertain the

[23] An almost literal parallel to this accusation is found in Psalms of Solomon VIII, 13: They (The Sadducees) have trodden the altar of the Lord with every uncleanness, and in the flow of blood they have defiled the sacrifice like profane flesh. As Schechter has correctly noted *ad loc.*, the issue here concerns a Halakic difference in interpretation of the biblical prohibition concerning the impurity of a זבה; *cf.* above, *ad loc.*, and p. 115. In view of these parallels and the one given above on p. 158, it is a bold piece of Apocalyptic wisdom for Gressmann (*op. cit.*, 493) to assert that מקדש here means not the Temple but the Law, particularly its regulations about sexual matters. He ought at least to have referred to the saying in the P. T. Yevamoth II, 3d: "He who observes the commandments about sexual matters is called 'holy,' קדוש"; Part V of Maim. Yad is called קדושה 'ס, "the book of sanctification" and similarly the work בעלי הנפש of his opponent RABD contains a section headed "Gates of Holiness" which treats of conjugal relations. In the Test. Levi IX, 9 the Armenian version paraphrases τὰ ἅγια with τὸν νόμον σου. It is, moreover, very improbable that the Armenian text is correct here, since one expects something about the defilement of the Temple in the Testament of Levi; besides, the defilement of sacrifices is expressly mentioned in XVI, 1. Furthermore, Gressmann has overlooked the fact that קדש can mean both "Temple" and "holy law" but מקדש can mean only the former. Moreover, in 12,1 there is a reference to the defiling of the "holy city" through the non-observance of the commandment about sexual matters which leaves no room for doubt about the meaning of מקדש in our passage. *Cf.* also 1,3; 6,12, where מקדש means nothing else than Temple.

[24] *Cf.* the list of ancient sources in Schürer, *Geschichte*[4], 449 ff. Whether the Sadducees or other heretics who deny the resurrection are meant in Mishnah Berakhoth IX, 5 (=Tosefta VII, 11) must remain an open question; the ancient texts read מינין and not צדוקין, which, however, does not exclude the possibility that it is the

belief that . . . there are punishments and rewards under the earth for
those souls that in life were devoted to vice or to virtue, and that for
the one kind eternal imprisonment is appointed but for the other the
possibility of returning to life, while the Sadducees state that the soul
perishes . . . together with the body." One does not have to make a
long search in our document to determine which of these two views
it represents, for at the very beginning, 2,2 ff., the members of the
covenant are informed that "the way of sinners"[26] leads to the angels
of destruction, who inflict divine punishment on those who scorn the
Law. In the matter of spirits and angels too, whose existence is affirmed
by the Pharisees but denied by the Sadducees, our document agrees
with the former.[27] Beside the "angels of destruction" it also mentions
the "watchers," עִירִים (2,18), who fell from heaven as a consequence of

Sadducees who are here designated as "sectarians" (מינין). On the other hand, there
can be no doubt that in Sanhedrin 90b, where a dispute is reported between R.
Gamaliel and the צדוקים over the belief in resurrection, צדוקים refers to no other
kind of sectarians than the Sadducees, who are expressly described as such in Avoth
de R. Nathan 26, ed. Schechter, and as men who deny the existence of reward and
punishment as well as resurrection. Geiger's attempt (*Urschrift* 130) to explain
these צדוקים as leading Romans cannot be taken seriously, and is rightly rejected
by Wellhausen, *Die Pharisäer und die Sadducäer*, p. 54, who, to be sure, makes
"the Jewish scholars" responsible for Geiger's fanciful notion. In his zeal to prove
too much, moreover, Wellhausen has the misfortune to commit a gross blunder. He
asserts that R. Eliezer ben Yose likewise disputed about resurrection with the
Sadducees, and not, as Geiger would have it, with the Samaritans (Rabbinowitz
ad loc., demonstrates that כותים is a late bit of censorship), and on the difficulty of
the text he remarks as follows: "These interpreters of the Talmud don't understand
a joke . . . it is irony when R. Eliezer ben Yose reproaches his opponents saying,
'You have falsified your Torah, you have never taken it into your hand at all.' "
The joke that Wellhausen unwittingly offers us is far too good for the interpreters
of the Talmud to have been able to misunderstand it. For Wellhausen makes this
Tanna speak German, since in Hebrew לא העליתם בידכם can only mean "You have
achieved nothing" and of course Geiger quite properly asks: of what falsification
is it said here that it did not avail the Samaritans? If, however, we take account
of the reading of the Samaritan text in Deut. 1:8 and 11:9, where להם is omitted,
one can understand the reproach of falsifications of the text made against the
Samaritans and it is rightly observed that they did them no good, because there
are still other passages from which the doctrine of immortality can be deduced.
Cf. Hoffmann in הפלס I, 268; Bacher, *Terminologie* 50, and Blau, *Studien* 93, are
to be corrected accordingly.

[25] *Ant.* VIII.1.3 (14).

[26] *Cf.* above *ad loc.*; Midrash Tehillim XL, 257, and the Slavonic Book of Enoch
XLII, 10.

[27] Josephus and the rabbinic sources do not speak of this difference but that is
no reason for doubting the statement in Acts 22:8. Moreover, the denial of the
existence of angels and a world of spirits fits in very well with the worldliness of
the Sadducees; *cf.* also below on the details of the angelology of our document.

their sins, and "the holy ones of the Most High" (20,8) who curse sinners. An important role is further played by the (bad) angel Belial (8,2 *et al.*) and his spirits (12,2), who mislead men into sinning. As a further difference between the sects mentioned above, Josephus[28] cites the doctrine of divine providence, through which everything is brought about, according to the Pharisees, while the Sadducees assert that good and evil are exclusively dependent upon man's own choice. Now there is no dogma in our document that is more strongly and decisively stressed than that of divine providence, as when, in eloquent words (2,7 ff.), the point is made that in the very beginning God foresaw and predetermined good and evil. If there is a basis of truth to the statement of the Church Fathers,[29] for which there seems to be some confirmation in rabbinic literature,[30] that the Sadducees, in contrast to the Pharisees, recognized only the Pentateuch as authoritative but not the Prophetic writings, we should then have a further point in which our document agrees with the Pharisees. For not only is a substantial portion of it based on citations from the Prophetic writings but it also expressly noted that (7,17) Israel was sent into exile because it scorned the words of the Prophets.[31]

Our investigation of the dogmatic standpoint of our document has led to the same result as that of its Halakah. In the preceding sections

---

[28] *Ant.* XVIII.1,3 (13); *cf.* below on the view of divine providence in our document.

[29] *Cf.* the pertinent data in Schürer, *Geschichte*[4], II, 480, although he declares this definite statement of the Church Fathers to be an error. When Charles, *Introduction* x, cites in support of this assertion Jesus' answer to the Sadducees (Matt. 22:32 and parallels), which attempts to prove the doctrine of resurrection from the Pentateuch and not from the Prophets, he overlooked the simple fact that the Sadducees sought to show the absurdity of this doctrine from the Pentateuch, and so it was natural that Jesus should oppose them with their own weapons.

[30] *Cf.* Tanḥuma V,19: "The sinners in Israel say that the Prophets and Hagiographa are not Torah and therefore we do not believe in them, but it is clear from Dan. 9:10 that they do belong to the Torah." The Samaritans can not be meant, since for them all Jewish Prophets, including Daniel, were deceivers, and Daniel's words would have proved nothing so far as they were concerned. Those who are probably meant are the Jews who, to be sure, held the Prophets in high regard and treasured them but still did not regard their revelations as "Torah," i. e. as binding doctrine, and it is in opposition to these Jews that reference is made, in the passage cited above, to the verse in Daniel which speaks of the Torah revealed by the Prophets. *Cf.* also below the words of Maimonides about the belief in angels as an absolute prerequisite for the belief in prophecy. On that premise, the Sadducees, who denied the former, could not believe in the latter.

[31] The antecedent of the pronominal suffix in דבריהם may be ספרי, in which case the translation would be "because they scorned the words of the prophetic writings." On the canon of the sect see below.

we have not only shown that this Halakah is in substantial agreement with that of the Pharisees but also that our document mentions almost only those religious regulations that Talmudic tradition regards as "rabbinic," and similarly there has been revealed a *full agreement with the theology of the Pharisees on all those points on which they differ from the Sadducees.* The interest in the minute observance of the Law, in "fencing it around" and extending it, which our document shares with the Pharisees, would hardly be conceivable without a corresponding theological background. Reward and punishment, God's awareness of every human action and His intervention in the life of the individual and of the nation through angels and spirits, are the necessary presuppositions for the view of life as a "continuous divine service!" The Sadducees, who had their roots wholly in this world and its pleasures, had more than enough in the written Law and had no desire the expand the Law. That in many questions of Law they took a more rigorous stand than the Pharisees is quite possible, even probable (they were too little concerned about the maintaining of the Law to undertake the modifications thereof that were categorically required by the circumstances of the time), but to characterize them on that account as zealots for the Law and their opponents as "progressives" is simply to turn the facts upside down. Greater zealots for the Law than the Pharisees can hardly be imagined; and therefore our sect, which exhibits exactly the same preoccupation, can only be regarded as a variety of Pharisaism. The agreement of our sect with the Pharisees in the four dogmatic teachings mentioned above is a further confirmation of the conclusion reached in the preceding section as to the Pharisaic character of our document.

*

*   *

Providence, reward and punishment, and the belief in the world of angels and spirits, however important they may be for the dogma of Pharisaism, do not exhaust Pharisaic theology. To become more fully acquainted with the theological standpoint of our document, we must therefore examine more closely its views about God, Torah, the Messiah, and the like.

Monotheism is nowhere specially stressed, to be sure, but it is simply presupposed. Opponents are accused of the worst sins of both moral and religious nature, with the sole exception of polytheism, because this no longer existed among Jews. Even our document's historiosophy ignores the idolatry in the ancient history of Israel because it was of no relevance to their present situation. Only in one place (20,9) is it said of apostate members of the covenant that "they placed idols on their hearts," שמו גלולים על לבם, and even in this passage,[32] as the context shows, we have merely a biblical phrase (Ezek. 14:3) העלו גלוליהם על לבם, employed in a figurative sense. Apostasy from the true teaching of the sect is counted against sinners as if it were idolatry.[33] Characteristic of the transcendental view of God is the extraordinary awe of the Tetragrammaton, which is missing throughout the whole document, even in citations from the Bible.[34] It is forbidden further (15,1) to name God in any way in swearing an oath, since this is almost the same as a profanation of God's name. God is so far above all earthly and worldly things that his name[35] may not be brought into connection with such things.

Of the attributes of God the following are mentioned, in 2,3 ff.: his wisdom, goodness, and punitive power — the same trio that appears in rabbinic theology as חכמה מדת הדין מ' הרחמים. "God loved wisdom and understanding and set them up before him; skill and knowledge serve Him. Long-suffering is in Him and abundance of forgiveness . . . but also powerful might and anger that are manifested

---

[32] But not in 20,23, where the reading proposed by Lagrange, שבו עד אל נָסָךְ "and they turned to an idol" is quite impossible because, in the first place, שב cannot be combined with עד and אל; because in the second place אל ש' or עד ש' is used only of returning to God, because this verb has in it the notion of arriving at the place where one belongs; and finally, because שב is the expression used in our document for the sect's entering into a covenant, and it is quite inconceivable that it should also denote the opposite.

[33] In rabbinic literature the expression כאלו עובד ע'ז, "this is as bad as idolatry," is often used with reference to serious sins; for example, Tosefta Bava Qamma IX end (of anger); Tosefta Avodah Zarah VI, 16 (of hypocrisy); ibid. 18 (indulgence toward unworthy pupils); Pesaḥim 118a (of profaning festivals); Sotah 4a (of arrogance); Niddah 13a (of onanism); Sanhedrin 92a (of lying); Arakhin 15a (of slander); Kethuvoth 68a (of lack of benevolence); Yerushalmi Nedarim IX, 41b (of unbridled passion); Semaḥoth II, 11 (of smuggling); Midr. Sam. XXIII, 115 (of heartlessness כופר בנ'ח); Midr. Ag. I, 158 (of unfriendliness toward proselytes). It is not without interest to note that in all these passages it is moral and not legal (or ritual) sins that are equated with idolatry.

[34] Characteristic of our document is 5,4, where the copyist first wrote ויהושע and then "corrected" it to ויושע in order to avoid pronouncing the abbreviated Tetragrammaton יהו.. It should be noted also that Fragment A simply omits י'י (7,11; 7,13; 11,18; cf. above, pp. 33–34, 69), while B substitutes אל for it (19,8; 20,19). In 9,5, however, where הוא is found twice for י'י, we do not have a substitute for the Tetragrammaton as I assumed ad loc., but an old variant, since Gen. Rabbah LV (3, p. 586, line 12, see variants ibid.), (so already in the ed. pr.!) has הוא instead of י'י as in the Masorah. [See below, p. 188, n. 146. — S. L.]

[35] And similarly his revealed word. It is for this reason that one may not swear by "The Torah of Moses" either.

in flames of fire." אל אהב דעת[36] חכמה ותושייה הציב לפניו ערמה[37] ודעת הם
ישרתוהו ארך[38] אפים עמו ורוב סליחות ... וכח וגבורה וחמה גדולה בלהביי[39] אש ...
It is probably no accident that wisdom stands at the head of the
divine attributes, for the words "God loved[40] wisdom" mean that
wisdom was present at the beginning of all existence, and through it
God directs all things. It is even probable that our document identifies
wisdom with the Torah, as Ben Sira did before it and many others
after him;[41] at any rate this is suggested by the term תושיה, which,
according to the Talmud,[42] is equivalent to Torah. The manner in
which these three attributes are spoken of makes it seem probable
that for our author wisdom, goodness, and punitive power are more
than mere attributes. Expressions like "he set wisdom before him"
and "long-suffering is with him" remind us very vividly of these
three hypostases[43] of Alexandrian Jewish philosophy and Palestinian
theology, and we shall probably not err in positing their existence in
our document as well.

[36] Since דעת occurs in the following sentence, it should probably be deleted
here. [Rabin renders: 'God loves discernment; wisdom and counsel He has set up
before Him; etc., etc. — H. L. G.]

[37] Not "cunning" but "cleverness"; cf. above ad loc.: Targ. Jonathan renders
ערום in Gen. 3:1 by חכים, while Onqelos has ערים in this passage, but in Gen. 27:35
and 34:13 renders מרמה by חוכמא "wisdom," probably in reference to Jacob and his
sons, to whom it does not wish to attribute deceitfulness. Cf. also Gen. Rabbah
LXVII, p. 758, on Gen. 27:35: במרמה בחכמת תורתו.

[38] Avoth V, 2, ארך אפים לפניו, where, however, אֹרֶךְ and not אָרֶךְ should perhaps
be read; cf. above, p. 8. On the synonyms for the goodness of God, cf. Bousset,
Religion des Judentums², 440. In our passage too "cleverness," "knowledge," and
"understanding" are only various expressions for "wisdom"; while "long-suffering"
and "forgiveness" denote God's goodness.

[39] This is taken from Isa. 66:15, and the text therefore needs no emendation;
Gressmann, op. cit., p. 501, is to be corrected accordingly.

[40] Not "loves," as it is incorrectly translated, since we are here concerned not
with what God does but with that which he did at the beginning of the world when
he chose Wisdom as the plumbline of his actions.

[41] Cf. Bousset, op. cit., 394 ff. and my Die Haggada bei den Kirchenvätern, pp.
2 ff., where this identification is attested also in rabbinic literature, and, further,
Schechter, Aspects of Rabbinic Theology, pp. 80 ff.

[42] Nazir 23b; Sanhedrin 26b, where three etymologies of תושיה are given, all of
which presuppose its identity with תורה, which indicates that this identification is
older than the interpretations there given. Cf. also Gemara, Kallah VI, ed.
Coronel, 15a.

[43] Cf., more fully, Bousset, op. cit., XVIII. As for rabbinic literature, it
should never be forgotten that the Rabbis frequently did not realize the implica-
tions of hypostasis-speculation and were anyhow too simple in their theological
notions to draw the conclusions that the Alexandrian Jews and later the Christians
drew from such speculations.

In unmistakable opposition to the Sadducees,[44] the deniers of divine Providence, the latter is asserted with extraordinary emphasis in 2:7 ff.: "And before they (the sinners) were created, he knew their deeds . . . and He knew the years of the duration, the number and exact periods of all that exists, has existed, and will exist. For all these times he caused to arise such as he designated by name and through his anointed ones he made known to them his holy spirit . . . yea, he named them exactly by their names": ובטרם נוסדו[45] ידע את מעשיהם . . . וידע את שני מעמד ומספר ופרוש קציהם[46] לכל הוי עולמים ונהיית עד מה יבוא[47] . . . ובכולם הקים לו קריאי שם[48] . . . ויודיעם ביד משיחו רוח קדשו . . . ובפרוש שמו[49] שמותיהם.

An almost verbal parallel to this passage is, Mekilta, Bo XVI, p. 60: מצינו[50] שמותיהן של צדיקים ומעשיהם גלוים למקום עד שלא נוצרו שנאמר בטרם אצרך בבטן ידעתיך . . . שמותיהן של רשעים מנין תלמוד לומר זורו רשעים מרחם תעו מבטן דוברי כזב. "We see from Scripture that the names and deeds of the righteous are known to God even before they are created, for it is said (Jer. 1:5), 'I noted you before I formed you in the womb.' We likewise see from Scripture that the names of sinners are known (even before they are created), for it is said (Ps. 58:4), 'The wicked turn away from the womb on, the speakers of falsehood go astray from their mother's belly on.' " In our document, as in the Mekilta, it is stressed that divine providence extends not only to the general

---

[44] Cf. above, pp. 160 ff.

[45] For נוסדו read נוצרו in accordance with Jer. 1:5, from which these words are taken. The confusion of ר and ד and that of צ and ס are mishearings and are so frequent that examples of their occurrence can be dispensed with.

[46] Not "the interpretation of their ends" but "exactness of their periods"; cf. above on 6,10, where there is a detailed discussion of the meaning of קץ in our document, and cf. further Mishnah Nedarim II,4, ופירושם "and the exact information." The suffix in קציהם refers not to the sinners previously mentioned but (more in accordance with Aramaic usages) to the following הוי וכו'; cf. also above, pp. 94, 132.

[47] Cf. The Slavonic Book of Enoch XXXIX, 1: "I have been sent to thee to make known to thee from the lips of God what was, is, and will be until the day of judgment." Cf. also IV Esdras V, 136: qui praesentes sunt et qui praeterierunt et qui futuri sunt.

[48] "Those who are called," cf. Exod. 31:2; Isa. 45:3–4.

[49] In view of the Mekilta passage here cited, we should read שם for שמו (which is due to the following שמותיהם). שֵׁם שָׂם is biblical, and is of especially frequent occurrence in the expression שׂוּם שֵׁם "to name a place for oneself," while בפרוש, "exact," is attested in the Mishnah, Sanhedrin VII,4.

[50] The Haggadah to which this saying of the Mekilta is appended concerns the pious who received their names from God before they were born, on which see also Pirqe R. Eliezer 32; Tanḥuma I,21; Exod. Rabba XL; Pirqe R. ha-Qadosh 35, ed. Grünhut; and Midr. Ḥaserot (Bate Midrashot, ed. Wertheimer, 1968, vol. 2, p. 229).

but also to the particular. God foresaw good and evil not only in the course of history but also in individual saints and individual sinners. The "chosen ones" whom God designated for all the ages[51] were known to him beforehand as individuals: "He named them exactly."[52]

Most instructive is the comparison between the strong stress laid on divine providence in our document and the doctrine of the freedom of the will that is taught with great emphasis by Ben Sira.[53] An absolute determinism was never taught by the Pharisees, and the same is true of our document. "Everything is predetermined by God except the fear of God," הכל בידי שמים חוץ מיראת שמים, is the pregnant form in which the Talmud[54] clothes the rabbinic doctrine of divine providence on the one hand, and moral responsibility on the other, and this, as we learn from Josephus,[55] was also the view of Pharisaism in his time. "The Pharisees," he tells us, "teach that all things are brought about by fate (i. e. divine providence) but it has pleased God that along with the will of fate the human will shall work with virtue or wickedness." If, however, our document stresses providence, and Ben Sira stresses the freedom of the will, this difference of emphasis is based upon the different historical circumstances. Ben Sira lived in a time of triumphant advance for Pharisaism; hence his warning to the representatives of this movement not to push this doctrine of providence

[51] This reminded us of the statement in the Haggadah that there are a number of pious men in every generation (according to some, 30, according to others, 36; cf. the collection of passages in Theodor's note on Gen. Rabba XXXV, 329; he has, however, overlooked the fact that Aphraates, *Hom.* XXII, 458, ed. Wright, cites a similar tradition from an Apocryphon of which nothing further is known; cf. my remarks in the *Jewish Encyclopedia* I, 665), because otherwise the world would have to be destroyed.

[52] The well known Tannaitic saying about the pre-existent name of the Messiah also means nothing else than that the individuality of the Messiah was pre-existent, and not only the idea of salvation. That שמו של משיח does not stand for the Messianic idea as many assert (cf. Klausner, *Messianische Vorstellungen*, p. 66) is clear from the remark in Gen. Rabba I, 4, p. 6, that "the name of the Messiah existed only in the idea of God," which makes sense only if שמו means something other than "idea," namely, as we have seen, "individuality"; of which it is said that it had only an ideal but not a real existence. On this last problem cf. my discussion in *Die Haggada bei den Kirchenvätern*, pp. 2 ff., which Klausner has overlooked.

[53] Cf. 15:11–20. In another passage, he describes God's free will, but this, strictly speaking, is not identical with divine providence.

[54] Berakhoth 33b; cf. also Niddah 16b, where it is explicitly stated that (somewhat differently in later legends; cf. my *Legends of the Jews* I, 56 ff.) the physical and spiritual qualities of a person are determined at birth, and only freedom of will is left to him.

[55] *Ant.* XVIII. 1,3.

to extremes, for otherwise freedom of the will would disappear. Our author is primarily concerned with opposing the Sadducees; hence his polemic against the doctrine of the freedom of the will, consistently maintained by them, which wholly negates divine providence.

Our document's philosophy of history is closely connected with the doctrine of divine providence. It culminates in the belief that God, who foresaw all things in the very beginning, has revealed himself at various times. Whenever the world is threatened with destruction because of the sinfulness of its inhabitants, the "chosen ones,"[56] קריאי שם, "whom God named explicitly," ובפרוש שם שמותיהם, appear and who then by their pious deeds save the human race from total annihilation. Sinners suffer the punishment they deserve, but the descendants of the pious people the earth anew. When the sinfulness[57] of the fallen angels and their descendants brought the flood upon the earth, it was Noah who saved it from complete destruction.[58] Among the descendants of Noah, in turn, it was the Hamites who were doomed to extermination because of their sins. But the continued existence of the world was not imperiled in spite of the sinfulness of the Hamites.[59] Abraham, the friend of God,[60] then appeared and his descendants Isaac and Jacob, who through their observance of the commandments became friends

[56] Cf. above, p. 165, where the biblical parallels to this expression are cited; cf. also in Berakhoth 54b the saying of R. Joḥanan that "God himself determines the worthy leaders of the people."

[57] It is viewed quite in the same way as in Test. Reuben V, 6; of actual intercourse between the angels and the daughters of men nothing is said in either source.

[58] The appearance of Noah is not directly mentioned but the whole account (2,11 ff.) is intended to show that at the same time as he punishes the godless God causes "his chosen ones" to appear, and in this case Noah is to be understood as the savior at the time of the Flood. In 2,8 this visitation is quite clearly presented as predetermined. One may further refer to Pirqe R. Eliezer III, where "the water of the Flood" is reckoned among pre-existing things. Cf. also Gen. Rabbah XXVII, 4, pp. 258–59, where a Tanna discusses with a gentile how the doctrine of divine providence can be reconciled with the biblical account of the flood (Gen. 7:6). Cf. also my remarks in מבול של אש (reprinted from הגרן VIII, p. 4).

[59] Cf. above on 3,1, where I have proposed the reading ומשפחת חם for ומשפחה הם, but where I now think that I was mistaken in identifying the Hamites in question with the Canaanites, for, although it is stated in Sifre Deut. 60, p. 125, that the latter were more given to idolatry and immorality than any other people, the context in our document requires an allusion to the corruption of the Hamites in the time of Abraham. It is therefore far more likely that what is meant by "the family of Ham" is the generation of the Tower of Babel, דור הפלגה. This rebellion against God is in Jewish legend (cf. my Legends of the Jews I, 179 ff.) attributed to Nimrod, whom Abraham vainly opposed; cf. also the Book of Jubilees, 11, where the birth of Abraham follows the increasing sinfulness of the Noachides.

[60] On this epithet of Abraham see above, p. 12, and Singer, Buch d. Jub., 151.

of God and confederates of the Most High.[61] The descendants of these
pious men, however, did not follow the example set for them by their
fathers. In Egypt, and especially in the wilderness, Israel appeared
rebellious and disobedient, but God sent the two pious brothers
Moses and Aaron at the same time as Belial caused the two magi-
cians Yoḥanah and his brother[62] to appear in order to mislead Israel
into sinning. But Moses' and Aaron's influence for good did not last
very long either. For hardly were Joshua, Eleazar[63] and the Elders
dead than Israel fell into idolatry, so that the Torah remained hidden
in the holy ark during the reigns of the Judges and Kings, and Israel
lived in such ignorance of the Law that even a pious king like David[64]
lived in polygamous marriage without knowing that it was forbidden
in the Torah. To punish Israel for its sins God gave it over to the
sword and gave its land over to devastation. Nevertheless he did not
wholly destroy it. In the reign of Josiah the King of Judah, there arose
in Israel, in the person of the high priest Zadok,[65] a "True Teacher"; he
found the book of the Torah that had remained hidden so long.[66] And
when, finally, after the destruction of the Temple, the people again
went astray and was punished for its sinful deeds by being affected
by the "Great King of the Greeks," God still did not forget His
covenant with the Fathers. In Damascus, where the pious remnant
of the people had fled from Judea, there appeared the "star of Jacob,"

[61] Cf. above, p. 12, and Bousset, op. cit., p. 357.

[62] Yoḥanah is an older creation of legend than his brother; the pagan writers
Pliny and Apuleius know only the former (cf. Schürer, II, 403), and in our document his brother is still unnamed. Originally the two persons contrasted were Moses
and Yoḥanah, and subsequently in order to make the parallel complete, a brother
was associated with the latter, just as Moses had Aaron by his side. I conjecture,
moreover, that much of what the Haggadah attributes to the brothers Dathan
and Abiram (cf. especially Targ. Jonathan on Exod. 14:3: the Midrashic source
for this is in שכל טוב II, p. 188) was originally applied to Yoḥanah and Mamre.

[63] Cf. above, p. 21, according to Seder Olam Rabba XII Eleazar died at the
same time as Joshua; but according to Bava Bathra 15a, after him. In Judg. 2:7
only Joshua and the Elders are mentioned at all. Is it out of priestly interest that
our document brings in the priest Eleazar? But the naming of Eleazar before Joshua
is biblical.

[64] Cf. above, pp. 21 ff.

[65] Our author gives his philosophy of history in 1,1–4,4; 5,17–6,10; 7,12–8,11;
on Zadok as the Teacher of Righteousness see below, Sections VI and VII.

[66] By the hidden things which God revealed to the remnant that was faithful to
the Law are to be understood the laws of the Torah that were unknown until they
were discovered by Zadok (5,5), so that all Israel (3,14) went astray. It cannot be
a protest against the calendar system of the Pharisees that is intended here because
our author reproaches all Israel on this score. Jubilees VI, 34 is hypothetical and
therefore no parallel to our passage.

the interpreter of the Torah, the last great leader, whose teaching is the only standard of law-abiding life and will remain so until the coming of the Messiah.[67]

*

*   *

Through divine providence, which is concerned with both the community and the individual, and which has determined, in particular, the fate of Israel according to a fixed plan, God is brought very close to man. At the same time, however, we find in our document a tendency to keep the Creator as far as possible from his creation. That hypostatizing speculations are not foreign to it we have noted on p. 164,[68] and from the same transcendental tendency (in part, at least) arises angelology, which seems to play an important role in the doctrines of the sect. We find in our document certain groups of angels as well as individual figures among them that stand out from the host of nameless heavenly beings and assume a definite character. The "angels of destruction," [ה]מלאכי חבל, who inflict divine punishment on sinners, (2,6) form a class of angels who are also frequently mentioned in rabbinic and apocalyptic literature. It is not without interest, however, to note that no trace is to be found in our document of the conception prevailing in the Book of Enoch[69] that these angels belong to the realm of evil over which Satan rules. Instead, these angels were meant by God from the very beginning of things to punish sinners, and in carrying out their duties they do not follow Satan in any way but fulfill the will of God. As in rabbinic doctrine[70] Gehinnom belongs to those things that existed before the world was created, so, according to our document the angels of destruction who inflict divine punishment on sinners in Gehinnom were also appointed to this task from the very beginning.[71] A class of angels quite unknown to

[67] *Cf.* below, Section VI.

[68] As was brought out above, p. 160, our document is in agreement with the Pharisees, who also taught the existence of the angel and spirit world. It should be noted, however, that angelology has almost no importance in tannaite literature. In the Mishnah the word מלאך does not occur at all, and in the Tosefta and in the halakic Midrashim hardly half a dozen passages about angels can be found.

[69] *Cf.* particularly LIII, 3: "and I saw the angels of destruction that prepared all kinds of instruments for Satan." The concept of a realm of evil is, however, not wholly unknown to our document, *cf.* below, what is said about Belial.

[70] Pesaḥim 54a and the parallels cited by Theodor to Gen. Rabba I, 4, p. 6; on the problem whether these pre-existent things are to be understood as real or ideal, *cf.* my remarks in *Haggada bei den Kirchenvätern* 2 ff.

[71] The "flames of fire in which are angels of destruction" are, of course, nothing but ever-burning Gehinnom.

rabbinic literature[72] but one that plays a great role in apocalyptic writers is that of "The Watchers," עִירֵי שָׁמַיִם (2,18), who came to their fall by not observing the commandments of God. That our document understands by "The Watchers" only the fallen angels cannot be said with certainty since the passage in question, in which this class of angels is mentioned, says only that the fallen angels belong to "the Watchers," but no more than that. In the Book of Enoch,[73] where this designation of the angels is frequent, it stands for a particular class of them[74] as well as for the fallen angels in general.

The angels appear in our document (20,8) as "The holy ones of the Most High,"[75] and it is said of them that they curse him who violates the covenant (who renounces the teaching of the sect). In the Testament of Naphtali VIII, 6 it is said, "But he who does not do what is right will be cursed by angels and men," so that there can be no doubt that it is the angels who are to be understood by "the holy ones who

---

[72] This is all the stranger because they are already mentioned in the book of Daniel. Neither Maimonides, Yesode ha-Torah II, 7 nor the Qabbalists (Zohar II, 43; *M. Azilut*) include "the Watchers" among the ten classes of angels, and the word עירין occurs only very sporadically in synagogal poetry (e. g. in Najara's יה רבון). It should here be noted at the same time that the division of the angelic world into ten classes does not occur in Maimonides for the first time, as is stated by the author of the article "Angelology" in the *Jewish Encyclopedia* I, 591, but earlier, in the Talmud Yerushalmi, Eruvin, I, 19d, where the saying "the camp of God consists of ten" is most simply explained to mean that God is surrounded by ten classes of angels (each class considered as a unit). It is true that this saying was interpreted differently at an early period, as is clear from Midrash Samuel XXIII, 116, which reads, "The camp of God consists of ten men, for when ten men are present in the synagogue they constitute the camp of God." (*Cf.* Avoth III, 6). The ten classes are also known to R. Moses ha-Darshan; see the quotation, from a manuscript in Gross, *Gallia Judaica*, p. 411.

[73] *Cf.* Charles' Index to his translation of Enoch, *s. v.* "watchers."

[74] Nevertheless the nature and the real meaning of this name cannot be determined. It should be noted, however, that both in the Gilgamesh epic as in Jewish legend, sleep appears as the criterion of mortals (*cf.* my *Legends of the Jews* I, 64), according to which "The Watchers who do not sleep" (Enoch LXXI, 7) are the equivalent of "immortals." "Watchmen" would be a false translation of עירים, since ער means "to be wakeful" and not "to watch" in the sense of "to guard." The designation of angels as "watchmen," צופים, is found in a saying of R. Meir, Yalkut Makh. on Isa. 196; its source has been lost, probably a Pesiqta (as appears from Yalkut M. Ps. I, p. 204), which Bousset, *op. cit.*, 371, has overlooked. The designation of angels as "watchmen," שומרים, appears also in Exod. Rabba XVIII, 5 = Aggad. Shir V, 39, ed. Schechter.

[75] *Cf.* Ben Sira XLII, 17 קדושי אל, whereas in the Bible only קדושין occurs with this meaning. קדושין is frequent in the liturgy; similarly in the Book of Jubilees XVI, 11; XXXI, 14, and Test. Job X, 19, οἱ ἅγιοι, which has been misunderstood by Kohler, *Semitic Studies*, p. 334.

curse sinners." We may not, indeed, identify these angels with the "angels of destruction" mentioned above; rather it is the "good" angels who are meant, who, though they are otherwise friendly toward men, have no sympathy with apostates but curse them. Similarly it is said in the Book of Enoch[76] "and behold, he comes with myriads of holy ones to give judgment." Here, as in our document, the "holy ones" are witnesses of the divine judgment upon the individual and the community.

The more important datum on the position of the angels is the passage 5,17. It reads: "And in ancient times Moses and Aaron arose through the Prince of Light, while Belial in his evil design caused Yoḥanah and his brother to arise; This came about when Israel was saved for the first time," כי מלפנים[77] עמד משה ואהרן ביד שר האורים ויקם בליעל את יהנה ואת אחיה במזמתו בהושע ישראל את[78] הראשונה. Whatever angel is to be understood by the "Prince of Light,"[79] it is at least certain that quite unusual importance is attributed to him. It was he who caused Moses and Aaron to carry out their mission of delivering Israel, and he is furthermore the antipode of Belial, the ruler of evil, and is thus the ruler of good. The conflict between Michael and Satan-Belial in rabbinic and apocryphal literature[80] certainly forms an interesting

---

[76] I, 9; cf. also Shabbath 119b.

[77] A new section begins with מלפנים or as we probably ought to read, ומלפנים. כי is a variant of the preceding מאשר which found its way into the text, and in the wrong place.

[78] Equivalent to את הפעם הראשונה, "the first time." This construction, instead of the usual בראשונה or בפעם הראש', is rare, to be sure, but not unheard of; cf. e. g. Eruvin II, 9 את יום ראש חדש, "on the new moon," instead of ביום ראש חדש in a saying of R. Dosa (floruit ca. 70 C. E.).

[79] Cf. above ad loc., on the identity of this angel with Uriel. Cf. further Slavonic Enoch XXII. "And God said to *Urevvil*, Bring the books out from my treasure ... and expound them to Enoch." It looks as if this mysterious name concealed our *Uriel*. Uriel also figures in the Slavonic Apocalypse of Abraham (edit. Bonwetsch), as Abraham's teacher and guide. Application may further be made of the fact that Qabbalah identifies Uriel with Metatron, also known as Raziel — angel of the divine mysteries — and explicitly connects him with the giving of the Law; cf. *Tiqqune Zohar* LXX, 296 and *Tiqqunim min Zohar Ḥadash*, Wilna 1876, pp. 82 ff.

In connection with my attempt, *ibid.*, to identify סוריאל with Uriel, reference should be made to Origen, *C. Cels.* VI, 30, where it is stated that the Ophites included among the seven chief demons Suriel, to whom they attributed the shape of a bull. It is not certain that the bull's shape is connected with the name סוריאל = ישׁור אל (Michael has the shape of a lion, Gabriel that of an eagle, etc.) and if it were, such an Ophitic speculation would prove nothing about the origin of the name Suriel; cf. Avoth de-Rabbi Natan, p. 51.

[80] Cf. for example, Judas IX; Deut. Rabbah, end, on Michael and Satan at the death of Moses, and more fully Lücken, *Michael*, p. 22.

parallel to the conflict between the Prince of Light and Belial; but
even of Michael, the guardian angel of Israel, it is merely said that he
interceded for his nation and was its spokesman before God,[81] but not
that he directed the destiny of Israel, as seems to be assumed of the
Prince of Light in our document. The mission of Moses makes one
think first of all of the revelation of the Law, when, therefore, it is
said that Moses and Aaron arose through the Prince of Lights, it
looks as if this angel were among other things the mediator of the Law.
In that case we should have an undoubtedly heretical teaching before
us, since Pharisaic Judaism never regarded the revelation of the Law
as anything other than a direct act of God.[82] It must, however, be

[81] *Cf.* Charles on Test. Levi V; Bousset, *op. cit.*, p. 337.

[82] In rabbinic literature no doubt exists about the fact that the revelation of
the Ten Commandments as well as that of the other laws was a direct one. "Israel
said, 'we wish to see our King . . . . . and God granted their wish,'" says the
Mekilta, *Baḥodesh* II end, p. 210; and legend expressly states that the revelation
at Sinai embraced not only the Law, but also the divine oneness and uniqueness;
cf. my *Legends of the Jews* III, 17. With regard to the other Mosaic laws it is remarked in Mekilta, Ki Tissa I, beg., p. 340: "And God spoke to Moses neither
through an angel nor through a messenger," and even more definite is the statement in Sifre Zuṭa 84, ed. Horovitz, Lipsiae, p. 276: "His (Moses') prophecy was
not through an angel," and similarly Avoth R. Nathan I, ed. Schechter, p. 2. In the
Talmud and in the Midrashim the immediate revelation of the Law to Moses is
so frequently mentioned that it would be superfluous to adduce instances, and
here we shall only point out that, according to a widespread legend, the angels
actually attempted to prevent the revelation of the Law; *cf.* my *Legends*, III,
109–114. Also in the passage Sanhedrin 38b where with reference to Exod. 24:1 it
is said that by יי Metatron is to be understood (see the correct interpretation of
Naḥmanides in his Bible commentary *ad loc.*; the interpretations of Rashi, R.
Ḥananel and Abulafia in יד רמה *ad loc.*, are untenable); it is further said that Israel
did not wish to have this archangel as a "messenger of God" at all, and God granted
their wish by revealing the Law Himself. Even in the very late Hekaloth (Yalquṭ
Reuveni end Mishpatim; my *Legends*, III, 114) nothing is said about "the angel of
the Torah" revealing it to Moses but, as is clear from a comparison of this passage
with Shabbath 89b and *Beth ha-Midrash* II, 116, only that this angel made known
to Moses the mysterious power of the Torah, שמוש, by means of which he was able
to impress the Torah on his memory as not to forget it again as he had done before.
In Josephus, *Ant.* XV.5,3 there is a word-play on מלאך, which in Hebrew means
"angel" as well as "messenger." God, he says, revealed the most important teachings and laws through Moses and the Prophets whom (in accordance with biblical
usage, Ḥag. 1:17) he designates as "angels or messengers." In *Ant.* III, 5,1 and 4
Josephus expressly states that the Law was given directly (by God), and in section
8 of the same chapter he stresses the fact that the writing on the tablets came from
the hand of God; so that Josephus could not possibly have attributed the giving
of the Law to the angels, unless we understand by this the teachings and precepts
of the Prophets. *Cf.* also Maimonides, *Moreh* III, 45: "No Torah without Prophets;
but prophecy is not possible without the mediation of an angel." These words,

admitted that the expression ביד שר האורים is far too vague for us to draw from it conclusions concerning the activity of this angel, since it may only mean that this Prince of Light gave his help to Moses and Aaron. In that case our document would only be giving expression to the belief which was prevalent in the Bible and in later literature that the angels assist the pious.

*

*   *   *

More concrete and clearer than the figure of "the Prince of Light" is that of his antipode, Satan. The purer and more perfect the doctrine of God became, the more difficult it became to explain the existence of evil. God, the source of goodness and justice, could not be the immediate author of sin; yet man is only like "clay in the hand of the potter,"

---

which remind us strongly of Josephus, are applicable, however, as Maimonides himself further explains, only to the other Prophets but not to Moses. The statement of several recent scholars (Bousset, *op. cit.* 377; Charles, Book of Jubilees I, 27) that Judaism knew only an indirect giving of the Law is characteristic of their method. For them Jewish means not what is in the Bible, still less what is in rabbinic literature, but only the phantastic notions of the Apocalyptic writers; we are often justified in asking in their writings whether we are not dealing with Christian, even anti-Jewish material, but still they are regarded by these scholars as the only authoritative sources for what is "Jewish." In the Pentateuch (Num. 12:8; Deut. 34:10), the direct and immediate giving of the Law is positively asserted, and so long as we have no convincing proof for the assumption that this view was later abandoned, it is against every principle of sound criticism to assume such a downgrading of the Law and the lawgiver, since the later development of Judaism moves in exactly the opposite direction, namely that of glorifying the Law and everything connected with the revelation of the Law. The appearance of angels in the post-exilic Prophets as mediators of the divine revelation to them has nothing to do with our problem — a fact overlooked by Charles, *loc. cit.* The existence of angels is also presupposed in the Pentateuch (Exod. 23:20), and it is for this reason that the uniqueness of the revelation made to Moses, as an immediate one, is stressed in the above mentioned passage. The same view is found in Ben Sira (XLV, 3 ff.), who describes the revelation of the Law in the following words: "And he (God) caused him to hear his voice and caused him to approach the darkness, and he placed in his hand the commandment, the law of life and discernment, that he might teach his statutes to Jacob and his laws to Israel." When, therefore, there is mentioned in the Book of Jubilees (*cf.* Charles *loc. cit.*) the writing down of the Law "through the angel of the Presence," this does not mean that the angel rather than God himself revealed the Law — a view which cannot possibly be ascribed to this book, if only because it explicitly states (I, 4 ff.) that God instructed Moses — but the sense is as follows: God himself revealed to Moses both the Ten Commandments and the other laws, but only the former were written by the Angel of the Presence. Thus it is not the revealing of the Law that is done by an angel but the writing of it after Moses had received it orally from God. The idea that is here

and can do nothing at all without the participation of God.[83] We therefore already find in the Bible (I Chron. 21:1) the figure of Satan, who seduces men into sin, and in the apocryphal literature he becomes more and more important, although the views about him vary in detail in the various passages.[84] In our document Satan usually appears under the name of Belial, which also occurs elsewhere;[85] it therefore seems proper first to examine the Belial passages more closely.

"And during all these years[86] Belial was sent against Israel." Although this statement is based on Prov. 17:11, "And a cruel angel[87] will be sent against him (the wicked man)," ומלאך אכזרי ישלח בו, what is probably meant in our passage is that during these years Belial will carry out his evil work "freely and unchecked" (משולח). This idea is developed in the following lines (4,15). Belial snares Israel with his three nets: immorality, dishonest acquisition and defiling of the Temple. The "builders of the wall" further Belial's undertaking by misleading the people, so that he can thrust Israel into perdition at will (משולח). It is also possible that the expression משולח was chosen

---

expressed is that the *whole Law* is of heavenly origin and not only the Decalogue. A similar view is perhaps to be found in the Hekaloth passage mentioned above: after Moses had orally received the Law from God he was unable to fix it in his memory (*cf.* the similar passage in Jubilees XXXII, 25), to say nothing of writing it down from memory. He therefore received the book of the Law from the angel of Torah. It is not altogether impossible that Josephus too (*loc. cit.*) wished to express the same idea: only the Decalogue was written down by God (*Ant.* III,5,8), the other laws by angels. Probably, however, Josephus, in agreement with the Midrash, meant that God himself revealed the Decalogue to Israel but gave the rest of the Law to it through his messenger = Moses. For rhetorical reasons Josephus uses the plural "messengers" for the singular. The revelation of the Law through angels can be attested with certainty only in the writings of Paul (Gal. 3:19 *et al.*), and here we are probably dealing with a tendentious doctrine of Paul. The abrogation of the Law through Jesus is made more plausible on this view; the Son of God is a higher authority than the angels; they revealed the Law, and he abolished it. *Cf.* also Ḥagigah 3b and Yoma 52a top.

[83] *Cf.* the fuller discussion, pp. 165 ff.

[84] Bousset, *op. cit.*, Chapter XVII; he should have emphasized more forcefully the fact that the devil plays no role at all in Tannaite literature, and that the name Belial, for example, does not occur anywhere in the entire Talmudic-Midrashic literature.

[85] Especially in the Testaments of the XII Patriarchs, *cf.* Charles' Index *s. v.* "Belial." It should be noted, incidentally, that Belial again becomes prominent in Qabbalah, especially in the combination אדם בליעל, which is equivalent to קליפה "husk" = "evil." *Cf. Mass. Aẓilut.*

[86] I. e. during the present world-order; *cf.* above, pp. 17 and 29 ff.

[87] Belial is the head of the angels of destruction and it was therefore natural to identify the "cruel angel" with him.

to indicate that Belial, in contrast to the other evil spirits,[88] who are restricted to the place of damnation in order that they may not do any harm to men, can accomplish his destructive work freely and unhindered. Belial, however, is not only the one who misleads men into sinning but he is also the enemy of Israel, and therefore sought to prevent the liberation of Israel from slavery in Egypt. It was through the Prince of Light that Moses and Aaron rose, awhile Belial maliciously caused Yoḥanah and his brother to arise. Here the same role is assigned to Belial that Masṭema plays in the Book of Jubilees. "And the prince Masṭema raised himself against thee and wished to let thee fall into the hand of Pharaoh and always helped the sorcerers of the Egyptians," it is said in this book[89] (XLVIII,9). What is more, the redemption from Egypt was possible only because (ibid., vs. 15) the prince Masṭema was bound and confined behind the Israelites to prevent him from accusing them. We also find in rabbinic literature the statement that Samael (= Belial) sought to prevent Israel's crossing the Red Sea by saying to God, "they are at present still idolators and thou wouldst divide the sea for them?" But God, in order to silence Samael's accusations against Israel, incited him against Job, so that he left Israel in peace for a short time while he was accusing Job. In the meantime Israel was saved from the Egyptians.[90]

Satan, observes a Baraita (Bava Bathra 16a), descends and misleads "man into sinning," and then ascends and through his accusation brings down God's anger upon the sinner, so that he receives permission "to take such a person's soul." Of these three tasks assigned to Satan, only the first and last are found connected with Belial in our document; he is the seducer and the inflicter of punishment, but it is highly probable that the role of accuser is also given to him even though this is not explicitly stated.[91] As we have seen, he snares men in his net, and all those who enter the covenant and do not remain faithful to him "God will give over into the hand of Belial for destruc-

---

[88] Cf. the Book of Jubilees X, 3, 13; cf. also the passages cited in the text concerning "the confinement" of Masṭema.

[89] Cf. also XLVIII, 18 with reference to Exod. 4:29; in Nedarim 32a too it is said that it was Satan who wished to slay Moses.

[90] Exod. Rabba XXI, 7, and, in briefer form, earlier in Gen. Rabba LVII, 4, p. 615. In the latter passage it is assumed that Satan's opposition was directed against Israel's exodus from Egypt so that Job's year of punishment coincided with the year of punishment of the Egyptians; cf. Eduyyoth II, 10. In Exod. Rabbah the legend of Satan's opposition is combined with the accusation against Israel (cf. my Legends of the Jews III, 17 ff.).

[91] The name Masṭema for Satan (16,5) would not prove anything about this role even if this passage were genuine — which is, however, very doubtful (cf. pp. 94–95 and 133) — since it doubtlessly means "adversary" and not "accuser."

tion."[92] This execution of punishment by Belial, however, is not to be thought of as eschatological; rather death and suffering are conceived as the instruments of Belial, so that it is said of the sinner who falls victim to them because of his deeds, "he is given over into the hand of Belial." This becomes clear from the description[93] of the visitation by the Great King of Greece as "giving over sinners into the hand of Belial," from which one sees that for our document every misfortune is to be considered as punishment by Belial. Punishment after death probably does not come under this head; in the only passage where it is mentioned, it is the "angels of destruction"[94] who function as those who inflict it and not Belial.

As Belial made use of various instruments to inflict punishment, so also he did to seduce men into sin. The spirits of Belial rule the man who preaches apostasy from God (12,2) and to these spirits probably also belongs the impulse toward sin, יצר אשמה,[95] (2,16) which brings about the fall of angels as well as of men. In the Testaments of the XII Patriarchs these spirits of Belial play a great role,[96] but Philo also speaks[97] of the many hosts of evil inmates (of men) who must be driven out in order that the sole good (God) may move in, and he therefore admonishes men with the words, "So do thou strive, O soul, to become a house of God." Of these words of Philo we are reminded by the following passage (16,4) in our document: "And on the day on which a man purposes to turn to the Torah of Moses, the angel of enmity, מלאך המשטמה,[98] leaves him." The bad angel always accompanies[99] the sinner, and leaves him when he turns to the good.[100] Never-

---

[92] The text of A, 8,2 is to be corrected in accordance with B, 19,14, but even B is not quite free of error; cf. my observations on באלה החקים, p. 35.

[93] Cf. the passages cited in the preceding note.

[94] Cf. pp. 170 ff. on these.

[95] This is merely a somewhat different expression for "the evil impulse," יצר הרע, of the rabbinic sources.

[96] Cf. Issachar VII; Dan I; Joseph VII; Benjamin III.

[97] De Somniis I,XXIII, ed. Mangey, I,643.

[98] In the book of Jubilees one finds "Prince Maṣṭema" (X, 8) as well as "Prince of Maṣṭema" (XVIII, 9; cf. Charles, ad loc.), while in our document we have "angel of Maṣṭema." There is nothing strange in Satan or Maṣṭema being described as an angel since, whatever views one may hold about the lower orders of evil spirits (cf. more fully below), there can be no difference of opinion as to the fact that their prince is an angel. In rabbinic literature the expression מלאך המות, "angel of death," occurs very frequently, and this is no other than Satan; cf. Bava Bathra 15a.

[99] Maimonides, Moreh III,23, discovers in the statements of the Talmud, Ḥagigah 16a, about the two angels who accompany every man the doctrine that Satan as well as "the good impulse" is always found in the company of men.

[100] I. e. as soon as he has undergone a change; similar is the statement in Qiddushin 49b, הרהר תשובה ... ע"מ שאני צדיק.

theless I have grave suspicions about the genuineness of this passage, for, apart from the reasons given above for excluding it as a later gloss, it is further to be noted that the constant designation of Satan in our document is "Belial," and it would be very strange to find him in this passage as "Mastema" or "angel of Mastema." It is true that in the book of Jubilees "Belial" occurs together with "Mastema," so that our document would differ from this book only in using "Belial" as the usual designation of Satan, and "Mastema" occasionally, whereas the use of these names in the Book of Jubilees is exactly the reverse. Nevertheless it is very doubtful whether "Belial" is at all known to the Book of Jubilees as a proper name. Sinners are described (XV, 33) as "sons of Belial," but this locution is already present in Deut. 13:14,[101] and so there remains only the passage I, 20, where Moses prays to God, "may the spirit of Belhor (= Belial) not have power over Israel to complain against them before Thee and to lure them away from all the paths of righteousness that they may be corrupted far from Thy face." If one reflects, however, that the spirits of Mastema who seduce men to sin are mentioned in many[102] passages in this book, Belial in this passage is very suspect, and it is probable that the Greek translator, on coming across the uncommon name "Mastema" for the first time, was prompted to replace it by the familiar "Belial," but discontinued it on finding how frequently Mastema is named.

The demonology of our document also seems to differ in several other respects from that found in the Book of Jubilees. In this book[103] the evil spirits are the descendants of the fallen angels, whereas in our document no trace of this mythological view can be found, even though the fall of the angels is not passed over in silence. In general, one cannot fail to recognize its tendency to attenuate the mythological element. In the Book of Jubilees[104] and in the Ethiopic Enoch[105] the intercourse of the fallen angels with the "daughters of men" is still treated quite literally, whereas in our document (2,18) it is said that

---

[101] On the basis of this passage, Tannaitic exegesis (Sifre Deut. 93, p. 154; Midr. Tann. 6; Sanhedrin 111b) explains בליעל as a compound of בלי 'without' and על 'yoke.' בני בליעל, according to this derivation, "sons of lawlessness," and it is therefore very fittingly used in the Book of Jubilees as a designation of the Hellenists.

[102] Cf. X, 7; XI, 5; XIX, 28. In the Testaments, there are frequent references to Belial and his spirits but none to Mastema; a designation of Satan that is confined solely to the book of Jubilees.

[103] Cf. X, 5; also Enoch XVI, 1.

[104] Cf. V, 1; VII, 21 and Charles' note on IV, 15.

[105] Cf. XV. 8–11: XVI. 1.

"the Watchers of heaven came to their fall because they did not keep the commandments of God," without mention of sexual intercourse. Our document appears to conceive of the fall of the angels as do the Testaments of the XII Patriarchs,[106] where on the one hand it is said that they came to their fall through sensual desire, while on the other hand the manner of their satisfying it is described in the following peculiar way. "So then did they (the women) enchant the Watchers before the flood. And they saw them constantly and began to desire them and conceived the deed in their minds and changed themselves into men, and when they (the women) lay with their husbands, they (the Watchers) appeared to them. And the women began to desire them in their imagination and so they bore giants." Accordingly, in our document the giants appear as the sons of the Watchers, although there is no reference to actual intercourse between the latter and the women. A very similar view has been preserved in rabbinic literature,[107] although the official doctrine of the synagogue wholly rejected this myth at a very early date.[108] "Do not fall through thine eyes, for it is the eyes that cause one to fall, as Azza and Azzael also came to their fall only through their eyes[109] . . . God gave them an evil impulse, and they came down. Question: But what pleasure could these angels have from carnal intercourse even if they were moved by the evil impulse? Answer: Their pleasure was in their clinging to the women. Question: In Scripture, however, (Gen. 6:4) it is said, 'and the women bore (children) to them.' Answer: Since the angels clung to the women as these lay with their husbands, they bore children who resembled the angels."

A further relation between our document and the Testaments in respect of demonology is indicated by the antithesis of "The Prince of Light" and Belial (5,18); similar to the contrast of "God and Belial." For example, it is said in Test. Levi 19:1, "Choose ye between light and darkness, the law of God of the work of Belial." But it

---

[106] Test. Reuben V,6. The text is, however, not quite correct.

[107] Mass. Kallah, ed. Coronel 8a; also in the Wilna edition of the Talmud, Kallah R. III, 53a.

[108] *Cf.* more fully my *Haggada bei den Kirchenvätern*, 75–76; Theodor in his notes to Gen. Rabba XXVI, 247, and Charles on the Book of Jubilees IV, 15; *cf.* further Philo, *Quaest. Gen.* I, 92.

[109] This is an interesting parallel to עֵינֵי זְנוּת, "The eyes of fornication" in our document, 2,16, which caused the fall of the angels; accordingly the reading עֵי = עָנִין is to be rejected. The expression used a little earlier, יצר מחשבות, is also found in Test. Judah XIII, 2, and is derived from Gen. 6:5 and not, as Charles states *ad loc.*, from I Chr. 28:9.

should not be overlooked that in our document Belial does not yet appear as the counterpart of God, for God is too elevated to permit of any angel or spirit being represented as his antipode, for which reason it is the Prince of Light and Belial who are contrasted; whereas in the Testaments the importance of Belial has become so great that he measures himself against God and is described as his opponent and equal.

Apart from the designation of Satan as Belial, there are no other names for him to be found in our document, and the cryptic names that Gressmann[110] thinks that he has discovered in it have no real existence. The impetuous spirit and spreader of Lies," רוח מבוהל[111] ומטיף כזב (8,13), or as the parallel (19,25) reads, "he who moves with the wind and is like a storm, drips deceit among men," הולך רוח ושקל סופות ומטיף אדם[112] לכזב, is not Satan but the leader of the opponents. The statement of Gressmann that "a little earlier the spreader of lies was called Belial" is based on a misunderstanding; the words (8,2) "to deliver them to destruction at the hand of Belial" refer to the afflictions of the Jews at the hands of the Greeks (8,11), as was noted above, and have nothing at all to do with the "spreader of lies." Still less is there any occasion for finding Satan in "the dripper, to whom they cry, be ever dripping." הוא מטיף אשר אמר הטף יטיפון.[113] The statement of Gressmann that this person is identical with the one "who ensnares Israel in three sins" is pure phantasy and has absolutely no support in the text itself. In this passage, as in 8,12, their opponents are described as those "who build the wall, but smear it with white-

---

[110] *ZDMG*, Vol. LXVI, 493.

[111] Gressmann, *loc. cit.*, reads מחובל, "corrupt," but there is no basis for this emendation, since an impetuous spirit (*cf.* Eccles. 7:9 אל תבהל ברוחך) is quite appropriate in this place. If, however, we should read מחובל, we should probably have to render it "disturbed" or "mad" as in Job 17:1. *Cf.* above, p. 75, on the idea of sin as madness.

[112] Schechter is right in not taking account of the easy emendation שקר for שקל, for, though Mic. 2:11 reads, הולך רוח ושקר כזב, our document cannot have cited the Prophet's words here, for otherwise the following סופות would be simply unintelligible. When Charles, p. 36, asserts that the original text read, הולך רוח ושקר ומטיף כזב, and ושקר was first corrupted to ושקל and then amplified to ושקל סופות, he not only ignores the peculiarities of our document, the style of which is chiefly characterized by the amplification and rephrasing of biblical verses, but he also forgets the first principle of text criticism, according to which the *lectio difficilior* must be regarded as the original one. We must therefore read וְשָׁקֵל סופות, "is like storms," and compare Test. Judah XXI end, "And they will be false Prophets like stormwinds," which is a parallel to our text in wording and content.

[113] *Cf.* p. 18 on the interpretation of this verse to which we should add that אשר אמר probably refers to Mic. 2:11.

wash, in following idle prating,"[114] as a result of which they are caught
in Belial's net. But that, as Gressmann claims, "the man of scorn"[115]
(1,14) and "the man of lies" (20,15) are none other than Belial, whom
our document imagines as a "devil in human form,"[116] is a wholly
unfounded notion. For even if it were to be granted that in our document Belial, who seduced[117] to sin, is characterized as a "spreader of
lies," it by no means follows that "the man of lies" or "the man of
scorn" is none other than Satan. One need only apply this method[118]
to any rabbinic text to see at once how absurd it is.

In Gen. Rabbah XXXVIII, 7, p. 356 (line 10), the expression
ארכיליסטיס "brigand-chief" is used of Satan, and in this book therefore Satan should equal ארכיליסטיס. But we read in XLVIII, 6, p. 480,
"A brigand-chief, ארכיליסטיס, rebelled against the king. Then the king
said, 'I will give a reward to the man who seizes him.' Then there
arose one who seized him. Then the king said, 'Both of you wait until
morning.' And both were fearfully expectant. One trembled and said,
'What reward will the king give me?' The other trembled and said,
'What judgment will the king pronounce over me?' " If the Midrash
in Gen. Rabbah were extant only in fragments like our document,
a bit of apocalyptic writing might be read into its text, such as: God,
the king, offered a great reward for the capture of Satan, the brigand-
chief etc. Unfortunately the conclusion of this midrashic passage has
been preserved. It read: "Just so anxious will the Jews and the idolators someday be. The Jews will be anxious, for 'Trembling they seek
refuge in God and in His grace at the end of days' (Hos. 3:5), and the
idolaters will be afraid, for it is said (Isa. 33:14), 'In Zion sinners will
tremble.' " The brigand-chief is therefore a quite ordinary mortal, who

[114] Our document interprets צו in Hos. 5:11 as "the babbler" or "crier" (מטיף),
and a very similar interpretation is given in Eliahu Rabbah VIII, 43, ed. Friedmann: ואין צויה אלא כרוז "when the term צו is used in Scripture, it is equivalent to
"cry out."

[115] "The man of lies" in Ps. 140:12 is identified in the Haggadah with the
serpent = Satan; cf. Gen. Rabbah XX, 1, p. 182, which can be adduced as a parallel
to the designation of Satan as a "man of scorn."

[116] Gressmann, by the way, errs in assuming that this conception of Satan as a
false prophet who seduces men into falling away from God, by his lying words is
quite unknown elsewhere, since it is found in the Testament of Job X, where Elihu
very clearly appears as the incarnation of the devil, probably on the basis of an
old legend which identifies him with the false Prophet Balaam; cf. Yer. Sotah V, 20d.
The appearance of Satan in human form is very common in Jewish legend as a
whole; cf. my Legends of the Jews, I, 200, 272 et al.

[117] Cf. above, pp. 175 ff.

[118] In our document 8,17 ראשונים = The Three Patriarchs, but in 1,16 = the early
generations; Gressmann ascribes this to different sources.

is interested in people's *denarii*, and not in their souls! In another passage of this Midrash (LXXVII, 2, p. 911) it is remarked of the man with whom Jacob fought (Gen. 32:25) that he appeared to Jacob as "a brigand-chief," driving camels and sheep before him. This certainly refers to a flesh and blood ארכיליסטיס and not to Satan. Gressmann, however, is not content with referring to Satan all the passages in our document that speak of the "spreader of lies," because Satan is allegedly so described in one passage, but he goes even further and claims that this devil in human form was credited with miracles with which he represented himself as a false Messiah; since, when it is said in 1,15 that he lured the Israelites into the trackless wilderness and there caused the everlasting mountains to be swallowed up, one is reminded of the miracles that Deutero-Isaiah predicted of the messianic age. One really fancies one is in the presence of a *Barnabas* or *Origenes redivivus* when one reads this allegorizing. The words of our document permit no doubt to anyone who can and will see that they are aimed at the activity of "the man of scorn" (whoever he may be) who is breaking down the Law and the customs of the Fathers. "He leads the people into a trackless wilderness" (ויתעם בתוהו לא דרך, a literal quotation from Ps. 107:40). The wilderness is the life of lawlessness; just as in a Baraita (Sanhedrin 97a bot.) the history of the world is divided into three periods: (a) the period of the wilderness, תוהו, from the creation to the revelation of the Torah, (b) the period of Torah, and (c) the Messianic period. In a Haggadic interpretation of the words תהו ובהו at the beginning of the Bible, it is stated (Gen. Rabbah II, 5, p. 18) that "the wilderness" means the (lawless) deeds of sinners. Lawless activity is further described in words taken from Hab. 3:6 as that which attempts "to pull down the high places of the world," that is, to tear down the laws; just as the Tannaim and Amoraim[119] saw in this prophetic utterance an allusion to the contempt for the Torah shown by gentiles, who do not even observe the commandments given to Adam, the so-called seven "Noachic commandments" and of whom it can rightly be said that they pull down "the eternal hills," גבעות עולם. Our document, moreover, leaves us in no doubt as to how it understood these words, for in the following verse the words ולסור מנתיבות צדק correspond to בתוהו לא דרך, while להשח גבעות עולם is a parallel to ולסיע גבול אשר גבלו ראשונים. The "paths of righteousness" are, of course, only a somewhat different expression

---

[119] *Cf.* Bava Qamma 38a; this interpretation, however, is already presupposed in the tannaite sources Mekilta, Baḥodesh I, p. 206; V, p. 221; Sifre Deut. 311, p. 352; Midr. Tann., pp. 190, 211.; *cf.* also Megillah 28b, where the parallel to גבעות עולם, namely הליכות עולם, is explained as "The Halakoth."

for the biblical נתיב מצותיך, "the path of Thy commandments"
(Ps. 119:35), and "the removing of the boundaries that the ancients
fixed" is in our document, as in apocryphal and rabbinic literature
and in Philo, a metaphor for the neglect of traditional customs.

We may therefore declare without qualification that our document
does not know of any "devil represented as a human being,"[120] much
less of such a devil as an anti-Messiah. The demonology of the document contains nothing that could not perfectly well have emanated
from a pharisaic source. Belial is essentially the same figure as that
which is known to us from rabbinic literature by the name of Satan
or יצר הרע,[121] "the evil impulse."

*

*   *

"And on the day when Man undertakes to turn to the Torah of
Moses, on that same day 'the persecuting angel' departs from him."
These words, although they probably do not belong to the original
document,[122] admirably characterize its point of view. "Whenever the
words of the Torah," says a midrash,[123] "find the heart open to receive
them, they move into it and remain there, so that the evil impulse,
יצר הרע, has no power over it." The only defense against Belial is (15,7)
"the firm resolve to turn to the Torah of Moses with heart and soul."
It is for this reason that admission to the sect consists of the "Censor"
imposing upon the newly admitted member an oath to observe the
Torah of Moses in accordance with the teachings of the sect.[124] In
view of the strict legalistic character of this sect the fact that the
Torah of Moses, that is the Law, is the basis of its faith is just what
one would expect. It is significant for the standpoint of our document
that it derives Halakot only from the legal parts of the Pentateuch.
The prohibition of polygamy is motivated by the legal prescriptions in

[120] Even if Gressmann were right in believing that Belial was meant by "the
man of lies" and similar terms, there would still be no warrant for taking metaphorical expressions literally.

[121] It is interesting to note that in the rabbinic sources יה'ר means Satan as well
as sensual desire (cf. for example, Soṭah 8a; Yerushalmi Qiddushin IV, 66c); similarly
in our document, in 1,16, יצר אשמה is used in the meaning of sensual desire.

[122] Cf. p. 176. The expression לשוב אל תורת משה occurs also in IV Esdras V, 133,
"qui conversionem faciunt in legem ejus." Gunkel's rendering, "die nach seinem
Gesetze wandeln," is therefore wrong. Cf. also Simonsen in the Lewy Festschrift,
p. 272.

[123] Avoth de-R. Natan XIII, 30, ed. Schechter.

[124] Cf. 15,10, "And no one shall impart the laws (of the sect) to him until he
has appeared before the Censor, etc."

Deut. 17:17,[125] whereas the passages in Gen. 1:27 and 7:9 are mentioned only as a "support," אסמכתא, for which reason they are not cited with the formula כתוב or אמר. This is in accord with the rule that prevails in the Talmud[126] אין למדים דבר קודם למתן תורה, "only the laws revealed to Moses are binding, but not the practice of the earlier righteous men."[127] Herein the affinity of our document with the point of view of the Rabbis is particularly evident: the Book of Jubilees, on the other hand, traces the bulk of the Law back to the pre-Mosaic generations, and even (Jubilees XXVIII, 6) goes so far as, on the basis of Laban's statement in Gen. 29:26, to lay down a law, forbidding the marrying off of a younger daughter before an older one! Other Halakoth for which our document invokes the authority of the Pentateuch are: the prohibition of uncle-niece marriages, which is derived from Lev. 20:19 by the hermeneutic rule of הקש (5,8), which the Rabbis employ frequently;[128] the requirement of תוספת שבת, an "extension of the Sabbath" (10,16), which, in agreement with the Rabbis,[129] is stated to be implicit in Deut. 5:12; and finally the prohibition against offering on the Sabbath, apart from the daily burnt offering of the community, anything but the special Sabbath burnt offering of the community (11,18),[130] the midrashic deducing of which from Lev. 23:38 is of a piece with rabbinic exegesis.[131]

---

[125] In the view of the sect, this biblical passage means that even the king is forbidden to marry several women, let alone commoners; we have therefore here a קל וחומר.

[126] Yerushalmi Moed Qatan III, 82c; cf. also Mishnah Ḥullin VII, 6, where this principle is already presupposed. R. H. Chajes discusses this principle at length in his work תורת נביאים 29c.

[127] In accordance with this postulate, the Yerushalmi, ibid., asserts that the halakic seven days' mourning cannot be derived from the seven days' mourning for Jacob (Gen. 50:10); the LXX to latter passage renders אבל שבעת ימים by τὸ πένθος.

[128] Cf. above, pp. 19, 153 ff.

[129] Cf. p. 56. R. Moses ha-Darshan writes שמור ... לעשות שמירה על שמירתו, which agrees almost verbally with the derash in our document; cf. A. Epstein, Moses ha-Darschan, Vienna 1891, p. 49. Cf. also Mek. de-Rabbi Simeon, ed., Hoff. p. 161: ושמרו שצריך להוסיף מחול על הקדש ... מלפניו ומלאחריו. Regarding the duration of this "extension," the responsa of R. Ḥayyim Or Zarua, No. 185, cite a passage in the Yerushalmi — wanting in the printed text! — according to which it is two hours˙ According to our understanding of 10,15 (see above, ad loc.), our document requires 108 minutes. Cf. further Moed Qatan 5a.

[130] [The German edition has only das Verbot, irgend ein anderes als das tägliche Gemeindeopfer am Sabbath darzubringen, which is clearly a slip. Instead of rendering it faithfully, the wording in the text accords with the author's actual, and obviously correct, understanding of the cited passage 11,18; see his observations on it above, p. 69.]

[131] Cf. above ad loc.

But while the actual Torah[132] is for our document only the Pentateuch, there can be no question but the Prophets and the Hagiographa
were included in the sect's canon; and, as has already been pointed out
on p. 161, its opponents — the Sadducees — are reproached with
despising the words of the Prophets.[133] Yet the source of the Law is
for it exclusively the Pentateuch and does not include the Prophets.
The view which prevails in our document and among the Rabbis is
that the Law was revealed solely through Moses, so that the laws
mentioned in the Prophets are not to be understood as newly revealed.
It was merely that the prophets, who were of course at the same time
outstanding doctors of Law, often cited the Mosaic laws according to
the authoritative interpretation that was known to them from tradition. Hence on the one hand there is the principle[134] דברי תורה מדברי
קבלה לא ילפינן, "Passages in Qabbalah (the Prophets and the Hagiographa) cannot serve as sources for laws," and on the other hand the
authority of prophets is frequently invoked for Halakoth, on the
assumption that their writings embody authoritative interpretations of
Mosaic laws.[135] Further, just as the great doctors of Law have authority to make ordinances as need arises, so, according to the Rabbis,
the prophets, as the empowered leaders and teachers of their times,
made various ordinances[136] which are binding as "teaching of the
fathers" though not as "Law." Accordingly the assertion, frequently
encountered among Christian scholars, that rabbinic Judaism does not
esteem the Prophets and the Hagiographa so highly as the Pentateuch
because it does not recognize them as a source of law, contains a
twofold error. In the first place, we have seen that the Pentateuch
itself is not a source of law throughout; yet no-one will seriously claim

---

[132] We find תורה at 5,2; 7,8; 7,15; 7,18 and 16,8 and תורת משה at 15,2; 15,12;
16,2 and 16,5; and if 7,15 is compared with 7,18 it becomes apparent that תורה =
ת' משה. Torah also means the Pentateuch in rabbinic literature; cf. Blau, Zur Einleitung, pp. 40 ff.

[133] The expression בזה דבריהם (7,18) is strongly reminiscent of the liturgical
formula בחר ... בדבריהם in the benediction preceding the reading from the Prophets.

[134] Copious material on the subject is furnished by R. H. Chajes, op. cit., under
the heading of תורת נביאים או דברי קבלה. The conclusions arrived at there are right
in the main, though they need to be corrected in detail. — It may be remarked
that the rule דברי תורה וכו' which is cited in the text is not to be found either in
tannaitic sources or in the Yerushalmi and doubtless represents a rule of the
Babylonian Amoraim, though the idea on which it is based certainly did not
originate with them; cf. e. g. Yerushalmi Yevamoth II, 4a = Gen. Rabbah VII, ed.
Theodor, p. 52.

[135] Bava Qamma 2b; cf. the preceding note and Taanith 9a.

[136] Such ordinances are ascribed in the talmudic literature to Joshua, Boaz,
Samuel, David, Solomon, "the old Prophets," or "the Prophets"; they are listed
and discussed in detail in Bloch, שערי תורת התקנות, Vol. I.

that the First Book of Moses was less sacred to the Rabbis than the Second or the Third. And in the second place, the Rabbis take the view that the Prophets were assigned a different task from Moses; the latter is first and foremost the proclaimer of the Law; while the former are preachers who exhort the people to observe the selfsame Law, which they seek to explain and bring home to them but to which they add nothing and from which they would not think of taking anything away. If such a thing as a conflict between Law and Prophecy exists, the Rabbis at any rate were certainly not aware of it. On the contrary, the Prophets were in their estimation the most authoritative expounders of the Law. It is therefore a completely baseless assertion that the Rabbis do not recognize the Prophets as legal authorities; even a hasty glance at the Mishnah, which collection of laws contains no fewer than 145 quotations[137] from the extra-pentateuchal books of the Bible, will suffice to convince one of the baselessness of that assertion. For good measure, however, here are a few important Halakoth which the Mishnah deduces from the Prophets and the Hagiographa.[138]

Shabbath V, 9. Rabbi Akiva said: How do we know that an idol renders a person who carries it unclean? Because it says (Isa. 30:22), "You will treat . . . your graven images and . . . your molten images as unclean . . . like a menstruating woman (דוה)." Hence an idol renders anyone who carries it unclean, just as a menstruating woman does.

Sheqalim I, 5 (anonymous Mishnah): If pagans or Samaritans wish to contribute the half-shekel to the Temple, it is not accepted from them, because it says clearly in Ezra 2:3, "It is not proper for you (the enemies of Judah and Benjamin) to build a temple for our God with us."

Gittin IV, 5; Eduyyoth I, 13 (the school of Shammai): A man who is half slave and half freeman[139] cannot marry a bondwoman because

---

[137] That is, about half the number of quotations from the Pentateuch, which is 308. Cf. the compilation of quotations from the Bible in Aicher, *Das Alte Testament in der Mischna*, Freiburg 1906, and Pinner, *Talmud Babli, Traktat Berachot*, Berlin 1842.

[138] The Talmudic age knows no distinction between the second and the third division of the canon; cf. Blau, *Zur Einleitung, loc. cit.*, and Malter, *JQR* NS I, p. 482. But it may be added that it was not Maimonides who coined the term מדבר ברוה״ק for the Hagiographa, inasmuch as R. Menaḥem b. Solomon already employs it in his Bible commentary שכל טוב, II, p. 321.

[139] Such half slaves are mentioned frequently in Talmudic literature. It was certainly quite a common thing for a slave to be owned in partnership by two or more persons, and if one of them enfranchised the slave he forthwith acquired the status of a partly free person. When Holtzmann, *Tosephta Trakt. Berakot*, p. 73, regards the half slave as a creation of rabbinic casuistry, he betrays a lack of familiarity with the realia.

he is half free or a freewoman because he is half slave. Yet the world was created for men to procreate in; for it says (Isa. 45:18), "He did not create it as a waste but formed it for habitation." Accordingly the master of this half-slave is compelled to manumit him but is given a note for half his value.

Soṭah IX, 9. With immorality on the increase, Rabban Joḥanan ben Zakkai abolished the ordeal of the water of jealousy on the basis of the prophetic words (Hos. 4:14) "I will not punish your daughters for being unchaste, nor your daughters-in-law for committing adultery."

Menaḥoth XIII, 10. Priests who have served in the Temple of Onias may not perform the service in the Temple of Jerusalem; for it says (II Kings 23:9), "However, the priests of the high places did not offer at the Lord's altar in Jerusalem."

Yadayim IV, 4. Judah, an Ammonite proselyte, inquired at the House of Study (in Javneh) whether it was permissible for him to marry a Jewess. Rabban Gamaliel said, "You may not; for Scripture says, 'An Ammonite or a Moabite shall not be admitted to the community of the Lord.' " But Rabbi Joshua countered: "Are there any Ammonites and Moabites today? Sennacherib, the king of Assyria, mixed all the nations up, as it is written (Isa. 10:13), 'I remove the borders of peoples.' "

As from the Mishnah, many instances of laws being deduced from non-pentateuchal books of the Bible can be cited from the other Tannaitic collections, the Tosefta and the Tannaitic Midrashim; but the foregoing data ought to suffice.

It is questionable whether our document takes the same position as the Rabbis in this matter, but it is certain that it does not exhibit a higher regard than they for the non-pentateuchal writings as sources of Halakah. As has already been observed, the references in the legal portion of our document to prophetic texts have all the character of props, אסמכתא. To be sure, the Halakah of our document rests essentially upon tradition rather than Midrash, so that the fact that the authority of the Prophets is not invoked is not remarkable. Nevertheless, two circumstances make it probable that our sect made far less use of the Prophets as sources of Halakah than the Rabbis. Both forbid carrying on the Sabbath. But whereas the Talmuds[140] explicitly

---

[140] Yer. Shabbath I, 2b; Bavli Horayoth 4a and Yom Tov 12a; cf. my Geonica I, p. 81. The Rabbis of course regard the words of the Prophet in the light not of a new revelation but merely of an authoritative interpretation of the מלאכה that is prohibited in the Pentateuch as including the act of carrying.

base the prohibition upon Jer. 17:21, our document (11,7) maintains a complete silence about the source. Further, the Tannaim[141] frequently cite the pious judges and kings as authorities for the correct interpretation of the Law, whereas our document (5,2) emphasizes that even pious David[142] was ignorant of the Law, the Torah having fallen into oblivion after the death of Joshua and only having been rediscovered in the reign of Josiah. But that is tantamount to declaring that none of the Prophetic writings that antedate the reign of Josiah can be used as a source of law. The passage against David even gives the impression of being directed against the tannaitic inference[143] from II Sam. 12:8 that a king may take eighteen wives. That is precisely why our document makes the point that when it comes to Law, neither David nor his Prophet Nathan is to be treated as an authority.[144] Accordingly, the prophetic passages cited in our document in connection with legal matters merely illustrate the ethical content of the Law. That the Prophets are the competent teachers of religion and ethics is, in the view of our document too, not to be questioned.

The prohibition of vengeances (Lev. 19:18) is illustrated by a concrete case, 9,2; but the writer adds that this pentateuchal law imposes no duties toward sinners, since God himself is said by the Prophet Nahum (1:2) to wreak vengeance upon his adversaries and to lay up wrath for his foes. The words of the Prophet are not cited as source of a Halakah but are quoted as a commentary to the penta-

---

[141] Cf., e. g., Mishnah Berakhoth, end; Sheqalim VI, 6; cf. also above, p. 184, n. 135. The few halakic derashoth of Shammai include one on II Sam. 12:9. Cf. Qiddushin 43a and Bacher, Monatsschrift LII, pp. 708 ff.

[142] As was demonstrated on p. 22; the view that our document is anti-Davidic is untenable. Rather, David is adduced as an illustration of the fact that prior to "the finding of the Torah" even the God-fearing were not versed in the Law. Incidentally, the Tannaim (Sifre Numbers 46, p. 51) make a similar reproach against David; cf. also Sotah 35a: "David came to grief because he forgot a law which even school children know."

[143] Cf. Sanhedrin II, 4 and the derivation of this Halakah from Nathan's words in Bavli Sanhedrin 21a. Cf. above, p. 184, n. 136.

[144] Since this Prophet says plainly "and if it (the wives) was not enough, I would have given you thus and thus more," our document must assume ignorance of the Law, which forbids polygamy, not only in David but also in Nathan. It follows that no downgrading of David is intended but on the contrary, as was explained in detail above, David is singled out as a model pious man in the age before the finding of the Law. How our document reconciled the above utterance of Nathan, which the Bible represents as a revelation by God, with its view of the illicitness of polygamy, cannot be said for sure. Presumably it made the words כהנה וכהנה refer not to the נשי that are mentioned a little before (so the Talmud, Sanhedrin 21a) but to בית, which likewise occurs in this verse.

teuchal prohibition. It may be remarked in passing that rabbinic literature offers an almost verbal parallel. According to Gen. Rabbah LV, 3, p. 586,[145] Israel said to God, "You have written in Your Torah (Lev. 19:18), 'You must not take revenge of or lay up wrath for those of your own people,' but You Yourself are vengeful and rancorous, as it says (Nah. 1:2) 'He is vengeful and prone to anger; he wreaks vengeance upon his adversaries and lays up wrath for his foes.'"[146] God's reply was, "What I have written in the Torah is 'You must not take revenge of or lay up wrath for those of your own people,' and I am only vengeful and rancorous toward the heathen." For the ungodly heathen[147] our document substitutes "the sinners,"[148] which is very characteristic of its bigotry. The sinner forfeits the right to God's love; consequently one owes him no indulgence, and the prohibition of vengeance does not apply to revenge upon him.

Again, when, with a reference to Prov. 15:8, the sending of offerings to the altar with an unclean man is forbidden (11,18–19), it is not a case of basing a Halakah on the verse in question. As was shown on p. 70, the members of the sect, who kept away from the Jerusalem Temple because the laws of purity were in their view not properly observed there, are enjoined in this passage to beware of even having others represent them in the Temple,[149] and the prohibition is reinforced with the quotation from Prov. 15:8, "The sacrifice of the wicked is abhorrent to the Lord, but the prayer of the upright is his

---

[145] Cf. also Koheleth Rabbah to 8:4; Avodah Zarah 4a; Eliahu Rabbah VII, 40.

[146] For the Tetragrammaton of the Masoretic Text, Gen. Rabbah reads both times הוא [This reading is found in the printed editions only. The Yemenite ms. used by Theodor is a copy of the ed. Venice, see Albeck's Introduction, pp. 115–116. — S. L.] from which it would appear that הוא in our document is not (cf. p. 40) a deliberate alteration but a variant reading.

[147] Cf. also Mekilta Baḥodesh VI, p. 226: I am a zealous God for punishing idolatry, but otherwise I am gracious and merciful; further, Mekilta de-R. Simeon [ed. Hoffmann] 105; ed. Epstein-Melamed, p. 147. For פלוספוס in Mekilta de-R. Ishmael, M. de-R. Simeon has אנריפס סבא, who is doubtless identical with the אנ' ההגמון in Midrash Tannaim 215. סבא is probably corrupt for שר צבא.

[148] Charles writes: "The implication here is, that no consideration is due to an enemy." But even if it did not make our document contradict Prov. 25:21, it would surely be absurd to attribute to it the view that the Bible forbade vengefulness only toward "friends." The enemies of God are of course the ungodly heathen and the sinners, to whom man too owes no indulgence. According to a statement in the Talmud, Pesaḥim 113b, "your enemy" in Exod. 23:4 means a sinner, since one must love every Jew.

[149] Hence the expression להרשותו, which is borrowed from legal terminology (הרשה, 'to empower').

delight."[150] The "wicked" are equated with such as do not belong to the sect, and "their" sacrifice with offerings sent through them, and the moral is drawn that it is better for the sectarian to limit his worship to prayer. The Mishnah, like the other Tannaitic collections (to say nothing of the Amoraim), very frequently quote texts from the Prophets and the Hagiographa for the purpose of stressing the religious or ethical content of a Halakah. Thus Mishnah Peah VII, 3 teaches: He who places a basket under a vine to catch any grapes that may fall off, which ought to be left to the poor (Lev. 19:10), robs the poor; and of him Scripture (Prov. 22:28; 23:10) says, "Do not remove the border of the needy."[151] The quoted verse is no more made the basis of a Halakah here than in the above passage of our document; it is cited only as an apt formulation of the ethical significance of a Halakah.

Similarly, as was demonstrated above on 16,14, the latter passage does not derive a Halakah from Mic. 7:2 but, in typical Midrashic fashion, applies the words of the Prophet opprobriously to people who only satisfy the letter of the Law without caring about its spirit, giving as an example of such persons one who seeks to evade the obligation placed upon him by Deut. 23:26.

In view of the three cited passages, it is most improbable that the words אשר אמר לא תושיעך ידך לך in 9,9 constitute a reference to I Sam. 25:26; for in that case a Halakah would actually be derived from a text in the Prophets, a thing unexampled anywhere else in the document. Far more probably, we have here a quotation from the sect's

---

[150] For 'but the prayer of the upright is his delight' (ותפלת ישרים רצונו) the document has 'but the prayer of the righteous is like a pleasing offering' (ותפלת צדיקים כמנחת רצון); which, however, is hardly due to confusion with 15:29, as one might suppose. צדיקים for ישרים is also found in Joseph ben Naḥmias's commentary to the passage and is therefore a variant, while כמנחת רצון is probably a Haggadic interpretation of רצונו. In the language of Midrash our passage would read רצונו זו מנחה. Since רצון occurs very frequently with reference to offerings, it is not strange that רצונו in our verse should, in the Haggadic manner, be considered equivalent to כמנחת רצון.

[151] The Rabbis read — or interpreted? — עוֹלָם for עולם; for further details, see Geiger, קבוצת מאמרים, ed. Poznański, 54; Barth, *Jahrb. d. jüd.-lit. Gesellschaft* VII, 137; and my observations in the Addenda to Geiger, p. 384. To the quotations from medieval commentators adduced by me should be added Roqeaḥ in Grossberg, חצי מנשה, p. 43, who is doubtless the source of פענח רזא; the emendation proposed by me, *loc. cit.*, is confirmed by Roqeaḥ.

[152] Cf. above, pp. 49 f. on this Mishnah of the sect. The formula of quotation אשר אמר does not, of course, prove that that work enjoyed canonical standing; see further below.

Mishnah, ספר ההגו,[152] where a certain Halakah in question, which is also found in rabbinic literature, was formulated as follows: "Your own hand must not afford you redress," לא תושיעך ידך לך. This law is elucidated in our document, which explains that only a court of law has authority to require an oath.[153] This hypothesis — which would otherwise be difficult to account for — explains the divergence of the wording of the phrase in our document from that in the passage in Samuel: the document's source, ספר ההגו, did not quote the verse but adapted a phrase from it in formulating its prohibition against taking the law into one's own hands. Our exegesis also obviates another difficulty. If it were a case of basing a Halakah on I Sam. 25:26, we should have the remarkable phenomenon of David and Nathan being stigmatized as ignorant of the Law,[154] but the words of Abigail — who moreover, just like David, manifested her ignorance of the Law, not to say her defiance of it, by her polygynous marriage — carrying such weight as to be made the source of a Halakah.

The above discussion will surely suffice to place in its proper light the assertion of Charles — Introduction 9 and 11 — about the difference between "apocalyptic" and "legalistic" Pharisaism in the evaluation of the Prophets. An essential difference between our sect and rabbinic Pharisaism, quotes Charles, is that the Rabbis almost never base Halakoth upon the Prophets because they did not hold them in high esteem, whereas in our document the Pentateuch and the remaining parts of the Bible are of equal rank and accordingly Halakic conclusions[155] are also based upon the extra-pentateuchal writings. One really does not know whether to wonder more at the ignorance of rabbinic Literature or at the grotesque misjudgment of our document that are reflected in these words. It is not without interest for the method that is usual in the treatment of Jewish theology in many circles, to observe how Charles arrives at such a result. He proceeds in a purely mechanical fashion, assembling all the biblical passages in our document that are expressly designated as quotations,[156] and

---

[153] *Cf.* on this above, p. 121.

[154] See above, pp. 22 and 187.

[155] As an example of a Halakah based on the Prophets, Charles cites the prohibition of carrying on the Sabbath, though it is just the rabbinical work, not our sectarian work, which cites Jeremiah 17 as a source for it. And that is offered as proof of the higher valuation placed upon the Prophets by our sect! See above, pp. 186–187 for the true state of affairs.

[156] The introductory formulae are כמה שנאמר=כאשר אמר in Tannaitic literature (Sotah VIII, 1; Sifre D. 301) and כאשר כתוב or ככתוב (written כ'כ), the last form being of frequent occurrence in rabbinic literature. The understood subject of אמר is probably הכתוב, as may be inferred from the rabbinic phrase אמר הכתוב and

discovering that the Pentateuch is cited ten times, the Prophets eleven times, and the Hagiographa once, and concludes: obviously, for our sect the Prophets have equal authority with the Pentateuch. Which goes to show that statistics may prove as fatal to a theologian as theology to a statistician. By this statistical method it can be proved with equal cogency that the redactor of the Mishnah Tractate of Avoth was no protagonist of legalistic Pharisaism, inasmuch as it contains twenty-two quotations from the extrapentateuchal parts of the Bible against only six from the Pentateuch. For that matter, the author of the Mishnah Order of Moed — about a seventh of the total volume of the Mishnah — cannot have esteemed the Pentateuch very highly, considering that only fifteen[157] passages from the Pentateuch are cited in it as against twenty-seven from other books of the Bible. The Pharisees of the Mishnah must have rated the first Book of Moses particularly low, since it is cited in the Mishnah much less frequently than, for example, Psalms or Isaiah.[158] Even more certainly must the post-Mishnaic tannaitic compilations have been authored by men who represented the apocalyptic branch of Pharisaism. Surely, Leviticus would not have been neglected by "genuine" Pharisees in favor of Isaiah, as it is, for example, in the Mekilta, which offers 176 quotations from Isaiah as against a mere 111 from Leviticus.[159] The absurdity of such statistical wisdom is so evident that we may spare ourselves the effort of going into it any further. There is not a trace of a difference, in rabbinic literature, in the degrees of reverence for the Laws and

---

הכתוב אומר; though it might conceivably be אל 'God' or the name of the author of the book quoted from, since א', משה אמר אל, and אמר ישעיה also occur in our document. In rabbinic literature אמר הקב'ה is found employed by Tannaim and רוה'ק 'א, שכינה 'א by Amoraim. The prefacing of משה 'א to a Pentateuch quotation is also rabbinic (Sifre D. 1; Yoma 69b; Yevamoth 49b), but no "legal" passage is cited in this way. In such cases the Babylonian Talmud says רחמנא 'א, "the Merciful One says." For this reason, the very formula משה אמר marks the passage 5,8, which is suspicious on more than one count (see above, p. 158), as unusual. The formula ביד יחזקאל, זכריה corresponds to על ידי in rabbinic literature; cf. Sheqalim I, 5; Tamid III, 7; Middoth IV, 2; Avoth VI, 6, while כתוב בדברי has a parallel in the liturgical formula ובדברי קדשך כתוב לאמר. Unknown to rabbinic literature is the expression ואשר אמר introducing a new section (8,14; 9,2), which is to be rendered 'and as regards the scriptural words . . .' Charles in his Introduction has collected the formulas of citation but without giving the rabbinical parallels, though Bacher's *Terminologie* would have furnished him with the necessary data. The parallels from the New Testament are not selected with care; καθὼς γέγραπται can render ככתוב just as well as כאשר כתוב.

[157] More exactly 13, since Yoma III, 8; IV, 2 and VI, 3 quote the same verse.

[158] Cf. the index in Aicher, *op. cit.*

[159] Cf. the index of passages in Friedmann's edition of the Mekilta.

for the Prophets. The Mishnah, as a collection of laws which contains hardly one per cent of Haggadah, naturally quotes the Pentateuch, and particularly the legal portions of it, much more frequently than the parenetic and historical books of the Bible. But as was pointed out on p. 185 the Mishnah nevertheless bases not a few Halakoth on extra-pentateuchal writings of the Bible. In the Tosefta, which was redacted not long after the Mishnah but which, although essentially a Halakic compilation, contains more Haggadah and Halakic Midrash than the Mishnah, the ratio of extra-pentateuchal to pentateuchal quotations is about 13 to 16;[160] and in the Mekilta, which was composed at about the same time as the Tosefta but contains more Haggadah than Halakah, the non-pentateuchal quotations far outnumber the penta-teuchal.[161] In the exclusively Haggadic Midrashim the relationship between the two groups of quotations is the very opposite of what it is in the Mishnah; for example there is roughly one quotation from the Pentateuch for every three from the other parts of the Bible in Pesiqta Rabbati and Tanna de-Be Eliahu Rabbah.[162]

The document we have been studying, which contains more Hag-gadah than Halakah and almost no Halakic Midrash, naturally quotes from non-Pentateuch books of the Bible more often than from the Pentateuch; but that is no more indicative here of a preference for the Prophets to the Pentateuch in contrast to the attitude of the Mishnah than it is in the Mekilta. It is questionable whether the document agrees with the Rabbis in recognizing the Prophets and the Hagiographa as sources of law;[163] what is not questionable is that rabbinic literature has no less regard for the Prophets than our document.

Very problematic is also the inclusion of various pseudepigrapha like the Testament of Levi[164] and the Words of Jeremiah to Baruch

---

[160] See the index in Zuckermandel's edition. [The German text has the ratio reversed, by a slip of the pen.]

[161] See the index at the end of Friedmann's edition of the Mekilta.

[162] See the indices of biblical quotations in Friedmann's edition of the midrashim.

[163] See above, pp. 185–186.

[164] A quotation from a work of this character occurs in 4,15, but it is not to be found either in the Greek or in the Aramaic text of the extant Testament of Levi, which makes it very doubtful that our document knew the Testaments of the XII Patriarchs. It would seem, rather, that the latter book is a parenetic re-working of an older collection of legends, and that the older collection is what our author had before him. Levi appears as a Prophet not only in the Testaments of the XII Patriarchs but also in the Legend of Asenath and in the Midrash, so that our author probably learned of this role of Levi from a source independent of the Testaments. If one discounts the interpolation in 16,3, a direct use of the Book of Jubilees by our author also becomes very problematic.

and the Words of Elisha to Gehazi.[165] It is a mistake to assume that a common method of citing is a sign of equality of rank among sources. The pseudepigrapha in question are indeed quoted from with the introductory formula אמר, and were doubtless held in high regard by our sect. But there is no warrant for concluding that they were regarded as canonical or even semi-canonical. On the same evidence, one would have to conclude that the author of the Mishnah accorded canonical status to the Fast Scroll or to the Hillelites' collection of Halakoth.[166] One might even go a step further and declare for a fact that Maimonides included the Prayer Book among the canonical works because he quotes a passage from it with the very citation formula שנאמר with which he everywhere else, in accordance with mishnaic and talmudic usage, introduces quotations from the Bible.[167] So long as the assertion that our sect's canon of Scriptures diverged from that of the Pharisees rests upon no stronger proof than a single quotation from a Testament of Levi,[168] one can only vigorously dissent from it.[169]

---

[165] Gressmann, *ZDMG*, LXVI, 495, discovers such a work, attributed to the joint authorship of Jeremiah and Elisha, referred to in our document 8,20. He cites as a parallel for such a joint attribution Judg. 5:1, which states that the Song of Deborah was sung by Deborah and Barak. He has, however, overlooked a trifling difference between the two cases. Deborah and Barak were contemporaries and colleagues, so that there is nothing remarkable about the statement in Judg. 5:1. But the assumption that two men who lived a couple of centuries apart should have been made joint authors of a work is so grotesque as to be unacceptable except as a joke. In any case, *cf.* my observations on the passage, in the light of which it is probable that 8,20 refers to a passage in the Apocalypse of Baruch. A pseudepigraphon attributed to Elisha is not otherwise known, but that is no reason for assuming that none ever existed.

[166] *Cf.* Taanith II, 8 הכתוב במג' תע'; Ḥagigah I, 5, where first the Hillelite Halakah I, 2 and then the scriptural text Deut. 16:17 are cited as נאמר. The reading אמרו in Lowe's edition is a later correction.

[167] *Yad*, Mattenoth Aniyyim X, 3: שנאמר שועת עניים וכו', where the quotation is from the prayer *Nishmath* (Sephardic version!). The term without any statement of source presupposes the reader's acquaintance with the source. The phrase אמר עליהם לוי בן יעקב, on the other hand, does not dispense with an indication of the source, since it does name the author. Medieval authors similarly refer to profane source with such formulae as אמר אפלטון, אמר אריסטו, etc. It is well known that verses from Ben Sira are introduced by the words דכתיב, שנאמר (Zunz, *Gottesdienstliche Vorträge* 2, p. 107; *cf.* p. 402), which however, does not, in my opinion, prove anything for the canonical dignity of that work. If quotations from Homer occurred in the Talmud, they would in all probability be cited with the formula אמר המירס or דכתיב בספר המירס. See also Sifre Numbers 42.

[168] The reference to the pseudepigraphon "the Words of Jeremiah etc." (8,20) probably originated with a reader, not with the author of our document.

[169] There is as little warrant for attributing to the author of the Epistle of Jude a canon which included the Book of Enoch merely because he cites that pseudepigraphon as the prophecy of Enoch.

A difficult question, on the other hand, is that of the nature of the Bible text of our document, inasmuch as the divergences from the Masoretic Text are so numerous even in direct quotations[170] from the Bible that copyists cannot very well be held responsible for all of them, though it must be admitted that they are not entirely free from blame for some of them.[171] It will therefore be profitable to subject the relation between the Masoretic Text and our document to a fairly close examination, in order to get an accurate idea of these divergences.

I) 3,21: ‏הכהנים והלוים ובני צדוק... מעליהם יגישו לי חלב ודם‎. MT, ‏והכהנים הלוים בני צדוק... מעלי המה... ועמדו לפני להקריב‎ :44:15 Ezek. ‏לי חלב ודם נאם אד' י"י‎.

Our document's interpretation of these words of Ezekiel,[172] takes the particle ‏ו‎ which is prefixed to ‏הלוים‎ and to ‏בני צדוק‎ into account, since, unlike MT, it finds three classes of men named in this verse. The possibility, however, cannot be entirely precluded that it was just the interpretation that gave rise to the divergence from MT; in no case did the sect alter its Bible because of the interpretation, but our document may have quoted it in accordance with the sense that this Midrash reads into it because it was going to quote the Midrash. In any case, ‏מעליהם‎[173] is simply due to the negligence of a copyist, the sect's Bible having the reading ‏מעלי הם‎ MT = ‏מעלי המה‎. A copyist is perhaps also responsible for ‏יגישו‎ for ‏להקריב‎; the author may have cited only the beginning and the end of the verse,[174] a copyist partly restoring the missing part and probably introducing ‏יגישו‎ from the preceding verse.

---

[170] I. e. such as are introduced by the usual terms ‏אמר, כתוב‎, and others. Indirect quotations, i. e. biblical phrases and clauses which are not qualified as quotations, prove nothing for the Bible text of the author; inasmuch as the biblical wording was often deliberately varied, either for the purpose of displaying the writer's own stylistic virtuosity or because the special application made a slight modification necessary. Thus at 1,15 (see above *ad loc.*), ‏גבעות‎, "hills," has been changed to ‏גבהות‎, "loftiness," because loftiness is a more suitable designation of the Law, and similarly at 1,16 (see *ad loc.*) ‏הסיע‎ is a deliberate alteration of ‏הסיג‎. The like phenomenon may be observed in rabbinic literature, as also even in the oldest portions of the liturgy; cf., e. g., the phrase cited above (p. 193, n. 167) from the prayer *Nishmath*, namely ‏שועת עניים‎, for which Job 34:28 has ‏וצעקת עניים ישמע‎. In the Talmud, even substantially altered verses from the Bible are introduced by the usual formulae; see ‏הליכות עולם‎, no. 101, and Naḥmias, Commentary to Avoth, p. 71b.

[171] See below for such mistakes. An interesting mutilation of a Bible verse is ‏אשר תשפך וכו'‎, 8,3; for which B 19,16 has the correct reading.

[172] *Cf.* above, *ad loc.*

[173] [Rabin reads ‏מעלי הם‎ in the manuscript.]

[174] Such abridged quotations are not rare in rabbinic literature; see above, n. 170.

II) 4,14: פחד ופחת ופח agrees perfectly with MT.

III) 4,20: אשר אמר הטף יטיפון is not a quotation but, as was observed *ad loc.*, an ironic allusion to אל תטיפו יטיפון (Mic. 2:6). That being so, the form הטף in contrast to תטיפו in the Bible passage alluded to is in no way out of order.

IV) 5,2: לא ירבה לו נשים as against MT (Deut. 17:17) ולא ירבה לו נשים. Most likely our author had ולא in his Deuteronomy text, and the absence of the ו in our quotation is due either to the carelessness of a copyist or to the author's desire to strengthen the case for his interpretation of the verse. For since לא ירבה לו סוסים in the preceding verse cannot very well mean that the king must not acquire more than one horse, and ולא would suggest very strongly that that ought to be the implication of לא ירבה in this case if it is in the other, our author might very well have omitted the ו in order to negate the analogy in advance.

V) 5,8: ומשה אמר אל אחות אמך לא תקרב שאר אמך היא. MT (Lev. 18:13): ערות אחות אמך לא תגלה כי שאר אמך היא. Actually, the expression לא תקרב is not found at all in connection with prohibited degrees of kinship except [in the general heading Lev. 18:6 and] in the case of an aunt [by marriage] (Lev. 18:14).[175] However, the wording of our document in the very next line[176] ואם תגלה בת האח את ערות וכו', shows very clearly that its author's reading in Lev. 18:13 agreed with that of MT. His wording in 5,8 is therefore not an exact quotation but a paraphrase.

VI) 6,13: מי בכם יסגיר דלתו ולא תאירו מזבחי חנם. MT (Mal. 1:10): מי גם בכם ויסגר דלתים וגו'. In the orthography[177] of our document, דלתו[178] probably stands for דלתים; but the absence of גם is a true variant. In Ezra 1:3, MT also reads מי בכם without גם.

VII) 7,11–12: אשר אמר יבוא עליך ועל עמך ועל בית אביך ימים אשר באו מיום יביא יהוה עליך ... אשר לא באו למיום. MT (Isa. 7:17): סור אפרים מעל יהודה וגו'. However, Schechter rightly observes that יבי is to be read in our document instead of יבוא and that the omission of לא before באו can

---

[175] Leviticus 18 does use the expression, but not of a prohibited degree of kinship but of the temporary prohibition of intercourse with a menstruating woman (18:19).

[176] Probably כן is to be supplied after ואם. The reasoning is: Although the prohibitions are addressed to males, they apply mutatis mutandis to females (see above, p. 19), so that a woman who has carnal relations with her uncle is as guilty of incest as a man who does so with his aunt. Charles, *ad loc.*, reads אל תגלה, and fails to observe that אל must be followed by the jussive. While the indicative often does duty for the jussive in ל"ה verbs, Isa. 47:3 nonetheless has תגל and not תגלה.

[177] See above, p. 4.

[178] דלתו is probably a misunderstanding of דלת'; the sign of abbreviation being mistaken, as frequently, for a ו. *Cf.* above, p. 4, n. 9, and Perles, *Analekten*, p. 32. [But see Rabin.]

only be a copyist's error, since the context demands לא באו,[179] and למיום for מיום may also be a clerical error. The absence of the Tetragrammaton is explained by the document's principle of avoiding it entirely.[180]

VIII) 7,14: והגליתי את סכות מלככם ואת כיון צלמיכם מאהלי דמשק. MT (Amos 5:26–27): ונשאתם את סכות מלככם ואת כיון צלמיכם ... והגליתי אתכם מהלאה לדמשק. The divergence is considerable, but it hardly reflects a variant reading in the author's text of Amos 5:26. What he cites is rather his own "actualization" of his Bible text than the text itself. In the word "Damascus" he finds an allusion[181] to the activity of his sect in Damascus. As Amos 5:27 stands, however, it is "you" — that is, apparently, "the house of Israel" (5:25) — which is to be exiled thither. Consequently our document, though it introduces the sentence with the words "as it says," substitutes for אתכם (to which it probably attributes the sense of "*for* you" and which it can therefore omit as unimportant) the phrase את סכות ... צלמיכם, which it borrows from the preceding verse. The latter phrase, in turn, the document goes on to interpret as meaning "the books of the Torah and the books of the Prophets"; these will find a refuge in Damascus, in the bosom of the sect, with its authentic doctrine. Hence also the alteration of מהלאה לד' to מְאַהֲלֵי ד', "those who tent in Damascus."[182] The sentence as quoted therefore means: "I will cause the books of the Torah (סכות מלככם) and the books of the Prophets (כיון צלמיכם) to migrate, pitching their tents in Damascus." Without a doubt, a fanciful interpretation of the Prophet's words; but not more fanciful than many a midrash in rabbinic literature and not a few allegories of the Church Fathers.

IX) 7,16: והקימותי את סוכת דוד הנפלת. MT (Amos 9:11): ביום ההוא אקים את סכת וגו'.[183]

X) 7,19: דרך כוכב מיעקב — identical with MT (Num. 24:17).

XI) 8,9: חמת תנינים יינם — identical with MT (Deut. 32:33).

XII) 8,14–15: ...לרשת את הגוים האלה כי מאהבתו את לא בצדקתך כי מאהבת ...מרבכם. MT (Deut. 7:7–8) אבותיך ומשמרו את השבועה וברשעת הגוים (9:4–5): "י אתכם ומשמרו את השבועה אשר נשבע לאבתיכם ה א ל ה. As ...לא בצדקתך ... לרשת את ארצם כי ברשעת הגוים ה א ל ה

---

[179] 14,1 quotes correctly אשר לא באו, but this passage also has מיום for MT's למיום.

[180] *Cf.* above, p. 163, n. 34.

[181] Our document itself hardly regards it as more than an allusion.

[182] I now consider very doubtful my surmise *ad loc.*, that there is an allusion here to the sense 'house of a study' of the word אהל. I withdraw my emendation (*ibid.*) of מאהלי to אהלי.

[183] The variant may be a consequence of our document's pronounced fondness for the perfect consecutive.

regards the document's apparent variant הגוים האלה for ארצם, it is no doubt merely a case of abridged citation. Perhaps the words כי ארצם ברשעת are actually to be added before 'הג' הא. Again, מאהבתו for מאהבת י"י accords with the document's practice of avoiding the Tetragrammaton. את אבותיך for אתכם, on the other hand, is either a deliberate alteration or a genuine variant, but in no case a copyist's error, as is proved by the following מאהבתו את אבותיך=באהבת אל את הראשונים. That it is no mere copyist's error is further evident from the fact that B (19,27), which usually follows MT, here agrees with A.

XIII) 9,2: לא תקום ולא תטור וגו' — identical with MT (Lev. 19:18).

XIV) 9,5: נוקם הוא לצריו ונוטר הוא לאויביו. MT (Nah. 1:2): נקם י"י. לצריו ונוטר הוא לאיביו. As was observed before, the document's variant הוא for י"י is also attested in rabbinic literature.

XV) 9,8: הוכח תוכיח את רעך. MT (Lev. 19:17): הוכח תוכיח את עמיתך. The substitution of the common רעך for the comparatively rare עמיתך is indicative of a cautious view of the reader's proficiency in Hebrew.

XVI) 9,9: אשר אמר לא תושיעך ידך לך; MT (I Sam. 25:26): והושע ידך לך. As was surmised on p. 189, the source quoted in the document is not the passage in I Sam. but a similar one in ספר ההגו, the official law book of the sect.

XVII) 10,16: שמור את יום השבת — identical with MT (Deut. 5:12).

XVIII) 11,18: מלבד שבתותיכם. MT (Lev. 23:38) שבתות י"י. The divergence of our document does not reflect a variant reading but results merely from its principle of never using the Tetragrammaton.[184]

XIX) 11,20: זבח רשעים תועבה ותפלת צדיקים כמנחת רצון. MT (Prov. 15:8): ישרים רצונו . . . תועבת י"י . . . זבח . . . תועבה for תועבת י"י is of course still another example of the avoidance of the Tetragrammaton.[185] But צדיקים for ישרים is doubtless an ancient variant, as was pointed out above. It was also explained there that מנחת רצון embodies a haggadic interpretation of רצונו.[186]

XX) 16,6: מוצא שפתיך תשמור — identical with MT (Deut. 23:24).

---

[184] But the statement made on p. 69 that י"י is elsewhere replaced by אל is inaccurate. The document itself, to be sure, employs this designation of God exclusively, but only B substitutes it for the Tetragrammaton in quotations from the Bible, never A.

[185] A further possibility: תועבה may be a misreading of תועב' ה', תועב' being an abbreviation of תועבת and ה', a surrogate for יהוה. The Tetragrammaton is commonly represented in the latter manner in rabbinical writings in the Middle Ages, and Perles, Analekten, 16 ff. and 92, assumes that this notation was occasionally employed in the Hebrew vorlage of the LXX.

[186] It is not certain that our document read רצון, since this graph can also be read רצונו.

XXI) 16:10: אמ[ר על א[שה]187 להניא את שבועתה is not an exact quotation but a paraphrase of ושמע אישה . . . לא הניא אתה (Num. 30:12).

XXII) 16,15: איש את עב[דו יצוד]ו חרם. MT (Mic. 7:2)
אחיהו יצודו חרם. The document, in quoting, deliberately substitutes עבדו
for אחיהו for the reason explained on p. 100: it interprets the verse as a
condemnation of the unkind treatment of a laborer (properly פועל).[188]

XXIII) 19,5: כאשר אמר בין איש לאשתו ובין אב לבנו. The actual quotation consists of the first three words (following "as it says"), whose
source is Num. 30:17; the other three being merely modeled by the
author of our document on the בין אב לבתו of MT — unless לבנו is
simply a scribal error for לבתו, which is also possible.

XXIV) 19,7: חרב עורי . . . נאם אל . . . ותפוצינה. MT (Zech. 13:7) is
identical except that it has י"י צבאות and תפוצין. By this time we are
familiar with the elimination of the Tetragrammaton, and תפוצינה
differs only orthographically from תפוצין.[189]

XXV) 19,12: להתוות התיו על מצחות נאנחים ונאנקים does not purport
to give the exact words that occur in Ezek. 9:4 — והתוית תו על מצחות
האנשים הנאנחים והנאנקים — but only to allude to recall the incident.

XXVI) 19,15: כמשיני גבול . . . עברה. . . . היו . . . MT (Hos. 5:10) has not
only the normal spelling כמסיני for the aberrant כמשיני[190] of the document but also עברתי for עברה. Its author, however, may have read
עברתי; but somewhere in transmission this may have been written
עברת,[191] which may have been turned into עברה by a copyist.

XXVII) 19,22: see XI.

XXVIII 19,26: see XII.

XXIX) 20,16–17: אין מלך ואין שר ואין שופט ואין מוכיח בצדק. The
first four words are quoted from Hos. 3:4 and agree with MT, while the
rest does not quote but merely employs the diction of Isa. 11:4.

Although barely a quarter of the quotations agree with MT,[192] the

---

[187] My restoration. Schechter reads משה, and my objection to it is not valid if
אמר משה (5,8 ff.) is not, as I have surmised, part of a later interpolation. [Rabin:
אמ[ר ל[אישה.]

[188] [The reading found by Rabin in the manuscript is רעיהו.]

[189] Rabbinical writings also exhibit such orthographic departures from MT in
quotations from the Bible.

[190] We have the same confusion of the root סונ with נשו in MT of Job 24:2
(נבולות ישינו). Qimḥi on our Hosea passage cites from Deut. 27:17 משיג גבול, but that
is probably a typographical error. Another passage in our document — to be sure,
also another fragment! — has מסיני הגבול (5,20).

[191] לאהבו (19,2) stands for לאהבו.

[192] Of the 27 quotations (not counting XXVII and XXVIII, as duplicates of
XI and XII), only the following seven agree word for word with MT: II, X, XI,
XIII, XVII, XX, XXIII. [See p. 377, n. 106 for additions by the author.]

possibility of genuine variants has to be considered seriously in only the following four cases:

I) Ezek. 44:15, where our document may have read יגישו לי for יקרבו . . . להקריב.

VII) Isa. 7:17, where our document probably read מיום for למיום.

IX) Amos 9:11: והקימותי for אקים.

XII) Deut. 7:8: אבותיך — deliberately substituted? — for MT's אתכם. It was shown above that the other cases of non-agreement with MT are not due to divergent Bible texts but to certain peculiarities of our document. It should also be observed that none of the departures from the Masoretic Text are supported by the LXX; our document, on the contrary, always agrees with MT against LXX. It reads (7,17) כיון צלמיכם, like Amos 5:26 MT, against the Septuagint's כיון כוכב אלהיכם. It reproduces (4,20) the MT reading in Mic. 2:6, אל תטפו יטיפון, with a minor variant,[193] whereas the LXX has a totally different text. And it cites (19,8) from Zech. 13:7 הך את הרועה, as against the LXX reading אכה.

As the document's Bible text agrees with that of the Masorah, so its method of exegesis is exactly the same as we find applied in rabbinic writings. Especially interesting is a comparison between the Halakic midrash of the Tannaim and that of our document; they are in fact identical. Our document (3,2) understands the biblical injunction לא ירבה לו נשים (Deut. 17:17) to prohibit the taking of two wives; this is intelligible in the light of the exegetical rule that wherever the Bible uses a plural form without specifying the number it means two.[194] The prohibition of uncle-niece marriages is inferred (5,9) from Scripture by the application of analogy, of which Tannaitic Midrash also makes extensive use.[195] The requirement of an extension of the Sabbath is justified (10,16) by a reference to שמור את יום השבת (Deut. 6:12). The point, as we learn from rabbinic sources, is that שמר means "to guard" as well as "to observe," and the sentence is taken to mean "Guard the Sabbath day," i. e., obviate the danger of its being profaned by beginning the Sabbath observance even before the Sabbath itself

---

[193] For the reasons for it see pp. 18 and 195.

[194] E. g. Sifra on Lev. 4:15, ed. Weiss 19b; Sanhedrin 13b: — זקני; שנים — וסמכו שנים; Sifre Deuteronomy 93, p. 154: אנשים אין פחות משנים. The rule מעוט רבים שנים is not found, to my knowledge, before the Middle Ages (in the book קנה, ed. Wilmersdorf, 3a), but the idea is Tannaitic, as is proved by the above passages. We do find in Yer. Yoma II, 40a מעוט רבים ג'; but it means that the word רבים implies at least three, but a simple plural in itself only two; see ibid., several Tannaitic utterances, all of which are premised upon this rule. [This rule is found in much earlier sources than the book of קנה, see my note in הלכות הירושלמי להרמב'ם, p. 19, n. 7. — S. L.]

[195] See above, p. 154, n. 197.

begins.[196] That only the Sabbath burnt offering[197] may be offered on the altar on the Sabbath is deduced (11,18) from the words מלבד שבתות י"י in Lev. 23:38. As was observed *ad loc.* on pp. 69 ff.,[198] the reasoning is that the verse in question explicitly adds, to the enumeration of the festivals and the communal offerings prescribed for them, the communal Sabbath offering and the various freewill offerings, which therefore are also offered on the festivals, but it is nowhere indicated that sacrifices other than Sabbath burnt offerings are offered up on the Sabbath. The rule which is applied here is, in halakic terminology, אין לך בו אלא חידושו:[199] "Nothing can be added to an exception." That is to say, in the present instance, since the offering up of any sacrifices on the Sabbath is an exception to the general prohibition of labor on the Sabbath, the exception cannot be extended beyond that which is expressly mentioned in the Bible, namely Sabbath and Festival sacrifices. It follows that the paschal lamb may not be offered on the Sabbath, let alone (as some would have it) the Festival peace offerings (שלמי חגיגה).

More variegated and much freer than the Halakic is the Haggadic Midrash in our document. This phenomenon has also a parallel in rabbinic literature. In the latter, Haggadic Midrash knows no limits but those of the Haggadist's imagination, whereas Halakic Midrash is correlated with life. It is therefore not surprising that our document makes plentiful use of typological exegesis. In this connection, however, we must not suppose that the plain meaning — the פשט[200] — of the Bible simply did not exist for it. The view that prevails in sectarian as in rabbinic literature is rather that the word of God has more than one meaning. The usual introduction to a haggadic application of

---

[196] See pp. 55, 108, 183; further, Moed Qatan, 5a where ושמרתם את משמרתי (Lev. 18:30) is interpreted to mean עשו משמרת למשמרתי, "Make a guard for my law."

[197] [See above, p. 183, n. 130.]

[198] See also Sifra *ad loc.*, where the words are interpreted to mean that on a festival which falls on a Sabbath, both festival and Sabbath offerings must be offered; our document, to be sure, infers from them rather that none but these may be offered on a Sabbath.

[199] The formulation is amoraic (Temurah 13b; Yerushalmi Soṭah III, 18c has דבר שהוא יוצא לחידושו אין למדין הימנו), but the rule itself is frequently applied in Tannaitic Midrash.

[200] The validity of the פשט is also recognized by Philo, though for him the allegorical meaning is of greater importance; *cf.* my exposition in *Jewish Encyclopedia* I, 404, where the radical allegorists in Alexandria, who disregard the plain meaning entirely, are also referred to. The well known saying אין מקרא יוצא מידי פשוטו, "Scripture cannot be stripped of its plain meaning" (Yevamoth 11b), applies only to the legal parts of the Bible.

Scripture in tannaitic literature is אמר על, "to which may be applied."[201]
Now, the same formula occurs in our document (8,9) where it is said
with reference to the persecutions of the Jews by the Greek rulers
אשר אמר אל עליהם חמת תנינים יינם וראש פתנים אכזר, and the interpretation
is added that "The serpents are the kings of the peoples, and the head
(ראש) of the asps is the head of the Greek kings."

Just as repetitions and superfluous words and clauses in the Bible
are particularly favored by Philo for allegorical exegesis and by the
Rabbis[202] for typological, similar phenomena appear in our document.
"Terror, and trench, and trap upon you, inhabitant of the land!"
cries the Prophet (Isa. 24:17): our author (4,15) discovers here the
three nets that Belial spreads over Israel. The sons of Zadok are
described by Ezekiel (Ezek. 44:15) as "priests . . . Levites . . . sons of
Zadok." In this unusual expression our author (4,2) sees a sketch of
the leaders of the sect, who are described, according to their various
activities, as priests, Levites, and sons of Zadok.[203] On the strength of
sundry biblical metaphors, literal statements in the Bible are interpreted metaphorically. God is a source of living water (Jer. 2:13),
and his instruction water for the thirsty (Isa. 55:1); so our document
(6,4) makes of the "well song" (Num. 21:17 ff.) a song in praise of the
Torah as taught by the founder of the sect. Substitute Moses for the
founder of the sect and those to whom Moses mediated the Torah for
the sect, and you have the interpretation of the "well song" in rabbinic Haggadah.[204] [It goes like this: *"The well dug by princes* — That
is the Torah, which was already observed by Abraham and Jacob.
Hollowed out by nobles of the people — That is Israel, who received the
Torah at Sinai. *With the scepter* (meḥoqeq, also "lawgiver") — That is
Moses. *With their staffs* (משענתם, connected with נשע 'to lean') — That
means that they leaned upon Moses in all things and agreed to all
that he enjoined upon them with at God's behest."] Num. 24:17 says
of a leader of Israel "A star arose from Jacob." Our author (7,14–19)
cites this verse as proof that כוכב אלהיכם, "the star of your God"[205]
(Amos 5:26), is none other than the founder of his sect.

The foregoing discussion demonstrates very clearly that both the

---

[201] E. g. Yoma III, 11; Taanith III, 8; Peah V, 6 and many other passages.

[202] R. Ishmael, it is true, asserts of such locutions דברה תורה בלשון בני אדם; but
his opposition is mainly directed against the practice of such midrash in Halakah.

[203] See p. 15, and further below, Section VII, p. 261.

[204] Midrash Aggadah, ed. Buber, Vol. 2, p. 129; see also Eruvin 54a and Tanḥuma
IV, 128, where probably the Haggadic interpretation תורה=באר is already presup-
posed. The Alphabet of Rabbi Akiva, letter ס, has an exposition of the Song of the
Well that agrees with that in our document almost word for word.

[205] The Bible text really means 'your god the star.'

Halakic and the Haggadic Midrash in our document move exactly in
the framework which rabbinic literature sets up for them. Very instructive for the relation of our document to rabbinic literature is the
fact that both are, in contrast to the Alexandrian allegorists and their
disciples the Church Fathers, innocent of an esoteric allegory. The
essential difference between Alexandrian allegory and rabbinic Haggadah is[206] that the latter never went beyond the world of the real,
whereas the former aimed primarily at the *reinterpretation of the real*.
The Alexandrians sought in the Bible the feeling and the thinking of
man, ethics, and philosophy; the Rabbis sought the destiny of Israel.
The four rivers that issued from Eden (Gen. 2:10) are explained by
the Midrash (Gen. Rabbah XVI, 4, p. 147) as the four world empires —
the Babylonian, Medo-Persian, Greek, and Roman; but for Philo
(*Alleg. Leg.* I, XIX; I, 56 ed. Mangey) they are the four cardinal virtues. Our document follows the example of the Rabbis, but with a
sharply narrowed horizon. It is no longer the history of Israel which
it looks for in the Bible, but the history of the sect.

*   *

*

The narrow-mindedness of the sectarian, however, manifests itself
not only in the interpretation of the biblical prophecies about the
future of Israel as referring to the history of the sect but also in the
ethics and theology of our document. We find in it (6,20) the Pentateuch command to love one's neighbor (Lev. 19:18), but with the
significant variant אחיהו for the רעך of the biblical phrase. It is not
love of one's fellow man, or even of one's fellow national, that is
enjoined but only of one's covenant brother, the member of the sect.
And even he forfeits his claim on the love of his fellow partisans when
he fails to observe the law (9,5); for God also hates his enemies, the
sinners; therefore, no kindly consideration for such.[207] How differently
the command to love one's neighbor is understood by the protagonists
of "legalistic Pharisaism"! The decapitation of a criminal, says the
Talmud,[208] is performed with a sharp sword, not with an ax, which
breaks the neck. For the Bible says, "Love your neighbor as yourself"; accordingly one must select the easiest death for him. The
Talmud, then, holds that even he who has forfeited his life by his

---

[206] See my observation in *Jewish Encyclopedia* I, 405, and Treitel, *Monatsschrift* LV, 551.

[207] [The point of 9,5 is understood quite differently, and much more plausibly,
in the author's note *ad loc.*, above p. 40.]

[208] Kethuvoth 37b.

misdeeds still has a claim to our love. Even the Book of Jubilees,[209] despite its exclusivist point of view, counts the duty of loving one's fellow among those which Noah urged upon his children; in other words, it is a law for mankind, not only for Jewry. That without a doubt is also the view of Slavonic Enoch LXVI, where the command is included among the admonitions of Enoch. In the Testaments of the XII Patriarchs the duty of loving one's neighbor figures three times, each time in a different formulation. Issachar V, 2: Love the Lord and your neighbor. Issachar VII, 6: I loved the Lord with all my heart, and also *every man*. Dan V, 3: Love the Lord all your lives,[210] and each other with all your hearts. On this last passage, Charles comments as follows: "In Lev. XIX, 18 certainly, and in our text possibly, the sphere of neighborhood is limited to Israelites. In our Lord's case there is no limit of race or country." We shall leave in abeyance the question whether the Canaanite woman whose plea for healing was answered by Jesus with the words "It is not meet to take the bread of the children and cast it to the dogs" had as high an opinion of his "boundless" love as Charles, but he certainly does a grave injustice to the author of the Testaments who, as we have seen, writes explicitly "every man," which cannot possibly mean only every Jew.[211] We have also seen that that is also the view that prevails in the Slavonic Book of Enoch. How broadminded Pharisaic Judaism is in

---

[209] VII:20, where the so-called Noachic laws are listed. "And to praise their Creator," *ibid.*, is doubtless a misunderstanding of the Hebrew original by the translator. It probably read והזהירם על ברכת השם, but that means "he admonished them against blasphemy." ברכה for קללה is also rabbinic, and the prohibition of blasphemy is also one of the Noachic laws in rabbinic tradition; see Sanhedrin 56b. The duty of loving one's fellow also figures in Jubilees XX, 2, which also stresses its universality.

[210] So the Greek text; which, however, can hardly be right. Presumably the Hebrew read בכל חייך, paraphrasing בכל נפשך, which Sifre to Deut. 6:5 interprets to mean אפילו הוא נוטל את נפשך. What the author meant in our passage is therefore "*with* all your life," "devoting your whole life to him." [That the author of Dan V, 3 had Deut. 6:5 in mind is also evident from the parallel "with all your hearts" at the end of the verse.]

[211] Issachar V, 2 and Dan V, 3 simply quote Lev. 19:18, where the Hebrew text has לרעך. In Issachar VII, 6 the narrator does not repeat the biblical command but relates that he fulfilled it, and here he substitutes what the author of the Testaments believes to be an equivalent expression ("every man"). Like the Rabbis, the author understood "your neighbor" to mean "your fellow man." In Jubilees XXXVI, 14, Isaac charges his sons Jacob and Esau, "Love, my sons, every man your brothers," which is an inaccurate rendering of a Hebrew בני אהבו איש את אחיו "My sons, love one another." Perhaps אחיו was preferred here to רעהו (despite לרעך in the verse of Scripture which served as model) because Isaac's sons were mutually hostile brothers, and it was fitting to urge them to behave toward each other like loving brothers. *Cf.* further XX, 2, and above, note 209.

its understanding of the love of one's fellow man is seen best of all in the famous dictum of Ben Azzai: "This is the basic idea of Torah: On the day that God created Adam, he created him in God's image" (Gen. 5:1). The duty of loving men follows from resemblance to God; one must love God and one's fellow man, who is created in God's image.[212] Our document therefore contrasts sharply with both the Rabbis and the apocryphal authors in limiting the love of one's neighbor to one's fellow covenanter.

Our document also occupies a narrow sectarian position with regard to "the Patriarchs," whose significance it, like rabbinic literature, strongly underscores. "Mindful of the covenant with the ancients," it says in one of the opening sentences, "he left Israel a remnant, and did not give them up to utter destruction." Even the text of the Bible is altered for the sake of throwing the forefathers into bold relief, so that Deut. 9:5 plus 7:8 becomes (8,14): "It is not for your righteousness[213] and uprightness of heart that you come to supplant these peoples, but because he (i. e. the Lord) loved *your forefathers* and abides by the oath." But, the document goes on to say, this[214] — the covenant with the Patriarchs — holds good only for the converted among the Israelites, who have turned back from the way of the people. Because of his love for the ancients who were devoted to him, he also loves those who have come after them, for the covenant of the fathers is theirs." In the Tannaitic sources are to be found two distinct views about the significance of the fathers for the history of Israel. The Midrashim from the school of R. Akiva[215] teach that הכל בזכות

---

[212] Sifra to Lev. 19:18. A wealth of data on the rabbinic understanding of loving one's neighbor is mustered by Theodor in his commentary on Gen. Rabbah XXIV, 236, but strange to say it does not include any of the three passages from the Apocrypha that have just been cited in the text. Both Ben Azzai and Rabbi Akiva regard the command to love one's neighbor and the teaching that man was made in the divine image as complementary doctrines.

[213] [The German edition has *Beschaffenheit*, but the context and the Hebrew original show that that is an error for *Rechtschaffenheit*.]

[214] See the discussion of this passage on pp. 36–37. On the העיר/העיד which is dealt with there, a reference may be added; Jubilees I, 12, where we find again "and I will send witnesses to them to witness against them." Singer, *Buch d. Jub.*, p. 204, infers from this the Christian character of Jubilees, on the ground that only a Christian would say witnesses (μάρτυρες) for Prophets. However, he, and Charles, *ad loc.*, as well, failed to note that the author of the Book of Jubilees here echoes Neh. 9:30 ותעד בם . . . ביד נביאיך.

[215] Mekilta de-R. Simeon 32 [ed. Epstein-Melamed 38]; Sifre Deut. 96, p. 157 and 184, p. 225. This strong stress on the merits of the fathers is most probably of anti-Christian motivation: the claims of the true children of Abraham are upheld against

אבותיך, "All [the kindness that God shows to Israel] is because of the merits of the fathers." A Midrash from the school of R. Ishmael, on the other hand,[216] says in so many words בשכר מצוה אתם חיים אין אתם חיים בזכות אבות, "It is as a reward for pious deeds that you live, not for the merits of the fathers." [In the view of our document, the covenant is vital for the survival of Israel, but it only benefits the elect, that is, the adherents of this sect. A consequence of God's love for the fathers is love for their descendants, yet not for "the body of Israel" but only for a small fraction of it. This declaration that the "covenant of the fathers" would do no good to the greater part of the Jewish people has nothing in common with the liberalism of the foregoing dictum of the school of R. Ishmael; it is, on the contrary, informed with sectarian bigotry. God's love is only for the offspring of the Patriarchs, and only the members of the sect have the right to be called offspring of the Patriarchs.

The context in which the fathers (אבות) and the ancients (ראשונים) are spoken of (8,17–18) shows quite clearly that the latter expression, no less than the former, designates the three Patriarchs.[217] Of the no-

---

those who call themselves children of the Patriarchs after the spirit. Among the Amoraim the view prevailed that the merits of the fathers had ceased to be of importance for the history of Israel since the Exile; cf. Shabbath 55a; Lev. Rabbah XXXVI, ad fin., p. 851. Bousset, being unaware of all this, inevitably came to an altogether erroneous conclusion about "the merits of the fathers"; see his discussion, p. 415. He also had the misfortune to misunderstand the sources he did employ. It does not say at the beginning of the Eighteen Benedictions that the Lord "brings a redeemer . . . for their (the fathers') sakes" but "for his (the Lord's) sake." A measure of familiarity with the Bible might have saved him, since the phrase למען שמו is not so uncommon. See Schechter, Aspects 170 f.

[216] Midrash Tannaim 62.

[217] In Berakhoth 16b we read: "The epithet 'fathers' may be applied only to the three Patriarchs." The meaning is not that other great men of Israel's history must not be designated as "fathers," but that the title of honor "our father" may not be added to the name of any individual other than one of the three Patriarchs. The source of the above passage in the Babylonian Talmud is Massekhet Semaḥoth I, 13, which has the right reading אבינו. It was probably originally a direction governing the formulation of prayers, its purport being that God was to be addressed only as the God of the three fathers of the nation because he had linked his name only with theirs; cf. Gen. R. LXXXII, 3; Yelam. in Jellinek, Beth ha-Midrash VI, 81; Pesaḥ. 117b. Although the last named passage concedes that David shared the honor with the three Patriarchs, the Babylonian liturgy [in the benedictions following the reading of a lesson from the Prophets] only goes as far as saying "O Lord, the Shield of David." The Palestinians, to be sure, said אלהי דוד "God of David" even in the daily prayers; see Yer. Rosh ha-Shanah IV, 59c; Midrash Samuel XXVI, 126, and Schechter JQR X, 657; but the view reflected in the Babylonian practice is doubtless the older one, since it is also found in Philo, On Abraham X (ed. M. 8;

tion, which figures so prominently in the Book of Jubilees,[218] of the great significance of the seven pre-Mosaic patriarchs Adam, Seth, Enosh, Mahalalel, Enoch, Noah, and Shem for the religious evolution of the human race, there is not even a trace in our document, in which

---

ed. C. 48): "For he joined his own name with theirs — those of the three Patriarchs — and assumed the designation which is composed of those three . . . he granted the human race a suitable appellation with which it could have recourse to prayer and not be left without hope." The last sentence shows quite clearly that Philo is speaking of the liturgical formula "God of Abraham, Isaac, and Jacob." Philo's observation shows, incidentally, how the phrase is to be understood: it recalls, not the merits of the Fathers (so Bousset 415) but God's acting in history, most clearly manifested in his relationship with those saints.

Exceptions were later made in Palestine not only in the case of David, which has already been referred to, but also of other great men. In Midrash Tannaim, p. 172, we read that Rabban Gamaliel's disciples said to him, "You are worthy of having God's name connected with you." (שיחול) is equivalent to יחד; cf. Bacher, Terminologie I, 69. [The correct explanation was given by H. Yalon in אלמה of Dr. Lewin, Jerusalem, 1936, p. 146. — S. L.]. He thereupon prayed etc. In Kallah II (in Wertheimer's Bate Midr., 1968, Vol. 1, p. 231) there actually occurs the version ברוך יי אלהינו ואלהי אבותינו אלהי אברהם אלהי יצחק ואלהי יעקב ואלהי ר' עקיבא. (The Babylonian Talmud — Avodah Zarah 18a bottom — also has אלהא דמאיר "God of Meir," but there it is a non-Jew who is advised by R. Meir to designate the true God by that appellation.) These exceptions notwithstanding, the rule that אבות, "the Fathers," by itself means only the three Patriarchs is warranted. אבות הראשונים, on the other hand, is applied to other great men as well: In Mekilta Bo XI, 11b, ed. Horovitz, p. 38, line 6, in the variant, to Abraham and Jacob; in Mekilta de-Rabbi Simeon (Hoffmann 7; Epstein-Melamed 8), to all the pious down to the time of Moses (in Mekilta Bo I, p. 7, therefore, אדם הראשון is evidently a false resolution of א"ה= אבות הראשונים); in Mekilta Wayassa II, 163 and Sifre Deuteronomy 97, p. 159, for the three Patriarchs; in Sifre Zuṭa 83 [Leipzig, 275] and 98 [ibid., 284], for the three Patriarchs and all the other pious of the pre-Mosaic period; in Tosefta Tevul Yom I, 10, to the Tannaim R. Eliezer and R. Joshua; in Tanḥuma V, 24, to the three Patriarchs; in Avoth de-Rabbi Nathan, ed. Schechter, p. 26, to Abraham, Joseph, and Jonah; ibid., p. 40, to all the pious of the pre-Mosaic era; in TP Berakhoth I, 2c; Yoma VI, 43d, to the three Patriarchs; in Ekah Rabbati V, 160, to the three Patriarchs; in Pesiqta, ed. Buber, p. 98a [Mandelbaum, p. 166], to the three Patriarchs; in Midrash Tehillim I, 16, to the Tannaim.

Besides אבות הראשונים, the designation אבות העולם likewise has a twofold application: to the three Patriarchs and to great men in general. Examples: Mishnah Eduyyoth I, 4, Shammai and Hillel; TP Sanhedrin X, 27d, the three Patriarchs; Sheqalim II, 47b and parallels, Rabbis Ishmael and Akiva; Midrash Tehillim XVI, 120; VII, 66; Tanḥuma to Exod. 25:3; Shir ha-Shirim Rabbah I, 14, Midrash Tadshe II, 17, ed. Epstein; Yalquṭ Makiri (from an unspecified source), Isaiah 195, all with reference to the three Patriarchs. See also Y. M., ibid., 215. This passage, as becomes evident from a comparison with Y. Shimeoni Jeremiah 292, is derived from Yelammedenu. The name of the Mishnah tractate Avoth (אבות) is doubtless shortened from אבות העולם, just as Ben Sira gave his song in praise of the great men of the past the caption שבח אבות עולם. In Midrash Tehillim LXXVII, 343 we

none of them is even mentioned.[219] The document therefore agrees in this regard with the Rabbis; for whom only Israel's forefathers Abraham, Isaac, and Jacob are the bearers of the divine plan of salvation, though they do recognize as a historical fact that great and pious men had been active before Abraham too.[220] Our document's

---

find for the three Patriarchs a combination of the two terms in the shape of אבות העולם הראשונים. In Mishnah Sukkah V, 4, אבותינו stands for the sinners at the time of the destruction of the Temple, and in Avodah Zarah 5a and Midrash Tannaim 189 for the generation of the wilderness. In Mekilta Bo, Petiḥta, p. 3, האבות הראשונים is to be read for האבות, as can be seen from Bo XI, 11b, ed. Horovitz, p. 38, line 6, in the variants.

Bacher in his *Terminologie* gives only one example of אבות from the Mekilta in the Tannaitic section, and documents אבות העולם with Tanḥuma I, 90 in the amoraic section. The lexica to the Talmuds and Midrashim do not know at all the various applications of the word אבות in rabbinic literature; *cf.* also Aggadat Shir, ed. Schechter, 14: אבות = Noah and his sons. In Zevaḥim 113a, Berakhoth 57b, and Qiddushin 66a, אבותינו is employed as a designation of former generations and of individual men of the past, and the correctness of the interpretation of Berakhoth 16b given above follows from these passages. *Cf.* further Derek Ereẓ Zuta I end.

[218] The basic tenor of this work is, of course, that the Mosaic institutions date from the earliest ages and are connected with the earliest history of the race. However, it is no accident that it names just seven men as the actual bearers of the early revelations, (XIX, 24) but this doubtless reflects the concept of "the seven pillars of the world" (see my expositions in *Jewish Encyclopedia* IV, 14), the instruments of divine revelation. The Book of Jubilees seems to posit two such chains of revelation: the first comprises the seven proto-Patriarchs that have just been named; and the second has Abraham for its first link and will be completed by the Messiah as seventh, the intermediate ones being Isaac, Jacob, Levi, Amram, and Moses.

[219] The following biblical personages are referred to: Noah's sons, 3,1; Abraham, Isaac, and Jacob, 3,2–3; Levi son of Jacob, 4,15; Moses, 5,8, etc.; Aaron, 5,18 and in the frequent designation of the Messiah as משיח מאהרן וכו'; Eleazar son of Aaron, 5,3; Joshua, 5,4; David, 5,2; Isaiah son of Amoz, 4,13; Ezekiel, 3,21; Zechariah, 19,7. In 8,20–21 Jeremiah, Baruch son of Neriah, and Elisha and his attendant Gehazi are named, but the authenticity of this passage is very doubtful; see p. 193, n. 198. The same applies to 1,6, where Nebuchadnezzar the king of Babylon occurs; see below, p. 260. One cannot say for sure who is meant by Zadok, 5,5. There occur further in quotations from the Bible: the sons of Zadok, 3,21; Ephraim and Judah, 7,13; 14,1 — meaning in both cases not the individuals but the ethnic groups descended from them — and finally Seth, 7,21. Other proper names: Judah — house, land, and princes of — 4,11; 6,5; 8,3; Javan — head of the kings of — 8,11; Mizraim — land of — 3,5; and Damascus, 7,19. יהוה, 5,18, is derived from the apocryphal literature.

[220] *Cf.* Singer, *Buch der Jub.*, 128, who already makes the point that the men named are also counted among the righteous in the rabbinic sources, with the exception of Enosh and Mahalalel. To which it may be added that the rabbinic sources say nothing in disparagement of Enosh. According to them idolatry originated in the age of Enosh, but he was not himself guilty of it; see my *Legends of the Jews*

term for the three Patriarchs, ראשונים (1,4; 8,17), "ancients," is very similar to the אבות הראשונים of the rabbinic sources;[221] for which, to be sure, the shorter אבות is more common, just as our document at 8,18 says simply ברית אבות.

Our study of *the theological views of the document* has therefore led to the certain conclusion that they *agree by and large with Pharisaic doctrine*, though in a number of details the bigotry of the sectarian is unmistakable.

I, 122. Philo, *De Abrahamo* II, 9, similarly describes Enosh as the forebear of "the pure, refined race." The piety of Mahalalel figures in a Midrashic fragment in Buber, Aggadath Bereshith XXXVII, and the Slavonic Book of Enoch knows of a Book of Mahalalel. Aggadath Bereshith, *loc. cit.*, explains the name אנוש with the words שנולד בדור אנוש, "because he was born in an incurable (אָנוּש) generation." Incurable here means sinful, which confirms my interpretation of פשע אנוש, 3,17, above on p. 14. The passage further goes on to show that rabbinic tradition made not Enosh but his generation the originator of idolatry. See further my observation in הצופה IV, 28.

[221] *Cf.* above, p. 205, n. 217. In the Bible neither אבות הראשונים (Jer. 11:10) nor ראשונים alone (Lev. 26:45) means the three Patriarchs. In the Talmud ראשונים means "former generations" but not the biblical period, which is דורות הראשונים; see e. g. Sanhedrin 69b.

VI

Messianic Doctrine

The doctrine of a Messiah is not central in the theology of this document. The center of its theology is rather, as in Rabbanism, the Torah. It is even very doubtful that the sect attached as much importance to Messianism as the Pharisees. But inasmuch as conclusions as to the nature and origin of the sect must base themselves largely on an interpretation of the Messianic passages in the document, a close examination of them is indispensable.

In several passages the Messiah is referred to by the phrase "the anointed one from Aaron and Israel," a description which, despite the alleged Priest-Messiah of the Testaments of the XII Patriarchs, still awaits an explanation. Another problem to be solved is the relation of the Messiah to "the teacher of truth,"[1] מורה צדק, about which the document is not clear. A number of passages suggest that the Messiah is identical with "the teacher," so that the sect appears to have expected a return of the latter, but in other passages they seem to be two different persons. In order to find a satisfactory solution for this problem, we propose to subject all the messianic passages in our document to a searching examination.

1,5–11: ובקץ חרון שנים . . . פקדם ויצמח מישראל ומאהרן שורש מטעת לירוש את ארצו . . . וידעו כי אנשים אשימים הם ויהיו כעורים וכימגששים דרך שנים עשרים ויבן אל אל מעשיהם כי בלב שלם דרשוהו ויקם להם מורה צדק להדריכם בדרך לבו. "And in the age of wrath he (God) remembered them and caused the root that he had planted to sprout from Israel and Aaron so that they possessed his land in safety and enjoyed the fruitfulness of its soil undisturbed. They became aware of their sin, and they realized that they were guilty people and that they had been like the blind and like them that grope their way for twenty years. Then God noted their deeds, namely that they sought him wholeheartedly, and raised up for them a 'teacher of truth' to guide them in the way that is pleasing to him." In our note on this passage we made the point that, contrary to the general view, there is nothing Messianic about this passage: the Messiah is always designated in this composition as

---

[1] When governed by הורה, צדק means that which is true or right, in our document the true interpretation of the Torah.

"the anointed *from Aaron and Israel*"; "the root that sprouted *from Israel and Aaron*" cannot mean the Messiah. "The plant of righteousness" as a designation of Israel is common to the Book of Enoch (X, 16; XCIII, 2, 10) and the Book of Jubilees (I, 16), while the original of the Testaments of the XII Patriarchs (Judah XXIV, 4)[2] — which followed Isa. 61:3 more literally — called Israel "the plant of God"; accordingly, "the root that he (God) had planted" in our passage cannot be anything but Israel.[3] The first exhortation in our document — 1,1–2,1 — does not, contrary to what is generally assumed, contain any allusion to the origin of the sect but only a reflection upon the history of Israel and Judah in the period of the monarchy. Israel — meaning the kingdom of that name — was, says our document, given up to destruction,[4] but God, remembering the covenant with the Fathers, suffered "a remnant," i. e. Judah, to survive. This idea of "the remnant," taken from the Prophets, is expressed in our document in words strongly reminiscent of Ben Sira XLVIII, 15: "For all that," says this sage, "the people (the kingdom of the ten tribes) did not repent . . . until they were plucked out of their land. . . . Yet a small remainder was left[5] for Judah, and still David's house had a prince." According to our source, however, the grace of God manifested itself not only in that about the same time as sinful Samaria was destroyed the state of Judah enjoyed undisturbed prosperity[6] under Hezekiah, but more especially in the saved remnant's discovering, during Israel's "time of wrath,"[7] the true way to God. For in this period, in the opinion of our source (which bears some resemblance to that of modern Bible criticism), the Torah, which had fallen into oblivion after the death of Joshua, was established once again as a code of law.[8] It was

---

[2] That this passage in the Testaments originally referred not to the Messiah but to Israel is to my mind evident from the context. *Cf.* also IV Ezra IX,22.

[3] For the מטע of its biblical source our document employs מטעה in accordance with later usage; see the Talmudic lexica and further Midrash Shemuel XXV,122, ed. Buber, מטעת שלו נקצצת, "his (Samuel's) planting was cut down," meaning that Saul, whom Samuel had anointed, fell in battle. In Yalqut Shimeoni, Psalms 765, and Yalqut Makiri, Psalms I, 282, מטעת has become corrupted to מעיל.

[4] The words לחרב . . . הסתיר in 1,3–4 are taken from Ezek. 39:23; which shows that וממקדשו is a later addition.

[5] וישאר ליהודה in the Hebrew Ben Sira = השאיר שארית in our source.

[6] לירוש means here "to possess," not "to take possession of." Cf. Ps. 37:11, where ירש has this meaning, and it is highly probable that this verse was in the mind of the author.

[7] *Cf.* above, pp. 29–30 and p. 132, n. 102.

[8] See on this subject in greater detail above, p. 21.

only when the Torah came to light again under Josiah that the people
of his realm realized how sinful their previous way of life had been.
Just as the reigns of the twenty kings of Judah appear in Assumption
of Moses II, 5 as "twenty years," so our document speaks of the period
covered by the reigns of the twenty kings[9] from Saul to Josiah (with
Ishbosheth included) as the twenty years of straying and groping.
Only under pious King Josiah did there arise for them "the Teacher
of Truth," who led Israel upon the path that is pleasing to God. One
cannot say with certainty whether Josiah himself is meant as this
Teacher or, as is more probable, the High Priest[10] who discovered the
Torah in Josiah's reign; but it is certain that מורה צדק in this passage
means none other than the man who reinstituted the Torah in the
reign of King Josiah.[11] This, however, is not meant to imply that the
expression never stands for any other person. On the contrary, its
application in our document parallels exactly that which we find in
the rabbinic sources. Inasmuch as nobody has thus far called attention to the use of the expression in other sources, the essential data
on the subject are given below.

* *
*

The oldest rabbinic source in which "the Teacher of Truth" is
referred to is the passage in TB Bekhoroth 24a in which the Palestinian Rabbi Joḥanan — *fl.* 250 — declares that a certain question of
law must be left undecided for all time, or rather עד יבוא ויורה צדק,
"until he comes and teaches the truth." In Hos. 10:12,[12] from which

---

[9] Alternatively, the reference might conceivably be to the twenty kings (including Tibni) from Jeroboam I to Hoshea. The first three kings, Saul, David, and
Solomon, are, though not altogether after our author's heart (V,5), in a class by
themselves, and cannot very well be counted together with those graceless monarchs.
On either of these interpretations, the age of the Judges would not be included in
the long period of error for the reason that at least the first phase of it counted
as part of the "good" old times. More probably, however, the age of the Judges
might be counted as one "year" and Josiah taken to represent the twentieth "year,"
not counting Ishbosheth.

[10] In V,5 he is called צדוק, for which I conjectured (on p. 21) חלקיה=בן צדוק.
Attention may be called to the fact that one manuscript of Seder Olam actually
has צדוק as father of חלקיה; A. Neubauer, *Medieval Jewish Chronicles* I, 165.

[11] According to Sifre Deut. 48, p. 112, it was Shaphan, who owes his title הסופר
(II Kings 22:8–10, 12) — taken in its later sense of Torah scholar — to this
circumstance.

[12] The medieval commentators oscillate between the interpretation of יורה as
"early rain" and as the verb meaning "he will teach"; *cf.* Rashi, Ibn Ezra, and
Qimḥi *ad loc.*

these words are quoted, the subject of יורה is י״י, at the end of the preceding clause; but R. Joḥanan hardly propounded the view that the Lord will one day decide all unsettled or controversial questions of law, since such a role is not ascribed to him anywhere else. To be sure, there is a statement by another Palestinian, R. Abba b. Kahana, a younger contemporary of R. Joḥanan, to the effect that,[13] "God is going to assign to the righteous a place closer to the Divine Glory than that of the ministering angels, who will ask them, 'What has God taught you?' (מה הורה לכם)." But this instruction by God which the ministering angels will in the age to come have to receive second hand from the righteous is surely identical with the Halakoth that "God teaches daily in the Celestial Academy" (Gen. Rabbah XLIX, 2, p. 501), and has nothing to do with the settling of controversial questions of law. In the above statement, therefore, R. Joḥanan can only have meant either Elijah or the Messiah, from whom, indeed, such an activity might be expected. Now, in no fewer than eighteen passages in the Talmud[14] Elijah appears as one who, in his capacity of precursor of the Messiah, will settle all doubts on matters ritual and juridical. There is, therefore, no reason for doubting the correctness of Rashi's interpretation of the statement of R. Joḥanan to which we have referred. The phrase עד יבוא ויורה צדק is accordingly equivalent to עד שיבוא אליהו ויורה צדק "until Elijah comes and teaches the truth." Neither in that passage nor any other in the Talmud nor anywhere in rabbinic literature is there any basis for R. Gershom's view that יורה צדק means the Messiah.[15] The two poles of the Messiah

---

[13] TP Shabbath VII, 8d; see also Sifre Deut. 310, p. 351 = Midrash Tannaim 189.

[14] Inasmuch as the passages have never been listed completely until now (not in Rabbi Z. H. Chajes's paper ברור אליהו in his collection of studies titled תורת נביאים, 3c ff., either), I list them herewith: 1. Berakhoth 35b; 2. Shabbath 108a; 3. Pesaḥim 13a = TP III,30b; 4. Pesaḥim 70a; 5. Mishnah Sheqalim II,5; 6. Ḥagigah 25a; 7. Yevamoth 35b; 8. Yevamoth 41b; 9. Yevamoth 102a; 10. Giṭṭin 42b; 11. Mishnah Bava Meẓi'a I,8; 12. Mishnah Bava Meẓi'a III,4; 13. Mishnah Bava Meẓi'a III,5; 14 and 15. Menaḥoth 45a; 16. Avoth de-Rabbi Nathan (ed. Schechter), 98 and 101; 17. Megillath Taanith VIII, 1; 18. TP Berakhoth 2c and the *locus classicus* Mishnah Eduyyoth VIII,7, where it is explained that Elijah's mission consists in "settling the controversies" (להשוות המחלוקת), that is to say, in putting an end to the differences of opinion among scholars. (Perhaps לכשיבוא אליהו is also to be read for לכשיבוא משה in Niddah 70b. However, there are other passages in which legend asserts that Moses will function as a teacher "in time to come." See, e. g., Sifre Deuteronomy 355, p. 418 = Aggadath Bereshith LXVII, 133 and my *Legends of the Jews* III, 481.

[15] The commentary, by the way, has been shown by Epstein (see *Steinschneider-Festschrift*) to be not the work of R. Gershom himself but a product of his school.

concept are: (1) the figure of a purely human, national Messiah and (2) the superhuman instrument of salvation, a mighty king — מלך המשיח — and wise judge or the destroyer of evil and judge of the world. A teaching role is attributed to the Messiah only in one passage, Gen. Rabbah XCVIII, 9, p. 1260, where the blessing of Judah (Gen. 49:11) is expounded as follows: "He washes his garment in wine — The Messiah will elucidate the words of the Torah; and his vesture in the blood of grapes. — The Messiah will elucidate where they — Israel — have misconstrued the law." A comparison with the corresponding parallel in the Tanḥuma[16] on Gen. 49:11 demonstrates clearly that the interpretation in Gen. Rabbah represents a revision of an old Haggadah. This old version does not interpret this verse with reference to the teaching activities of the Messiah, but rather, in keeping with TB Yoma 26a, to "the lawgivers of Judah (Ps. 60:9)" who succeed in arriving at the correct conclusions. Hence, the Amora R. Ḥanin[17] rightfully objects to this revision, remarking: "Israel will not need the instructions of the King Messiah in the days to come; they will receive instruction directly from God Himself; it will be the Messiah's mission to ingather the exiles and to instruct the heathens in the thirty[18] commandments. Only in a very late Midrash, the so-called Alphabet of R. Akiva,[19] do we hear of a new Torah[20] which God will reveal through the Messiah. The older sources know neither of a new Torah, nor of the Messiah's mission as a teacher. To assume Christian influence here is more than questionable; the abrogation of the law at the time of resurrection, עתיד לבוא, is already

---

[16] The sentence אין יין אלא תורה . . . אל בית היין has been misplaced; it belongs to the scriptural words: He washes his garment *in wine,* כבס ביין.

[17] Gen. Rabbah *ibid.*; Midrash Tehillim XXI, ed. Buber, p. 177, reads תנחומא instead of חנין. It is possible, and even probable, that this Amora was not acquainted with the mentioned revision of the old Haggadah, as presented in our text. The juxtaposition of his doctrine with the doctrine of the Messiah as the instructor of Israel may be attributed to the editor of the Midrash. It is well known that the last paragraphs of Gen. Rabbah have undergone heavy revision; the anonymous doctrine about the Messiah's teaching mission to Israel may be dated rather late.

[18] "The Minimum of Torah" incumbent even on non-Jews; see Joel, *Graetz — Jubelschrift*, pp. 174–175.

[19] Letter ז; Jellinek, *Beth Ha-Midrasch* III, p. 27. This Midrash served as source for Yalquṭ on Isa. 26:2 – N. 429 in *ed. princ.*, and in later editions 296, which has been overlooked by Weiss, *Dor* I, p. 229, as well as by Klausner, *Messianische Vorstellungen*, p. 83.

[20] *Cf.* also Midrash Tehillim CXLVI, ed. Buber, p. 535 ולעתיד לבוא הוא מתיר את כל מה שאסר, "in the days to come He — God — will permit again all that He has forbidden. However, ולעתיד לבוא does probably not refer to the messianic era, but rather the time after the resurrection.

assumed in the Talmud[21] as a generally accepted doctrine, and later writings seem to have confused, in this as in so many other cases, "the messianic era," ימות המשיח, with "the days to come," עתיד לבוא. As we have seen,[22] early allusions to the Messiah's teaching activities may be traced in older sources; the doctrine of "the new Torah to be revealed through the Messiah" may thus be explained without assuming Christian influence.

Whereas the biblical phrase עד יבוא ויורה צדק finds its application in the Talmud only once, it is employed very frequently in the post-biblical literature of the Rabbanites and the Karaites. It is of particular interest for the meaning of the expression מורה צדק in the present document to note that its manifold employment in later literature is the same as in the sectarian fragments. The Gaon Rav Hai b. Naḥshon (d. 896) remarks with reference to the fixing of the Jewish calendar that "it became accepted by all of Israel, from one end of the earth to the other, to be valid up to the Messianic era, when he — Elijah — will teach the truth." The words: קבלו כל ישראל מסוף העולם עד סופו עד זמן המשיח עד יורה צדק[23] call to mind the words in our document (6,10/11) that the laws as having been promulgated by the founder of the sect shall remain unalterable "up to the advent

---

[21] Niddah 61b (and note of Z. Chajes ad loc.) where certainly, as Weiss, Dor I, p. 229 noted already, the era discussed is only the time after the resurrection, and not "the messianic era," ימות המשיח. What Klausner, Messianische Vorstellungen, p. 53, says with reference to TB Sanhedrin 97b and Shir Hashirim Rabbah II,13, is correct but not new, since Weiss, op. cit. ibid., has already stated this correctly. However, Klausner is mistaken in quoting Sifre Deuteronomy 160, p. 211, and in attributing the partial change of the law to the Tannaim: [This is an old mistake. See חרב פיפיות, ed. Rosenthal, Jerusalem 1958, p. 63, and the reply, ibid., p. 71. — S. L.] the reference in point deals with changes of script and not of laws; see Tosefta Sanhedrin IV,7 and parallels. See also TP Megillah I,70d, and against this Midrash Mishle IX, p. 61, ed. Buber.

[22] See the reference in Gen. Rabbah, loc. cit., and in addition Midrash Hag. Schecht. 738. Midrash Tanḥuma, ed. Buber I, p. 139 contends that the Messiah "will excel even Moses," which means merely to extol his prophetic gift, as this passage was correctly interpreted by Maimonides, Hil. Teshuvah IX, 2. On basis of later Midrashim the author of ספר חסידים, ed. Wistenetzki, p. 268, assigns to the Messiah the function of a teacher; we may perhaps have to assume Christian influence on this mystic; see John 4:25; in Pesiqta Rabbati XV,71b the Messiah is addressed as רבנו.

[23] Pinsker, לקוטי קדמוניות II, p. 149; Harkavy, in his addenda to the Hebrew edition of Graetz, History III, p. 506, maintains that this sentence cannot be attributed to the Gaon Rav Hai b. Naḥshon of Sura, but belongs to his contemporary Hai b. David, the Gaon of Pumbeditha; however, see my remarks Geonica I, p. 163 and Bornstein, מחלקת, p. 144.

of him who teaches the truth." Whereas the Gaon still employs the biblical expression [24] עד יורה צדק, his Karaite contemporary Daniel al-Qumisi uses the term מורה צדק in discussing an intricate point of law, which may ultimately be dependent for its decision on "the advent of the Teacher of Truth,"[25] עד יבוא מורה צדק. Both expressions, the biblical עד יבוא יורה צדק and its circumscription by עד יבוא מורה צדק are found alongside each other in postgaonic literature without discrimination; both expressions are employed, as the above mentioned talmudical phrase עד שיבוא אליהו, to indicate an indeterminate point of law. R. Yehudah b. Barzillai al-Bargeloni — *fl.* about 1100 — writes in his commentary on *Sefer ha-Yeẓirah* that in consideration of the fact that no Talmud has been preserved on the tractates of the order Tohoroth, some difficulties in the Mishnah of this order will have to remain unsolved until the Teacher of Truth[26] will arrive, כיון שאין היום גמרא לטהרות .... עד שיבוא מורה צדק. From among the authors of the twelfth century we may mention here the renowned Provençal Talmudist R. Abraham b. David of Posquieres (ראב"ד), and his Karaite contemporary Yehudah Hadasi, who both employ the expression עד שיבוא ויורה צדק. The latter writes:[27] "In cases of doubt — in religious practice — I am inclined to adopt the stricter opinion, until the Teacher of Truth will arrive," ודעתי נוטה אחרי המחמיר עד יבוא ויורה צדק לנו ..., whereas the former concludes the discussion of a difficult passage in the Sifra with these words:[28] "Understanding is beyond me ... until the Teacher of Truth will arrive": ונפלאת דעת ממני ..... עד יבוא ויורה צדק. The Karaite Aaron b. Elijah of Nicomedia remarks in his Code,[29] written in 1354, also regarding a legal problem: "This will only be decided when the Teacher of Truth will come," עד יבוא ויורה צדק. His Rabbanite contemporary R. Eleazar b. Matha-

---

[24] The words יורה צדק do not refer to the preceding משיח, as one would be inclined to assume, but merely say that the "Teacher of Truth" will appear in the Messianic era; see the elaboration on this point in our further discussion.

[25] Harkavy, in the appendix to his edition of Anan's *Code*, pp. 188–189; [Nemoy, p. 34].

[26] פירוש ספר יצירה, p. 50.

[27] אשכול, p. 112b; but when he says there, p. 70d, that there will be controversies in Israel up to the advent of the Messiah, עד שיבוא משיח בן דוד לא יבטלו המחלוקת מישראל, it does not imply that it will be the Messiah who "will teach the truth." Hadassi probably had the above mentioned Mishnah Eduyyoth VIII, 7 in mind, which assigns to Elijah the function of arbitrating controversies להשוות המחלוקות. Hence משיח represents the Messianic era, and not the Messianic person.

[28] In his commentary on Sifra.

[29] *Gan Eden*, p. 41a.

thiah deplores that on account of so many Halakhic problems left unsolved and undecided, the Babylonian Talmud is not capable of enlightening Israel on all points; this will only be realized with the advent of the Teacher of Truth: ובמחשכים ישבנו כמתי עולם עם תלמוד בבלי עד יבוא מורה צדק לנו.[30]

The references listed may prove sufficient to demonstrate the employment of the terms עד יבוא מורה צדק and עד יבוא מורה ויורה צדק respectively in the sense in which it occurs in this document. We have found that this terminology is thus generally recognized and rather prevalent. We also noted that it is none other than Elijah who is expected, in the Messianic era, to clarify all doubtful points of Halakah. Hence this Prophet was given the eponym מורה צדק, and is referred to by this title, even when this reference is not applied to his teaching activity. The Palestinian Gaon Ben-Meir concludes his famous epistle, which he addressed in 921 against the Babylonian authorities, with the following words: מלך ברחמים רבים יחזיר את לבב עמו ישראל וישבור מעליהם עול ברזל ויביא להם מורה צדק ונזכה ותזכו להקביל [פני] משיח במהרה,[31] "May the King — God — in His great mercy rehabilitate the heart of His people Israel, break the bands of their yoke, and bring unto them the Teacher of Truth, so that we and you — recipients of this epistle — may soon deserve to welcome the Messiah." The important events in the days to come are, according to rabbinical doctrine:[32] Israel's return to God, תשובה, is the first prerequisite for salvation, which will then be followed by Israel's liberation from the yoke of the gentiles — through the instrumentality of the Ephraimite Messiah, then Elijah will appear heralding the advent of the (Davidic) Messiah, who then will arrive himself. Hence it seems beyond doubt that "the Teacher of Truth," who will appear after the rehabilitated Israel has been set free from the yoke of the gentiles, can be no other than Elijah. Since the advent of Elijah is identical[33] with the inception of the Messianic era, it has been customary to employ the congratulatory phrase: "May you live to see the advent of the Teacher of

[30] Berliner-Hoffmann, *Magazin* IV, p. 147; see also his older contemporary ריטב"א on Shevuoth 28a.

[31] Bornstein, מחלקת, p. 56; see also *ibid.*, p. 45 where להתבשר ברגלי המבשר corresponds to מורה צדק — the (joyful) herald is, of course, Elijah.

[32] Compare also the discussion of Saadia, a contemporary of Ben-Meir, in his האמונות והדעות, ch. VIII, ed. Cracow 1880, p. 160.

[33] The appearance of the Ephraimite Messiah indicates the conclusion of the old era rather than the ushering in of the new era. Incidentally, the activities of this Messiah do not represent any essential part of the rabbinical Messianology; neither Maimonides, in Hil. Melakhim XII, nor the very ancient source quoted by R. Tobiah b. Eliezer in his לקח טוב on Num. 24:17 mention him.

Truth!," as can be seen in a congratulatory epistle to Maimonides, published recently,[34] in which a life of happiness is invoked upon him עד ביאת מורה צדק.[35] The Karaite Aaron of Nicomedia[36] prays for the advent of the מורה צדק, and, indeed, the Karaite prayer book contains the phrase at the conclusion of the evening prayer:[37] והראנו את פני משיחך ואליהו נביאך וקרב לנו צמח בן דוד עבדך, "show us the face of Thy Messiah[38] and of Elijah Thy Prophet, and bring nigh to us the scion of David, Thy servant." Obviously Aaron of Nicomedia refers by מורה צדק, to the same who is mentioned as אליהו הנביא in the prayer book. Yet it seems that later on the phrase ביאת מורה צדק as reference to the Messianic era became misconstrued: "The Teacher of Truth" became identified with the Messiah. This misunderstanding was facilitated by the growing conception of the Messiah as a "teacher." Corroboration for this identification I can find with certainty only in a later author,[39] who out of sheer ignorance called the Messiah מורה צדק.

Although מורה צדק stands par excellence for the Prophet Elijah, yet important scholars were also honored with this title.[40] This custom cannot be corroborated from documents prior to the eleventh cen-

---

[34] *Herman Cohen Festschrift*: Judaica, p. 252.

[35] According to a prevailing view, resurrection will take place with the advent of the Messiah — see e. g. Hai Gaon, in the collection טעם זקנים, p. 60. Therefore the wish to be present in the messianic era is not identical with the wish to stay alive and experience this time; yet "to see the advent of Elijah" means: to stay alive to experience the Messianic days. Hence the custom to employ the phrase עד ביאת מורה צדק in a wish; the Ashkenazim, however, use today the phrase עד ביאת הגואל, "till the advent of the Redeemer."

[36] גן עדן, p. 128b.

[37] This prayer commences with the words אנא אלהי, in ed. Vilna, 1891, vol. I, p. 28.

[38] Perhaps the reference is made to the Ephraimite Messiah, for this reason the order is: משיחך, then אליהו, and ultimately the scion of David. See further on. Yet I know of no instance in which the Karaites took over from the Rabbanites the role played by the Ephraimite Messiah. Is it possible that the whole sentence here hails from Rabbanite provenance?

[39] The anonymous author of the apocryphal biography of Maimonides — *REJ* IV, pp. 175–176 — remarks that the Talmud has 18 inexplicable problems, which will have to wait for their solution until the מורה צדק will arrive. These 18 problems, which Neubauer, *ibid.*, is at a loss to ascertain, are doubtless identical with the 18 legal cases we have listed above, p. 212, n. 14, which the Talmud leaves in abeyance עד שיבוא אליהו; our anonymous author, however, most certainly identifies the מורה צדק with the Messiah, probably on basis of misunderstanding the passage in Bekhoroth 24a.

[40] Similarly משה is employed as honorific for outstanding sages in the Babylonian and the Palestinian Talmud; see Kohut. *Arukh Compl., s. v.*

tury. Rashi[41] refers to his teacher R. Isaac b. Yehudah with this honorific. Rashi's colleagues, R. Eliakim[42] and R. Samuel[43] ha-Cohen as well as R. Abraham[44] b. David of Posquieres bear the same title. Most probably this title originated at a much earlier date,[45] a thesis which may be corroborated by the following circumstances: the employment of מורה צדק as honorific can be traced to Spain and Egypt in the twelfth century; Maimonides[46] is addressed by this title in Egypt, and the Spaniard ibn-Zabara commends a town for possessing "sages, scholars and teachers of truth": כי קהלם חכמים ונבונים ומורי צדק שומרי אמונים.[47] It is nigh impossible that a title which made its debut in Northern France[48] in the eleventh century would have gained vogue in Spain and Egypt[49] within the span of two generations. It should be pointed out further that the scholars just mentioned as well as many others[50] bore the title מורה צדק to designate their activity as "teachers of religious practice"; this usage has been preserved to our own time.[51] In the Talmud, as early as the terminology of the

[41] Yoma 16b.

[42] מעשה הגאונים, p. 17, 54, 65. The same scholar is probably also meant by this title מורה צדק in Pardess, p. 36. Epstein, *Steinschneider Festschrift*, p. 126, demonstrated that in the talmudical commentary ascribed to R. Gershom, the often mentioned מורה צדק is none other than this R. Eliakim.

[43] ספר האורה, p. 146.

[44] See the poem of R. Zeraḥia ha-Levi in his commentary on the tractate Qinnim. R. Eleazar of Worms mentions in רקח, p. 250 his teacher, probably R. Yehudah the Pious with the title מורה צדק.

[45] The responsum in שערי תשובה, No. 99, attributed to R. Hai Gaon, mentions a כהן מורה צדק; however this responsum is doubtless the fabrication of a Qabbalist of the thirteenth or fourteenth century. The expression עד יורה צדק which appears in תשובות חכמי צרפת is an allusion to Hos. 10:12.

[46] *Responsa*, No. 127, ed. Lichtenberg (p. 23b).

[47] ספר שעשועים, ed. Davidson, p. 145. See also חובות הלבבות, VI, 2 and מוסרי הפילוסופים, I, 2 where the translators ibn-Tibbon and al-Ḥarizi render מורה צדק for the original ولا مرشل.

[48] Literary communication between Northern France and Spain was of rather infrequent at this time; there was hardly any contact between Northern France and Egypt.

[49] Also in his son's מלחמת השם and in the epistle by R. Hillel of Verona, Maimonides is called מורה צדק, yet they may be rather alluding to him as the author of מורה נבוכים, which is certainly the case with the panegyrical poem on the *Guide for the Perplexed*; see יד קובץ על, I–II.

[50] *Cf.* מעשה הגאונים, No. 65: וכן הורו כאן מורי צדק, "and thus decided here the teachers of truth," referring to the scholars of Speyer who flourished about 1100: *cf.* also מחזור ויטרי, p. 105: למורי צדק, where, however, most probably we ought to read למורי and not למורי, referring to Rashi, who also elsewhere is just called המורה.

[51] In Vilna, one of the largest Jewish communities, for more than a century there has been no communal rabbi. The religious guidance is provided by the מורה

earlier Tannaim, the title מורה — usually מורה הלכות[52] — designates not
the scholar חכם, סופר, or the teacher רבי, רבן, but the authority who
decides[53] in applying the law to actual practice. The almost exclusive[54]
usage of this title in this document, in exactly the same connotation
as in rabbinical literature, is in keeping with its strictly legalistic
character.

After this long excursus, which was, to be sure, necessary for the
understanding of the document, we shall now return to our earlier
point in discussion. We have seen[55] that מורה צדק in 1,11 refers
neither to the Messiah nor to the founder of the sect, but to the
Restorer of the Torah during the reign of King Josiah, who in this
document is probably identified with the contemporary high priest.
The origin and provenance of this title from Hos. 10:12 is evident
from 6,7. There the words עד עמוד יורה הצדק are certainly reminiscent
of the biblical עד יבוא ויורה צדק.[56] Since, as we have seen, both this

---

צדק — popularly called "Mats," מ"ץ — and such a figure is mainly concerned with
Halakic applications. Cf. Maggid, עיר ווילנא, p. 102 ff. In a lamentation on the
massacre of Jews in Schneidemuehl (1654), special mention is made of מורי צדק
הרבנים; cf. Brann, in Festschrift Lewy, p. 579.

[52] R. Gamliel in Tosefta Niddah V, 15 and his colleague R. Yoshua, Giṭṭin 58a —
but not in the parallel passage Tosefta Horayoth II, 6 — are the earliest Tannaim to
whom this usage can be traced. For just מורה I could only find one reference, Nedarim
49b, where R. Yehudah b. Ilai is called מורה, most certainly in consideration of his
position as מוריינא דבי נשיאה; cf. Menaḥoth 104a. Graetz, Geschichte III[5], 759, assumes
that καθηγητής in Matt. 23:8 is a translation of מורה.

[53] Cf. Jer. Sanhedrin IV,22a, where it is said of a very subtle scholar: לא הוה
ידע מורייה, "he could not properly decide the applicability."

[54] The Founder of the Sect is in 6,7, called דורש התורה = ἐξηγητὴς τῶν νόμων;
see also Josephus, Ant. XVIII,6,2; in rabbinical sources the title is דרשן; so in reference to Shemaiah and Avtalyon — Pesaḥim 70b; to R. Akiva — Eliahu Zuṭa I,
p. 168, ed. Friedmann, and to Ben Zoma, Sotah IX, 15.

[55] Cf. above, p. 211.

[56] I am put hard to understand how in view of this fact Gressmann (ZDMG
LXVI, 501) can contend that our document speaks of a "Teacher of Justice," to
be corroborated by reference to Joel 2:23, המורה לצדקה. Not only has he failed to
notice the prevalent expression מ"ץ in rabbinical literature. He has also ignored the
corresponding connotation of צדק in phrases like חקי הצדק in our document —
20,11; 20,33 — which removes all doubts about the meaning and origin of מורה צדק.
Note the substitution of עמד for יבוא in our document, in keeping with the eschatological designation of the word עמד in other passages — 12,24; 20,1. This usage
can also be demonstrated elsewhere; cf. Ezra 2:63; Neh. 7:65; and I Macc. XIV, 41.
We have already satisfied ourselves earlier that יורה is not a proper name, nor could
it possibly be such; my suggested emendation there — to read מורה instead of יורה —
I herewith retract, since in this passage the words of Hosea are quoted, therefore,
the verbal form יורה is called for, although it is incorrect grammar. The whole expression is eliptical for עד עמוד אליהו ויורה, just paraphrasing the biblical expression.

biblical expression and its derivative עד יבוא מורה צדק are tantamount
to the meaning of the rabbinical "until the advent of Elijah," עד
שיבוא אליהו, there are no warranted or plausible grounds to invest it
with a different meaning in our document. The change from the biblical צדק to הצדק is purposeful in this passage and not a dittography.[57]
Every significant teacher of the law can, just as in rabbinical literature, bear the title מורה צדק, e. g. Zadok in 1,11. However, Elijah is
just the one of whom the Prophet Hosea announces "that he will
then come and teach the truth." This very substitution of יורה הצדק
here, for the usual מורה צדק in our document, alludes to the distinction between the status of Elijah and that of other teachers of the
law. But the Founder of the Sect occupies a singular position: he is
the "Exegete of the Torah," דורש התורה (6,7; 7,18), whereas other
teachers have to contend themselves with the title דורש or דרשן[58]
respectively. However, despite his exceeding importance he is never
called the "Teacher of Truth," for this title is reserved for Elijah
exclusively. However, the founder of the Sect is distinguished from
other teachers, and in this capacity he is called "the distinct teacher,"
מורה היחיד[59] (20,1;14;32). The passage 20,32 is particularly instruc-

---

[57] The preceding word is יורה — ending with letter ה.

[58] Cf. above, n. 54, where details are given on this ancient title. The quotation
from Josephus cited, ibid., makes it probable to assume that originally the accepted
title was דורש התורה.

[59] In the Mishnah — e. g. Taanith I, 4 — the expression יחידים refers to a distinct degree of piety. The term יחיד may have obtained the connotation of dis-
tinctiveness already in Gen. 22:2 and in Judg. 11:34; cf. Ehrlich, Randglossen, ibid.
Gressmann writes (ZDMG, LXVI, 494: "The heretofore accepted translation of
מורה היחיד as the distinct (=unique) teacher is unjustifiable from the grammatical
point of view." However, this remark can only prove that Gressmann has never
heard of כנסת הגדולה (the assembly) or יצר הרע (the evil impulse), otherwise he could
not have maintained that the combination of a noun lacking the article, with an
adjective possessing the article, is grammatically untenable. Actually, this construction is not only permissible in post-biblical Hebrew, but even the only correct form
if, as in this case, emphasis on the attribute is intended. Segal, Mišnaic Hebrew,
has forty passages from the Mishnah alone confirming this rule, and hundreds more
could be marshalled from other Tannaitic sources. A few rare instances could be
culled even from biblical Hebrew; cf. Gesenius-Kautzsch § 126, and Driver, Tenses,
p. 209. It would have behooved the theologian Gressmann to realize that for the
Jews, God is not יחיד, but אחד; thus "the teacher of the Only One" would have to
be called מורה האחד. As for the meaning of יחיד in the sense of "distinct," cf. also
Sifre Deut. 313, p. 355, and Num. Rabbah III,6: ה ל ו ד ג לשון אלא יחיד אין.
Note also epitheta in Jewish and Arabic usage יחיד הדור, חד בדרא — Kethuvoth 17a;
very often in post-Talmudic literature יחיד אל זמאן. In Test. Benjamin IX, 2 μονογενής
is probably derivative of יחיד, which is the way this word is rendered by the
Aramaic versions of John. — In regard to the article in יצר הרע, its presence may
be explained by euphonic reasons: to avoid the succession of two ר'; therefore, the
article here, whereas יצר טוב is the usual form in the contrasting phrase.

tive for the relationship between מורה היחיד and מורה צדק. For here
the pious and the just are commended for being "those who follow
the ancient instructions by which the disciples of the Distinct Teacher
were guided, hearkening to the voice of the Teacher of Truth": והתיסרו
במשפטים הראשונים אשר נשפטו בני אנשי היחיד והאזינו לקול מורה צדק.[60] Here,
clearly, an admonition is addressed to the late generation to follow in
the footsteps of the former generation, and as these agreed to obey
"the Distinct Teacher," so in turn the latter-day sectarians are to
obey their teachers. The founder of the sect is, according to this
passage, distinguished from all other teachers by being referred to as
"the Distinct Teacher,"[61] whereas all others are merely called just
teacher, or teacher of righteousness.

Summing up our investigations of the meaning of מורה צדק and
יורה צדק respectively in our document, we reach the following conclusion: In keeping with the talmudical interpretation of Hos. 10:12
the Prophet Elijah has been assigned the ultimate mission to restore
the unity of law and doctrine in the messianic era; in this restoring
capacity Elijah bears the title מורה צדק [יורה], "he who will teach the
truth." All other teachers of the law are either, as in the Talmud,
just called מורה (20,28),[62] or, as in post-Talmudical literature, they
bear the honorific title מורה צדק. In our document, known historical
personalities are referred to by their title: the Restorer of the Torah
in the days of King Josiah is called מורה צדק (1,11), whereas the
Founder of the Sect is "the Distinct Teacher," מורה היחיד [יורה]
(20,1;14) or "the Distinct," היחיד[63] (20,32). Far from identifying the
Founder with the Messiah, our document employs a designation for
him which distinguishes him only gradually from other teachers; it is
conveniently suggested that his authority as teacher of the law is inferior to Elijah's authority. He will ultimately, at the End of the

[60] On the translation rendered in the text, we should like to add the following
remarks: והתיסרו, "to accept obligations," in the Aramaic form ייסר, Meg. Taanith
XII and thence Taanith 12a. For בני we certainly ought to read בם. The meaning
of נשפט, to act in compliance with the ordinance (משפט), can be derived from the
primary meaning of שפט without undue strain, although it cannot be traced elsewhere. The terminology chosen here is probably an allusion to the biblical יסר
למשפט. The designation אנשי היחיד is, of course, short for אנשי מורה היחיד.

[61] For מורה the copyist wrote in 19,35 first יורה, which he subsequently struck
out, whereas in 20,14 he left it uncorrected; he thought of the biblical application
of the term מורה, the עד יבוא ויורה of Hosea.

[62] Here the reference cannot possibly mean the Founder of the Sect, for in that
case it could only have said המורה or מורה הצדק, the "teacher," a term much too
broad and general. Among medieval authors, Rashi is referred to by this title, as
pointed out earlier.

[63] Perhaps for היחיד, instead of מורה היחיד, the copyist is responsible?

Days, decide all doubts and controversies, but until then prime authority is vested in the Founder of the Sect.

*   *

*

The title משיח is mentioned for the first time in 2,12, where it is said that "God will make known to them His holy spirit, the spirit of truth, through His chosen one," ויודיעם ביד משיחו רוח קדשו והוא אמת.[64] It has already been remarked on the passage that one has to read here מְשִׁיחָו, "his anointed ones," which in the frame of reference of our document relates to the ancestors, who were the bearers of divine revelation during the many generations that preceded the era of Moses. The tenor of the content of the passage in point dispels all doubts concerning the validity of our interpretation. The whole paragraph[65] deals with a trait of divine justice and providence, i. e., that even at times of retribution — such as the Deluge, the scattering of the builders of the tower of Babel, etc. — the world was not destroyed entirely, but a few elect survived to whom He revealed His truth.

We deem it very doubtful that משיחו of 6,1 refers to the Messiah. Most probably it speaks of the Highpriest Zadok (5,5) as the holy anointed one, who, according to our document, is identified with the Restorer of the Torah in the days of Josiah. Therefore the sinners are being chastised with these words: "And at the time[66] when the land was laid desolate there arose those who removed the landmarks and led Israel astray so that the land was made into a desert. For they preached rebellion against the commandments [given] by God through Moses, and also through His holy annointed one," ובקץ חרבן הארץ עמדו מסיגי הגבול ויתעו את ישראל וַתֵּשַׁם הארץ כי דברו סרה על מצות אל ביד משה וגם במשיחו הקודש [הקדוש67]. A tannaitic statement (Sifre Deut. 48, p. 112; Midrash Tannaim 43) says: "But for the activities of Shafan[68] (II Kings 22:12) in the days of Josiah, the Torah would

---

[64] The last two words are not, as could easily be assumed, a gloss on רוח קדשו, but serve as emphasis respective ואת אשר שנא התעה in the following line; cf. similarly 20,12 והוא ברית וכו', which emphasizes ברית ואמונה.

[65] Cf. above, p. 167.

[66] About this meaning of קץ, cf. p. 29. It is not referring to the time when the Temple was destroyed, but to the reign of Alexander Jannai during which Palestine was visited by many troubles; cf. below, Section VII.

[67] Thus Schechter on the text. Yet this emendation is not absolutely necessary. ו instead of Kamez is prevalent and goes back to the pronunciation of Kamez as O.

[68] Cf. above the reason for this glorifying of Shafan. In the cited Tannaic sources, as also in Sukkah 20a, similar statements are made about Ezra and other Men of the Great Assembly.

have been lost for Israel." Our document is therefore entirely justified in referring to the Restorer of the Torah as "the holy anointed one through whom the commandments of God were given" — for if not for his activities, the Mosaic revelation would have come to naught. Only, in contrast to the rabbinical tradition, the Restorer is identified here with the contemporary anointed Highpriest. We notice, however, that our document speaks of divine commandments given "through Moses, and *also* through His holy anointed." The word גם, "and also," expresses the difference between the two: the Revelation proper occurred through Moses. The designation of the Highpriest as משיח finds its parallel not only in the Bible but also in tannaitic literature,[69] as e. g. Mishnah Horayoth II — eight times! — Tos. Shevuoth I, 6 and in many other passages, although the eschatological usage of this word was certainly prevalent at the time of the redaction of the Mishnah. We should remember that according to rabbinical tradition[70] with the exception of Aaron and his sons, Zadok was the only Highpriest actually to be anointed. Hence the designation of משיח for the Highpriest was chosen deliberately for a good reason. It must be borne in mind, though, that the Rabbis were apparently referring to the Zadok who served as Highpriest in the reign of David,[71] whereas the present document seems to extol the glory of another Zadok. However, it belongs to the nature of legends to bestow rich embellishments upon their darlings; our document may here have derived inspiration from a legend which bequeathed upon the latter-day Zadok[72] what rightly belonged to the former. Another possibility is indicated by the words "the commandments [given] by God through Moses and Aaron." Aaron was already designated in the Bible as "the holy one of the Lord" (Ps. 106:16), and in rabbinical literature[73] as "the anointed one of God," משיח י"י; this again is a very apt description

---

[69] It is probably a pure coincidence that the word משיח is not to be found in the Mishnah in its eschatological meaning; the most ancient documents of Christianity and extra-Mishnaic Tannaite literature attest to the prevalence of such connotation in contemporary usage of his word.

[70] Pirke Rabbenu ha-Qadosh, ed. Grünhut, 87–88.

[71] This tradition means to signify only that at the time when the hereditary office of the Highpriest was transferred from the Aaronide family of Ittamar to the Aaronide family of Eleazar — the first Highpriest of the latter family, Zadok was initiated by anointment.

[72] Cf. above, p. 21; about the equation חלקיה=צדוק discussed there, see also Smend, *Weisheit des Jesus Sohn des Sirach*, p. 493 and further below in this present study.

[73] Midrash Tehillim, ed. Buber II, p. 25; there, Ps. 2:2 is explained as reference to Korah's rebellion against Aaron.

of the man who was the first to have been initiated into his high office by anointment. Aaron's participation in the revelation of the divine commandments is assumed[74] in numerous places in the Pentateuch. With this in mind, the words כי דברו סרה על מצות אל ביד משה וגם במשיחו הקודש can plausibly be explained without any forcing. If, however, we want to understand the passage in point to mean[75] that sinners arose inciting to "rebellion against the commandments given by God, and against His holy Messiah," it would still not follow that the Messiah, whose advent was expected by the sect, would be a personality that had already appeared once in the history of Israel and would return again in the end of the days to be revealed in his full glory.[76] For our document charges the opponents only with inciting Israel with heresies to rebel against the Messiah, either by categorically denying the belief in his advent, or by circulating an interpretation of his expected activities which is at variance with the sectarian doctrine. A similar charge is raised in the Book of Enoch (CVIII, 6) against "the sinners, the blasphemers . . . ., who commit evil and pervert whatever God hath announced about the things to come by mouth of His Prophets." In the light of the Enoch passage one would be inclined to read בִּמְשִׁיחָו, "His anointed ones," indicting the perverters for preaching rebellion against the divine commandments revealed through Moses and "His holy anointed ones," i. e., the Prophets. Although the term משיח in the sense of Prophet cannot be traced elsewhere, it stands to reason that this honorific is ap-

---

[74] In thirteen passages of the Pentateuch we find the formula וידבר/ויאמר ה' אל משה ואל אהרן לאמר. Some Tannaim — beginning of Torath Kohanim and parallel references — explain this inclusion of Aaron to mean merely that God enjoined Moses to inform his brother about the commandment, but not that Aaron was partner in the revelation proper of the commandment; see Friedmann's note on the first section of the Mekilta.

[75] This explanation would face great difficulties, as instead of the במשיחו of our text, על משיחו would be expected. Even if we admit the construction of דבר סרה with 'ב — in the Bible על and אל respectively — it seems rather strange to find the construction with על and 'ב employed in one sentence interchangeably.

[76] Cf. Sanhedrin 98b, according to which the Messiah will be a person who will impress himself upon the life of Israel with great significance by his very first appearance. I have elaborated on this point in my Die Haggadah bei den Kirchenvaetern und in der Apokryphischen Literatur, p. 5, explaining from this point of view the employment of "revelari" relative to the advent of the Messiah. "The hidden Messiah," משיח הנחבא (Midrash Tehillim XXI), on the other hand, originates in the concept of the Messiah's disappearance shortly after his advent, and his subsequent reappearance. Cf. Pesiqta R. Kahana, ed. Buber, V, p. 49b [ed. Mandelbaum, p. 92] and parallel references.

plicable[77] to them as well as to the "fathers," with regard to whom, as was demonstrated earlier, it is used both in the terminology of our document and in rabbinic literature. Accordingly, we may raise the possibility that the term משיחו refers to the afore-mentioned Moses.

The first undoubted mention of the Messiah is in the passage 12,23. There the constitution of the community is introduced with the following preamble: "The following is the constitution of the community in compliance with which it ought to conduct itself during the period of corruption until the advent of the Messiah of Aaron and Israel," זה סרך מושב המֹחֹנֹה להתהלך בֹו[78] בקץ הרשעה עד עמוד משוח אהרן וישראל. A phrase bearing striking similarity is to be found in 6,10. There we read about the regulations promulgated by the founder of the sect (מחוקק) "in compliance with which they ought to conduct themselves during the period of corruption until the advent of him who will teach the truth in the end of the days, and without them — these regulations — nothing will be accomplished," להתהלך במה בכל קץ הרשיע וזולתם לא ישינו עד עמד יורה הצדק באחרית הימים. The similarity between these two passages gave rise to the fallacy that the Messiah was identical with the Teacher of the Truth. Such mistaken identification was made possible only by completely ignoring the parallel application of these two terms in Talmudical literature.

The Tannaim and Amoraim[79] employed a stock phrase for expressing unlimited duration: "Thus it will remain until the advent of the son of David,"[80] עד שיבוא בן דוד. The phrase conveys the same meaning implied in the phrase under discussion, עד עמוד משיח, "until the advent of the Messiah." However, if an opinion concerning a legal controversy was to be declared as authoritative, the Talmud employs another stock phrase based on the words of Hosea עד יבוא ויורה צדק, as we elaborated above. Correspondingly our document reads[81]

---

[77] As explained in an earlier remark, מֹשִיחוֹ in 2,12 corresponds to נביאיך in Neh. 9:30, whence the equation משח=נביא can be demonstrated. In the Middle Ages the honorific משיח is also applied to great luminaries, such as Maimonides; see אגרות קנאות, ed. Leipzig, the beginning.

[78] The dotted letters are illegible in the manuscript and filled in by me; cf. p. 84.

[79] PT Ḥagigah II, 77d; Bavli Soṭah 48b and ARN, ed. Schechter 103. Cf. also the Baraitha in Eruvin 43a הריני נזיר ביום שבן דוד בא, "I take upon myself to become a Nazir with the advent of the son of David," i. e. "on the ultimate day," but not as long as the present state of affairs prevails.

[80] As is well known, this is the abbreviation for משיח בן דוד, the Messiah.

[81] Instead of יבוא our document reads עמד and for צדק it reads הצדק; cf. above, on these variants.

עד עמד יורה הצדק. The Talmud and our document understand the designation יורה צדק as clear reference to the Prophet Elijah, the messianic herald who will ultimately clear up all controversial issues.

Hence it is evident why in the passage 6,11 — which deals with the authority of the מחוקק — the phrase appears as עד עמד יורה הצדק; until the advent of Elijah, the מחוקק will represent the highest authority. In 12,23, however, where the stress is put upon the unlimited validity of the community's rules and regulations, the fitting expression is עד עמד משיח. Rabbinic literature provides us with clear distinctions to demonstrate how unwarranted would be any identification of משיח with יורה צדק merely on grounds of the close relationship between these two formulae. The rabbinical sources employ both עד שיבוא אליהו and עד שיבוא בן דוד although אליהו and בן דוד are entirely different persons. The Tosefta Soṭah XIII, 2 comments on the passage in Ezra 2:6 עד עמוד הכהן לאורים:[82] "this expression is equivalent to the figure of speech: it will remain like this until Elijah will come, or: till the dead will be resurrected עד עמוד כהן לאורים ותומים, כאדם שאומר לחברו: עד שיבוא אליהו, או: עד שיחיו המתים.[83] In the parallel references, (PT Qiddushin IV, 65b and Bavli Soṭah 48b), however, we read בן דוד for אליהו. The advent of Elijah, the advent of the Messiah, and the resurrection of the dead, represent the three essential criteria for the future order of the world; hence the three designations בן דוד, עד שיבוא אליהו and שיחיו המתים for the time to come. The meaning of these phrases is not in the words proper, but in their common denominator: the new order of the world. Therefore we also read in Seder Olam Rabba, ch. XVII: "Elijah went into concealment and will reappear only at the advent of the Messiah," נגנז אליהו ולא נראה עוד עד שיבוא מלך המשיח. According to the generally accepted tradition,[84]

---

[82] Similarly in I Macc. XIV, 41: "that Simeon should be their priest forever, until there should arise a faithful prophet." *Cf.* also my remarks in *Jewish Encyc.*, I, p. 637, *s. v.* Antiochus, in reference to a similar term in the Megillath Antiochus.

[83] The expression is also to be found in Mekilta, Ki Tissa (ed. Friedm.) 104b; [Hor.-Rab., p. 343]; Mekilta R. S. [Hoffm. 161], speaking of the era which starts with Creation and will conclude with resurrection, מיום שברא הקב׳ה עולמו עד שיחיו המתים, i. e. for the duration of the present state of world order. Most probably this expression is older than the other two. According to an ancient conception the activities of Elijah and the Messiah belong, still, to the present, existing world order. The term עד שיחיו המתים is found also in Sifre Numbers 139, p. 186; Tanḥuma, ed. Buber, I, p. 8; Avoth R. N., ed. Schechter, p. 99, and Mid. Agg., ed. Buber, II, p. 122.

[84] The advent of Elijah prior to that of the Messiah is assumed not only in the writings of the primitive church; it is maintained also in the Bab. Talmud, Eruvin 43b. By the way, we should like to point out that Maimonides, Melakhim XII,2 alludes to this passage of the Seder Olam, a reference which eluded the commentators on that work, including Ratner.

Elijah will appear as herald and precursor of the Messiah, and there-fore our passage reads here עד שיבוא מלך המשיח, meaning "the time to come."

*   *
*

The designation of the Messiah as "the Anointed of Aaron and Israel" occurs twice in Fragment A[85] and twice in Fragment B.[86] Hence we are quite justified in assuming that this designation constitutes part of the original teaching of the sectarian doctrine, although we may find difficulty in determining its exact meaning. Usually it is understood as being related to the doctrine concerning the Messiah's descent from Levi (=Aaron) and Judah (=Israel) in the Testament of the XII Patriarchs. Upon closer scrutiny, however, this inter-pretation (that the sect expects a priestly Messiah who will also on his mother's side, be a descendant of a non-priestly family, so that all Israel will share in him; hence his designation Messiah of Aaron and Israel) appears to be untenable. For corroboration of the usual interpretation reference is made by those who maintained it to the passage, 5,2–6 where David, the ancestor of the Messiah whom the Pharisees are expecting, is rebuked for his keeping many wives. How-ever, we have demonstrated above that our document nowhere even remotely approaches stigmatizing David as a sinner. On the contrary, it endeavors to exonerate David from this charge and explicitly extols the king's conduct. It is, furthermore, natural to imagine the Messiah as a scion of royal and priestly stock. The Haggadah[87] expresses this expectation in the statement that King David, the Messiah's ances-tor, was a scion of Miriam, the sister of Aaron and Moses. This, then, would be sufficient to explain a משיח ליהודה ולוי, and even, with some forcing,[88] a משיח מלוי ויהודה, as expounded in the Testaments, but never the משיח אהרן וישראל of our document. It would be possible to imagine that the German Constitution had a paragraph: "The Ger-man Emperor must be a German and a Prussian"; but it would be meaningless to say "a Prussian and a German," for every Prussian is *eo ipso* a German. An Aaronide is an Israelite of the first order; hence

---

[85] 12,23 and 14,19, where אהרן וישראל ought to be preceded by the word משיח.

[86] 19,10; 20,1; in contrast to A we read in B משיח instead of משח, and in the latter passage מאהרן and not אהרן. We shall elaborate on this further on.

[87] Already in Tannaitic sources: Sifre Num. 78, p. 75; *cf.* also Soṭah 11b; Exod. Rabbah I,17. The latter two references stress that Jochebed, Amram's wife, the mother of Miriam, Aaron and Moses, was the ancestress of both the priestly and royal lines.

[88] In case one is inclined to accept the usual view regarding the messianology in the Testaments — *cf.* further on in the text.

a משיח אהרן is automatically also simultaneously משיח אהרן וישראל. Emphasis on the fact that the priestly Messiah is also an "Israelite" would be ridiculous. Besides this objection, we ought to bear in mind that according to Jewish law maternal ancestry is of no consequence,[89] and the identification of the Messiah with reference to the distaff side is hardly plausible. To be sure, the Testaments do make mention in several passages[90] of the Messiah as scion of Levi and Judah. However, in spite of the dominant scholarly opinion that this dual genealogical identification of the Messiah belongs to the original Jewish part of this pseudepigraph, the matter appears highly doubtful to me. The Messianology of the Testaments cannot be discussed here, but we cannot help referring to several passages in the Testaments which allegedly corroborate the doctrine of the priestly Messiah, but which, upon closer critical scrutiny, must be given a different interpretation.

In Reuben VI,7 we read: "For the Lord gave dominion to Levi and Judah with him also unto me — Reuben — and Dan and Joseph, to become rulers." Charles discovers here the priestly king, and therefore declares the conclusion of the verse starting with "and Judah" as "foolish interpolation." How could it ever have happened, we wonder, that anybody would dare be so foolish to add not only the name of Judah, which might conceivably make sense, but even Reuben, Dan and Joseph, if the original had only been "Levi"? In fact, this passage is not dealing with the subject of the Messiah at all. It lists the tribes which, at one time or another, will exercise dominion over Israel, until the royal dynasty will be established. First comes Levi — Aaron and Moses were the first leaders of Israel; then Judah — represented by Othniel,[91] the first judge; then Dan, forebear

---

[89] Cf. Sifra on Lev. 24:10, ed. Weiss 104c; Lev. Rabbah XXXII,3, p. 742, and Tanḥuma, ed. Buber III, p. 103; Bava Bathra 109b.

[90] Cf. Volz, Juedische Eschatologie, p. 203 ff.; and Charles, Testaments of the XII Patriarchs, particularly his comments on Reuben VI; Levi VIII; Judah XXIV; Dan V; and Joseph XIX.

[91] In Judg. 3:9 he is described as a brother of Caleb, the Judean. Also Ebzan — Judg. 12:8 — is reported as inhabitant of the Judean town Bethlehem. The Haggadah identifies Ebzan with Boaz, David's forebear; cf. elaboration on this point in my Die Haggadah bei den Kirchenvaetern, I, p. 10, where I demonstrated, with references to patristic literature, that this identification was known in Christian circles. Concerning the Judah mentioned in Judg. 1:2 who was bidden to initiate the attack upon the Canaanites, the Haggadah, Jewish and Christian (cf. my Haggadah, p. 2), identifies him with Judge Othniel, who, among other names, was also called Judah. Josephus seems not to have known the name Othniel, strange as it seems, for he calls this judge by the designation Keniazua — קני, קנז — father or grandfather of Othniel.

of the epic hero in the era of the judges, Samson. Finally Joseph's
Manasseh and Ephraim, the tribe which produced many judges during the preroyal period.[92] Reubenite judges are not mentioned in the
Bible. However, it stands to reason that the report in the Testaments
derives from an otherwise unknown Haggadah[93] which relates one or
more judges, whose genealogy is not specified, to Reuben. It is also
possible that we are dealing here with a misunderstanding on part of
the Greek translator. The original Hebrew may have read: וללוי נתן
הממשלה וליהודה גם לוי[94] ולדן וליוסף, "and He gave dominion to Levi,
and also to Judah, as well as Dan and Joseph"; a change from לו to
לי, against the author's intention, bestowed the rank on Reuben. We
also recall that according to the Haggadah[95] the tribe of Reuben
held hegemony in Israel even prior to the Exodus from Egypt;
thus its claim as a "ruling" tribe seems to be justified.

Another passage in the Testaments which is cited, erroneously, to
support the notion of the priestly Messiah is Reuben VI,10–12. It
reads: "And approach Levi in the meekness of your heart that you
may receive the blessing out of his mouth; for he will bless Israel and
Judah, since he was chosen by the Lord to rule over all the people.
And you shall prostrate yourselves before his seed, for he shall give
up his life for you in wars visible and invisible, and he will reign over
you evermore." In a note on this passage Charles relates the "wars
visible and invisible" to the activities of the Maccabees, who as
leaders of the rebellion against Israel's foes fell on the battlefield,
but who also as members of the priestly family led the spiritual battles

---

[92] Besides Joshua, also Gideon, Abimelekh and Jephtah are traceable to the
tribes of Joseph. Judg. 4:5 stresses that Deborah resided in the mountains of
Ephraim, probably implying that she belonged to this tribe; however, cf. Judg.
3:2 and 10:18.

[93] A tradition, reported in the name of the Tanna R. Eliezer b. Hyrkanus (fl.
about 100 C.E.), states: "All tribes but Shimeon produced judges and kings (Sukkah
27b)." The Apocryphal Midrash Tadshe essays to demonstrate the correctness of
this statement by quoting detailed proofs from the Bible (ed. Epst. ch. VIII), but
with dubious success for neither Gad nor Reuben is given its due. The Haggadah in
the Testaments seems to acknowledge this rank and honor only for the six outstanding tribes: Reuben, Levi, Judah, Dan, Joseph (Manasseh and Ephraim). In
the Midrash Tadshe the correct reading is דבורה מאפרים וברק מקדש נפתלי.

[94] Rhetorical and poetic form for וגם ליהודה.

[95] Cant. Rabbah IV,7, where it is contended that Simeon is to succeed this tribe
and then Levi in the person of Moses. In light of the Haggadah concerning Simeon,
which was mentioned in the previous note and which finds its parallel also in the
Testaments (Simeon V,6), we can well understand why Simeon is ignored in the
present passage dealing with leadership. Cf. also Levi VIII,11 ff., where Moses
appears as the representative of Levi's hegemony.

of Israel. What he fails to explain, however, is why anyone has to give up his life in leading spiritual battles for Israel. Demons and evil spirits can inflict death, but only on those who follow them; those who combat them are safe with their lives! However, if we take the trouble to retranslate this passage into Hebrew, we shall notice at once that the "wars visible and invisible" owe their existence to a translator's error; that this passage definitely refers to the "Messiah out of Judah." In Hebrew it would probably read thus: ובנפש שפלה תנשו אל לוי לקבל ברכת שפתיו כי הוא יברך ישראל ויהודה אשר בו בחר אלהים להיות מלך על כל הגויים, והשתחוו לפני זרעו כי הוא ימות במלחמות נראות ונפלאות אשר ילחם לנו והוא יהיה מלך לעולם ביניכם. It is the purpose of this passage, first of all, to admonish the tribes to do obeisance to the priests, for the divine blessings pronounced over Israel and Judah come forth out of their mouth, according to Num. 6:23 ff. Moreover, they are enjoined "to prostrate themselves before Judah," the royal tribe, for it is destined to rule — in the messianic era — over all the nations and, furthermore, because this tribe is ready to lay down its life for Israel "in awful and enormous wars." It is hard to determine whether ἐν αὐτῷ . . . ἐξελέξατο refers to Levi or Judah, above in the text, since it represents a verbatim translation of the Hebrew אשר בו בחר, and this Hebraism makes for ambiguity in the Greek version. However, the Greek translation has transparently preserved the Hebrew אשר בו instead of ובו, thus making it abundantly clear that the chosen royal station refers to Judah and not to Levi.[96] Judah is also justifiably mentioned as a tribe of valiant warriors, for it was this tribe mainly who led in battle during the era of the Judges, and even more so in subsequent periods. Unfortunately the Greek translator took נוֹרָאוֹת (awful) to read in its *defecto* spelling נִרְאוֹת (visible). This mistake led, in turn, to interpreting נִפְלָאוֹת as "invisible," which in other contexts would be possible,[97] but not in this passage, which speaks of "awful and enormous wars."

The proponents of the thesis that the priestly Messiah belongs to the Jewish material of the Testaments do not hesitate to force emendations wherever the plain reading of the text at hand does not

---

[96] It would also be the worst of taste first to demand obeisance before Levi, and then to request prostration before him only because of his prospective kingship in the messianic era.

[97] *Cf.* Ben Sira 3:21 (Ḥagigah 13a; PT Ḥagigah 2.1; Gen. Rabbah 8, p. 58), where פלאות resp. מופלא is synonymous with מכוסה; also T. Onk. Gen. 18:14 and Deut. 17:8 has יתכסי, "hidden," "invisible," for the textual יפלא. *Cf.* also Midrash Tannaim 102 top, and לקוטים ממדרש דברים זוטא, ed. Buber, p. 28, top. [Devarim Rabbah, ed. Lieberman, p. 116.]

bear out their preconceived thesis. Thus Charles reads into Levi VIII,14 ἐν τῷ 'Ιούδα, against the unanimous reading in all the manuscripts, ἐκ τοῦ 'Ιούδα, without taking into consideration that this passage can by no stretch of the imagination be taken to pertain to a priestly messiah. "Into three realms," it says there, will your — Levi's — seed be divided. . . . The first "will be great! indeed greater than this you will not find. . . . The third will be called by a new name, for a king will rise up from out of Judah and establish a new priesthood[98] before all the nations."[99] It is generally accepted that the "first realm" refers to the leadership of Moses, the most outstanding scion of the stock of Levi, wherefore it is said that "even greater than this you will not find." How, then, can this characteristic of Moses be reconciled with the doctrine of the priestly Messiah, who cannot be thought to be inferior to Moses or any other mortal? The ms. reading ἐκ τοῦ 'Ιούδα must, of course, be kept. This passage wants to stress that the — Judean! — Messiah will establish a new priesthood, implying a distinct accusation of the Hasmonean dynasty as usurpers. The Messianic restoration of a pure priesthood forms part and parcel of Pharisaic expectation for the messianic era, as we shall demonstrate later.[100]

The passages under discussion from the Testaments, along with many others, the discussion of which would, however, lead us too far afield, demonstrate satisfactorily that the concept of the priestly Messiah is not the dominant one in this pseudoepigraph, and, hence this idea is no part of its original.[101] The most probable interpretation is the contention that the priestly Messiah is a Christian creation. Christ as Priest is a topic to which the Letter to the Hebrews —

---

[98] The new priesthood ὁ δὲ τρίτος ἐπικληθήσεται αὐτῷ ὄνομα καλόν certainly sounds reminiscent of Isa. 62:2, וקרא לך שם חדש; it means that the future priesthood will be holier and better than the present one. Contrary to Charles' view, neither this passage nor Levi XVIII,2 has any connection with the Hasmonean title כהנים לאל עליון.

[99] The Greek reads κατὰ τὸν τύπον τῶν ἐθνῶν which goes back to לעיני הגוים, for עין is here being understood in the sense of τυπος. This meaning of עין is prevalent in post-biblical Hebrew, and it can even be found in some biblical passages. The correct translation is implied in the doublet εἰς πάντα τὰ ἔθνη. Charles' conjecture that the original Hebrew had למליץ, which was mistaken by the Greek translator as לצלם, does not require disproof.

[100] Cf. pp. 233–234; 238 ff.

[101] In some places — see the Index in Charles' ed. — it is especially emphasized that Levi has greater importance than Judah. This merely indicates that the spiritual leaders of Israel have higher rank than the political heads, but this is entirely irrelevant ot the Messianic problem. Ben Sira represents a quite similar view.

V,1 ff. — already devotes an elaborate discourse. It would, therefore, come as no surprise to us if a Christian editor of the Testaments introduced into that text this concept of the priestly Messiah, which was known to them from the Pauline works. Jesus' claims to the Davidic throne are hardly justified by the alleged Davidic stock of Joseph, if the doctrine of the virginity of Mary is to be maintained. Hence it was quite natural for a perceptible effort to appear in some Christian circles to base the Messianic claims of Jesus on the priestly descent of Mary.[102] Thus the priestly Messiah was introduced into the Testaments.

Irrespective of his Jewish or Christian provenance, one thing is clear about the priestly Messiah of the Testaments: a messiah "out of Levi and Judah" or "out of Judah and Levi" is unknown to this pseudepigraph. The original, composed about the time of John Hyrkanus' reign, spoke either of a Messiah expected "out of Levi," and the additional "out of Judah" was interpolated at a time when great expectations of the Hasmoneans turned into disappointment and the old belief in a shoot of David revived again;[103] or the words "out of Levi" come, as discussed earlier,[104] from the hand of a Christian interpolator who saw in Jesus a priestly messiah rather than "the shoot of David." It never, however, occurred to anyone to depict the Messiah as the heir of both the priesthood and the monarchy.[105]

The Messiah had to be either one or the other, but not both. The conjunctive "and" in the designation "out of Judah *and* Levi" or "out of Levi *and* Judah" is surely due to the hand of a copyist who conscientiously tried to include *both* of the sources that he used, in his combined version.

Even if we would concede that during the flourishing of the Hasmonean dynasty the hope was harbored in some circles that this glorious family was yet destined to play a role in the end of days, akin to the one that it had played in the critical days of Judah the Maccabee, it still would be incongruous to find such aspirations

---

[102] This point is often mentioned in the Apocrypha of the N. T.; perhaps it was known already to Luke (see 1,5).

[103] It is possible, yet less probable, that the interpolation "and out of Judah" was added by a Christian who adhered to the generally accepted concept of Jesus as a scion of the house of David.

[104] For a Christian who believes in the virginity of Mary, Jesus according to the flesh was of "priestly blood," although generally paternal lineage was the decisive one — for Jesus according to the flesh had no father.

[105] That the Messiah would be the rightful heir of the Davidic kinship was quite clearly stated in Test. Judah XXIV and XXII,3. The latter passage contains an allusion to II Sam. 7:12, unnoticed by Charles, *ad loc.*

reflected in the document under discussion. Whatever one may think about the origin of our sect, one thing is certain: it disavowed any communal ties with the Judean potentates, שרי יהודה (8,3 ff.), and even steered clear, completely, of the Temple at Jerusalem. Either the Hasmoneans are looked upon as corrupters of the people, for whom our sect has nothing but hate and contempt; or the document belongs to an era in which the Hasmoneans had already degenerated into insignificance. In either case a "priestly messiah" against the backdrop of the Hasmonean dynasty is completely inconceivable. As far as the sect was concerned, in the time of their flowering, the Hasmoneans could have been only a thorn in the eye and during the period of their decline they offered no inspiration for the messianic ideal. The notion that a "priest messiah" is found in the Testaments, which has been invoked as parallel to our text, represents no corroborative evidence, even if this "priest-messiah" in the Testaments were based on warranted assumptions, which, as we have demonstrated, is not the case. The Jewish revision of this pseudepigraph shows that even in circles where the splendid accomplishments of the Maccabeans briefly stirred the imagination to devote serious thought to the possibility of a priestly messiah, the course of subsequent events — the fall of the Hasmoneans — forced a complete return to the time-honored faith in the Davidic Messiah. Are we then to assume that our sect was ready to view the Hasmoneans during their time of decadence as fitting ideal for their messianic aspirations?!

Summing up the conclusions from our investigation on these matters, we obtain the following picture: a "messiah from out of Levi and Judah" or "from out of Judah and Levi" is unknown in the Testaments. The priestly Messiah is most probably a Christian concept. If there is any warrant at all for his Jewish provenance, such a concept could only have emerged at the time of the flowering of the Hasmoneans, to be again abandoned during their decline. The present document cannot possibly contain the doctrine of a Hasmonean "priestly messiah," and the double title "Messiah out of Aaron and Israel" is equally impossible. For a proper understanding of the messianology in our document, we have to achieve clarity on several points regarding the evolution of the Messianic hope.

*　　　*

*

In one of the oldest Messianic Prophecies in the Bible, the version of the olive trees by Zechariah (4:3 ff.), both of the sons of oil appear as the bearers of salvation. the anointed of David, משיח בן דוד, and the anointed of Aaron, הכהן המשוח. One hopes not only for the renewed splendor of the Davidic kingdom but also for a worthy representative of the priesthood, for a high priest who would not be inferior to his great predecessors. In the course of history the image of the priestly Messiah was gradually displaced by the Davidic Messiah; the less an aspiration can be realized, the greater its idealization. The stark realities of the growing control and influence over the Jewish community that was gained by the hierarchy under the leadership of the High Priest weakened the ideal image of the priestly Messiah and relegated it to insignificance. The "priest-messiah" was not, however, entirely abandoned and banished from later Jewish eschatology. This concept was least likely to disappear in circles which saw in the dominant priestly families the incarnation of sin and apostasy, and hence awaited a pious priesthood, pleasing to the Lord, as a prime requisite of the messianic era. These aspirations found their expression in the expected image of a high priest complying with the ideal of the pious loyalists; for on most occasions it had been the head of the priesthood who disappointed the loyalists by the secularity of his conduct.

The striving to model the future in terms of the golden era in the past constituted an important factor in the maintenance and further development of the "Priestly Messiah." A critical study of the Messianology of the prophecy of Micah (7:15): "According to the days of thy coming out of the land of Egypt will I shew unto him marvellous things," demonstrates the great significance of "parallel correlation between future and past," that is, of the redemption to come, גאולה, with the past redemption from Egypt, גאלת מצרים, for the definition of eschatological hopes. The particular events which are forecast as bound to occur at the Messianic redemption reflect to the largest possible extent a recurrence of events known from the redemption at the Exodus from Egypt. "All plagues which God brought upon Egypt, He will bring in the future upon Edom (the representative of the gentile world in the Messianic era[106])" וכל מכות שהביא הקב"ה על המצרים, הוא עתיד להביא על אדום, is a prevalent dictum of the Haggadah.[107] "Just as the first Redeemer disappeared for temporary

---

[106] Edom, or Esau, is an eponym applied already during the Tannaite period to the Roman Empire, subsequently to Christendom, whereas Ishmael was applied to the realm of Islam.

[107] Tanḥuma Bo, ed. Buber II, p. 43 and parallels cited there note 48. Cf. Mishnah Eduyyoth II,10 and Seder Olam ch. 3 in re the duration of punishment for Gog and Magog. Cf. also Ferdinand Rosenthal, *Vier apokr. Buecher*, p. 64, note 2.

seclusion after his first manifestation, so the last Redeemer will disappear for a time after his first manifestation," מה גואל ראשון נגלה להם וחזר ונכסה מהם — כן גואל אחרון נגלה להם וחזר ונכסה מהם is an observation noted in several passages of the Midrash;[108] on the basis of this concept the Messiah is called משיח הנחבא[109], "the secluded Messiah." During the forty years trek of Israel through the desert, nobody needed sunlight during the day or moonlight during the night; the cloud pillar of the Shekhinah provided them with light — just so it will recur in the days to come כל ארבעים שנה שהיו ישראל במדבר לא נצרך אחד מהם לא לאור החמה ביום ולא לאור הלבנה בלילה ... מפני ענן השכינה ואף לעתיד לבוא כן ... This is said as early as the Tannaitic collection ברייתא דמלאכת המשכן[110]. Another miracle which occurred to Israel in the past and is to recur in the day of the Messiah is "the provision of Manna (Exod. 16) which God will bestow upon Israel"[111] הקב"ה נגלה להם ומוריד להם את המן למטה. Regarding this miracle it is explicitly stated "that there is nothing new under the sun" (Eccles. 1:9), but that "just as in the days of thy exodus from the land of Egypt will I shew unto him marvellous things (Mic. 7:15)." All these passages demonstrate the tendency to expect for the Messianic era miracles and events which will feature a recurrence, a second edition of those that occurred at the exodus.

This parallelism finds its expression not only in forecasting details of the Messianic situation in terms of what is remembered from the days of the exodus, but it is also applied to the division of functions assigned to the several Messianic personages. We may trace the enigmatic figure of the Messiah ben Joseph, משיח בן יוסף, to details of this parallelism. This Messiah was conceived as precursor of the primary Messiah, משיח בן דוד, to accomplish the work of redemption; however, in spite of his initial success and many triumphs, he will succumb to the onslaught of overwhelming powers hostile to Israel,

---

[108] Pesiqta R.K., ed. Buber 49b [ed. Mandelbaum, p. 92] and parallels cited there note 115. *Cf.* also Aggadath Shir ha-Shirim, ed. Schechter, p. 30, on II,8, featuring similar activities of Elijah.

[109] *Cf.* above, p. 224, note 76; the Pesikta has both נחבא and נכסה.

[110] Ch. XIV, p. 84, ed. Friedmann; *cf.* Yalquṭ Makhiri on Isaiah, p. 241.

[111] Pesiqta R.K., ed. Buber, p. 49b [ed. Mandelbaum, p. 93] and parallels cited there note 122; Ḥagigah 12b: "in the third celestial sphere are the mills in which the Manna will be prepared for the righteous." The Munich Codex and other good versions attest to the reading לעתיד לבוא after לצדיקים — *cf. Var. Lect.*, Rabbinowitz, *ad loc.* — but in view of the indeterminancy of this phrase it need not indicate "Messianic era." Further allusions to the Manna as Messianic desert are to be found in the Proem to the Sibyllines 87 and Baruch (Syriac Apocalypse) XXIX,8.

a defeat which will cost his life. There are various theories about the source of this conception:[112] that it was borrowed by the Jews from the Samaritans, and the suffering Messiah of the Synagogue represents, allegedly, a concession on part of the Judeans to the "The Tribes," the Northern Kingdom under the Ephraimite leadership of Joseph's scions; or that this conception was a reflection of the tragic revolt of Bar-Kokhba; or even that it was a creation of scholarly circles which misinterpreted Zechariah 12. We can refute these theories on the origin of this Messianic figure, the Messiah, son of Joseph, because all of them rest on the flimsiest of foundations, which can stand no critical inspection. Nowhere do we find atoning power ascribed to the Messiah, son of Joseph; wherever the sources[113] refer to atoning suffering of the Messiah, it clearly pertains to the suffering of the primary Messiah, never to the Messiah, son of Joseph. In the light of the enmity between Judeans and Samaritans, a Messianic figure of Samaritan provenance could only be conceived by Jews as "antichrist," a role which definitely does not hold for the Messiah, son of Joseph.[114] The Ten Tribes were considered as "*Lost* Ten Tribes"; controversy arose relative to the future, whether or not they will reappear at the time of redemption;[115] this excludes conceding the acceptance of a Messiah, son of Joseph, in consideration for Ephraimite emotions about messianic leadership. Bar Kokhba was certainly considered a Judean, else his messianic claims would not have been accepted; concerning the regard in which he was held after his unsuccessful revolt we can only judge on basis of the scanty reports in rabbinical sources,[116] which tend to see in this inspired warrior an impostor.

[112] *Cf.* Joseph Klausner, *Messianische Vorstellungen*, p. 86 ff. where the references in point are listed. This messiah is perhaps already alluded to in Midrash Tannaim 218=Sifre Deut. 353, p. 414. "Joseph" these sources maintain, "was the first in Egypt, and he will again be the first in times to come." Joseph stands here for the Ephraimite Messiah.

[113] *Cf.* e. g. Pesiqta Rab. XXXVI, ed. Friedmann 161b — perhaps under Christian influence?!; Sanhedrin 98a; Ruth Rabbah V on 2:14; Midrash Tehillim ch. II, ed. Buber, p. 28; Midrash Konen, in Jellinek: Beth Ha-Midrasch II, p. 29.

[114] *Cf.* in the following on "the four builders," one of whom is the Messiah ben Joseph.

[115] *Cf.* Sanhedrin X,3 and Yevamoth 16b bottom.

[116] *Cf.* e. g. PT Taanith IV,68d reporting unfavorable remarks on Bar Kokhba. It is quite questionable though if the meaning "liar," ascribed to the alternate version of his name, Bar Kozba, is ancient ascription. It is worth noting that whereas Christian writers refer to him by the name Bar Kokhba, the rabbinical sources almost [The name Bar Kokhba is found only once in early rabbinical sources. See Ratner Seder Olam Rabbah, p. 146, n. 80. — S. L.] never call him by this name, probably to avoid conferring on him a designation of "star-messiah" [the rising star = Messiah, *cf.* Num. 24:17 and PT *ibid.*].

Hence it does not stand to reason that they conceived the figure of Messiah, son of Joseph as precursor of the primary Messiah in order to save the messianic image of Bar Kokhba, i. e., that he was not the true redeemer but rather his herald, the Messiah, son of Joseph. Nor is this Messianic figure the creation of a midrash on Zechariah 12, for this chapter was originally not considered as a Messianic message;[117] only in the days of the Amoraim, when the Messiah, son of Joseph had already achieved his definite role in the warp and woof of messianology, was this prophecy interpreted by some as implying a Messianic message.[118]

Thus we find in the parallelism between occurrences at the exodus and their recurrence in the Messianic era the only satisfactory answer to the question of origin of the Messiah, son of Joseph. Folklore has preserved information about a faded memory of events which we find confirmed in the Tell El-Amarna Letters, contemporary with the era of the Exodus. Sons of the tribe Ephraim, under the leadership of the Ephraimite יגנון, forced their exodus from Egypt prior to the appearance of Moses, but ultimately suffered defeat from their pagan opponents and were totally annihilated.[119] *This widespread tradition is responsible for the emergence of the concept and figure of Messiah, son of Joseph.* Just as in the days of the first redemption the Ephraimites made a premature attempt to shake off the Egyptian yoke, so also it will recur in the days of the ultimate redemption. An Ephraimite משיח בן אפרים[120] will try to bring about the redemption, but his attempt

[117] Cf. Joseph Klausner, *op. cit.*, p. 88.

[118] Klausner, *ibid.*, p. 93 with reference to Sukkah 52a requires correction. The Dosa mentioned in the text is not Rabbi Dosa ben Hyrcanus — on whom see J. I. Halevy: *Doroth Harishonim* I, p. 570 ff., to correct Klausner's statements accordingly — nor any other Tanna, but an Amora by that name, probably דוסא בר טבת, cf. Shir ha-Shirim Rabbah VII,8.

[119] The earliest source referring to the premature exodus of the Ephraimites is the Tannaitic Midrash, the Mekilta on Exod. 13:17, ed. Friedmann, p. 24a [ed. Horovitz-Rabin, p. 76 bottom and parallels cited in line 16]; RSBY, p. 37 [ed. Epstein-Melamed, p. 45]; also Sanhedrin 92b in the name of Rav; Tar. Jonathan Exod. 13:17; Pirqe R. El. XLVIII; Exod. Rabbah XX; Shir ha-Shirim Rabbah II,7. In the latter passage reference is also made to a premature unsuccessful exodus in the days of Amram, an attempt perhaps originally identical with the Ephraimite adventure, cf. Pirqe R. El., *ibid.*, where the Ephraimite initiative is traced to the beginning of Egyptian oppression שעבוד — which occurred, according to Haggadah tradition (see my *Legends* II, p. 261) in the days of Amram; see also Book of Jubilees XLVI, 6 ff., which is probably also reminiscent of events reported and described in the Tell El-Amarna letters.

[120] So in Midrash and later literature instead of the talmudic משיח בן יוסף; since יוסף and אפרים are somehow identical in genealogy, the meaning of the patronym is the same.

will be doomed to failure. Moses had been destined to be the first redeemer, and the Davidic Messiah is destined to be the last. The attempt of the Ephraimite יננו[121] to anticipate Moses in his redemptive task miscarried — the same will recur with the abortive attempt of the Ephraimite Messiah to carry out the task preordained for the משיח בן דוד.

The first redemption was mainly the achievement of Moses, but not exclusively his accomplishment; his success was shared by his brother, the Highpriest Aaron. The Midrash[122] states: "God announced the goodly message to Israel that wherever their way will lead them, they will be escorted by a king and a priest. In Egypt they were under the leadership of Moses[123] and Aaron; the same applied to their exodus, as it is said (Ps. 77:21): "Thou leadest Thy people like a flock, by the hand of Moses and Aaron." שבישרן הקב"ה שכל מקום שהן הולכין הן משתמשין במלך וכהן. כיצד במצרים מלך וכהן, שנאמר ויאמר ה' אל משה ואל אהרון וגו' (שמות ז, ח), וביציאתם, נחית כצאן עמך ביד משה ואהרן (תהלים עז, כא). In keeping with the parallelism discussed above we may assume without hesitation that besides the royal Messiah, מלך המשיח, a priestly Messiah must also play a role in the messianology. This would be tenable even if the source material would not explicitly mention the function of a priestly Messiah. However, the role for the priestly Messiah can be corroborated from references in the rabbinical and pseudepigraphical literature. In the light of such material it is very puzzling how this exegesis could have been ignored when the various efforts were made to explain the term משיח אהרן וישראל in our present document. The importance of this topic recommends itself for a more detailed and elaborate study, to collect the data and references, and to investigate the relationship of the priestly Messiah as represented in our document to these references culled from Jewish literature elsewhere.

*   *

*

---

[121] This name occurs only in Pirqe R. El., *loc. cit.*; other sources mention the Ephraimite exploit without naming its leader. Yalkut Shimeoni I §227 reads נוון (the proud?) for יננו.

[122] Tanḥuma, ed. Buber I, p. 188.

[123] Moses is also elsewhere entitled "King"; *cf.* Philo, *De Vita Mosis* I §148; II § 2–3; II § 187; *idem, De Praemiis et Poenis* IX,54; Midrash Tannaim, p. 213; Seder Olam VII, ed. Ratner, p. 34 and other passages, *ibid.*; Schürer, *Geschichte* III, p. 472 points out that the Alexandrian Demetrius as well as Justus of Tiberias start their histories of Jewish kings with Moses; see also Ibn Ezra on Gen. 36:31 who interprets מלוך מלך לבני ישראל as referring to Moses.

The earliest direct reference in rabbinical literature to the priestly Messiah is found in an opinion of the Tanna Rabbi Simeon the Pious,[124] in which he explicates "the four builders" in the Apocalyptic vision of Zechariah (2:3–4): "They are: the Messiah, son of David; the Messiah, son of Joseph; Elijah; and the Priest of Righteousness" — משיח בן דוד, משיח בן יוסף, אליהו, וכהן צדק. Other Midrashim (Pesiqta R. K., ed. Buber 51a [ed. Mandelbaum, p. 97]; Pesiqta Rabbati XV, ed. Friedmann 75a; Shir ha-Shirim Rabbah on 2:13) identify "the four builders" as: אליהו, ומלך המשיח, ומלכי צדק, ומשוח מלחמה. Without committing ourselves yet about the congruity of these two versions, it is obviously safe to assume that the מלכי צדק of the Midrashim is identical with the כהן צדק mentioned in the Talmud. Rashi in his commentary identifies כהן צדק with the king-priest of Salem, Melchizedek (Gen. 14:18),[125] a contemporary of Abraham; on basis of this identification the Munich Codex reads מלכי צדק also in the talmudical passage. Rashi and R. Ḥannanel, ibid., and David Qimḥi on Zech. 2:3 agree with the editions[126] reading כהן צדק. It is therefore beyond any doubt current to read כהן צדק. Most probably the מלכי צדק of the Midrashim originated in the explanation presented by Rashi on the Talmudic passage. This is also evident from Kalir's reference to "the four builders," which must have come to him from a Midrash, since he was not acquainted with the Babylonian Talmud. In his well-known elegy אנכי אנכי for the fast on the ninth of Ab,[127] in which he elaborates on the expectations for the messianic era, "the four builders" are the following: "the Tishbite, Menaḥem, Neḥemiah, with whom is included the

---

[124] Sukkah 52b; the date and biography of this Tanna cannot be determined, although we possess a rather extensive collection of sayings — almost all reveal a mystic tendency — transmitted in his name; cf. Bacher Agadah der babylonischen Amoraim, 76; idem, Ergänzungen und Berichtungen, p. 9. I tend to dispute that R. Simeon the Pious of whom some Halakhic opinions are mentioned in the Palestinian Talmud, is identical with this Aggadist. The Halakhist was most probably an Amora. A "man in Jerusalem whose name was Simeon, and the same man was just and devout, waiting for the consolation of Israel," a contemporary of Jesus, is mentioned in Luke 2:25; in the days of the fall of the Second Temple there flourished a שמעון הצנוע; cf. Tosefta Kelim, I,6.

[125] The Haggadah identifies him with Shem, Noah's son. On basis of this widespread opinion — cf. my Haggadah bei den Kirchenvaetern, p. 103 ff. — Rashi tries to explain [ad loc. Sukkah 52b] in a forced manner how Shem came to be considered a "builder."

[126] The same reading is to be found in Eliyahu Rabbah XVIII, ed. Friedmann, p. 96; Yalquṭ Shimeoni II § 568 on Zech. 2.:3. Cf. Yalquṭ Makhiri on Micah, p. 33.

[127] In the Roman Maḥzor; this elegy contains important material for messianology during the first half of the Gaonic period.

glorious priest"[128] תשבי ומנחם וגם נחמיה, תפארת מכהן עמם מנויה. Hence Kalir found also in his source material the Highpriest כהן צדק = תפארת מכהן as the fourth in the quartet of builders. Even if one would accept the reading of the Midrash and assume מלכי צדק as the original version, it would yet not warrant the conclusion that the Haggadah assigned this pre-Mosaic priest a messianic[129] role. However, we may safely maintain that Melchizedek stands for the symbolic name or appellation for the messianic highpriest, just as both Messiahs have been designated by symbolic names.[130] The Haggadah finds the name of the first priest at Jerusalem (Gen. 14:18) to be the most appropriate appellation for the Highpriest who will officiate at the Temple restored by the Messiah. Moreover, the biblical words (Ps. 110:4): "Thou art a priest for ever, after the order of Melchizedek" may well have inspired this appellation. Direct proof for our contention that Melchizedek merely stands for the symbolic appellation of the Priest of Righteousness who will serve in the Temple in the days of the Messiah, can be adduced from a passage in Avoth de-R. Nathan A–XXXIV (ed. Schechter, p. 100). Here the Midrash interprets the vision of the two olive trees "Upon the right side of the candelabrum and upon the left side thereof... These are the two anointed ones Zech. 4:11–14)" as follows: The two olive trees stand for Aaron (i. e. the Highpriest, scion of Aaron) and the Messiah. Yet I still know not which of them is the more beloved in the sight of God, till the Bible reveals (Ps. 110:4): 'The Lord hath sworn, and will not repent, thou art a priest for ever, after the order of Melchizedek,' whence we see[131] that the king Messiah is more beloved than the priest of righteousness." כשהוא אומר: נשבע י"י ולא יינחם אתה כהן לעולם על דברתי מלכי צדק הוי יודע שהמלך המשיח חביב יותר מכהן צדק. This passage[132] also demonstrates that Rashi's explanation for כהן צדק (loc. cit., Sukkah) is untenable, for in this Midrash כהן צדק is being identified with אהרן, i. e.

---

[128] The "Tishbite," of course, is the prophet Elijah; Menahem, "the Comforter," an appellation for the Messiah in Talmud and Midrash; whereas Nehemiah, "God's Comfort," appears in post-talmudic times as appellation for the Ephraimite Messiah.

[129] About the reverence of Melchizedek among the Gnostics, cf. Friedlaender, Antichrist, p. 88 ff., and idem., REJ, V, p. 1 ff. There is no trace of such reverence in Jewish literature; therefore we can ignore it here entirely.

[130] The Messiah commands a great number of such appellations; cf. Sanhedrin 98b.

[131] The Midrash does not reveal how this preference is indicated in the cited verse. Probably the Midrash takes the preposition in the sense of a comparative "higher than." We should then translate accordingly: "Thou art a priest for ever higher than the order, or office, of Melchizedek."

[132] Also quoted in Yalqut Makhiri on Ps. 110:4.

the priest of righteousness will be a scion of Aaron. The identity of משוח מלחמה mentioned in the Midrashim with the משיח בן יוסף of the Talmud is explicitly attested in Num. Rabbah XIV[133] as well as in Aggadath Shir ha-Shirim on 4:11.[134] In the light of these cross-references there is no longer any doubt about the common origin of the tradition recorded in the Talmud and the Midrashim. The intended meaning[135] of this tradition: the work of salvation will be carried out by the following four persons: first comes Elijah, heralding the Messiah; then the Messiah scion of Joseph, anointed for war, will defeat the gentiles, and ultimately the Messiah proper, משיח בן דוד, and the fourth[136] the Priest of Righteousness, כהן צדק, who is also called Melchizedek.

Up to this point we have only demonstrated that the rabbinic tradition assigns to the Highpriest a significant function in the process of eschatological salvation. A critical investigation of the source material is bound to yield more detailed characterization of the per-

---

[133] There it is said: משוח מלחמה שבא מאפרים, "the oil anointed at the time of war, who is a descendant of Ephraim." Besides this one, the Midrash also knows of a "Messiah of the sons of Manasseh," who is mentioned nowhere else; he is probably the product of the academy. For the Talmud knows only of the designation משיח בן יוסף, whereas the Midrashim of Palestine employ exclusively the designation משוח מלחמה and משיח בן אפרים. Hence the theory originated that the משיח בן יוסף belongs to the tribe of Manasseh, in contradistinction to the משוח מלחמה, "the anointed in war," who will be a scion of Ephraim.

[134] Ed. Schechter, p. 36; ed. Buber, p. 32. The editors were not aware that their reading of ד'א is a scribal error for דו'ח = דבש וחלב. The correct reading is found in the commentary קמחא דאבישונא on the Maḥzor by R. Yoḥanan Treves — Passover, Morning-prayer צאינה וראינה. The Yalqut Makhiri on Isaiah, p. 88, already has the corrupted reading ד'א. In passing we should like to draw attention to the fact that passages from a manuscript commentary on the Maḥzor which Schechter cites in his notes on Aggadath Shir ha-Shirim are to be found in the quoted commentary by Treves.

[135] Similarly Friedmann in his note 92 on Pesiqta Rabbati, p. 75a and his introduction to Seder Eliyahu, p. 9. — Yet his interpretation of משוח מלחמה as army chief under the Messiah is untenable, as we shall point out later on.

Bruell, *Jahrbuecher* IX, p. 155, sees in these "four builders" an amalgamation of various Messianic types, viz. the Pharisaic בן דוד, the Sadducean priestly Messiah כהן צדק, the Essene אליהו, and the Zealots' messiah as a warrior hero. This explanation is extremely forced. Heroic exploits and military valor are characteristic for the Messiah also according to the Pharisaic doctrine. Nor is the Messianic significance of Elijah of specifically Essene provenance. With regard to the Sadducees, that this party maintained any belief at all in the coming of the Messiah seems to me to be more than doubtful.

[136] Kalir, *loc. cit.*, has three Messianic personages, and in addition the associated high priest. This presentation is quite correct, for the activities of the כהן צדק will commence only after the process of salvation has been accomplished by these Messianic personages.

sonality traits expected of the כהן צדק. The designation משוח מלחמה for
the Ephraimite Messiah in later Midrashim has so far defied any
plausible explanation. This designation cannot possibly refer[137] to the
Ephraimite Messiah in his function of "field marshal," second in
command to the supreme Messiah, משיח בן דוד. All sources converge
on the point that the activities of the Messianic scion of Joseph will
precede, from the temporal aspect, the Messianic scion of David, and
will terminate with the former's violent death prior to the advent of
the latter, the Messiah proper. Moreover we ought to consider that
the designation משוח מלחמה is frequently employed in Tannaitic and
Amoraic literature;[138] it is a technical term always referring to the
Kohen (priest) who accompanies the army to war and admonishes
the warriors before the battle (in compliance with the biblical directives, Deut. 20:2). Hence we are puzzled and wonder how the Messianic scion of Joseph would qualify for a priestly title and function?!
The order and sequence in which "the four builders" appear in the
Midrashim is also most remarkable. This arrangement respects neither
the chronology of their activities nor their rank, status or importance;
אליהו, משוח מלחמה, מלך המשיח, מלכי צדק, or as in the Talmudic passage,
מלך המשיח, משוח מלחמה,[139] אליהו, מלכי צדק, are the only possible orders
of listing them according to a meaningful sequence. The arrangement
of the Midrashim אליהו, מלך המשיח, מלכי צדק, ומשוח מלחמה is obviously
strange.

In order to solve this problem we have to recall, first of all, that
the Haggadah[140] identifies Elijah with Phineas, the son of Eleazar and
the grandson of Aaron, who is reputed[141] to have been the first משוח
מלחמה in history, in the campaign against the Midianites (Num.
31:6). What could have been more natural[142] than to assign Elijah-

---

[137] Such is Friedmann's interpretation, cf. note 92 in his Pesiqta Rabbati 75a
and Introduction to Seder Eliyahu, p. 9. This contention has rightly been rejected
by Dalman, Der Leidende ... Messias, p. 7; however Dalman's own interpretation
of this designation is equally untenable.

[138] Mishnah Soṭah VII, 2; ibid., VIII, 1; Makkoth II, 6; Tosefta Soṭah VII, 17;
Sifre Deuteronomy 193, p. 234, and many other references.

[139] The two Messianic personages belong together; therefore, it does not follow
from the Talmudic passage that the Messiah descending from Joseph ranks higher
than Elijah.

[140] This identification already in the pseudo-Philonic Liber Antiquitates Bib-
licar [composed ca. 100 C. E.], ed. Basel 1528, p. 48; [Ch. 48, 1, ed. G. Kisch, p. 239];
cf. also my Legends of the Jews IV, pp. 53–54.

[141] Tosefta, Soṭah VII, 17.

[142] This tendency of the Haggadah to assign to prominent historical personalities
functions for the Messianic era similar to those which they performed in their re-

Phineas a function for the end of the days which he had already performed in his very first appearance. The "anointed in war" to Moses will serve as "anointed chief in war" to the Messiah. This implication of the designation משוח מלחמה is also applied in the Pesiqta Rabbati VIII (ed. Friedmann, p. 30a) to the vision of Zechariah (4:11): "this refers to the two anointed ones (משיחים), one anointed for military office, the other for royal office, to reign over Israel," אילו שני המשיחים, אחד משוח מלחמה ואחד משוח למלך על כל ישראל. There is obviously no need to elaborate and prove that this passage does not refer, by the designation משוח מלחמה, to the Messianic scion of Joseph;[143] the whole Jewish literature knows of no other interpretation of these two olive trees of Zechariah's vision but that they represent the priesthood of Aaron and the kingship of David.[144] However, whereas the "olive tree" of Aaron is generally related to the High-priest of the Messianic era, here the Pesiqta relates it to the priestly descendant of Aaron, anointed for his Messianic military office. Indeed, the role assigned to the Messianic chaplain transcends by far the circumscribed office that this designation might suggest. The Messianic משוח מלחמה is not a military officer under the Messiah, assigned to combat his foes. The משוח מלחמה will actually be the Messiah's partner in the process of salvation. The Messiah is "the Prince of Peace" (Isa. 9:5), before whose advent the war-Messiah will already have broken the yoke of the gentiles and have destroyed them;[145] therefore, in a certain sense the משוח מלחמה is really the active Messianic savior,

---

spective historical setting can be traced and corroborated in Jewish literature; cf., e. g., the dictum of R. Joshua, Niddah 70b, Yoma 5b, and also my *Legends of the Jews* II, p. 30, and III, p. 35.

[143] Friedmann, *loc. cit.*, explains correctly דהיינו כהן ומלך without, however, drawing our attention to the fact that elsewhere in the Midrashim, even in the Pesiqta, p. 75a, the designation משוח מלחמה is a title of the messianic scion of Joseph and not of Aaron.

[144] Cf., e. g. Sifra on Lev. 7:35, ed. Weiss 40b; Sifre Zuṭa, ed. Horovitz, p. 57 [Leipzig, p. 253]; Avoth dR. Nathan A ch. XXXIV, ed. Schechter, p. 100, and many other references. A sublime poetic application of this interpretation is found in the hymn for Ḥanukkah, שני זיתים, by Ibn Gabirol. The author of רוקח, in his commentary on the Haphtaroth רמזי הפטרות, comments on this verse of Zechariah's vision (הפטרת בהעלותך) that the בני יצהר are identical with the two messianic personages, drawing on this passage in the Pesiqta without, however, interpreting it correctly.

[145] There is a wide difference between the rabbinic and the Apocryphal literature relative to the fate of the gentiles in the Messianic era. Tanḥuma, end of Shofetim [19 — on Deut. 20:10] contends that the gentiles will first voluntarily surrender to the Messiah ["make him an answer of peace . . . be tributaries unto him and serve him"], but subsequently, in a spell of madness, they will rise up in rebellion against

and the Midrash, on this account, accords to him the status of the most prominent scion of Aaron. This significance, however, is due him only on account of his office as military Messiah personifying the legendary identity of Phineas-Elijah, who has always stood for the annihilator of the gentiles. "Elijah," it is related in Gen. Rabbah LXXI, p. 833: "will destroy the foundation of the gentiles,"[146] שעתיד לגדד משתיתן של אומות העולם. In Tanḥuma (end Mishpaṭim, ed. Buber II, p. 88)[147] it is emphasized that Elijah will accomplish in the days to come what originally had been assigned to an angel at Israel's first entry into the promised land (Exod. 23:23) to destroy the gentiles: בעולם הזה שלחתי מלאך לפניהם, והיה מכרית אומות העולם, אבל לעולם הבא אליהו זכור לטוב הוא אני משלח לכם, with proof text Mal. 3:24. The emphasis in the Pesiqta Rabbati IV, ed. Friedmann 13a, therefore, is readily understood: "Just as God wrought the redemption from Egypt through a Levite and Prophet, so also Israel will be redeemed from Edom through a Levite[148] and Prophet, Elijah." שתי (read שני) נביאים עמדו להן לישראל משבטו של לוי, משה ראשון ואליהו אחרון . . . ; משה גאלם ממצרים . . . ואליהו ינאלם לעתיד לבוא . . . מאדום . . . . . . תשועת עולם for the redeemer proper is Elijah — not the Messiah.

Whereas in this passage Elijah is presented as "the Messianic Moses," he appears in Midrash Tehillim XLIII (ed. Buber, p. 267) in parallelism with Aaron. "You sent" reads the Midrash, "to that generation — at the exodus from Egypt — two Redeemers, as it is said (Ps. 105:26): 'He sent Moses His servant, and Aaron whom He had chosen'; thus may You also send to this generation correspondingly[149] two redeemers: the Prophet Elijah of the house of Aaron, and

---

him and all of them will be destroyed, leaving only Israel in being. In contrast to this opinion, the existence of the gentiles in the messianic era is assumed in Midrash Tehillim II, ed. Buber, p. 25 = Yalquṭ Makhiri, Isaiah, p. 86 (where erroneously מדרש רות is referred to as source instead of מדרש תהלים). The passage in the Pesiqta, discussed here in our text, agrees essentially with the opinion of the Tanḥuma; for this reason it is stated explicitly that the Messiah will reign "over Israel."

[146] [The correct explanation is given by Kutscher in *Tarbiẓ* XVI, 1945, p. 48. — S. L.]. For the discussion in point it is irrelevant that according to the Midrash here [on Gen. 40:19: גד גדוד יגודנו] Elijah is not of priestly descent, but a scion of Gad.

[147] *Cf.* also the old edition of Tanḥuma, end Mishpaṭim (18) which incorrectly reads מבריח instead of מכרית. In Megillah 17b it is assumed that the Messiah will appear only after the ingathering of the exiles and the punishment of the sinners; these tasks, too, will be performed by Elijah.

[148] Levite in this context is not to be contrasted with priest. The intended meaning is obviously the common descent of Moses and Phineas–Elijah from Levi, even though the latter is a priest whereas the former is a Levite.

[149] *Cf.* above, p. 234, on parallelism between the Messianic era and the Exodus.

the Messiah, scion of David." ולא שלחת הגאולה לדור ההוא אלא על ידי שנים
גואלים, שנאמר: שלח משה עבדו אהרן אשר בחר בו. וגם לדור הזה שלח שנים
משיח בן דוד ... אליהו הנביא מבית אהרן ... כנגדן. In the literary sources
discussed earlier, Elijah, just like his prototype Moses, is Israel's
Redeemer from the yoke of the gentiles and the victor over them, his
priesthood being relegated to the background. Although he bears a
priestly title, משוח מלחמה, but the function assigned to this Messianic
"war-anointed" are not of a priestly kind.[150] In the literary source[151]
discussed immediately above, on the other hand, Elijah's messianic
function is described as bearing relationship to his priestly descent.

A similar concept provides the basis for an opinion demonstrably
prevalent during the middle of the second century:[152] the Messiah
will be anointed by Elijah. David was anointed by a Prophet, by
Samuel. David's son, Solomon, was anointed by a Highpriest, Zadok,
in the presence of a Prophet, Nathan (I Kings 1:34 and 39). The
Davidic Messiah, however, will be anointed by Elijah, who is both

---

[150] This is reflected mainly by the notion applied later, as we shall yet demonstrate, which transferred this designation to the Messiah, scion of Ephraim.

[151] The Targum Jonathan on Deut. 30:4 reads: "The divine logion, מימרא, through the high priest Elijah, will forgather you from where you have been driven unto the utmost part of heaven, and from thence will he fetch you and bring you nigh through the Messianic king מימרא יתכון יכנוש מתמן שמיא בסיפי מבדריכון יהון אין דמלכא משיחא ידוי על יתכון יקרב ומתמן רבא כהנא דאליהו ידוי על אלהכון דיי. This passage does not say clearly that Elijah himself will be the victor over the realm of the gentiles; however this seems to be the meaning. Elijah will forgather the scattered exiles and restore them to the Holy Land. There the Messiah will then establish his kingdom over them. This then corresponds to the opinion represented by the Pesiqta.

[152] Justin Martyr, Dialogues VIII and XII; in the literature of Midrash and Talmud there is no trace of the concept that the Messiah will be ceremoniously anointed. J. Klausner, *Messiasidee*, p. 62, cites Kerithoth 5a and Sifra on Lev. 8:10, ed. Weiss 41b, but his argument rests on an erroneous interpretation, for these passages deal with the anointing of holy vessels, not of the Messiah. In Sifra on 7:35, ed. Weiss 40b, and Sifrei Zuṭa, ed. Horovitz, p. 57 [Leipzig, p. 253], it is indeed stressed explicitly that the Messiah will not be anointed. The anointing of the Sanctuary is known to the Kalir, *cf*. his elegy וילון; he ascribes this function to the Messiah. The anointing of the Messiah by Elijah is first mentioned by mediaeval authors; *cf*. Jellinek, *Beth Ha-Midrash* VI, p. 142; this notion is also present among the Sabbatians, who instituted a holyday on the date on which "Elijah" anointed Sabbatai Zevi, *cf*. Freimann, עניני שבתי צבי, p. 95. In folklore this tradition of the Messiah's anointing by Elijah seems to have had a strong hold; even the Karaites have absorbed it into their messianology. Thus wrote the Karaite Yephet ha-Levi regarding Isa. 52:13: הנה ישכיל עבדי ירום ונשא וגבה מאד; the term ירום indicates that the Messiah will ascend to the throne of Israel after having been anointed by Elijah: והו גלוסה עלי כסא ישראל פי וקת ימסחה סידנא אליהו עה'ש, *cf*. A. Neubauer, *The LII Chapter of Isaiah*, pt. I, p. 21.

a Prophet and a priest. This legend is related to another[153] which recounts "that Elijah will eventually restore to Israel a basket of Manna (Exod. 16:33), a vessel of purifying water (Num. 19:17), and a vessel of anointer oil (Exod. 30:22)." In other words: the holy oil for the anointing of the Messiah will be in the possession of Elijah, the messianic Highpriest, as well as the purification waters which would be required to purify both the Temple and the priests. The basket of Manna, originally "laid up before the Lord" with the Ark of Testimony in the holiest of holies by Aaron (Exod. 16:34) as a testimonial of the exodus, will be replaced there by the Messianic Highpriest.

The same circles which saw in Elijah-Phineas the Messianic High-priest, gave rise to his designation "the righteous priest,"[154] כהן צדק. We may conclude now that the tradition concerning "the four build-ers" represents a latter day combination of earlier doctrines con-cerning "the two saviors," Elijah and the Messiah. These two figures bore various designations, the factor of change being the varying conception of the Messianic activities of Elijah:

1) אליהו ומשיח בן דוד
2) משוח מלחמה ומשיח בן דוד
3) משיח (בן דוד) וכהן צדק

---

[153] Mekilta Wayassa V, ed. Friedmann, 51b [ed. Horovitz-Rabin, p. 172], משלשה דברים שאליהו עתיד להעמיד לישראל: צלוחית המן, וצלוחית של מי נדה, וצלוחית של שמן המשחה. Cf. also my remarks in *Jewish Encyclopedia* I, p. 626, where I have traced this legend in the Sibyllines II, 188.

[154] Palestinian recensions of the Tefillah designate the Messiah as משיח צדקך, perhaps with reference to Jer. 23:6 and Isa. 11:5; quite possibly this designation כהן צדק derived from משיח צדקך. However, we ought to bear in mind that in the prayer texts משיח צדקך is also applied to David — so in the Trishagion for Sabbath morning ממקומך מלכנו תופיע — so that the Messianic designation כהן צדק may have been derived from Ps. 132:9 צדק ... כהניך. — The Karaite Aaron of Nicomedia writes in his גן עדן, Tefillah, p. 74a: וביאת בן דוד משיח צדקנו וכהן שהוא משיח צדק. I know of no rabbinical literary source where משיח צדק is used for כהן צדק. Pesiqta Rabbati, ed. Friedmann, 36, p. 161b, and 37, p. 164a, reads משיח צדקי and משיח צדקנו respec-tively for messianic designation, and similarly משיח הצדיק in Ag. Shir ha-Shirim, ed. Schecht., p. 36 (see also ibid., p. 81). As an epithet for Elijah we can trace כהן צדק with certainty only to the Paitan Abraham ben Isaac ha-Cohen (fl. about 1110), who employs it in the Piyyut for Grace after the feast in honor of a circumcision: הרחמן הוא ישלח לנו כהן צדק אשר לוקח לעילום עד הוכן כסאו כשמש ויהלום. However it is quite possible that the proper name כהן צדק, traceable to the eighth century, is actually a by-name, כינוי, for Elijah כהן צדק (אליהו); cf. my *Geonica* I, p. 55 for similar application of the name מבשר in the Gaonic period. We have to take into consideration the possibility that כהן צדק is a condensation of כהן מורה צדק; on מורה צדק=אליהו, see below, p. 256.

Now we have seen already that the designations משוח מלחמה and כהן צדק are honorifics for Elijah. Then there emerged the doctrine of a Messiah, the scion of the house of Joseph, to whom the function was assigned to defeat the gentile foes. Apparently on account of this military office, the designation משוח מלחמה, originally Elijah's honorific, was transferred to him. Thus we may explain how in the Talmudic passage (Sukkah 52b) the designation משיח בן יוסף is substituted for the more original משוח מלחמה. Even in the above quoted Midrashim, which retained משוח מלחמה over against the Babylonian text משיח בן יוסף, this designation is no longer applied to Elijah, but to the Josephite Messiah. In the course of time the designation כהן צדק as an honorific for Elijah was no longer understood by some circles. We must recall that there were opinions abroad which refuted[155] the attribution of priestly descent to Elijah; it stands to reason that these circles then affixed this honorific for Elijah to the Highpriest of the messianic era, a personage who is otherwise unknown. The sequence in which "the four builders" are listed in the Midrashim: אליהו, מלך המשיח, מלכי צדק, משוח מלחמה, becomes plausible as the outcome of the three aforementioned combinations:

1) אליהו ומלך המשיח
2) מלך המשיח ומלכי צדק[156] (כהן צדק)
3) מלך המשיח ומשוח מלחמה[157]

whereas in the Babylonian Talmud, Sukkah 52b the designation משוח מלחמה has been substituted by משיח בן יוסף. Hence the pair משיח בן דוד and משיח בן יוסף instead of משיח בן דוד ומשוח מלחמה; due to his preeminence, the Davidic Messiah precedes the Josephite.

*　　*
*

The hope for Elijah-Phineas, "the Zealot for the Lord," must have been cherished with particular intensity in circles which waited not only for redemption from the gentiles, but which, and perhaps pri-

---

[155] *Cf.*, e. g., Gen. Rabbah LXXI, p. 834, and many other references. For elaboration on this point see Friedmann, Introduction, Seder Elijah, pp. 2–6.

[156] The identity of מלכי צדק with כהן צדק has been demonstrated above, p. 240.

[157] In two versions of the original Haggadoth on Elijah and the Messiah, the order of listing was chronological: אליהו ומשיח and משיח וכהן צדק respectively. In a third version we find, in keeping with their eminence, precedence given to the Messiah, and משוח מלחמה at the end. However it could possibly represent a scribal error, committed by a later copyist who mistook משוח מלחמה as meaning quite literally "field marshall" and therefore altered the sequence.

marily, hoped for the destruction of the sinful rulers of Israel in the
Messianic era. In the light of these aspirations, our sect recognized
two Messianic leaders. Corresponding to "the two anointed ones that
stand by the Lord of the whole world" in Zechariah's vision (4:14),
which the Pesiqta Rabbati VIII, 30a interprets as שני המשיחים, אחד
משוח מלחמה ואחד משוח למלך על ישראל, this sect was looking forward to
the advent of the Messiah of Aaron, משוח אהרן, i. e. Elijah, and the
Messiah of Israel, משוח ישראל, i. e. the Messiah of David's royal dynasty. The designation of משוח אהרן for Elijah-Phineas is far more
natural than the nomenclature employed in the Midrash. Firstly, it
indicates[158] more clearly the priestly descent of this redeemer; and,
secondly, it relates these two messianic figures more definitely to the
apocalyptic vision of Zechariah. The designation משוח ישראל, instead of
the common משיח בן דוד, must not be construed as a sectarian expression of opposition to the Davidic Messiah, who was expected
according to the Pharisaic doctrine. This designation merely emphasized that the gentile world would have no share in "this king of
Israel." His task, in the words of the Pesiqta, would be exclusive,
"to reign over Israel," משוח למלך על ישראל. The multitude of the
gentiles will be destroyed by the משוח אהרן, i. e. Elijah, so that at the
advent of the Messiah proper, only Israel would exist.[159] The sequence
משוח אהרן before משוח ישראל, therefore, does not point to the superiority
of the former over the latter. It merely describes the chronological
order of their appearance[160] and it represents the same functional
sequence that we meet in rabbinical literature: אליהו ומשיח or משוח
מלחמה ומשיח בן דוד. In the light of this analysis we have to reject the
dominant opinion which seems to find references to only one Messiah
in our document, who unites both priesthood and kingdom in his
person. The messianology of our sect is much more congruent with
the rabbinical doctrine of two distinct Messianic personages, two

---

[158] Cf. the designation for Elijah, אליהו הנביא מבית אהרן, in Midrash Tehillim
XLIII (cited above, p. 245) which comes very close to his designation משוח אהרן in
our document.

[159] According to the doctrine of the present document, 19,10, all who would
not accept and follow the precepts of the sect would be doomed to annihilation in
the days of the Messiah. We may assume that the gentiles will not fare any better.
The phrase ויתגברו על כל בני תבל in our document, 20,33, is, however, too inconclusive
for proof that all gentiles will be overwhelmed and destroyed. See above, p. 243
[and below, p. 255].

[160] One cannot conclude from 5,3 that there is a preference for the priesthood
over the kingship. This rhetoric of our document follows biblical usage; cf. Josh.
14:1; 21:1. Likewise, discussions in rabbinical literature mention "priesthood and
kingship," but not vice versa; see e. g. Sifre Zuṭa, ed. Horovitz, p. 57 [Leipzig,
p. 253], and cross references there.

saviors and redeemers: Elijah and the Davidic Messiah. משוח אהרן וישראל is simply a contraction or abbreviation[161] for the properly formal משוח אהרן ומשוח ישראל. Taking into consideration orthographic peculiarities of our document — cf. above, pp. 3–4 — one could make out a good case for the reading (משוחָ(י) אהרון וישראל; in that case we may dispense with the supposition that this phrase represents a contraction.[162]

In the light of the demonstrated agreement between our document and the rabbinic sources on the function and significance of the priestly Messiah in the process of salvation, the many messianological references in the Testaments of the XII Patriarchs must now appear in a quite different light. The admonition of Simeon (VII,2–3) reads: "and do not rise up against these two tribes — Levi and Judah — for out of them salvation will sprout. For the Lord will bring forth out of Levi a Highpriest, and out of Judah a king [God and man]; and they [he] will save [all the gentiles and] the people of Israel." After removing the Christian interpolations,[163] we recognize in this passage none other than the conception that is well known to us of the messianic Highpriest Elijah, who will join with the Davidic Messiah in completing the work of salvation. The same idea is also expressed in the following words of the Testament of Levi II,11: "and through you — Levi — and Judah, the Lord will be made manifest among men," i. e. through Elijah and the Messiah God will restore his abode among men.[164] A phrase in the Testament of Naftali (VIII,3) clearly

[161] Similar contraction we find in the Papyri published by Sayce and Cowley: plate A, line 9, בעל דגל וקריה contracted from plate E, line 11, בעל דגל ובעל קריה.

[162] On basis of the above mentioned legend about the anointing of the Messiah by the priest Elijah, one may tend to interpret משוח אהרן וישראל in the sense that the Messiah will obtain his Messianic recognition from the priests and the other tribes of Israel. This recognition will become manifest in his anointing by the priest Elijah. One could see in this symbolic act a rebuke of the Hasmonean dynasty whose royalty had been acknowledged by the priests, but not by the tribes of Israel; see PT Horayoth III, 49c.

[163] Cf. Charles' notes, loc. cit., who sees in all words which I bracketed Christian interpolations, except in οὗτος σώσει, "he will save." However, if one assumes that the words θεὸν καὶ ἄνθρωπον do not belong to the original text, the genuineness of οὗτος σώσει becomes very doubtful, since only the phrase θεὸν καὶ ἄνθρωπον would entail the singular form σώσει.

[164] "In the beginning the principal abode of the Shekhinah was among men; yet on account of their sins .... the Shekhinah removed to heaven where it remained until Moses erected the Holy Tabernacle," Pesiqta de R. Kahana, ed. Buber, 1b and parallel references. With the destruction of the Temple the Shekhinah returned to the heavenly abode — Rosh Hashanah 31a — so that it can be rightfully said of the Messianic era that God will return to establish His abode among men. Charles interprets the passage ὀφθήσεται τοῖς ἀνθρώποις literally, which is definitely incorrect.

alludes to the joint enterprise of priestly Elijah with the Davidic Messiah. It says of the tribes Levi and Judah "that through them[165] God will become manifest to take His abode among men, to save the generation of Israel, and to ingather the righteous[166] who are scattered among the gentiles." This phrase is strongly reminiscent of the paraphrase by the Targum Jonathan on Deut. 30:4 (cited above, p. 245): "The divine logion, through the Highpriest Elijah, will forgather you from wherever you have been driven unto the utmost parts of heaven, and from thence He will fetch you and bring you nigh through the Messianic king." In these as also in all other passages[167] in the Testaments where reference is made to Levi and Judah as the bearers of Messianic salvation, Levi always precedes Judah. It would be wrong to infer from this phenomenon, as Bousset, Charles and other scholars do, that in this pseudepigraph the priesthood is held in higher esteem than the — Messianic — kingship, or even, that the Messiah is primarily a Priest. The order of precedence is based on the conception of the Messianic functions assigned to the Priest Elijah who, functionally and chronologically, will have to precede the Messiah. Therefore, Levi is mentioned before Judah.

Although the Messianic significance of Elijah is held in highest esteem in rabbinical and apocryphical literature, official recognition of his messianic status is nonetheless wanting. The basic prayers[168] of the liturgy contain pleas for redemption, for the restoration of the Temple and its services, and for the advent of the Messiah, but not for the coming of Elijah. Yet it would be erroneous to assume that this has always been so. We have good grounds to believe that the earliest versions of the basic prayers did not ignore the mission of

---

[165] The text reads τοῦ 'Ιούδα, emended by Bousset to αὐτῶν, as the context undoubtedly requires.

[166] The phrase δικαίους ἐκ τῶν ἐθνῶν does not refer to "the pious gentiles" but to the pious Jews scattered among the gentiles. The ingathering of the exiles, קבוץ גליות, is an essential element of Messianic hope, to which a Berakhah among the eighteen of the Tefillah is devoted; cf. also Ben Sira 33:13, 51:6 (H. Sup.).

[167] Cf. e. g. Test. Gad VIII, 1; Jos. XIX, 11; see also Dan I, 10–11 with clear reference to Elijah, which remained unnoticed by Charles, although he points as parallel to Luke 1:17. This latter passage, however, does not speak of the Messiah, but of Elijah-John as the one to convert many children of Israel back to God. Also some other tasks which, in this passage, are assigned to the savior, e. g. the punishment of Israel's enemies, are identified with Elijah rather than with the Messiah.

[168] In the eighteen Berakhoth, עמידה, which are said on weekdays; in its condensation, הביננו; and in the grace after meal, ברכת המזון. Also the Mussaf for the oldest version of New Moon and holydays used to contain the prayer יעלה ויבוא, in which the Messiah is mentioned; see Elbogen, Monatsschrift LV, p. 431 ff., and my remarks in הצופה מארץ הגר III, p. 18 ff., and IV, p. 97–98.

Elijah. This is evidenced by the mentioning of Elijah's promised coming in one of the Berakhoth after reading the Prophetic lesson (Haftarah).[169] The peculiar text and structure of this Berakhah suggest the assumption that it dates from Hasmonean or Herodian days. It reads: "Make us to rejoice, O Lord our God, in the Prophet Elijah, Thy servant, and in the kingdom of the house of David, Thine anointed. Soon may he come and gladden our hearts. Suffer not a stranger to sit upon his throne, nor let others any longer inherit his glory" שמחנו י'י אלהינו באליהו הנביא עבדך ובמלכות בית דוד משיחך במהרה יבוא ויגל לבנו על כסאו לא ישב זר ולא ינחלו עוד אחרים את כבודו. The "strangers" and the "others" who ascend to the Davidic throne could not well refer to the Roman emperor. In that case, the terminology "strangers" and "others" would be very odd, for we would expect זדים and רשעים respectively instead of זר and אחרים; more important, it would be entirely out of character to describe the Roman emperors as actually occupying the Davidic throne. However, these objections vanish if we assume that this Berakhah was composed in the Hasmonean or Herodian era. Both these dynasties could justifiably be called "strangers," who were usurpers of the throne of David.[170] If this interpretation is correct, we thus have in this Bera-

---

[169] This Berakhah is already referred to in Talmudic literature: see Pesaḥim 117b, and part of it is cited in Midrash Tehillim XVIII, ed. Buber, p. 154. Derenbourg in *REJ* II, p. 290, contends that the version cited in the text that follows must be traced to Christian provenance and must be understood as combating Christianity, whereas the version of the Berakhah which does not mention Elijah — so in Seder R. Amram Gaon and Maimonides — must be considered the original one. However, Derenbourg overlooked the simple fact that the Amram-Maimonides version corresponds *verbatim* to the Berakhah צמח דוד of the Babylonian tradition. Hence it could not have been the original version of the Palestinian tradition, which the Berakhah after the Haftarah obviously represents. The Babylonian Gaon R. Amram certainly offered the Babylonian version, whereas Mas. Soferim XIII,12 [ed. Higger, p. 247] and Midrash Tehillim presented the Palestinian, i. e. original, version. The view that this Berakhah was composed prior to 70 C.E. is made plausible by the negative evidence that it mentions neither the restoration of the Temple nor the ingathering of the exiles, while these pleas are present in all other messianic prayers. See also Duenner, הנהות on Sanhedrin 32b, and Mueller on Mas. Soferim XIII,13. The latter draws our attention to the affinity between these seven Berakhoth after the reading of the Haftarah and the Berakhoth after the reading from the Torah on the Day of Atonement by the high priest in the Temple. Is David in these Berakhoth identical with the Messiah? See also Mas. Soferim XIX,7 [ed. Higger, p. 331] where Elijah and the Messiah are mentioned: אליהו הנביא במהרה יבוא ואצלנו המלך המשיח יצמח בימינו.

[170] The singular זר assumes neither in biblical nor later literature the connotation "gentile." It means a man who does not belong to a specified family. Thus an Israelite is called זר in juxtaposition to a Levite or a priest. Anyone who does

khah a Pharisaic text from about the beginning of the Common Era, in which Elijah appears in partnership with the Messiah as the bearer of salvation. Later on a tendency developed to dogmatize only the eschatological expectation of the Davidic Messiah. Jewish folklore, however, did not relinquish its time-honored hope for the Messianic advent of Elijah. On the contrary, the people tenaciously held on to this belief and even intensified and sublimated it. This elevation of Elijah by popular conception found expression in the Haggadic rabbinic sources which we have discussed and also in the pseudepigrapha.[171]

Our present document offers amazingly little information about the specific functions assigned to the two Messianic personages. Perhaps we may draw certain conclusions from the designation משוח ישראל for the Davidic Messiah: he will reign as "the Prince of Peace" over Israel. Correspondingly we may take as implication of משוח אהרן that this priestly Messiah will carry out the task of bringing the gentiles and the sinners of Israel to justice.[172] Concerning the passage 14,19 where the phrase [משוח] אהרן וישראל is followed by the clause ויכפר עוננו it has been observed already, ad loc., that the state of the text does not permit us to determine the meaning of these two words. We may conjecture that the missing words may be rendered: עד אשר ישלח אל משיח וכו', "till God will send the Messiah of Aaron and — the Messiah of — Israel, and then He will atone for our transgressions."[173] We may also consider another possible conjecture: to read the verb as a passive, וִיכֻפַּר עוננו, "and our transgression will be atoned for." In that case the atonement for our transgressions will not be effected by one

---

not descend from David is a זר in relation to this family. The dictionaries translate אל זר (Ps. 44:21; 81:10) with "God of an alien people." This is entirely incorrect, for the phrase means, rather, "a false God." Or, parallel to the use of זר in אש זרה ["unlawful fire"], it means "unlawful God," i. e. a God whose worship is disapproved by Jewish norms.

[171] Under the influence of folklore and legend, Elijah has attained a place of honor and glory in Jewish hymnology. The hymns at the conclusion of the Sabbath pay especial homage to him. The Karaites included a petition for his early advent in their evening weekday prayers; see above, p. 246. In the Karaite version of the petition יעלה ויבוא — Karaite Prayerbook, ed. Wilna 1891, II, p. 196 — after וכרון משיח there follows the clause וכרון כהנת זרע אהרן, which however does not refer to Elijah, but to the messianic Highpriest, the כהן צדק of rabbinic literature. Rabbinic prayers petition for the restoration of the Temple and its services without mentioning the priests; cf., however, the section מלך רחמן of Mussaf on holydays והשב כהנים לעבודתם ולויים לשרם ולזמרם.

[172] See above, p. 243 and p. 248.

[173] The concept of divine forgiveness of Israel's sins at the time of Messianic redemption is prevalent throughout the literature, since it is often mentioned in the Bible.

or the other Messiah. A passage in rabbinic literature[174] would perhaps invite the suggestion that the Messiah does effect atonement:
"Happy the eyes that merit to behold the Messiah, whose lips utter
blessing and peace, whose talk is pleasantness . . . . whose tongue
spells *pardon* and *forgiveness*, whose prayer is pleasing savor, whose
entreaty is sanctity and purity." אשרי עין שזכתה לראותו לפי שמפתח שפתיו
ברכה ושלום ושיחתו נחת רוח . . . ולשונו מחילה וסליחה, ותפלתו ריח ניחוח, ותחנתו
קדושה וטהרה. However, the Jewish provenance of this Midrashic passage is very dubious.[175] Moreover, it engages in poetic description of
the Messianic personage, which cannot be taken as a literal statement. At best this enthusiastic paean shows what great effects are
expected from the prayer of so holy and pious a personage as the
Messiah. If we consider that vast importance is attributed[176] in rabbinic Judaism to the efficacy of the prayers of the pious, that such
effects would be expected from the Messiah's praying, is not at all
extraordinary. The Messiah as forgiver of sins[177] cannot be found in
any Jewish sources. Hence there are no warranted grounds for interpreting the present document to maintain that the sect believed in
the atonement of transgression through the Messiah.[178]

The only passage in Fragment A which gives some positive description of the work of the Messiah is the one which gives a Messianic interpretation of Num. 24:17:[179]

> I shall see him — but not now
> I shall behold him — but not nigh

---

[174] Pesiqta de R. Kahana, ed. Buber, p. 149a; [ed. Mandelbaum, p. 470] Pesiqta
Rabbati XXXVII, ed. Friedmann, p. 164a, where it reads לאפרים משיח צדקנו . . .
אשרי הדור שעיניו רואות אותו . . . אשרי עין שחיכתה לו, שמפתח שפתיו ברכה ושלום, ושיחתו נחת
רוח . . . אשרי עין זכתה בו, שמלל לשונו סליחה ומחילה לישראל, תפלתו ריח ניחוח וכו', whereas
Yalquṭ Makhiri on Isaiah, p. 251, quoting this passage in the Pesikta, omits the
words on pardon and forgiveness: ולשונו . . . סליחה.

[175] This we maintain in opposition to Friedmann in his notes, *loc. cit.*, and
Chwolson, *Das letzte Passamahl*, p. 83 ff., who argue for the Jewish provenance of
this Pesiqta. It is hard to believe that no Christian influence has affected this text
[e. g. אשרי הבטן שיצא ממנו].

[176] *Cf.* e. g. Bava Bathra 116a, bottom; Sanhedrin 95a with reference to
Abishai's plea for David; and Mishnah Berakhoth V,5.

[177] On Testaments XII Patriarchs Levi VIII, 14 see above, p. 231.

[178] See further also Dalman, *Der leidende Messias*, pp. 75–76, who missed the reference that in Berakhah eleven of the Amidah it is said of God that "He will justify
Israel in judgment," hence the plea וצדקנו במשפט; by the same token all of the
passages that he does adduce in re the concept of "justification" really refer not
to the Messiah but to the justifying power of God himself.

[179] See the interpretation of this passage above, pp. 34 ff.

> A Star shall shoot forth out of Jacob
> And a Comet jet forth out of Israel
> And shall smite the corners of Moab
> And destroy all the sons of Sheth

The text of Fragment A 7,18 reads: "The *Star* refers to the Exegete of the Torah; the *Comet* refers to the Prince of the *entire community*; when he emerges, he shall destroy all the sons of Sheth — the gentiles." Be it noted that in this passage, too, our document stresses that the Messiah is king only of Israel; or, from the precise viewpoint of the sect, the Messiah is king of the loyal remnant of the pious — "The Community," according to our document. The gentiles will, on the contrary, be destroyed. We found the same basic concept implied in the designation of the Messiah as משוח ישראל, above, p. 248, which indicated that only those of Israel will partake in the Messianic salvation. Our contention above that according to the doctrine of the sect it will be Elijah, the משוח אהרן, who will mete out punishment to the gentile world, can thus be harmonized with the indication that it will be incumbent on the Davidic Messiah to visit destruction upon the sons of Seth. Also some Apocalyptic Midrashim[180] identify the "Star of Jacob" with the Messiah, whereas the destruction of the sons of Seth which is mentioned in the same verse is a task which is assigned to the warrior Messiah, the son of Joseph. This may very well also be the doctrine of our document: the Messiah will not himself execute punishment; the day of doom will come about the time of the advent of the Messiah, in the Messianic era.[181] Other rabbinic Apocalypses have the warrior Messiah, the son of Joseph, conquer the gentiles except for a tiny but very significant remnant, Gog and Magog; the Davidic Messiah will then take over and complete their annihilation. Our document is thus correct in designating the lat-later Messiah as the Comet who shall reign as prince over the entire community and "destroy completely all the sons of Seth."[182] The

---

[180] *Cf.* e. g. the messianic Apocalypses in Lekaḥ Tov on Num., *loc. cit.* [ed. Padva, p. 258], where the defeat of the gentiles, with the exception of Gog and Magog, is assigned to Messiah ben Joseph, [who will be killed. In the time of ensuing calamity, Israel will "return and seek their God and David their King (Hos. 5:3)," ומיד נגלה עליהם מלך המשיח and King Messiah will appear immediately ואו יתקיים: דרך כוכב מיעקב] so that here too "the Star from out of Jacob" is identified with the Davidic Messiah.

[181] Similar cases in rabbinic literature where "Messiah" stands for the Messianic era have been referred to above, p. 226.

[182] *Cf.*, e. g., the Apocalypses of Zerubabel in Jellinek, *Beth Hamidrash* II, p. 56 ff.; the Apocalypses אותות המשיח in Jellinek, *op. cit.* II, pp. 60 ff.; and in many other passages.

passage in Fragment B (19,10), to the effect that "the sinners will be committed to the sword at the advent of the Messiah of Aaron and of the Messiah of Israel," is also no doubt to be understood in this sense. The judgment will commence with the advent of "the Messiah of Aaron" and be concluded with the advent of "the Messiah of Israel." However, quite plausibly the passage בבוא משוח אהרן וישראל may merely stand for "in the end of the days"=באחרית הימים.[183] That this phrase means the eschatological era without particular reference to the two Messianic personages would correspond to such usage elsewhere in our document: e. g. Fragment A 12,23 and 14,19; Fragment B 20,1. Yet I am not even convinced that we are dealing in 19,10 with a genuine passage. I am rather inclined to take it as an interpretative gloss on the preceding בקץ הפקדה, "in the period of visitation," which a reader related to the Messianic judgment day, whereas it really means the visitation upon Judea by "the chief of Greek Kings" — 8,11 and 19,23. It is remarkable that in the description of the period "when the glory of Israel's God will make itself manifest" there is no mention of the Messiah, although it certainly refers to "the days to come." It reads (20,33–34): "The pious will rejoice and be merry; their heart will take courage and they will overwhelm all gentiles of the world. God will grant them atonement, and they will behold His salvation for they put their trust in His holy name." ישישו וישמחו ויעז[184] לבם ויתגברו על כל בני תבל[185] וכפר[186] אל בעדם וראו ישועתו כי חסו בשם קדשו. Defeat of the gentiles, expiation of sins and the vision of divine salvation — but no word of the Messiah.

---

[183] Fragment A reads in both passages in which the Messiah is mentioned: משוח, whereas Fragment B spells consistently משיח. Perhaps the original formula had משוח אהרן ומשיח ישראל, which became in the contraction משוח and משיח respectively. However originally in the designation of Elijah it read משוח as in משוח מלחמה, who is the משוח אהרן, the priestly anointed. For the royal anointed, the Messiah proper, it read משיח. See also in the above cited Pesiqta Rabbati VIII, 30a, שני המשיחים where after משיחים it reads twice משוח, which one is inclined to see as derived from משוח מלחמה, for which our document has משוח אהרן.

[184] Not to be emended into ויעלז! The trust in God inspires joy and courage. עז =valiant; so in Bible and Mishnah.

[185] Literally "the children of the world." This expression was probably also in the Hebrew text of Enoch C,6 where "the children of the world" refers to the sinners. Charles and Beer, ad loc. cit., want to recognize in this expression the עם הארץ of rabbinic literature! In Enoch XV, 3 "the children of the earth" means בני אדם; cf. Gen. 6:6.

[186] To be read either וכופר or וְכִפֶּר, for this expression cf. 4,10 and above, p. 91.

The conclusions which result from our investigation of the Messianology of the sect can now be summarized as follows: The sect believed and hoped for the advent of the Messiah of Aaron and the Messiah of Israel. Both rabbinic and apocalyptic sources make it very plausible that the Aaronide Messiah is none other than Elijah, who was identified with Aaron's grandson, the Highpriest Phineas. The functions of these two Messiahs are not detailed. However, the designation "Messiah of Israel" makes it probable that this personage is conceived of exclusively as "the Prince of Peace," reigning over all of Israel. The task assigned to the "Messiah of Aaron" is the destruction of the gentiles. This Messianology corresponds to an outlook that was widespread in rabbinic literature. The "Teacher of Truth" and the "Excellent Teacher," who are mentioned in our document, have no bearing on the messianology of this sect. Just as in rabbinic literature, so in this document "Teacher of Truth" is an honorific for prominent sages and scholars. The "Excellent Teacher" is a designation used to refer to the founder of the sect. The only eschatological use of this term is to be seen in the passage (6,10) "until the advent of him who will teach the truth in the end of the days," עד עמוד[187] יורה הצדק באחרית הימים. Its meaning obtains cogency in the light of the Talmudical formula interpreting Hos. 10:12 to the effect that Elijah will come in the end of the days as the supreme ultimate teacher who will then summarily clarify all moot point of the Halakah, remove all doubts, and thus restore peace in Israel.

---

[187] The employ of עמוד for the Hosean יבוא is perhaps latently affected by the phrase in Ezra 2:63: עד עמוד כהן לאורים ותומים. Our document agrees with the leading sense of this phrase as transmitted in rabbinic literature and I Macc. XIV, 41 — cf. Dérenbourg, *Essai*, p. 60 ff. — where the priest to rise up is identified with Elijah-Phineas. In the light of our conclusion that משוח אהרן וישראל in our document represents a contraction meaning "the Messiah of Aaron and the Messiah of Israel," we now can understand why this phrase could not have been employed here (6,10), to make the passage read עד עמוד משוח אהרן וישראל. The function of teaching — in the meaning of יורה intended here — will be the exclusive assignment of one messianic personage, viz. משוח אהרן. It was, therefore, impossible for our document to use here the otherwise usual phrase for "the end of days," עד עמוד משוח אהרן וישראל. To be sure, this exclusive teaching assignment of Elijah does not exclude him from performing his other messianic function, that of the משוח מלחמה, the warrior Messiah. Yet it is quite conceivable that for our sect Elijah is to be exclusively "the messianic teacher." The true understanding and interpretation of the law rates so high with our sect that it added the honorific Messiah to "the last great teacher." Taken by itself, the designation משוח אהרן וישראל could also mean: Messiah for Aaron and Israel, in contradistinction to משוח or משיח respectively — see above, p. 255 — which would then designate the Highpriest, who is but "the anointed," scion of Aaron.

VII

The Genesis of the Sect

The character of our document can be determined despite its fragmentary state. It reflects the basic tendency of its provenance, the sect which maintained and practiced what may be called legal rigorism. Accordingly, the document focuses its primary interest on Halakhah. Its purpose is to demonstrate that one can only attain divine grace and the salvation promised by Him to the patriarchs by observant practice of the Torah as expounded in the teaching of the sect. To prove this truth, certain incidents and events, culled from biblical and post-biblical history, were cited in evidence. The readers to whom the document addressed itself were exclusively initiates of the sect, who were no less conversant with the details of its own history than with the content of the Bible. It was therefore quite sufficient for this didactic purpose to make no more than vague allusions and veiled references when referring to incidents from the past. This esoteric mode of communication leaves us with almost insurmountable difficulties when we attempt to reconstruct the history of the origin of the sect from the elusive statement of the text. The very nature of the text has, therefore, evoked numerous and mostly phantastic theories among the scholars who have dealt with the subject. It is, therefore, of value to investigate the "historical references" of our document before we can make some judgment concerning the history of the origin of the sect.

1,3–11. "For their perfidy . . . He committed them to the sword . . ., but He left a remnant of Israel, not relinquishing them entirely to destruction. In the era of wrath lasting 390 years (since He had delivered them unto the hand of Nebuchadnezzar . . .) He took account of them, and out of Aaron and Israel He made grow the roots which he had planted. . . . They recognized . . . that for a score of years they had groped like the blind, and God saw their deeds in that they sought Him with all their heart, He raised unto them a 'teacher of truth' to guide them in the way according to His own heart." במועלם אשר עזבוהו . . . ויתנם לחרב . . . השאיר שארית לישראל . . . ובקץ[1] חרון שנים שלוש

---

[1] Rabbinic tradition [Seder Olam XXX, Ratner p. 137, n. 15], counts only 52 years for "the rule of the Persians." Accordingly, 390 years after the destruction of the Temple by Nebuchadnezzar in the year 586 B.C.E. would bring us up to

257

מאות ותשעים (לתיתו אותם ביד נבוכדנאצר ...) פקדם ויצמח מישראל ומאהרן
שורש מטעת ... וידעו ... ויהיו כעורים ... שנים עשרים ויבן אל אל מעשיהם כי בלב
שלם דרשוהו ויקם להם מורה צדק להדריכם בדרך לבו. Almost all the scholars
who deal with the history of the sect, have made these first lines in
Fragment A, which do probably represent the introduction to the
scroll, the point of departure for their investigations. Controversy
has arisen only concerning the chronology employed here! As we have
pointed out earlier (pp. 209–211) this first admonition merely presents
a summary survey of the history of Israel and Judah up to the restoration of the Torah in the days of Josiah.[2] At this time God appointed
unto them a "teacher of truth" in the person of the incumbent High-
priest, who restored the Torah to its rightful place. At this juncture
they recognized that during the reign of "the twenty kings" — called
"twenty years" in the Midrashic-Apocalyptical idiom of our document
— "they had groped about like the blind." Hence we may infer that
the "390 years" are also related to this juncture in the days of Josiah.
Now we read in Ezek. 4:5–6: "For I have laid upon thee the years of
their iniquity, according to the number of the days, nineteen score
years and ten;[3] so thou shalt bear the iniquity of the house of Israel ....
I have appointed thee each day for a year." On basis of this prophecy,
our document employs the expression "the era of wrath[4] lasting

----

the year 30 B.C.E. Assuming however that our document knew the correct chronology, we would arrive for the year 390 after the destruction (586–390) at the year
196 B.C.E. In his Introduction, p. 22, Schechter contends that the date indicated here
corresponds to the period in which Simeon the Just [the elder] flourished, about
290 B.C.E. However, this remains inexplicable to me, for I cannot figure out on the
basis of any chronological system how 390 years after the destruction of the Temple
could coincide with 290 B.C.E.

[2] Cf. above, where we have elaborated on this point. It is noteworthy that the
words בלב שלם דרשוהו in 1,10 are literally reminiscent of II Kings 23:25 and II Chron.
34:3 where the Bible characterizes this pious king as seeking God whole-heartedly.
On the metaphor of the groping blind see also Midrash Tehillim on 146:8, ed.
Buber, p. 535, in conjunction with Isa. 59:10: הדורות האלו שהולכות בתורה כעורים
שנאמר: נגשה כעורים קיר.

[3] So MT; LXX reads 190.

[4] As pointed out on pp. 29–30, the term קץ means consistently in our document
a span of time, not a terminal point in time. On the other hand, Charles, ad loc., is
definitely wrong when maintaining that all combinations with קץ indicate the same
time. Here is a list of the various periods mentioned in our document:

a) "Era of Wrath lasting 390 years," i. e. from the exile of the ten tribes up to
the Maccabean Revolt. According to rabbinic chronology of traditional years
since creation, Samaria fell in 3205 and the Maccabean era started about
3590; cf. Yeḥiel Heilprin, Seder ha-Doroth on the years 3205 and 3590 respectively (ed. Warsaw, I, p. 118 and p. 144), primarily based on Seder Olam XXX.

390 years" to indicate more definitely the lapse of time between the destruction of Samaria and of Jerusalem. With regard to Israel's iniquity we read in a tannaic Midrash,[5] in conjunction with above cited prooftext from Ezekiel: "This indicates that during their years of settlement in the Promised Land Israel provoked God with idolatry for a span of 390 years." Since God "pays measure for measure", so Israel had to suffer divine wrath for the span of 390 years.[6] Our document could not use the קץ חרון for this "era of wrath"; it would have been misleading, since the text wants to emphasize and highlight that during the very "era of wrath" (between the fall of Samaria and the fall of Jerusalem) the remnant of Judah experienced the arising of salvation. The term קץ חרון, without any further modification, would mean the period after the destruction of the Temple. To avoid such a misunderstanding our document adds the modifier שנים שלוש מאות ותשעים to make it clear that this beginning of salvation

---

b) "Era of Wasteland" (5,20), the years of Civil War under Alexander Jannaeus; cf. further on.

c) "Era of Wickedness" (6,14 et al.), designating the present state of world affairs, in distinction to the messianic era; it corresponds to the rabbinic עולם הזה.

d) "Era of Former Visitation," קץ הפקודה הראשון (instead of הראשון read הראשונה; cf. above, p. 4 on this peculiar orthography), i. e. the time of the destruction of the first Temple, in distinction to the Era of Latter Visitation (19,10) with the advent of the messianic e ra.

[5] Seder Olam XXVI; this text relates Ezek. 4:5 to the ten tribe Kingdom of Israel only, whereas Seder Eliahu Zuṭa VIII, ed. Friedmann, p. 185, includes also the Kingdom of Judah: "410 years God abode in the First Temple; for all but 20 years, the kings of Israel and the kings of Judah worshiped idols." These twenty years probably represent the reign of Josiah; although he reigned for 31 years, he began the work of purification only in the twelfth year of his kingship; see II Chron. 34:3.

[6] Ekhah Rabbati, Petiḥta 21 (ed. Buber, p. 16). As was already mentioned in note 4, it had been believed originally that the Era of Wrath had terminated with the inception of the Maccabean era [390 years after the fall of Samaria]. Later on, after the destruction of the Second Temple and the ensuing Exile, it was held that the idolatrous period had lasted longer than 390 years. Hence this Midrash intimates: כל מי שיודע כמה שנים עבדו ישראל עבודה זרה — הוא יודע אימתי בן דוד בא, "He who knows the number of the years that Israel served idols can figure out when David's scion will come." The opinion of Seder Eliahu Zuṭa, mentioned in the previous note, which speaks of 390 idolatrous years of both Israel and Judah, may have been inspired by the aspiration to fix the advent of redemption about the year 200 C.E., for the sins of Judah and Israel will first have to be atoned. The allusion of our document in 20,15 probably refers to Ezek. 4:6. The basic idea in this instance is the requirement of a 40 year penitential period for 20 years of transgression; cf. Isa. 40:2 and Targum on Ezek. 4:5.

occurred during the period of wrath against Israel but not against
Judah. This dating modifier tells us, therefore, nothing whatsoever
about the founding date of the sect as "in the year 390." Had not the
hand of a latter-day scholiast interpolated a farther explanatory
gloss, no one would ever have thought that this date had anything to
do with the history of our sect. Such error could only occur by mis-
construing the syntax and not seeing that לתיתו אותם ביד נבוכדנצר
is an explanatory gloss on ובקץ חרון שנים שלש מאות ותשעים; although
the plural form שנים[7] for the otherwise required construct singular
שנת ought to have led to the correct interpretation. The grammatically
impossible form שנים as well as the obvious break in the stichic structure of our text make it clear beyond any doubt that the original
text read ובקץ חרון שנים שלש מאות ותשעים פקדם. Along came a reader who
identified the termination of "the era of wrath" with the destruction
of the Temple by Nebuchadnezzar, and therefore he enlarged our text
with the gloss לתיתו אותם ביד נבוכדנצר.

The first certain datum about the inception of the sect is found in
the Midrashic exegesis of Ezek. 44:15: "But the priests, the Levites,
the sons of Zadok, that kept the charge of My sanctuary when the
children of Israel went astray from Me, they shall come nigh Me to
minister unto Me, they shall stand before Me etc." The document
interprets this verse as follows:[8]

> THE PRIESTS are those of Israel who returned to God and
> went out of the Land of Judah
> THE LEVITES are those who joined themselves unto them
> and THE SONS OF ZADOK are the elect of Israel, men of
> renown
> THEY STAND in the end of the days.

---

[7] Cf. above, where we have already demonstrated that before the modifying
clause לתיתו it could then have been correct only to write שנת. It is, of course,
the easiest way out for a critic — such as Charles ad loc. — to delete the entire
clause from ובקץ up to פקדם as a gloss. The number 390 derived evidently from
Ezek. 4:5. Yet nobody who has had the passage from the Prophet before his eyes
could have possibly started this Era of Wrath with the destruction of the Temple.
Verse 5 refers exclusively to "the House of Israel," whereas verse 6 exclusively to
"the House of Judah." Hence the number 390 of verse 5 relates to the expiatory
period for the ten tribe kingdom of Israel, the 40 of verse 6 to the kingdom of Judah.
The interpolator of the clause לתיתו apparently no longer knew whence the number
390 in the text had derived; hence he attempted to connect the "era" with the
"wrath" manifest in the destruction of the Temple and the ensuing period of calamities. — This hypercritical method, which deletes whatever it cannot explain,
leaves unanswered the question why the text reads שנים and not שנת, if the entire
passage were really the work of the same hand.

[8] 4,2–4.

הכהנים הם שבי ישראל היוצאים מארץ יהודה [והלויים הם]⁹ הנלוים עמהם
ובני צדוק הם בחירי ישראל קריאי השם העמדים באחרית הימים.¹⁰

Aside from "the elect" to whom our document assigns a role only in the "Messianic era" we can here discern with some clarity a distinction between two periods in the evolution of the sect:

1) The founders proper of the sect, "the priests" in the Midrashic idiom of our document, are God-fearing Judeans who left their land to realize their ideal abroad.

2) Outside of Judea they were "joined" by new members, either Jews from Palestine or from the Diaspora — our document does not specify, who did not assume the rank of the leaders (the priests) of the new movement; these became disciples of the Judean veterans, or, in the idiom of our document: the Levites of these "priests."

What, then, were the ideals of these God-fearing Judeans, which could not be realized in their homeland, but demanded their exodus into strange lands? For an answer to this question we turn to the following passage (6,11 ff.)¹¹ — and it is indeed a sufficient answer¹² "And all who have been initiated into the covenant not to enter the Sanctuary as long as — Israel — do not live up to the Torah in keeping with the interpretation, for the duration of the Era of Wickedness — as long as this order of the world shall prevail! — not to enter the Sanctuary to kindle fire on His altar for nought, but be rather the lockers of its doors, as God said: O that you would shut the doors and

---

⁹ Thus we would have to complement before והנלוים; the almost identical lettering of הלויים and הנלוים is responsible for the scribe's mistake.

¹⁰ The last three words can only be conceived *sub specie messianis*, as evident from comparison with 6,10: עד עמד . . . באחרית הימים. Ezekiel's prophecy is interpreted in our document, in consonance with rabbinic exegesis (*cf.* Qimḥi to Ezek. 43:11), as to be projected into the Messianic era. The founders of the sect, as "the elect of Israel," are singled out by the Prophet as those who will be honored by God in the Messianic era. We are not told who "the elect" are. However, we would not err by assuming that this designation refers to the "Seven Shepherds" and the "Eight Princes" who will constitute the royal entourage of the Messiah, among them Abraham, Jacob, Moses, David and other pious personages; *cf.* Sukkah 52b.

¹¹ For detailed notes on this passage see above, pp. 30–31 and p. 155; [the emendation implied by us on p. 31 is unnecessary when we take as subject of ישמרו not the brethren of the covenant but their opponents].

¹² This sentence וכל אשר הובאו בברית לבלתי בוא אל המקדש וכו' represents a continuation of the preceding חקק המחוקק אשר במחוקקות הבאר את לכרות הבאים הם העם ונדיבי. The נדיבי העם, the noblest of the people are the followers of the מחוקק, the canonist, as well as the initiates who entered the covenant, etc.

not kindle fire uselessly on Mine altar! Moreover, those who entered the sect took it upon themselves to separate themselves from the sons of corruption and to shun all unlawful property, which is contaminated because it represents things that have been vowed and consecrated, or the property of the Temple or property stolen from the poor of the people by preying on widows or murdering orphans; to distinguish between the impure and the pure, to know what is sacred and what profane; to observe the Sabbath in keeping with its law, and the feast-days and the fastday according to their laws."

We infer from this program of the Sect[13] that its adherents knew that the Temple was in the hands of people who did not obey "the interpretation of the Torah," i. e., who did not recognize the sectarian Halakah. Consequently, the sectarians regarded themselves as constrained to give up visiting the Temple, lest they become accomplices to the pollution of the Sanctuary. Moreover, the judicial system and the regulation of the calendar, entailing the cycle of holy days,[14] lay in the hands of their enemies. The participants in this new covenant obligated themselves to shun their opponents and to accept neither their legal jurisdiction nor the dates that they assigned to the holy days. We may assume that this program had been drawn up in Judea, probably in Jerusalem (cf. 20,22 [וכל האנשים] מבית פלג אשר יצאו מעיר הקדש). For some time the spokesmen of the new movement were content with a policy of passive resistence: non-attendance at the Temple, ignoring of court jurisdiction, and contemning the dates of the calendar as proclaimed by the ruling officials. This policy of passive opposition could not last. The rulers "justified the wicked and condemned the righteous, transgressed the covenant — between God and Israel — and broke the law, conspired against the righteous and abhorred all who walked upright; they even persecuted them with the sword."[15] These sectarians could not remain any longer in Judea. The "righteous" Judeans who had entered the new covenant felt themselves compelled to emigrate.

They expatriated themselves to Damascus (3,19; 7,15 ff.). There

---

[13] See above, p. 155 for explanatory notes.

[14] Even the Sabbath is included in this passage, although its weekly celebration is independent of the fixation of the monthly cycle in the lunar calendar; cf. our commentary above, pp. 69–70.

[15] Cf. 1,19–21. Although this passage describes the sins of the Northern Kingdom of Ephraim, the ten Tribes, as has been elaborated above, p. 168, yet we have to bear in mind that in the Haggadah as well as in the Apocalypses it is always contemporary circumstances which color such "historical" descriptions. Is לריב עם in 1,21 an allusion to ירבעם? Cf. Ben Sira 47:23.

God "builded them a firmly established home[16] the like of which had heretofore not stood; those who hold on to Him are destined for life eternal, and all mundane glory will be theirs."[17] For it happened in Damascus that the Star out of Jacob arose unto them in the person of the Exegete of the Torah (7,18 והכוכב הוא דורש התורה הבא דמשק כאשר כתוב with prooftext Num. 24:17). To him and his loyal followers the words of the Bible (Num. 21:18) concerning the well are applicable:

"*the Well* — is the Torah;
  and *its diggers* — the converted of *Israel* who emigrated from Judea and have settled in Damascus. . . .
  and *the lawgiver* — מחוקק[18] — is the Exegete of the Torah. . . .
  and *the Nobles of the people* — those who come to delve into the Well, i. e., to study the Torah as mediated through the teaching which the Exegete had established and to live according to it during the whole era of wickedness . . . and all who entered the covenant agreed not to enter the Temple."

In Damascus, probably under the guidance of the canonist, they devised a new program for the sect in response to changed circumstances. This new program was recorded in the passage 6,19–7,4, where the new one follows after the Judean program (6,11 ff.). The revised program enjoins those "who entered the new covenant in the Land of Damascus," באי הברית החדשה בארץ דמשק.[19] This new program contains the following points:

a) to offer up[20] the sacred gifts in keeping with their — the sectarians' — interpretation להרים את הקדשים כפירושיהם.
b) to love each his brother like oneself לאהוב איש את אחיהו כמהו.
c) To support the poor, the wretched and the alien ולהחזיק ביד עני ואביון וגר.

---

[16] *Cf.* Zech. 5:11 לבנות . . . . בית, according to which our passage wants to express merely that God granted the emigrés safe residence at Damascus. We shall elaborate on this later on.

[17] Literally: all humanly possible glory; *cf.* 20,26, where בהופע כבוד אל refers to messianic blessings, whereas mundane bounty of the present world is called כבוד אדם.

[18] It is noteworthy that the Great Teacher of the sect is designated מחוקק as well as שבט (7,20); these words were already synonyms in the Bible (Gen. 49:10); see however above, p. 34.

[19] *Cf.* above, p. 31 and pp. 155 f.

[20] In Mishnah Zevaḥim V,6 *et al.* the verb הרים is employed as term only for sacrificial offerings from livestock. Our document, however, follows biblical usage which employs it as term for any hieratic gift.

d) to promote each the welfare of his brother ולדרוש איש את שלום
אחיהו.

e) not to commit an incest ולא ימעל איש בשאר בשרו.

f) to keep away from illicit women in keeping with the law[21]
ולהזיר מן הזונות כמשפט.

g) to rebuke each his brother as instructed[22] להוכיח איש את אחיהו
כמצוה.

h) not to bear grudge from one day to the next ולא לנטור מיום ליום.

i) to abstain from all impurities in keeping with their law ולהבדל
מכל הטמאות כמשפטם,

so that nobody make his spirit of sanctity detestable ולא ישקץ
איש את רוח קדשיו,

since it was God who made these distinctions for them כאשר
הבדיל אל להם.

Comparing the Damascene compact with the Judean, we can
clearly gauge the great change which the sect underwent from the
time of its inception up to its reconstitution at Damascus. In Judea
they merely represented a nonconformist group of protestants who
ostentatiously demonstrated their dissatisfaction with the prevailing
state of religious disloyalty. They fondly cherished the hope that
conditions may soon improve. Yet they meant to emphasize the
seriousness of their indignation: they announced solemnly that until
the situation improved as they hoped they would not participate in
public worship or recognize the official jurisdiction in matters of law.
In Damascus, however, we meet them as a sect which cares little for
the Jewish people as a whole; hence the Damascene compact contains
rules of conduct exclusively for the initiates[23] of the covenant, without
even the slightest mention of Jerusalem and the Jews who dwell
there. Their Damascene outlook is best epitomized in the following
passage (4,10):[24] "And even during the course of this era according to
the appointed number of its years, none shall any longer abide allegiance to the House of Judah, but each shall stand on his watch by
himself. The barrier (between Judea and Damascus) has been builded,
the Messianic time is far, far away!"

It is, therefore, not incidental that our document announces particularly severe penalties for those (20,10 ff.) "who utter error against
the righteous ordinances and reject the covenant and the compact

---

[21] For the connotation of זונות in this passage in the meaning of illicit marriages,
cf. also Yevamoth VI,5, Temurah 29b and Sifra on Lev. 21:7 [ed. Weiss 94b], where
the Tannaite definition of זונה is presented.

[22] Read כמצוה; cf. above, p. 155. n. 7.

[23] Cf. above chapter V, p. 156.

[24] Cf. above, pp. 16–17 for detailed commentary on this passage.

which they (the initiates of the sect) took upon themselves in the Land of Damascus, even this very new covenant." The wrath of the sect is focused with intensity on those who had joined this body but refused to participate in the radical step of making a complete break with the whole of Jewry. Hence also the emphasis in this passage — as in three other passages of our document: 6,19; 8,21; 19,33–34 — "that the new covenant was made at Damascus." The conservative sectarians who adhered to the program that was established in Judea are herewith being charged with defection. The new covenant[25] is the one which was made in Damascus; abiding by it henceforth constitutes the true sign that one is a member of the sect. Now it also emerges clearly who are meant as those who entered into the covenant but would not consider the observance of laws — promulgated by the Damascene Master — as binding upon them; for whom, therefore, grave punishment in the end of the days was predicted.[26] These words are directed at those of the members of the sect who clung to the Judean compact but ignored the teachings announced in Damascus. These people are, therefore, stigmatized as "the princes of Judah" (8,3 = 19,15), even those who "have entered the covenant for their conversion, and have yet not turned away from the way of the perfidious." The reference here is to individuals who have entered the covenant but would not take part in the radical step taken in Damascus of complete separation from all of Jewry; they are here viewed, therefore, as sharing in the sins of Israel.

*　　　*

*

Reliable data on the history of the sect are, as we have seen, rather scanty in our document. The first phase of the new movement consisted of the forming of an association by covenant in Judea. Members of this association obligated themselves to boycott the

---

[25] This term is derived from the ברית חדשה, "new covenant," in Jer. 31:30. In our document it is employed to stress the innovations of the Damascene platform, the new covenant as over against the old covenant of Judea, and not the relationship of the sect to all Israel (correct our note on 20,8 accordingly). In Judea the compact of the sect was but a ברית תשובה; only in Damascus did they resolve complete schism and secession from the rest of the Jews, and only then did they call their members initiates of the new covenant.

[26] Cf. Fragment A 8,1 ff., and its parallel in Fragment B 19,14 ff. Be it noted that the passage 7,21 presents a corrupted text, since by dint of a homoioteleuton a whole sentence was skipped. Instead of אלה מלטו בקץ it should read: אלה [ימלטו בקץ הפקודה כאלה אשר] מלטו בקץ. What then follows constitutes the threat of impending doom for the sinners; it is not a description of events which occurred already. Elaboration on this point will be presented later on.

Temple, not to recognize official jurisdiction in the realms of juridic and religious decisions and to reject the official fixation of the calendar as long as the authorities in power would not mend their ways of disloyalty to God and the law and base their behavior on exegesis of the Torah propounded by the sect. The second, more decisive phase took place at Damascus: the formation of "the New Covenant in Damascus" which postulated in its program complete secession from Jewry at large and obligated its members to the strict observance of all ordinances promulgated by the Teacher of the Torah in Damascus. The Founding Fathers of the "New Covenant" were dedicated pious nonconformists from Judea, who had exiled themselves in an attempt to realize their ideals on alien soil. The formation of the new covenant did not proceed without struggle. The postulate of complete secession from Judea, i. e., from Jewry at large, met violent opposition. It is against these Judeans who had formed the old covenant but refused to enter "the New Covenant" that our document fulminates with unrestrained fury.

These were charged particularly with the following offenses: polygamy, marriage with nieces and pollution of the Temple by cohabitation with menstruating women.[27] The Damascene terms of the New Covenant allude to the first two of the defectors' sins by admonishing its members not to commit incestuous trespass against relations and to keep away from illicit women in keeping with the law ולא ימעל איש בשאר בשרו להזיר מן הזונות כמשפט. The incestuous relations are certainly the nieces,[28] whereas the warning against intercourse with illicit women refers to polygamy.[29] The Judean compact indeed mentions "distinction between the pure and the impure"[30] the minute observance of which was highly cherished by the sectarians, in contradistinction to the dominant circles, but neither marriages to near relatives nor polygamy were forbidden in the original, Judean covenant. Since, as we have demonstrated above[31] polygamy and marriage with nieces were prevalent among both the Pharisees and the

---

[27] *Cf.* 4,20 ff. and our discourse thereon above, pp. 19–20 and pp. 22–24.

[28] *Cf.* above, pp. 31–32.

[29] Hence the reading זונות is to be maintained and not to be emended to זנות.

[30] The instructions concerning conduct with menstruating women belong to הלכות טומאה, hence this passage refers to the sin of the opponents, mentioned in 5,6–7 as "polluting ... not making the *distinctions* according to the Torah, and have intercourse with a woman during the period in which she sees the flow of her menstrual blood," which is alluded to in this passage as "*distinction* between the pure and the impure," i. e. that the wicked declare menstruation to be "pure" instead of "impure."

[31] *Cf.* chapter IV.

Sadducees, we are driven to the only possible conclusion, that the prohibition of such marriages, which was stressed in the Damascene compact but not mentioned in the Judean compact, was an innovation of "the Exegete of the Torah at Damascus." Hence it would be a fallacy to regard these restrictions concerning marriages as the original point of departure for the schism and first formation of the sect in Judea, for the original sectarians who made the first covenant in Judea, did not, as we have seen, make any such laws. The prohibition of polygamy and marriage with nieces was first promulgated later in Damascus. Aside from the prohibition of marriage with nieces and polygamy, the Halakah in our document is in complete accord with Pharisaic teaching, as we have demonstrated in detail in chapter IV. We, therefore, conclude *that the original sectarians in Judea emerged from the Pharisees. We think that this is the solution of the problem of the origin of the sect.*

"During the era of the desolation of the land there rose up the removers of the boundaries, and they misled Israel and the land became desolate; for they preached rebellion against the divine commandments transmitted through Moses, and against His holy anointed;[32] and they prophesied lies in order to cause Israel to backslide from God. And then God thought of His covenant with the ancestors, and He raised men of insight out of Aaron, and wise men out of Israel . . . who dug up the well — The Well that Princes digged — . . . the Well — that is the Torah." This description of the period during which the sect emerged — 5,20 ff. — corresponds best to the conditions during the years of warfare between Alexander Jannaeus and the Pharisees, "a succession of battles which lasted six years and cost the lives of as many as 50,000 Jews" (Josephus, *Bel. Jud.* I, 4, 4,). Josephus observes on this brutal campaign of Alexander: "He had little cause to rejoice over these victories so ruinous to his kingdom, his own people." The cause for the desolation of the land is ascribed in our document to "the removers of the boundaries," that is that calamity came because of the Sadducean teachers, who removed the boundaries that the ancients had defined.[33] During the reign of this godless king who attempted to introduce his Sadducean heresies even into the Temple practice,[34] certain Pharisees made a covenant to boycott the Temple and to ignore Sadducee jurisprudence. The

[32] On this designation, *cf.* above on 6,1 and p. 222.

[33] The Sadducees rejected the traditions handed down by the ancients [thus trespassing against (Prov. 22:28): "Remove not the ancient boundary which thy ancestors have set"]. Hence "removers of the boundary" is a felicitous designation of the Sadducees; *cf.* above, pp. 124–125.

[34] *Cf.* Josephus, *Antiq.* XIII 13,5 and Sukkah 48b.

active persecution by Alexander[35] of the Pharisees compelled many of
them to emigrate. These Pious made mostly for Egypt[36] and Damascus.
Megillath Taanith records a day of rejoicing on the seventeenth of
Adar, because "the heathens rose up against the remnant of the
scholars, ספריא, in Chalkis and Beth-Zavdai, but they were saved":
בשבעת עשר ביה קמו עממיא על פליטת ספריא במדינת בליקוס[37] בבית זבדי והוה פורקן.
Deriving probably from authentic sources, the scholiast notes
that the event occurred in the days of Alexander Jannaeus.[38] The
scholars fled before murderous bands of this persecutor to Syria, to
the district of Chalkis. However, the Chalkians attacked them and inflicted grave losses. Their remnant escaped to Beth Zavdai, from
which they made their escape under the cover of night. This Beth
Zavdai is certainly identifiable[39] with the modern Ez-Zebedani, a stop
on the railway between Beirut and Damascus, some 28 miles from
the latter terminal. This scholion would prove the statement in our
document that the scholars who emigrated from Judea settled in the
Land[40] of Damascus (6,5). Here they pursued their mode of living,
serving God and observing His laws without hindrance and amidst
great respect (3,19).[41] One among these emigrants to Damascus seems
to have been the famous leader of the Pharisees, Shimeon ben Shattaḥ;
the Talmud even reports[42] an episode about a business deal between

---

[35] *Idem.*, *Bel. Jud.* I 4,6.

[36] The leader of the Pharisees, Judah ben Tabbai, escaped to Egypt; *cf.* Yer.
Ḥagigah II,77d, and Frankel's note thereon in *Darkei ha-Mishnah*, p. 25.

[37] The *var. lect.* of this word — *cf.* Neubauer *ad loc.* (*Géographie*, p. 295) — dis-
pel any doubt that it refers to Chalkis, כלקיס [*cf.* Lichtenstein, *HUCA* VIII–IX,
p. 293].

[38] [שכששדר ינאי המלך להרוג את החכמים ברחו מלפניו והלכו להם לסוריא ושרו במדינת
כלקיס וכו'.]

[39] *Cf.* Dérenbourg, *Essai*, pp. 99–100; Graetz, *Geschichte*⁵ III, p. 571; Baedeker,
Palestine and Syria, latest edition, p. 338. It does not stand to reason to reject the
scholion entirely, as Dérenbourg does, and to project the incident of Adar 17 in the
days of Jonathan (I Macc. XII, 30–32) [who, after crossing the Eleutherus (Leontes?)
on his way to Damascus "turned to the Arabians who were called Zabadeans, smote
them and took their spoils"]. The scholiast did "edit," here and there, the source
material at his disposal, yet it would go too far to assume that he invented his data
entirely out of the air.

[40] Except for one passage (7,19), our document — *nota bene* — always refers to
"the Land of Damascus." Beth-Zavdai could well be designated as belonging to "the
Land of Damascus," but not to Damascus proper. The phrase היוצאים מארץ יהודה
of our document is strongly reminiscent of Josephus, *Bel. Jud.* I, 4,6 where it is
reported: "Such terror gripped the people that the next night 8,000 of Alexander's
opponents *fled right out of Judea* and remained in exile till his death."

[41] *Cf.* our commentary on this passage, above, pp. 262–263.

[42] Jerushalmi Bava Meẓi'a II, 8c; *cf.* commentaries, *ad loc.*, who interpret סירקאי as
Saracens, which seems to me very dubious; *cf.* Schlatter, *Verkanntes Griechisch*, p. 56.

him and an Arab, stressing that "to hear the Arab praise the Jewish God was worth more to him than all worldly gain." בעי הוה שמעון בן שטח משמעיה בריך אלההון דיהודאי מאגר כל הדין עלמא. Part of the population and around Damascus was Arab. Most probably even the place-name Beth Zavdai is of Arab origin.[43] In the light of the Judean refugees' precarious situation, it is easy to understand why Simeon ben Shattaḥ strove to impress the Arab.

The Pharisee refugees "remained in exile" reports Josephus (*Bel. Jud.* I 4,6), "till Alexander's death." He was succeeded by his widow Alexandra: "Woman though she was, she established her authority by her reputation for piety (*ibid.*)." The change of ruler surely occasioned the return to Palestine of many of the emigrés, for in the reign of the pious Alexandra the Pharisees had nothing to fear. However it is *a priori* most improbable that all the emigrés returned. Refugees who leave their native land in adulthood and then live in exile for a quarter of a century[44] are not always able to attempt, towards the end of their days, the daring experiment of returning. We may assume that a substantial part of these Judean refugees at Damascus never went home to Judea. We have even less grounds to assume that the new generation, i. e. the children born in Damascus to these Pharisee immigrants or those who left Palestine at a tender age, was eager to avail itself of the changed political situation in Jerusalem. It is much more reasonable to presume that the young, for whom Judea and Jerusalem were merely names, whereas they were living in a land in which they had grown up and which had made their parents welcome, remained, even as some of the emigrés returned to the Holy Land. "In the Land of Damascus" there had resettled not only laymen persecuted by Alexander Jannaeus, but also some of the leading spirits among the Pharisees. These men spurred the people on with concern for devotion to the study of the Torah and to single-minded opposition to Sadduceeism. It was here and in this atmosphere that around[45] 76 B.C.E. the sect was constituted which is reported on in our document. The Pharisees of Palestine gladly welcomed the peace overtures made by the government after the death of Alexander Jannaeus. The state of affairs was, indeed, not yet entirely satisfactory to them. The power of the aristocratic Sadducees in the Temple — and in the law courts — did not disappear entirely even in

---

[43] Dérenbourg, *Essai*, p. 99.

[44] Alexander Jannaeus reigned 103–76 B.C.E. His battles with the Pharisees started soon after the beginning of his reign.

[45] This represents the *terminus a quo*, whereas it is quite possible that one or more decades transpired until the New Covenant was actually established.

the days of Alexandra.[46] Yet the Pharisees felt themselves sufficiently master of the situation that they could allow the Sadducee aristocracy to retain some of their former prerogatives without feeling that they were compromising Pharisaic principles.

In the emigré settlement in Damascus the situation was entirely different. There were no political considerations or patriotic motives which could move these Pious to any compromises whatever with the Sadducees. Their slogan, as it were, was: *aut Caesar, aut nihil* — either all affairs of state, Temple, law-court, and academy are conducted in compliance with Pharisaic teaching, or we break all connection with a Jewish state in which godlessness reigns. We therefore prefer to keep away from the Promised Land and the Temple. Hence "the New Covenant of Damascus" may be defined as a compact of intransigents who rejected any compromise whatever with the Sadducees.

As an opposition movement it would probably not have lasted long. However, it was able to provide itself with an affirmative, positive basis by accepting as binding on all sectarians the Halakic interpretations of "the Exegete of the Torah." The Pharisaic Halakah which the Judean refugees had transplanted with them would, in the course of mounting schism between Damascus and Jerusalem, have grown completely petrified, had not "the Exegete of the Torah" created fresh means for the further development of the old Pharisaic Halakah. We have demonstrated above that the injunction against the marriage of nieces and against polygamy had its origin in the teaching of this "Exegete of the Torah." More important, however, than his various specific teachings are his methods. The basis for his prohibition of marriage with nieces was the application of the exegetical mode of analogy, היקש.[47] As demonstrated earlier,[48] this prohibition was the root of the further prohibition of polygamy. Without hesitation we may assume that many other points of difference and deviation from Pharisaic Halakah derived from the singular Midrash employed by this "*Darshan*." We must not overlook that also in contemporary Judea the Midrash rose to increasing significance. About this time the two Pharisaic leaders, Shemaiah and Avtalion,

---

[46] In his exposition of party affairs and their political activities during the reign of Alexandra, Josephus drew on anti-Pharisee source material and, therefore, exaggerated their power and influence on the queen. The scholiast on Megillath Taanith (Teveth 28) reports that about this time the Sanhedrin was composed of Pharisees and Sadducees [*cf.* also Acts 4:1; 5:17].

[47] *Cf.* pp. 127ff.

[48] *Cf.* on 4,20 and p. 129.

flourished there. They were the first to have been designated as *Darshanim*. The Talmud[49] has preserved a report which intimates that some scholars, dissatisfied with this method,[50] seceded and moved South, where they settled.[51] The Darshan at Damascus was probably influenced by the flourishing of the exegetic application of the Midrash which was dominant in Palestine. Yet he blazed his own trail in Midrashic exegesis; his very independence caused the break between Jerusalem and Damascus to widen, since we are dealing here with the most sensitive realm of authenticating the divine word by exegetic application. For the intransigents in Damascus, who maintained an attitude of the greatest strictness in legal matters, and especially in questions related to the purity of the Temple — this was, indeed, a stance much easier for them to adopt than for the Pharisees in Palestine, because the emigrés to Damascus, in their concrete situation of distance from Jerusalem did not participate in the Temple service — their former brothers in covenant, the Pharisees of Palestine, were the thorn in their eye. They no longer battled with the Sadducees — they were hardly any to be found among the Jews of Damascus — so the Pharisees were now stigmatized as their archenemies. "Because they preached falling away from the righteous laws, rejecting the covenant and compact that they — the members of the sect — took upon themselves in the Land of Damascus, even the New Covenant; therefore, neither they nor their families shall have a share in the house of the Torah."[52] כי דברו תועה על חקי הצדק ומאסו בברית ואמנה אשר קיימו בארץ דמשק והיא ברית החדשה ולא יהיה להם ולמשפחותיהם חלק בבית התורה. With these words the Pharisees[53] were excluded from the community because they refused to recognize

---

[49] Pesaḥim 70b.

[50] They charged the Pharisaic leaders with inconsistency since they had taught that the offering of the Paschal lamb, but not the offering of the holiday sacrifice, Ḥagigah, חגיגה, would supersede the Sabbath restrictions. So also the use of the method of analogy as the basis for forbidding marrying nieces is the consistent application of a hermeneutic rule; *cf.* above, p. 155. Inconsistency is a charge often hurled by a minority against the majority.

[51] Pesaḥim 70b; as Rashi, *ad loc.*, so correctly remarks, these secessionists refused to participate in the services at the Temple.

[52] 20,11–13. 20,13 — בית תורה is Hebrew for בית אולפנא employed in the Targum, just as (11,22) בית סנידו=בית השתחות. Charles, Introduction, p. 13, note 1 sees in בית התורה an opposition to the Pharisaic בית המדרש; thus he demonstrates that he knows neither the Aramaic בית אולפנא, nor the fact that בית המדרש occurs already in Ben Sira [LI, 23].

[53] 20,1–8 is a passage spoken about the renegades, following which it is stressed that the doom destined for them will be no less than for those who in their blindness had never entered the New Covenant at all.

the New Covenant and to accept the declaration that the covenant
that had been made in Judea was valid no longer.[54] Because of their
opportunism and their moderation, the Pharisees were branded as
those (8,12) "who do build up a wall, but then again daub it with
untempered mortar." This metaphor of a "wall" purposefully erected
by religious rigorism, we also meet in the Epistle of Aristeas 139:
"The wise legislator, having weighed everything in his wisdom, decided to hedge us around with an impenetrable fence and with iron
walls, lest we intermingle with other peoples, etc." Now the charge
is leveled against the Pharisees that instead of the iron wall, which
the Law ought to be, it had become in their bounds a wall of untempered mortar,[55] because they had not gone far enough in building
and strengthening it.

The result of our inquiry into the historical background of this
unknown sect may now be summed up as follows: During the bloody
reign of Alexander Jannaeus some pious Pharisees, both priests and
laymen, in Judea, most probably in Jerusalem, made a compact. The
terms of their covenant included avoidance of the Temple and re-
pudiation of both the juridic and religious decisions rendered by
Sadducee-teachers and judges,[56] but instead to follow the only true
Pharisaic exegesis of the Torah in all matters. This boycott would be
enforced as long as the Sadducees would predominate in public life.
This covenant could not be maintained for long in Judea. In those
times of persecution the covenanters, like so many other Pharisees,
had to leave Palestine to escape imminent death and, therefore, they
sought refuge in the land of Damascus, or, to use the exact place-
name of their settlement, which is the usage in rabbinic sources, in
Beth Zavdai. This colony of emigrés rejoiced not only in its economic
prosperity, but also in the spiritual renascence that it experienced.
The latter was largely due to the work of the "Exegete of the Torah,"
a teacher of the law who blazed new trails for the advancement of
Halakah. The death of Alexander Jannaeus posed for this community in Damascus the question of what their attitude should now
be. How should one react to the new state of affairs in the old homeland? There was no uniform attitude in the Damascus community

[54] This is the meaning of (8,31 = 20,8) המואס בראשונים ובאחרונים — the "former"
refers to the Judean compact, the "latter" to the Damascene (New Covenant).

[55] *Cf.* [Ezek. 13:5 and 10 and] also above, our commentary on 8,12.

[56] Legislative decision also included fixation of the calendar; *cf.* above, p. 262.
Regulation and fixing of the calendar was an official function of the authorities;
the opposition regarded Sadducee control of official authority as illegitemate and
that included acts regarding the calendar.

towards this challenge. Some were glad to go home again and they rejoiced even more over at the bright prospects that, under the protection of pious queen Salome Alexandra, the Pharisees now come to power, would restore a life according to true law in Palestine. However, other covenanters at Damascus, particularly the younger generation, who were devoted disciples of the "Exegete of the Torah," were strongly opposed to the policy of restoration as represented by the Pharisees in Palestine and refused to acknowledge their teachings as orthodox. It was no longer possible to unite the heterogeneous elements within the Damascene community. Thus emerged the New Covenant of Damascus; its slogan: break with Judea. In the course of time the secessionists developed into (20,5) "the congregations of perfect holiness" which lived up to "the teachings of the Exegete of the Torah," whose honorific was "The Excellent Teacher." These congregations had their peculiar constitution, though it seems that this document was not the work of the Exegete of the Torah, but rather a product of evolution. Hence this constitution contains elements[57] that are later than the teaching of the sect's original founder. This constitution is remarkable no less by its humanitarian attitude which it prescribed towards members of the community than by its extreme rigor[58] adopted towards renegades from the sect. The former as well as the latter are genuine criteria of sectarianism — brutal and unscrupulous towards opponents, but helpful and lenient towards the initiated brethren.

---

[57] *Cf.* above, p. 91 and p. 92, where we have drawn attention to some similarities between these elements and Jewish practices during the Gaonic era. We shall elaborate on this further on.

[58] *Cf.* 20,1 ff. It should be noted that בהופע (20,3) is not to be emended — with Charles — either to בהורע or to בהודע; *cf.* Makkoth 23b where הופיע is employed in the connotation of proving, becoming manifest — Rashi: נגלה והוכיח; prouver = ברוביר — as also here, where as requisite grounds for the renegade's expulsion it is demanded that his misdeeds are manifest and proven בהופע מעשיו. The renegade is also designated אנשי מעות (20,4–5) corresponding to the statement in the Mishnah (Ḥagigah I,7) that a scholar who departs from his Torah studies, תלמיד חכם הפורש מן התורה, is classified with those of whom Scripture (Eccles. 1:15) says: מעות לא יוכל לתקון, a crookedness not to be straightened. Our document, however, stresses that such a straying person is not yet entirely lost: if he mends his ways he may be readmitted to "the Congregation of Perfect Holiness," עד יום ישוב לעמוד במעמד אנשי תמים קדש.

VIII

The Language of the Document

For practical considerations we have heretofore referred to the present fragments as "the sectarian document," as if it were of uniform composition. Yet we have never had any doubt that the document is composite in character. One only has to compare the first discourse (1,1–2,1), written in excellent, natural Hebrew, with the dragging and artificial language of the pericope dealing with the community's constitution (13,1 ff.), to arrive at the conclusion that these two passages cannot possibly be ascribed to the same author. The contrast between these two passages is so great that we must rule out the existence of an editor who attempted to gloss over the differences and unify the document. It is most likely that these are fragments of diverse documents. On the basis of the historical background of the sect's origin and development, as we described it above, we are in a position to classify the major part of these *disjecta membra* according to their provenance.

1) The first pericope in the present document (1,1–2,1) presents a Pharisaic tirade against the Sadducees "who remove the landmarks,"[1] bitterly attacking their jurisprudence as well as their religio-moral conduct. Conditions of contemporary life are projected from the present into the past, a ruse often employed in Apocalyptic literature, in order to teach a lesson drawn from "history": that Israel can rely upon divine support only when, on their part, the Jews are loyal in their observance of the Torah and obedient to the will of God. The kingdom of the Ten Tribes, our Pharisaic proponent asserts,[2] perished because it was negligent in observance of Torah, whereas Judah was saved when it repented in the days of King Josiah and turned back to God from its sinful conduct. We notice in this discourse that its author is well informed about the conditions he is criticizing; he probably was an eye-witness of his opponents' daily life. It would not be far wrong to assume that this discourse may be traced to the early

---

[1] *Cf.* above, pp. 124–125.
[2] *Cf.* above, pp. 209 f.

years of Alexander Jannaeus' reign, when the Sadducees, favored by the King, attempted to impose the acceptance of their doctrines with the authority of the sword.

2) The second pericope (2,2–2,13) originated with the same author[3] as the first. It, too, is directed against the Sadducean doctrines; it takes special exception to their overemphasis on the freedom of will, a doctrine which is here contrasted with the Pharisaic doctrine of divine providence.[4]

3) The third and last discourse of this Pharisee is contained in the next pericope (2,14–3,21). It presents a brief overview of the course of history, from the Fall of the Angels until the day of the restoration of the true doctrine in Israel. Sin and its inevitable consequence, retribution, both result from the striving to follow after the impulses of one's own heart; the truly pious prefer obedience to God's commandments to their own inclinations and therefore merit divine reward.

In our document this historical review follows the analysis of the causes that led to the doom of the Ten Tribes (first pericope), but we have good grounds to assume that this represents no chronological sequence. The mention in the third pericope of the firm house in Israel which God erected for his loyal servants, a house stronger than any of its predecessors, may well be interpreted as reference[5] to the flourishing estate of the Hasmonean house. However, no Pharisee would have expressed himself with such enthusiasm for the Hasmonean dynasty during the reign of Alexander Jannaeus. Hence, we may rather assume that this discourse originated in the days of John Hyrcanus. The hostile collision between the Sadducees and Pharisees occurred, to the degree to which we know the story from the sources,[6]

---

[3] The thesis that these first three discourses, or sermons, are not to be attributed to different authors can be demonstrated by the similarity of the exhortatory introduction to all three: 1) "and now hearken all ye that know righteousness (1,1)"; 2) "and now hearken unto me, all ye that entered the covenant (2,2)," 3) "and now, children, hearken unto me (2,14)". I call these pericopes "sermons," for they bear the distinct signs of the spoken exhortation.

[4] Cf. above, p. 165.

[5] The expression "firm(ly established) house" is applied in I Kings 11:38 — cf. also I Sam. 25:28; II Samuel 7:11 and 16 — to the Davidic and Ephraimite dynasties respectively. It is therefore probable that our document is here, by this expression, referring to the Hasmonean dynasty. Cf. however I Sam. 2:35, which speaks of a priestly dynasty.

[6] Josephus, Ant. XIII, 10,5–6; Qiddushin 66a. In the latter reference two different historical notes were merged: the open rupture between John Hyrcanus and the Pharisees is ascribed to the persecution of the Pharisees by Alexander Jannaeus, "King Jannaeus," ינאי המלך. Since father and son bore the same Hebrew

under the reign of John Hyrcanus.[7] The second and third pericopes represent two Pharisaic discourses of this time, reflecting a bitter attack upon Sadduceeism. The first pericope, however, reflects a later day, the reign of Alexander Jannaeus, when the conflict between Pharisees and Sadducees was no longer merely theoretical. Therefore in the first pericope there is no longer any argument against Sadducean heresy but rather an attack upon the actual conduct of godless Sadducean potentates.

4) When this Sadducee administration gained power and mocked the feelings of the people and its popular leaders by adding insult to injury, by introducing the heretical practices of the Sadducees into the Temple service,[8] the "covenant" emerged. Members of the covenant pledged themselves to stay away from the Temple as long as the Sadducees were in charge. The program of this covenant — perhaps somewhat revised — is presented in the fourth pericope[9] (6,11–6,19); it stems from about the same period as the first pericope.

5) Besides these Pharisaic passages, which were composed in Palestine, probably in Jerusalem,[10] our document also contains a few fragments of the literary activities of members of "the new covenant in the land of Damascus." To these fragments we assign first of all the program (6,20–7,6) which, as we have demonstrated above, pp. 269–270, the Palestinian emigrants composed during the reign of Queen Salome Alexandra for the purpose of promulgating a set of rules for the Damascus colony.

6) Though this second program has no trace of any hostility in the relationship between the Damascene and Palestinian groups, the pericope 3,21–4,12 does contain a formal declaration of war by the members of the covenant at Damascus against Palestinian Judaism. It seems that at an earlier stage the intransigents at Damascus nurtured the hope that there would soon be a reconciliation with their former brethren in covenant. When they saw no prospect that their hope would be fulfilled, a formal schism was precipitated between the

---

name, יני = (יהונתן) יהוחנן [Ed. — cf. Dérenbourg, *Essai sur l'histoire et la géographie de la Palestine*, part I, p. 80, note 1, and p. 95, note 1], the confusion was bound to happen.

[7] The open rupture between John Hyrcanus and the Pharisees was of course the climax of a long development. Sadduceeism was extending its power long before this sect became the King's open favorite.

[8] *Cf.* above, chapter VII, p. 262.

[9] *Cf.* above, pp. 261–262.

[10] *Cf.* 20.23: "the house of Peleg (division, secession) who abandoned the holy city."

representatives of the opportunistic Pharisaism in Palestine and the irreconcilable Pharisaism in the land of Damascus.[11]

7) Among the refugees from the sword of Alexander Jannaeus there were, without any doubt, more men than women. When the schism occurred, the Damascene colony inevitably saw monogamy as the means required for its self-preservation. Intermarriage with the surrounding pagan population was prohibited by their tradition. The Jews of Palestine could hardly feel impelled to marry off their daughters to men whom they considered secessionists and who had "excommunicated" the main body of Jewry. Had polygamy not been ruled out, the Damascene colony would probably not have survived for more than one or two generations. For zealous representatives of the Torah such as these sectarians, there can be no law that is not directly rooted in Scripture. It is therefore quite natural that no other law receives so much attention and zealous apologetic defence in our document as the prohibition of polygamy, which was so vitally necessary for the survival of the sect. The Sermon on the Three Snares of Belial (4,14–5,7) is mainly devised to prove that the Torah bans polygamy.[12] This pericope must therefore be dated after the complete schism and secession of the Damascene colony from Palestinian Jewry.

8–9) The gulf between the colony and Palestine probably widened with the flourishing of the Exegete of the Torah, דורש התורה, who came from Palestine[13] to the land of Damascus in order to combat the Pharisees with their own weapons. Our document pays homage to him in two different passages (5,17–6,11 and 7,14–7,21).

The advent of the Exegete of the Torah, a person of decisive influence upon the development of the sect, coincided most probably with the flourishing in Palestine of Hillel[14] who so firmly established the

---

[11] *Cf.* the extended discussion of this point above, chapter VII, pp. 262 ff.

[12] Of the three cardinal sins — fornication, pollution of the Sanctuary, and misappropriation — our document charges the opponents in this pericope with only the first two. Pharisaic jurisdiction — during Alexandra Salome's reign there could hardly have been any Sadducee judges — is therefore recognized as "according to the Torah." Also the accusation of polluting the Temple is not hurled against the Pharisees, but directed, as demonstrated above, p. 158, n. 20, at the Sadducees. All this points towards the enjoining of monogamy as the first point of legal conflict between the Damascenes and the Judeans of the sect, a modification required, as we have seen, by the precarious social condition of the colony at Damascus.

[13] It is evident from the qualifying designation for the Exegete of the Torah (7,19) "who came to Damascus" that he hailed from elsewhere. We are probably justified in assuming that he came from Palestine, the seat of Jewish culture.

[14] It seems more probable that he was a young contemporary of Hillel the Elder than our conjecture, above, pp. 270–271, that he was already active in the days of Hillel's teachers.

authority of the Midrash. This dating is likely because there is both argument against a ruling of Hillel[15] (11,17) and elsewhere (13,6) acceptance of a ruling of this prominent Pharisee.[16]

10) The polemic against blasphemers who mock frivolously "the ordinances of God's covenant," and whom the sectarians are bidden to shun completely (5,11–17), may well have originated after the advent of the Exegete of the Torah; "the ordinances of God's covenant" is probably a reference to the doctrines of the דורש התורה, which the members of the covenant accepted as binding upon themselves.

11–12) The latest component of our document — at least in its Haggadic part — is perhaps the pericope on the punishment of apostatizing members of the covenant (20,1–13). This passage may be assigned to a period in which the Damascene covenant had dissolved into congregations. The eschatological discourse (20,13–34) may perhaps have to be dated even later, for it contains the sentence 8,38–39 = 20,15–16; alluding to Hos. 3:4: "And in that epoch the wrath of God will be kindled against Israel, as He has said: then there will be no king or prince, neither judge nor anyone to reprove in righteousness." This passage was undoubtedly composed after the year 70 C. E., for up to that time there had been Jewish kings and princes; the pious did indeed not approve of these Jewish rulers, but they certainly would not have ignored them to the extent of denying their existence.

13) The discourse on the Visitation upon the Land (Palestine) by the chief of the Greek kings (7,9–8,19 = 19,5–33) has been dated by some scholars as reflecting the catastrophe of the year 70. I have to take exception to this interpretation, for a description of these events could not possibly have omitted the most important event, the destruction of the Temple. It is much more plausible that "the chief of the Greek kings" is none other than Pompey;[17] for it is correctly emphasized that the princes of Judah who "hope for healing (8,3 = 19,15)," will be disappointed in their expectations. The advent of Pompey in Palestine brought the immediate joyous result of the end of Aretas' siege of Jerusalem.[18] However, the favor of Rome, which Aristobulus had wooed so zealously, became their undoing. The Pharisees saw in

---

[15] *Cf.* above on 11,18.

[16] *Cf.* p. 124.

[17] The reference to the Roman emperor as "the chief of the Greek kings" is basically not incorrect. Although Rome was a republic at this time, the powers and authority vested in Pompey were by no means inferior to those of a king. As first officer of the Roman republic he was actually "the chief of all Greek kings and rulers."

[18] Josephus, *Ant.* XIV, 2, 3 (29–35); *Bell. Jud.* I, 6, 2–3 (128–130).

Pompey's conquest of Judea the meting out of divine judgment on the
Sadducees, as is clearly attested by the Pharisaic author of the Psalms
of Solomon.

The intransigents at Damascus went even further in their assess-
ment of these events: they saw in them God's punishment of the entire
Jewish community in Palestine. Although mainly "the princes of
Judah," i. e., the Sadducees,[19] the adherents of Aristobulus would be
"given to extinction by the hand of Belial (8,2 = 19,14)," but "in that
epoch the wrath of God will be kindled against Israel," which the lax
Pharisees of Judea refused to see. These charges against the duped
and dazzled Judean Pharisees are strikingly demonstrated in the
Psalms of Solomon. As we can infer from our document, the Pharisees
viewed the fall of Aristobulus and the Sadducee aristocracy as provi-
dential intercession, without realizing that Pompey would bring doom
indiscriminately upon Sadducees and Pharisees alike, upon aristocrats
as well as upon the common people. Since this passage refers distinctly
to the compact of the Damascene colony,[20] which, in our view, was
promulgated during the reign of Salome Alexandra, we cannot possibly interpret the Visitation upon the Land by the chief of the Greek
kings as reference to Demetrius' defeat of Alexander Jannaeus in the
year 88.

In our attempt to analyze the non-Halakic parts of our document,
we paid no attention to the numerous interpretations and glosses.[21]
We should like now to draw attention to some of these. The words
בו חבו באי הברית הראשונים ויסגרו לחרב בעזבם את ברית אל ויבחרו (3,10–12)
ברצונם ויתורו אחרי שרירות לבם לעשות איש את רצונו are evidently a later
addition to No. 3, which a member of the Damascene colony appended
to the Pharisaic discourse. In the latter it is stressed that in spite of
Israel's straying, God will favor them, whereas the additional gloss
announces that even "the first members of the covenant became
culpable." The Pharisaic discourse dates, as we have noted above,
from the reign of John Hyrcanus, when the Jewish state flourished,
whereas this gloss was added after the annexation of the state by the

[19] Whatever one may think about the formation of this party, it cannot be
ignored that the vast majority of Jewish aristocracy — or "the princes of Judah,"
as our document calls them — belonged to it. The victory of the Maccabees drove
the aristocrats to seek closer ties with Phariseeism, for pronounced Sadducees had
little to expect from the pious Maccabees. The later rupture between the Hasmonean dynasty with the Pharisees allowed the aristocrats to return to their old
love. Therefore our document charges "the princes of Judah" with defection (19.16),
"for they are all of them rebels inasmuch as they entered the covenant of repentance and did not turn away from the way of the disloyal."

[20] Compare 8,5 and 19,17 with 7,1.

[21] Cf. below, chapter X.

Romans. The members of the second Damascene covenant saw in this
visitation divine punishment for "the first members of the covenant."[22]
We may also draw attention to the change in style which is noticeable
by the repetition and lumping together in this gloss of three expressions
for passions of the senses found in different parts[23] of the Pharisaic discourse: "chose their own desire, and went about after the stubborn-
ness of their hearts, by doing each man his own desire"; the interpolator thus destroyed the stichic structure of the original fluent
discourse.

An obvious addition is to be found in 7,6–9 (parallel passage 19,2–5).
The Damascene compact had been drawn up by the emigrants from
Judea. However, when a new generation grew up in Damascus, an
"amendment" had to be added. This addition stresses that the duties
of the new covenant will be incumbent even upon the new generation.[24]
Comparison between the two versions of pericope 13 bears out that
neither has preserved the original form of this passage. We need not
elaborate to demonstrate that the Midrash on Amos 5:26–27 in version A (7,14–21) is not part of the discourse proper on the visitation on
Judea by Pompey. The absence of this Midrash in version B, as well
as its defective contextual setting in version A, linking up neither
with the preceding nor with the successive lines, marks it clearly as
interpolation. Even if this interpolated Midrash be disregarded, our
text is yet interspersed with later additions. As biblical source of
authority for the punishment to be visited upon the wicked, version A
(7,10) cites Isa. 7:17, whereas version B (19,7) quotes Zech. 13:7.
This discrepancy can best be explained by assuming that the original
text contained merely the words כבוא הדבר אשר כתוב עליהם, without
any direct biblical reference.[25] Different prophetic passages were
inserted later on by different glossarists. Version B was treated to
still another addition: כאשר היה בקץ פקדת הראשון has been inserted
(19,11 אשר — ברית), citing Ezek. 9:4 as premise for these words.

Whereas the documentary analysis of the non-Halakic part of
these discourses may be carried out with relatively high degrees of
certainty, we find ourselves in an awkward position when looking for

---

[22] Cf. on this expression above.

[23] לתור ...= (3.11); ויתורו אחרי שרירות לבם =(3.2); בחר ברצון רוחו =(3.11) ויבחרו ברצונם
(2.20); בעשותם את רצונם =(3.12); לעשות איש את רצונו =(2.16); בלכתם בשרירות לבם

[24] Cf. also 15,5.

[25] Similarly the concluding phrase of pericope 3 had merely: כאשר הקים אל להם
(3,20), "as God had committed to them" — without any reference to a biblical
prooftext. The subsequent words: ביד יחזקאל הנביא לאמר (3,21) citing Ezek. 44:15
are an editorial addition for the sake of smoothing out the transition from pericope
3 to pericope 6 and of establishing a connection.

criteria that will provide us with operational means to trace the provenance of the halakic passages. However, we would be close to the truth in maintaining that the laws pertaining to purity rituals, Sabbath observance and dietary restrictions (10,10–12,18) derive from an ancient Pharisaic code which the Judean emigrants brought with them to Damascus. Of more recent date are the laws concerning the constitution of the community and its judicial affairs (9,1–10,10; 13,1–15,20). Hence we find, on the one hand, a broad agreement between our document and rabbinic sources with regard to religio-ceremonial laws, whereas, on the other hand, our sect and the rabbis differ, although not in essentials, about the regulation of civil and communal affairs.[26] The peculiar social and economic situation of a Jewish colony in a pagan country made it mandatory that laws intended to regulate civil and communal affairs of Palestinian Jewry had to be revised before they could have been effectively applied to the novel conditions, whereas the religio-ceremonial tradition could have been transplanted without any essential adaptation.[27]

We are now in a position to give a satisfactory reply to the question: did our sect possess a sanctuary in their midst? In a few passages, distinct reference is made to sacrifices.[28] Yet a sanctuary is mentioned nowhere in our document. Indeed, in one passage there is an express admonition not to dispatch sacrifices with impure men (11,18). This means, probably, only that they were enjoined not to participate, even indirectly, in the Temple service at Jerusalem. Such an injunction suggests that the sect possessed no temple of its own. In the light of our explanations above, these apparent contradictions can be explained quite simply. The ancient Pharisaic code of Halakah contained a number of rules concerning the sacrificial cult and, in particular, those that were directed against Sadducean practices.[29] When the sect promulgated its Damascene code, these sacrificial laws were also included. However, they no longer had any practical validity and application for our sect; their value was merely academic.[30]

---

[26] *Cf.* elaboration of this point above, chapter IV. Our thesis does not, of course, exclude the possibility that, on the one hand, some later clauses of (Damascene) Halakah were included in the older (Judean) code, and, on the other hand, that some earlier (Judean) Halakah was inserted into the later compendium.

[27] *Cf.* pp. 116 ff.

[28] *Cf.* above on 11,19.

[29] *Cf.* on 16,14.

[30] It is possible, even probable, that the (Judean) Pharisaic code of Halakah contained much more material about sacrifices than remained in our document, which preserved only as much about sacrifices as was relevant to polemics against the latter-day Pharisee; *cf.* above, p. 117

Similarly we may explain the Halakah regarding capital punishment. Our document refers to it (12,4), because it has been taken over from the ancient Pharisaic code, where it was applicable during the period of complete political independence in Palestine. Our sect, however, had settled "in the Land of Damascus," a Roman province,[31] where it could exercise no such authority.

Though our document is amorphous, featuring excerpts from various sources which are arranged without system and relationship, yet one can detect a certain uniformity with regard to diction and grammar. A prominent feature of our document's style is the employment of the imperfect with the WAW consecutivum. This feature is not restricted to only a few passages, but is a peculiarity of the entire document. Comparably we find that the use of certain terms, such as מורה, פרוש, and the like, is not restricted to particular fragments of divers sources, but occurs throughout the document. Hence we shall present here a list of lexigraphic peculiarities of our document, including even some words of biblical diction, which, however, are employed but rarely in the Bible.

1. אבות (8,18; 19,31) — designating the three patriarchs; this usage is prevalent in rabbinic literature, cf. above, pp. 205–208.

2. אובד — lost (biblical); in rabbinic literature אָבַד is used in this meaning, cf. האובד (9,10); האובד מן השדה (10,22); cf. ad loc. cit.

3. אֵד (?) (12,10) — pagan holy day; vernacular Aramaic and Mishnaic, cf. ad loc.

4. אחה (?) (20,7) in the form יֵאָח (R: יֵאוֹת) — to join; the root also is biblical, (Isa. 7:2) though hapax legomenon, but not rare in Mishnah.

5. אחרונים in the meaning ברית אחרונים (20,9), i. e., the Damascene covenant.[32]

6. אחר — יתאחר (11,23) — tarry; neither biblical nor rabbinic, but found in Ecclesiasticus (7:34; 11:11; 35:11); cf. below.

7. אוכר (R: אוכד 10,22) — harvested; cf. ad loc.

---

[31] It is of course possible that "the covenant" executed capital punishment in secret, disregarding the law of the land. This was certainly the case with the Essenes, who decreed capital punishment upon their members for infraction of their sectarian rules; they certainly could execute such sentences only in secret, since neither the Jewish Synhedrion nor the Roman Government would approve of autonomous sectarian jurisdiction. Cf. also Juster, Les Juifs dans l'Empire romain II, 157, and our discussion above, p. 118.

[32] Cf. above, end of ch. VII, p. 273. In a saying of R. Eliezer (Elazar?) (fl. ca. 70–100) ראשונים occurs in the meaning of "contemporaries of the destruction of the First Temple" and אחרונים "contemporary with that of the Second Temple"; cf. Yoma 9b, and Midrash Tehillim 137, ed. Buber, p. 526. TP Yoma I, 1, 38c, however, reads דורות האחרונים; cf. our document 1,12.

8. אומן — נאמנות — loyalty, confirmation; corroborated only in Pirqe R. Eliezer 19 = Midrash Tehillim 92, ed. Buber, p. 406.[33] Our document employs it three times (7,5; 14,2; 19,1).

9. אנוש (3,17) — incurable (biblical Jer. 15:18, Mic. 1:9, Job 34:6); in our document in figurative meaning "grave sin," פשע אנוש.[34]

10. האסף (19,35; 20,14) — to be ingathered, euphemistic for dying.[35]

11. אֶרֶךְ (?) — in the expression ארך אפים: long-suffering;[36] cf. on 2,4.

12. אורים (5,18) — luminescent beings, i. e., angels.[37]

13. מובה (11,8) — Mishnaic מבוי, cul-de-sac, cf. loc. cit. and p. 135, note 112.[38]

14. בדל (5,7) מבדיל — biblical, in the Mishnaic meaning of deciding (מורה) religious issues; cf. Lev. 10:10–11 parallelism להבדיל — ולהורות, and our document 6,17 and 12,19–20 להבדיל — להודיע.[39]

---

[33] Thus already in ed. pr. of PRE, corrupted in Yalquṭ Shimeoni II 843 to read נאמרת (already in ed. pr.) as emendation. Buber, loc. cit., note 59, explains נאמנות incorrectly as the plural of נאמֶנָת for it is linked in the text to the noun עדות, which is in the singular. In the terminology of medieval Jewish philosophers נאמנות has the meaning of "religion" or "trustworthiness," "credibility"; cf. Levias' dictionary, s. v.

[34] Cf. above on 3,17, and p. 207, n. 220; see further my remarks in הצופה IV, 28.

[35] Absolute only in Num. 20:26 and Isa. 57:1; elsewhere with the additional אל עמיו (אבותיו) or אל קברותיך, whereas in talmudic literature it appears only in the absolute form; cf., e. g., Sifre, Numbers 106, p. 105, Sukkah 5a — also Ecclesiasticus VIII,7; XL,28; XLIV,14 and the saying ascribed to Ben Sira (but not in our editions) in Kallah, ed. Coronel 7ᵇ [Kallah R., ed. Romm III (53a) also end of ch. on Isa. 57:1, ed. Cor. 9ᵇ; Higger, p. 229]. Often also in Gaonic literature and synagogal poetry; cf., e. g., our Geonica II, p. 87; JQR XIV, p. 308; אבקת רוכל, section מלחמת המות towards end; and Ibn Gabirol cited by Davidson, JQR n. s. IV, p. 68.

[36] Cf. also above, p. 164, n. 38.

[37] Cf. on loc. cit. and above, p. 171, n. 79. For our equation there of סוריאל = אוריאל+ר(ס)ש see as further reference Avoth R. Nathan, ed. Schechter, p. 51 (version A, note 37) where var. lec. for אוריאל are given as נוראל, סראל and סמאל; the latter is of course an "emendation" for the unintelligible סראל, whereas נוראל is to be found also elsewhere for אוריאל (נורא=אור); cf. Heilprin, ערכי הכנויים, s. v. ארגמן. In the Ethiopic Apocalypse of Barukh (Dillmann, Cat. Cudd. Aeth. Mus. Brit. XIX, Add. 16,223) Surjal = סוריאל is reported to have shown to Barukh Paradise and Hell.

[38] In the latter reference the usual form ומובאיו (Ezek. 43:11) is cited, which certainly has been affected by the preceding ומוצאיו as has been noted by the early grammarians; cf. Jonah ibn Janaḥ, Riqmah XI and p. 140; in the latter reference Judah b. David Ḥayyuj is quoted as author of this explanation, cf. Lewin, Jahrbuch der jüdisch-literarischen Gesellschaft 1909, and תחכמוני I, pp. 25 ff.

[39] According to Sifra (on 10.10, III 1.9, ed. Weiss, 46d) and Keritoth 13b, להורות is a terminus technicus for dealing with decisions on איסור והיתר, whereas להבדיל for those dealing with טומאה וטהרה or הקדש וחולין. This distinction is, however, purely

15. בהל — מבוהל — confused; similarly Giṭṭin 14b; cf. 8,13 and p. 179, note 111.

16. בון (10,6; 13,2; 14,7) מבונן — versed, erudite; always in conjunction with בספר ההגו.

17. בחון (13,3) — proved, experienced; cf. Jer. 6:27 which the Targum renders בחיר.

18. בית מושבת (11,10)[40] — Syr. ܟܘܪܣܝܐ ܕܒܝܬܐ = Lat. *sella familiarica*.[41]

19. בית העם (14,14) — community house or synagogue.[42]

20. בית פלג (20,22) — House of Secession, designation for the founding fathers of the sect.

21. בית השתחות (11,22)[43] = Targum בי סגידו or בי סינדתא.[44]

22. בליעל (4,13; 4,15; 5,18; 8,2; 12,2; 19,14) — name of Satan; does not occur in Talmudic literature, but is frequent in the

---

theoretical, for we find in Talmudic literature only the term הוראה in this meaning; cf. e. g. Horayoth I, 3. For הבדיל in our document, cf. also 9,23 and our remarks above, p. 44, nn. 118, 119.

[40] It applies here to the removal, יטול, of cleansing objects (see Beth Yosef on Tur 1 § 312 and § 355). The passage in point is accordingly to be translated: One is not allowed to pick up in the outhouse a stone (see Tos. Shabbath XIII, 17; Shabbath 81a; Sukkah 36b and Leḳeṭ Yosher, ed. Freimann I, p. 48) or sand (see Deut. 23:14) to cover the excrements (see Tosafoth Sukkah 36b). The Essenian doctrine "to abstain from work on the seventh day more strictly . . . . they do not even venture to remove any utensils or to go out and ease themselves; on other days they dig a hole a foot deep with their trenching tool (the hatchet presented to novices) . . . . then put the excavated soil back in the hole. . . ." (Josephus, *Bell. Jud.* II, 8.9) is not borne out by our passage; for the covering of excrement on weekdays could have been for reasons different from what is mentioned in the Torah. The Talmud mentions nowhere any restriction to apply Deut. 23:14 to the military camp only. The first rabbinical authority thus to limit its application is Maimonides (on contextual evidence in *Sefer Hamizvoth*, directive comm. 193; regardless whether the Ark is present or not in Yad, Hilkhoth Melakhim, VI, 15, on basis of Sifre Deuteronomy 257 (p. 281) and Tosefta Megillah VI, 25). Duran (זהר הרקיע, note 67) objects to Maimonides' restriction. Malbim's argument (ארצות החיים 2, 6 towards end) against Duran rests on a misunderstanding, since all Duran writes is: אם כן אין זה דין מיוחד במחנה המלחמה אלא להזהיר שכל מקום שיש ארון ושכינה או הזכרת שם שמים שיהיה נקי מכל לכלוך.

[41] Since in Deut. 23:14 שבת carries the connotation of sitting down for the purpose of defecation (Sifre, *loc. cit.*, and Berakhoth 25a) i. e. to defecate, there are no warranted grounds to consider בית מושבת (Mishnaic בית הכסא; like sella from sedeo familiarica) a translation from an Aramaic term.

[42] In 14,14 we probably ought to read בית העם. Particular stress is laid there upon the responsibility of the community for the maintenance of the בית העם. The expression is biblical (Jer. 39:8), whereas in Talmudic times the common people used to call the synagogue by this name, a practice condemned by the Rabbis; cf. Shabbath 32a bottom.

[43] Cf. below, pp. 374–375.

[44] However, designating only pagan temples; see our discussion below.

Pseudepigrapha and in the later mystic writings; *cf.* above, pp. 173–176.

23. בלוע (14,9) — practical, competent; *cf. loc. cit.*

24. בוני החיץ (4,19; 8,12; 8,18) — builders of the partition, derived from Ezek. 13.10 to designate the unaccountable teachers of the people; *cf.* on 8,12 (p. 36).

25. בני השחת (6,15; 13,14) — sons of Hell, the opponents of the sect and the pagans (?); *cf.* on 13,14.

26. מבקר (9,18(2); 9,19; 9,22; 13,6; 13,7; 13,13; 13,16; 14,8; 14,11; 15,8; 15,11; 15,14) — inspector; title of the superior officer in the sectarian community.[45]

27. בריאה (4,21; 12,15) — creation; in talmudic literature[46] usually יצירה, yet in biblical vocabulary only בריאה.

28. ברית (16,12) — marital covenant; biblical (Mal. 2:14), but not rabbinic, *cf.* on *loc. cit.*

29. ברית אברהם (12,11) circumcision; frequent in Tannaitic and Amoraic literature.

30. ברית החדשה (6,19; 8,21; 20,12) — a biblical term (Jer. 31:30) referring in our document to the new Damascene compact.

31. ברורים (10,4) — elected; judges selected by the community, the usage is biblical (I Chron. 9.22), talmudic (e. g., Mishnah Sanhedrin III, 1; IV, 4), and it is also frequent in Gaonic literature; *cf.* on 10,4 and p. 118, also p. 124, note 73.[47]

32. גאל — לגאולי — יגואלו (12,16) — polluting, tainting, in the sense of Levite impurity; in biblical vocabulary and also in the Talmud the word means only soiling, staining; *cf.* on 12,16. [Dan. 1:8 contradicts LG on this point.]

---

[45] The titles מבקר (9,18), המבקר למחנה (13,7), המבקר אשר לכל המחנות (14,8–9) refer to one and the same officer; the latter title is to be translated: Inspector of any settlement. On the title מבקר in Philo and the talmudic literature, see above, pp. 123–124; we should like here to add to our remarks above that the oldest text of authorization, סמיכה, which has been preserved (Sanhedrin 5a) contains a clause granting the right יתיר בכורות ידין) יתיר ידין יורה יורה) and התרת בכורות on basis of inspecting the animal is tantamount to בקור מומים.

[46] However בריאה occurs also, though by far less frequently than יצירה; *cf.* Yadayim II, 2; Miqwaoth VI, 7 כל שהוא מברית המים, where בריה is not to be translated as "creature," but "creation," as borne out by Tosefta Yadayim II, 18 שבריתו מן המים, cited in Zevaḥim 22a כל שתחילת בריתו מן המים: it is originally of the same creation (nature) as the water itself. In Gen. Rabba, ed. Theodor, 17,4, p. 155, בריאה is used, in a discussion by R. Yoḥanan b. Zakkai, to modify the ambiguous וייצר (Gen. 2:19); for further references see the dictionaries, *s. v.* ברא. In our document (4,21; 12,15) בריאה is best translated by "nature." See also Niddah III,7; *cf.* on 12,15.

[47] *Cf.* also Midrash Tannaim ed. Hoffmann, p. 95 (Deut. 17:1) and p. 104 (Deut. 17:15) מן הברורים שבאחיך =מקרב אחיך.

33. גבהות עולם (1,15) — Bible and Talmud use it in the figurative meaning as "pride" (Isa. 2:11, 17) גבהות — שח; in Hab. 3:6 שחו גבעות עולם; *cf.*, however, Tanḥuma, כי תשא section 27 on Exod. 33:11 פנים אל פנים: אין אנו יודעין אם השפל הגביה עצמו אם הגבוה השפיל, אמר ריב״ל: כביכול גבהותו של עולם הרכין עצמו, גבהותו של עולם שנאמר: וירד ה' באהל (Num. 11:25 ?), where גבהותו של עולם cannot mean "pride," but is used in the plain sense "height." Midrash and Talmud refer to God by the appellation גבוה (e. g., TP Sanhedrin VII, 25b, *ibid.*, Nazir VI, 54c; Qiddushin 28b, Bava Qamma 13a) but never גבהות.

34. גלגל השמש (10,15) — Sun-globe, mishnaic גלגל (ה)חמה; however, *cf. loc. cit.*

35. התגוללו (3,17; 8,5) — to dirty oneself, not in rabbinical sources, but in Ecclesiasticus, as we have observed on 3,17. Also מגולל (Isa. 9:4) seems to belong to this root rather than to גלל = to roll, wallow (knead), as reflected also by the Aramaic translators (Pesh. מפלפל; Targum איתגעלו) by rendering it: a garment stained (not rolled) with blood. In the Hebrew original of IV Ezra VII, 68 and in that of the Apocalypse of (II) Barukh XXI, 19 the reading was, as in our document, something like ויתגוללו בפשע.

36. גלה (2,14) עיניכם (2,2) אזנכם ואגלה (2,2) — uncover your ears, your eyes; biblical, e. g., I Sam 9:15; *ibid.*, 20:2, 12, 13; 22:8, 17; but not Talmudic.

37. דורש תורה (6,7; 7,18) — Exegete, interpreter of Torah. In Talmudic literature the term דורש is found infrequently, whereas דרשן is found frequently. The rabbinical form דורש is actually an abbreviation for the term דורש תורה, as we can see in the terminology of Philo νόμον ἑρμηνεύς and of Josephus[48] (*Ant.* XVII, 9,3 (214)) ἐξηγητής τῶν νόμων.

38. מדוקדק (16,2–3) — precisely explicated; neither biblical nor Talmudical in this meaning. However, the root and its derivatives in the meaning of "to do something assiduously" are frequent in talmudical literature, e. g., Mishnah Berakhoth II, 3.

39. ספר ההגו (10,6; 13,2; 14,7) — probably to be read ס', ההגות, or better yet: ספר הֶהֶגֶי. On this book see our discussion on 10,6. See also H. Graetz in *Monatsschrift* (*MGWJ*) 35, p. 287.

---

[48] Schürer, *Geschichte*[4] II, p. 375 cites from Josephus only the designation πατρίων ἐξηγηταί νόμων, whereas the form employed by Philo is wanting altogether. Hoffmann, *Die erste Mischna und die Kontroversen der Tannaim*, p. 7, refers to Philo as well as to the phrase by Josephus that is cited above.

40. הוה — (2,10) הוי עולמים and (2,10; 13,8) עולם נהיות — present and past events. הוי=הוה is both biblical and mishnaic; the noun נהיות is found only in Ecclesiasticus XLII, 19 and XLVIII, 25, where it probably refers to future events and not to present ones.

41. זכו (10,3) both the reading and the meaning of this word are uncertain; cf. loc. cit.

42. חוב (3,10) חבו — to be guilty, indebted; (13,9?) חובם, their debt. In mishnaic Hebrew this word is frequent in the more common form חייב (accountable, in duty bound); so also biblical (Dan. 1:10) וחיבתם. The Qal חב is preserved only in the old stratum of Mishnah, such as Bava Qamma I, 2.[49] The Talmud (ibid., 6b) remarks on this form of חב instead of חייב: האי תנא ירושלמי הוא דתני לישנא קלילא. The author, being a Jerusalemite, prefers the Qal.

43. חבל (2,6) מלאכי חבל — destructive angels; frequent in pseudepigrapha and talmudical literature. Instead of חבל, we ought probably to read חבלה; cf. ad loc. cit. [— Cf., however, Lieberman, Sifre Zuṭa, p. 121.].

44. חלל a) (11,15)[50] יחל השבת; b) (12,4) לחלל את השבת, (15,3) וחלל את השם — desecrate, profane. a) biblical (Num. 30:3; Ezek. 39:7),[51] in this form (יחל) and not rabbinic, b) the forms of חלל are common in Bible and Talmud.

45. חבור (12,8) council (company, compact, partnership). Cf. 14,8; rabbinic term: חבורה, as we probably have to read חבור here;[52] (cf. also חבר עיר in our Com. on TP Berakhoth III, p. 424) see our commentary on 12,8.

---

[49] Moreover: חבין לאדם in Eruvin VII, 11, Giṭṭin I, 6; לחוב Berakhoth I, 3, Sanhedrin IV, 5; תחובו Avoth I, 11. All these forms are evidently from old Halakoth. In the Aramaic-Targum, as well as in Syriac, חב, not חייב, is the common form.

[50] An amusing misunderstanding in Charles, p. 828, line 25. He translates: "No man shall suffer himself to be polluted (the Sabbath) for the sake of wealth or gain on the Sabbath." He then comments: "יחל=suffer himself to be polluted, i. e. ritually, by contact with the dead (Lev. 21:4). In Lev. 21:1–4 the exceptions are enumerated in which a man might submit to such defilement. What our text seems to demand is that even in these cases defilement should not be incurred on the Sabbath." What actually is meant by the passage we have explained on 11,15.

[51] As we have noted in our glossary, s. v. מובה, our text bears strong traits of Ezekiel's vocabulary and terminological influence. Here is another example: יחל occurs only with this priestly Prophet, who, however, also employs other derivatives of חלל; cf. also Chajes, Riv., Is. VIII, 211–13, on the dependence of our document on Ezekiel.

[52] We should like to point out that perhaps חבור (Hos. 4:17) is the same nominal form as employed here.

46. לחברם — one would be inclined to identify this word with the Arabic خَبَّر, "to explain, to make clear"; however, according to Nöldeke (*Persische Studien*, II, 24), this is a loan-word in Arabic. If the reading לְסִבְּרָם, which I proposed *ad loc.*, is to be rejected, perhaps the word לחברם is related to the Arabic خَبَّر, "sought after exact details"; this root might underlie אחבירה in Job 16:4.

47. חלק — (16,3) ספר מחלקות העתים the Book of Jubilees[53] (?? In reality the Book of Enoch is not mentioned??)

48. חרב (5,20) ובקץ חורבן הארץ — in the era of the land's destruction, which is not to be confused with the period of exile, for the latter would have been termed, as in rabbinic literature, ובקץ חרבן הבית.

49. טוב (1,19) טוב הצואר The fair (fat) neck, allusive to Hos. 10:11, as we have pointed out *ad loc. cit.*; *cf.* also Ecclesiasticus XXXVII, 11e טוב בשר, happiness.

50. טהרה, the purity of reputation, unquestionable status of the sectarian community, from which suspects of questionable or irreputable deeds were banished — *cf.*, however, on 9,21–23.

51. יחנה (5,18) name of a sorcerer contemporary with Moses. In talmudical sources (Exodus Rabba, 9,4; Menaḥoth 85a) he is called יוחני, in NT (II Timothy 3:8) and in the Pseudepigrapha: Iannes. The mentioning of Moses' opponent by the name of Iannes may be a disguised attack on (King Alexander) Jannaeus, or on King Ioannes[54] (Hyrcanus).

52. יכח — הוכיח — to produce evidence, to (re)-prove. a) reprove (7,2; 9,7–8; 20,17); b) prove (9,3; 9,18) — on the semantic development in biblical and Talmudical literature, see Bacher, *Terminologie*, I, pp. 39–40 (הוכיח Tannaitic), II, p. 49 (הוכיח Amoraic). (9,3) אשר לא בהוכח לפני עדים is a nominal infinitive, as in Job 6:25 (see Ehrlich, *Randglossen*, *ad loc.*).

53. ילד — (11,13) — assist in birth: biblical (Exod. 1:16, 17) and Mishnaic (Shabbath XVIII, 3 ff., Rosh Hashanah II, 5; Avodah Zarah II, 1).

[53] Biblical meaning: division, class (I Chronicles 27; II Chron. 8:14, 31:2, 35:4); Mishnaic מחלוקת, very frequent, *cf.* e. g. Sifra on 2, 10, ed. Weiss 10b, where it occurs four times.

[54] יחנה respectively יוחני or יוחנא are abbreviated forms of יוחנן or יהוחנן. Since the vernacular pronounced the ח in יחנה as hardly audible, the difference between ינאי — יהונתן and יהוחנן=יחני=יחנה was scarcely perceptible. In the Talmud we find ינאי both for Alexander Jannaeus and his father John Hyrcanus; *cf.* above, p. 275, note 6, (and our *Legends of the Jews* VI, p. 144.)

54a. יסד (יסר) (a) (2,7; 4,21; 10,6) — found, foundation. Figurative: fundamental doctrines of covenant (10,6) יסודי הברית; it corresponds to the talmudical יסוד הנביאים, prophetically ordained ritual (in opposition to מנהג נביאים, a ritual practiced by the prophets, see Sukkah 44a). *Ad loc.* 7,5 I conjectured that על פי כל יסורי ברית is to be read, on the basis of B 19,4 (וכמשפט היסודים), as יסודי ברית; this seems to me now more than doubtful, for יסר as verb (4,8) התוסרו and (20,31) והתיסרו (to bind oneself — biblical אסר) and as noun (7,5) יסורי and (7,8; 19,4) יסורים make a better case for יסורי; on this verb in Mishnah, see pp. 32, 101.

54b. יסד (b) (4,21) ויסוד הבריאה זכר ונקבה ברא to be translated as "the primeval creation" or as "law of nature"; *cf.* 27 in this glossary, on בראה.

54c. יעל (אל) (11,17); *cf.* the remarks *ad loc.*

55. יפע (20,3; 20,6; 20,25) בהופע — to become evident; *cf.* above, end of ch. VII.

56. יצר (2.16) יצר אשמה — the corruptive impulse; in rabbinic literature יצר הרע, evil impulse.

57. יחד — (20,1) מורה היחיד(י)ד, (20,32) אנשי היחיד (biblical: Deut. 33:5; I Chron. 12:17) the distinct teacher, or the teacher of the sectarian order; מורה צדק, teacher of truth; *cf.* above, pp. 211–222 on the meaning of מורה in our document. Here we should like to add that the honorific title "Morenu" in German Jewish tradition is not, as is erroneously stated in *Jewish Encyclopedia, s. v.*, derived from "our teacher" (מורה), but from "our master" (מר in Aramaic), as מורן=מרן,[55] frequent form of address to the Gaonim. On the other hand, it is quite possible that διδάσκαλος of NT and inscriptions, a honorific for scholars, was a translation of מורה, διδάσκειν; *cf.* LXX for להורות.

58. כבוד אדם (3,20) — gloria mundi; *cf.* the rabbinic העולם הזה; see below on נצח (חיי), with which it is contrasted, along with כבוד אל (20,26) gloria Dei, designating the order of the world to come.[56]

59. כבס (11,22) אל יבוא טמא כבוס — meaning is uncertain (see Mek. on Exod. 19:10 (p. 212), Yevamoth 46b); *cf. ad loc. cit.*

---

[55] Already recognized by S. D. Luzatto בתולת בת יהודה, p. 111, note 1; elaborated and corroborated by Kaufmann (*Monatsschrift* 39, p. 156=*Ges. Schriften* I, p. 26). For מר=מור *cf.* my *Geonica* II, p. 388 and p. 425; *cf.* also Yalquṭ Hamakhiri on Malachi, ed. Greenup, p. 51, citing Midrash Teh. 30, ed. Buber, p. 236.

[56] *Cf.* Schürer, *Geschichte*⁴ II, p. 377, and Juster, *Les Juifs dans l'Empire romain*, p. 451.

and p. 123. Perhaps we should read here: כביש, using the root

60. כבש in the rabbinical meaning: to press (subdue, violate) in sexual intercourse.[57] The context permits either meaning. There is a very early[58] Halakah (Berakhoth III, 4–5) on the requirement for ritual purification after the sex act; cf. also on 11,4.

61. כון (10,22) אל יאכל איש ביום השבת כי אם המוכן; rabbinic for food prepared before the Sabbath (Shabbath III, 6; XVII, 1; XXIV, 4; Beẓah I, 2; III, 4; Josephus, *Bell. Jud.*, II, 8.9); cf. ad loc. cit.

62. כי (9,15) as particle of contrast; biblical, but not rabbinic; cf. Num. 5:20; the passage should be translated: The same applies to any lost object which was found but its possessor cannot be determined[59] — this object shall belong to the priests; if, however, the finders cannot determine whether the lost object bears any indication of its possessor, then it is incumbent on them (the finders) to keep it (in trust).

63. כנה — (7,17) וכינוי "and the naming," the verb is also biblical (Isa. 44:5; 45:4; Job 32:21–22); the noun, however, כינוי, is only Mishnaic (Megillah IV, 9; Nedarim I, 1–2; Sanhedrin VII, 5).

64. לץ (1,14; 20,11) איש הלצון (אנשי) man (men) of scorn; biblical (Isa. 28:14; Prov. 29:8) designating the sinners, particularly the Sadducees, the opponents of the sect. Another historical document,[60] roughly contemporary with the text before us, calls the leader of the Sadducees during the reign of Alexander Jannaeus: איש לץ.[61]

65. מאד (9,1; 9,11; 12,10) — possession. From Mishnah Berakhoth

[57] Cf. (Esther 7:8) Aruch Comp. IV, p. 186b and p. 192b and the Gaonic responsum cited by D. Qimḥi on Gen. 38:26.

[58] Cf. above, p. 123.

[59] This Halakah would read in Talmudical terminology as follows: אם הוא דבר שאין בו סימן — לכהנים הוא ואם המוצאים אותו אינם יודעים אם יש בו סימן או לא — עליהם לשמרו. For rules about such cases, see Bava Meẓi'a II, 1.

[60] Qiddushin 66a; cf. on this: Friedländer, *JQR* n. s. vol. 4, p. 443 ff., whose discussion, however, has not convinced me to prefer the Talmudic version over Josephus (*Ant.* XIII 10,5–6). The Talmud probably merged here two reports; cf. above, p. 275 n. 6.

[61] The following לב רע is not to be connected with איש and not to be read "man of vicious heart," as Friedländer, loc. cit., has it, but rather: "a scoffer — a vicious heart." On לב רע cf. Avoth II.9, saying of R. Eliezer b. Hyrcanus whereas רע לב (Neh. 2:2; cf. Prov. 15:15; 25:20) means "troubled mood."

IX, 5 (= Sifre Deut. 32 (p. 55) and Midrash Tannaim, ed. Hoffmann, p. 25, bottom) we may deduce that this connotation of nominal מאד was prevalent during the Tannaitic period.

66. מחיר מות (16,8–9) — forfeiture of life; cf. ad loc. cit.

67. מיל (?) (10,16) — mile; cf. ad loc. cit.

68. מימי כזב (1,15; 8,13) — falsehood; verbatim: fickle waters; figurative here (1,15): heretic doctrine (cf. Avoth 1,11); not only rabbinic (cf. ad loc. cit.), but also biblical (Prov. 23:3), לחם כזבים; this cancels Charles' emendation (p. 801) to מאמרי כזב.

69. ממון (14,20) — money; common Aramaic.

70. מסר (3,3) וימסרו transmit, hand over. This root is prevalent in rabbinic literature, but its presence in Bible (Num. 31:5, 16) is doubtful.

71. מעט (10,9; 10,11; 13,1; 20,24). The last occurrence of this word is in the form למועט, "for few." It would be biblically למעט, whereas in rabbinical literature (cf. var. lec. on Tamid IV, 2) it is very frequent in the form here.

72. מצא (9,14–16) and (15,10) אל הנמצא לעשות בם — the candidate, literally, "he who is found ready." [See Bacher, Terminologie I מצא Nif.].

73. מרא (11,12) אל ימרא איש את עבדו — let no man provoke his servant; Aramaic (?) from מרא master; cf. ad loc. cit. and p. 111.

74. משח (2,12; 6,1; 12,23; 14,19; 20,1) משוח or משיח in the phrase משיח אהרן וישראל; cf. our elaboration in ch. VI, pp. 222 ff.; משיחו (2,12), his pious (ordained) men;[62] cf. ad loc. cit.

75. נדה (2,1; 3,17; 12,2) — impurity (figurative); biblical (Lev. 20:21; Lam. 1:17; Ezra 9:11; II Chron. 29:5) but not rabbinic.

76. נהג (19,3) in construct כמנהג התורה — this phrase is probably older than the use of the word מנהג to denote rabbinic ritual practice.[63]

77. נוע (14,15) to beg; the usage is also biblical (Ps. 59:16); cf. ad loc. cit.

78. נטע (1,7) מטעת planting, state of cultivation; biblical מטע (Isa.

---

[62] Besides the Talmudic material cited ad loc. cit., cf. also Pirqe Rabbenu Haqadosh, ed. Grünhut, p. 49, paragraph 62.

[63] On the relationship between מנהג and הלכה, cf. Perls in Lewy Festschrift, p. 66 ff. Possibly, however, both terms had originally identical meaning.

60:21; Ezek. 17:7; *ibid.*, 34:29), figurative for regeneration (prophetic imagery); our form is not infrequent in rabbinic literature (e. g., Pesaḥim 87b; Gen. Rabbah 15 (1); Midrash Tehillim 104, ed. Buber, p. 443); *cf. ad loc. cit.* and pp. 209 f.

79. נסג (7,13; 8,1) נסוגים (5,20; 10,18) גבול (משיגי) מסיגי removers of landmark, i. e., the Pharisees; *cf.* on (1,16) ולסיע גבול אשר גבלו ראשונים בנחלתם and pp. 124–125.

80. נצח in the term (3,20) חיי נצח — immortality, corresponds exactly to the term "who inherit eternal life" in Enoch XL, 9 (*ibid.* XXXVII, 4; LVIII, 3; *cf.* Dan. 12:2, Ecclesiasticus XXXVII, 26, NT ζῶν αἰώνιος), the העולם הבא of rabbinic sources, but older than these; חיי עולם, *cf.* Shabbath 33b; Berakhoth 21a, in place of which TP Berakhoth VII, 1 (11a bottom) has חיי עד.

81. נשא (5,1; 7,20) נשיא — prince, king; also biblical in the meaning "king," but not rabbinic. Some contend, erroneously, that the term was employed in 5,1 derogatorily in order not to call David by the title מלך but "only" נשיא — however, in 7,20 even the Messiah is called by this title!

82. נשא (13,14) אל ישא ואל יתן (*cf. ad loc. cit.*), — to trade; very frequent in rabbinic literature, as well as in various Aramaic dialects (שקלא וטריא=משא ומתן etc.) in the corresponding equivalent for נושא ונותן, but not biblical.

83. נשה (10,18) ישה — to press for repayment of debt; biblical, *cf.* p. 109, note 12.

84. נתר (13,10) יתר כל הרצובות קשריהם — perhaps (figuratively) to be lenient (Isa. 58:6); *cf. ad loc. cit.*

85. סאב (11,3) סואבים or מסואבים (?) — soiled; *cf. ad loc. cit.*

86. סבר (14,8) לסברם (?) — to explain them; *cf. ad loc. cit.* and also p. 89.

87. סמן (11,10) אל ישא איש עליו סמנים — spices; frequent in rabbinical literature and various Aramaic dialects (סמן, סממן), whereas in biblical literature only סם, in plural regularly סמים.

88. ספר (7,17); ספר תורה (5,2; 7,15); ספר ההגו (10,6; 13,2; 14,7) הנביאים — scriptures (books) of the prophets; in rabbinic literature simply נביאים, designating also the canonical books of the prophets.

89. סרך (7,6; 7,8; 10,4; 12,19; 12,22; 13,7; 14,3; 14,12; 19,4) — order; very frequent in our document, but not in rabbinic literature. *Cf.* on 7,6.

90. עבר (10,3) עובר דבר מן המצוה — who has transgressed against a

biblical commandment; in rabbinical literature[64] very frequently עוֹבֵר עַל, whereas the biblical syntax uses עָבַר אֶת or
עָבַר followed by a noun in the objective case to express
this meaning; cf. e. g. Num. 22:18; Deut. 17:2 לַעֲבוֹר בְּרִיתוֹ;
cf. on this term (16,12 and 1,20?) above 28 on בְּרִית. כָּל עוֹבֵר
(14,16?) — every transient, probably an Aramaism; עֲבוּרָא
is Judeo-Aramaic as well as Syriac.

91. עָגֵל (12,12) מֶעָגְלֵי דְבוֹרִים עַד כֹּל נֶפֶשׁ — larvae of bees; cf. ad loc. cit.

92. עֲזַב (5,6) וַיַעַזְבֵם לוֹ אֵל — and God abandoned (forgave) them to
him; biblical (Neh. 5:10), probably under Aramaic influence;
cf. ad cit. loc.

93. עִיד (3,2) וַיְעִידֵהוּ — and he praised him; biblical as noted ad loc. cit.

94. עִיר (2,18) עִירֵי שָׁמַיִם — celestial guardians; twice in Aramaic part
of Daniel (4:10; 14:20) and frequent in the pseudepigrapha;
cf. p. 170.

95. עִיר (12,1-2) עִיר הַמִּקְדָשׁ — city of the Sanctuary, probably term
for the mountain complex on which the Temple stood,[65]
whereas עִיר הַקֹדֶשׁ (20,22), the Holy City, is the term for
Jerusalem;[66] it appears as early as Neh. 11:1.

96. עָלָה (5,5) וַיַעֲלוּ מַעֲשֵׂי דָוִיד — they were pleasing; biblical and
Mishnaic.; cf. ad loc. cit.

97. עַם (1,21; 5,16; 8,8 = 19,20; 8,16 = 19,29) — people, probably in
the rabbinic meaning of עַם הָאָרֶץ, the ignorant, non-observant
populace.

98. עָנָה (6,19) יוֹם תַּעֲנִית — Day of Atonement (biblical הַכִּפֻּרִים יוֹם/צוֹם);
cf. ad loc. cit. and p. 108, n. 9.

99. עָצָה as לְהָעֵץ (3,5) to combat; derivative probably of the Syriac
אֶתְעֲצִי; not from the biblical עוּץ — to counsel.

100. עֶרָה (5,10) עֶרְוָה (5,9) הָעֲרָיוֹת prohibited sex relations; frequent in
Mishnah.

101. עָרַךְ (11,4?) יִתְעָרֵךְ? cf. below יִתְעָרֵב.

102. עָרַם (2,4) עָרְמָה וְדַעַת הֵם יְשָׁרְתוּהוּ — prudence; both biblical and
rabbinic; cf. ad loc. cit.

<hr>

[64] Cf. e. g. Mekhilta Yithro VII (ed. Friedmann 69a, ed. Horovitz-Rabin 228,9);
for the transgression of a prohibition the usual term is עָבַר עֲבֵירָה, e. g. Sanhedrin IX, 4.

[65] Cf. ad loc. cit. and Schürer's discussion, Geschichte[4] I, p. 153, note 37, of the
identity "Zion" and Temple Mountain.

[66] Cf. Kelim I, 8 on the superior sanctity of Jerusalem over other cities of the
Holy Land.

103. עשת (10,20) לעשות עבודת חפצי השדה — to plan, devise;[67] the root עשת is both biblical and Aramaic.

104. עת (10,5) לפי העת; *cf. ad loc. cit.*

105. פנה (9,10) אשר לא לפנים השפטים, that which does not merit (or require) the attention of the inner (court).[68] For similar meaning of לפנים in talmudic terminology, *cf.* Bava Meẓi'a 16a, וזו אינה צריכה לפנים, and Rashi's commentary *ad loc.*[69] (3,4) וייענשו לפני משגותם — they were punished according to their errors; not to be emended to לפי, but to be understood like the Aramaic כלפי — according (אל פני =כלאפי=).

106. פרץ (20,25), break, destroy; biblical and Mishnaic.

107. פרץ (1,18–19) ויצפו לפרצות — they yearned for frivolity; very frequent in this meaning in Talmudical literature (Aruch compl. VI, p. 443b); there are a few instances in Syriac also.

108. פרש (2,9; 2,13; 4,4; 4,8; 6,14; 6,18; 6,20; 16,2) פרוש; a frequent word in our document, its connotation corresponding by and large to the rabbinic usage; *cf.* above, p. 165, notes 46 and 49.

109. פתח (15,11) יתפתח בו — to be introduced to studies; *cf. ad loc. cit.*

110. פתה (13,6) פתי — unsophisticated; Sifra on Lev. 13:2 (ed. Weiss 60b), אעפ"י שוטה; *cf.* above, p. 124, n. 74, the conjecture that here פתי is a translation of הדיוט, ἐδιώτης.

111. פתר (13,8) בפתריה — according to its (correct) interpretations. In the Talmudic idiom (particularly the Jer. Talmud) פתר means the same as פרש (פשר): to interpret, explain (in general); whereas in the Bible פתר is used only for interpreting dreams.

112. צוה (7,2) כמצוה — as commanded; frequent in liturgy; *cf.* on 6,19.

113. צפף (1,18) ויצפו לפרצות — they yearned; not to be derived from

---

[67] Translate accordingly: One is not allowed to walk in the field in order to devise what work the field requires (read השדה for השבת). On rabbinic parallels to this Halakah, *cf. ad loc. cit.* and also Mekhilta R. Shimeon, ed. Hoffmann, p. 108; Midr. Hag. Exod. 20:10, ed. Margulies, p. 416; Yalquṭ Hamakhiri, Isa. 58:13, p. 234; *LeR* 34, 16, ed. Margulies, p. 814, on prooftext חפצך עשות of Isa. 58:13: לא יטייל אדם בשדה בשבת לידע מהיא צריכה.

[68] The words השופטים או מאמרם are a later addition, obviously in order to explain the obscure לפנים, which betrays itself as a gloss by maintaining the form לפנים, which now ought to read לפני.

[69] Rashi also cites a Gaonic explanation. Another Gaonic explanation is in our *Geonica* II, p. 104; *cf.* also *ibid.*, p. 10, line 32. Corroboration for the explanation proposed in the text is found in TP Kilayim IX, 32b, where לפני can only mean the interior of the academy.

root צפה; צפף is common Aramaic: to crowd, huddle, crave; cf. Schulthess, *Homonyme Wurzeln*, p. 60.

114. קדם יתקדם (11,23) — precede, anticipate.

115. קדש (20,8) כל קדושי עליון — the saints (angels) of the Highmost (Dan. 4:10); cf. above, p. 170.

116. הקים (3,21) to pledge, commit, promise solemnly; not to be derived from the biblical root קום — הקים, which means: promise, fulfill, but from the Aramaic (Syriac and Judeo-Aramaic) קיים or אקים — to confirm under oath; mishnaic: קיֵּים — to swear by somebody (Sanhedrin VII, 6) הקים — to put under oath[70] (Qiddushin 66a).

117. קץ (1,5; 2,9; 2,10; 4,5; 4,9; 4,10; 5,20; 6,10; 6,14; 7,21; 12,23; 15,7; 15,10; 16,2; 19,10; 20,15; 20,23) all carry in our document the meaning of "era, period"; also rabbinic; cf. our elaborate discussion of this term, above, pp. 29–30.

118. קרא (2,11; 4,4) קריאי שם — called (appointed) by name; cf. above, pp. 165 and 167.

119. קשר (13,10) קשריהם — cf. in our glossary no. 84, s. v. נתר.

120. ראה (5,7) ושוכבים עם הרואה את דם זובה — but lie with her that sees the blood of her flow; as noted already *ad loc. cit.* the term רואה דם is Mishnaic (e. g., Niddah IV, 6; Zavim II, 3), but רואה דם זובה is, to the best of our knowledge, attested nowhere (only רואה זוב as in Zavim I, 2).

121. ראש (8,11 = 19,23) וראש הפתנים=הוא ראש מלכי יון (Deut. 32:33) — the head (chief) of the kings of Greece, referring probably to Pompey; הראשונה (5,19) — for the first time;[71] cf. above, p. 171, note 78. ראשונים (8,17 = 19,29) — the ancestors = the three patriarchs.[72]

122. רב (2,16) כי רבים (תעו בם || וגבורי חיל נכשלו בם — the mighty ones; cf. also remarks on 13,7 and 14,12, as well as on 15,8; this meaning of רבים is only biblical.

---

[70] The expression הקם להם בציץ has been misunderstood by the early commentators, as Arukh (Aruch compl. VII, p. 117a) and Rashi *ad loc. cit.* It does not say: make them stand up — which situationally and philologically is impossible; rather it means: make them take a loyalty oath on the high-priestly frontplate. The Sadducee adviser of King Alexander Jannaeus insinuated that the Pharisees had contempt for the king לבן של פרושים עליך!; hence, he suggested, cause them to pledge their allegiance to you with a loyalty oath by the most sacred ציץ bearing the divine name. The advice would read in Aramaic: קיים עליהון בציצא. "To make them stand up" would have read העמידם. It would be absurd to imagine that the Pharisees would get up to honor their king only when he would wear the ציץ. Swearing on the ציץ also in Bel legend, Cant. Rabba on VII, 9.

[71] ראשונה in adverbial use is already biblical.

[72] Probably also 1,4 and 6,2; see our glossary *s. v.* אבות.

AN UNKNOWN JEWISH SECT

123. רוח (3,18) רוי פְּלָאֲו — the fulness (lit. satiety) of his wonders; cf. ad loc. cit. [Ed. — However, רזי פלאו is now better established as emendation].

124. רוח appears in our document in some unusual connections. Besides (2,12) רוח קדשו, which one would tend to identify with רוח הקדש in rabbinic theology, our document employs (5,11; 7,4) רוח קדשיהם, רוח קדשיו to designate the moral impulse of man, which would roughly correspond to the rabbinic יצר טוב; this is also the meaning of רוח קדשו in 2,12. The apposition רוח קדשו והוא אמת represents the Hebrew equivalent for πνεῦμα τῆς ἀληθείας of the Pseudepigrapha, as we have elaborated ad loc. cit. A rather unusual expression is (3,3) רצון רוחו, connoting probably sensual passion. Our version of 3,6–7 is: יכרת זכורם במדבר דבר להם בקדש עלו ורשו ור ע ו א ת ר ו ח ם; it is emended on the basis of the hapaxlegomenon in Hos. 12:2 רעה רוח.

125. רום in (6,20) להרים את הקדשים to offer up the holy offerings for the priests,[73] corresponds more to biblical than to rabbinic usage.

126. רעב as in 11,4 יתרעב=אל יתערב to fast; like הרעיב in rabbinic usage; cf. ad loc. cit. See, however, p. 114, according to which we perhaps ought to read יתערך — to perform military service.

127. רעל an obscure word מרעיל in 10,11, 13; perhaps we should read, with Schechter, מטביל,[74] or מגעיל[75] (purification, cf. on 10,11). It is indeed possible to see in מרעיל a denominative of רעלה=veil, hence it would mean: to cover (as with a veil) entirely.[76] Such a denominative of רעלה is known in the Mishnah! Cf. Shabbath VI, 6: רעולות "veiled."

---

[73] The Bible uses the term קדשים for sacrifices exclusively, whereas rabbinical literature uses this term to designate also offerings due to the priests, such as תרומה, חלה and the like; e. g. of Kethuvoth 24b (a Baraitha!) — and in Derekh Erez Zuṭa 1,6 and 3,12 (ed. Hig. 1,14, p. 64 and 2,3, p. 90) קדשים is also used in this connotation.

[74] So Schechter reads here, and translates correctly "Immersion," for we have to treat מטביל of course as noun (as also warranted by the closely following (10,19) משכים).

[75] Cf. above loc. cit.; see, however, Barth's view on נעל in his Wurzelstudien.

[76] Cf. p. 148, note 166. Later on I noticed that the same interpretation has been suggested by Böhl in the Theol. Tijdschrift, XLVI, p. 33. Taking our point of departure from the elementary meaning of the root רעל as "dangle, swing," we may translate the passage אל ירחץ איש במים צואים ומעוטים מדי מרעיל: "Nobody shall take a ritual bath in (soiled) water (and) such as insufficient to dangle therein."

128. רפה (רפא) in (12,5) ואם ירפא ממנה, if he lets up on it; differing merely in spelling of cognate א for ה from the biblical רפה, to be lax.

129. רשה as in (11,20) להרשותו לטמא את המזבח granting him (authority as an agent) to taint the altar; this usage appears often in rabbinical terminology.

130. שכל as משכיל in (12,21) ואלה החקים למשכיל, these are the ordinances for the enlightened; probably a title of the מבקר; cf. ad loc. cit. and also p. 124, note 73.

131. שטם as name of Satan מלאך המשטמה (16,5); cf. pp. 176 ff.

132. שגה as הקודש שוגים (4,6 emendation, cf. ad loc.), those who are passionately devoted to the Sanctuary.[77]

133. שוב. The members of the sect call themselves (4,2; 6,5; 8,16 = 19,29) שָׁבֵי ישראל those of Israel who returned (unto God); derived probably from the biblical (Isa. 59:20) שבי פשע ביעקב, which is reflected almost verbatim in (2,5; 20,17): שבי פשע.

134. שלם (4,8–10) שלום הקץ, at the completion of the period (as verb in (10,10) עד לא ישלימו ימיהם, before they complete their days). The expression קץ שלום occurs in Midrash Haggadol on Exodus in a somewhat different meaning, citing an otherwise unknown Midrash.[78] The verbal ישלימו ימיהם, "to live their days to the end," corresponds to the rabbinical השלים שנתו.[79]

135. שם the name — God (15,3) very frequent in rabbinic literature.

136. שכם (10,19), on the morrow: למשכים; occurs once in rabbinic literature, in a very ancient Mishnah (Bikkurim III, 2) from the days of the Temple.[80]

137. שמע in (6,3) וישמיעם, and he assembled them; biblical and Mishnaic,[81] but rare.

---

[77] This is probably the correct reading for הקודש שוגים; שנה דבר is biblical: to be passionately and exclusively devoted to something; cf. Ehrlich, *Randglossen*, on Prov. 5:19; also the interesting note of Epstein on the usage of this root in the mouth of Eldad ha-Dani (Collected Writings of Abraham Epstein (Hebrew), Mosad Harav Kook, 5710, vol. I, p. 101 (former ed., p. 71); cf. also Ibn Naḥmias on Prov. 5:19). Maimonides uses שנה in this connotation in Hilkoth Teshuvah 10,3.6 (cf. RABD's scholium thereon and Guide for the Perplexed III, 51).

[78] Cf. ed. Mar., p. 39, 24. Probably quoting from Yelamdenu.

[78] According to biblical usage one would expect ימלאו ימיו.

[80] Cf. D. Hoffmann, *Die erste Mischna und die Kontroversen der Tannaim* (Berlin 1882), p. 15 f.

[81] Cf. above, *loc. cit.* and also Sanhedrin 47a.

138. שער in (10,16) גלגל השמש רחוק מן השער, the gate through which the sun passes departing and returning; no rabbinic parallel.

139. שפט in (9,15; 12,15 *et al.*) משפט ordinance, rule for conduct, character; this is similar to the biblical usage (e. g., Judg. 13:12); *cf.* above on 12,14–15.

140. שקל as (19,25) שקול (שוקל), equal; *cf.* above, p. 179, note 112.

141. תבל as (20,34) בני תבל, sons of the world, i. e., sinners.[82]

142. תמם in (20,2–7) עדת אנשי תמים הקדש, "the congregation of men of perfect saintliness," was the designation assumed by the sectarians in the course of their development.[83]

143. תור as (14,11) איש בתרו each in his turn; biblical and rabbinic.

144. תורה for Pentateuch, *cf.* p. 184: בית תורה (20,10, 13) house of study, corresponding to בית מדרש in Ben-Sira (51,23 = מז, נא) and rabbinic literature; this designation in our document is probably a translation of the (אולפנא) בית יולפנא frequent in the TP.[84]

This roster of lexical peculiarities and characteristics[85] in our document can be divided into three classes:

a) new words and idioms which occur neither in biblical nor in Talmudic-Midrashic literature;

b) rabbinisms

c) biblical purisms.

The first class (a) includes:

עשת	103	התגוללו	35	יתאחר[86]	6
פנים	105	דורש התורה	37	אורים	12
פתי	110	ספר ההגו	39	מבונן	16
צפף	113	נהיות	40	בחון	17
יתקדם	114	חבר	45	בית מושבת	18
מרעיל	127	סרך	89	בית פלו	20
שער	138	עגלי	91	בית השתחות	21
(בני) תבל	141	עיר המקדש	95	גאולי	32
				גלגל שמש	34

[82] Conceived probably in contrast to (3,20) חיי נצח; *cf.* the Talmudic terms בן העולם הבא and בר עלמא דאתי, which make it possible to posit the existence of terms like בר עלמא הדא and בן העולם הזה.

[83] This designation for the sectarian congregation goes back probably to the expression (7,4–5) כל המתהלכים באלה בתמים קדש על פי יסודי ברית אל, all that walk in these in perfect saintliness in accordance with all tenets of divine covenant (i. e. of the Damascene compact). The reading תמים קודש, meaning saintliness, is doubtful in the references, for it could just as well be read קדוש, to be understood תמים קדוש, as: saintly integrity.

[84] My note on 20,10 is to be corrected accordingly.

[85] On the exegetical terminology of our document see p. 190, n. 156. To our re-

Out of these twenty-five new words only three derive from roots which cannot be traced in Hebrew (89; 91; 113). Since the latter two certainly have Aramaic roots, it is a likely assumption that the first (89) derives from some Aramaic dialect. This assumption is supported by the occurrence of this root in the Aramaic fragments of the Testament of Levi (*cf.* above on 7,6). No. 21 may also probably be traced to an Aramaic origin (see glossary 21), and even 103 as well.

Rabbinisms (b) include:

הקים	116	כינוי	63	אבות	1
קץ	117	מאד	65	אח	4
רואה דם	120	ממון	69	נאמנות	8
הרשה	129	מסר	70	האסף[87]	10
השלים	134	מטעה	78	ברית אברהם	29
שלום	134	נשא ונתן	82	דקדק	38
השם	135	סמנים	87	חב	42
משכים	136	עריות	100	התוסר	54a
שקול	140	פרצות	107	יסוד	54b
תורה	144	פתח[88]	109	הופיע	55
		פתר	111		

It is worth noting that in this class there are but a few words that cannot be found in Tannaitic[89] literature. Proven Aramaisms of this class are 38; 42; 54a; 69; 70; 87; 116; 129.

Biblical purisms (c): Our document shares with most pseudepig-

---

marks on the peculiar usage of אשר, we should like to refer to Eccles. 7:28, where אשר introduces a quotation or proverb (logion).

[86] In extant printed texts of the Talmud it occurs in Bava Bathra 16b, but not in the manuscripts; *cf.* Rabbinowicz, *Diqduqe Soferim, ad loc. cit.*

[87] But also biblical, *cf.* Isa. 57:1.

[88] Perhaps already biblical in the meaning of "disclose, explain"; *cf.* Leopold Loew, *Gesammelte Schriften*, vol. V, p. 71, who refers to Ps. 119:130; *cf.* also Giṭṭin 88a bottom: שוב אינן פותחין and Luke 24:32: διήνοιγεν ... τὰς γραφάς. This latter reference has been cited by Charles (5,2) to explain his translation of (3,16) פתח לפניהם as "opened before them"; however this is decidedly incorrect, since פתח in this passage connects with the following digging of the water well, as we have demonstrated in our commentary thereon. Also in Derekh Ereẓ Zuṭa II the word בפתחיה ought to be translated "expositions," since "doors," is impossible in this context.

[89] Except for יסוד, הופיע, מטעה, which occur only in Aramaic sayings, and for נאמנות, which can be corroborated only from Pirkei R. Eliezer. However, three of these four words (נאמנות, יסוד, מטעה) have doubtful readings.

rapha[90] the mosaic style of *opus musivum*. This style is characterized, among others, by its preference for purism. This characteristic accounts probably for the employment of biblical words and idioms[91] in our document at a time when, as we may safely assume, this vocabulary was already obsolete and archaic, and hence alien to rabbinic literature. This class includes:

חיי נצח	80	יצר אשמה	56	אובד	2
ויעידהו	93	כבוד אדם	58	מובה	13
יום תענית	98	כבוד אל	58	מבדיל	14
רוח קדשיהם	124	לצון	64	ברית (נישואין)	28
שבי	133	נוע	77	הוכח	52

In some of these expressions we cannot help noticing the strenuous attempt at unusual and rare diction.

The mosaic style (opus musivum) of our document is not the only characteristic which it shares with the Apocrypha and the pseudepigrapha. We have pointed out earlier that two peculiar Hebrew words in our document (35, 40) are also found in the Hebrew Ecclesiasticus (Ben-Sira). A careful comparison of the vocabulary of these two books demonstrates that a rather close contiguity of diction exists between them. The following roster of linguistic parallels does not attempt to be complete; it will be sufficient, however, to demonstrate the correctness of our contention.

Ben Sira		Our Document	
3,22	שהורשית	להרשותו	11,20
3,13	עזוב לו	ויעזבם לו	5,6
4,28	עד המוות	עד מחיר מות	16,9
4,28	היעצה	להיעץ[92]	3,5
5,6	רחמים ואף עמו[93]	ארך אפים ועמו רוב סליחות	2,4
5,15	מעט והרבה	אם ר[ב ואם] ל[מעֹט]	15,13
7,30	אהוב עושך		
35,13	ברוך עושך	divine creator	
43,7	וחפץ ע[וש]ה	מצות עושיהם	2,21
46,13	ורצוי עושהו	לקול עושיהם	3,8
47,8	אוהב עושהו		

[90] Infrequent also in Tannaite and Amoraic literature; *cf.* the compilation of J. Weisse in his biography of Yedaiah Ha-Penini Bederesi in Slucki's edition of בחינת עולם (Warsaw 1863). The oldest prayers in the liturgy were, however, largely in musive style.

[91] Some of these are not based directly on biblical passages, but derive from biblical usage.

[92] =לְהֵיָעֵצה, not to be emended to להתיעץ.

[93] *Cf.* also Ecclesiasticus XVI, 11.

Ben Sira		Our Document	
7,34	אל תתאחר ⎫		
11,11	הוא מתאחר ⎬	יתקדם או יתאחר	11,23
35,11	אל תתאחר ⎪		
38,16	תתחר בגוי עם ⎭		
9,8	בעד אשה השחתו רבים	ולא לתור במחשבות . . . זנות	2,16
12,14	ומתגלל בעונותיו	והם התגוללו בפשע אנוש	3,17
		בהופע מעשיו	20,3
12,15	עד עת עמד⁹⁴ לא יופיע	בהופע כבוד אל	20,25
15,13	רעה ותעבה שנא יי	ואת אשר שנא התעיב⁹⁵	2,13
19,1	ובוזה מעוטים	עד עשרה אנשים למועט	13,1
11,31	ובמחמדיך יתן קשר ⎫		
13,12	על נפש רבים קושר קשר ⎬	יתר כל חרצובות קשריהם⁹⁶	13,10
30,19	ואין נהנה⁹⁷ מהונו	ואם להניא	16,11
34,28	יין נשתה בעתו וראי	ואל ברוי פלאו	3,18
38,12	גם לרופא תן מקום ולא ימוש	וממקום . . . אל ימש⁹⁸	13,2
37,11	ואכזרי על טוב בשר	ויבחרו בטוב הצואר	1,19
40,28	טוב נאסף ממסתולל ⎫		
44,14	גויותם בשלום נאספה ⎬	מיום האסף 19,35; 20,13–14	
41,21	מחשבות מחלקות⁹⁹ ומנה ⎫		
42,3	ועל מחלקות נחלה ויש ⎬	על ספר מחלקות העתים	16,3
42,17	קדושי אל	כל קדושי עליון	20,8
42,19	מחוה חליפות נהיות	לכל הוי עולמים ונהיות	2,9–10
48,25	עד עולם הגיד נהיות	ויספר לפניהם נהיות עולם	13,8
43,6	וגם ירח ירה¹⁰⁰ . . . ממשלת קץ	קץ¹⁰¹	6,10
	ואות עולם		
44,19–20	אברהם . . . שמר מצות עליון	אברהם . . . בשמרו מצות אל¹⁰²	3,2

---

⁹⁴ Instead of עמד read מעד, corresponding to 12,15b ואם נמוט לא יתכלכל.

⁹⁵ Emended for התעה, which makes no sense here; cf. also IV Ezra VI, 4 and Box's note thereon.

⁹⁶ "Their wickedness" must be the meaning here of קשר, for "their bonds" after חרצובות (cf. Isa. 58:6) does not yield satisfactory meaning.

⁹⁷ Cf. also 40,23 where we probably ought to read יהנו instead of ינהגו, as Bacher proposed.

⁹⁸ Emended for ובקום, although we do not exclude the possibility that ובקום may stand as abbridged for ובקום למשפט.

⁹⁹ [Ed. — Division, apportioning, distribution.]

¹⁰⁰ Thus we emend to ירה for ירח which makes no sense. Accordingly we translate: "The Moon prescribes the seasons, the rule of periods in signs to the world." This verse is a poetical paraphrase of Gen. 1:14 and 16; לממשלת קץ corresponds to the biblical לממשלת היום and לממשלת הלילה there (cf. Lev. R. XIX, 5).

¹⁰¹ See our remarks on 6,10 (cf. also Ben-Sira XXXIII, 10).

¹⁰² In our document (20,8) we find קדושי אל=קדושי עליון of Ben Sira XLII, 17, as already noted.

Ben Sira		Our Document	
44,21	בשבועה הקים לו	הקים אל להם . . . לאמר	3,21
46,8	גם הם בשנים נאצלו	על כן ניצל[103] אברהם ביום דעתו	16,6
48,10	הכתוב נכון לעת	אשר היה כתוב עליה	1,13
		ועל הנשיא כתוב	5,1
50,27	בפתור לבו	ויספר לפניהם נהיות עולם	13,8
		בפתריה	
6,8	כפי עת	לפי העת	10,5

The many points of vocabulary contiguity between Ben-Sira and our document, which are not always of the nature of loan-words,[104] suggest the inference that the sectarian scripture was composed at a time not much distant from the writing of Ecclesiasticus. The century which separates between the Ben-Sira era (about 180 B. C. E.) and the inception of our sect (reign of Alexander Jannaeus) was politically eventful, but it was uneventful in literature. It is not amazing to find such contiguity between literary creations which originated at the beginning and the end of this period.

Other works of the Apocrypha and Pseudepigrapha which bear linguistic affinity with our document are the books of Enoch. There is no doubt that we would see much greater contiguity between our sectarian document and these books if we were in the possession of their Hebrew originals, for comparison. However, even a comparison with the extant translations of the books of Enoch demonstrates that they share a number of words and idioms with our document. These include:

Our Document		Enoch (I Ethiopic; II Slavonic)
6,15	הון הרשעה	wealth of your sins I 103, 5[105]
3,20	חיי נצח	the lot of eternal life[106] I 37, 4
19,4	יסודים	who keeps the foundations of his fathers II 52, 9[107]

---

[103] Thus we emend for the נימול of the text, and translate accordingly: "Abraham was elected on the day that he acknowledged God." There is nothing exceptional in the spelling of ניצל instead of נאצל. [But see above, p. 95.]

[104] It is by no means a rhetorical mannerism of the Greek translator to render עושהו of B.S. XLVI, 13 with κυριος. At that time the direct original connotation of the word κυριος was no longer felt, and became by dint of its frequent use (as attested by our document and Ben Sira) a synonym for both אדוני and אל.

[105] Cf. above, p. 155, n. 5.

[106] The Hebrew term in Enoch is not חיי עולם, for this rabbinic term is an abbreviation of חיי העולם הבא (Soṭah 7b).

[107] Cf. above ad loc. cit.

10,16	השמש רחוק מן השער	the sun ... rising, setting ... portals I 72, 3[108]
2,20–21	בעשותם את רצונם וגו'	taking counsel of their own will II 7, 3[109]
20,34	בני תבל	children of the earth I 100, 6

What we have contended earlier[110] concerning the relationship between Ecclesiasticus and our document applies also to the relationship to it and the books of Enoch. This interdependence is evidence not so much of the borrowing but of their common provenance in the same literary period. The dependence of our document on the Book of Jubilees and on the Testaments of the Twelve Patriarchs, which represent Pseudepigrapha closely related to each other, has been irrefutably demonstrated by Solomon Schechter, in the Introduction[111] to his edition. As we have elaborated above,[112] the position of our sect on law differs from those of the two Pseudepigrapha; our document's dependence on them is to be explained by their great nearness in time.[113]

Our investigations of the language of the document have *thus completely confirmed the conclusions reached in the previous chapters: our document presents a work of the first century B. C. E.*

---

[108] The corresponding rabbinic term is חלון.

[109] This has been emphasized above loc. cit.

[110] Cf. above, p. 11.

[111] Cf. particularly the references in his Index.

[112] P. 302.

[113] Hence the usage of archaisms in our document:

למשכים (10,19) which occurs once in an early Mishnah (Bikkurim III, 2; cf. Hos. 6:4).

גלגל השמש instead of גלגל החמה of Talmudic literature, but in conformity with Hillelite usage; cf. on 10,15.

דורש התורה instead of דורש of rabbinic literature, but in conformity with Philo and Josephus; cf. above, p. 286.

מורה. As we have already emphasized, pp. 218–219, it occurs very often in our document, but it is rare in the Talmud-Midrashic literature. The term seems, however, to have been prevalent during the first century C. E., as we may infer from the frequent use of διδάσκαλος in the N.T. מורה הלכה is, however, rather frequent in rabbinic literature; cf. above, loc. cit., and further Pesikta (di RK) 25 (ed. Buber 158b; ed. Mandelbaum 354–5). In a Genizah fragment containing excerpts from Eliahu Zuṭa, I found the reading למורים for the לחכמים in the printed edition (ed. Friedmann, p. 173 bottom).

IX

The Critique of the Literature

Solomon Schechter's publication of our document caused a sensation of the first order when it appeared (*Fragments of a Zadokite Work*, Documents of Jewish Sectaries, vol. I, Cambridge, 1910). In the light of the surprising nature of its contents, no other reaction could have been expected. In the four years which have passed since this sensational stir, considerable literature has appeared in the attempt to solve the highly intricate problems which Schechter put before the world of scholarship. However, in my investigations I could not take this literature into account, since most of it was published after the major part of the present study was already in the hands of the printer. Later reading of the various scholarly observations and discussions has given me no cause to change my views concerning the sect and the text of the sectarian fragments. Yet I deem it useful for the serious student of the problems which occupy us in connection with this document, to discuss some of the relevant bibliography.

1) Adler, *Athenaeum*, Feb. 4, 1911: when the Pharisees came to power under Queen Alexandra (78 B. C. E.), many Sadducees fled to Damascus; our document is the work of this circle of refugees (the present form of the text may, however, be six or seven centuries later than the original records!); it warns the Sadducees to beware of any compromise with the Pharisees. The "root" which God is "planting" after a period of wrath lasting three hundred and ninety years, refers to John Hyrcanus; he and his son Alexander Jannaeus (!) are designated as the divine Messiahs. The "chief of the kings of Iawan (the Greeks)" who "comes to wreak vengeance upon them (the princes of Judah)" is Pompey, who occupied the Holy Land not long after the victory of the Pharisees.

The untenability of this interpretation becomes evident from our conclusions above concerning the Halakah and the theology of the document. These sectarians were not merely remote from the outlook of the Sadducees, as we have amply demonstrated; they were indeed in opposition to the Sadducees. It is noteworthy that Adler was not even aware of the contradiction in which he involved himself. Pompey defeated the head of the Sadducees, Aristobulus, and appointed the

Pharisee Hyrcanus high-priest and ethnarch over Judea. Hence the punitive action of Pompey was directed mainly against the Sadducees. The Pharisees, as we are informed by the Psalms of Solomon, were so pleased by this turn of events that they interpreted the Roman conquest of Jerusalem not as a national calamity but as triumph of true religion. How is it, we ask in perplexity, that a Sadducee could conceive of the terrible plight which befell his party as a favorable turn of fortune?!

2) Bacher, "Zu Schechters neuesten Genizah-Funden," in *Zeitschrift für hebräische Bibliographie*, 1911, pp. 13–25. Bacher accepts Schechter's thesis that our document is of Sadducee origin. He sees the historical cause for the Zadokite secession, of which our document is supposedly an account, in the prevailing of the Pharisees over the Sadducees in the administration of the Temple affairs during the last decades before its destruction. The document proper, however, could not have been written earlier than the end of the first century C. E., for it makes use of the Book of Jubilees and the Testaments of the Twelve Patriarchs.

Bacher's basic premises are partly uncertain and partly incorrect; hence his conclusions must needs be unwarranted. The predominance of the Pharisees in Temple affairs is not to be dated, as Büchler (*Die Priester und der Cultus*) and, in his footsteps, Bacher maintains, from the year 63, but as we conclude from reports in the Talmud and evidence in the NT (*cf.* Epstein, *Monatsschrift* XL, pp. 139 f.), from a much earlier time. Definitely fallacious is Bacher's argument that our document's dependency on the cited Pseudepigrapha constitute as *terminus a quo* the second century C. E. for its written record. It is the consensus of scholars in the field that only the era between John Hyrcanus and Herod can be considered as the time when the Book of Jubilees was composed, and that the Testament of the Twelve Patriarchs is not only in content but also in time of origin very closely[1] related to that pseudepigraphic chronicle.

Although we cannot accept Bacher's historical interpretation of our document, we are glad to observe that we find ourselves in agreement with him on some textual interpretations — such concurrence confirms the validity of our common conclusions.

3) Blau, *Jüdische Ehescheidung* (Budapest, 1911, I, pp. 58–67) discusses[2] in detail the marital laws in our document. He arrives at

---

[1] *Cf.* Schürer, *Geschichte*[4] III, p. 339 ff. and p. 371 ff. Singer's opinion that the Book of Jubilees is Judeo-Christian and anti-Pauline cannot be taken seriously.

[2] In the Hungarian journal *Magyar Zsidó Szemle* (1913) Bacher returns to this topic. Because I know no Hungarian, I cannot comment on this article.

the conclusion that it maintains an absolute prohibition of divorce and of polygamy (4,20 f.). According to our interpretation of the passage in point, the latter prohibition is absolute, whereas the former is not forbidden; as a matter of fact, the term לְמָגְרַשׁ (13,17) evidently mentions divorce. Blau does not try to fix an exact date for the origin of the sect, but he is convinced that it antedates the advent of Jesus.

4) Böhl's "Neugefundene Urkunden einer messianischen Sekte im syrisch-palästinensischen Judentum" (*Theolog. Tijdschrift* XLVI, pp. 1–35; 93) contains a verbatim German translation of our document, following closely Schechter's rendition into English, except for a few instances in which he follows Lévi (*cf.* below).

5) Büchler, *cf.* below, ch. **X.**

6) Chajes; "I frammenti d'un libro sadduceo," in *Rivista Israelitica* VII, pp. 203–213; and: "Ancora dei frammenti d'un libro sadduceo," *ibid.* VIII, pp. 1–7. The sect originated shortly before the Maccabean religious uprising, as a protest against the Hellenist party, which had gained control over Temple and state. The sectarians emigrated to Damascus, where they stayed not only during the religious persecutions under Antiochus Epiphanes, but even after the glorious Maccabean victories. The document dates from the first century B.C.E., and contains, besides the old anti-Hellenist parts, also later anti-Pharisee passages, for the Damascene "emigrants" were pious Sadducees, who first combated the Hellenist party, and after their defeat they fought the Pharisees. The "teacher of truth" and "the root which God implanted" refer to the Hasmoneans Jonathan or Simeon, and one of these priestly brothers also appears as משיח אהרן וישראל.

Our proofs for the anti-Sadducee character of our document in the preceding chapters render a refutation of Chajes' arguments superfluous. We should just like to remark here that the משיח אהרן וישראל refers most definitely to an eschatological and not to a historical personage.

7) Charles, *Fragments of a Zadokite Work*, translated and edited with introduction, notes and indexes, Oxford, 1912.[3] This sect, or party, as Charles prefers to call it, originated about 196 B.C.E. out of the circle of the Sadducees, in the wake of a religious revival which stirred the Jewish people for twenty years. When this Sadducee reform party realized that its struggle with the Hellenists and its combat against the secularist tendency of the Sadducees were to no

[3] Published as separate work, then also included in: *The Apocrypha and Pseudepigrapha of the Old Testament in English*, ed. R. H. Charles, vol. II (Oxford 1913) p. 785–834.

avail, its followers emigrated to Damascus under the leadership of "the Star," about the year 176 B. C. E. Before long, however, they returned to Palestine where they sought to spread their doctrine among the inhabitants of the Holy Land, in opposition to the older Sadducee party as well as to the Pharisees. In opposition to the former, our sect preached the commitment to certain traditional Halakoth; they charged the latter with turgidity of their tradition and fossilization of the Law.

We have analyzed some examples of the method employed by Charles, which led him to entirely untenable results concerning the origin of the sect. However, it may be in order to present here a survey of the anti-Pharisaic attitudes which Charles contends to discover in our document:

a) The attacks on the "builders of the wall" (4,19; 8,12) are directed against the Pharisees who erected a "hedge around the Law." As we have demonstrated above, citing the Letter of Aristeas, the designation "builders of the wall" is not applicable to the Pharisees and furthermore it is not employed in our document as a derogatory term against opponents; rather the opponents are reproached with "daubing the wall with plaster," i. e. with laxity in the observance of the law (cf. on 8,12).

b) Our document prohibits divorce, whereas the Pharisees do permit it. This contention contains a twofold error: the early Pharisaic Halakah permits divorce only in case of adultery;[4] our document forbids polygamy but not divorce. We may assume that polygamy was practiced more frequently among the wealthy and worldly Sadducees than among the poor and ascetic Pharisees; the latter expressed themselves in rather derogatory terms about this old practice — or malpractice! — as we can learn from the talmudic-midrashic literature.

c) The charges of robbing the Temple (6,15) are directed against the leader of the Pharisees Shimeon ben Shettaḥ who, according to a late rabbinic legend,[5] granted absolution of their vows to a great

---

[4] Cf. Blau's very painstaking investigation of this topic in his monograph Die jüdische Ehescheidung, pp. 31–40, in which he proves irrefutably that Matthew held the same view as the early — Shammaite — Halakah. Blau failed to deal with the opposite opinion presented by Halevy in Doroth Harishonim Iᶜ, pp. 723 ff., according to whom the controversy between the schools of Shammai and Hillel did not revolve around a legal but an ethical principle, but this omission is insignificant, since Halevy's opinion is untenable.

[5] Berakhoth 48a and parallels; the whole tenor of presentation betrays the legendary character of the episode reported.

number of Nazirites, thus depriving the Temple of due offerings. If we would date, as does Charles, the first appearance of our sect during the flourishing of the Hellenists, then it would be most natural to connect this charge with the report (II Macc. IV, 32) on Menelaus, the Hellenist leader, who misappropriated and sold golden vessels of the Temple in order to curry favor with the Greeks with the money thus gained. Charles' bias, however, could not forego the opportunity to bring charges against the hated Pharisees and to accuse them of robbing the Temple, notwithstanding the folly of such a claim against men who revealed the utmost scruples in all affairs concerning the Temple.[6] Charles graciously allows the possibility of interpreting the respective passage in our document differently: "to hold aloof . . . from the wealth of the Sanctuary" may represent an attack, in the light of the Sadducean contention that the daily burnt offering should be offered at the personal cost of the High Priest, on the Pharisaic view that its cost should be provided as national sacrifice by the Temple treasury. Irrespective of the absurd assumption that our document would brand the expenditure for sacrifices as "robbing the Temple," this contention of Charles contains a twofold error. The source material which reports the controversy between the Sadducees and the Pharisees concerning the financial arrangements for the daily sacrifices, makes the true nature of their difference abundantly clear: according to the Pharisees the daily offering was a public (צבור) affair in every respect and hence its cost *must* be borne by the public treasury, whereas the Sadducees maintained that it was *permissible* for *an individual* (יחיד) to donate the offering (*cf.* scholia on Megillath Taanith I, 1; Menaḥoth 65a). Charles may have acquired his misleading information that according to the Sadducees it was incumbent on the High Priest to provide the daily sacrifice, by consulting the *Jewish Encyclopedia*, Vol. X, 632, *s. v. Sadducees*; the author of this article must have confused the daily public offering (Num. 28:1–8) with the daily meal-offering (חביתים) of the High Priest (Lev. 6:12–16)! Concerning the "robbing of the Temple" alluded to in our document, one needs only recall the charges mentioned in the talmudic literature as well as in Josephus[7] to recognize that such crimes were perpetuated by the noble priests who administered the Temple treasury and who

---

[6] If somebody inadvertently misappropriates or misuses Temple property he must offer an atoning sacrifice and he furthermore has to pay compensation of its value with an additional fifth of it as fine; *cf.* Meʻilah V, 1.

[7] *Cf.* above on 16,14; see also Josephus, *Ant.* XX, 8,11 on the wall erected by the priests, the costs of which were probably defrayed from the Temple treasury.

probably did not always conduct their offices without deriving some personal gain.[8]

d) Another difference between the Damascene Sect and the Pharisees can be demonstrated, according to Charles, in their respective attitude towards the Prophets: whereas the Pharisees single out the Pentateuch from the other biblical books as the only authoritative source of law, the sectarians do not maintain such a distinction. We have already shown that this opinion is unwarranted.

e) The Damascene Sect, according to Charles, was, like the Sadducees, opposed to the Pharisaic institution of the Eruv, i. e., the combination of several private precincts (within a yard) in order to justify carrying objects from one house to another on the Sabbath (referring to 11,7). This is a double error! There is no trace of an Eruv to be found in the sectarian document. Even if we would assume that Charles' contention were valid and that the sect objected to the institution of the Eruv as insufficient for consolidating the several private domains (to be considered as partnership to justify carrying within this area on the Sabbath) — the sectarians would, in their intransigence, still be closer to the Pharisees than to the Sadducees, who maintained that the institution of the Eruv was altogether unnecessary.

f) Again Charles holds that our sect (12,15), concurring with the Sadducees (Yadayim IV, 7), extends the force of contamination (Levite impurity) from direct to indirect contact, against the Pharisaic practice. We have demonstrated above that this opinion is based on ignorance of the pertinent Halakah.

g) Charles finds in our document an accusation against the Pharisees, charging them with disregard for the restrictive laws against sexual intercourse with a woman in the state of hemorrhea; as a result of this disregard the offenders pollute the Temple by entering it without first purifying themselves (5,7). In his note to the passage in question Charles refers to the "Pharisaic" Psalms of Solomon VIII, 13 where "the Sadducean priests are charged with similarly profaning the altar and Temple ... But the charge here is brought

---

[8] As early as Hasmonean times the priests appropriated the tithe for the Levites to themselves (TP Maaser Sheni, end; TB Soṭah 47b–48a) so that we may conclude that men who dared to deprive poor Levites of their livelihood would not have too many scruples when abusing Temple funds. *Cf.* also Sheqalim I, 4 R. Yoḥanan ben Zakkai's protest against the priests who saw themselves exempt from contributing the annual half-Shekel tax, the main income of the Temple treasury. We may safely assume that these priests had been following a Sadducee doctrine.

against the Pharisees." Any unbiased scholar would draw the conclusion: the almost literal similarity between this sectarian passage
and the Pharisaic reference in the Psalms of Solomon suggests that the
sectarian charge is not brought against the Pharisees but against the
Sadducees. Not so Charles; he manages to have the sect level the
charge of disregarding a biblical injunction (Lev. 15:19) about purity
against the Pharisees, whose very name probably derives from their
strict observance and abstinence in matters of purity!

The shortcomings in the introduction to Charles' *Fragments of a
Zadokite Work* are even more evident in his translation and attending
notes. We dare say that wherever he deviates from Schechter's translation, he misunderstands the text. We shall cite a few examples in
order to corroborate this harsh judgment.

1,14–15 Charles renders:

> When there arose the scornful man,
> Who talked to Israel lying words
> And made them go astray . . . . . .

In his note: "The text reads מימי בזכ 'waters of lying,' which I have
emended into מאמרי כזב and so translated." He failed to know that
not only the rabbinic idiom possesses many such terms (evil, lying,
troubling water) for heretic doctrines (*cf.* our remarks to 1,15), but
even the biblical idiom employs such imagery, and our passage has
imitated Jer. 15:18: as a liar, as waters that fail אכזב מים לא נאמנו.
Ibid. Charles renders להשח גבהות עולם:

> to bring low the pride of the world,

referring to Isa. 2:11, 17 and remarking: "But these words seem to be
interpolated." This reference, indicated by Schechter, may be misleading. We have pointed out (on 1,15) that it ought to be translated:
"to bring low the height(s) of the world" alluding to Hab. 3:6 (see our
glossary, No. 33).

1,19 Charles renders ויבחרו בטוב הצואר:

> They chose the best of the neck,

remarking that the text is certainly corrupt, and suggests:

> They laid waste the best of the flock

ignoring the distinct allusion to Hos. 10:11, as we have pointed out
on the passage.

1,20 Charles renders ויעבירו ברית:

> and transgressed the covenant, i. e., ויעברו ברית.

This emendation[9] is correct but not original, since it was proposed by Schechter, whom Charles accuses: "Schechter emends the text into ויעברו בברית and translates 'transgressed the covenant.' But this means 'entered into a covenant' (*cf.* Deut. 29:11). This clause is practically equivalent to the text." He misunderstood Schechter's ויעברו ב' to read ויעברו בברית!

2,10 Charles cites Lévi's comment to relate עד מה to the Syriac עדמא, without mentioning that Schechter has already communicated this suggestion on p. LIX in the name of Montgomery.

3,2 Charles conjectures that the lacuna ויע ... הב ought to be restored as ויעלה אהב on basis of I Chron. 27:24 עלה המספר במספר and II Chron. 20:34 הועלה על ספר, in the sense of "to be recorded," for the root עלה, and thus translates: "And he (Abraham) was recorded friend"; as if in these references the root עלה alone, and not the whole phrase, carries the connotation "to be recorded!"

4,20 Charles deletes בשתים as a dittograph from the following שתי, whereas it represents a contextual necessity.

5,11 Charles believes that he has found another parallel for רוח קדשיהם טמאו in "Late Hebrew Testament Naphtali X, 9," he then mentions: "Schechter compares Wertheimer, בתי מדרשות, II, p. 14" (ed. 1950, I, p. 203), as a second (!) reference, without realizing that Schechter referred exactly to the self-same concluding passage of Hebrew Testament Naphtali, in the Wertheimer edition!

6,7 והמחוקק הוא דורש התורה as designation of the sect's founder, Charles claims, represents a characteristic original title in our document; whereas the Talmud (Sanhedrin 5a, ref. to Gen. 49:10) calls the princely successors of David's scion Hillel by this title, for "they (the patriarchs of the Sanhedrin) taught the law of the Torah in public."

7,5 Charles emends נאמנות into נאמנת; we have cited rabbinical references for נאמנות in our Glossary above, No. 8.

8,18 Charles emends בשונאי into בשונאו without mentioning that Schechter anticipated him in this.

9,13 אשר אין בעלים Charles renders: "which has [not] an owner," noting: "The negative is here an intrusion . . . . The אין was inserted by an unintelligent scribe, in the place of a lost לו or לה. Schechter . . . . has failed to observe this intrusion and therefore to see the meaning of the text." The passage undoubtedly needs no emendation, the אין בעלים corresponding in idiom and meaning to the biblical אין גואל (Num. 5:8).

---

[9] The "deletion" of the mater lexionis Yod is not actually necessary, since our document offers more instances in which a Yod was written to indicate a Shewa, as we have observed above, p. 4.

10,11 Charles: "The text reads מרעיל, which I have emended into מרחץ, 'for a bath.' Schechter emends into מטביל and translates 'for the immersion of a man.' But is this rendering possible?" It certainly is, in biblical as well as in Mishnaic usage. It is Charles' emendation which is impossible, since מרחץ can never mean "bath" but only bath-house.

10,20 Charles: "The text reads חפצי; with Lagrange I have changed it into חפצו 'his business.' " This emendation is to be found in Schechter's edition!

11,15 אל יחל איש את השבת Charles renders: "No man shall suffer himself to be polluted (the Sabbath)," remarking on his deletion: "a scribe's slip. Schechter would emend (!) יחל into יחלל . . . but the sense would then be unsatisfactory." He fails to recognize that יחל stands for יחלל (Num. 30:3), in the sense of "desecrating" the Sabbath; it is used as *terminus technicus*, among other passages, in the Mishnah Eruvin IV, 5 as we have pointed out *ad loc. cit.* His reference to Lev. 21:4 and his interpretation here is unadulterated nonsense.

12,12 Charles emends מעגלי דבורים (an Aramaism, see our commentary, *ad loc. cit.*) into מגאלי דבורים — the defilement of bees!

12,19 Charles tacitly reads עִירֵי, cities, for עָרֵי!

13,9 Charles emends כל מדחובם into כל המחיבים "all that have incurred guilt"; but the Hebrew חַיֵּב and Aramaic חַיֵּב can only mean: to pronounce somebody guilty.[10]

14,9 Charles: "Here I have changed the MS reading בעול into בעל בכל סוד" without noticing that this emendation would represent a most unidiomatic Hebrew. His rendition: "a master in every counsel" would correspond to the Hebrew בעל כל סוד. In Lev. 21:4 the noun with preposition בעמיו belongs to the predicate יטמא and not, as some expositors would have it, to the subject בעל.

15,4 Charles "restores" (עֹנֶשׁ) מות (ולא ישא) ("I restore the lost word by עונש, *cf.* Prov. 19:19). This is impossible, since neither in biblical nor in rabbinical law is the transgression (by commission or omission) of an oath punishable by death.[11]

16,7 ואשר אמר מוצא שפתיך תשמור להקים כל שבועת אסר, Charles renders: "As to what he said: 'That which is gone forth from thy lips thou shalt keep' to make it good — No binding oath . . . ." But להקים belongs to the following sentence! להקים . . . אשר יקים איש על נפשו.

---

[10] In talmudic usage those who have incurred guilt can be designated as המחויבים, but this idiom never occurs as an absolute; it is always modified as "incurred guilt" (to be punished by) death or other penalties מחויבים מיתה, מחויבים מלקות etc.

[11] See above on 16,8.

19,19 ויתגברו להון corresponds to Jer. 9:2 גברו לאמונה נפשו but Charles: "I have emended יתנכרו (8,7) into יתגבהו or יגבהו (cf. B יתגברו) on the strength of Jubilees XXIII, 21."

20,4 Schechter reads אנשי מעות and translates: "the men of perversion," which is quite possible, since מעות is a quite acceptable form. Charles, however, exclaims in wonderment: "How he (Schechter) can explain this Hebrew construction in אנשי מעות I cannot see." How could he, indeed, with all due fairness, expect of a Schechter the most elementary rudiments of Hebrew philology and grammar!

8) Hugo Gressmann, "Eine neuentdeckte jüdische Schrift aus der Zeit Christi," in *Internationale Wochenschrift für Wissenschaft, Kunst und Technik* V, pp. 258–266; *idem, ZDMG* LXVI, pp. 491–503.

Our document is an Apocalypse, full of mystifications to an extent which calls into question, for example, whether Damascus, which is mentioned many times as the place of residence of the sect, is not rather to be interpreted as a cryptonym. The "Man of Mockery" certainly stands as a cryptonym, as does the "Man of Lies," which refers to Satan. When, moreover, the opponents of the sect are charged with "polluting the Sanctuary," we may see in this not a reference to the Temple, but rather to the Law, particularly to regulations pertaining to sexual relations. When, further, it is said of the "Man of Mockery" that he makes Israel to go astray in the trackless wilderness and makes the eternal mountains sink low (1,15), this is an allusion to Satan as anti-Christ, who will perform the miracles prophesied by Isaiah for the messianic era. With such inventive flair for allegory, Gressmann merrily expounds our document, until all is dissolved into vague apocalyptic reveries, without the least explanation relating the text to any historic context. We are at least indebted to Gressmann that he has spared us the extension of his allegorizing to the halakic sections of the document, although he would undoubtedly not have encountered any difficulties in doing so had he only willed it. He admits that our document contains Halakic passages; in his elaborate discourses he actually devotes a whole sentence to inform his readers that "precepts pertaining to oaths, testimony, judges, priests, administration, etc., but above all to the Sabbath, have been indiscriminately compiled" in this fragment.

We have already dealt with this approach and have demonstrated the vacuity of such Apocalyptic sophism. Hence we would not deem it necessary to pay attention to it in our review of the literature on the document, had his approach not been so typical for the interpretative method applied by German scholarly circles in their

approach to works dealing with Jewish literature and theology. The
major part of our document presents Halakah. Even the Aggadic
part aims essentially at admonitions not to forget the significance of
Halakah for the religious life. Yet in an investigation which claims
scholarly merit, the significance and content of Halakah is entirely
ignored! Since Halakah represents the major bulk of the material
under discussion, one cannot even apply here the cheap excuse, so often
heard in the circles of Christian scholars, that a general impression of
the subject matter — in Judaistic studies — would be sufficient. Even
if it be conceded that Aggadah — in the broadest sense of the term —
could be correctly understood by scholars who disregard Halakah,
we should yet expect by any scholarly standards that the student of
subject matters like our present document would be sufficiently
equipped with philological and topical knowledge of the aggadic
literature. How little Gressmann could meet such standards will be
demonstrated by the following examples.

Gressmann explains the expression מורה היחיד (20,1; 20,14; *cf.*
also 20,32) as Teacher of the Only-One, i. e., the unique God; the
customary conception according to which it would mean: the unique
(distinct, excellent) teacher is rejected by Gressmann as "ungram-
matical," since it would then have to correspond to the Hebrew
המורה היחיד. We have already demonstrated (above, p. 289; glossary,
No. 57) that מורה היחיד represents the form regularly found in Midrash and admissible in biblical morphology and syntax. We may
add that Gressmann is mistaken also in his assumption that in talmudic literature יחידי means: worshiper of the unique God. Had he
consulted instead of Dallmann's school-dictionary the *Arukh* or the
dictionaries of Levy or Jastrow, he would have readily found that
even in Esther Rabbah on (יחידי) איש יהודי (2,5) it does not bear this
connotation, but rather refers to a Jew (יהודי) who acknowledges the
uniqueness of God (ייחודי)[12] by reciting Deut. 6:4; *cf.* W. Bacher,
Terminologie I, p. 70 [ערכי מדרש, p. 48, note 5].[13]

Dallmann's *Dictionary* is the source of two other errors of Gressmann. פרצה in rabbinical literature does not mean licentiousness; this
meaning is rendered in Hebrew as well as in Aramaic by פריצות and

---

[12] In a parallel version, Midrash Panim Acherim (ed. Buber), p. 82, the reading is
מאי י ה ו ד י, שייחד שמו של הקב"ה; hence the יחידי in Esther R. stands for שייחד שמו.
[13] יַחַד in the meaning "to acknowledge," "declare the divine uniqueness," is,
as Bacher stresses correctly, derived from philosophical literature, and hence an
Arabism; *cf.* also Makhiri on Isa. 43:13 (ed. Schapira, p. 141) quoting Tanḥuma (?)
מעידין עליך... שאתה יחידי, probably a late gloss for המיחדין שמך.

פריצותא respectively. פרצה means: rent, cleft, breach, rupture, even in Gen. Rabba 26,5 (on Gen. 6:2, ed. Theodor-Albeck, p. 247) where Levy and Jastrow, blindly followed by Dalman, translate incorrectly: licentiousness.

Gressmann is also mistaken when he, relying on Dalman, contends that in rabbinic idiom עלה means: to be accounted as, to be counted for, to count as. In the well-known Halakah in Moed Qaṭan III, 5 שבת עולה is an ellipsis for עולה במספר שבעה[14] and this, again, is a biblical (I Chron. 27:24) usage. The root עולה in the meaning: to suffice, to be credited, with regard to sacrifice or other religious acts (e. g., Zevaḥim I, 1) is always constructed with the dative case of persons, probably an ellipsis for עלה ביד.

It is not at all surprising that Gressmann ventures to comment on our document in spite of his insufficient training in the realm of rabbinics, since, it seems, he assumes that there exists a sort of "apocalyptic Hebrew" which can dispense with all rules of Hebrew grammar. Thus he explains the ספר ההגו of our document as "Book of Meditation," and he reads הֶהָגוֹ. Accordingly, Gressmann takes it as linguistic possibility to attach the definite article to the absolute infinitive! We could go on citing amusing samples of Gressmann's conclusions, but those already given have amply demonstrated our point.

9) Juster, *Les Juives dans l'Empire Romain*, Paris, 1914, I, pp. 26 ff. and pp. 492 ff.; II, p. 157. — The sect of our document originated around 4 B. C. E., according to Juster, since the calamities which are mentioned in these fragments refer to the Roman outrages which the Jews of the Holy Land suffered during the "War of Varus" פולמוס של [אם] וירוס (Severus). The disastrous effect of these persecutions are described in the works of Josephus and in rabbinic literature. The "Man of Falsehood" is none other than the well-known Judah, the Galilean, who ventured about this time to lead a rebellion against the Romans. The present document was written about sixty years after these events. All precepts and doctrines presented in the document are to be traced back to the founder of the sect.[15]

---

[14] In mishnaic usage במנין is probably expected rather than במספר. The Talmud knows also the construction עולה מן המנין; *cf.* TP Bava Bathra 6, 15c.

[15] The evidence for this contention is based on the emphasis in 6,10 that at the end of days the precepts of this teacher will have to be followed exclusively. In the Bible it is stressed that the commandments given through Moses must be observed without any additions or curtailment. If we would follow Juster's argument we would either have to ascribe the Talmud to Moses, or to charge the latter-day Jews with disregard for the Torah!

Juster bases his opinion essentially upon a textual emendation: in 1,5 he reads for the duration of the "era of wrath" 590 years instead of 390; thus he manages to arrive at his dating. Without the slightest doubt, however, the span of 390 years relates to Ezek. 4:5 [where the Septuagint reads 190]. Nor is there any plausible reason for changing the number given in our document for the time which transpired between the demise of the sect's founder and the mendacious leader (20,14–15): "and from the day that the Distinct (Teacher) passed away until all men of war who returned with the Man of Falsehood expired: about forty years," for the span of forty years again has reference to this prophetic passage (Ezek. 4:6). Hence there is no peg on which Juster can hang his hypothesis.

Of special interest is Juster's reference to a report in patristic literature about Chobaa near Damascus, where a settlement of Ebionites was situated; these sectarians observed the laws, and may well have been the descendants of our Damascene sect; we are hard put to determine the characteristics of his sect, since there is no sufficient ground for conclusions, in spite of some Sadducee Halakah in our document.

10) Kohler, "Dositheus, the Samaritan Heresiarch, and his Relations to Jewish and Christian Doctrines and Sects," *American Journal of Theology*, XV, pp. 404–435.

In his perspicacious and erudite introduction, Schechter has weighed the possibility whether our document be of Dosithean provenance. He thought that he had found some points of contiguity between our document and the doctrines of Dositheus, but he cautioned against any hasty conclusions, basing his warning partly on the glaring contradictions which we find in the patristic reports on the Dosithean heresies. This careful advice did not benefit Kohler. In this paper on Dositheus he maintains with absolute certainty that our document bears Dosithean character — without ever referring to Schechter's observations on this topic! Moreover, he allegedly finds Samaritan influences throughout this fragment. We take it for granted that no serious scholar will have the slightest doubt about the untenability of this hypothesis, yet we should like to draw attention to Kohler's method of demonstration.

In Kohler's view the Samaritan attitude of the sect is borne out by its expectation of a Zadokite messiah, in opposition to a Davidic messiah (such playing out David's messiah against Aaron's messiah exists only in the imagination of some scholars, as we have expounded in Chapter VI above). Kohler, in making this point, either ignores or

does not know of the well-known fact[16] that in the Samaritan tradition
the messiah will be a scion of Joseph. If, then, our document teaches
the expected advent of a priestly messiah it is as much in opposition
to the Samaritans as well as to the Pharisees.

For Kohler the very beginning of our sectarian fragment points to
Samaritan provenance, since it mentions the "era of wrath," which
commenced with the destruction of the Temple by Nebuchadnezzar.
The Samaritans divide Israel's history into an "era of grace" and an
"era of wrath." Let us, for the moment, disregard that the term
קץ חרון of our document hardly corresponds to the Samaritan term
panuta (reflecting the Hebrew הסתר פנים, *cf.* Deut. 31:18 and Ḥagigah
5a–b). Would anybody seriously assume that in the eyes of the
Samaritans the "era of wrath" would begin with the destruction of
the anathema, the Temple in Jerusalem! Actually the Samaritans make
it quite explicit that the *panuta* commences with Samson's death and
lasted throughout the monarchy of the First Commonwealth.

Kohler concedes that the high esteem in which the Prophets are
held in our document is not consonant with the Samaritan doctrine.
He contends, however, that this should not keep us from assuming
that some Samaritan sects followed the Pharisees in accepting the
sanctity of prophetic scriptures. Kohler seems to have forgotten that
the canonization of the Prophets stands diametrically opposed to
Samaritan doctrine. The Prophetic promises of the future glory of
Jerusalem and the expected salvation of Judea could not possibly have
been recognized as valid by any Samaritan sect. This impossibility
cannot be removed by the attempt to make our sect see in these
references to Jerusalem and Judea a mere allegory; for our document
makes it clear beyond any doubt that the sect believed firmly in the
sanctity of Jerusalem and its Holy Temple. The pollution of the Temple
is the gravest sin with which our document charges the opponents.
Can anybody imagine that a Samaritan sect would thus accuse the
Pharisees?

In another instance Kohler has the temerity to tell us that since,
according to the church fathers and Samaritan writers, Dositheus held
very strict views concerning the observance of the Sabbath rest, the
dietary laws and the rules for purity, our document must be ascribed
to him. Had Kohler bothered to compare in detail the Halakah of
Dositheus with that of our document, he would have seen clearly that

---

[16] I deem it superfluous to demonstrate this and other assertions about the
Samaritan doctrine made in the text, since the material is easily accessible in
Montgomery's *The Samaritans*.

they not only disagree but even contradict each other, as we have incontrovertibly demonstrated above, pp. 138 ff. Kohler, however, is not satisfied with merely discovering alleged contiguity[17] between the Halakah of our sect and that of the Dositheans. He goes even further, to maintain summarily that the Halakah in our document, e. g., the numerous rules concerning the Sabbath, is pointedly directed against the Pharisees. We have demonstrated above the *complete agreement* of this sectarian Halakah with rabbinic Halakah. We would not expect of Kohler a profound appreciation of Halakic issues; yet we deem it inexcusable of him to attempt to transform a situation in which the agreement between our document and the rabbinic source material is so obvious into one of opposition.

"Let nobody send an alien (non-Jew) to carry out his affairs on the Sabbath Day" reads our document (11,2). Kohler notes on this passage: *cf.* the rabbinic opinion, according to which it is not unlawful to make the non-Jew one's agent for something forbidden for a Jew to do on the Sabbath (Maimonides, Hilkhoth Shabbath VI, 1). What, however, does Maimonides really say? "On the basis of biblical law one is not restricted from instructing the non-Jew to perform work on Sabbath, but such is forbidden by enactment of the Soferim (in Maimonides' terminology equivalent to a very early Halakah)." By what justification may we introduce a differentiation between this legislation and the passage in our document which makes no mention or allusion that these rules for conduct on the Sabbath are to be considered of biblical origin? By the way, what kind of scholarly method in the study of Halakah is this, to refer to so late an authority as Maimonides? We have already called attention to the Mekhilta which sees in this injunction, of doing no work on the Sabbath even through a non-Jew, a biblical prohibition.

Here is another interesting case illustrating how Kohler twists data inconvenient to him. It concerns the pronouncing of the divine name in an oath. The Mishnah (Sanhedrin X, 1) states that "he who pronounces the (divine, ineffable) name (Tetragrammaton) literally, forfeits his share in the world-to-come." The Jerusalem Talmud ob-

---

[17] As an example for such contiguity Kohler cites the following: in our document the consumption of honey is forbidden (12,12) and the Dositheans prohibit the consumption of eggs. This is a double error! Our document does not forbid honey, but honey-worms (*cf. loc. cit.*); but assuming the injunction to be against eating honey, as Kohler does by mistake, there would yet be no point of contiguity between the prohibition of honey and of eggs. Honey, if forbidden, would fall under the category of דבר הבא מן הטמא, whereas eggs would come under אבר מן החי. Hence there is no kinship between the two cases.

serves on this Mishnah (28b top): "like those Samaritans do when they swear." Anybody familiar to the least extent with the talmudic style and who would not *per fas et nefas* try to put his own favorite notions into the Talmudic text, will doubtless understand that, according to this talmudic remark, the Samaritans pronounced the Tetragrammaton literally when taking an oath. All commentators interpret in this way. This interpretation, accordingly, is offered by Schechter, who also points out that the prohibition on this point in our document (15,2) proves that it cannot have originated in a Dosithean-Samaritan provenance. Kohler, however, for whom Geiger represents the highest authority in the field of Talmud,[18] understands this Talmudic passage, following Geiger, as if it had stated: "one ought to follow in an oath the Samaritan practice,[19] substituting a surname (השם) for the Tetragrammaton." Even if we would disregard the linguistic difficulties for this interpretation (כגון always introduces an illustration to the preceding sentence), it is entirely implausible that the Amoraic author of this illustration would recommend the alleged Samaritan practice, since such an oath would have no validity in court (Shevuoth 35a, 38b)!

In his strenuous efforts to discover Samaritan Halakah in our document, Kohler exposes an embarrassing lack of critical judgment in the handling of his source material. Our document prohibits polygamy, and this prohibition is also observed by the Samaritans — in recent times, since early records know nothing of such a restriction.[20] Ergo, quoth Kohler, our document bespeaks affinity with the Samaritans. By the same kind of reasoning one may arrive at the conclusion that our fragment hails from a Franco-German provenance, for the

---

[18] However high in esteem one tends to hold Geiger as historian, theologian, and literary historian, he certainly was no great talmudist, let alone halakhist. In my notes on Geiger's Hebrew discourse (קבוצת מאמרים, ed. S. Poznanski, pp. 378 ff.), I have pointed to many glaring errors in Geiger's reading of talmudic texts. His talmudic studies in German demonstrate even more obviously how far he was from mastering this subject.

[19] Kohler refers to *Urschrift*, p. 266, where nothing relevant to the discussion in point is mentioned. Geiger does discuss this talmudic passage in the Hebrew journal אוצר נחמד, vol. 3, p. 118 = קבוצת מאמרים, p. 99; *cf.* my remarks on this discussion there, p. 394.

[20] Kirchheim in כרמי שומרון, p. 20, proposes an emendation in Hadassi 41° (not 96 as he indicates mistakenly), item 96; instead of ואינו נושא אשה he wants to read: ואין נושאין שתי נשים. This is entirely unacceptable because Hadassi himself states only a few lines earlier that the Samaritan High priest practices celibacy: גם ... כהן שלהם ... כמסונר (כצ'ל!) וקדוש יחיד ובדד יושב בלי אשה. Whether or not Hadassi is reporting the truth is a different question. Anyhow, he cannot be cited as corroboration for a Samaritan restriction against polygamy.

Jews in these lands have accepted monogamic restriction for the past millennium! It stands to reason that even in prohibiting polygamy the Samaritans followed the practice of European Jewry.[21] For the latter point we refer to the parallelism of allowing the husband of a childless couple to take another wife, as practiced by the Samaritans and formerly also by European Jews (cf. Shulḥan Arukh, Even ha-Ezer I, 10). Had the Samaritans considered polygamy as licentious, as it is presented in our document, they would not have made an exception even for a childless couple.

The injunction against marrying a niece[22] may have been an old Samaritan practice; there is no documentation for it. Such a restriction in the early church does not prove anything! The passage in our document (5,7–8) opposing the marriage with a brother's or a sister's daughter is certainly a later interpolation and is no part of the original text (cf. above, chap. III). It is, however, incorrect when Kohler contends that such marital union is recommended in the Book of Jubilees (IV, 15 ff.). In this Apocryphal passage we merely find a descriptive report on the pre-Noachide generations, of righteous men marrying the daughters of their father's brother; cf. above, pp. 142 ff. Confusing cousins with nieces is not the worst error committed by Kohler in this treatise.

11) Krauss "Die Ehe zwischen Onkel und Nichte," in *Studies in Jewish Literature*, Berlin, 1913, pp. 165 ff.

The objection in our document (5,8) to the marriage with nieces is traced by Krauss to Roman influence: This thesis seems to us rather improbable.

12) Lagrange, "La secte juive de la nouvelle alliance au pays de Damas," in *Revue Biblique*, IX, pp. 213–240.

This careful and erudite work is divided into two parts. First Lagrange presents us with a painstakingly precise rendition into French of our document, which is based to a large extent on Schechter's English version. In the second part he offers a profound discussion of

---

[21] The gradual decrease in Samaritan population may have been propitious for such a reform.

[22] The מינים, who are branded in הלכות גדולות (ed. Hildesheimer, p. 609) as objectors to marriage with nieces, are, of course, the Karaites and not, as Kohler writes, "certain sectaries." Kohler's alleged authority for this identification is Poznanski, who, however, has identified them correctly (*Kaufmann Gedenkbuch*, p 173). If further proof for the validity of this identification were needed, it suffices to refer to Meshullam ben Kalonymos' polemics against the Karaites (*Hermann Cohen Festschrift, Judaica*, p. 576) where the same arguments as are to be found in הלכות גדולות are advanced. On anti-Karaite passages in the responsa of Rav Yehudai Gaon, the author of הלכות גדולות, see our remarks in *Geonica* I, p. 111, note 2.

pertinent problems arising out of our document. He analyzes critically the various opinions about the inception of the sect. Finally he proposes his own solution of this problem!

Whereas we find ourselves in agreement with everything he argues in criticism of the divers theories on the origin of our sect, we cannot accept the thesis which he proposes. Lagrange contends that during the reign of John Hyrcanus priests and Levites formed an Apocalyptic movement. In his words, this movement was "stricter than the Pharisees and more 'priestly' than the Sadducees." These reactionaries established themselves in the beginning only as a school. When after the fall of the Hasmonean dynasty the Herodians introduced an anti-traditional policy, this school grew into a sectarian movement. The catastrophe of the year 70 C. E. intensified the fanaticism of this sect. This intensity reached its peak during the Bar-Kokhba Revolt: the leader of this uprising (Bar-Koz(i)ba) is referred to in our document (20,15) — as a play on his name — as "Man of Falsehood," איש הכזב. It was against this leader that the sect announced and affirmed its belief in the advent of a priestly Messiah. Our document was recorded during this era of revolt or shortly after it, although the *terminus a quo* for the origin of the sect was more than two centuries earlier. In the previous section we have stated our views on the Halakah and theology of our sect. In view of this we have to reject also the interpretation advanced by Lagrange.

13) Landauer, in *Theologische Literaturzeitung*, 1912, pp. 261–264, reviews Schechter's *Sectaries*.

In the course of this review he offers a number of philological remarks on our document.

14) Lévi, "Un écrit sadducéen antérieur à la destruction du Temple," *REJ*, LXI, pp. 161–205; *REJ*, LXII, pp. 1–19.

Idem, "Document relatif à la 'Communauté des fils de Sadoc,'" *REJ*, LXV, pp. 24–31.

Idem, "Notes sur les observations de M. Leszynsky," *REJ*, LXII, 1–200.

As indicated already in the title of his first paper, Lévi takes our fragment for a Sadducean document. The historical background he describes as follows: when in 162 B. C. E. the family of Zadok lost the office of high-priest to Menelaus,[23] the old hereditary line came to

---

[23] Menelaus was not, as generally assumed on basis of II Macc. III, 4, a Benjaminite, but a Priest from the stock of בני בנימין, which is also mentioned in rabbinic sources as a priestly family. The priestly R. Eliezer ben Zadok, an eyewitness of the destruction of the Temple in 70 C.E., reports that he is a descendant of the family סנואה בן בנימין (Eruvin 41a, Taanith 12a, Tosefta Taaniyoth IV,6 [ed.

an end. Our sect arose to defend the legitimate claim for the holy
office of Zadokite descendants and to restore the priestly leadership
to them. When the members of the Zadokite sect realized that for the
time being they had little prospects for success, they emigrated to
Damascus, just as about the same time Onias IV, the legitimate heir
to the high-priestly office, bade his time in Egypt. The Maccabean
victory, however, signified for this Zadokite sect the triumph of a
new usurper, a scion of the Hasmonean and not of the Zadokite stock.
Hence this dynasty, and their main popular supporters, the Pharisees,
become the target of violent sectarian attacks. Our document emerged
from the Zadokite provenance, representing not only the political
claim of this priestly family, but also reflecting its religio-legal practice,
which is here defined in exclusivist terms. Although this corpus of
theological and Halakic doctrines was committed to writing a few
generations later, our document contains in its present form the old
Zadokite tradition.

In the light of our earlier discussion defining the tenor and character of our document, we cannot accept Lévi's thesis about the sect's
origin. Nonetheless we should like to mention that his paper offers
many instructive and interesting points, as e. g., his refutation of
the Dosithean hypothesis. His translation is elegant and careful.

Zuckermandel, p. 220₄; ed. Lieberman, p. 338₂₉]; scholia on Megillath Taanith,
Av 15 (ed. Lichtenstein, p. 77; TP Sheqalim IV,1, fol. 47d; TP Megillah I,6,
fol. 70c). The Tosafoth to Eruvin, *loc. cit.*, מבני, identify סנאה with the family by
the same name listed in Ezra 2:35 = Neh. 7:38, in consequence of which they see
themselves forced to assume that this Tanna was a matrilinear Benjaminite. Their
assumption is, however, untenable since in Jewish sources nobody traces his genealogy on the distaff side. The entirely incorrect textual version in TP Taaniyoth
IV, 6 (68b) reading יוסי for צדוק originated perhaps in the difficulty observed by
the Tosafoth, though little is gained by this "emendation," for ר' יוסי is listed in
TP Taaniyoth IV, 2, 68a as a Rechabite. It is, however, entirely unwarranted to
consider the ancestor of R. Eliezer (the reading of סנ(ו)אה is dubious; *cf.* Rabbinowitz, Var. Lect. on the Talmudical passages referred to) a Benjaminite on account
of the patronymic בן בנימין, for it may as well have been the name of a priestly
family. The following considerations make it abundantly clear that the cited passage
in II Macc. is not referring to a scion of the tribe of Benjamin: in the good, old
days, during the administration of the pious Onias, the "Benjaminite" Simeon
was chief of the Temple. It would be rather strange to surmise that such high office
of the Temple should be held by a layman. Moreover, the author of this book who
makes every effort to blacken Menelaus, would not have missed the chance to
inform us of such an infamy as the usurpation of the highest priestly office by a
layman. Hence it can hardly be surmised that at any time it would have been
possible for a layman to serve in priestly offices of the Temple, let alone the supreme
office of high-priest!

In his second paper Lévi publishes a small fragment from the Genizah — containing altogether 25 words! — which he identifies as the inquiry of a legal opinion addressed to the "Community of the Sons of Zadok" towards the end of the first millennium C. E. This would accordingly signify that a remnant of our sect survived to this date. There can, however, be no doubt about the identity of this fragment. It is part of a Piyyut, as Schechter has convincingly and correctly demonstrated (*JQR*, NS, IV, p. 449). This Piyyut was most probably composed of the Sabbath of the weekly portion "Emor," which has as lesson from the prophets the section Ezek. 44:15 ff. Hence the mentioning of these verses and the sons of Zadok in this Piyyut.

Nonetheless I should like to present here the text[24] published by Lévi, with my translation, in proof of my conclusion that no connection exists between our document and this Genizah fragment.

The priest ...	... כהן
The time when My learned teachers[25] will instruct us	הֵעת יורונו מְבנָיִי
As the congregation of Zadok's sons (did of yore)	כּעדת בני צדוק
So that the rules of taint and pure	וְעל חוק טמא וטהור
They will decide[26] according to My laws	כמשפטי ישטפוני
As also (discriminate) between sacred[27] and profane	וביֹן קדיש(ו) וחול
They will surround[28] the balustrades	והֹם יסובו דוכניי
Praising in chant, in My tent (temple).	בשיר יהללו אוהלֹי[29]
God grants might to His people (Ps. 29:11)	יי עז לעמו יתן

It is evident that this fragment represents merely a paraphrasing of Ezek. 44:23–24 in the well-known style of the Payyetanim.

In his third discussion of our document, Lévi refutes some of Leszynsky's contentions; *cf.* below.

16) Leszynsky, "Observations sur les Fragments of a Zadokite Work," *REJ*, LXII, pp. 190–196.

---

[24] The fragment, as Lévi emphasizes, is rather damaged. I have indicated by dots above the respective letters how I propose to restore the text.

[25] Not מְבָנִי (from the sons) as Lévi reads, which makes no sense in Hebrew.

[26] As Lévi noted, we ought to read ... ישפט instead of ... ישטפ (see Ezek. 44:24).

[27] The spelling קדיש for קודש is to be found elsewhere in mediaeval manuscripts.

[28] The priests ascend the דוכן for pronouncing the priestly blessing, עולים לדוכן. The Levites arrange themselves in choral and orchestral position for the chanting of Psalms (Arakhin II, 5). Our passage refers, however, neither to priests nor to Levites but to any crowd of Israelites who would surround the Levite choir and ensemble and join in the chanting. Hence the correct expression יסובו is employed.

[29] אוהל for the Temple, biblical as well as rabbinic; *cf.* on our text 7,15.

Idem, "Die Fragmente einer sadduzäischen Schrift," in his book *Die Sadduzäer*, Berlin, 1912, pp. 142–167; 305, 308.

Idem, "Der neue Bund in Damaskus," in *Jahrbuch für jüdische Geschichte und Literatur*, Berlin, 1914, pp. 97–125.

Besides some emendations of textual readings in the fragments, in his first essay Leszynsky advances the peculiar opinion that the "members of the Covenant" [החדשה] באי הברית in our document are really not the members of the sect. Since the subsequent discussions of Leszynsky reveal that he gave up this untenable opinion, we deem it unnecessary to deal with it; Lévi has pointed to the absurdity of this contention in *loc. cit.*, pp. 197 ff.

In the second of his discussions, listed above, Leszynsky devotes himself to a more thorough study of our document. His striving to come to grips with the sectarian Halakah is most laudable. As in many other endeavors, however, good will alone is not enough; hence his conclusion — that the fragments of our document represent remnants of a Sadducee work composed in the last century before the destruction of the Second Temple — is entirely untenable. It would lead us too far afield to deal with all the unwarranted and basically incorrect contentions in this discourse. We shall limit ourselves to the arguments which he marshals against our discussions, in a postscript on pp. 305 ff.

The rabbis not only recommended monogamy for ethical reasons; they even tried to restrict polygamy by law. The first step in this direction is to be recognized in the commandment that the high priest must practice monogamy, as mentioned in two passages of the Talmud (Yevamoth 59a top and Yoma 13a, codified by Maimonides in איסורי ביאה ה' XVII, 13, criticized by RABaD, *ad loc.*, on weak grounds), which certainly derive from an old tradition. Zipser, *Flavius Josephus . . . gegen Apion*, p. 29, believed that he found in Josephus' *Contra Apionem* I,7 the opinion that polygamy was forbidden for priests; as Grünbaum (*Priestergesetze bei Flavius Josephus*, p. 29) has correctly seen, however, the words ἐξ ὁμοεθνοῦς γυναικός do not lend themselves to such interpretation. Earlier in this thesis we have already drawn attention to significant legal restriction of polygamy in the Amoraic period; there we have also irrefutably demonstrated that the Sadducees practiced polygamy. According to Leszynsky, the prohibition of polygamy in our document is of Sadducee origin!

He attempts to refute my interpretation of the passage (11,1–2) dealing with drinking water from a river or lake on the Sabbath. I have, in my comment on this passage, demonstrated that the Book of Jubilees, the Falashas and the Karaites prohibit not only the drawing of water on the Sabbath, but, in general, the use of

water for bathing or any other purpose. Since our passage reads
"and goes down to take a bath, he may drink where he stands . . .,"
our document obviously permits bathing on the Sabbath. Hence I
explained the Halakah in point which forbids the drawing of water
from the river ("but he may not draw water into any vessel") in the
light of Mishnah Eruvin VIII, 7 אין — אמת המים שהיא עוברת בחצר
ממלאין הימנה בשבת, referring to the same action as discussed in our
document. Leszynsky disapproves by noting: "The over-sophisticated
distinctions which he (Ginzberg) has introduced would never have
entered the mind of the Sadducee who lacked Talmudic training; he
would certainly not have distinguished between drawing water on the
Sabbath with a vessel, which would be prohibited because by this mode
the water would be transferred from one 'domain' to another — a
violation which would be equally committed if the water would be
scooped up by hand!" Obviously, Leszynsky did not bother to look up
the passage in the Talmud to which I have referred above; otherwise
he would not have given me the credit for over-sophisticated distinction which is due to the Mishnah and the Talmud. Had he studied the
reference properly, he would not have raised the question why scooping
up water by hand would be permissible, whereas drawing water in a
vessel would be forbidden — the Talmud makes this distinction clear.
It is allowed to incline the head towards the water (river) and drink
the water scooped up in his hands, whereas it is prohibited to drink
the water drawn up in a vessel. The underlying rationale for this
distinction: since water scooped up by hand can be held only for a
few moments, there is no concern lest he transfer the water from the
river to the bank, but such a fear is realistic when water is drawn
from the river by means of a vessel. This very distinction between
hand and vessel is assumed already in the Mishnah Eruvin X, 6, as
the Talmud (Eruvin 99a) plausibly observes. Hence it violates every
principle of sound criticism when Leszynsky misconstrues the words of
our document, when they do agree almost verbatim with the Mishnah,
for the capricious fancy of an unproven theory!

In this context we should remark, however, that river water is not
permitted without Halakic qualifications. Already in the Mishnah
(Eruvin X, 14) and the Talmud thereon (104a bottom) we find
precautions against the eventual use of drinking water for prohibited
purposes as watering planted soil.

Discussing the passage (10,10) of the sectarian Halakah which
disqualifies מים צואים (soiled water) for ritual purification, I have
pointed out (above, p. 51) that although this strict view is not
held by the Talmudic Halakah, yet this view is not entirely unknown
in rabbinic literature. Criticizing my interpretation, Leszynsky again

has not taken the trouble of first looking up the references cited from rabbinical sources. Otherwise his statement that "the slightest resemblance to Pharisaic ordinances is not to be found here" is inexplicable. Since I have merely indicated briefly the pertinent references in my remarks above, *ad loc.*, I shall take this opportunity to reiterate in greater detail.

The Halakah that muddy or slimy water is disqualified for purifying immersion in a ritual bath is the tacit assumption in Mishnah Miqwaoth II, 10 in which the early Tannaim R. Eliezer and R. Yehoshua attempt to determine the exact quality of such water. In the talmudic passage Zevaḥim 22a to which I have already referred above, it is stated explicitly: ואי אין פרה שוחה ושותה ממנו — אפילו למקוה נמי אין משלים (if a cow would not bend down and drink from such water, it would not even qualify to make up the required volume of water for a miqweh); according to this passage such slimy water would not only be disqualified for purifying the hands, but even for complementing the miqweh water. Although this distinction[30] is made in Ḥullin 106a, it applies, according to the Tosafoth, *ad loc. cit.*, not to slimy but to fetid water, a disqualification which cannot be detected by sight. Now there is no reason why we should understand the expression מים צואים in our document other than slimy water which, as we have just seen, is also disqualified by talmudic Halakah. If, however, by מים צואים any kind of soiled water is to be understood, then there exists merely a difference in degree between the rule promulgated by the Tannaim and the stricter rule of the sectarian Halakah.

In my discussion of the passage on legal maturity (10,1–2), I have pointed out that in spite of the later dominant opinion according to which majority is reached at the age of thirteen, there is ample evidence in rabbinic sources of the earlier Halakah which admits legal maturity only at the age of twenty. Leszynsky does not attempt to refute this opinion entirely; he assumes, however, that since the early (Tannaitic) literature cannot yield such evidence, we are dealing here with a Sadducee doctrine, which again became accepted during the Amoraic period.

Even if we disregard Leszynsky's peculiar logic, which would have us accept that there was a revival of Sadducee doctrines long after the extinction of Sadduceeism, the premise of his criticism here is fundamentally incorrect. There is no doubt at all that we are dealing

---

[30] *Cf.* the elaborate discussion of this question in the scholia ראש יוסף on Ḥullin 106a by R. Joseph Teomim, and in משנה אחרונה on Miqwaoth II, 10 by R. Ephraim Yitsḥaq.

here with an old Pharisaic tradition, as appears clearly from the following observations.

A Baraitha (Rosh Hashanah 18a) reports that the members of a certain Jerusalemite family would never survive the age of eighteen; this was taken by R. Yoḥanan ben Zakkai as evidence that they descended from the high-priest Eli whose progeny had been cursed (I Sam. 2:33) never to reach manhood. The assumption here implied is that R. Yoḥanan ben Zakkai would not consider an eighteen-year-old to have already reached manhood.

Regarding the above-mentioned (p. 45) Aggadah which reports that nobody under twenty is subject to heavenly punishment, Leszynsky maintains that it originated with the Amoraim of the third century. It is to be found, however, already in tannaitic sources[31] (Midrash Tannaim, ed. Hoffmann, p. 160). Moreover, traces of this old Halakah are detectable not only in Aggadah but also in Halakic literature, as, e. g., Mishnah Niddah V, 9 to which I have referred earlier. Leszynsky remarks on this reference: "First of all, the school of Shammai[32] speaks of the age of eighteen, not of twenty." Had Leszynsky read the Mishnah properly, he could have spared himself this objection. R. Eliezer (a follower of the school of Shammai) notes that the controversy between the schools of Hillel and Shammai is to be resolved by understanding that women reach legal maturity at eighteen,[33] whereas men only at twenty. No profound acumen is required in order to recognize that the school of Shammai, with its

---

[31] There is no doubt as to the Tannaitic character of this passage in Midrash Tannaim. This is proved by the terminology, e. g. פרק and קונס; in Amoraic terminology קנס connotes a specifically juristic usage, whereas in Tannaitic sources this root is synonomous with ענש.

In Midrash Mishlei ch. I (ed. Buber, p. 42) R. Yishmael is quoted as the authority for the statement שמעשרים שנה ומעלה מחשבין לו עוונותיו. We have to bear in mind, however, that this Midrash quite often ascribes later sayings to earlier authorities.

With regard to Gen. R. 58, beginning, Rashi and Naḥmanides on Gen. 23:1 read with the printed text, בת ק' כבת ז' לגוי בת מאה כבת כ' שנה לחטא which is the only correct reading, and not as the later emended (cf. ed. Theodor-Albeck, p. 618) בת ק' כבת כ' לגוי ובת כ' כבת ז' לחטא. This later emended version is apparently preferred by Leszynsky; only he blundered by quoting בת ק' כבת ז', a version which does not exist anywhere.

[32] Against the accepted rule ב"ש וב"ה — הלכה כב"ה (cf. Tos. Eduyyoth II, 3; Eruvin 6b) it appears that the later Tannaim and Amoraim were inclined to follow in this question the school of Shammai; cf. Niddah 47b and Yevamoth 8a, where R. Judah the Prince, Rav and Samuel talk about the age of eighteen.

[33] The earlier maturity of women is assumed here and elsewhere; cf. Niddah 45a and Gen. R. 18 (ed. Theodor-Albeck, p. 160) נתן בה בינה יותר מן האיש.

stricter approach, would reduce the age level for the legal maturity
of men by two years, whereas the school of Hillel would raise it by
two years even for women. The age of twenty, as the time of the
completion of maturity for men, is assumed by both schools; the same
assumption as to age level is implied in the Talmudical statement
(Qiddushin 29b) that a man is in duty bound to marry before reaching
twenty.[34] Leszynsky has not only overlooked these details, but has,
moreover, thoroughly misunderstood the Mishnah. As a result of his
misunderstanding he charges me with having been misled by the
amoraic discussion in Bava Bathra 155–156. In interpreting the
Mishnah the view of the Amoraim remains for me the surest guide,
and I never fear that I will be misled by them.

Leszynsky has not only failed in the proper understanding of
Mishnah Niddah V, 9, but also in the proper understanding of the
discussion of this passage in the Talmud (Bava Bathra 155b). He
notes: "The Mishnah teaches absolutely nothing about attaining
legal majority at the age of eighteen or twenty, but just the very
opposite: whoever has not developed physical indication of adolescence
at the age of eighteen or twenty respectively is to be considered ab-
normal, and consequently cannot, for example, undertake to perform
the levirate marriage.[35] The Amoraim erroneously tried to use this
Mishnah as evidence to settle a question which arose only in the days
of Rava: if somebody who has not yet reached twenty can legally
dispose of his real estate." As many words, as many errors. First of all,
the Amora Samuel ruled as early as a century before Rava that nobody
under the age of twenty could dispose of real estate. The later Amoraim

---

[34] In the Apocryphal addition (Baraitha) to Avoth V,21 the age of eighteen is
indicated as terminal for marrying, בן י"ח לחופה, which may possibly be traced to
the Shammaite tradition, discussed previously, that complete adulthood is reached
at eighteen. We have to bear in mind, however, that according to the Talmud the
proper age for marriage is prior to complete maturity; cf. Mekhilta Mishpatim III
on Exod. 21:10 (ed. Friedmann, fol. 78b; ed. Hor.-Rab., p. 258) חייב אדם להשיא את
בנו קטן, and Yevamoth 62b bottom והמשיאן סמוך לפרקן, which indicate the age
18–20, in agreement with the early Halakah that the terminal age for legal majority
is twenty. Child-marriage is definitely frowned upon in rabbinic Halakah, as pointed
out in the Tosafoth on Sanhedrin 76b (on text-word סמוך לפרקן). A contrary statement is found in Lam. R. I,2 end (ed. Buber, p. 44), that in earlier times boys
in Jerusalem would be married off at the age of twelve (cf. scholium of R. Samuel
Strashun ad loc.), which is incompatible with statement in Niddah 41a and also
in Qiddushin 30a which indicate sixteen as earliest age for marriage (according to
others even eighteen).

[35] This controversy is probably connected with the above mentioned inclination of later authorities to accept the Shammaite tradition in this point; cf. above.

enter the discussion merely on the point whether eighteen or twenty
is the age of legal majority (Bava Bathra 156a). Moreover, Leszynsky
errs in stating that the Amoraim make use of Mishnah Niddah V, 9
to settle the question of the legal age for disposing of real estate.
The subject of the discussion in Bava Bathra 155b is the question of
the evidence for considering a person סריס: whether the absence of
adolescent physical signs is sufficient, or whether direct indications of
abnormality are required. Since the Mishnah is not clearly committed
on this point, both opinions may be considered as warranted; the
Talmud decides for the latter opinion in order to harmonize this
Mishnah with Mishnah Yevamoth X, 9. Whatever the case may be,
the Mishnah Niddah V, 9 is invoked to establish that nobody can be
declared a סריס before having reached the age of twenty, regardless
of what may be the indications of his abnormality. From this requirement as to age I concluded that even the later Halakah was still aware
of the great significance marked by the age of twenty in the stages of
human development: this is the age of attaining complete maturity —
prior to this term no indication of abnormality can be accepted as
proof. Since the Halakah elsewhere (Niddah 45b *et al.*) considers
twelve and thirteen as the respective terms for coming of age, we
may conclude that the Halakah under discussion is influenced by an
earlier view which held that majority is not attained before the age
of twenty. The earliest Amoraim, Rav and Samuel[36] — who are to be
counted, in a certain sense, as the last of Tannaim — consistently
infer from our Mishnah that the סריס reaches majority only at the
age of twenty. This passage in the Talmud, which I did not include
in my references above (pp. 45–46), was unknown to Leszynsky; hence
his mistake in claiming that nobody before Rava detected in our
Mishnah the view that legal majority is attained at twenty.

    Indeed, I doubt if the term of thirteen for coming of age was known
in the Mishnah; thirteen as the age of majority is mentioned for the
first time in the Tosefta.[37] In Mekhilta Mishpatim III on Exod.
21:11 (ed. Friedmann, fol. 79a, bottom; ed. Horovitz-Rabin, p. 260;
Mekhilta de RSbY, ed. Epstein-Melamed, p. 168) R. Eliezer ben
Hyrcanus is cited as being of the opinion that a אמה העבריה is to be

---

[36] *Cf.* Yevamoth 80a and TP Yevamoth X, end, which offer the various versions of controversy between Rav and Samuel.

[37] Schürer, *Geschichte*[4] vol. II, p. 497 errs in stating that documentation for the
legal age of thirteen can be found only in the post-talmudical literature. This terminal age is not only implied in many Talmudic passages (e. g. Yoma 82a) but
explicitly listed in Tosefta Niddah VI,2, which reads: בן י״ג ויום אחד שהביא שתי
שערות — הרי הוא כאיש לכל דבר.

emancipated at the age of twenty, i. e., when coming of age.[38] Unfortunately, our text reads ויצאה ... בגרעון כסף which is an erroneous
solution of the abbreviation ב״כ, which actually stands for (בת כ'),
בת עשרים!

It is furthermore incorrect of Leszynsky to impute that I could
find the term of twenty as qualifying age for judges only in the
Amoraic literature. The Tanna R. Yehudah (ben Ilai) observed
(Exod. Rabbah 1,30) that Moses came of age (Exod. 2:11) when he
reached twenty, and at that time he was humbled by his opponents
(Exod. 2:14): who appointed you judge over us? בן כ' שנה היה משה
באותה שעה; אמרו לו: עדיין אין אתה ראוי להיות שר ושופט עלינו. A misunderstanding of the situation is responsible for the conflation with the
apocryphal Baraitha Avoth V, 21 which resulted in the later modification לפי שבן מ' שנה לבינה. Correctly understood, this Tanna alludes
to the doctrine that a judge qualified to participate in a trial for
capital punishment has to be at least twenty years old. The conflation
in the text citing R. Yehudah was partly caused by the subsequent
statement of R. Neḥemiah בן מ' שנה היה; this in turn is to be understood as follows from Tanhuma (on Exod. 2:6), that Moses' life
was divided into three equal periods of forty years each. The Tanhuma
(loc. cit.) reads pithily מי שמך לאיש ועדיין אין אתה איש, מלמד שהיה פחות
מבן עשרים, which reflects R. Yehudah's opinion.

We have demonstrated that whereas our opinion about the age of
legal majority in the early Halakah is warranted, Leszynsky's contention that our text reflects such a Sadducee Halakah is entirely unfounded. As a matter of fact, we can prove that the Sadducees fixed
the age of majority prior to the age of twenty. Josephus reports
(Ant. XV 3,3) that Aristobulus[39] officiated as high-priest on the
Feast of Tabernacles when he was but seventeen years old. Could
anybody imagine that Herod would have dared to put a minor into
office — let alone the office of a high-priest? Had Herod been so
insolent as to defy the tradition, would such a provocation not have
aroused a storm of indignation among the noble priests, the majority
of whom were Sadducees?[40]

---

[38] Possibly or even probably R. Eliezer refers to אילונית who bears no סמנים,
hence reaches majority only at the age of twenty; cf. Niddah loc. cit. In this
Mishnah, however, R. Eliezer holds that women mature and come of age two years
earlier than men.

[39] This reference in Josephus already has been pointed out by Wiener: Biblisches
Realwörterbuch II, p. 269; Grünbaum's objections (Priestergesetze bei Flavius
Josephus, p. 36) are irrelevant.

[40] When we, therefore, find among the Tannaim here and there (Tos. Ḥagigah
I, 3 (ed. Zuckermandel, p. 232₁₄; ed. Lieberman, p. 376₂₀); Tos. Zevaḥim XI, 6 (ed.

Even if we would, for argument's sake, agree with Leszynsky that the Halakah that one attains his legal majority at the age of twenty is to be considered as Sadducean, we would then find in the sectarian Halakah of 10,1 proof for the non-Sadducean character of our document. In this very passage witnesses in capital cases only are required to have attained the age of twenty, but not those in any other cases, whereas in the Halakah here in question any witness must be at least twenty years old, since we have no grounds for assuming that the Sadducees would admit a minor to testify in any matter. For anyone who is free of the *idée fixe* that the entire literature of the Second Commonwealth is the work of the Sadducees, it is obvious that our document, i. e., this sectarian Halakah, essentially agrees with the accepted rabbinic Halakah: that nobody under twenty can function[41] as judge in capital cases.

The sectarian Halakah concerning the qualifying age for judges *terminus a quo* has its counterpart in 10,7–8 for the *terminus ad quem*: "Nobody of sixty years and over shall function to judge the congregation." As a parallel I have referred (above) to the rabbinic Halakah in Sanhedrin 36b which also disqualifies senescent judges. Leszynsky remarks on my reference: "the *only* passage which is pertinent ... is so singular and unparalleled that I feel that all experts will certainly agree with my view that this reference represents an error in transmission; the Baraitha אין מושיבין בסנהדרין זקן וסריס ומי שאין לו בנים I emend to [מי שאין לו] זָקֵן וסריס ומי שאין לו בנים, i. e., not the senescent but the beardless is disqualified." Even at the risk of being banished from the circle of experts I voice strongest objection against this "emendation." First of all, this is not the *only* passage which disqualifies senescent judges. The Mishnah Horayoth I, 4 and parallel Sifra, Dibbura-de-Hovah 4,3 (on Lev. 4:13, ed. Weiss, p. 19a) also know this Halakah;

Zuckermandel, p. 496₄); TP Sukkah III end, fol. 54a; TB Hullin 24b) the opinion that nobody under twenty is to be admitted to the Temple service, we are not justified in relegating this Halakah to Sadducee provonance, for we are dealing here with Pharisaic rigorism which insists on completely mature men for officiating in any public function of Temple service as well as in the synagogue. The order of service in the synagogue is certainly of Pharisaic origin, yet it requires that the precentor be at least twenty years old; *cf.* the above references and also Midrash Mishlei on I,4 (ed. Buber, p. 42).

[41] *Cf.* above. We should like to draw attention to the stricter view in rabbinic Halakah concerning the qualification of witnesses as compared with the qualification required for judges; this distinction has already been made by Leopold Löw (*Die Lebensalter*, p. 155). Hence we are justified in assuming that the Talmudic disqualification of judges under the age of twenty would *eo ipso* include the respective disqualification of witnesses, in complete agreement with the Halakah of our document.

in these two texts emendation is out of the question.[42] Furthermore it is implausible that a beardless judge is to be disqualified, because this would be redundant in this passage. The lack of beard-growth serves as indication[43] either of a סריס or of impotence. This very passage, however, disqualifies both of these, the סריס or the childless, from serving as judge. Finally, we should like to point out that such an emendation could, from the textual aspect, only read: מי שאין לו זקן סריס, but not סריס מי שאין לו זקן ומי שאין לו בנים וכו', ומי שאין לו בנים וכו', as Leszynsky proposes.

There would be no cogent reason for us to discuss Leszynsky's third discourse, since it merely presents a popularization of the researches into our document which appear in his book on the Sadducees. Yet I cannot help citing a few sentences which throw a peculiar light on this author's Halakic theories and on his critical approach. He maintains that the precepts in our document dealing with the Sabbath are thoroughly non-Pharisaic, even though the latter-day Pharisees did reaccept some Sadducee doctrines and did reintroduce some of their Sabbath practices. We have already demonstrated in all minute details how all precepts in our document dealing with the Sabbath are not only in complete agreement with the Pharisaic Halakah, but how some among these betray a pronounced anti-

---

[42] The readings in the Mishnah vacillate; cf. N. N. Rabbinowicz, *Var. Lect loc. cit.*, and above, p. 119, n. 46. Certainly Maimonides (cf. above) read או after זקן. Even if we read, with the usual text, only זקן שלא ראוי לבנים, it can only mean: a senescent judge who can no longer beget children; it would be incorrect to interpret: a Zaken = member of the Synhedrion who is impotent and cannot beget children, for the Mishnah states explicitly that the judgment of the entire court will be invalidated שהיה אחד מהן גר או ממזר או נתין או זקן (או) שלא ראוי לבנים, concluding עד שיהיו כולם ראויים להוראה. It can, therefore, not possibly include Zaken = Synhedrist (senatus, senator) as qualified and in the same breath exclude a senescent Synhedrist (Zaken = senex). Zaken connotes here an old man (senex), not a honorific (senatus). Moreover, as I have already stressed, this Halakah can only read: שהיה אחד מהן גר או...או שלא היה ראוי לבנים and nothing else. The Baraitha quoted in Sanhedrin 36b is most certainly an explanatory Tosefta on our Mishnah, supplementing the phrase שלא היה ראוי לבנים in the sense that it intends to disqualify both the impotent סריס and the father bereft of all his children. *Cf.* also the scholium of R. Samuel Strashun *ad loc. cit.* for the correct interpretation of this Mishnah.

[43] *Cf.* Tos. Yevamoth X, 6 (ed. Zuckermandel, p. 252₆); Yevamoth 80b. Had the beardless been disqualified for the lack of dignified countenance expected by protocol of a public personage, the Talmud would certainly have employed the phrase מי שלא נתמלא זקנו. Even the conclusion of the Baraitha (Sanhedrin 36b) which reads: וחילופיהן במסית (cf. Tos. Sanhedrin VII, 5 and X, 11, ed. Zuckermandel, p. 426₆ and p. 431₄) indicates that the זקן, or, according to Leszynsky, מי שאין לו זקן, cannot serve as judge because he is susceptible to feeling pity; it would be silly to contend that according to the Talmud the lack of a beard is identical with lack of feeling!

Sadducee spirit (*cf.* pp. 124–126). As far as Leszynsky is concerned, however, their Sadducean character is indubitable! Proof: the sect of the New Covenant adamantly refused to employ a non-Jew to perform any kind of work on the Sabbath, as Pharisee Jews were wont to do *at all times*. We do not pretend to being as omniscient as scholars such as Leszynsky, and therefore we shy away from sweeping statements which report without any doubt on what the Pharisaic Jews were wont to do at all times. This much, however, I do know for certain; that all pertinent Pharisaic literature, from the Mishnah[44] up to the Halakic authorities of our own generation, forbid the work performed by a non-Jew for a Jew on the Sabbath at least as rigorously as this is enjoined in our document. Or have the thousands of Jews, who would not even ask a non-Jew to open a letter for them on the Sabbath,[45] learned this practice from our sectarian document?! Leszynsky relies for the validity of this statement (which he has probably derived from A. Geiger) that the Pharisees adopted some of their opponents' laws on the testimony of the Pharisee Flavius Josephus — we really know little about the extent of his Phariseeism — who reports (*Bel. Jud.*, II, 8,9) that washing after defecation was a custom peculiar with the Essenes, whereas this is a common talmudic precept. This example, however, would prove nothing for this thesis, if he would understand the words of Josephus correctly. The Essenes are to be considered "hyper-Pharisees" in questions of religious observance; hence it is most probable that many a pious custom practiced by the Essenes would tend to become, in the course of time, an accepted common practice among the Pharisees. This testimony of Josephus does not prove anything of what Leszynsky wants to demonstrate: that the Pharisees gave up any of their own opinions and practices in favor of adopting the doctrines and precepts of their archenemies, the Sadducees. By the way, I have no doubt that Josephus reports here that *bathing* and not *washing* was the Essene practice after defecation, and it was this custom of bathing which the Pharisees took over from them.[46] The rationale which

[44] Such is the case already in the earliest documents of the Mishnah, as we have emphasized above, p. 110. The early origin of this injunction is also indicated by the notion of some Tannaim to credit it with biblical authority; *cf. loc. cit.* and p. 318.

[45] *Cf.* the abundant literature on this question cited in Coronel, זכר נתן, p. 34a ff.

[46] The precept in point presented in Yoma III, 3 concerns only those within the Temple precinct; hence it does not apply here. Were it applicable, Josephus would appear rather incompetent as a reliable reporter of the Pharisaic way of life, because Mishnah Yoma is certainly not later than the composition of Josephus' historical writings.

Josephus advances for this custom, that the Essenes considered defecation as tainting with impurity, makes the purifying bath, not merely washing, a requisite.

17) Margoliouth, "The Sadducean Christians of Damascus," *Athenaeum*, 1910, pp. 657–658.

Idem, "The Two Zadokite Messiahs," *Journal of Theological Studies*, 1911, pp. 446–450.

Idem, Expositor, 1911, pp. 499–517 and *ibid.*, 1912, pp. 212–235.

Idem, Jewish Review, III, pp. 361–364.

Idem, International Journal of Apocrypha, X, 37 (April 1914, pp. 36–37).

In the five articles which Margoliouth devotes to our subject, he attempts to demonstrate that our document originated in Judeo-Christian circles. The "Messiah out of Aaron and Israel" is John the Baptist, whose followers believed him to be the predicted Messiah (according to the NT, however, he was only the (priestly, Luke 1:5) precursor (*ibid.*, 1:17; John 1:15; Matthew 3) of the Messiah!), whereas the Teacher-of-Truth was Jesus. Paul, the apostle of the mission to the heathens, appears in our document as *Belial*, because he was anathema to the "Johannian Christians," who remained loyal to the observance of the law. These Johannian Christians were recruited from among the ranks of the Sadducees, or, more correctly, from among the Boethusians, a subdenomination of the Sadducee party.

We deem it unnecessary to subject this figment of the imagination, a Johannian-Christian-Boethusian-Sadducean sect,[47] to any critical discussion, since Margoliouth does not offer even the flimsiest of evidence for the presence of any Christian doctrine[48] in our docu-

---

[47] This would be the proper name for Margoliouth's supposed sect. In any event, even with regard to the two Messiahs it would be decidedly incorrect to assign similar functions to both, as Margoliouth does. If he reserves the typological reference to the "Messiah out of Aaron and Israel" for identification with John the Baptist as Judge, it would follow that the typological reference to the other Messiah would make Jesus into only the Distinguished Teacher.

[48] The "only Christian element" which Margoliouth supposedly finds in our document is the Pentateuchal commandment of altruistic love! *Cf.* also above, p. 202 ff., where we have demonstrated that the sect, in sectarian narrow-mindedness, confined the application of altruistic love only to conforming fellow-sectaries. The meaning of the phrase (2,13): ובפרוש שמו שמותיהם we have elucidated above — yet, according to Margoliouth, this phrase is an allusion to Jesus; according to Margoliouth, again, Jesus was not even identified by the sect as the Messiah! *Cf.* also Bava Bathra 75b, where the saying is quoted that "the righteous bear the divine name"; even if John would be identified as Judge, the phrase ובפרוש שמו שמותיהם in our document would refer to the righteous at large, not particularly to the Boethusians.

ment. Moore and also Ward have already thoroughly refuted this theory, but have failed to stress that Margoliouth merely tries to apply the thesis advanced by Singer (*Das Buch der Jubiläen, oder die Leptogenesis*, Stuhlweissenburg, 1898) concerning the Book of Jubilees, to our document. These two texts do have a certain affinity, but, at least with regard to our text, the thesis is wrong. The identification of the apostle Paul with Belial has already been suggested by Singer; Margoliouth offers no explanation as to why our document (4,15) charges this Belial with the practice of whoredom (i. e., polygamy), when Paul was so completely averse to matrimony (I Corinthians 7)!

18) Montgomery, in *The Biblical World*, 1911, pp. 373 ff., discusses Schechter's theories of our document, without offering anything new.

19) Moore, "The Covenanters of Damascus, a hitherto Unknown Jewish Sect," *Harvard Theological Review*, 1911, pp. 330–337.

The title of Moore's discourse points to his view: the provenance of our document is to be found in the circle of "a hitherto unknown Jewish Sect." This sect is to be identified neither with the Pharisees nor the Sadducees, neither Dosithean nor Judeo-Christian, but represents a strictly law-observant direction within Judaism which has much in common with the hitherto known sects, but yet distinctly separatist. Moore's discussion is distinguished in its lucidity and sound critical judgment. Some details,[49] however, warrant correction.

20) Poznanski, in *Jewish Review*, II, pp. 273–281 and *ibid.*, pp. 443–446, doubts the Sadducee character of our document and demonstrates the untenability of Margoliouth's theory (17).

---

[49] E. g. the statement that a Karaite court consists of ten judges (p. 351, note 55) is a mistake, see above, pp. 150–151. Moore is also mistaken when he contends (note 109) that Rabbi (Yehudah ha-Nasi) called Shimeon bar-Kokhba a liar = bar Kozba, for the Midrash text of Ekhah Rabba on Lam. 2:2 in the usual editions is corrupted. In the critical text edition of Buber, p. 101 (and there note 57a): אמר רבי יוחנן כד הוה חזי רבי עקיבה לבן כוזבא, הוה אמר: דרך כוכב מיעקב'...כוכבא מיעקב — זה מלך המשיח. Hence it was not Rabbi who called bar-Kokhba by the name bar-Kozba, but R. Akiva who called bar-Kozba by the name bar-Kokhba, a honorific based on Num. 24:17; the Kozbian (see I Chron. 4:22) was considered "the star." The validity of this reading is corroborated by the tradition in TP Taanioth IV, 8 fol. 68d, according to which we ought to read the Midrash: א'ר יוחנן [אמר רבי שמעון בר יוחיי: עקיבה] רבי היה דורש: דרך כוכב מיעקב אל תקרי .כוכב' אלא .כוזב'. The copyists omitted the words in brackets, which led to the conclusion that Rabbi (Yehudah ha-Nasi) pronounced this verse over the hero. The word "Rabbi," however, in the mouth of R. Shimeon refers to his teacher, R. Akiva. This is also supported by the fact that the Palestinian Amora R. Yoḥanan distinguishes himself as transmitter of R. Shimeon's sayings (see Bacher, *Tannaim*, under: Shimeon b. Yoḥai), as in this case.

21) Revel, *The Karaite Halakhah*, Philadelphia, 1913, pp. 44–57, discusses the relationship of our sectarian Halakah to Karaism. He reaches the conclusion that despite numerous points of agreement between the two Halakic systems there are distinct and essential differences between the two sectarian traditions. We have described the true situation in our comparative analysis, and hence see no need to discuss Revel's conclusions.

22) Schechter, Reply to Dr. Büchler's Review of Schechter's "Jewish Sectaries," in *The Jewish Quarterly Review*, New Series, IV, pp. 449–474. An elaborate rebuttal concerning the character of our document, particularly refuting Büchler's argument that the fragments are spurious; *cf*. next section.

23) Segal, "Notes on Fragments of a Zadokite Work," in *JQR*, New Series, II, pp. 133–141.

Idem, "Additional Notes on Fragments of a Zadokite Work," *ibid.*, III, pp. 301–311.

Segal's "Notes" deal mainly with linguistic aspects of the Fragments, offering a number of textual emendations. In one passage, however, he presents his opinion on the origin of the sect: in the wake of the complete Maccabean victory under Simon there emerged an opposition party. Its membership was composed of rather diverse elements: the ancient nobility of priests, or Zadokites, as we may call them; the descendants of the Hellenists; also some Pharisees and Hassideans. These were united for some time in the common cause of restoring the Zadokite family to its legitimate position. The career of this party was, however, of brief duration. The Sadducees joined forces with the Hasmoneans, and the Pharisees lost their interest in restoring the Zadokite priesthood. Were it not for the advent of the "Unique Teacher," or the "Teacher of Truth" as he was also called, this party would have disappeared entirely after its factional split. This new leader, however, gathered the loyal remnant around himself and transformed the original party of loyalists into a sect which withdrew from the Temple and rejected the Calendar and jurisdiction of the Hasmoneans because these had usurped the office of the High Priest and had accepted the doctrines of the Pharisees. Towards the end of John Hyrcanus' reign these separatists suffered from bloody persecutions in which their leader was martyred; because of his martyrdom he was proclaimed the Messiah by his enthusiastic followers. The sect emigrated to Damascus only in the next generation, towards the end of Alexander Jannaeus' reign. The present sectarian document, however, was composed in 63 B. C. E., at the time when Pompey conquered Palestine.

This opinion conforms essentially with Lagrange's historical interpretation; it thus suffers from the same basic mistake of ascribing the halakic sections of our document to Sadducean provenance which, as we have amply demonstrated, is decidedly erroneous.

24) Strack, "Die israelitische Gemeinde des neuen Bundes in Damaskus" (*Die Reformation*, 1911, N. Y.) presents the content of our document, based entirely on Schechter's interpretation.

25) Ward, in the *Independent*, 1910 (pp. 1337 ff.), published a short notice of this document; in *Biblia Sacra*, 1911 (pp. 429–456) he devoted an elaborate review to it. In the latter paper he adduced weighty arguments against Margoliouth (above, #17, p. 334) who ascribes Judeo-Christian character to the sect. My conversation with him about the Pharisaic provenance of the sect has convinced him and he has completely accepted this interpretation.

X

The Karaite Hypothesis Disproved

"Quot homines — tot sententiae"; this remark by Terence best characterizes the wide variety of opinions concerning our document, since, as we have seen in the previous chapter, almost every scholar disagrees with the interpretations advanced by all the others. There is, however, complete agreement on one point, that our document does indeed report real events which did occur at some time and that this text is not a forgery, tendentiously presenting phantasies as facts in the interest of some party or sect. The only opinion which dissents from this consensus is that of Büchler (*Jewish Quarterly Review*, N. S. III, pp. 429–485). He dates[1] the fragments as composed in the late seventh or early eighth century C. E. and identifies their content as a bungled fabrication by an antirabbinist sectarian — of whom there was a goodly number during this period — who intended, just as the Karaites did later on, to "reconstruct" Jewish history of the First and Second Commonwealth in such fashion as to insinuate that the Rabbanites were heretics. The emigration from Judea to Damascus, which was frequently mentioned in our document, never occurred; the sectarian author, who resided in the vicinity of Damascus, introduced this episode only in order to justify the antirabbinist doctrines of his own environment. He was suggesting by this alleged invention, that he and his fellow sectarians were the true representatives of Israel, for their doctrines had been handed down to them by their ancestors, who had settled in Damascus as early as the days of the Temple in order to teach and practice there the true Judaism. In Büchler's view the efforts of the several scholars to date and interpret the historical allusions in our document are futile; the document recorded no real

[1] To my knowledge, except for journalists to whom an opinion is the more attractive to the degree to which it is more improbable and bizarre, Büchler is the only scholar who denies the authenticity of our document. One of this ilk (S. D. in *Jewish Chronicle*, 1912) has had the temerity to reproach Schechter for having prefaced his edition of the fragment with an introduction that, according to S. D., would have better been left unwritten, as it has only served to mislead the scholarly world. Our sages would have seen in this impertinence a Messianic symptom, according to their dictum: בעקבות משיחא חוצפא יסגא (Soṭah 49b).

338

facts, for it contains only some mystifying games played with dates taken from the Bible.

The arguments which Büchler uses to make his case that our document is spurious are vitiated by a basic methodological error; even if the supposed data to which he refers were correct in detail, the case would still remain unproved. Büchler's demonstration moves in a vicious circle: agreements between Talmudic sources and passages in our document lead him to the conclusion that the sectarian material is necessarily secondary and dependent on the Talmud; in Büchler's method of argument disagreements prove the same thing, that the sectarian material is of a late date, especially in all those instances where sectarian views concur with those to be found among the Karaites. Moreover, Büchler uses in an indiscriminate way the self-evident rule that Halakah has undergone evolution. Nobody denies that some Halakoth of Tannaim who flourished during the second century C. E. were unknown to earlier generations; yet it is uncritical to state: this or that Halakah is late because we have no textual evidence that it was known in the days of the Temple. The activities of the Yavneh Academy — not to speak of even later generations — consisted predominantly in standardization and clarification of controversial Halakoth and in their midrashic demonstration, rather than in innovating positive or negative commandments. Hence we are justified in considering a Halakah reported by the Tannaim — and even by the Amoraim — as belonging to the common store of early tradition, so long as there is no evidence that these Halakoth arose out of the contemporary and immediate circumstances of those who announced them.[2] This applies in particular to cases in which the Tannaim dispute details of certain halakic norms; such Halakoth must be dated as early, since contemporary Halakah is usually reported in general formulation without any exact definition of particulars. Or will Büchler contend that any Halakah which is not cited in the controversies between the schools of Shammai and Hillel is to be dated as

---

[2] Leszynsky (*Sadduzäer*, p. 306) remarks: "Since Ginzberg, however, ignores the development of rabbinic Halakah, we have to consider that he has failed to prove his thesis of the sect's non-Sadducee character." The discussions in our present book amply demonstrate that I have paid serious attention to the development of Halakah. I do ignore the thesis presented by Leszynsky that there was rapprochement between latter-day Talmudic rabbinism and the Sadducee mentality and that Sadducee influence is reflected in the Mishnah. This notion is not even discussable. I have no doubt at all that competent Halakic scholars have totally removed from their agenda of subjects worthy of investigation this chimera fabricated by Geiger's fancy.

originating in the period after the destruction of the Temple?! In compliance with the Talmudical dictum גברא רבא אמר מילתא — לא תחיכו עליה (Berakhoth 19b), we shall investigate Büchler's theories in detail without entering into any further discussion concerning the origin and development of Halakah.

In his research into the fragments Büchler has made three determinations which convinced him that our document is spurious:

a) the Halakah shows Talmudical and Karaite influence;
b) the language betrays Arabisms and artificial affectations of the post-talmudical period;
c) the so-called historical data are so vague and of such indeterminate nature that they can hardly be considered reports of real events.

Büchler saw correctly that our judgement on the question of date is essentially predicated upon the proper understanding of the sectarian Halakah. He therefore devotes a detailed investigation to the Halakic aspects of our document. We shall follow his lead and analyze in detail his arguments in favor of a very late dating.

The passionate injunction against polygamy in our document (4,20) finds its only parallel in Karaite literature, Büchler argues (p. 434), whereas the Talmudic-Midrashic literature knows of no such restriction, in spite of the fact that the rabbis themselves practiced monogamy and at times even went on record with derogatory remarks[3] about polygamy. This argument is incorrect in more than one respect. We find among the Karaites no example[4] of an absolute prohibition

---

[3] *Cf.* Schechter's Introduction to 4,20, where he refers to Avoth d'R. Nathan 9; Büchler quotes this reference without giving credit to Schechter; I have listed other references in rabbinic literature elsewhere. The reference, cited by Leszynsky, *Sadduzäer*, pp. 305–306, to the opinion of Rabbi Simeon in Sifrei Deut. 215 (=Midrash Tannaim, p. 128, where this opinion is ascribed to R. Ishmael) is irrelevant to the case in point. This Tanna is not critical of polygamy as such, but only of marriage with a woman taken captive in war. The Tanna deduces that such a union would lead to aversion from the juxtaposition of יפת תואר to שונא אותה; this text is correctly expounded by Pardo and Najar in their commentaries *ad loc.* The version מי שיש לו שתי נשים in Midrash Tannaim, *loc. cit.*, (this passage is not cited by Leszynsky) is not reliable. The passage in Gen. Rabba ch. 23 (ed. Theodor-Albeck, p. 222) quoting R. Judah's criticism of Lamekh's marriage to two wives, does not reflect, as Leszynsky and Büchler contend, a rejection of polygamy. The sin of the generation of the flood, according to this passage, was not polygamy but the sterilizing of wives in order to preserve their beauty.

[4] Büchler's citation of *REJ* XVI, p. 185, is of no help to his argument, for the facts given there mean something else. I took this reference into consideration when I said there might have been a Karaite rigorist who demanded the absolute pro-

concerning polygamy. Some demand such a restriction in a case when the marriage with a second wife diminishes the rights of the first wife. Such a restriction, in due protection of the first wife, was already suggested by a Palestinian Amora *ca.* 300 C. E., as we have demonstrated above. There is, thus, no proof for exclusively Karaite influence which is the source for this restriction of polygamy in our document. On the other hand, we refer only to the evidence cited above for the prevalence of polygamy among leading Pharisees,[5] in support of the legitimacy of such marriages, according to Pharisee doctrine. How Büchler can conclude that our document must be dated very late because the sectaries charge their opponents, the Pharisees (and also the Sadducees), with practicing polygamy is an argument which I fail to follow. When the early church prohibited polygamy, the Christians who were thus restricted in their matrimonial freedom were at that time nothing other than a Jewish sect. If this Jewish sect condemned polygamy, near the end of the Second Temple, is it not rather probable that the same restrictive attitude prevailed in our Damascene sect barely one century earlier? Such a monogamous trend would only demonstrate the kinship of certain sectarian doctrines among Jews. The attempt to refute such an analogy by arguing that the earliest church abandoned the ancient Semitic practice of polygamy in sensitive consideration for the neo-Christian proselytes of Greco-Roman origin is based on the assumption that influences other than Jewish introduced monogamy into the Judeo-Christian sect. This assumption, however, is doubtful and unwarranted as far as the early church is concerned.[6] If, for argument's sake, we would admit that the early

---

hibition of polygamy. However, in light of the evidence from the entire Karaite literature, which knows of no such prohibition, we must conclude that this Rabbanite R. Tobiah did not really know the Karaite marriage code, or that he reported incorrectly.

[5] There were not many instances of polygamy among the rabbis. The reports about Rav and R. Naḥman (Yoma 18b) were difficult for the later Amoraim to explain. Rav's personal practice makes it certain, however, that his meaning in Gen. Rabba, ch. 61 (4) was not that he wanted to reject polygamy, as Leszynsky, *op. cit.*, p. 144, has tried to argue. The reading רב is however doubtful; *cf.* Pseudo-Rashi, *loc. cit.*, and Theodor-Albeck, p. 661.

[6] Our document correctly cites Gen. 2:24 and 7:2 to prove that the Bible considers monogamy as the natural and divinely approved form of matrimony. This view is clear in many other passages in the Bible, such as Proverbs etc. In later times those Essenes who did not practice celibacy were probably strictly monogamous, for they permitted marriage only for the purpose of procreation (*cf.* Josephus, *Bel. Jud.* II 8,13; Mishnah Yevamoth VI, 6 which rules that the commandment of פריה ורביה is fulfilled by him who has begotten two children). We have pointed out already that according to the unanimous tradition of the Talmud a High Priest

church introduced monogamous restrictions in considerate sensitivity of proselytes unaccustomed to polygamy, then this argument may just as plausibly be applied to the monogamy that was decreed in the Damascene sect, for our fragments demonstrate beyond doubt that our sectarians engaged in missionary work among the Gentiles.

Büchler cites yet another matrimonial law in our document for which, again, he argues that the only parallel is to be found in Karaite literature; it is the prohibition of marriage between uncle and niece (5,6), a form of marriage which was regarded as especially commendable by the Pharisees and which was practiced even by the Sadducees. The latter contention of Büchler rests upon a misunderstanding, as we have pointed out, for there is no direct evidence for Sadducee approval of such a marriage. Moreover, we have cited (pp. 23–24) several passages in Tannaitic literature which seem to reveal that the attitude of frowning upon marriage between uncle and niece was not unknown to the respective authors during the second and third century C. E. Most probably the Sadducees did not hold so restrictive a view,[7] for they seem to have agreed in this matter with the Pharisees. Whatever the truth may be, it is in any case entirely out of the question to date the sectarian prohibition of marriage between uncle and niece in the Karaite period, as Büchler is trying to convince us. He himself admits[8] that such a restriction already prevailed in the earliest church, and that the Falashas have always frowned upon such mar-

---

was restricted to one wife. Essene as well as priestly influence cannot be ignored in the early church as well as in our sect. Even if one is not inclined to accept the socio-economic explanation that I proposed for our sect's rejection of polygamy, there is no reason to imagine that this is a borrowing from non-Jewish practice. It is to be noted, also, that the Falashas practice monogamy; cf. Abraham Epstein, כתבי רא׳׳ע, Jerusalem 5710, vol. I, p. 171 (ספר אלדד הדני).

[7] Josephus, *Ant*. I, 12,1; that Sarah was Abraham's niece is a view that was also held by the rabbis and the church-fathers; cf. my *Die Hagadah bei den Kirchenvätern*, I, pp. 98–100; (see Lauterbach's note in *HUCA* VII (1930), p. 326, note 22).

[8] Büchler errs when he presumes to find this restriction in the *Altercatio Simonis J. et Theophili*, VII, 28. The Jews are charged there: similiter aequam luto mixtam volutas, sororem tuam tibi in conjugio copulas; this refers neither to the potion of "bitter water" for the suspected wife (Num. 5:11–31), for this ordeal had been abolished by Rabban Yoḥanan b. Zakkai before the destruction of the Temple (Soṭah IX, 9), and hence could not have been observed by the Christian apologists; nor does it refer to marriage with a niece (a niece is not "soror") or to a levirate childless widow. The correct interpretation of this passage was given fifteen years, ago in my *Die Haggadah bei den Kirchenvätern* I, p. 3, note 4. There can, to be sure, be no doubt about the early date of the Christian prohibition of marriage with nieces; cf. the material in Krauss, *Studies in Jewish Literature*, p. 168 and p. 174.

riages. We have argued above, on the basis of textual criticism, that the passage in our document which prohibits marriage with nieces probably represents a later addition. If this argument of ours is rejected, we see no plausible reason why such heretic doctrine could not be preached and practiced by a Jewish sect a century before the emergence of Christianity, especially since proof-texts may be cited from the Bible, as the Karaites correctly emphasize.[9] Krauss (*Studies in Jewish Literature*, p. 174) refers to the Roman codes which consider marriage between uncle and niece as incestuous; we cannot agree with him that this Roman legislation brought its influence to bear upon Jewish heretics, but we note with keen interest that a nation of highly developed culture such as the Romans held the same view in this matter as the Jewish heretics.

[9] *Cf.* above, pp. 153–154. It is quite amusing to read Leszynsky's discourse (*Jahrbuch für jüdische Geschichte* XVII, p. 111) on the rationale of the prohibition, in our document, to marry nieces; he writes "The reason advanced for this prohibition is quite startling: it says that although the laws of the Torah against incest are addressed to men, they apply correspondingly also to women — a line of thinking which indeed appeals to us. It is only a step from such a rule to the conception that men and women are equal before the religious law." Leszynsky seems to be blissfully ignorant of the fact that such equality is already taught in the Mishnah (Qiddushin I, 7), with the exception of a few commandments the mandatory observance of which would impose great hardships on women: moreover, this equality is emphatically stated in the Sifra on Lev. 18:6, to the effect that the rules concerning incest apply equally to men and women. Besides, it would be foolish of our document to emphasize that incestual relations are forbidden for both sexes alike when the Torah states explicitly that in some cases both parties to the intercourse will suffer death punishment.

What our document really wants to say, as we have expounded, is the following: by the hermeneutic rule of analogy (היקש) the prohibition of intercourse with an aunt would conversely also apply between uncle and niece. This rule, indeed, existed later among the Karaites — but they cannot possibly be suspected of having promoted the legal equality of women, because they maintained, contrary to the Talmud, that a woman always remains under potestas patris!

I should like to take this opportunity to point out that the medieval codifiers ignored the Talmudical recommendation that it was a meritorious deed to marry a niece. R. Jacob b. Asher does not mention it in his "Tur." In the Shulḥan Arukh of R. Yoseph Caro it is conspicuous by its absence in two obvious paragraphs, so that R. Mosheh Isserles saw himself compelled to add it in his scholium (Even ha-Ezer 2,6 and 15,25). These two glaring omissions may be due to the influence of environmental Christian practice. Although Caro composed his code in Mohammedan Palestine, he collated and summarized the religious practice of Iberian Jewry a generation after their expulsion from Christian Spain. Moreover, Islam (Qoran, Surah IV, 23: forbidden unto you are . . . . your brother's daughters and your sister's daughters) may also have influenced this omission (see *in loco*, Estorre Parchi כפתור ופרח, ch. 5 end, ed. Edelmann, p. 13).

I should like to point out that in this discourse on the marriage
between uncle and niece Büchler presents the opinion of Rashi[10] as
the undisputed interpretation by Halakic authorities, according to
which the Talmud encourages a man only towards marriage with his
sister's daughter (since the fondness for his sister will ensure special
devotion to her daughter, according to Rashi), whereas no mention
is made of his brother's daughter. Büchler fails to present the controversy of Halakic authorities[11] on this point. Rashi's grandson, R.
Shemuel ben Meir,[12] and Maimonides,[13] among others, extend this
Talmudical encouragement to both fraternal and sororal nieces. This
opinion is not only supported by the Midrash,[14] but also by talmudic
data reporting on outstanding men who were married to their brothers'
daughters; when the daughters of the priestly R. Shemuel b. Abba
were released from captivity, their uncle שמן בר אבא was asked by his

---

[10] Cf. above, where we have already listed some of the medieval rabbinic opinion.
Rashi and his grandson Rabbenu Jacob Tam favor the marriage with a sister's
daughter, in stricter interpretation of the Talmudic term בת אחותו (Yevamoth 62b.
In Sanhedrin 76b Rashi is uncommitted).

[11] R. Sherira Gaon, in גבול מנשה, ed. Grossberg, Frankfurt am Main, 5659,
p. 15 (cf. אוצר הגאונים, ed. Lewin on Yevamoth, p. 142, שלג; ibid., ed. Taubes on Sanhedrin, p. 438) Halakoth Gedoloth, ed. Hildesheimer, p. 609, Hil. Temurah (against
the heretics who forbid marrying a brother's daughter, as Othniel b. Kenaz did).
Even R. Yehudah he-Ḥasid seems to be rather undecided, cf. ספר החסידים, ed. Ms.
Parma 1099 and 1116; ed. Ms. Bologna 488 and 477, and his Will. On possible
Karaite influence: A. Epstein, כתבי רא"ע. Jerusalem, 5727, p. 240. R. Yechezkel
Landau's criticism (Noda Bihudah II, Even ha-Ezer, Resp. 79) is not valid,
since the Talmudic text does not contain the term מצוה; it merely advises and
recommends. The term מצוה occurs in Maimonides, R. Nissim's commentary on
Nedarim 63b et al.

[12] Cited in Tossafoth on Yevamoth 62b, והנושא; cf. also ibid. 99a ספק, and
תוספות ישנים on ibid. 62b, who point to the possible conflict between marrying a
brother's daughter and the difficulties which might ensue if a levirate marriage
were later required (i. e., the father might be obligated to marry his daughter!).

[13] Maimonides in the Yad, Hil. Issurai Biah 2,14 means simply permissible
relatives, as he states more explicitly in his Commentary on the Mishnah, Nedarim
VIII, 7 and in the Guide for the Perplexed, 3,42 end. This general recommendation
is found in Talmudic literature; see next note. The controversy has been analyzed
by R. Menaḥem ha-Meiri, Beth ha-Beḥirah on Yevamoth (ed. Albeck, p. 235; ed.
Dickman, p. 230); and by R. Meir b. Todros Halevi Abulafia, יד רמה, on Sanhedrin 76b (ed. Warsaw, p. 146b) where he proposed a social reason over against
Rashi's psychological reason for preferring a sister's daughter.

[14] Gen. Rabba XVIII, 23, ed. Theodor-Albeck, p. 164; see also TP Kethuvoth
I, 5 (25c), which proposes a broader meaning of the term בת אחותו in the Talmud.
The Midrash is quoted by R. Joseph Caro, כסף משנה, on Maimonides, loc. cit.

teacher R. Ḥanina to marry one of his nieces.[15] The controversy actually revolves around the meaning of the term בת אחותו, which may be taken in the literal restricted sense, as e. g. Rashi does, or as a general term for niece or other permissible relatives. In rabbinical terminology the latter meaning may be the intended one, since we find also in other languages, e. g. Judeo-German "Schwesterkind," such term referring to male and female alike.

According to Büchler, not only do the marital laws in our document bear the hallmark of Karaite influence, but also the dietary laws. In proof he cites the rules concerning fish and locust (12,13), which agree with Karaite practice but not with Talmudic tradition. Our sect is permitted to consume fish only after splitting them alive and draining them of blood. The Karaites prohibit the consumption of fish blood, whereas both the Talmud and the Book of Jubilees permit it; ergo, our sectarian rule is Karaite Halakah. This line of deduction, however, is erroneous. It rests on the premise that the blood of fish is permissible for consumption. There is support for this view in a Talmudic opinion; but it is prohibited in the Mishnah Kerithoth V, 1.[15a] Since, as we have shown above our document concurs with the earlier Halakah, there

---

[15] Kethuvoth 23a; on the family see Bava Meẓi'a 73b. The uneasiness about a Cohen's marrying a captive girl was aggravated by her being his niece. Such uneasiness has prevailed. See also Mishnah Nedarim VIII, 7 and IX, 10; Tos. Qiddushin I, 4 (ed. Zuckermandel, p. 335₁).

[15a] In keeping with the common usage of the Mishnaic idiom, the term אין חייבין עליהן in reference to the blood of fish (Kerithoth V, 1) can only mean: the Torah has not made the consumption of fish blood punishable by כרת, although, it may be inferred, it is forbidden and may possibly be punishable by מלקות. The inference that the term אין חייבין עליהן implies permission to consume fish blood is impossible, because the Mishnah uses this term to rule on דם התחול and דם תמצית as well, and these, as is also stressed in the Baraitha (Kerithoth 21b, 22a), are clearly forbidden; we must therefore regard all the varieties of blood consumption cited in this Mishnah to be prohibited by biblical law and even punishable. Thus we reach the conclusion that this Mishnah does not concur with the Tosefta Kerithoth II, 18 (and Sifra X, 11 on Lev. 7:26; also Talmud Kerithoth, *loc. cit.*) which permits the consumption of fish blood (*cf.* also above, pp. 79 ff., p. 126). In the Talmudic discourse, *loc. cit.*, Rav proposes to differentiate between cases in which fish blood is permissible and those in which it would be forbidden, in order to harmonize the Baraithoth with the Mishnah; his attempt at harmonization is obviously not satisfying. The opinion of the Mishnah is also represented in Targum Jonathan on Lev. 7:27, which paraphrases the prohibition to consume כל דם by including all living כל אדם מן דכל חי, i. e., even דם דנים ודם חגבים, as forbidden and punishable by כרת, according to this verse. This paraphrase of the Targum does not derive from Karaite influence; we have noted above (p. 148, note 168) that according to the earlier Karaite authorities the blood of locust is not prohibited for con-

is no proof here for the Karaite provenance of this sectarian prohibition. In any event, even if this is not so, this prohibition of the eating of fish blood bears more affinity with heretical opinions cited in early Midrashim than it does with Büchler's Karaite parallel. The Midrash[16] tells of a preacher, known for his Judeo-Christian tendencies,[17] who flourished at the beginning of the fourth century, who instructed an audience at Tyre to have fish slaughtered as fowl has to be slaughtered, since both fish and fowl are mentioned together in the same verse (Gen. 1:20). According to this opinion, the blood of fish would indubitably be strictly forbidden for consumption, since the blood of fowl is subject to such prohibition (Lev. 17:13–14). In contrast, the dominant opinion in the Talmud[18] is that the requirement to slaughter fowl was not a biblical law but that it was promulgated by the rabbinical authorities. Hence, when our document requires the draining of blood from fish by splitting them, this sectarian Halakah agrees essentially with the opinion advanced in the Midrash,[16] which, by analogy, puts fish and fowl into one category, although the sect does not extend the rabbinic requirement of slaughtering fowl to apply also to fish.

The Karaites, however, do not only maintain that the Torah prohibits the consumption of fish blood,[19] but even insist that the killing of fish requires a certain procedure, corresponding to the slaughtering procedure of Sheḥitah, an opinion which stands in

---

sumption, whereas the latter-day Karaites may well have derived their stricter rule from the Targum in point. This paraphrase of the Targum elucidates also the text of Seder Eliahu Rabba ch. 16 (ed. Friedmann, p. 73), which ought to read: מ"מ, כל דם כל בשר העבודה, אף דם החי אסור באכילה שנאמר whereas the interpolation from ונקרש ונתמצה to אף זו, which has been inserted on basis of Kerithoth 21b, is to be deleted; even the biblical text interpreted here ought to read, as in the Targum, 7,27 (instead of 17,14), at least in the proof text מכל מקום, כל דם :שנאמר. The presentation of the injunction against the consumption of blood in Josephus (*Ant.* III 11,2) is quite remarkable; taking his departure from Lev. 3:17 he combines the injunctions against the consumption of blood and certain fats, noticing: "Moses forbade the consumption of blood completely . . . . forbidding also the fat of goats, sheep and oxen."

[16] Gen. Rabba 7 (ed. Theodor-Albeck, pp. 50–51); Pesikta (ed. Buber 35b, ed. Mandelbaum, p. 63); Pesikta Rabbathi, ed. Friedmann 61a, and parallels cited there.

[17] Theodor, *loc. cit.*. and Bacher, *Aggadah d. palest. Amoräer*, p. 711.

[18] Ḥullin 20a and the cross references and parallels indicated there; also TP Nazir 4 (53c).

[19] *Cf.* above pp. 79, 148.

obvious conflict[20] with the sectarian prescription in our document. Anan, one of the earliest Karaite authorities, is known to have permitted the consumption of fish only if they were caught by a Jew, or, according to another version, when killing by מליקה (Lev. 1:15), known from fowl, is applied to them.[21] Our document, however, requires merely splitting of live fish to drain them of blood. Büchler and other scholars are also in error when they cite Pirqei de R. Eliezer, IX (ed. Warsaw 21b) as evidence for the opinion that at the time when this Midrash was composed, coinciding with the inception of the Karaite movement, the consumption of fish blood was considered forbidden. We have already demonstrated that the passage in point means that the blood of fish, in contrast to the blood of fowl, need not be "covered." Employing a phrase reminiscent of Deut. 12:16, 24, the Midrash states: דגים וחגבים נאכלין שלא בשחיטה, (אבל העוף אינו נאכל אלא בשחיטה) אלו שנבראו מן המים — דמן נשפך כמים, ואלו שנבראו מן הארץ — דמן לכסות בעפר. According to an early Midrash, the biblical phrase מה מים מלכסות — אף דם פטור מלכסות means פטורין מלכסות כמים דם . . . תשפכנו so that the terminology in Pirkei R. Eliezer[22] expresses the opposites דמן לכסות בעפר and דמן לשפוך כמים.

<hr>

[20] See above p. 79.

[21] *Cf.* the passage quoted by Hartwig Hirschfeld, *JQR*, from Qirqisani's *Kitab al-Anwar wal-Maraqib*, according to which Anan, in keeping with later Karaite authorities (e. g., Judah Hadassi: Eshkol ha-Kofer 89c bottom) juxtaposes the "gathering" of fish with the slaughtering (שחיטה) of other animals. Shahrastani, in 'Kithab al-Milal w'al-Niḥal" (in Sacy, *Chrestomathie Arabe*, vol. II, p. 498), contends, on the other hand, that the Ananite Karaites distinguish themselves from the Rabbanite Jews by killing fish on the back of the head (מן אלפא), which certainly is meant as a reference to מליקה. The text I consulted, the Cairo edition of Shahrastani (in the volume of Ibn Hazm's work by the same title, vol. II, p. 54, 1902–1903), reads, however, אלחיואן instead of אלסמך; which would signify that Anan prescribes מליקה for killing animals and not for fish, an opinion which is also reported by Karaite authors (e. g., Nicomedia, גן עדן, Sheḥitah XII). It is quite possible that Anan juxtaposes fish with birds and animals, in which case the correct reading in Shahrastani would approximately be: אלחיואן ואלסמך. *Cf.* also Anan's Code, ed. Harkavy, p. 67, where he mentions אסיפה only with regard to locust. The opinion ascribed by Shahrastani to the Ananite Karaites can actually be traced to Anan himself, as explicitly stated by Nicomedia, *loc. cit.*

[22] We have pointed out above (p. 80, note 263) that the extant text of Pirqei de R. Eliezer cannot possibly be correct. It would maintain that blood of all animals, except fish, requires "covering." This stands in clear contradiction to the Mishnah Ḥullin VI, 1 and the simple wording of the biblical passage (Deut. 12:24). The emendation which I proposed above has already been suggested by R. Wolf Ein-

Büchler's interpretation of the sectarian Halakah on locust (12,14) is also untenable. He claims that locusts must be killed, according to our document, by scorching or drowning, whereas it correctly means that locusts may be fried or boiled alive, since they present no blood problem (p. 80): "All the various kinds of locust shall be put into fire or water when still alive, for this is in keeping with their nature." Our document here stresses the very difference between fish and locust; the former have to be drained of blood first, hence fish must be split while still alive, whereas locust may be put straight into fire (for frying) or water (for boiling), each in keeping with its nature.[23] The very phrase יבואו באש ובמים is not accidental; although the dietary laws apply no restriction to the consumption of locust (i. e., they may be eaten alive); yet "aesthetic considerations" in the legal restriction of בל תשקצו enjoin against such a practice (cf. above, pp. 80 ff. and notes, for references).[24] There is similar phraseology in a responsum of R. Hai Gaon (*Geonica* II, p. 45) דמיתי שליפי חגבים ושאגדו להון בדודי, instead of the less circumlocutory דמיתי שליפי חגבים ואוכלם, to avert misunderstanding that locust may be consumed alive. The exclusive validity of our explanation of 12,14 is demonstrated by comparison to the preceding ruling on eating fish. Corresponding to

---

horn in his commentary *ad loc.*; it is, however, unsatisfactory. Midrash Hagadol Bereshith, ed. Schechter, p. 44, seems to have read a passage from Pirqei R. Eliezer about the creation of birds from רקק, i. e., a mixture of water and soil (Ḥullin 27b), which would mean accordingly אלו שנבראו מן הארץ: these birds which were — also — created from the soil. *Cf.* also Pinsker לקוטי קדמוניות, pt. II, p. 75, citing from Abu Yaaqub's commentary on the Bible, that the blood of domestic animals (הבתיים) has to be covered. Such opinion cannot possibly be imputed to Pirqei R. Eliezer, for there in ch. XI clear reference is made by the words וכולן שחיטתן to the distinction between domestic animals on the one hand, and wild animals and birds on the other hand. Parenthetically, I know of no other instance in Karaite literature in which this opinion of Abu Yaacub is represented; the Karaite codes speak of כיסוי, just as do the Rabbanites.

[23] The nature of locust, i. e., they have no blood; *cf.* Anan's Code, ed. Harkavy, p. 67, who also observes relative to locust: ואף על גב דדם לא אית להון.

[24] Shabbath 90b, end of chapter. Anan, *loc. cit.*, prohibits the consumption of locust for a different reason and stresses, quite as in our document: אילו מייתו אדאית להו (=דסליק) בהו חיי ומטוי להו או דצליק. In this sentence מטוי corresponds to our יבואו באש and צליק to יבואו במים in our document. Harkavy, however, misunderstood the term צליק and translates "splitting"! Tos. Terumoth IX, 6 reads אוכל אדם דגים וחגבים בין חיין בין מתים — ואינו חושש, which means that one prepares for human consumption fish and locust which are still alive, without saying anything in particular about the fact that creatures are consumed alive. Maimonides, Sheḥita 1,3 writing: דגים וחגבים אינן צריכים שחיטה, אלא אסיפתן היא המתרת אותן ... לפיכך אם מתו מאליהן בתוך המים — מותרין; ומותר לאוכלן חיים agrees almost verbatim with Anan's formulation, *loc. cit.*, about the "gathering" of locust.

the formulation והדגים אל יאכלו כי אם נקרעו חיים we ought to expect
וכל החגבים . . . אל יאכלו כי אם באו באש או במים if our document intended
to rule that locust must be killed before consumption. In any case,
it is clear that with regard to locust the rules set forth in our document
are so much at variance with the Karaite Halakah[25] that no possible
connection between the two codes can be established.

Büchler engages in an elaborate discourse on the controversy
between Pharisees and Sadducees concerning the rules on menstruation. He attempts to prove that the charges made in our document
(5,7) against the opponents of the sect, i. e., that they pollute the
sanctuary by violating the precepts of the Torah by having intercourse with a זבה, refer to the Rabbanites. The Karaites taunted the
Rabbanites for being lax in observance of the biblical commandment
(Lev. 12:4), which they interpret in the most literal and rigorous
meaning.[26] The analogy between the sectarian and the Karaite basis
of Halakic criticism is untenable for several reasons. First of all, as we
said above (pp. 22–23), the textual data clearly indicate that the controversy between the Damascene sect and their opponents does not
revolve around the interpretation of Lev. 12:4, which was the point of
contention between Karaites and Rabbanites; in that case our text
ought to have read instead of דם זובה either דם נדתה or דם לדתה. Qirqisani, in his account of Karaite controversies with the Rabbanites,
lists various points of differences on menstrual law, but he omits
mentioning their disagreement over what is to be inferred from Lev.
12:4. Büchler feels compelled to conclude from this that Qirqisani
based himself on a Zadokite source; that our document could not have
been known to him; and that if the passage in point from our document,
had he known it, would have been completely misunderstood by
Qirqisani! I fail to understand such line of reasoning. Secondly, we
have already referred above to an almost verbatim parallel to our
document's 5,7 in the Pharisaic Psalms of Solomon. If we would
accept Büchler's contention of our document's Karaite origin (or at
least of the Karaite origin of the passage in point), it would follow
that the Psalms of Solomon could have been composed no earlier than
the eighth century. Moreover, the Mishnah Horayoth I, 3, reports
a halakic controversy between the Pharisees and Sadducees con-

---

[25] Büchler overlooked the simple fact that the early Karaites (cf. Anan, loc. cit.)
knew only the "gathering" of locust; killing them in water is mentioned only by
the later authorities (as e. g., Eshkol ha-Kofer 89d).

[26] This rigorous attitude is represented by Anan in his Code, ed. Harkavy 51
and 64; Büchler failed to note this reference.

cerning laws of זבה; it is most probable that our sectarian passage
as well as the passage in the Psalms of Solomon refer to this controversy and charge the Sadducees with the consequent pollution of
the Temple.

In the heat of arguing his case, Büchler loses sight of contradictions among his own points, because of his compulsion to prove the
charges of the sectarians in our document against their opponents are
antirabbanite in nature. The pollution of the Temple, expressed in the
charge וגם מטמאים הם את המקדש, is not to be understood as referring to
the Temple, but to any synagogue, since the latter is also called מקדש,
possessing, according to Karaite doctrine, the same degree of sanctity
as the Temple precinct.[27] If this were true, it would be nonsense to
accuse the opponents, i. e., the Rabbanites, that they pollute the
synagogue by misinterpreting the Torah and, in consequence, by
having intercourse with הרואה דם זובה. The Rabbanites permit[28] all
who are tainted with all manner of טומאה to enter the synagogue. Any
anti-rabbanite critic would have taunted them much more effectively
by attacking their very permission to admit tainted persons to the
synagogue (מקדש according to Karaites). By the way, I know of no
reference whatsoever in rabbinic literature[29] which designates a synagogue as המקדש, the Sanctuary. Concerning our sectarian document,
the house of prayer (synagogue) is referred to as בית השתחות[30] (11,22),
whereas מקדש, which occurs ten times (1,3; 4,1; 18; 5,6; 6,12; 16;
12,1.2; 20,23) refers exclusively to the Holy Temple in Jerusalem.

[27] Büchler refers to Anan's Code, 53, though this seems to be a misprint for 35;
he ought to have pointed, however, to the reference in 22–23, where Anan equates
the synagogues with the Temple (cf. Harkavy, op. cit., p. 200, on 21).

[28] In this respect there is no difference between a synagogue and any other
house, according to Talmudic-rabbinic opinion. Subsequently, under Karaite influence, there developed the practice of keeping women away from the synagogue
for the duration of their menstrual impurity. The earliest reference to this practice
is the apocryphical ברייתא דנדה (ed. Horowitz תוספתא עתיקתא, pp. 30–33, and my
Geonica II, p. 38; cf. further H. Graetz, Geschichte⁴, vol. V, p. 550 and S. Pinsker,
לקוטי קדמוניות II, p. 32).

[29] The Talmud in Megillah 29a interprets the biblical expression (Ezek. 11:16)
מקדש מעט in Haggadic fashion as reference to the houses of study and prayer. The
Mishnah Megillah III, 3 concludes from a textual observation on Lev. 26:31 that
consecrated sites retain their sanctified character even when their buildings lie in
ruins; the biblical expression מקדשיכם here is not taken as reference to synagogues.
The only reference in which מקדש seems to stand for synagogue appears in the work
of the Karaite Sahl b. Mazliah (cf. S. Pinsker לקוטי קדמוניות II.).

[30] This is to be distinguished from בית העם (14,14?), which probably means
Community Hall, Meeting House, a term popularly applied in talmudic times to
the synagogue (Shabbath 32a).

Sundry other "anti-rabbanite" laws concerning purity, recorded in our document 12,15–18, are, according to Büchler, unknown during the Talmudic period, but traceable to Karaite Halakah. "All wood, stones and dust which are defiled by the taint of a dead human body . . . ," whatever is taught here in our document concerning natural materials in the raw such as wood, stones and dust stands not only in contradiction to the talmudical-rabbinic Halakah, but also, as we have pointed out in our discussions, to the Karaite Halakah. However, it would certainly be erroneous to contend that the teaching in our document is that all varieties of ritual contamination, from whatever source, apply to raw materials; the terminology used in this passage, בטומאת האדם, is certainly an allusion to Lev. 5:3, where the terminology refers, according to unanimous tannaitic tradition,[31] to the ritual taint caused by a dead human body. The phrase לנאולי שמו בהם is certainly a corruption; it must represent an explanatory gloss or paraphrase of בטומאת האדם, indicating that the source of contamination was a human corpse, לנאולי טומאת מת בהם.[32] Above (on p. 81) we have already referred to the Targum Jon. for Num. 19:14 which agrees with the ruling in this passage in our document. We should like now to add another reference from the Tosefta, which not only considers raw materials contaminable by ritual taint, but also holds that even the soil of the ground (מחובר) as liable to be מקבל טומאה. The implements used at the execution of criminals, such as the sword, the rope, the stone, or the gallows, are contaminable, as the Tosefta (Sanhedrin IX, 8; ed. Zuckermandel, p. 429, line 25)

---

[31] *Cf.* Sifra on Lev. 5:3: בטומאת אדם — זה טמא מת; Rashi on Lev. 5:3 reads ו טומאת מת (from direct contact with a corpse), whereas RABaD in his commentary on Sifra reads זה טמא מת (derivative contact from one who was contaminated by a corpse) and explains accordingly, which appears, however, to be incorrect.

[32] The abbreviation טמ', standing for טומאת מת is customary and very frequent in rabbinic literature. The letters ט and ש by dint of their similitude are liable to be confused by a scribe or copyist. The proposed emendation to read instead of שמו in the document rather טומאת מת=טמ' is graphically plausible, particularly when we bear in mind that the mark indicating an abbreviation is graphically hard to distinguish from the letter ו.

I cannot accept Schechter's proposed emendation to read rather יגואלו כמוהם, because this reading would render the continuation of the sentence כפי טומאתם וכו' superfluous.

We should like to observe, by the way, that in rabbinic literature the term טומאת אדם is never employed in the sense of טומאת מת, but rather in contradistinction to טומאת בגדים: the former לטמא אדם contaminates human (live) bodies, whereas the latter לטמא בגדים only garments and certain vessels. In Kelim XI, 1 we read לטומאת הנפש in the biblical sense (Num. 5:2; 19:11, 13) =טומאת נפש אדם; hence טומאת האדם in our passage may stand for טומאת נפש אדם.

סייף שנהרג בו, סודר שנחנק בו, אבן שנסקל בה, ועץ שנתלה עליו — כולן טעונין טבילה, ולא היו קוברין אותן עמו; all these implements had to be purified by submersion, but were not buried with the corpse of the person who was executed. This ruling states, in other words, that the court did not have to provide new implements for every execution. They were stored at the place of execution in readiness. Since they came into contact with the corpse of the executed, it was incumbent on the court to purify them, lest people would inadvertently touch them in their state of taint and become contaminated. This practice is also borne out by a previous passage in this Tosefta (line 19), reporting that "a heavy stone was there for execution by stoning," evidently placed on location for repeated use at executions. When the later Halakah ruled that the ground and whatever is solidly attached to it cannot be ritually contaminated, this passage of the Tosefta, which in the Erfurt version reads כולן טעונין טבילה, had to be emended, as other mss. and editions read, to כולן טעונין קבורה: now the ruling was that all implements of the executioners had to be buried,[33] although not together with the executed. In the next phase, the Amoraim (Sanhedrin 45b) introduce an even more radical emendation by deleting טעונין טבילה altogether and by reading נקברין עמו instead of ולא היו קוברין...עמו. We find the evidence of these emending activities in the talmudical discourse, where according to another Baraitha the version אין נקברין is presented. The strenuous efforts at harmonizing the versions by interpretative methods cannot satisfy; even granted that עמו can mean "with him" or "next to him," it would hardly be plausible that the one term in the same Halakah would be employed not only in two different, but in this case even opposite connotations. Hence we must conclude that the Erfurt version טעונין טבילה is the only correct reading; it contains traces of the early Halakah, which held that raw materials and even the ground and all that is attached (מחובר) to it are contaminable by ritual taint of a human corpse.

Most probably it is this early phase of the Halakah in point which is tacitly assumed in the controversy between the Sadducees and Pharisees concerning the current of a liquid on the ground (ניצוק, cf. Yadayim IV, 7). The commentaries have observed the difficulty in the light of the accepted Halakah which arises with the Pharisaic

---

[33] This opinion is ascribed in a Baraitha (Sanhedrin 46b) to R. Yose and his colleagues. I have my doubts, however, whether this Baraitha is of Tannaitic origin. Considering the Midrash (Sifrei Deuteronomy, paragraph 221) on Deut. 21:23 ותלית אותו על עץ — בעץ התלוש, ולא בעץ המחובר, we may conclude that here, as quite frequently in the Talmud, the cited Baraitha contains Amoraic additions. Cf. Midrash Tannaim, p. 132 and TP Nazir VII (55d).

retort, אמת המים הבאה מבית הקברות, since such a current is מחובר and would not be contaminable, even if a human corpse is lying in its flow; hence it would not represent a parallel to ניצוק. Moreover, we must pay attention to the wording of the Mishnah: a current which flows *from* a cemetery — not one which flows over a cemetery. The accepted Halakah, however, rules out the possibility that a current flowing naturally is contaminable. All these difficulties dissolve, however, if we accept that the controversy reported in this Mishnah tacitly assumes that even מחובר לקרקע is contaminable. Hence the Pharisees point to the special case in which a current is not contaminable, i. e., when it flows from a cemetery, but not over it. This case represents a perfect parallel to ניצוק: the upper part of the current is contaminated by corpses in the cemetery, but as soon as it flows outside the burial ground it obtains purity, because we (Pharisees) do not consider the entire flow of the current as conjunctive and transmissible of contamination; in other words: ניצוק אינו מטמא, which is what the Pharisees want to maintain. We cannot trace the exact time at which the revision of this Halakah of מחובר took place. The terminus ad quem is the era of R. Eliezer b. Hyrcanus, who already took the revised Halakah for granted (*cf.* Kelim XV, 2). It is clear from the controversy[34] between the Tanna and his colleagues that a number of specific points were yet under dispute; only R. Eliezer held the view that מחובר לקרקע — כקרקע, whereas his opponents granted this inviolability by impurity only to the natural ground proper, but they held that anything else, however solidly attached to the ground, is liable to contamination. Our document reflects the early phase of this Halakah, which did not discriminate between קרקע and מחובר לקרקע — the ground and whatever is attached to it are both liable to ritual contamination.

We would assume that the early Halakah knows of טומאת מחובר only with regard to contamination by a human corpse. The biblical statement (Num. 19:14) וכל אשר באוהל יטמא שבעת ימים, which the Jon. Targum renders: מכל דבמשכנא ואפילו קרקעיתיה ואבנוי וקיסוי ומנוי (*all* that is within the tent, even its ground, its stones, wooden chips, and vessels); the Mishnah (Oholoth XV, 5) states: שארצו שלבית כמוהו (see also Tosefta, *ibid.* XV, 4, ed. Zuck., p. 612[26]); Midrash Hagadol formulates it: לעשות קרקעו שלבית כמותו and the Sifre Num. (para. 126, ed. Hor., p. 162₄) שומע אני אף הקש והחריות והעצים והאבנים והאדמה במשמע (the early Halakah) — all these refer to טומאת מחובר whose subject is

---

[34] This is discussed elaborately in Bava Bathra 65b–66b; *cf.* my interpretation of this Talmudic passage in ראב'ן, ed. Raschkes (Jerusalem, 1914), vol. II, p. 26d.

exclusively טומאת מת as the verse commences: זאת התורה אדם כי ימות באוהל,
from which it is inferred that אדם is the subject of this טומאת מחובר
(Rashi on Num. 31:19).

We should like to point out that the cited Apocryphic ברייתא דנדה
(above, p. 81) is not the only source which holds to the opinion that
a woman during her menstrual period would contaminate the ground
on which she walks, the stone on which she sits, etc.; the Falashas, too,
know of such a tradition and they remove the menstruating woman
for the duration of her period from the contaminable dwelling to a
special abode.[35] Our document, however, teaches that the natural
ground and attached raw materials are affected in טומאת מחובר
only by a human corpse, as we have already emphasized above
(p. 82).

However, this view is not, as Büchler contends, to be found only
among the latter-day Samaritans; it is in keeping with the early
Halakah. Moreover, Büchler states that even if we want to explain
טומאת האדם[36] in our document as meaning contamination by a human
corpse, we could find only a single parallel in a Halakah of Yavneh;
the earlier Tannaim know nothing of an object, contaminated by a
human corpse, which can communicate its taint to a person. This is an
erroneous statement. R. Tarfon — an eye-witness of the catastrophe
in 70 C. E. — attests to the application of the principle חרב הרי הוא
כחלל in interpreting an early misunderstood Halakah,[37] but even
the schools of Shammai and Hillel discuss the Halakah that כלים
הנוגעין במת מטמאין אדם as a well-known and established principle, which

---

[35] See A. Epstein, *Eldad Ha-Dani* (p. 172; ed. A. M. Haberman, Jerusalem,
5710, vol. I, p. 173) and my remarks in: *The Students' Annual of the Jewish Theological Seminary*, New York, 1914, p. 150, note 47, where I have demonstrated that
the Mishnah, too, knows of this tradition of separate housing for women (see also
Maimonides, *Guide* 3,43 and Naḥmanides on Gen. 31:35 and Lev. 12:4). Josephus
Ant. III, 11,3 (261) even reports that a menstruating woman may not remain
in town. The rabbinic Halakah is decidedly opposed to such a practice (Kelim
I, 8), but the Karaites do accept this rigorous separation (Anan's *Book of Laws*,
ed. Harkavy, 41). *Cf.* also Y. H. Schorr, החלוץ VIII, pp. 51–59, but his wild ideas are
not to be taken seriously.

[36] In explaining this expression Büchler refers us to Lev. 5:3 and 22:4–5, where
it means ritual taint of various origins. However, in the former reference it means,
according to Tannaitic tradition, contamination by a human corpse; in the latter
reference it is not even mentioned at all! In Lev. 7:21 it also means contamination
by a human corpse, according to the Sifra *ad loc.* (=Zevaḥim 44a).

[37] Oholoth XVI, 1; Tosefta *ibid.* XV, 12 (Zuckermandel 613, l. 23); Shabbath
16b–17a and Meiri *ibid.* (ed. Wien, 1866, p. 10; ed. Lange, Jerusalem, 5725, p. 64).

they used as the premise in the endeavor to decide a derivative controversy.[38]

Our discourse on these instances of טומאת האדם in tannaitic litera-ture ought to suffice to demonstrate the untenability of Büchler's contention[39] that the Halakah in our document reflects the influence of an anti-rabbanite movement in the eighth century. Furthermore, we have noted that even in the one single case in which the sectarian tenet is in agreement with Karaite teaching — opposition to marrying nieces — this agreement is merely coincidental and does not reflect any historical relationship between the earlier and the latter-day heretics.[40]

Aside from the alleged anti-rabbanite Halakah, Büchler contends that our sectarian document contains direct borrowings from the Talmud. He cites the following proofs:

a) The discussion of who is authorized to make the determination of the status of someone suspected of leprosy (13,5).

This Halakah corresponds, as Schechter, *loc. cit.*, already noted, to a parallel in rabbinic sources ascribed to Hillel, whence it is borrowed. Büchler presents his case as if in rabbinic sources this Halakah was

---

[38] Tosefta Oholoth XV, 9–10 and R. Simson Sens' commentary on Mishnah Oholoth XV, 9. The words דבר אחר at the beginning of XV, 10 (613, 1. 10) in this Tosefta are not introducing a new passage in addition to the discussion between the two schools, but rather the continuation of the Hillelites' argument: "More-over . . ."; the Hillelites employ the same terminology for an additional argu-ment in Tosefta Berakhoth VI, 1–2 (139, 1. 15). Zuckermandel, *Gesammelte Aufsätze*, vol. I, p. 54, maintains that the well-known tradition which ascribes to R. Shimeon b. Shetah (Sabbath 14b and parallels) the contaminability of metal implements גזר על כלי מתכות will merely indicate that he was the author of the Halakah חרב הרי הוא כחלל. I doubt such a possibility since it was already assumed in Tannaitic sources, such as Mishnah and Sifrei, that this Halakah was of biblical origin; hence it seems most improbable that a Baraitha be credited with still pre-serving the historical report on the rabbinic authority who introduced this Halakah.

[39] Büchler does not even mention that this Halakah is recorded already in the Mishnah (Oholoth I, 3 — a pre-Akiva tradition!). He refers to the non-canonical source, Sifrei Num. 130. The passage in the Sifra (on Lev. 5:2) which he quotes, has been correctly explained by Israel Lewy, as cited in Horovitz, *Der Sifre Zutta*, p. 7, note 5. This passage has no bearing whatsoever on our topic, since it deals only with a controversy on the case of ביאת מקדש; nobody, however, calls into question the validity of the Halakah that כלים שנגעו במת מטמאין אדם.

[40] Even were we to admit that this coincidence could be viewed as historically coherent, it could then only mean that the Karaites revived an early heretic doc-trine. Our elaborate discourse on the relationship between heretic and Karaite Halakah would still be valid.

handed down as a tradition traced back to Hillel. As a matter of
fact, these sources maintain exactly the opposite. They relate[41] that
Hillel came from Babylonia to Palestine for the purpose of investigating whether three Halakoth (the first of which concerned persons
who contracted leprosy) at which he had arrived by the Midrashic
method of applying hermeneutic rules would be confirmed by traditions prevailing in the Holy Land; he was gratified to discover that a
traditional practice corresponded to the Halakic conclusion reached
by his use of midrash.

It violates all the norms of responsible criticism to rely on talmudical sources only as long as they yield confirmation of our hypotheses, but to declare them unreliable as soon as they do not furnish
support for the desired conclusions. True enough, the existing text of
the cited Talmudical passage may be corrupt and its meaning disputable — yet we see no valid reason to doubt its historical value:
either this entire report about Hillel is a latter-day invention, or things
actually happened as recounted in the tannaitic-amoraic tradition.
The sources reveal no trace of attempts to restrict priestly prerogatives, duties or functions allegedly proposed by Hillel's Halakah con-

---

[41] *Cf.* Sifra on Lev. 13:36 (IV, 9, 16, p. 67a); Tosefta Negaim, end of first
chapter (619, l. 17); TP Pesaḥim VI (33a); Büchler, *ibid.*, note 71. Büchler deletes
in his quotation the characteristic sentence ודרש והסכים ועלה וקיבל הלכה. The correct
explanation thereof is already to be found in the commentary on Sifra, קרבן אהרן,
by Ibn Ḥayyim, cited by Weiss in his notes. A. Geiger, *Jüdische Zeitschrift*, II,
pp. 47 ff., and A. Schwarz, *Die Controversen der Schamaiten und Hilleliten*, p. 18,
mention the incorrect explanations of former commentators without quoting Ibn
Ḥayyim's correct one! We deem it unnecessary to refute the ridiculous caprice of
Geiger to make Hillel, according to this report, take over the "Leitung der Gesetz-
lehre." The correct explanation of the phrase דרש והסכים, as meaning דרש והסכים
להלכה, has been amply corroborated by W. Bacher, *Die älteste Terminologie der
jüdischen Schriftauslegung*, under סכם (הסכים) both in Tannaitic (I) and Amoraic (II)
terminology. The expression קבל הלכה is already recorded in the Mishnah (Peah
II, 6) as quotation from the mouth of Nahum the Scribe, who belonged to the
next to the last generation of the Second Temple. R. Eliezer b. Hyrcanus and his
colleague R. Yehoshua (Yadayyim IV,3; Eduyyoth VIII,7) expressed themselves
in similar terms: מקובל אני .... הלכה; hence there can be no doubt about the meaning of our passage here. See also Y. I. Halevy, *Doroth Harishonim*, II, p. 176;
III, p. 34, correcting Z. Frankel, *Darkai Hamishnah*, p. 40 who claims that
according to this report the Palestinians summoned Hillel to come from Babylon
and instruct them. This error is old: RABaD (on Sifra, *ibid.*) has Hillel invited to
teach in the Holy Land.

We should like to remark that Bacher is mistaken in stating (*Terminologie*, I,
p. 165 in note on קבלה) that there is no passage in which קבלה means תורה שבעל פה
(oral tradition); *cf.*, however, Avoth R. Nathan (B 42, ed. Schechter, p. 117) where
היה ר' מאיר אומר בקבלה can only mean: R. Meir explained this on basis of a tradition.

cerning the authorized declaration on the status of a person suspected
of leprosy. Hillel merely provided a *derash* as exegetic rationale for
deriving this Halakah from the biblical verse (Lev. 13:37). Our document records the early Halakah without citing Hillel's exegesis.
Büchler is very inaccurate when he talks here of "priestly privileges"
with respect to the authorized declaration of the status of a leper;
the Halakah in point, cited in our document and in the talmudical
sources, tends to restrict "priestly privileges."

How could anybody imagine, we wonder, that our document which
so zealously protects the prerogatives of the priests (*cf.* 10,5; 13,2),
could possibly have succumbed to Talmudic influence and have cur-
tailed their traditional functions? Even had we not known from
talmudic sources that this Halakah constitutes a very early component
of tradition, we could have established that this was so from the
evidence in our sectarian document.

By the way, we should like to note that this restriction of priestly
functions was probably due to circumstances prevailing outside the
Holy Land (חוצה לארץ), where learned Priests could no longer be
found, and it was, therefore, no coincidence that Hillel had to concern
himself with this question when he was still in Babylonia. I doubt
very much whether the biblical laws about leprosy were, according to
Talmudic Halakah, to be observed after the destruction of the Temple,
despite the evidence of Maimonides' codified ruling[42] to the contrary:
טהרת מצורע זו נוהגת בארץ ובחוצה לארץ בפני הבית ושלא בפני הבית.[43] The
Tosefta rules that these rules were applicable in the Holy Land and
abroad (VII, 15 and VIII, 1), without mentioning its dependence on or
independence of the Temple בפני הבית ושלא בפני הבית. Thus we may
conclude that according to the Tosefta the existence of the Temple
is indispensable for the application of this Halakah. Besides these
normative rules, the Tosefta presents a descriptive report[43a] from
the tannaitic period about R. Tarphon who purified three leprous
persons. R. Yehudah, who reports the episode, recounts that he learned

---

[42] טומאת צרעת 11,6 based on Tosefta Negaim VII, 15 (627, l. 33) and VIII, 1
(628, l. 7) for "abroad," and VIII, 2 (628, l. 13) for the view that the Temple is
unnecessary to the purification of a leper. In his Commentary of the Mishnah,
end of Negaim (XIV, 13, ed. Dérenbourg, p. 178) Maimonides cites these normative
Toseftoth and also the descriptive report of R. Yehudah when calling on R. Tarfon,
ibid., and Sifra on Lev. 14:4 (V, 1, 13, p. 70c).

[43] In his Commentary on the Mishnah, Maimonides reasons: לפי שאין לה (טהרת
מצורע) קשר בדבר מזה, וייטהר המצורע בו, ויישאר מחוסר כפרה; except for the atoning
sacrifices, he sees no necessity for predicating the purification process upon the
existence of the Temple.

[43a] Tosefta Negaim VIII, 2 (628, l. 13) and Sifra on Lev. 14:4 (V, 1, 13).

on this occasion seven Halakoth, among them ומטהרין בפני הבית ושלא
בפני הבית ומטהרין בגבולין (628₁₃). This report may relate to R. Tarphon
in his younger days, before the destruction of the Temple.[44] In the
light of my previous doubts, I have my reservations whether our text
concerning R. Yehudah's seven Halakoth is correct. The seventh,
ומטהרין בגבולין, makes little sense, particularly after the sixth Halakah
allegedly already states that the existence of the Temple is dispensable.
Since a leprous person can be purified outside of the Holy Land, there
is certainly nothing gained by explicitly stating it may also be done
בגבולין, anywhere in the Holy Land outside of Jerusalem. I suspect
that the entire passus of the sixth Halakah has been added as a later
gloss; R. Yehudah reported only that R. Tarfon purified lepers
outside of Jerusalem. The conflation is probably due to a misunderstood reading of (הלכות) ש' as שבע instead of the correct שש; to justify
the incorrect seven, another Halakah, *in re* the dispensability of the
Temple for such purification, was inserted. R. Tobia b. Eliezer cites
in his commentary the following amoraic statement:[45] אמר ר' יוחנן:
מיום שחרב בית המקדש אין טומאה ממצורע. This statement is found nowhere
in Talmud or Midrash.[46] In any case, it is most probable that our
document originated during the time when the Temple existed and
when these laws were being observed without any qualification.

b) Sale of sacrificeable animals to gentiles.

In discussing the laws regarding this situation Büchler develops
his thesis even further. He claims to find in our document not only
a Halakah of Hillel but even Halakoth of talmudic authorities who

---

[44] *Cf.* R. Shimshon of Sens on Sifra, *ibid.*

[45] לקח טוב on Exod. 4:6 (p. 21) and on Lev. 13:2 (p. 70). The latter is based on
the Sifra, *ibid.* (IV, 1, 9), corresponding to our passage in the document: ללמד שאין
טומאה וטהרה אלא מפי כהן; הא כיצד? חכם שבישראל רואה את הנגעים, ואומר לכהן, אע"פ שוטה
(לקח טוב — אע"פ שאינו בקי) אמור טמא — והוא אומר: טמא — אמור טהור, והוא אומר: טהור.
On basis of this Halakah, he writes in לקח טוב: והיינו דאמר ר' יוחנן: מיום שחרב בית המקדש,
אין טומאה ממצורע, פירוש ... טומאה ממצורע ליכא כלל — שאין בהם מורה. The importance
of the מורה is derived in the Sifra on Lev. 14:57 (V, 7, 16, p. 74d): חנניה בן חכינאי
אומר: ולמה בא .להורות? ללמד שאינו רואה את הנגעים עד שיורנו רבו. RABaD cites this
passage *ad loc.*: להורות — מלמד שאינו רואה את הנגעים עד שיורנו. וכן גרסינן בחגינה ירושלמי
פ' אין דורשין: אמר רב, אין אדם רשאי לומר דבר בנגע הצרעת אלא אם כן ראה או שמש. כיצד הוא
עושה? בתחילה רבו פותח לו ראשי פרקים ומסכים; למדנו שאע"פ שהוא תלמיד ותיק ויודע ומבין את
הכל מדעתו — אינו רשאי לעשות בהם מעשה אלא על ידי פתיחת רבו; ומפיק טעמיה הכא מדכתיב
.להורות — עד שיורנו רבו. On the cited text from TP Ḥagigah II, 1 (77a) see B. Ratner,
Ahavath Zion Virushalaim, Ḥagigah, p. 62.

[46] *Cf.* on this passage Reifmann, רוח חדש, p. 21, who overlooked the discourse
by R. Zalman of Wolozin in תולדות אדם (Dyhrenfurt, 1800), p. 36a: *cf.* also R. Jacob
David in his annotations on the Sifra (ed. Warsaw, 1866), p. 56a, note 16. The
Karaites hold the view that nowadays the laws concerning leprosy are inapplicable

belong to a much later period. True enough, the Talmud knows of a prohibition against selling certain things to a gentile; its parallel is recorded in our document (12,8): No man sell "clean"[47] beasts and birds to gentiles, so that they may not offer them as sacrifice." As we have demonstrated, *loc. cit.*, this Halakah is predicated on the existence of the Temple. Büchler has not only misunderstood the character of this decree but he also misinterpreted the discussions regarding it in the Talmud. Hence he arrived at the conclusion that this rabbinical decree was promulgated after the destruction of the Temple. The Talmud (Avodah Zarah 7b) cites a Baraitha reporting on a controversy between Nahum, the Medean and his colleagues concerning details of this decree. The more lenient opinion of Nahum, the Medean was refuted with the words נשתקע הדבר ולא נאמר (the matter is now obsolescent). Büchler quotes all of this Baraitha, in his own translation — but he omits the expression נשתקע הדבר which is of such decisive significance for our discussion. This expression cannot mean anything else but the factual statement that this matter (decree) has been obsolete for such a long time that nobody can know any longer the subtle distinction which you are stating ולא נאמר. Consultation of dictionaries will prove that this is the only correct explanation of this expression, as e. g., נשתקע השם (no longer traceable, fallen into oblivion). This meaning emerges clearly from Tannaitic sources[48] which employ the full expression נשתקע הדבר ולא נאמר עכשיו.[49] This Nahum the Medean is known to have been a judge in Jerusalem before 70 C. E., and he survived the destruction of the Temple. Shortly after the catastrophe of 70 he must have left the Holy Land,[50] or he must have died soon thereafter, for he is never mentioned as being in the circle of scholars

---

because we know of no כהן מיוחס; *cf.* Nicomedia, נן עדן, paragraph טומאה וטהרה, ch. V; *cf.* Maimonides in his Code, Terumoth VII,9 and RaDBaZ thereon. See my note in גנזי שכטר, I, p. 78.

[47] *Cf.* above.

[48] Sifra on Lev. 11:33 (III 7,7, p. 53d); Tosefta Kelim B.Q. II, 2 (570, l. 29). We may consider the possibility of reading עד שבאו instead עכשיו, though not necessarily.

[49] *Cf.* Y. I. Halevy, *Doroth Harishonim*, Ic, p. 237, who does not cite the passage in Sifra.

[50] It is remarkable that only Babylonian authorities know whatever little that is reported in the Talmud about the life of Nahum, the Medean. R. Nathan (the Babylonian) mentions Nahum, the Medean as one of the official judges in Jerusalem (מדייני גזירות בירושלם) — Tosefta Bava Bathra IX, 1 (410, l. 17); Kethuvoth 105a. The Babylonian Amora R. Aha observes (Avodah Zarah 7b) in a remark to Abayye: נברא רבא אתא אתא מאתרין, a great man Nahum came from here. On basis of this remark one would be inclined to explain Nahum's toponym, "the Medean," as referring to his Babylonian origin.

who carried on under R. Yoḥanan b. Zakkai. Furthermore we should like to point out that he did not yet bear the title Rabbi, whereas *all* scholars who were his contemporaries and survived the destruction of the Temple, who continued their activities in the Beth Hamidrash, are mentioned with the title Rabbi.[51] Hence we *may* conclude that he flourished before the year 70. We therefore reach the conclusion that this rabbinic decree antedates Nahum by several generations, since his colleagues point out in the discussion of some detail of this law that the circumstances attending this decree are no longer known. It would therefore be erroneous to contend that such a directive in our document must have been derived from talmudic legislation.

c) Traffic with the banished.

The ruling in our document prohibiting all traffic with anyone who had been excommunicated serves Büchler as proof that our sect derived this ruling from the Talmud, since this rule bears the imprint of later legislation; Büchler maintains that the earliest possible date for such a rule would be the tannaitic period. It is hard to understand how Büchler could have arrived at such an idea in view of the passage in Ezra 10:8. Without the institution of the ban, Ezra would have been unable to constitute the Jewish community;[52] the rigorous observance of ostracism is of absolute necessity for a minority to keep its members under control when it cannot count on enforcement by authority of the state. Thus Josephus reports (*Bel. Jud.* II, 8,8) that the Essenes would rather see a banished member starve to death than transgress the ban and save him from starvation. The same type of rigorous communal discipline prevailed in the early church; it is especially evident in the words of Paul (I Cor. 5:5 ff.). Even if we had not found anything explicit in our document about the application of a ban to insubordinate or delinquent members of the sect, we would have assumed as a matter of course their employment of such methods. On the other hand, it would run counter to all historical

---

[51] Z. Frankel, דרכי המשנה, p. 71, note 7 is partially to be corrected. R. Simeon of Miẓpeh bears the title Rabbi as well as R. Ẓadoq, R. Dosa b. Hyrcanus, R. Simeon הצנוע and many others — because all these scholars were still active after the year 70. H. Graetz (*Geschichte der Juden*[5], III, p. 759, note 20,5) overlooked that in the NT the honorific Rabbi is used exclusively in respectful address, but not as a title of status.

[52] *Cf.* Schürer, *Geschichte*[4], II, p. 507 ff., who refers to the practice of banishment in the days of Jesus, reflected in many NT passages. Wiesner's contention (*Der Bann*, p. 11) that the "isolation" from the community under Ezra was nothing but an administrative edict of regional expulsion, without any bearing on the later application of a ban, requires no refutation, since it is completely unfounded.

information and judgment if we would attribute to the Tannaim the initiative for such measures of enforcing communal discipline.

Not being satisfied in ascribing the rules of ban and excommunication to talmudic origin, Büchler goes further and maintains that the reason offered in our sectarian passage — "until then let no man be amenable to any traffic with him in property affairs or in work, for all the holy ones of the Highmost have cursed him" (20,7–8) — indicates that this sectarian edict is of a much later provenance than the talmudic legislation. The notion that the saintly angels take part in the malediction pronounced with the ban is first found in the Gaonic responsa and in Pirqei de R. Eliezer, which work dates from the Gaonic period.

We should like to make the following observations on Büchler's arguments: it is very doubtful that the term כל קדושי עליון (all the holy ones of the Highmost) is meant as a reference to angels, although this term can elsewhere be shown to refer to angels. Here it might possibly refer to the sectarians in good standing; just one line above they are called אנשי תמים הקדש, men of perfect holiness, or men of holy perfection. Moreover, we have already pointed out that the talmudic sources know of the concept that angels condemn the sinners with maledictions. It is the same concept with which we meet here in our document. It demands that the sinner be entirely cut off and excluded from the community "for the holy ones of the Highmost have cursed him" on account of his transgressions. Proof for the validity of this interpretation is offered in the passage of our document (12,22) which is also based on this concept, employed here as a warning: "And in keeping with this ordinance shall the seed of Israel walk — and they shall not be cursed (לא יוארו)." Malediction by angels may be traced to the employment of this concept in the Song of Deborah (Judg. 5:23), where the inhabitants of Meroz are cursed because they did not participate in combatting Israel's enemies. The Talmud (Moed Qaṭan 16a) interprets that Meroz is the name of an angel כוכבא=מלאך, (cf. Commentary on Mashqin by R. Shelomoh b. HaYathom, ed. Chajes, ad loc.); hence the passage in Judges is understood to express the curse of an angel, uttered by their appointed accurser (cf. also Galatians 1:8: But though we, or an angel from heaven, preach any other gospel unto you than that which we have preached — let him be accursed).

d) Formula of Confession (20,28–29).

"And they confess before God (and they say): we have acted wickedly, we and also our ancestors, by walking capriciously against the laws of the covenant." Büchler first emends our text in a most

untenable way and then, on the basis of this "text," he makes his case
for a very late dating of the document! He reads our passage in point:
חטאנו הרשענו ועוינו; on the basis of his emended reading he finds Gaonic
influence in this formula of confession. Schechter's facsimile of the
text admits no doubt that the reading of the third word is not ועוינו.
There is room for certainly no more than three letters. We shall not
engage in discussing here our proposed reading ונם (the scribe may
possibly have written first ואנו, then have preferred ואנחנו), but ועוינו
is in any case graphically impossible. Even if we were to assume, for
the sake of argument, the validity of Büchler's proposed emendation,
his inferences are nevertheless fallacious. There is no possible connection between such a formula and the confession recommended by the
Gaonim. In the matter of the Gaonic form of the confession, Büchler
has overlooked the observation[53] of R. Menaḥem Hameiri (on Yoma
86b) that this form is recommended not as the text of the formal
public prayer, but as a substitute form used in private prayer by those
who did not wish to recite the detailed roster of sins arranged in
alphabethical order, such as אשמנו or על־חטא. The passage from Meiri's
חיבור התשובה,[54] which Büchler does cite, would certainly have to be
read [ועל דרך זה היה נוסח הוידוי] של הרבה גאונים instead of בימי הגאונים.
Even in this citation it remains a moot question whether by Gaonim
Meiri meant the exact term referring to the heads of the Babylonian
Yeshivoth, or the looser use of the term as an honorific referring to the
great European luminaries in the talmudic studies. The latter opinion
seems more plausible, since opposition to reciting the detailed confession in the על חטא or אשמנו forms first arose among Spanish and
French scholars,[55] whereas the Gaonic prayer texts contain the על־חטא
and the Gaon Rav Amram indeed expressly attests that this prayer was
customarily recited in the Yeshivoth.[56] In any case, whatever may be

---

[53] *Beth Habbeḥirah* (ed. Jerusalem, 5645, p. 78a; ed. Benei Beraq, 5726, p. 257).

[54] *Book of Repentance* (ed. New York, 1950), p. 198 and p. 402.

[55] *Cf.* R. Aaron of Lunel, *Orḥot Ḥayyim*, H. Yom Hakkippurim, pp. 106–107; R.
Zidqiah dei Mansi, *Shibbolei Halleqet* (ed. S. Buber, 1886), p. 296.

[56] *Cf.* Or Zarua (ed. Zitomir, 5622), vol. II § 281 (p. 128a): בסדר רב עמרם כתב.
מנהג בשתי הישיבות לומר בערבית ושחרית ומנחה... ועל חטא הבא באל״ף בי״ת. The same
quotation from Seder R. Amram Gaon is in Mordekai on Yoma, § 727. In the
printed edition of Seder R. Amram Gaon and its Mss. this sentence is not found.
For זה הודוי in Seder R. Amram Gaon (ed. Coronel, vol. I, p. 47a, top; ed. Frumkin,
vol. II, p. 342) the reading in Manhig, p. 59a (No. 53) is הודוי זוטא, i. e., אשמנו; this
designation reveals that the Gaonim called על־חטא most probably ודוי רבא; *cf.*
I. Elbogen, *Gottesdienst*, p. 537, who cites this designation from Siddur Rashi
(ed. Buber, p. 96): לפיכך צריך כל יחיד לומר... ודוי זוטא, ודוי רבה, ואשמנו, ועל־חטא.
[*Cf.* also R. Asher, Yoma VIII, § 25; R. Nissim, *ibid.*, on Alfasi (96b); Kol-Bo

the elaborations preferred by some authorities, all of the various views agree that the basic obligatory formula of the confession is חטאנו עוינו הרשענו ופשענו; yet in the formula reconstructed by Büchler through emendation the significant term פשענו is missing. It is therefore clear that the formula of confession in our document is independent not only of the Gaonic tradition, but even of the mishnaic formula. The latter, prescribed for the High Priest on the Day of Atonement,[57] reads either חטאתי עויתי ופשעתי or עויתי פשעתי וחטאתי, and is different again from biblical formulae (I Kings 8:47; Ps. 106:6; Dan. 9:5; II Chron. 6:37), which follows the general pattern of חטא, עוון, רשע (*cf.* Yoma 36a). Büchler tends, contrary to his bias towards post-Geonic dating, to follow rather the biblical pattern. However, even leaning on this biblical formula, it would be strange indeed that the sect should disarrange the traditional sequence found nowhere else — to mention עוון as last. Büchler's emendation thus appears all the more indefensible.

e) Proof-texts for halakhic Midrash.

Büchler concludes his "demonstrations" that our document borrows from talmudic Halakah with some observations on the essential differences in midrashic exegesis between the rabbinic literature and our sectarian document. The Halakic midrash of our document is based on texts from any book of the Bible, whereas the Talmud uses texts from only the five books of the Torah as sources of Halakah. The midrashic method employed by Anan for Karaite Halakah follows the same principle as our document — hence it follows, in Büchler's view, that our document must be dated close to the Karaite period.

The double fallacy at the basis of this thesis has been discussed at length. Here I should only like to add that whereas Büchler knows of just one single example in the Talmud where Halakah is derived from a prophetic book, I have on hand the work מקור ההלכות והדינים by R. Abraham Efron (Wilno, 1901) in which no less

---

§ 68; R. Yiẓḥaq Gaiath (ed. Bamberger), p. 59]. The *genre* of alphabetical rosters of confession is very old, as attested by Rom. 1:29; *cf.* J. Rendel Harris, *The Teaching of the Apostles*, pp. 82–86. Elbogen's discourse on ודוי requires many essential complements and corrections. R. Saadiah Gaon has אשמנו, but no alphabethical על חטא, according to Frumkin, *Seder R. Amram Gaon*, II, p. 331 (*Siddur R. Saadiah Gaon*, Jerusalem 1941, p. 259; p. 261; p. 409).

[57] *Cf.* Yoma III, 8; IV, 2; and the remarks by R. Aaron of Lunel, *loc. cit.*; *cf.* also R. Saadiah Gaon, אמונות ודעות, ch. V, end of § 6 (ed. 1880, p. 123; ed. 1864, p. 92; ed. 1878, p. 145): חטאתי ועויתי, אמור: ועל כן מנהגנו לומר לחולה קרוב לפני מותו, ופשעתי, ותהא מיתתי כפרה לכל עוונותי.

than two hundred Halakoth are listed which the Talmud derives
from proof-texts in the Prophetic books and the Hagiographa.[58]

f) Methodology of Aggadic Midrash.

As far as Aggadic Midrash is concerned, our document offers
(6,4 ff.) an allegory of the Song of the Well (Num. 21:17–20) which
invalidates Büchler's "distinction" between rabbinic and sectarian
Midrash, since the almost verbatim agreement with talmudic parallels is so obvious, as we have pointed out elsewhere. The same
applies to the rather fantastic interpretation of Amos 5:26–27
(cf. above, p. 196). With regard to this "Pesher" (7,14 ff.) Büchler has
asserted that in all of rabbinic literature there is no Aggadic homily
which is even remotely similar to this type of interpretation. Since he
does not present any further discussion on the "peculiarity" of this
Midrash, we need not develop this point any further. True enough,
this interpretive handling of the passage in Amos sounds fantastic
and far-fetched — but are there not hundreds and thousands of
examples to be found in rabbinic and Alexandrian as well as Christian
literature of the interpretation of biblical passages in a comparably
fantastic and far-fetched manner, which is in no way other than the
strained and forced methodology of the sectarian Midrash under
discussion. Moreover, by dividing this sectarian Midrash into its
component parts we are able to adduce exact parallels to every one of
its elements from the whole range of Jewish literature.

Amos said, as quoted in our document,[59] והגליתי את סכות מלככם
which our document takes as an allusion ספרי התורה הם סוכת המלך.
The biblical סִכּוּת is read (or interpreted?) as if it said סוּכַּת or סָכּוֹת;
the Septuagint, Symmachos, the Vulgate and the Peshitta also "read"
סָכּוֹת in, or into, this passage. Hence our document is here in con-

<hr>

[58] Efron's compilation of biblical passages which serve as proof-texts and basis
for Halakic derivation is neither complete nor exhaustive. He confines himself
almost exclusively to the Babylonian Talmud, without any attention to the Palestinian Talmud, or to Tannaitic source material such as Mishnah, Tosefta or the
Halakic Midrashim! We should like to draw attention particularly to the fact that
there is *not a single book* in the Bible which has not been used as the source of
Halakah in the Tannaitic-Amoraic literature. Since Efron gives inaccurate references
or none at all to the Prophetic books Obadiah, Jonah, Micah, Habakkuk, and
Haggai, we should like to add the following references to his list:

Obad. 1:7 — cited by R. Eleazar b. Pedath in Sanhedrin 92a;
Jonah 3:8 — cited by R. Yoḥanan in TP Taanith II, 1, 65b;
Mic. 4:12 — cited by R. Mathana in Bava Meẓi'a 89b;
Hab. 2:5 — cited by R. Ḥiyya b. Yosef in Bava Bathra 98a;
Hag. 2:12 — cited by Rav in Pesaḥim 16b.

[59] See above.

formity with a very early tradition of exegesis. This exegetical "tabernacle" is then interpreted in the allegorical sense — the Torah which shelters and protects its observers. Philo[60] follows about the same direction of thought when he says that the tabernacle (σκηνη) represents divine virtue (ἡ θεῖς ἀρετή). The Torah, however, is not only the protection of the King (ספרי התורה הם סוכת המלך), but even the protection of all Israel — the prophet says מלככם merely because "the King" is tantamount to the entire community (המלך הוא הקהל); in this allegorical representation סוכת מלככם stands for סוכת קהלכם.[61] Rabbinic sources know of a similar logion: ראש הדור הרי הוא ככל הדור — the leader of the generation is equivalent to the whole generation;[62] such a logion is to be found, also, in medieval authors.[63]

Just as סוכת המלך stands as allegorical representation for Torah, so the expression (Amos 5:26) כיון צלמיכם is taken as an allusion to the prophetic books וכיון הצלמים הם ספרי הנביאים. They read this word as כֵּיוָן, in the Aramaic connotation of "correct," "orthodox." That this phrase was an allusion to the Prophetic books was so self-evident to the sectarians that it required no further demonstration. More difficult was the exegesis of צלמיכם, the modifier of כיון; even this was interpreted along a customary line. The Prophetic books, the orthodox doctrine כיון, were treated by Israel like transient shadows, silhouettes without substance — which were dealt with with contempt: וכיון הצלמים הם ספרי הנביאים — אשר בזה ישראל את דבריהם. Thus we have the contrast of כיון, the rightly and soundly established, over against צלם, the insubstantial shadow.[64]

Even the conclusion of this Midrash, on כוכב אלהיכם אשר עשיתם לכם follows traditional homiletics: והכוכב הוא דורש התורה הבא דמשק again with a proof-text (Num. 24:17): כאשר כתוב: דרך כוכב מיעקב. According to the Aggadic tradition[65] אין כוכבים אלא צדיקים, stars are symbolic of

---

[60] *Quis Rerum Divinarum H.*, XXIII (ed. M. I., p. 488).

[61] [The author revises here his earlier view of צלמים. *Cf.* p. 34.]

[62] Tanḥuma IV (ed. Buber, p. 129 and parallels cited in his note 369); *cf.* the formulation in RaSHI on Num. 21:21: [כי הנשיא הוא הכל] נשיא הדור הוא ככל הדור.

[63] R. Joseph b. Meir Zabara, ספר שעשועים (ed. Israel Davidson), p. 74.

[64] The words in our document הצלמים ... בזה are certainly intended as distinct allusion to the biblical expression צלמם תבזה (Ps. 73:20), which helps us to understand that our passage is not upbraiding Israel for treating the prophets like idols, but as shadowy vague silhouettes.

[65] *Cf.* above; for the stars as allegory, or as symbol for righteousness, *cf. ibid.* and TP Nedarim III, 8 (38a bottom); Leviticus Rabba 30, 2 (ed. Margulies, p. 692 and parallels cited there); Pes. R. Cahana, ch. 27 (ed. Buber, p. 179b; ed. Mandelbaum, p. 405); Sifrei Deuteronomy 47 (ed. Friedmann, p. 83a); Midrash Tannaim on Deuteronomy (ed. Hoffmann), p. 40.

righteous persons, so that כוכב אלהיכם is interpreted as the God-sent
Righteous Teacher of Torah who made his advent in Damascus.

Thus we arrive at the following Midrash: And I shall cause the
Tabernacle of your King (i. e., the Torah) and the rightly established
doctrine which you treated as if it were a fleeting shadow, and also the
Star sent to you by your God (the Exegete of the Torah) to reach
those who have pitched their tents[66] in Damascus. Evidently there
is nothing in this Midrash which cannot be traced to multiple parallels
in rabbinic literature — whereas this entire method of interpretation
is alien to Karaism. Büchler's contention that the only kinship with
the midrashic method of our document can be found in Anan's work
is an absurdity unbecoming any serious scholar.

g) Literary criticism: opus musivum.[67]

An essential criterion for investigating the authenticity of any
historical source material is found in a comparative study of form,
language, style and composition between the document in question
and any corresponding material which has been established as genuine
and reliable. Hence it is important from the methodological aspect to
analyze and compare the linguistic character[68] of our document, as

---

[66] On מהלאה=מאהלי, *cf.* above, p. 34. The Aggadah very often employs the
device of metathesis for such associative exegesis; *cf.* Waldberg, דרכי השינויים, pp.
4a ff.; Philo also knows of this device in exegesis: e. g. *Legum Allegoria* I, XXI, where
he interprets Gen. 2:13 נחון=ניחון as "the goring river," by associating the word
by metathesis with גונח (נגחן). In Aggadic exegesis the vowels אהו״י are considered
equivalent (*cf.* Waldberg, *op. cit.*, pp. 6a ff.); hence מהלאה>מאהלי and thence מאהלו.

[67] *Cf.* above, pp. 299–300.

[68] *Cf.* above, *loc. cit.*, for extended discussion of this point; there we also have
defined the relationship of our document to the Pseudepigrapha. We should like
to supplement our observations there with pointing to the usage of אין with ל
and the infinitive ("one may not") in Ben-Sira (10:23; 39:21; 39:34) as well as in
our document (4,11). On 11,23 תחזר=יתאחר in Ben-Sira 38:16 see further on. Below
(pp. 376–381), I present a compilation of the peculiar fashion in which our document cites quotations. I have drawn attention (p. 193, n. 167), to the habit of rabbinic
literature to quote non-biblical phrases as if they were written in the Bible; I have
referred there, at the end of the note, to Sifrei Numbers 42 (ed. Friedmann, p. 13a,
note 23; ed. Lurie, p. 24, note 13 of R. Eliahu, the Vilna Gaon; ed. Horovitz, p. 47,
line 10). Hannaniah, the Dean of the Priests (see W. Bacher, *Aggadah der Tann.*,
I, 4, 3), is reported by this tradition to have declared that the significance of peace is
equivalent to the creation of the world, גדול השלום שקול כנגד כל מעשה בראשית, the
proof-text cited: שנאמר: יוצר אור ובורא חושך עושה שלום ובורא את הכל. This quotation is not the biblical verse (Isa. 45:7), but its paraphrase in the יוצר-benediction [*cf.* Ginzberg, *Commentary on the Pal. Talmud*, I, 1,8, p. 201]. Later copyists wanted to cite a biblical proof-text; therefore they substituted Amos 4:13
or Isa. 45:7. Hannaniah's logion requires equivalence of peace and world creation,

Büchler has done, in order to determine its provenance and date of composition. Unfortunately, he reached totally unwarranted results, for he began with basically false premises regarding with both the language of our document and the sources to be adduced as comparative material. His initial bias led him to assume that the mosaic pattern of style in our document — or more exactly: in its Aggadic parts — was unknown in early Jewish literature and emerged only in post-talmudic works, if we disregard Ben-Sira (the authenticity of which being rather doubtful). This is not the proper opportunity to discuss the authenticity of the Ben-Sira text, yet we cannot help registering our amazement at Büchler's opinion on the subject. To our knowledge, there seems to be almost unanimous scholarly agreement that the Hebrew text discovered in the Genizah is genuine; since the publication of R. Smend's elaborate and painstaking work *Die Weisheit des Jesus Sirach* (Berlin, 1906) any other judgment is hardly conceivable. Regardless of the question of the authenticity of these Hebrew fragments, the mosaic-pattern of style is so dominant in Ben Sira that it is no less clear in the Greek version than in the original Hebrew. This early example of a peculiar literary mode, the mosaic style, is paralleled throughout the Apocrypha and pseudepigrapha. Although this style originated in Hebrew literature, it left its characteristic imprint of mosaic pattern even upon those works of this genre which were originally composed in the Greek language, e. g., the Epistle of Jeremiah, which consists essentially of a patchwork of biblical quotations. The early church adopted this literary genre from the synagogue. Quite a number of books of early Christian literature are nothing but

---

when "He makes peace — (thus) He creates everything" — hence there is no doubt that the emendation proposed by R. Eliahu of Vilna, which is partly corroborated by Yalquṭ Shimeoni I, § 711, is the only valid reading. This is not only warranted by the context, but also confirmed by the Midrash on Lev. 26:6, cited by RaSHI and the Yalquṭ Shimeoni I, § 672, with the proof-text וכן הוא אומר: עושה שלום ובורא את הכל. Numbers Rabba 11 cites this Midrash anonymously — גדול שלום שהוא שקול כנגד הכל (not as in Sifra, Mid. Hag. Lev., p. 658 and Mid. Hag. Num., ed. Rab., p. 97), but in order to indicate that he is not quoting from the Bible, but citing a prayer text, he says אנו אומרים instead of the Sifrei's שנאמר, because at that time they thought that a term traditionally employed to introduce a biblical quotation would be misleading when citing from a prayer. Cf. also Avoth R. Nathan B 12 (ed. Schechter, p. 49, note 9), where this prayer text is cited by Rabban Gamaliel with the introductory term הרי הוא אומר.

Another example is presented by Midrash Aggadah (ed. Buber II, p. 5) which cites: שנאמר: גאל ישראל — ה' שפתי תפתח, joining the conclusion of the גאולה-benediction with the beginning of the Amidah. Cf. more examples in the notes of R. Eliahu Gutmacher on Berakhoth 30a (ed. Romm, p. 44d); [cf. also Ginzberg, *Commentary on the Palestinian Talmud* I, Berakhoth I, 8, p. 164.]

a collection of scriptural quotations and allusions. One only has to read such a work as the strongly anti-Judaic apocryphon V Ezra to realize that there is hardly a verse that has not been culled from the prophets.

The mosaic style is thus not, as Büchler contends, a criterion for the late date of our document; it is an example of a literary form which is traceable to centuries before the common era.[69] Büchler's erroneous notion that the mosaic pattern of style is a product of the Arabic period can be explained only by his mistake in drawing his comparative material solely from talmudic (tannaitic and amoraic) material, without adducing the Apocrypha and pseudepigrapha, to which field of literature our document belongs. This grave methodological error has been further aggravated by Büchler's failure to include all of the relevant literature from the talmudic period.

Our criticism of this failure refers particularly to his disregard of liturgical compositions from the period under discussion. As we have pointed out earlier the style of these prayer texts distinctly bears the same characteristics of mosaic pattern as our document and the Apocryphal and pseudepigraphical literature. Although it would seem superfluous to demonstrate this peculiarity of early Jewish liturgy, we ought to give at least one example.

The first benediction of the Amidah is probably the earliest Jewish liturgical composition. This prayer is put together entirely in biblical phrases. Since the respective biblical parallels and allusions of the Amidah text have not yet been completely traced (R. David Abudraham was, as far as we know, the only commentator who has paid attention to this phenomenon), we should like to demonstrate the mosaic pattern of its composition by analyzing the first benediction (Avoth).[70]

I Chron. 29:10 (Ab. Ps. 119:12)	ברוך אתה ה'
	אלהינו
Ezra 7:27	ואלהי אבותינו[71]
Exod. 3:16	אלהי אברהם אלהי יצחק ואלהי יעקב
Deut. 10:17	האל הגדול הגבור והנורא

[69] The early stages of this opus musivum style can already be found in the latter books of the Bible.

[70] [Cf. Ginzberg, Commentary on the Palestinian Talmud, vol. IV (Berakhoth V), p. 177 ff.]

[71] Cf. Mekiltha R. Yishmael, Bo 16 (on Exod. 13:3; ed. Friedmann, p. 19a; ed. Horovitz-Rabin, p. 60): ומנין שאומרים ברוך אתה ה' אלהינו ואלהי אבותינו, אלהי אברהם אלהי יצחק ואלהי יעקב? שנאמר (שמות ג, טו): ויאמר עוד אלהים אל משה כה תאמר אל בני ישראל: ה' אלהי אבותיכם, אלהי אברהם אלהי יצחק ואלהי יעקב וגו'.

Gen. 14:19–20	אל עליון
Isa. 63:7[72]	גומל חסדים טובים
Ruth 4:9 (Ab. Isa. 45:7; Deut 8:17 Targ. Onk.)	קונה הכל[73]
Jer. 2:2 (Ab. Lev. 26:42)[74]	זוכר חסדי אבות
Isa. 59:20	ומביא גואל
Ezek. 37:25	לבני בניהם
Ezek. 20:9, 14:22 (Ab. Isa. 63:16)	למען שמו
Isa. 63:9	באהבה
(Ab. Isa 33:22; Ps. 145:1)	מלך
Deut. 33:29 (Ab. Ps. 37:40)	עוזר
Deut. 33:29 (Ab. Isa. 63:8; Jer. 14:8)	מושיע
Deut. 33:29; Ps. 33:20	מגן
I Chron. 29:10 (Ps. 119:12)	ברוך אתה ה'
Gen. 15:1	מגן אברהם

h) Literary criticism: diction and vocabulary

Büchler sees other evidence of the late date of our document's composition in a number of expressions and words which he characterizes as products of medieval Hebrew. As a particularly gruesome example of corrupt diction he cites, first of all, the passage 13,2–4 which reads: ובקום עשרה אלימש איש כהן מבונן בספר ההגו
על פיהו ישקו כולם
ואם אין הוא בחון בכל אלה ואיש מהלויים בחון באלה
ויצא הגורל לצאת ולבוא על פיהו כל באי המחנה

Büchler's criticism is directed foremost at the improper application of biblical phraseology, as Gen. 41:40 על פיך ישק; Josh. 16:1 (and in many other biblical passages) ויצא הגורל; and לצאת ולבוא in Deut. 31:2 et al.

We should like to retort with the following observation:

[72] חסדי ה' אשר גמלנו ורב ט ו ב = גומל חסדים טובים.

[73] קניתי את כל; this expression circumscribes in later usage what in the Bible is termed קונה שמים וארץ. In consideration of the biblical expression which has been retained in the summary of the Amidah for the Eve of Sabbath (מעין שבע), one would tend to see in קונה הכל a later version. We should like to point out, however, that Ben-Sira already knows the versions (33:1; 45:23; 50:22; 51:4 in the Hebrew supplement) אלהי הכל and יוצר הכל. The latter patterned after Jer. 10:16; cf. also the coinage בורא את הכל in the very early יוצר-benediction (cf. p. 366) and Ben-Sira 24:8.

[74] Cf. also II Chron. 6:42 זכרה לחסדי דויד עבדך; R. David Abudraham's reference to Lev. 26:42 represents neither a philological nor a topical parallel to the formula of which the text of Amidah, in the pattern of opus musivum, is composed. There is a distinct difference between the invoking of divine remembrance with regard to the "deeds of lovingkindness" and the appeal to divine remembrance of His covenantal commitment.

על פיהו ישקו כולם = Gen. 41:40 — all the oldest translations, such as the Septuagint, Vulgate, Peshitta etc., have understood this phrase, whatever its origin may be, as an expression of order and obedience, and it is employed exactly in this sense here in our document.[75]

לצאת ולבוא is employed here in the same meaning as in the biblical passages, e. g., I Sam 29:6; II Kings 19:27 *et al.* I fail to see Büchler's point of criticism.

ויצא הגורל. The metaphorical usage of גורל is biblical (e. g., Isa. 17:14 = חלק), and hence there is nothing corrupt or strange in our passage, where it is used to mean "appointment."[76]

אל ימש is criticized by Büchler because he contends that in the Bible the stem מיש or מוש is never used without a local modifier. This is decidedly an error, for Exod. 13:22 and Nah. 3:1 employ this word in the same syntax and connotation as our passage, and the same holds for Ben-Sira[77] 40:10.

ובקום is not necessarily the infinitive of קום but, so I surmise, an Aramaism (Syriac קוּם) for the Hebrew[78] מקום = station.

מבונן Aramaism is perhaps also traceable in[79] מבונן = "versed," "erudite"; in vulgar Aramaic the stem בַּיֵן means "to teach," and in Hebrew the verba mediae ו and י use the Polel instead of Piel. The

---

[75] The tannaitic tradition, according to R. Shimeon b. Gamaliel (Gen. Rabba 90, 3, ed. Theodor-Albeck, p. 1102; Lev. Rabba 23, 9, ed. Margulies, p. 540; see their notes for parallels), understands ישק as a kiss of homage.

[76] R. Eliezer ha-Qalir (in his מלכיות for R. H. כי מלכי אנסיכה, line ל) even employs the expression ליום זה פור הפיל (for this allotted day) = ליום זה גורלו יצא, which aroused the irate criticism of R. Abraham ibn Ezra (Kohelet 5:1 כי המשליך גורל לא ידע מה יהיה).

[77] *Cf.* Smend, *op. cit.*, *ad loc.*, who reads with Cowley-Neubauer: לא תמוש (*cf.* Prov. 17:13). It would be easier to read תמוש or even תשוט, for ט and מ are easily interchanged by copyists of Hebrew Mss. The Greek ἐγένετο proves that the translator had no negative לא in his text.

[78] The early tannaite Tradition, according to R. Eleazar of Modin (Mekiltha R. Shimeon on Exod. 17:7, ed. Epstein-Melamed, p. 118), the term מקום was a designation of the celestial court: מיכן לבית דין הגדול ב"ה שנקרא מקום. R. David Hoffmann explains שנקרא מקום — ונקרא מקום מפני שהוא מכוון כנגד מקדש של מטה referring to Deut. 17:18. This explanation is untenable, for it assumes an identification between the celestial Temple and the celestial Court which cannot be supported by any source and which seems most improbable.

We should like to observe that Syriac קום is also a term referring to administration, which would be very appropriate in our passage. In the light of Isa. 46:17, ממקומו לא ימיש, however, it is more probable that we ought to read וממקום עשרה לא ימש; *cf.* also Ben-Sira 38:12: וגם לרופא תן מקום ולא ימוש מאתך כי גם בו צורך which also ties in topically.

[79] *Cf.* also Hosanna for Sabbath of Tabernacles (Qalir?) אום נצורה כבבת בוננת בדת נפש משיבה. The poetical form בוננת stands for מבוננת, but not for בוננה.

Hithpael (Hithpolel) התבונן means "to be attentive" as well as "to be understanding," and hence it is quite plausible to assume that the author who composed our document availed himself of the intended ambiguity[80] offered by בון, although its biblical connotation[81] is "to be attentive." In any event, Büchler's claim that מבונן here carries the meaning of "erudite," which may be traced to a homiletic interpretation in the Sifre,[82] is entirely unwarranted. It seems much more probable that the Tannaim and the authors of the Targum versions were familiar with the root בונן in the sense of "instructing," "teaching," which they applied to this biblical reference.[83]

Moreover, Büchler is guilty of a worse oversight in stating that בחון in the meaning of "versed," "experienced" is to be considered a word peculiar to the diction of our document. This very word in this very same meaning is sound biblical usage, rendered in the Targum as בחיר.[84] This word in our passage may quite justifiably be read as a *qetul* form; as such it occurs in Talmud and Midrash in the sense of "tried," "tested."[85]

Büchler errs also when he observes that נהיות presents an otherwise unknown noun in Hebrew literature. It occurs twice in Ben-Sira.[86] Comparison between verse 12 and verse 19 in Proverbs 13 will yield that נהיה corresponds to באה,[87] hence this connotation "future events"[88] in Isa. 41:22, where נהיות = באות.

Büchler's objection to יהותו (13,12) is a point well taken, since this reading is quite impossible; yet it is equally certain that we have to

---

[80] *Cf.* J. M. Casanowicz, *Paronomasia in the Old Testament* (Boston, 1894).

[81] Deut. 32:10; the versions have ἐπαίδευσεν αὐτον; docuit; Onkelos אלפינון פתגמי אוריתא, and similarly Jonathan and Yer., whereas the plain meaning requires: compassionate, encompassing attention and care.

[82] *Ad loc. cit.*, 313 (ed. Fink. p. 355), יבוננהו בעשרת הדברות; מלמד שהיה הדיבור יוצא מפי הקב"ה, והיו ישראל רואים אותו ומשכילים בו, ויודעים כמה מדרש יש בו, וכמה הלכה יש בו, וכמה קולים וחמורים יש בו, וכו'. Even here, the meaning of "observation and attention" is also implied, see also Mekiltha R. Yishmael, Yithro 9 (ed. Friedmann, p. 71b; ed. Horovitz-Rabin, p. 235) on Exod. 20:18; *cf.* also Targum, Josh. 1:3; I Kings 3:21.

[83] *Cf.* the versions (note 81); Sifra 12,14 (4) on Lev. 2:13 and the discussion of it in Menaḥoth 21a; Arukh BN and dictionaries.

[84] Jer. 6:27 *et al.*; *cf.* above, p. 284 (17).

[85] Pesaḥim 87b; Eliahu Zuṭa 9 (ed. Friedmann, p. 186).

[86] *Cf.* above p. 287.

[87] Ben Sira 42:19 τὰ ἐσόμενα; Isa. 41:22 τὰ ἐπέρχομενα.

[88] Hence its meaning in Ben Sira: future events. In our document its definite meaning is difficult to establish. Passage 13,8 נהיות עולם may satisfactorily be rendered as "events of yore"; it would be equally satisfactory to translate "concealed events to be expected in the future." In passage 2,10 ונהיַת (?) the rendition "future events" as well as "past events" is possible.

read יחוסו instead, which can be established[89] by comparing 13,12 with 14,3.

Definitely erroneous is Büchler's observation on pebble, flint= סלע[90] in 11,11 as a quite unusual connotation. He fails to pay attention to סלע = Sela, name of a certain weight/coin in Aramaic vernacular as well as in Mishnaic idiom;[91] hence it can not be doubted that the word סלע would not evoke exclusively the association with rock in an Aramean or Aramaic speaking Jew. It seems that Semitic languages do not distinguish emphatically between rock and stone (weight/coin); the Hebrew צור and the Aramaic טירנא connote rock as well as flint, sharp-edged stone-wedge, as (Josh. 5:2): חרבות צורים, "flint knives" and the Talmudic (Ḥullin 48b) טירנא "petrified-like tubercles."

Summing up these observations, we need go no further in order to disprove Büchler's contention that words like בחון, מבונן, נהיות or the connotation of "pebble," "flint" for סלע point to a Hebrew jargon which probably was at some time idiomatic with the Samaritans (!).

No less absurd is Büchler's thesis that there are Arabisms in our document. He refers to the already discussed form (13,12) יהות as probably an Arabism — as if under Arab influence the Hebrew root היה could become transformed into יהה. Büchler translates (20, 3,6) בהופע מעשיו: "when his actions will be revealed," remarking thereon: "not used before the Arab period." I know of no passage in medieval Hebrew from the Arab period in which הופיע connotes "reveal." On the other hand, I do recall a passage attributed to the Amora R. Yoḥanan (flourished in the beginning of the third century) in which the expression צפונות מופיע, "he uncovers the hidden"[92] occurs — ergo, the Amoraim of the third century, accordingly, bear in their vocabulary Arab influence! As we have noted already above, בהופע מעשיו actually means here: when his (bad) actions have become evident — a meaning alien to any connotation of הופע in the Hebrew literature of the Arab period; attested, however, in talmudic literature. In the Mid-

---

[89] The emendation (cf. ad loc. cit.) כפי היותו or כפי הייתו is graphically more likely than כפי יחוסו; but the passage 14,3 requires a qualification about the status and community relationship of the novice — יחוס is the word that the context makes us expect.

[90] I suspect that this passage would demand the reading of קלע instead of סלע. In ancient times a clod, קלע ועפר, is the material which served the functions of our contemporary toilet paper. See Anan's Code (ed. Harkavy, p. 26): צריך לקנוחי בקלאי שפיר; the correct old spelling is קֶלַע as in Syriac, not קלא as in Talmud and in Anan's Code.

[91] Cf. e. g., Mishnah Kelim XII, 7: A sela, disqualified as coin, which has been designated for use as a weight.

[92] Gen. Rabba 90, 4 (Theodor-Albeck, p. 1103).

rash[93] הופע is defined by the parallelism with מעיד עליו; thus its true meaning can no longer be doubted.[94]

The passage (9,10) לפנים השפטים או מאמרם cannot mean: before the judges or those vested with their authority (derived from Arabic أمير אמר), since *muammarun*, which Büchler probably had in mind, does not connote throughout "vested with authority," but rather "vested with governmental authority," a meaning which does not fit well for the passage in point. But why invent an Arabism, when the simple Hebrew מֵאֲמָרָם "on their behest" (biblical אֹמֶר mandate, command) would fill the bill completely. Above (p. 294, n. 68) we have already pointed out that the passage השופטים או מאמרם is nothing but a qualifying gloss of the preceding לפנים; a gloss, however, cannot possibly serve as proving ground for characterizing the linguistic or historical provenance of the entire document!

According to Büchler the passage (6,10) זולתם means, as in medieval Hebrew, "and others." Were that the case, our document would present here an absurd statement. Under the influence of Arabic, our medieval writers employed זולת, in the sense of the Arabic *gair*, as "and others also." Given this meaning, the passage in point would read: "And the Nobles of the People, they that have come to dig the Well ... and others also will obtain nothing." It would stress then the exact opposite of what was intended, since emphasis is laid upon the exclusive privilege of the Nobles who drew from the Well of the Exegete of the Law to obtain the highest and choicest, the True Doctrine! As we have stressed (above, p. 30 on 6,11) that זולתם refers to the true doctrine and its laws, hence the passage means: "and without them (the true laws) they will obtain nothing."

The passage (9,1) כל אדם אשר יחרים אדם מאדם presents a number of difficulties, which we have tried, *ad loc. cit.*, to solve by emendation. The validity of the solution that we proposed may be disputable; Juster, among others, (*Les Juifs dans l'Empire romain*) accepted it. In any case, there is no warranted reason to conceive of

[93] *Ibid.* 85, 26 (ed. Theodor-Albeck, p. 1045); *cf. var. lect.* line 7.

[94] *Cf.* parallels *ibid.* line 5; Rashi (Makkoth 23b), with his keen feel for linguistic subtleties, has rejected his teacher's explanation הופיע=נשמעה בקול גדול, but has accepted הופיע=נגלה והוכיח with reference to French ברובי״ר=prouver. The term in point cannot possibly connote in this passage a mere "revealing" of the Holy Spirit, because then the rabbinic comment, "on three occasions the Holy Spirit revealed itself," would make no sense. According to the rabbis, the Holy Spirit ceased to reveal itself only after the death of the last prophets; *cf.* Tosefta Soṭah XIII, 2 and parallels. Up to that time, it was a common phenomenon, hence Rashi as well as his teacher correctly observe that הופיע in this passage cannot merely mean "revealed itself."

אדם מאדם as an Arabism; at most, such a construction would mean איש מאנשים, which is poor Hebrew style, though it does reflect rather closely an Arabic idiom.

The "House of Prostration" (11,22), בית השתחות, has been related to the Falasha designation מסגד for synagogue (above, p. 71). I am now very much in doubt whether this name derived from Arabic, as Epstein[95] and Büchler contend. Even granted the Arab origin[96] of the Falashas, as Halévi maintains, it would be strange indeed to assume their using a name for their house of worship which is employed neither by Arabic speaking Jews nor by the Arabs themselves.[97] We have already referred to a papyrus from Elephantine (P. 13485) which records the designation מסגדא. Since the religious customs and attitudes of the Falashas betray unquestionable traces of Egyptian-Jewish influence, we may justifiably assume that their use of the name מסיד for their house of worship is also of that origin. It follows, therefore, that the name בית השתחות in our document is no Arabism but a translation of the Achaemenid or Judeo-Aramaic מסגדא, which word was later relegated to disuse in Jewish circles because it referred too specifically to the sanctuaries of the pagans. We should like, however, to point out that neither Tannaitic nor Amoraic sources employ a specific term to designate a Jewish house of worship; the term בית הכנסת means primarily, community-house, which led people to use the designation בית עם, as we have noted above (p. 284, n. 42). How then are we to explain that the "classical people of praying" have no specific term for their house of prayer? The simplest explanation would probably be that מסגדא, or its Hebrew equivalent בית השתחות, was in ancient times the customary term that Jews used for their house of worship. However, this designation fell into disrepute, as we have just mentioned, because it was used in the generic, non-specific sense to include even pagan houses of worship. Moreover, talmudic

[95] Abraham Epstein, *Eldad the Danite* (ed. Presburg, 5661, p. 166; ed. Jerusalem, 5710, p. 169).

[96] Our increasing knowledge of the religious life of the Falashas points more and more clearly to its relationship to old Egypto-Jewish traditions.

[97] In Arabic the customary designation for synagogue is (בית) הכנסת=אל־כניס or בי כנישתא respectively. We also find פֻּהר (fuhr) with its very obscure etymology; *cf.* Ignaz Goldziher, *MGWJ*, XXIX, p. 310, note 2. Further *cf.* Leop. Loew, *Gesammelte Schriften*, V, p. 22 who refers to the usage of Meskita = מסניד in Sicily during the middle ages. In Dutch, the term Kerk(e) = church is employed by Jews and Christians in reference to the Snogha, the synagogue (*cf.* Kerkebestuur for synagogue commission).

Judaism tended more and more to eliminate[98] prostration at the prayer service. The term was thus progressively superseded by the designation בית הכנסת (synagogue), which in most instances was also used as place of public prayer. In contradiction to Büchler's thesis, the employment of בית השתחות in our document demonstrates thus not the late but rather the very early date of its composition.

In a later stratum of our document we therefore find the early term בית השתחות replaced by בית העם.[99]

As parallel to this development of the term בית השתחות we should like to point to the vicissitudes of the term אגורא. In rabbinic literature it designates exclusively: altar of idolatry (in contrast to מדבחא: altar in the Holy Temple), whereas in the Judeo-Aramaic of the Elephantine papyri it refers to the Jewish house of worship, i. e., altar, in the narrow, specific meaning.

The passage (11,22) יתקדם או יתאחר presents to us, according to Büchler, a definite Arabism, but he gives no reasons for this assumption. We, on our part, assume that there are no reasons to see an Arabism in this usage. True enough, the Arab says jata qaddamu au jata aḥaru (observed already by W. Bacher, in *ZHB*, 1911, p. 22); this, however, is no cause for denying the genuine Hebrew character of this usage, which is morphologically a *hithpa'el*. Bacher, *ad loc. cit.*, refers to the lexicographical works which cite passages in Ben-Sira[100] and Talmudic literature for the Hebrew usage of התאחר. Since Büchler does not recognize the authenticity of the Hebrew Ben-Sira, and since the only Talmudic reference cited (Bava Bathra 16b) has התאחר in the printed editions only, but not in the manuscripts, we should like to adduce parallels to this form from elsewhere in rabbinic literature. It occurs in Midrash Tehillim 18,11.[101] Furthermore, the usage in the Babylonian Talmud of the frequent root תרח or תרה demonstrates that התאחר = אתחר was once a much-used term, for there is no doubt that the root תרח is nothing but a metathesis of תחר.[102] The form

---

[98] *Cf.* above, p. 71; we further add here reference to TP Berakhoth, ch. IV, 1, 7c middle. [*Cf.* the author's *Commentary on the Palestinian Talmud*, New York, 1941, vol. III, pp. 116–123], which tells us that in the Land of Israel it was customary on public fastdays to pray (lying) on the stomach, רביעין על מעיהון.

[99] *Cf.* above, p. 284.

[100] Ben-Sira 7:34; 11:11; 35:11.

[101] Ed. Buber, p. 143; Yalquṭ Ha-Makhiri, p. 111; Yalquṭ Shimeoni, Sam. § 160.

[102] This view probably underlies the comment by RaSHI on Bava Qamma 80b, top; *cf.* also *Arukh*, *s. v.* תרה (A. Kohut, *Ar. Compl.*, VIII, p. 276a). Both explain תרח by התאחר.

התאחר=אתחר can also be traced in Syriac, as shown distinctly by ܐܬ݂ܚܪ.[103] The passage in Ben-Sira 38:16 has a marginal reading in the form of תחחר, which represents a secondary formation derived from התאחר (hence R. Smend's emendation to read תתאחר is unwarranted).

For התקדם I cannot offer at present any references in the old Hebrew literature. Since the Ethap'el of קדם is frequent usage in Syriac, we may quite justifiably assume an Aramaism. Of course we need not have recourse to either Aramaism or Arabism, for this form of the root קדם is morphologically genuine Hebrew.

i) Literary Criticism: Terminology

Büchler tried to show the presence of Arabisms in the technical terms which our document employs in introducing biblical quotations. We have already pointed to the various such introductory formulae that are employed in our document.[104] Our inspection has shown that they differ terminologically from the formulae used for the same purpose in rabbinic sources. This difference, taken by itself, is of no relevant consequence, if we consider that the introductory formulae in tannaitic literature differ from those in amoraic literature.[105] Büchler, however, advances the thesis that introductory formulae like כאשר

---

[103] J. Barth, *Etymologische Studien*, p. 12, derives this Syriac word from the Hebrew-Arabic root שאר, which is entirely unacceptable, as has already been pointed out by Fränkel, *Beiträge zur Assyrologie*, III. We should like to remark, by the way, that ܐܬ݂ܚܪ, to get spoiled, belongs to ܚܫܟ, to become black.

[104] *Cf.* above, p. 190, n. 156.

[105] *Cf.* e. g., the introductory clause in use in traditions handed down by the school of R. Yishmael, מגיד הכתוב, in contrast to the school of R. Akiva (ספרי דבי רב), which uses the formula מלמד הכתוב (*cf.* W. Bacher, *Terminologie*, I, p. 32; Heb. ed., p. 62). The expression אמר הכתוב=אמר רוח הקדש, which is frequent in writings in Palestine of the Amoraic period, is never used in the Babylonian Talmud. The Hebrew equivalents of the formulae introducing biblical proof texts in the N. T. cannot possibly be determined with any certainty. The term Μωσῆs ... εἶπεν (Acts 3:22) corresponds exactly to the terminology of our document (5,8; 8,14) and of rabbinic sources (Sifrei Deut. § 1; Yoma 69b; Yevamoth 49b). On the other hand, the formula: ὅπως πληρωθῇ τὸ ῥηθὲν διὰ τοῦ προφήτου Ἡσαίου (Matthew 13:35) may correspond either to לקיים מה שנאמר על ידי [בידי] ישעיה הנביא or to לקיים מה שנאמר בדבר[י] ישעיה הנביא. The former usage is found frequently in rabbinic source material, and occurs also in our document (see farther below), whereas the latter usage cannot be traced to any rabbinic terminology. Hence it seems most probable that the idiomatic term אמר ביד corresponds to ῥηθὲν διὰ, a Greek periphrasis or paraphrasis.

These brief observations suffice to demonstrate that Charles' remarks on this subject (*Fragments of a Zadokite Work, Apocrypha and Pseudepigrapha*, vol. II, p. 789) need correction.

כתוב, אשר אמר, ואשר אמר "occur only in Arabic"; hence our document cannot possibly have been composed prior to the Arab conquest of Syria. Since Büchler deems it unnecessary to disclose his Arabic sources which would demonstrate the alleged parallels to this terminology of our document, we deem it unnecessary on our part to examine here the formulae by which biblical proof texts are introduced by Jewish authors writing in Arabic. At this point we should like to list a complete roster of the formulae[106] used to introduce biblical proof-texts in our document and juxtapose parallels in rabbinic literature, with the purpose of detecting idiomatic characteristics of the sectarian style.

Document		*Rabbinic Equivalent*
1) (1,13)	אשר [היה] כתוב עליה	שעליה נאמר הכתוב[107]
2) (4,13)	כאשר דבר אל ביד ישעיה הנביא	כמו שאמר הקב"ה על ידי ישעיה[108] / כמה שנאמר ברוח הקודש על ידי ישעיה
3) (4,15)	אשר[109] אמר עליהם לוי בן יעקב	שאמר עליהם לוי בן יעקב
4) (5, 1)	על הנשיא כתוב	cf. (1
5) (5, 8)	ומשה אמר[110]	
6) (6, 7)	הוא דורש התורה אשר אמר ישעיה	זהו דורש התורה שאמר עליו י'
7) (6,13)	אשר אמר אל	cf. (2 שאמר הקב"ה
8) (7, 8)	כאשר אמר	ככתוב; כמה שנאמר; כאמור
9) (7,10)	בבוא הדבר אשר כתוב בדברי ישעיה בן אמוץ	כשיתקיים המקרא שכתוב על ידי ישעיה
10) (7,11)	אשר אמר	שאמר
11) (7,14)	כאשר אמר	cf. (8
12) (7,16)	כאשר אמר	cf. (8
13) (7,19)	כאשר כתוב	ככתוב; כמו שכתוב
14) (8, 9)	אשר אמר אל	cf. (7
15) (8,14)	ואשר אמר	כתוב; ומה שכתוב; ומה שאמר
16) (8,20)	הוא הדבר אשר אמר[111]	cf. (21 זה מה שאמר
17) (9, 2)	ואשר אמר	cf. (15

[106] Cf. pp. 194 ff. for a roster of biblical proof-texts cited in our document; by mistake two items (1,13 = Hos. 4:16; 6, 7–8 = Isa. 54:16) were omitted.

[107] Cf. Aggadath Shir ha-Shirim, end: על אותה שעה אמרו.

[108] Amoraic terminology.

[109] This relative pronoun refers to the preceding מצודות.

[110] Cf. above, p. 190, n. 156.

[111] Cf. Lev. 10:3: הוא אשר דבר ה'; Exod. 16:23: הוא אשר דבר ה' לאמר.

18)	(9, 5)	ואין כתוב כי אם	112לא נאמר אלא; אין כתוב אלא
19)	(9, 7)	אשר אמר [אל] לו	שאמר לו הקב"ה
20)	(9, 8)	אשר אמר	cf. (10
21)	(10,16)	כי הוא אשר אמר	על זה נאמר; שנאמר cf. (16
22)	(11,18)	113כי כן כתוב	שנאמר
23)	(11,20)	כי כתוב	שנאמר; שכן הכתוב אומר
24)	(16, 6)	ואשר אמר	cf. (15
25)	(16,10)	אשר אמר	cf. (15
26)	(16,15)	כי הוא אשר אמר	cf. (21
27)	(19, 5)	כאשר אמר	cf. (7 and (8
28)	(19, 7)	בבוא הדבר אשר כתוב ביד	cf. (9
29)	(19,11)	אשר אמר יחזקאל ביד יחזקאל	cf. (17 and above, p. 102
30)	(19,15)	כאשר דבר	ככתוב
31)	(19,21)	אשר אמר אל	cf. (7
32)	(19,26)	ואשר אמר	cf. (15
33)	(20,16)	כאשר אמר	cf. (8

This comparative roster yields at a first glance that for introductory terms the Tannaitic literature as well as our document employ predominantly the two verbs אמר[114] (20 times) and כתב (8 times).

In six instances (3; 5; 6; 10; 29) we find, as is also frequent in Talmudic-Midrashic literature,[115] that the biblical author himself is the subject of the predicate אמר. In these instances (7; 14; 19) the divine author (אל) is the subject of this predicate; this usage does not only correspond to the frequent introductory formula of Babylonian Amoraim[116] when citing prooftexts: אמר רחמנא;[117] but also to the frequent

---

[112] Both in tannaitic and amoraic terminology.

[113] In early liturgical texts the introductory formula to biblical quotation is not infrequently וכן כתוב בתורתך, replaced in turns by בתורתך כתוב לאמור [cf. the author's Commentary on the Palestinian Talmud, vol. IV, pp. 222 ff.]. When, however, a biblical proof-text is adduced for establishing a Halakah or for authenticating it, the term שנאמר is employed exclusively. The Mishnaic ככתוב (Taanith III,3) is not introducing a Halakic proof-text from the Bible, but merely indicating the case.

[114] The frequent usage of this word in introducing quotation is also traceable to the biblical terminology (Exod 16:23; Lev. 10:3) הוא אשר דבר; hence הוא אשר אמר; cf. items 16; 21; 26.

[115] W. Bacher, Terminologie, II, s. v. אמר, who cites only amoraic references; but see also tannaitic: cf., e. g., Sifre Deut. § 9 = Midrash Tannaim, p. 7; ibid., § 342 = Midrash Tannaim, p. 207.

[116] Cf. p. 190, n. 156.

[117] Cf. Bacher, op. cit., II, s. v., who surprisingly fails to stress that the formula אמר רחמנא introduces only quotations cited from the legalistic part of the Pentateuch.

The designation רחמנא with reference to God (the Merciful) is found in the TP in the following passages: Sanhedrin 20a (twice) = Horayoth 47a; Bacher, loc. cit., is to be corrected accordingly.

tannaitic use of אמר הקב״ה when introducing paraphrases[118] of biblical statements. The Amoraic formula רוח הקודש אמרה[119] was probably based on an older expression such as אמר הקב״ה or אמר אלהים.

The most frequent term in rabbinic literature for introducing biblical quotation is the passive form שנאמר; this term is unknown in our document.[120] Instead the sectaries use frequently (8; 11; 12; 21; 26; 33) the active form כאשר אמר.[121] The rabbinic formula is probably of much later date, for it is an ellipsis of שנאמר בתורה, which in turn corresponds to the frequent אמרה תורה. The latter seems to have superseded אמר אל, in order to avoid as much as possible pronouncing a divine name.

Rabbinic literature has no example of the usage of opening a pericope by introducing a biblical citation with אשר אמר or ואשר אמר respectively[122] (this occurs five times in our document: 15; 17; 20; 24; 25). In such a case the rabbis would either omit an introductory formula, or they would use כתוב (or Aramaic: כתיב).[123] This sectarian term can be traced to the biblical formula הדבר אשר אמר, just like the biblical (Exod. 4:12)[124] אשר תדבר, which stands elliptically for הדבר אשר תדבר; or (Lam. 2:17) אשר זמם, which stands for הדבר (דברו) אשר זמם (parallel to אמרתו אשר צוה) et al. Most probably our sectarian author bore in mind an introductory formula employed by Jeremiah in a few passages (14:1; 46:1; 47:1; 49:34) אשר היה, which, however, is always followed by דבר.[125]

These biblical antecedents demonstrate sufficiently that Büchler's contention of Arabism represented by the terminological idioms in our document כאשר אמר and כאשר כתוב is entirely unfounded; taking into consideration the "opus musivum" style of our document (cf.

---

[118] Frequent in this application; cf. e. g., Sifre Deut. §45; §319; §320 et al.

[119] Abundant references in Bacher, op. cit., II, s. v. רוח הקודש.

[120] Found, however, in many passages in the NT.

[121] Terms like καθώς εἶπεν and καθώς ἐλάλησε may reflect either כאשר אמר or the rabbinic כמו שאמר.

[122] In the passage 9,2 we ought perhaps to read הוא אשר אמר; cf. above, ad loc. cit. It is quite possible that (8,14) ואשר אמר is a modifier of לא הבינו in line 12; in this case we have for the usage of ואשר only the one reference, 16,6. Even this passage can, without undue difficulty, be considered as a posterior clause of וביום אשר יקום וכו' in line 4. Thus it is rather doubtful whether our document ever introduces a new paragraph with ואשר.

[123] Cf. W. Bacher, Terminologie, both Tannaitic and Amoraic sections, s. v.

[124] Cf. also Gen. 44:9 אשר ימצא אתו, which stand elliptically for האיש אשר ימצא אתו.

[125] According to the usual exegesis of these passages in Jeremiah, the phrase אשר היה דבר ה' אל ירמיהו stands for the regular דבר ה' אשר היה אל ירמיהו; this exegesis can hardly be correct, for such a transposition seems implausible. It is much more probable that אשר היה stands for הדבר אשר היה.

above, pp. 299–300), we find nothing unusual in the employment of the relative pronoun אשר as in biblical phrases (Josh. 11:9; Judg. 3:4; I Kings 21:11 and Dan. 9:13), instead of the post-biblical כמו שנאמר; כשהוא אומר; כדכתיב; כמו שנאמר *et al.*

Besides the introductory formulae which employ the root אמר we find biblical quotations introduced in our document with the following usages of the root כתב:

(1,13; 5,1) כתוב עליו corresponding to biblical usage (Ps. 40:8), whereas rabbinic sources[126] employ the later עליו הכתוב אומר; *cf.* p. 377.

(19,7) ביד זכריה הנביא (אשר כתוב) corresponds basically to the formula frequent in early liturgical texts ככתוב על יד נביאך (introducing the Treshagion), though it may possibly bear closer affinity to biblical usage (Exod. 31:18 כתובים באצבע) than to ביד as it occurs in rabbinic sources;[127] *cf.* pp. 377, 9; 378, 28.

(7,10) אשר כתוב בדברי ישעיה finds its parallel[128] in an early liturgical text: the Qedushah is always concluded with a hagiographical verse, introduced by the formula ובדברי קדשך כתוב לאמור.

(7,19) כאשר כתוב is exclusively biblical. The abbreviation כ"ב in 19,1 is perhaps כ"כ, which is frequent[129] in rabbinic literature for ככתוב, which, in turn, occurs once in the Bible (Neh. 8:15).

(11,18) [כי] כן כתוב can be traced to Talmudical (Rosh Hashanah 34b) and liturgical texts; in these texts, however, it has a different meaning and application (*cf.* above, p. 378, n. 113).

(11,20) כי כתוב is not known in rabbinic sources (p. 378, 23).

---

[126] *Cf.* Bacher, *op. cit.*, I, *s. v.*

[127] In biblical usage, the verbs צוה; ענה; יעד; דבר as predicates to God as the subject are connected with their object by the preposition ביד, in order to express the divine operation through the prophet. There is nowhere, however, an idiomatic term such as כתוב ביד משה introducing a quotation from the Torah. *Cf.* also (3,21) כאשר הקים אל להם ביד יחזקאל הנביא לאמור הכהנים והלויים ובני צדוק.... Büchler translates correctly: "as He promised to them through Ezekiel, saying . . ." (see above, p. 295, on הקים in the meaning of "promise"), but adds that this represents an Arabism. I find it absolutely impossible to find any warrant for this assertion. Is כאשר (as) not good Hebrew? We should like to point out, parenthetically, that כאשר in this passage is probably a pronoun relative to the preceding כבוד אדם (glory of man *which* He promised. . . .)

[128] To the best of my knowledge we find nowhere ובדברי נביאך כתוב, which would represent the exact parallel to this term in our document.

[129] This is Schechter's emendation for the reading כב; his view is quite acceptable, but not beyond any doubt, for כב might just as well represent כאשר כתוב.

(9,5) ואין כתוב כי אם is known from rabbinic usage (*cf. ibid.* 18) as
אין כתיב אלא or אין כתוב אלא, Hebrew and Aramaic respectively.
The Aramaic אלא in these terms stands for the Hebrew כי אם
in our document.

(19,15) כאשר דבר and (4,13) ביד . . . כאשר דבר (*ibid.*, 30; 2) are not
known in rabbinic source material, though these terms are
frequent in biblical literature.

If one can draw any conclusion at all for the date of the composition
of the document from the characteristics of the terminology used in
the formulae introducing biblical quotations, then one must be per-
suaded that they are obviously earlier than tannaitic literature; they
are, like other elements in our document, much more akin to biblical
diction — much closer, indeed, than any of the earliest documents of
rabbinic literature. We have to caution, however, that biblical purism
in a Hebrew document cannot be accepted without any further evidence as proof of its early date. On the other hand, we have to point
out that Büchler is caught in a vicious circle by his method of determining the date of the composition of our sectarian document by
linguistic analysis. Its biblical style is an indication of its lateness, so
Büchler argues, for this style is unknown in early rabbinic literature.
However, any correspondences, parallelisms or congruences between
this sectarian document and early rabbinic literature are, according to
Büchler, proof that our document is dependent on rabbinic sources.

It would indeed be most instructive to obtain from Büchler his
literary portrait of a Hebrew author who actually might have composed
a document during the first century B. C. E.; Büchler would have
him writing neither in biblical diction or style, nor, even less, in
rabbinisms — but *tertium non datur*!

j) Historical Criticism

Büchler's fundamental mistake in dealing with the language of our
document consists, as we have seen, in that he has used only talmudic
literature for comparative purposes and has ignored the Pseudepigrapha, to which provenance this sectarian composition actually
belongs. The same type of bias misleads Büchler when investigating
historical allusions in this fragment. Proceeding hence to the construction of a historical frame of reference, he derives from this scanty and
uncertain material the thesis that the author of our document knows
nothing to report about the alleged emigration from Jerusalem, nor
about the pollution of the Temple there, which was the real reason for
the emigration of the sectarians. In other words: our document was

composed at a date when the live memories of the real events in Jerusalem, has been blurred in the folk-memory into oblivion. The author of this document imagined an "emigration" from Judea to Damascus but, since this was poetic license and not based on fact, he could fill in the picture with only some general charges against the godlessness of the Jerusalemites.

Applied to other areas of Jewish literature, Büchler's "critical method" would yield, for instance, the following results: the Psalms of Solomon are the literary fruits of anti-rabbinic polemics on the part of Karaite authors writing in Greek, who portray their opponents, the Rabbanites, as godless and frivolous and themselves as righteous and loyal. The desecration of the Temple by the irreverent and its violation by Israel's enemies have nothing to do with the real, historical Sanctuary which once stood in Jerusalem. The Karaites charge their opponents with gross negligence of the purity laws which, according to Karaite doctrine, ought to be strictly observed in every synagogue;[130] as punishment for this scandalous disregard, the synagogues of the Rabbanites are being burnt down by Christians and Mohammedans. Had the author of this apocryphon lived in the days of Pompey's conquest of Jerusalem, he would have given us concrete details about domestic conditions and foreign relations in Judea and Jerusalem of his day.

By the same token, there is hardly any cogent argument to maintain the authenticity of the Mishnah in the light of Büchler's "critical method."

The well known historian Rhamberg (*Die Erhebung der Geschichte zum Range einer Wissenschaft*, p. 37) has correctly observed that "it would be well nigh impossible for an historian to disengage himself completely from the circumstances, outlook, ideologies, influences and modes of thinking of his own day." The literary product of the author himself, though concerned with another, non-contemporary era, represents a historical document of his own days. Accordingly, were the Patriarch R. Judah the main editor and author of the Mishnah, this document ought to reflect relevant information about the political status of the Patriarch; about prevailing views on political, social and religious affairs; on economic conditions and many other aspects of contemporary life in Palestine. However, "Rabbi" made no claim to be a historian, and the Mishnah was not intended as a history of Pales-

---

[130] Büchler maintains that our document employs the term "sanctuary" for synagogue.

tine or of the Jews; hence we are not surprised by the lack of historical data in this work of R. Judah ha-Nasi.

Likewise, the author of the Psalms of Solomon had no intention to reflect a portrayal of the contemporary situation; he clearly imitated the lyricism of the Psalms as means of expressing gratitude and homage to God for protecting the righteous and punishing the wicked. The historical elements, if any, are so elusive and vague that scholars disagree widely over the date of the book's composition; the prevailing opinion places it in Jerusalem shortly after the conquest by Pompey.

What warranted grounds do we possess to justify the premise that the Aggadic elements of our document would yield more definite and extensive historical data than the Psalms of Solomon? Or do its Halakic passages offer more material which is more clearly laden with historical information than the Mishnah of R. Judah ha-Nasi? If we take into account that the bulk of Aggadah in our document represents exhortatory sermons (*cf.* above, pp. 274 ff.) which were actually delivered before the sectarian congregation, and not literary compositions, we should marvel rather at the relative abundance of historical data than at their paucity. The intimacy of the esoteric circle made it superfluous for the preacher to offer detailed explanations of his allusions when he referred to the acts perpetrated by the Sons of Perdition who misappropriate tainted wealth of vows and consecrations and who wax fat on the treasures of the Sanctuary and on possessions snatched from widows and orphans (6,14–15). He did not refer to events of the past long gone by, but to scandals and outrages committed daily which were known to his audience no less than to himself. Only by failing completely to appreciate and discern the character of our document, as Büchler has done, can one reach the conclusion that our document is spurious because it lacks in abundance of historical data.

The character of our document is determined by its practical purpose: to exhort the sectaries to *meticulous* observance of all the laws. There is, therefore, no reason for this text to give a history of the sect. Nevertheless, one can detect important historical evidence in the Halakic passages of our document. By its very nature the Halakah, regulating the mode of practical living, affords us a glance into the lives of the people who are its concern. Büchler recognized that the Halakah of the document contained important historical allusions; his preconceived ideas about the character of our text, however, prevented him from properly assessing this material. His conclusions concerning the historical data explicated from the Halakah (*ibid.*, pp. 457–467) are untenable, as the following analysis will demonstrate.

k) Historical Evaluation: the Temple Service.

The affairs of the Temple and the sacrificial service are mentioned in many passages of our document in the tenor of routine, part of the daily life. It is not quite clear, however, whether these affairs refer to the Sanctuary at Jerusalem, or possibly to a local sanctuary of the sect itself. Above, on p. 281, we have attempted to prove that our document knows of no other Temple and Altar than those at the chosen site of Jerusalem. If our contention is correct, it would follow that our document could not have been composed much later than 70 C. E. On the other hand, even if the view advocated by most scholars were correct, according to which the sect maintained its own local sanctuary at Damascus, we would still arrive at approximately the same *terminus ad quem* for the composition of our document.

The temple at Leontopolis survived the Temple of Jerusalem by only three years. We have no reason to assume that the Romans would have been more favorably inclined towards the Jewish sectaries of Damascus than towards the Jews of Judea and Egypt.[131] It is, of course, inconceivable that a Jewish sanctuary would have existed[132] during the Christian rule in Syria.

Let us now see how Büchler presents his case. He argues that the sectarian sanctuary could not possibly have been established in the pre-Christian era or during its early beginnings; besides the illegiti-

---

[131] As far as the Samaritan temple on Mt. Gerizim is concerned, we have to bear in mind that Hyrcanus did not destroy it utterly; this building is mentioned as existing as late as the year 484, although its use for Samaritan services ended after the Hasmonean assault on it (*cf.* Juynboll, *Historia Samaritana*, p. 113; and Montgomery, *The Samaritans*, pp. 83 f. and p. 111). Montgomery points to a contradiction in Procopius, *De Aedificii* V, 7 who stresses that the Samaritans no longer have a temple on Mt. Gerizim, and yet mentions their temple on Gerizim in an earlier passage. He simply fails to notice that in the former passage the chronicler was discussing the building, or whatever had remained of it, whereas in the latter passage he was making a statement about its religious function. Even Hadrian, who was favorably disposed towards the Samaritans, did not permit them to resume services at that site (*cf.*, e. g., Adler-Seligsohn, *Nouv. Chronique Samaritaine*, p. 46, about the temple of Jupiter on Mt. Gerizim).

[132] The Romans were not opposed to a "Temple to the Jewish God" as such, but they would not tolerate the "Sanctuary of the Jews." The Christians, however, would permit neither, because their hatred was directed both against the Jews and their religion.

macy[133] of such a sanctuary outside of Jerusalem when the legitimate Temple still existed, no such Jewish sanctuary of Damascus is reported in the writings of Josephus, although he presents us with a detailed description of the large Jewish population in this important city and its marked influence there around 70 C. E. The weakness of Büchler's argument needs no further analysis; it seems that Büchler was himself aware of it. Investigating his argument of illegitimacy, we note that the Jews of Egypt were not sectarians, and that the Sanctuary at Jerusalem was no less dear to them than to their Palestinian brethren — and yet they had no religious scruples about establishing a temple at Leontopolis. What then could have been more natural for Jews[134] who were dissatisfied with the state of affairs in Judea, particularly with the administration of the Temple affairs at Jerusalem, than to erect a puristic sanctuary in their new homestead?! Büchler's *argumentum ex silentio* from Josephus is almost funny. This historian describes the situation of Jews during the great war against the Romans (66–70), whereas our document refers to the sanctuary of a Jewish sect which would have been established in Damascus more than a century[135] before Josephus. What certainty does Büchler have that a sanctuary which, according to our document, had been erected in Damascus by Judean immigrants, would remain standing for more than a century, so that Josephus' silence about it proves that our document must be spurious?! We are even in a position to point out why this sectarian sanctuary at Damascus, if indeed it ever existed, could not have endured for any length of time. When these Judean emigrants settled at Damascus (about 88–87) they were ruled by the Seleucid dynasty.

[133] According to the dominant opinion of the rabbis, any sanctuary besides the Temple at the divinely chosen site in Jerusalem would *always* be illegitimate; *cf.* Megillah 10a. We should like to remark, by the way, that the term בזמן הזה in this Talmudic passage is not to be taken literally; it actually means לאחר החורבן.

[134] *The Odes of Solomon* (ed. Rendel Harris, Cambridge, 1909, IV, 1–4) report the sinful aspiration of some people who would have liked to transfer the Sanctuary of Jerusalem to another site. R. Harris (*ibid.*, p. 57) thinks that this castigation is directed against the Jews who wanted to see in the temple at Leontopolis an adequate equivalent to the Temple at Jerusalem. This opinion is most improbable. The Egyptian Jews, as far as we know, never denied the primacy of the Central Sanctuary at Jerusalem. This charge would, however, properly fit our sect, which even claimed that it would be sinful to send sacrifices to Jerusalem (*cf.*, above, p. 281). In light of the Odes' mystic tenor we would have to query, however, if the "sacred site" is to be understood literally.

[135] *Cf.*, above, p. 272; the emigration out of Judea in the wake of persecution by Alexander Jannaeus is to be dated about 88 B. C. E.; *cf.* Schürer, *Geschichte*[4], vol. I, p. 382.

A short time after the sectarian community arrived, Damascus passed into the hands of the Nabatean king.

This Jewish colony in Damascus would probably not have met with any opposition to the erection of a Jewish sanctuary, either from the last Seleucid king, Antiochus XII, or from the Nabatean king, Aretas III. We may safely assume, however, that the Romans, who conquered Damascus in 65, would have closed such a sanctuary. Although Judaism as such was recognized by Rome as a "tolerated religion," such recognition would not be extended to separatist splinter groups which represented potential cause for social unrest and friction with the majority of the Jewish population.[136] Therefore such a sanctuary could possibly have existed and functioned at Damascus in the year 85 B. C. E., and yet be closed and abandoned around the year 70 C. E. Hence no conclusion can be drawn, as Büchler has done, from Josephus' silence about a sectarian sanctuary at Damascus.

1) Historical Evaluation: the Socio-Economic Situation.

Büchler also adduces proof for the incompatibility of the social life and the economic conditions reflected in the sectarian Halakah with the socio-economic situation which prevailed in Jewish communities during the Roman rule. On basis of this Halakah and the sectarian constitution of the community, he draws the following picture:

The sectarians, living in the land of Damascus among the Gentiles,[137] were mostly urban residents, though a minority of them belonged to the rural population of this district. They possessed fields, plantations and vineyards, fowl and cattle, slaves and gentile laborers. In the vicinity they could find reptiles, fish, locust and honey for food. This mode of living, opines Büchler, is vividly reminiscent of Bedouin behavior and it fits the political situation of Jewish tribes throughout Arabia in the days of Mohammed. Moreover, the constitution of the sectarian community presumes[138] jurisdictional autonomy, the use of penal execution and disciplinary institutions, all of which would be unthinkable under Roman rule but which would fit well the situation of free Jews in pre-Islamic Arabia. The proscribing of killing any

---

[136] *Cf.* our remarks above, p. 384 about the Temple on Mt. Gerizim. What the Romans denied the Samaritans they certainly would not grant the sectarians in Damascus.

[137] By the same token it could be said that the gentiles resided among the sectaries; all that is reflected in our document is that the sectaries had some limited relationship with their surrounding world.

[138] *Cf.* our discussion above, p. 282, according to which the jurisdictional autonomy of the sect is not as certain as Büchler would have us believe.

pagan for profit or the confiscating[139] of his property without permission of the "Israelite council" (12,6–8) would also be compatible with the Jews of wildest Araby and not of a community living in settled conditions. In brief: this sectarian community, by all indications, did not exist at a time when the Second Temple was still standing but much later, probably about the beginning of the seventh century. Under Arab rule we would also find nothing strange about a "Jewish sanctuary," since the Samaritans probably also enjoyed such a privilege.

It is truly remarkable to be treated by Büchler to so many situational details which he discovered in our document. More remarkable yet are the many contradictions in which he entangles himself. He finds our sect to be a community of Jewish Bedouins, akin to Jewish tribes which flourished in pre-Islamic Arabia, who were their own masters; therefore there is nothing strange in their autonomous jurisdiction.

He fails, however, to notice that our document states unequivocally that our sect had its moorings in the land of Damascus. This land was under Christian rule till the year 635, when it was conquered by the Muhammedans. Independent tribes of Jewish Bedouins are unimaginable both under Christian and under Muhammedan[140] rule; pagan Arabs were never the lords of Damascus. A Jewish sanctuary in Christian Damascus is certainly inconceivable, and Büchler would not even attempt to make such a situation plausible.

Büchler's contention that the Arabs had permitted the Samaritans to offer sacrifices at Shechem is entirely unfounded;[141] even if this were so, the existence of independent sectarians in Damascus in the seventh century would remain untenable in the light of the problems

[139] According to our interpretation of this passage, *ad loc.*, it legislates an injunction against accepting charity gifts from pagans. This is also prohibited by rabbinic law; besides the literature cited *ad loc. cf.* also ברייתא דישועה, § 15 (ed. Schenblum, p. 46; ed. Eisenstein, p. 249a) that he who accepts gifts from pagans (as Gehazi did from Naaman) postpones the advent of salvation (causes the Messiah to tarry).

[140] Tribes of Jewish robbers are reported here and there among Muhammedans, as described by Benjamin of Tudela (ed. M. N. Adler, English index *s. v.* "Jews," "fighting men") and Eldad the Danite (ed. A. Epstein, Jerusalem, 5710, p. 52). These reports indicate that such tribes existed only in mountainous regions and deserts, but never in cultivated settlements like the land of Damascus.

[141] The Samaritans were not again permitted to slaughter the Paschal Lamb until the reign of Mahmud I (1730–1754), and even he allowed it only on Mt. Gerizim, but neither at the site of their former altar and temple, nor as a formal sacrifice, which would require an altar; *cf.* Adler-Seligsohn, *Nouvelle Chron.*, p. 106 and Montgomery, *The Samaritans*, pp. 139 ff.

raised by Büchler himself. The Muhammedans might possibly have tolerated a Jewish sanctuary at Damascus; it seems, however, most improbable that during the centuries of their brightest glory and most triumphant conquest they would have suffered the unrestricted freedom within their realm of autonomous Jewish Bedouins. Hence we are not at all surprised to find Büchler, at the conclusion of his investigations, shyly advancing the possibility (note 146) that all that is reported in our document about Temple and sacrifice is nothing but "invented detail." Does Büchler think us gullible enough to accept the notion that a seventh century author possessed so large and modern a talent to dissemble and to create an impression of antiquity by inventing sacrificial laws and temple service? But besides these "invented details" concerning the temple and its sacrifices, employed as "antique" window-dressing, how could we possibly ignore the sectaries' primary charge against their ungodly opponents: the pollution of the Temple; this charge constitutes the major motif in the aggadic parts of the document. Are all these passages to be taken as purely inventive without base in any reality?

The probing question *cui bono* is of no less significance for the historian than for the jurist; Büchler does not attempt to offer the slightest reason for this ingenious swindle which he has posited. If anything is certain in history, it is the fact that the author of our document lived at a time when the Temple still existed. What is in doubt is only the location of the temple: does our author refer to the Temple, which was at Jerusalem, or to a sectarian sanctuary at Damascus? If the latter opinion is correct,[142] then we may safely assume that the Damascene temple was erected between the years 85 and 65 B. C. E., under the rule of Aretas III. This date would coincide with the time of the emergence of our sect, as we have demonstrated above. Under Nabatean rule over Damascus, the Judean emigrants enjoyed complete autonomy there, including independent penal jurisdiction. The sworn enemies of Alexander Jannaeus and his son Aristobulus would find only goodwill and encouragement from Aretas, who carried on a continuous warfare with these Hasmoneans.

This situation makes the political and communal autonomy of our

---

[142] *Cf.* p. 384, where we have doubted that this assumption is necessary but have conceded that it is possible. The sectaries simply ignored the existence of the Temple at Jerusalem, for it was being constantly polluted and desecrated. Only from such a perspective could strictly observant Pharisees sanction the conduct of Temple Services outside of Jerusalem and beyond the borders of the Holy Land. *Cf.* Megillah 10a שמעתי שמקריבין בבית חניו בזמן הזה, and our remarks above.

sect sufficiently plausible. The cogent reasons advanced for our dating makes the fantastic hypothesis of Jewish Bedouins in Damascus at the rise of Islam quite unnecessary.

Büchler, however, advances other reasons besides political autonomy for the Bedouin character of our sect. In 19,3 we read: "And if they dwell in camps אשר היה מקדם הארץ [כסרך] [כחוקי] [כחוקי]." These "camps (מחנות)" are here described as having been customary with the sect in the past. From this Büchler concludes that מחנות cannot possibly connote settlement or something sedentary, for such a characterization would be meaningless — at all times people lived in villages, hamlets, or similar settlements. This term rather refers to a nomadic type of dwelling, to "movable camps." The sect, or at any rate part of it, *once* dwelt in Bedouin fashion, but later on it abandoned this mode of living. This turning point in the life of the sect is seen by Büchler in the word מקדם. It is very strange that Büchler has overlooked the fact that מקדם usually means "since ancient times." The phrase is therefore to be translated: And if they dwell in מחנות, as customary on earth ever since ancient times, etc." ואם מחנות ישבו כחוקי הארץ אשר היה [ו]מקדם.

We already pointed out above,[143] *ad loc. cit.*, that the expression כחוקי הארץ represents a rather clumsy paraphrase of כסרך הארץ, the expression found in version A (7,6), which in turn corresponds to the biblical דרך כל הארץ (Gen. 19:31), and to the talmudical[144] דרך ארץ and דרכו של עולם respectively.

We can indeed demonstrate with certainty that מחנה and מחנות never have the meaning "nomadic camp" in our document. In the passage (13,4) על פיהו כל באי מחנה we can establish by its parallel[145] (14,10) על פיהו יבואו באי העדה that the term מחנה is synonymous with עדה, congregation or community.[146] Hence in the above passage (7,6; 19,2) ואם מחנות ישבו is to be translated accordingly: when they dwell in communities, e. g., organize themselves socially as sectarian community. These words introduce a passage which stresses the binding

---

[143] *Cf.* our remarks above. The explanation of אשר היה מקדם as reference to the biblical time of wandering through the wilderness, is untenable; if this was meant, our document would hardly have used the expression מקדם.

[144] Aramaic אורח ארעא; the frequent connotation of דרך ארץ and ארעא אורח ארעא in rabbinic literature as decent, decorous conduct or decency is secondary — its primary meaning is route, routine, conventionalism and conformity to mores and accepted conduct, the τάξις order and social discipline. Hence decency in the habitual behavior of the people.

[145] *Cf.* also 13,12–13: אל ימשול איש מבני המחנה להביא איש אל העדה, no member of the congregation has the right to admit somebody to the community.

[146] In the meaning district, quarter of a city — already biblical, *cf.* I Chron. 9:18.

character of the preceding precepts not only for the Damascene colony, באי הברית החדשה בארץ דמשק (6,19), but also for all future sectarian communities which will emerge from its midst and establish themselves elsewhere. In the light of this specific terminological connotation we understand now why our document uses this term מחנה when discussing the constitutional statutes of the community (13,1 ff.), so that the word occurs on these two leaves (13;14) no less than nine times, whereas in the Halakic passages, where the reference to the social settlement is not constitutional or socio-structural, but rather a situational reference to the place occupied by the sect, the term עיר, "city," is employed.[147]

m) Historical Evaluation: the Dietary Restrictions.

Dietary laws restricting the consumption of fish and locust (12,13–15) serve Büchler as further proof[148] for the sect's nomadic mode of living. The Mishnah (Ḥullin III, 7) lists the prohibited and permitted kinds of fish and locust. If we would adopt Büchler's method of research and inference, we ought to reach the conclusion that the Jews in Palestine at the time when this Mishnah was recorded (second century C. E.) lived like Bedouins!

Büchler has moreover failed to notice that the passage in point presents not so much sectarian legislation as it does sectarian exegesis of biblical verses (Lev. 11:43 and 46), an observation which would admit the possibility that these rules are theoretical-normative rather than applicable-descriptive. Moreover, the rivers of Damascus were famous in early antiquity (e. g., II Kings 5:12); no reason is known to presume that there were no fish in them. Consumption of locust is mentioned not only in the Bible but also, quite often, in Jewish sources of the tannaitic-amoraic period.[149] Hence there is no justifica-

---

[147] In the rules pertaining to the sabbatical district limits (10,21; 11,15) the terminology is revealingly exact. Our document does not use the term חוץ למחנה, as we would have expected according to biblical pattern in this *opus musivum* style, but חוץ לעירו; because עיר is the spatial, local framework in which the social organization מחנה is situated. The same exactness in terminology applies to the Sanctuary, the precinct called מחנה in the Bible and Talmud (מחנה שכינה וכו' etc.). Here (12,1) it is called עיר המקדש and not מחנה המקדש; whereas (9,11) the term ממאד המחנה is employed, because it is an elliptical expression for ממאד בני המחנה, referring to the property of the sectaries, the members of the congregation.

[148] Büchler also includes here the dietary laws pertaining to the consumption of honey. We have, however, demonstrated *ad loc. cit.*, pp. 78–79 that this is a misunderstanding of the technical term employed in our document.

[149] *Cf.* p. 348.

tion whatever to reach any conclusions about the nomadic life of the sect because of laws pertaining to the mode of their consumption.[150] Whence does Büchler know that Bedouins love fish? Guidi (in: *Della sede primitiva dei populi semitici*) observes that there are no proto-Semitic names for the various kinds of fish, and the early Semites certainly were nomads!

n) Historical Evaluation: Administrative Structure.

We have demonstrated so far, that there is nothing in the references and description about socio-economic conditions in our document which would not fit the historical situation of the first century B. C. E. We have seen that the existence of a Jewish temple at Damascus and the large autonomy granted to the sectaries could not have easily been possible in any other but the Nabatean[151] era. This finding will be further supported by a closer look at the precise character of the sect's administrative structure.

Our document shows ample evidence of the privileged status accorded to the Priests, who had large prerogatives both in court and council (10,5; 13,2 f.). To the best of our knowledge, this is consonant with the situation during the Second Temple, when Priestly precedence was accepted by Jews irrespective of their particular shade of belief, whether they were Sadducees, Pharisees or Essenes.[152] The destruction of the Temple in 70 C. E. brought in its wake the gradual decline of the Priestly status; what had been their prerogatives were now reduced to insignificant gestures of courtesy. Even these amenities in the synagogue, in consideration of their Priestly descent, might be

---

[150] *Cf.* above, p. 80.

[151] This era = 85–63 B. C. E. (*cf.* below, p. 407). Some scholars claim that Damascus remained in Nabatean dependency until 106 C. E.; *cf.*, however, the arguments against this opinion in Schürer, *Geschichte*[3], vol. I, p. 789. Even if this were true, we could not possibly date the conditions described here in the period of Roman supremacy over the Nabateans. Such autonomy as was enjoyed by the sectaries is implausible in a state that was vassal to the Romans.

[152] The attitude of the Pharisees towards the priests is reflected in Josephus' glowing praises of them. His own priestly pedigree no doubt made him exaggerate but we may accept the general tenor of his references to the priests as quite typical of Pharisee opinion (*cf.* also H. Graetz, *MGWJ*, XXXVI, 97–118). Even the Essenes recognized the prerogatives of the Aaronic priests, as indicated by Josephus (*Bel. Jud.*, II 8,5; ἱερεύς in this passage can only mean an Aaronite, for otherwise Josephus would have qualified: "priest of the sectarian order"; hence also in *Ant.* XVIII 1,5 (22) he means to say: they elect … (Aaronic) priests; *cf.* Schürer, *Geschichte*[4], vol. II, p. 666).

challenged by a worthy scholar who would be granted precedence over a Cohen.[153]

The quorum of ten judges sitting in court[154] (10,4) can be traced directly only by the Amoraic period, as we have pointed out above, pp. 84–85. It seems, however, most probable that the college of seven[154] for municipal affairs, שבעה טובי העיר, which is mentioned in the Mishnah and which perhaps was the same as the Court of Seven to which Josephus refers, represents a later development of the ancient decemvirate "Edah."[155]

[153] Cf. Giṭṭin V,8 (Maimonides' commentary, ibid.) concerning the honors given the priests in the synagogue for the sake of peace in the community. We need not stress that such preferential treatment of the priests goes back to the days when they laid claim to this status by dint of their real leadership and actual authority. A trace of such deserved claim can still be found with the Tannaim, R. Shimeon b. Yoḥai (TP Giṭṭin 5, 47b) and R. Yishmael (Bavli Giṭṭin 59b). The latter, himself, a Cohen, mentions the priestly prerogative to be the one delegated to pronounce the benediction over food; this practice was also followed by the Essenes (Josephus, Bel. Jud., II 8,5). In Amoraic days the scholars claimed this honor which originally belonged to the priests (cf. Giṭṭin 59b). The strong influence on the Jews which some churchfathers attribute to their priests (cf. the material in Juster, Les Juifs d. l. Emp. Rom. I, p. 453, note 7) refers to the Jewish spiritual leaders rather than to the Aaronic priests.

[154] In smaller communities the council was not only an administrative executive but also the juridical authority; hence the שבעה טובי העיר appear in tannaitic sources as magistrates, whereas Josephus (cf. above, p. 47) describes them as a septemvirate court of magistracy and jurisdiction (cf. Ant. IV, 8,14 (214–215); 8,38 (287); Bel. Jud., II, 20,5 (571)). Since in our sect the distribution of charity was administered by the מבקר together with the judges (14,13), it follows that this sectarian community, too, combined court and magistracy into one body politic. Similarly, the (12,8) חבור probably constituted the supreme judicial and executive authority, corresponding in function and status to the Synhedrion. [Translator's note: I could not find the term שבעה טובי העיר in the Mishnah or in Tannaitic sources; cf. Dimitrovsky's RaShBA on Megillah, p. 128, note 1; Ratner, AZJ, Megillah, p. 67.]

[155] In every version of the Tannaitic tradition the term עדה in the legal parts of the Pentateuch always is interpreted to mean the supreme institution of Synhedrion (e. g., Horayoth I, 5). Although this interpretation is somewhat too sweeping, it cannot be doubted that this term עדה means in many biblical passages the communal representation in council rather than the community at large. Also the term בעדה, prescribing divorce procedure in the Assuan Papyrus, stands for בפני בית דין; cf. Sulzberger, JQR, N. S., vol. 3 and Funk, JBJLG, VII, p. 378.

The decemvirate as magistracy in biblical times is attested by Eccles. 7:19, a passage pointedly interpreted in a Midrash (Exod. Rabba 15,20) to adduce biblical reference for the decemvirate college of intercalation. The "foremost ten" also figure institutionally in ancient Phoenician municipalities (Schürer, Geschichte⁴, vol. II, p. 253), hence one has to proceed cautiously in drawing conclusions about dating the composition of Ecclesiastes from the fact that it mentions a decemvirate. It seems, rather, that decemvirate councils represent a good old Semitic tradition, whereas under Persian influence (e. g., Esther 1:14;

Also the office of the מבקר, although unattested in Pharisaic Judaism, is not unknown in Jewish antiquity. Josephus reports of the Essenes that "except for doling alms they undertook *nothing* on their own without specific directives by their overseers[156] (ἐπιμεληταί) (*Bel. Jud.*, II, 8,6). Büchler (p. 464) let himself be misguided by Kohler[157] and contends like him that the status of the מבקר corresponds to that of a bishop in the Didascalia. Since this document cannot be dated earlier than the third century C. E., as is evident to any competent scholar, it would follow as corollary that our sectarian document could not belong to the pre-Christian era. True enough, Büchler would not admit that there were Christian influences on our sect; he does maintain that both documents absorbed Syrian practices, hence their kinship in these matters.

I can hardly believe that Büchler has engaged in any close study of the Didascalia, because he would soon have discovered that there is no similarity at all between the bishop's office in that document and our מבקר. There the congregation is instructed (ed. Gibson 35b): "Love thy bishop like a father, pay him respect like a king, and venerate him like God." The latter exhortation is not meant as hyperbolic expression,[158] but in the literal sense, and therefore it is of

---

Ezra 7:14) such councils were reduced to septemvirates. It would also stand to reason that for purely administrative functions a septemvirate body was found sufficient, whereas for judicial functions a decemvirate was required, i. e., the addition of two Levites and an expert מופלא. *Cf.* also Funk (*MGWJ*, LV, pp. 33 ff. and 699 ff.), who proposes a different explanation of the institutional relationship between the septemvirate college and the decemvirate *Edah*; it should be mentioned here that he overlooked my explanation in *Geonica* I, p. 207.

[156] By "overseers" is meant the respective commissioner of the various corporations and settlements, but not that each corporation had several officials. Also our sect had *one* מבקר (13,7 f.) for every community. The term המבקר אשר לכל (14,8) המחנות is not a superior official (the inspector general of all communities) but a qualification: the overseer of whatever camp (community). There was no High Commissar of the sectarian communities — the supreme office lay in the hands of the חבור; *cf.* 12,8.

[157] *Cf. American Journal of Theology*, XV, p. 416. By his comparative study between our document and the Didascalia, Kohler finds them in agreement (!) with each other; from this finding he concludes that our document must be rather early, since the Didascalia is an Essene composition! We should like to point to another curiosity in this study: none of his quotations "culled" from the Didascalia can be found in this work; without noticing he cited from the Constitutiones Apostolorum, which abstracts many passages from the Didascalia, but was composed centuries later.

[158] *Cf.* the well-known Midrash of R. Akiva (on Deut. 6:13): "(Alongwith) God you shall fear (the scholars of His Torah)"; *eth*=along with; *cf.* Bava Qamma 41b.

far-reaching theological and juridical significance. The bishop's status as representative of God on earth has been vested with the authority to forgive sins (*op. cit.*, 23a), and he has been charged to take upon himself the sins of all of his flock, even as Jesus vicariously atoned for all sinners (*ibid.*, 30a). As benefice for this responsibility, the bishop receives from his community food and clothing and all other provisions (*ibid.*, 29b), as formerly were supplied to the priest, for he is now Levite and highpriest (*ibid.*, 32b). As absolutist king, the right is his to appoint presbyters and deacons; since a secular king, who rules only over their bodies, is empowered to choose his own officers, how much more is the bishop entitled to such power, since he rules over body and soul (*ibid.*, 34b)! This obviously implies that the bishop is entrusted with the disposition of charities for the needy and the clergy (*ibid.*, 32b), and with the dispensing of justice (*ibid.*, 18a).

What are the parallels in our document to this privileged status of the bishop? The judges and magistrates[159] of the community are to be elected by the community itself (10,4–5); the מבקר has no power of appointment and he is not even a member of the court (13,2; 14,13). The administration of charities for the needy was not entrusted exclusively to the מבקר; he had to distribute them together with the judges (14,13). Unlike the bishop, the מבקר could claim no benefice in recognition of his functions; Jews would not pay teachers and judges in any way. The early Christians first accepted this Jewish tradition; when, however, the clergy assumed the status of the former Jewish priesthood, the ensuing benefits were accepted by the church. The bishop represents, as we have shown, the Highpriest, whereas the מבקר remains a layman who, regardless of his own learning, must respect the prerogatives of the priest (13,5). Kohler (AJT XV, p. 418) quotes a passage from our document according to which the מבקר would be authorized to exclude somebody from "the sphere of purity," corresponding to similar authority vested, according to the Didascalia, in the bishop. This alleged kinship between the two documents, how-ever, does not really exist; even if there is such a parallel, it would not provide us with any grounds for the dating of our document.

Under certain circumstances,[160] a sinner can be excluded from the "sphere of purity," according to a precept of our document (9,21).

---

[159] *Cf.* above, n. 154, where we stressed that the judges also acted as magis-trates. We should point out that the council of judges in our document requires a decemvirate, whereas the church councils in the Didascalia (III, 9a) are duo-decemvirates.

[160] We find in 9,18 f. that the מבקר kept book on suspected members, enabling him to submit the necessary evidence in court. Thus the מבקר more nearly represents the office of prosecutor rather than that of judge, whereas the bishop acts as the

Kohler understands this punitive measure to mean "excommunication." On basis of this interpretation he finds a parallel between our sectarian and the early Christian office-holder: just as the מבקר was vested with the power of excommunication, so was the bishop, according to the Didascalia. At closer scrutiny Kohler ought to have noticed that neither in the cited passage nor anywhere else in our document[161] could he have found support for the authority of the מבקר to exclude somebody from the "purity." Moreover, he misunderstands the passage in point; the "setting apart from the purity" has nothing to do with excommunication, as we have already demonstrated (ad loc. cit., p. 45, notes 120 and 122, cf. below p. 288). Excommunication is mentioned in our document (12,3–6), but it is a power given to the judges and not to the מבקר.

Another passage in our document (20,2 f.) speaks of the case of a sinner who is expelled and then readmitted; the מבקר is not referred or alluded to throughout this discourse. Hence we may conclude that the passage (15,5–11) which discusses the activity of the מבקר as admitting sinners is not concerned, as Kohler reads it, with an excommunicated veteran sectary seeking readmission, but with the initiation of novices, as borne out by the context. In the Didascalia the bishop is vested with the competence to exclude and restore members of the church, whereas our document charges the מבקר only with the admission of new members.

These considerations prove that the alleged parallelism between the bishop of the Didascalia and our מבקר is pure fantasy.

o) Historical Evaluation: Validity of Witnesses.

Büchler's contention that there is similarity in the rules concerning the character and the validity of witnesses between our document and the Didascalia is again entirely unwarranted. He must have studied a

---

presiding judge. We should like to point out that according to the Didascalia (IV, 14b) the bishop may not be younger than fifty — the older the better, whereas our document stipulates (14,9) that the מבקר can only hold office between thirty and fifty (cf. Num. 4:3 e. a.); at fifty his age disqualifies him from office. If בעול in 14,9 has the meaning of "espoused," as many do propose, then we would have found at least one point in common for the מבקר with the bishop; for, according to the Didascalia (IV, 15a) the bishop must be married. We have demonstrated, however, (above, p. 89), that this explanation of בעול is untenable.

A metaphor common to our document (1,7) and the Didascalia (beginning) is the expression "divine plantation (מטעת = dei plantatio vinae)" meaning the pious. We have noted already that this metaphor is rather frequent in apocryphal literature.

[161] Cf. also below.

most peculiar version of the Didascalia. In the available printed editions nothing is mentioned about the qualification and admissibility of witnesses. We only find some general instruction for the bishop to investigate the veracity of testimonies, since there are always evil men who try to promote strife and hatred among the members (x; *ed. cit.*, 37a ff.).

Our document records a similar admonition[162] against accusations by a witness behind the back of the accused (9,2 ff.). However, the characteristic injunctions[163] which make it incumbent on every member to report transgressions, even as a solitary witness and the eventual consequences of such a testimony, are entirely absent from the Didascalia. In the later revision of the latter work, the so-called "Constitutiones Apostolorum," some rules pertaining to witnesses can be found,[164] and one of them even resembles a rule recorded in our document; but in contrast to the latter (9,20–23) the Christian code rules that three witnesses are necessary for the indictment of the accused.

p) Historical Evaluation: Essene Correspondence.

The similarity between the office of the מבקר and that of the ἐπιμελητής is not the only point of contact between our sect and the Essenes. Both sects followed the practice of admitting only adult males[165] to their order. It seems also that both considered the age of twenty as the earliest term of adulthood for a candidate seeking entrance into the sectarian community.[166] If a father[167] wished to enter

---

[162] The context proves that we are not dealing here with false charges in court but, as the expression (9,4) להבזותו indicates, with personal defamation of a person out of court.

[163] About these *cf.* above, pp. 44–45, 119–120.

[164] See CA II, 21; differently (?) II, 48. In the Didascalia (X, 37b) the biblical law pertaining to witnesses is interpreted allegorically; the three witnesses correspond to the Father, the Son, and the Holy Ghost. This would suggest that this document, too, demands three witnesses to make testimony valid, an opinion held also by the pseudepigraphical Testament of Abraham. *Cf.* also Harris, *Mesopot. Codex of the Didascalia*, p. 217: three deacons are to be appointed, as it is said (Deut. 17:6; Matthew 18:16): at the mouth of two witnesses, or three witnesses . . . shall the word of the Lord be confirmed; *cf.* Josephus, *Ant.* IV, 8,14.

[165] *Cf.* Philo (ed. T. Mangey) II, p. 632.

[166] Text 10,1–2 and our elaborate discussion of this passage above. We do not rule out the possibility that the phrase 'אשר לא מלאו ימיו וכו does not refer to the age limit but to the candidate's trial period, interpreting "the fullness of his days" in a special sense, corresponding to the trial period for novices of the Essene order.

[167] *Cf.* 15,5 where the line ought to be completed: אשר לא מלאו ימיהם.

the sect together with his children, he was in duty bound to take the covenantal oath for the minors, who were then raised in the life of the sect until they came of age. The Essenes would also, as is known,[168] admit children to be trained in their sectarian doctrine. It is important to stress that the Essenes demanded of their novices an oath at admission, whereas the Pharisees were satisfied with a promise of the new member of their sect, without making him take an oath.[169]

Another correspondence between our document and the Essene doctrine is to be seen in their common attitude of avoiding any oath which demanded the pronunciation of the divine name; this we have pointed out previously. The reluctance to employ the divine name is so pronounced in our document that in biblical quotations which include the Tetragrammaton אל is used instead, or the divine name is entirely omitted.

These points of correspondence do not, of course, lead us to ascribe our document to Essene provenance. Our sect rejects essential Essene doctrines, such as common ownership of property, objection to slavery, etc. The similarities which do exist,[170] are, however, evident and obvious and they show that our sect belongs to the era during which Essenism was still a vital force.[171]

In the light of this plausible historical contiguity, Büchler's argument on this point, the avoidance of the divine name (p. 466), sounds embarrassingly lame and clumsy. He assumes that our sect's reluctance to use the divine name was defined in opposition to certain other sectaries (of the ninth century?) who insisted on pronouncing the Tetragrammaton as spelled, instead of the customary אדני. Such an opposition would, indeed, have been demonstrated by the consistent and conspicuous use of אדני, but not by such shy avoidance as is found in our document. How would Büchler explain the precept (15,1) that in the formula of an oath[172] the theonym אל is not to be employed,

---

[168] Josephus, *Bel. Jud.*, II, 18,2.

[169] This distinction is clearly indicated by the term המקבל (Demai II, 3; Tos., *ibid.*, II, 2–14; Bekhoroth 30b).

[170] The lacuna in the passage 14,21–22 probably recorded the punishment for a member who speaks disrespectfully of Moses. The Essenes would sentence to death anyone who blasphemes the legislator Moses (Josephus, *Bel. Jud.*, II, 8,9). The prohibition against mentioning even "the Law of Moses" in an oath (15,2; *cf.* above, p. 93) follows also from the deferential veneration of the legislator himself, for otherwise it would merely have read ואת התורה אל יזכור.

[171] It is during this very period that Essene elements penetrated into Talmudic Judaism.

[172] Probably an abbreviation for אלהים as is frequent in Rabbinic sources.

whereas throughout our document just this theonym, and not אדני
is recorded![173]

Any unbiased scholar will concede on this point that our document represents the Essene attitude of avoiding the divine name,
especially in the taking of oaths. Such pious sensitivity would point to
a dating of our sect at a time when the Essenes were still a vital and
powerful force.[174]

We cannot take seriously Büchler's contention (on 15,1) that the
theonyms in this passage, אל and אד respectively, stand as abbreviation
of אלהים and אדני respectively and that this derives directly from the
Mishnah Shevuoth IV, 13. This Mishnah deals with the application
of theonyms to the witnesses' oath (שבועת העדות, Lev. 5:1), whereas our
passage rules on the defendant's oath (Shevuoth VI, 1 שבועת הדיינים).
His learned reference is apt to create the impression that such spelled-
out abbreviations of theonyms were a rare phenomenon to be found
only in his cited Mishnah and our sectarian passage. In reality this is
nothing unusual in talmudic literature (e. g., Tosefta Berakhoth
VII, 20, ed. Lieberman VI, 20, p. 39[96]; Jer. *ibid.*, IX, 1,12d), in
keeping with corresponding sigla for the Tetragrammaton (Tosefta
ibid.; *et al.*).

The avoidance of pronouncing the divine name at the occasion of
administering an oath to witnesses (שבועת העדות) recommended in our
document (9,11), displays the consistent application of the Essene
doctrine to which we have referred already above.

p) Historical Evaluation: Adjuration of Witnesses.

The employment of this oath as a means of detecting a thief represents an ancient practice. It is already assumed in the Bible (Prov.
29:24), and the elaboration by the Midrash[175] is based on this verse.
The latter passage demonstrates clearly that in the amoraic period the

---

[173] A differentiation in this respect between אל and אלהים would be untenable,
since only the ineffable Tetragrammaton was considered the "magnificent name."

[174] Philo, the early Christians as well as the Pharisees (*cf.* above on 15,1) are all
influenced by the Essenes in their aversion to swearing by the divine name. Philo may
also have been affected in this attitude by Stoic doctrines.

[175] Lev. Rabba 6,2 (ed. Margulies, p. 128). The invocation of the Ḥazzan is
based on the injunction (Lev. 5:1): If a person sin, and hear the voice of adjuration,
and is a witness, whether he has seen or *known* of it — if he do not utter it, then he
shall bear his iniquity. Hence we prefer to read at the end of this Midrash, with
Yalq. Makhiri Prov. (ed. Grünhut, p. 86b, bottom) מאן ידע גנב לשמעון instead of
מאן גנב לשמעון of our text (*cf. var. lect.* Lev. Rabba, p. 130, line 3). The Midrash,
of course, cites only the opening of the adjuration formula invoked by the Ḥazzan
upon all who possess information about the theft and do not come forward to testify.

earlier practice, to have the interested party[176] administer the oath to persons expected to possess pertinent testifiable information, was replaced by a public conditional curse, invoked by the Ḥazzan in the synagogue upon all persons who possess such information but reserve their testimony. The procedure adopted in our document represents a procedure intermediate between the practice alluded to in the Bible and the one customary during the talmudic and gaonic periods. In biblical times, adjuring was the concern of the injured party, as clearly borne out by the passage Judg. 17:2; hence the Halakah[177] states that the law of the Torah (Lev. 5:1) is to be applied exclusively to such cases. In our document it is also the injured party who invokes the maledictory adjuration, but not upon a certain person or persons whom he suspects of being privy to the theft,[178] but upon anybody who could bear witness to the crime. The rabbinical legislators, who pre-

---

The curse of adjuration was: מאן ידע גנב לשמעון ולא סהיד — יקום בארור. The whole context of the Midrash שמע קול מכריז corresponding to ונפש כי חטאה ושמעה קול אלה (Lev. 5:1), and again והלא כבר נתנה תורה, the apophasis has already been pronounced by the Ḥazzan in the name of the Torah, i. e., the formula of adjuration.

[176] According to Shevuoth IV, 12 only the interested party can have the adjuration administered to witnesses who refuse to testify. Maimonides (Shevuoth IX, 6) codifies that adjuration can be demanded by בעל דין עצמו או שלוחו; the latter is not, however, an agent in the usual sense, but one authorized by power of attorney (ibid. 33b בא בהרשאה), an authority not held by the adjuring Ḥazzan. Cf. R. Yomtov Lippman Heller, Tosefoth Yomtov, ad loc.; [R. Akiva Eger, ibid., Tosefoth RAE (34).] Sifra on Lev. 5:1 (Hova Parasha VIII, 4) states explicitly: שלח להן ביד בנו, ביד עבדו, ביד שלוחו... יכול יהו חייבין, תלמוד לומר... עד שישמעו מפי התובע.

[177] According to Shevuoth IV, 10 and Sifra, loc. cit., the adjuration of witnesses must be specific. In the Talmud (ibid., 35a), however, what this Mishnah means by specification is defined as referring to the whereabouts of his witnesses, but not to addressing them personally by singling them out from a group of people present. If we would assume for our document an adjuration formula as follows: משביע אני עליכם בני המחנה העומדים כאן we would obtain a valid שבועת העדות according to the Halakah. The specification stipulated here in the Talmud is, however, subject to various interpretations (cf. R. Nissim b. Reuben Gerondi in his scholia on R. I. Alfasi, loc. cit.). If our proposed emendation of the text (assuming a homoioteleuton) is accepted: וכל האובד ולא נודע מי נגבו ממאד מאר המחנה (המחנה) אשר נגב בו ישביע בעליו בשבועת האלה, then we would find here that the requirement to specify the whereabouts of the adjured witnesses is stipulated in the sectarian Halakah. Under no circumstances may we read ישמיע for ישביע, since twice in this passage שבועת העדות is mentioned. Bava Meẓi'a 28a deals with a loss not incurred by theft, whereas our document is clearly speaking of a case of theft.

[178] According to Shevuoth IV, 10 the law in Lev. 5:1 requires adjuration of witnesses who refuse to testify and of nobody else; a general adjuration in a public place addressed "to whom it may concern" is not binding on anybody. Cf. the previous note, where we have observed that the modification in the Talmud, loc. cit., demands only specification of locality, not the identity of the witnesses addressed.

served the pronunciation of the divine name in oaths at court,[179] were no less reluctant than our sectaries to employ theonyms in oaths generally. They therefore substituted a public ban (חרם) for the old adjuratory formula of שבועת העדות; this ban was pronounced against everyone who reserved testimony in the particular case. The public ban is, of course, in its juridical aspect, an entirely different institution[180] than the original שבועת העדות; as coercive means, however, both are equally effective and, hence, the supplanting of the former by the latter.

Aptowitzer's discussion of the "Ban for obtaining evidence" (*JQR*, N. S. IV (1913/14), pp. 46 ff.) is to be corrected accordingly, since it contains facts which are untrue from the perspective of both Halakah and history. As we have seen,[181] the introduction of this public ban, was already taken for granted in the Midrash; it was not a novelty in Gaonic literature, as Aptowitzer contends. This ban cannot be conceived as a mere transformation of the שבועת העדות; it is a different act entirely, which could replace a specific oath only by virtue of its similar coercive force and effect. The Gaonim[182] stress explicitly that the public ban was introduced as substitute of the oath in order to avoid an oath by the divine name and the Torah; moreover, it offers wider possibilities, for it can be put into effect even in cases where Halakah provides no basis for adjuration. The Gaonic responsum[183] from which Aptowitzer wants to adduce proof for his contention that it was the Gaonim who introduced the "witness ban," on the basis of an explanation evolving from the biblical law (Lev. 5:1),[184] offers no

---

[179] *Cf*. above, pp. 92–93, n. 320.

[180] The adjuration of witnesses who refuse to testify (שבועת העדות) is exclusively the concern of the interested injured party, whereas the ban (חרם) can only be decreed and pronounced by the court. Adjured witnesses who continue to refuse their testimony are liable to sacrificial atonement for contempt of שבועת העדות (Lev. 5:1 ff.); no such consequences are incurred by this ban (except for the curse). When the Midrash applies the biblical verse to the case in which witnesses suppress their testimony, in spite of the threat contained in the Ḥazzan's public ban, we are dealing, of course, with an Aggadic interpretation, like many others presented there.

[181] *Cf*. also R. Abraham ibn Ezra on Lev. 5:1.

[182] חמדה גנוזה, no. 23 and many others; see also Aptowitzer, *loc. cit.*

[183] See שערי צדק, 87b, No. 17.

[184] Aptowitzer himself is surprised that for the practice of this ban the Geonim can find no antecedent in the Talmud; nay more, it conflicts with the Talmud. The Halakah in the Talmud stipulates that שבועת העדות must be administered in a specific situation, whereas this Gaonic ban is publicly pronounced "to whom it may con-

hint of such evidence! Captivated by his preconceptions about our sect, Aptowitzer identifies the procedure for eliciting testimony in our document with his gaonic "witness ban." The sectarian legislation, however, as we have demonstrated, is much closer to the practice in biblical times.[185]

q) Historical Evaluation: Self-Imposed Oaths.

Besides the maledictory oath, related to evidence of the past, our document (16,6) records a formula of oath asserting exclusively a future commitment (Num. 30:3; Deut. 23:24). Büchler (*op. cit.*, p. 465) errs, however, when he maintains that this legislation were original with our sect. It is already taken for granted in the Talmud (Nedarim 8a). In complete agreement with rabbinical legislation our document teaches that the force of an oath inheres only in such self-imposed commitment which merits religious approval. Even the derivation of this precept from a biblical passage (Deut. 23:24) adds nothing new; it is already reflected in the Jon. Targum *ad loc.*, as Büchler failed to notice.

Büchler also overlooked the early rabbinical concept of a biblical term (Num. 30:2) employed in our document (16,7). It is clearly defined in the Sifre[186] and the Jon. Targum (*loc. cit.*, למיסר איסר ממדעם דהתירא). It definitely refers to something otherwise permitted or commanded, but not to a self-imposed commitment to violate something "prohibited." Neither our document nor rabbinical legislation

---

cern." Were it only this point of specification which keeps the ban from serving the function of the original adjuration, we could easily see how this could be corrected: as we have pointed out it would be enough to insert in the ban the required specification of place. Aptowitzer, however, has missed the most essential characteristic of the שבועת העדות; it must come from the interested party personally (above, p. 400, note 180), whereas the ban is exclusively an instrument of the court. This fundamental distinction makes it impossible, regardless of how one may adjust the text, to have the ban considered as a transformation of the adjuration שבועת העדות.

[185] *Cf.* p. 122, where we referred to Philo and Targum Jonathan, who interpret Lev. 5:1 as enjoining the duty to inform the authorities about perjuries committed. The same interpretation is probably intended by the Tanḥuma (ed. Buber, III, 9) which derives from this verse the duty to inform on anyone who blasphemes God. The perjurer is considered a blasphemer, because he confirms the truth by appealing to the divine name, and then perverts this truth, thus committing a sacrilege by his perjury.

[186] Num. 153 (ed. Friedmann 56a; ed. Horovitz, p. 200 and *ibid.* reference to parallels).

recognize an oath to commit a sin (*cf.* above, p. 97). In one aspect,[187] however, the rabbinic legislation differs from the sectarian: the latter seems to teach the indissolubility of a binding oath by stressing (16,8) עד מחיר מות, even at the price of death, whereas the former encourages dissolution in cases of great stress. This indissolubility of such oaths — but not of vows (נדר) — is also taught by the school of Shammai (*cf.* above). The Karaites maintain[188] the indissolubility of both oaths and vows. Since our document does not mention vows (נדר) at all,[189] it clearly follows that this sectarian legislation corresponds to the Shammaite and not to the Karaite opinion.

r) Historical Evaluation: Public Confession.

In our document the sinner is required to pronounce his penitent confession (15,4) in front of the Priest (9,13). The early rabbinic literature rejects such practice with indignation. We refer, how-ever, to the Didache[190] which prescribes: ἐν ἐκκλησίᾳ ἐξυμολογήσῃ τὰ παραπτώματα σού. Such public confession of sins in the syna-gogue, at the time when the Didache was composed, assumed that there was a procedure at the presentation of the sin-offering in the Temple which was similar to the procedure recorded in our document.

*
*   *

We have now concluded our investigation concerning the authen-ticity of these sectarian fragments. We should now like to sum up, briefly, the results of our study with respect to our document's lan-

---

[187] *In re* the question of what our document rules in a case when the obligation of such an oath would endanger life, the oath may be broken or dissolved, *cf.* above, p. 96 on 16,8. In addition to the Rabbinic references cited here, *cf.* also *Eldad the Danite* (ed. A. Epstein, Pressburg, p. 50) ואינם נשבעים בשם עד שתצא נשמתם.

[188] Even Aaron of Nicomedia, who otherwise frequently follows the Rabbanites, also argues against the dissolubility of vows and oaths; *cf.* Gan Eden, Nedarim 173a. Only the very late Karaite authors, like Afendoppolo (supplement to Bachjatzi's אדרת אליהו, pp. 225a ff.), accept in principle the Rabbanite doctrine of their dissolu-bility.

[189] From the two words found before long gaps at the beginning of two successive lines (16,18–19) הנודר followed by a lacuna, and לשופט followed by a lacuna, Büchler reaches the conclusion that according to our document the taking of a vow was punishable!

[190] II 14; it ought to be noted that the two first words (in ecclesiam) are not found in the corresponding text of the Constitutions of the Apostles; the Latin translation thereof deletes the entire passage.

guage, diction and style, to its theology, eschatology and Messianology, to the form and content of its Halakah and Aggadah, and to the historical references which the document contains regarding the political and socio-economic conditions of the sect.

a) The Hebrew[191] of our document is uninfluenced by any trace of Arabism in either its words or grammatical structure. On the other hand, one cannot fail to notice the influence of Aramaic. In one passage (10,11 [11,10?]) we even find a Greco-Latin loan-word.

b) In style our document is much closer to the Apocrypha and the Pseudepigrapha than to rabbinic literature. This stylistic kinship may be ascribed to the fact that the sectarian tract is much closer in content to the Apocrypha and Pseudepigrapha than it is to the rabbinic sources. The Book of Jubilees and the Testaments of the XII Patriarchs, which were at the disposal of our sectarian author in their Hebrew original, served as literary pattern for our document; the author was most probably influenced, also, by other Pseudepigrapha such as Ben-Sira and the Books of Enoch. In some cases we can trace the acquaintance of Jews with the Hebrew originals of the Pseudepigrapha until the late middle ages.[192] It is most improbable, however, that a Jewish author of the Talmudic period, let alone of the Gaonic days, would hold the authority of the Pseudepigrapha in such high esteem as the author of our document did. The high authority which these works enjoyed in Christian circles, led early to the Jewish attitude which regarded them as heretic anathema, or in the most favorable view, as unreliable literature. The attitude of our Jewish author to the Pseudepigrapha is only plausible during the flourishing of this literature, i. e., from the first century B. C. E. to the second century C. E.

c) That our author was close to the pseudepigraphical tradition is borne out by his version of the legend about Moses' opponents in Egypt, which is definitely earlier than the versions handed down to us in the NT and in rabbinic sources.

---

[191] *Cf.* above, pp. 372 ff.

[192] It is well known that R. Saadiah Gaon (*fl.* ca. 900) still knew the Book of Jubilees. In the *Rivista Israelitica*, 1908, pp. 13–16, I have adduced proof from medieval Jewish literature for the late use of quotations from the Testaments of the XII Patriarchs. (The Hebrew "Testament of Naftali" is not original, but a late Hebrew revision of the Greek text).

d) The theology of this sect is, as we have demonstrated in detail (pp. 134 ff.), anti-Sadducee. Some individual remains of Sadducee doctrines persisted even after 70 C. E., probably as late as the Gaonic period.[193] During the talmudic and gaonic period, however, they were so insignificant that nobody bothered to combat them, whereas our document not only does battle with the opponents of the sect because of their Sadducee heterodoxy, but accuses them of abusing their power and position. To the best of our knowledge, there is no indication in either Jewish or Christian sources of Sadducee power and position after the destruction of the Temple in 70 C. E.

e) Both the theology of our document, in general, so also its Messianology, in particular, point to an era in which the legitimacy of the High-priest was a burning problem for the Jewish people. Our sect expected the ultimate advent of the "annointed of Aaron," i. e., the legitimate High-Priest, and the "annointed of Israel," i. e., the legitimate King (cf. Section VI). After the destruction of the Temple, the eschatological hope of the Jewish people concentrated on the restoration of the Temple by the Messiah; the personality of the High-Priest was relegated to the background. The great interest of our sect in the High-Priest demonstrates that our document was composed at a time when the High-Priest played a significant, perhaps even the most significant, role of any person in the contemporary life of the Jewish people.

f) The Halakah in our document is completely independent[194] of Karaite influence (influences which Büchler erroneously believed that

---

[193] It is definitely incorrect to see in Karaism a direct continuation of Sadduceeism. It may be correct, however, to say that men like Anan and other founding fathers of this anti-Rabbinic movement collected whatever relics of Sadducee tradition were available when they founded their own anti-Rabbanite party. We have to bear in mind that the possible contiguity between Sadduceeism and Karaism is restricted exclusively to the legal and expository aspect of Judaism; the theological tenets and doctrines of the latter are completely in keeping with Rabbanite tradition. This observation indicates that the Karaite attitude reflects merely the Sadducee antagonism against the practical aspect of Pharisee Judaism — but not their dogmatic opposition. Our document, on the contrary, centers its attack almost exclusively on Sadducee theology.

Juster (Les Juifs d. l. emp. rom. I, p. 374) finds in the known Novella of Justinian about the Jews a direct allusion to the Sadducees' denial of resurrection and angelology. I doubt the validity of Juster's interpretation in point. About anti-Rabbinic opposition during the Talmudical period, cf. Brüll, Jahrbücher, I, p. 225.

[194] Cf. our elaboration of this argument above.

he had found in this text); it is presented in a literary form which is different from any pattern known from Talmudic sources.[195] This can easily be demonstrated, e. g., by the laws of the Sabbath; almost the entire sectarian Halakah for the Sabbath can be corroborated in the Talmud (*cf.* pp. 107–115), but not a single rule, however, corresponds *verbatim* with the respective rabbinic formulation of the Halakah. This original form of the sectarian Halakah presents unanswerable challenge to all who, like Büchler, contend that our author derived his Halakah directly from the Talmud; hence their compatibility in content. Only in one single instance in our document do we find a Halakah corresponding to the rabbinic source not only in content but even in form: it is a rule taught by the ruling pair Shmaiah and Avtalion, two leading Pharisees of the first century B. C. E. Is this a coincidence or is it evidence for our thesis that our sect emerged at the time when these two Pharisees were flourishing?

g) Not only the form but also the content of this sectarian Halakah is evidence of its age. Our document offers rules and laws which are concerned with many areas of daily religious life. Parallels for every detail can be adduced from the Talmud. Despite the many-sidedness of the sectarian Halakah, there is not a single instance in which a law of the sect is paralleled in the rabbinic sources by a decree promulgated by a Tannaitic or Amoraic authority. Indeed, the Halakic material in our document actually represents the earliest elements of Tannaitic tradition, i. e., those rudiments of the Pharisaic tradition which had already crystallized by the time when Christianity was first consolidated.[196] The few actual differences between the sectarian and the "standard" Halakah are but of such nature that the former represents the earlier attitude, whereas the latter reflects a later stage of development under Tannaitic cultivation.[197] As an example we refer to the sectarian Halakah that even the ground contracts ritual taint from a corpse, which was already antiquated during the period of

---

[195] This observation appears even more remarkable when we consider that the early Karaites, for all their venomous and violent opposition to Rabbinism and Talmud, continued to study and write in the Halakic terminology of the Rabbanites; Anan's Code is actually Talmudic in form and diction, and Karaite only in content.

[196] E. g., sabbatical limits of dwelling district (10,21; 11,5); extension of the Sabbath (10,15); injunction against carrying in a blind alley on the Sabbath (11,8) and many other Halakoth.

[197] The prohibition of polygamy is to be explained on grounds of developments inside the sect, whereas the opposition against marrying a niece belongs to the provenance of the early Halakah.

Yavneh (end of first century C. E.), but had been the accepted view in earlier times. The aversion to oaths appealing to the divine name, and sundry other practices concerning oaths, show Essene influence which effected both the sectarian and Pharisaic Halakah.

Is it at all conceivable that our sect could have flourished at the beginning of Islam, centuries after the Talmud had been concluded; that this sect ignored the entire Halakic process which had evolved through the days of the Amoraim and even the Tannaim and that the sect revived a mode of living patterned on the Pharisees and the Essenes which was antiquated by close to a millennium? All known anti-rabbinic sects and movements dismissed Talmudic traditions for good and all, irrespective of their amoraic, tannaitic or sopherite provenance, making "tabula rasa" with one radical sweep; a return to the earliest Halakah, of the kind recorded in our document, after the vicissitudes of centuries had transformed all the premises for such a life, seems utterly implausible.

There is no such historically consistent return. Thus the Karaites abolished the Amidah-prayer, which was essentially composed by the Sopherim — yet the late amoraic practice[198] to have lessons from Pentateuch and Prophets read publicly on Sabbaths and Holidays was retained. If we were to assume a date as late as the beginning of the eighth century C. E., we would face a historically unique eclectism which is unthinkable. The evolutionary or historio-genetic theories about the Talmud's process of growth during the span of a millennium is modern, and we can hardly credit a Jewish sect of the gaonic era with such a critical approach.

The fact that our document knows only the early Halakah finds its natural explanation when we accept the thesis that our sect emerged at the time when this was the authoritative Halakah, flourishing in daily life.

h) Historical information on the political situation of the sect is admittedly scarce in our document. Nonetheless, these allusions afforded scholars an opportunity to misinterpret them. These references

---

[198] Tracing the fixed prophetic lessons in the Sabbath and holiday liturgy (Haftaroth) to Christian influence is a brain-storm of Venetianer (*ZDMG* LXIII, pp. 103 ff.); it is not to be taken seriously, but it is true that these passages were chosen rather late (*cf.* Elbogen, *Der jüdische Gottesdienst*, pp. 174 ff.). The Karaites did not follow the Rabbanites exactly in fixing their schedule of Haftaroth. We must, however, admit that we possess only scanty information about the order of Haftaroth as they existed in the Gaonic period; it may turn out that differences between various Rabbanite traditions and practices are preserved in the Karaite rite.

indicated that our sect not only possessed a temple, but also enjoyed full autonomy. We have already amply demonstrated that these data cannot possibly have been inserted by a resourceful author of the seventh or eighth century who was interested in inventing them for the sake of sectarian polemics.

The laws pertaining to service and sacrifices in the sanctuary, as also those concerning the execution of criminals, bear not the slightest traits of polemics. Actually they correspond to rabbinic tradition in talmudic source literature. Even if we credit an author of antiquity with such refined trickery as to dress up his document with antiquated Halakah in order to create the impression that his work is very, very old, such an assumption would not explain all that is recorded in our document about the Temple and its service. As a matter of fact, the regulations and rules about the sanctuary constitute but a minor and insignificant part of the sectarian Halakah; it is in the sectarian Aggadah that this topic assumes significance, in the elaborate and detailed history of the sect. The pollution of the Temple is distinctly reported as the immediate cause for the elder generation to emigrate from Judea and to seek voluntary exile in the Land of Damascus. The relevancy of the Temple for the sectarians is now supposed to be pure invention — seven hundred years after its destruction. However, is it conceivable that with all his learned skill, our ingenious impostor falls into a foolish trap: he tries to connect the emergence of the sect with fabrications and figments of his imagination which were irrelevant to this generation, when he could have made it more plausible for his own time by citing doctrines as essential as monogamy, opposition to marrying nieces, etc., as motives for the origin of the sect?

If, however, our sect actually possessed a temple, enjoying autonomy, then the historical situation fits only the conditions which prevailed during the first half (85–63) of the first century B. C. E., when Damascus enjoyed the liberal rule of the Nabateans, granting autonomy and religious freedom.

i) Neither the Halakah nor the Aggadah, neither theological doctrines nor historical references in our document find their satisfactory explanation if we consider these sectarian fragments as spurious. We have amply demonstrated that they are the genuine literary product of a sectary who flourished during the first century B. C. E. The sect whose history and doctrine are recorded in this document, emerged around 76–67 within the Pharisaic colony of Judeans at Damascus, whither they had fled from Alexander Jannaeus' persecutions. In the beginning the Damascene refugees differed only on political grounds from their fellow Pharisees in Judea. Gradually there evolved, however, also religious and particularly halakic distinctions which set them more and more apart, until a schism and rift consolidated the sect of exiles. The Damascene sect branded both the Pharisees and the Sadducees as backsliding sinners and considered its own sect as the only true Israel.[199]

---

[199] *Cf.* at length, pp. 270–273. I fail to understand what Büchler means by his statement (*op. cit.*, p. 458) that the sect called itself Israelites, but never Judeans. Not Apocrypha or pseudepigrapha, or Rabbinic literature ever call the Jewish people by any other name but Israel, and this commonly accepted usage is followed by our document. They felt even more justified in adopting this name for themselves since they disclaimed the fulfillment of the divine promise to the patriarchs (8,14 ff.) for anybody but themselves, the true Israel, the only true remnant of the chosen people. Hence Büchler's attempt to find in the sectarian designation of themselves as Israel a trace of Samaritan aspirations make no sense at all. His line of reasoning would make Bar-Kokhba a staunch Samaritan, since he had imprinted on his coins לחרות ישראל! Another reference to Samaritan identification of our sect is proposed by Büchler on the mentioning of Ephraim in our document (7,9 ff.). What this passage means is that the future punishment of sinners will be more horrible than anything that has happened since Ephraim left Judah (Isa. 7:17); the Prophetic expression סור אפרים is paraphrased here in our document, just as in the Targum, *loc. cit.* In the passage 14,1, however, the Prophetic phrase is quoted without any paraphrase. The claim that the sectarians themselves see in the name Ephraim a designation of their own identity is entirely unwarranted.

Indexes

Index

411

Source Index

For other sources see general index